QUALITATIVE RESEARCH
IN THE STUDY OF LEADERSHIP

Related Elsevier Series

Advances in Global Leadership, Vols 1–4

Monographs in Leadership and Management, Vols 1–4

Qualitative Research Methods in Psychology

Related Journals

The Leadership Quarterly

Organizational Dynamics

QUALITATIVE RESEARCH IN THE STUDY OF LEADERSHIP

KARIN KLENKE
Leadership Development Institute (LDI), U.S.A.

Emerald

United Kingdom – North America – Japan
India – Malaysia – China

Emerald Group Publishing Limited
Howard House, Wagon Lane, Bingley BD16 1WA, UK

First edition 2008

Reprints and permission service
Contact: booksandseries@emeraldinsight.com

British Library Cataloguing in Publication Data
A catalogue record for this book is available from the British Library

ISBN: 978-0-08-046410-7

Awarded in recognition of
Emerald's production
department's adherence to
quality systems and processes
when preparing scholarly
journals for print

Dedication

To Will,
    My children Max and Katja
    and Dubby and Walker

Contents

Preface...xv
Foreword...xxi

PART I: FOUNDATIONS OF QUALITATIVE RESEARCH 1

1   QUALITATIVE RESEARCH AS PARADIGM 3
    Introduction...3
       Leadership Research: Past Traditions and Current Trends 3
    What is Qualitative Research?..6
       Defining Qualitative Research 7
    Characteristics of Qualitative Research 10
       Strengths of Qualitative Methods 12
    Qualitative Research as Paradigm 12
    Philosophical Assumptions Underlying Qualitative Paradigms...........................14
       Ontology 15
       Epistemology...16
       Axiology..17
       Methodology..18
    Major Research Paradigms in Qualitative Research 19
       Constructivism 21
       Interpretivism..22
       Symbolic Interactionism..25
       Pragmatism 26
    Summary..29

2   QUALITATIVE RESEARCH AS METHOD..31
    Introduction...31
    Qualitative Research as Method...32
    Quality Standards in Qualitative Research 36
       Understanding Reliability and Validity in Qualitative Research 37
    Strategies for Enhancing Quality and Rigor in Qualitative Research 41
    The Quantitative–Qualitative Debate: One More Time 44
    The Role of Ethics in Qualitative Research..49
    Summary..52

PART II: MAJOR QUALITATIVE TRADITIONS IN LEADERSHIP RESEARCH 55

3   CASE STUDIES IN LEADERSHIP RESEARCH 57
An Illustrative Leadership Case Study 57
Introduction to Case Study Research 58
    Case Study Defined.. 59
    Role of Theory in Cases Studies 60
The Architecture of a Leadership Case Study 62
    Case Study as Method of Choice 63
    Selecting Cases: Single and Multiple Case Studies................................... 64
Data Collection and Analysis in Case Study Research 66
    Data Collection Methods.. 66
    Data Analysis Techniques.. 66
Interpreting the Findings of Case Study Research 69
Quality Assessments in Case Studies 69
Selected Case Studies in Leadership Research.. 72
    Leadership Theory in Case Studies 79
Summary.. 84

4   CONTENT ANALYSIS IN LEADERSHIP RESEARCH 87
An Illustrative Leadership Content Analysis Study 87
Introduction... 89
    Defining Content Analysis 89
Designing a Content Analysis Study 90
Content Analysis Procedures 90
    Qualitative and Quantitative Approaches to Coding................................. 92
    Types of Coding.. 93
Data Collection and Analysis 96
    Use of Software in Content Analysis 98
Quality Criteria and Validation Issues.. 99
    Intercoder Agreement in Content Analysis... 99
        Measuring intercoder reliability 100
    Validity in Content Analysis 103
Examples of Content Analysis in Leadership Research................................ 104
Summary.. 114

5   QUALITATIVE INTERVIEWING IN LEADERSHIP RESEARCH 117
An Illustrative Qualitative Interviewing Leadership Study........................... 117
Introduction... 119
    Defining Interviews 119
Types of Interviews and Interview Questions 121
    Structured Interviewing.. 122
    Unstructured Interviewing 125
    Semistructured Interviewing... 126
        Role of the interviewer in in-depth interviewing 130

Focus Group Interviews..131
Telephone Interviewing...133
Internet Interviews 134
Virtual Focus Groups Interviews 135
Data Collection and Analysis 136
Reliability and Validity in Qualitative Interviews...138
Applications of Qualitative Interviewing Studies in Leadership Research 139
Ethical Consideration in Qualitative Interviewing..149
Summary...150

6   MIXED METHODS IN LEADERSHIP RESEARCH 153
An Illustrative Mixed Methods Leadership Study..153
Introduction..155
Mixed Methods Design Consideration 156
Defining Mixed Methods Research...156
Types of Multimethod Designs 159
Selection of Empirical Studies Employing Mixed Methods Design....................160
Data Collection and Analysis 160
Applications Of Leadership Studies Combining Different Qualitative Methods
(Within Qualitative Mixed Methods Studies)..161
Applications of Leadership Studies Combining Qualitative Methods and
Quantitative Methods (Between Mixed Methods Designs) 170
Summary...181

**PART III: UNDERUTILIZED QUALITATIVE METHODS
IN LEADERSHIP STUDIES...183**

7   GROUNDED THEORY, ETHNOGRAPHY, AND HISTORIOMETRY 185
Grounded Theory 185
An Illustrative Grounded Theory Leadership Study 185
Introduction to Grounded Theory...186
Data Collection and Analysis in Grounded Theory 188
Category development in grounded theory 189
Quality and Rigor in Grounded Theory 192
Applications of Grounded Theory in Leadership Research.................................193
Summary 197
Ethnography 198
An Illustrative Ethnographic Leadership Study..198
Introduction to Ethnography...200
Defining ethnography..200
Types of ethnographic studies 201
Data Collection and Analytic Processes in Ethnography 203
Data collection 203
Data analysis and interpretation 204
Strengths and weaknesses of the ethnographic method...................................205
Applications of Ethnography in Leadership Research..205

Historiometry...213
  An Illustrative Historiometric Leadership Study...................................213
  Defining Historiometry...213
  Data Collection and Analysis in Historiometry....................................214
  Applications of Historiometry in Leadership Research.........................214
  Summary...218

8 PHENOMENOLOGY AND NARRATIVE ANALYSIS.............................221
  An Illustrative Phenomenological Leadership Study.............................221
  Introduction to Phenomenology...222
    Defining Phenomenology..222
    A Brief History of Phenomenology: Husserl, Heidegger, and Gadamer.......223
    Data Collection, Analysis, and Interpretation......................................226
      Bracketing and phenomenological reduction....................................228
      Delineating units of meaning..228
      Clustering of units of meaning to form themes.................................229
      Summarizing, validating, and modifying each interview....................229
      General and unique themes for all interviews and composite summary.......229
    Validity and Quality in Phenomenology..231
    Applications of Phenomenology in Leadership Research.....................232
    Summary...238
  Narrative Analysis...239
    An Illustrative Narrative Analysis in the Study of Leadership.............239
    Introduction To Narrative Analysis...240
    What is Narrative?..242
    Data Collection and Analysis in Narrative Inquiry.............................246
  Quality Criteria...246
  Applications of Narrative Analysis in Leadership Research..................247
  Summary...254

9 BEYOND WORDS: SIGHTS AND SOUNDS IN QUALITATIVE RESEARCH.........257
  Introduction...257
    Defining Image-Based Research..260
    Leadership, Aesthetics, and Art...261
  Image-Based Leadership Research...263
    The Aesthetics of Leadership..264
  Image-Based Research as an Emergent Methodology............................266
  Image-Based Sources of Data..268
  Analyzing Visual Data...269
    Content Analysis of Visual Data..271
    Iconography...272
  Quality Issues in Image-Based...274
    Alternatives to Validity and Quality Standards in Image-Based Research.......276
  Examples of Arts-Based Research...280
  Summary...285

PART IV: EMPIRICAL QUALITATIVE LEADERSHIP STUDIES 287

10 CONTENT ANALYSIS OF THE WRITINGS OF MARY PARKER FOLLETT..289
  Overview of the Study 289
  Approach to the Text 290
    Initial Questions 291
  Collecting, Exploring, and Analyzing the Data..291
    Data Collection Process 291
    The Seven Text Sample/Hermeneutic Unit 291
    Locating and Securing the Texts 293
    New Questions That Shaped Approach to Text 294
    Mining for Gold 295
    Phase One: Word Crunching..295
    Phase Two: Autocoding 299
    Phase Three: Coding Line-by-Line...299
      Code worthiness..300
    Phase Four: A Necessary Pause 301
    Phase Five: Hand Coding..302
    Phase Six: Code Comparisons Between Atlas/ti and Hand Coding....................304
    Phase Seven: Returning to Atlas/ti...307
  A Folletian Framework for Understanding Leadership 308
    Tracing Leader, Leaders, Leadership Across PDs 308
      Leader and leaders...310
      Leadership 311
  Implications for Contemporary Leadership Theory...312
      Hope and Optimism 312
      Shared Leadership/Team Leadership 313
      We-Power and Empowerment..313
      Followership...314
      Invisible Leader 315
  Summary...316

11 CALLING AND LEADER IDENTITY: UTILIZING NARRATIVE ANALYSIS TO CONSTRUCT A STAGE MODEL OF CALLING DEVELOPMENT...................317
  Introduction and Theoretical Background 317
    The Development of Calling in the Management Literature 318
    Empirical Research on Calling and Related Constructs 318
    Relating Calling to Identity..319
    Narrative Theories of Identity Development 320
    Narrative Identity and Leadership 321
  Research Design 322
    Interview Protocol...322
  Findings..324
    Themes—Individual Level 325
    Themes—Universal 325

Stage 1: precall antecedents—awaiting 325
Stage 2: Recognition of the call through spiritual awakening and
involvement—awakening 326
Stage 3: Realization of the call through experience, mentoring,
and/or preparation for vocational service—actualizing 326
Stage 4: Struggle to separate from previous roles and identities/dealing with
precall stage issues-anguishing 327
Stage 5: Identity integration and role merger of faith and work/subsequent
wrestling with preferred roles/possible selves—acceptance 328
Calling Narratives—Three Prototypes 329
Type I calling narrative 331
Type II and type III calling narratives 331
A General Psychological Structure of Calling and Leader Identity Formation 332
The Impact of the Childhood and Early Adult Years 332
Awakening to the Call 333
Interpersonal and Identity Conflict 333
Interpersonal Conflict and Resolution 334
Identity Conflict and Resolution 334
Identity Integration and Role Merger of Faith 334
Discussion 335
Conclusion 338

12   LEADERSHIP IN AT-RISK COMMUNITIES **341**
Introduction 341
Myles Horton: An Exemplary Leader in At-Risk Communities 342
The Role of Context in Leadership 343
At-Risk Communities as a Context for Leadership 344
Research Design 346
Data Sources for the Study 346
Results of Content Analysis and Case Study 347
Phase 1—Content Analysis Coding 347
Phase 2—Case Study Coding 351
Content Analysis and Case Study Convergence of Findings 352
Discussion 354
Level 3 S-Codes 354
Level 4 P-Codes: a Grounded Theory of Leadership in At-Risk Communities 356
Communal residence 356
Radical subordination 357
Responsibility 358
Reconciliation 359
Reframing 360
Restoration of people and community 361
Replacement 362
Level 5 Worldview—Horton's Foundational Concepts 362
A Model of Leadership in At-Risk Communities 363
Summary 364

13 EPILOGUE **367**
Contributions to the Study of Leadership 368
The Debate over Methods 369
Underutilization of Methods 372
The Future of Qualitative Research in the Study of Leadership:
Challenges and Opportunities 378
Summary 384

References **387**

About the Authors **449**

Index **451**

PREFACE

This book is about the use of qualitative methods in the study of leadership. It reflects my transformation as a leadership scholar from a quantitatively trained organizational scientist to an eclectic researcher who is comfortable with both qualitative and quantitative paradigms and methodologies. Questions about leadership that address what and when types of issues such as what are the effects of a coaching intervention on executive health or when should a leadership succession plan be implemented are readily answered by quantitative methods. On the other hand, questions about why types of leadership issues such as why do some leaders mysteriously change after their ascension to power or how do certain leadership attributes that are originally an asset turn into a liability often cannot be answered by quantitative designs. Crossing the great paradigm divide for me was an enormous challenge which involved unpacking philosophical assumptions and previous training in quantitative methods and statistics. At the same time, it was a profound learning experience that broadened my own research repertoire significantly and allowed me to take a fresh look at the way we study leadership, an ageless phenomenon.

It was a journey that was supported by my work as chair of numerous qualitative doctoral dissertations, my role on the editorial boards of a number of leadership journals, both qualitatively oriented such as *Leadership* published by Sage in the United Kingdom and *The Qualitative Report* as well as journals that publish both qualitative and qualitative leadership studies such as the *Journal of Management, Religion, and Spirituality* and the *Leadership and Organizational Development Journal*, and as Guest Editor of special issues of journals devoted to specific leadership topics published in, for example, the *Journal of Organizational Analysis* and the *Journal of Management Systems*. My foray and transition into the qualitative domain was solidified by opportunities to teach introductory and advanced qualitative methods courses, lecturing at universities in the United States and abroad, and bringing a qualitative research perspective to practicing managers through workshops and seminars.

The content of the book reflects a dual concern for students of leadership studies at all stages of scholarship ranging from graduate students to seasoned researchers and practitioners as consumers of qualitative leadership research. I believe that it is important for practicing managers to develop an understanding and a sense of the complexity of qualitative research which may entail suspending previously held assumptions about qualitative research as being less rigorous compared to quantitative research. Hopefully, after reading this book, both scholars and practitioners develop a new appreciation of the potential and limitations of qualitative research in a specific context, namely the study of leadership, which begs for answers to many why and how types of questions surrounding the role of leadership in contemporary organizations, communities, and society at large.

This book is not intended as a how-to-do qualitative research text although some chapters (i.e., Chapter 4 on content analysis) are more detail oriented than others (i.e., Chapter 7 on grounded theory and phenomenology). Again and again, it has been shown that the how-to-approach is not always practical. For example, decades of repetition of the how-to-approaches has not helped leaders to become more effective. Likewise, for the various qualitative methods described in the book such as interviews or ethnography, numerous how-to, procedurally oriented treatises that take the reader from the A to Z of the research process are available. Instead, the book situates qualitative leadership research in the larger context of leadership studies as an academic discipline taking into account the multifaceted nature of leadership as a relational phenomenon, the context-dependent nature of leadership research, and the prevailing methodological trends.

GENERAL ORGANIZATION OF THE BOOK

The book is divided into four parts. Part I consists of two chapters which provide the philosophical, theoretical, and methodological assumptions underlying qualitative research. These two chapters introduce qualitative research as paradigm shift evidenced in leadership research as empirical qualitative leadership studies have slowly gained credibility and legitimacy over the past two decades. Ten years ago, it was unlikely that major publication outlets for leadership researchers such as the *Journal of Applied Psychology* or the *Academy of Management Journal* accepted qualitative manuscripts for publication; today, most quantitatively oriented journals welcome well-designed and rigorously executed qualitative submissions.

Part II represents an assessment of those qualitative methods that have been most frequently utilized in leadership research. Part II (Chapters 3–6) includes four chapters that cover case studies, content analysis, qualitative interviewing, and mixed methods. These methods cover a range of approaches ranging from purely qualitative studies such as thematic content analysis discussed in Chapter 4 to quantitatively focus qualitative studies as found in some of the mixed methods research presented in Chapter 5.

Part III examines qualitative methods that I believe hold considerable promise to advance the field of leadership studies but have been infrequently utilized for a variety of reasons including time constraints, costs, and concerns about rigor and quality standards in qualitative research that these methods raise in the minds of those who still question the legitimacy of qualitative studies in empirical leadership research. Part III covers a range of methods including grounded theory, ethnography, and historiometry (Chapter 7), phenomenology and narrative analysis (Chapter 8), and nontext-based qualitative approaches that utilize works of art, film, photography, choreography, and other image-based sources of data (Chapter 9).

Finally, Part IV presents in-depth three empirical studies that employed content analysis, a mixed method design in which case studies were nested in a content analysis, and narrative analysis. More specifically, Martin (Chapter 10) content analyzed over 1400 pages of the writing of early management scholar and political philosopher Mary Parker Follett whose ideas anticipated many concepts and ideas that are part of the contemporary leadership landscape such as followership, empowerment, shared leadership, complexity theory, and invisible leadership. Not only is the study remarkable because of the size of the database, but it also combines hand and computer-assisted coding to trace Mary Parker Follett's thoughts and writings about leader, leaders, and leadership through her books, papers, and lectures and discusses the implications of her work for contemporary leadership theory. In a comprehensive set of detailed analyses, Martin was able to synthesize Follett's work and demonstrate that leadership in its many different manifestations emerged as the unifying thread of Mary Parker Follett's work, both in theory and practice. Chapter 9 complements Chapter 4 on content analysis and brings to life many of the principles, procedures, and issues described in the methods chapter.

Markow (Chapter 11) used a qualitative method, narrative analysis that is greatly underutilized in leadership research. Leaders tell stories that capture their life experiences in the form of narratives that portray their passions, crucibles, successes, and failures to frame their leadership practices and give them meaning. The author conducted qualitative interviews with church leaders using a standardized interview protocol designed to elicit respondents' descriptions of their sense of calling, identification of significant people who enhanced or hindered their calling, life themes, and future scripts. The results revealed three types of calling narratives modeled after a suffering-crisis-transformation plot. The author concluded that a leader's calling narrative is an essential component of self-identity. This research reinforces many aspects of narrative analysis described in Chapter 8.

In Chapter 12, Wallace examines a topic which has received none or very little attention in the leadership literature. Instead of examining leadership in political elites, formal organizations, or multinational firms, the author focuses on leadership in at-risk, distressed communities where situational contingencies bear little resemblance to most contexts in which leadership is typically studied. The purpose of this research was to develop a grounded theory of leadership in poverty stricken, at-risk communities by an in-depth study of a single leader who served as an exemplar and developed leaders in these settings for decades. The database in this study consisted of the writings of and interviews with Myles Horton that were content analyzed. In addition, three case studies comprised the hold out sample that was nested in the content analysis. The study provided the unique opportunity to compare the results and convergence of the results derived from two different qualitative methods. The emergent grounded theory of leadership in at-risk communities identifies seven foundational principles, which, taken together, converge on a small set of higher order values that reflect the needs and contextual realities of leaders and followers in at-risk communities. Wallace's research illustrates concepts and analytic techniques described in Chapters 3 and 4 while at the same time venturing into a topic of global relevance and importance given the efforts that are made currently made worldwide to alleviate poverty.

Collectively, these three application chapters demonstrate that carefully designed and rigorously executed qualitative leadership studies can add new dimensions to the extant literature and open multiple windows for future research.

In the Epilogue (Chapter 13), I revisit themes that are woven into the chapters throughout the book such as the lingering paradigm wars over the relative superiority of qualitative and quantitative research methods, the popularity of mixed methods designs as a means of enhancing credibility and legitimacy of qualitative research, and the need of leadership scholars to avail themselves of the less utilized qualitative methods and venture beyond text-based data sources to take advantage of image-driven, technology-enhanced ways of studying leadership using works of art, film, dance, and other performing arts or photography.

Each chapter covering the qualitative methods presented in this book is structured to share a number of common elements and conventions. For example, each chapter opens with a representative study illustrating the specific qualitative methods discussed in the chapter. Each chapter also describes the major design features, data collection, and analysis procedures germane to the method followed by a review of major published leadership studies illustrating the defining features of a given qualitative method. These studies are summarized in tables with yet a smaller subset of them singled out for a more detailed discussion. Furthermore, these selected applications are discussed in the broader context of the extant leadership literature as well as the more immediate context in which the study was conducted. As the research presented in this book spans a time span of over two decades, the sample studies are ordered chronologically from the most recent to the earliest as I was interested in detecting temporal shifts in terms of the relative importance of topics, the increased popularity of certain methods in response to current events such as 9/11 or hurricane Katrina which spurred qualitative research, the emergence of new methods, and shifting quality criteria over time. Where appropriate, each chapter also features the special dynamics governing the interactions between researchers and research participants or unique ethical consideration requiring the researcher's attention, as for example, in e-mail interviews.

Broadly speaking, this book is targeted to students of leadership—whether they are graduate students, established scholars, or practicing managers who want to continue to remain current in cutting edge leadership research. Hence, the book is appropriate for use as the primary text in graduate course in research methods in leadership studies and related disciplines such as organizational psychology, educational administration, health care management, and public administration, to name a few. The book is also appropriate for leadership scholars who, like me, are interested in broadening their research repertoire and venturing into new territory. The book is also likely to be of interest to practitioners in many fields as there is hardly an industry or area of management in the profit or nonprofit sector that is not concerned with individual, team, or organizational leadership. Throughout history, the fate of civilizations and millions of individuals have depended on the quality of leadership of a nation, organization, or community. Today, managers from all walks of life want to know whether leadership does make a difference. Qualitative research along with its quantitative cousin provides some answers to this quintessential question. As the world in which leaders and managers operate is becoming much more difficult than it once was, continually shaping and renewing itself through forces such as globalization, rapidly changing technologies, changing workforce dynamics, and changing conceptualizations of leadership, qualitative research has much to offer. This book presents a tapestry of qualitative methods with warp and weft threads waiting for students of leadership to weave their own distinctive fabric using these methods to advance the study of leadership and breathe a breath of fresh air into a discipline on the cusp of a paradigm shift.

I acknowledge my gratitude to my PhD students, past and present, in helping me fine tuning my qualitative research skills. In addition, my thanks go to my editor, Zoë La Roche at Elsevier Sciences, for her guidance and input that brought this project to fruition. Finally, I thank my husband Will for his insights, the extraordinary leadership challenges he experienced, and the profundity of his thought which provided the necessary intellectual and emotional climate for the work on this book.

Karin Klenke

Richmond, Virginia, USA, September 2007

FOREWORD

One standard for assessing the growth and legitimacy of qualitative research is to note the more specialized books on the topic that have emerged in recent years. In addition to the more general references on qualitative research that are available (e.g., Denzin & Lincoln, 2005; Marshall & Rossman, 2006; Maxwell, 2005), we now have discipline- or field-based books targeted to specific audiences, such as qualitative research for social workers (Shaw & Gould, 2001), qualitative research for public relations and marketing communications researchers (Daymon & Holloway, 2002), qualitative research for health science investigators (Crabtree & Miller, 1992), and qualitative research for educators (Hatch, 2002). So it does not come as a surprise that we now have a qualitative book, *Qualitative Research Methods in the Study of Leadership*, for those who study leadership. We need good examples of qualitative studies in the leadership field, and this book provides an excellent resource on the topic.

Those who conduct leadership studies using qualitative research will find in this volume a primer on the basic features of conducting this form of inquiry, an argument for its use in leadership studies, examples of standard and under-utilized and innovative methods, and numerous examples of actual leadership research projects (e.g., the "ripple effect" of mentoring in an undergraduate leadership program, followers' dominant fantasies about their leaders, drawings of Bedouin women, and content analysis of the writings of Mary Parker Follett). Any one of these features would make this volume valuable; together, they provide a book that will be extremely useful in the leadership field.

Where, then, is qualitative research in the study of leadership going? asks the author of this book in the epilogue. The chapters, one by one, unfold answers to this question. The discussion begins by noting that the leadership literature has largely been quantitative in orientation and that a qualitative approach would provide a deeper understanding of leadership and the way it plays out within particular settings or contexts. The past 25 years have seen slow but gradual growth in the use of qualitative research methods in leadership studies. Because qualitative research has advocates with varied perspectives, one finds in this book a definition of qualitative research and, true to qualitative thinking, a presentation of multiple perspectives on the definition. But there is a need for greater awareness among leadership researchers of the rich diversity of methods that are subsumed under qualitative research. A number of predictors are encouraging increased qualitative research in leadership, including the greater credibility and legitimacy qualitative leadership research has achieved, the willingness of gatekeepers such as journal editors to entertain qualitative submissions, the addition of qualitative research method courses in doctoral programs in organizational leadership, and the migration of some qualitative research methods to the Internet. Technologies that enhance the rigor of qualitative research have helped legitimization.

I was delighted to learn that many chapters in this book emphasized the philosophical underpinnings of qualitative research. This turn should warm the hearts of many qualitative researchers who feel that this form of inquiry is really about philosophical ideas rather than methods. Indeed, when qualitative research emerged during the 1960s and 1970s to challenge quantitative approaches, it was the philosophers who led the way and created philosophical distinctions between quantitative and qualitative research practices (e.g., Lincoln & Guba, 1985; 2000). My hunch is that when *quantitative* research first began in the late 1800s and early 1900s, philosophers were very much in the forefront of discussions about how to proceed with scholarly inquiries. So, I would suggest that those in leadership who use qualitative approaches should look closely at the philosophical paradigms being raised in this book and ask whether these paradigms play a role in bringing you to qualitative research. Whether you make them explicit in your research studies is an open question but one you should be prepared to answer when presenting a qualitative study at a conference or summiting it for journal publication. I also remembered reading this collection of chapters as to how leaders need to learn a new language when they learn qualitative research. Terms such as triangulation, paradigm, and method, for example, require embracing and understanding of a new vocabulary.

It is the strong methods discussion that quickly takes hold in this volume of writings. Much discussion in the last fifteen years has been devoted to identifying different methodological procedures for conducting qualitative research (Creswell, 2007; Denzin & Lincoln, 2005). These methods discussions place emphasis on the phases of the research process related to data collection, data analysis, and quality considerations (e.g., validation, evaluation, generalizability) and on the use of different procedures depending on the "type" of qualitative research being undertaken. The reader will be treated in this volume to useful procedures that seem well-suited for leadership research, such as case studies, content analysis, interviewing, appreciative inquiry, and mixed methods approaches. The last approach involves the use of both quantitative, numeric data as well as qualitative text data in combination to address research problems.

Turning to case studies, it is not surprising to learn that case studies of leaders or their organizations have been undertaken using qualitative research based on single and multiple case study procedures. Content analysis in leadership research highlights the importance of language, and often this analysis involves the leader and the followers and the creation of a linguistic map found in the relationship between leaders and followers. Leadership research using content analysis includes diverse topics such as charismatic leadership, speeches of political leaders, leader emergence during the Polish solidarity movement, and women's leadership styles. Content analysis also has a well-worked out system for checking for inter-coder agreement that deserves close attention in this book. Turning to interviewing, the leadership researcher will find useful discussions about the types of interviews available that run from more structured to unstructured approaches. A sample interview guide is provided as a model for designing interview questions. The expected increase in the use of virtual focus group interviews and other new technologies for qualitative interviewing online is suggested. Despite the intuitive appeal of qualitative interviewing as a primary research method in the study of leadership, the number of empirical studies that utilized this methodology is relatively small although several examples are mentioned.

Combining methods by mixing qualitative and quantitative methods is becoming increasingly popular in the social, behavioral, and health sciences (Creswell & Plano Clark, 2007). In leadership research, there are two types of mixed methods studies reviewed here: (1) those that triangulated method by combining different qualitative methods, referred to as within qualitative mixed methods and (2) those that combine qualitative and quantitative methods. In this book, the leader researcher will find many examples of both approaches to mixed methods research although the use of multiple qualitative methods is called multimethod research in other writings on the topic (Morse, 2003). The reason for mixed methods studies in the leadership literature is, in part, because of continued pressures on qualitative researchers to build objectivity, generalizability, and replicability into their research designs to provide greater legitimacy for a qualitative study. Readers will see that mixed method designs have the ability to reduce some of the problems associated with single methods. On the other hand, mixed methods research makes considerable demands on the researcher who has to be skilled, competent, and experienced in both types of methods.

Moving beyond the more traditional methods of qualitative research are several approaches that the authors characterized as "underutilized" in the leadership area. Qualitative methods—grounded theory, ethnography, and historiometry (biographical material, such as personality profiles of eminent leaders)—require prolonged engagement with the research participants and are used less frequently in leadership studies. The leader researcher will find the procedures of data collection and analysis as well as helpful sample studies in this book. Empirical studies using phenomenology and narrative analysis are also found infrequently in the leadership literature. To apply phenomenological research, the leader–researcher needs to understand the underlying philosophical assumptions of this approach found in authors such as Husserl (1970). Despite the scarcity of phenomenological studies in leadership research, the few studies reviewed illustrate the basic philosophical assumptions, procedures, data collection, and analytical methods used, and they represent fairly recent studies suggesting that scholars may be becoming more interested in applying phenomenology to leadership phenomena. Also, narrative research, as a method of qualitative inquiry, is edging its way into the social sciences including leadership studies. Because the story is offered as a scholarly explanation and realistic depiction of a human episode, the researcher needs to include evidence and argument in support of the plausibility of the narrative story. Another underutilized approach is image or arts-based leadership research. In many ways, image-based leadership research today, like qualitative text-based research 20 years ago, is in its infancy, controversial, and often labeled nonscientific. Visual representations (e.g., works of art, photographs, cartoons, graffiti, and film) are considered legitimate text that communicates meaning about leadership. Images can be collected in leadership qualitative research in the form of documentaries, the performing arts, freehand sketches of informants, photography, and computer visuals. It is useful to reflect on the ways that arts can inform leadership: through using art as a metaphor for leadership (e.g., the leader as artist, leadership an orchestra, and management as a theater ensemble); using specific artistic methods that support leadership practices (e.g., a business leader with some education in the visual arts could ask his or her team to paint a picture of their team); and using arts-based methods to generate artistic content (e.g., a leader with some knowledge and understanding of architectural design may use this knowledge to create work spaces that reflect organizational values). Images of leaders and leadership can be located in sources as diverse as Egyptian hieroglyphs, sculptures of contemporary leaders and historical statues, tributes to leaders found in musical scores or in leaders' self-presentation in films. Although no art-based studies were located in the leadership literature that apply image-based methods to a particular leadership issue or problem, the examples presented were intended to illustrate how leadership researchers may design an arts-based study.

Readers should not overlook the last three chapters. It is in these chapters that the specifics of conducting qualitative research in leadership areas provide the most detailed guidance for practice. In the chapter of Mary Parker Follett, one finds painstaking coding of hundreds of pages of documents and the weaving by the researcher between hand coding and coding using a qualitative computer software program. Leadership emerges as the unifying thread of Follett's body of work. The results of this comprehensive content analysis show that Mary Parker Follett was a trailblazer and original thinker whose ideas and concepts expressed or anticipated many contemporary leadership constructs such as followership, conflict management, authority, control, and power and leadership theories including contingency theory. In a second applied paper, the idea of a "calling" and "identity" in the Christian tradition has long been used to address topics about one's place and purpose in the world. This chapter uses a narrative analysis, and from a structural standpoint, the author takes the reader through fascinating multiple layers of analyses, always building toward larger abstractions, until the study ends with an overall psychological structure of calling and identity. It shows the complexity of using both narrative analysis as a method as well as the "layered" approach to qualitative data analysis in a sophisticated and rigorous study. A "layered" approach also emerges in a chapter on at-risk communities. Myles Horton (1905–1990), a little-know leader from Appalachia, was a suitable candidate for exploring leadership in at-risk communities. Horton became instrumental in training leaders for the American Labor Movement, the Civil Rights Movement, the approaches used by the Appalachian people to address economic and social problems, and the training for the poor in developing countries in how to organize themselves to address issues of poverty. Working from various sources of data, a study of Horton's work was offered as another picture of how qualitative data can be "layered" in the analysis phase through five levels with each level offering a more general level of abstraction, ending in a broad theory that explains the activist's life.

How, then, does this volume of writings speak to us about conducting qualitative leadership studies? It points out a need, asks the reader view both philosophy and methods as important, and highlights some traditional approaches to qualitative data collection, analysis, and quality control as well as several exciting and innovative underutilized approaches. It takes the reader into many useful examples so that the specific workings of a qualitative researcher can be seen, and, most importantly, it provides a new "take" on qualitative inquiry that can help promote emerging forms of research in the field of leadership.

John W. Creswell

University of Nebraska-Lincoln, October 2007

REFERENCES

Crabtree, B. F., & Miller, W. L. (1992). *Doing qualitative research*. Newbury Park, CA: Sage.

Creswell, J. W. (2007). Qualitative inquiry and research design: Choosing among five approaches (2nd ed.). Thousand Oaks, CA: Sage.

Creswell, J. W., & Plano Clark, V. L. (2007). *Designing and conducting mixed methods research*. Thousand Oaks, CA: Sage.

Daymon, C., & Holloway, I. (2002). Qualitative research methods in public relations and marketing communications. London: Rutledge.

Denzin, N. K., & Lincoln, Y. S. (2005). *The Sage handbook of qualitative research* (3rd ed.). Thousand Oaks, CA: Sage.

Hatch, J. A. (2002). *Doing qualitative research in education settings*. Albany, NY: State University of New York Press.

Husserl, E. (1970). *The crisis of European sciences and transcendental phenomenology* (D. Carr, Trans.). Evanston, IL: Northwestern University Press.

Lincoln, Y. S., & Guba, E. G. (1985). *Naturalistic inquiry*. Beverly Hills, CA: Sage.

Lincoln, Y. S., & Guba, E. G. (2000). Paradigmatic controversies, contradictions, and emerging confluences. In N. K. Denzin & Y. S. Lincoln (Eds.), *Handbook of qualitative research* (2nd ed, pp. 163–188). Thousand Oaks, CA: Sage.

Marshall, C., & Rossman, G. B. (2006). *Designing qualitative research* (4th ed.). Thousand Oaks, CA: Sage.

Maxwell, J. (2005). *Qualitative research design: An interactive approach* (2nd ed.). Thousand Oaks, CA: Sage.

Morse, J. M. (2003). Principles of mixed methods and multimethod research design. In A. Tashakkori & C. Teddlie (Eds.), *Handbook of mixed methods in social & behavioral research* (pp. 189–208). Thousand Oaks, CA: Sage.

Shaw, I., & Gould, N. (2001). *Qualitative research in social work*. London: Sage.

Part I

FOUNDATIONS OF QUALITATIVE RESEARCH

1

QUALITATIVE RESEARCH AS PARADIGM

INTRODUCTION

Leadership Research: Past Traditions and Current Trends

Historically, leadership research has been grounded in the objectivist, positivist, quantitative paradigm since the inception of leadership studies as a field of scholarly inquiry. Both the work of Sir Francis Galton conducted in the study of individual differences more than 100 years ago and the emergence of social psychology, particularly the study of small group behavior, more than 80 years are often viewed as the beginnings of leadership studies. Leadership as a topic and as an academic discipline has received attention in thousands of empirical studies, theoretical work, books, and popular press articles, yet it can be argued that we still do not understand leadership particularly well (Barker, 1997). Burns (1978) concurs when he states that we know too much about leaders and far too little about leadership.

During the history of the discipline, research has relied heavily, at times almost exclusively, on the traditional social science repertoire of quantitative methodologies to help us identify and understand leadership problems and develop solutions that can be scientifically tested, verified, and replicated. Positivism ruled along with the assumption that knowledge can be conventionally summarized in the form of time- and context-free generalizations. According to Lee (1991), the positivistic approach involves "the manipulation of theoretical propositions, using the rules of formal logic and hypothetico-deductive reasoning so the theoretical propositions satisfy four requirements: falsifiability, logical consistency, explanatory power, and survival or the ability to survive attempts aimed at its disconfirmation through controlled empirical testing"

(p. 351). Hesse (1980) points out that the basic posture of the positivistic paradigm is both reductionistic and deterministic.

Recently, the quantitative paradigm has come under scrutiny and resulted in a call for alternative paradigms and methods of inquiry that are resonating in the leadership research community. The interest in qualitative research has been fostered by a general dissatisfaction with the type of information provided by quantitative techniques (Van Maanen, 1988b; Weber, 2004). This dissatisfaction stems from several sources: the complexity of multivariate research methods, the distribution restrictions inherent in the use of these methods (e.g., multivariate normality), the large sample sizes these methods require, and the difficulty understanding and interpreting the results of studies in which complex quantitative methods are applied (Cepeda & Martin, 2005, p. 851). Although quantitative methods are ideal for testing hypotheses, especially with large samples, permitting the development of sophisticated causal models and allowing for replicability across settings, they are poorly suited to help us understand the meanings leaders and followers ascribe to significant events in their lives and the success or failure of their organizations. As a result, until fairly recently, qualitative studies in leadership remained relatively rare (at least as measured by published journal articles), especially within North America. Instead, the paradigm that still guides leadership research is the quantitative model heavily subscribing to survey and questionnaire research as the dominant data collection method.

However, quantitatively generated leadership descriptors often fail to lead to an understanding of the deeper structures of the phenomena we study. Several authors (e.g., Bryman, Stephens, & à Campo, 1996; Conger, 1998; Steiner, 2002) argue that qualitative studies must play a more pivotal role in management and leadership research. The study leadership is particularly well suited for qualitative analyses because of multidisciplinary nature of the field which has to be more open about paradigmatic assumptions, methodological preferences, and ideological commitments than many single disciplines. Moreover, the study of leadership is context-dependent. Stripping qualitative research (and leadership) of its context, according to Guba and Lincoln (1994), through appropriate controls or randomization may increase the theoretical rigor of a study but "...detracts from its relevance, that is, applicability or generalizability, because their outcomes can be properly applied only in other similarly truncated or contextually stripped situations (another laboratory, for example). Qualitative data, it is argued, can redress the imbalance by providing contextual information" (p. 106).

However, despite the talk of a paradigm shift away from logical positivism, with its emphasis on reification of verifiable data, utilization of reductionistic research methods, and postulation of a priori hypotheses that can be subjected to statistical analyses, qualitative leadership research is only increasing at a slow rate. This will continue to be the case as long as the widespread conviction persists that only quantitative data are ultimately valid and of high quality (Sechrest, 1992). Yet, it is widely recognized that rigid adherence to the dominant paradigm leads us to become prisoners of that paradigm and can result in dysfunctional consequences. For example, managers who applied the total quality management (TQM) model in the 1970s were pioneers and trailblazers; if they were still doing TQM in the 1980s, it was a good idea; but TQM in 1990s was corporate suicide. Likewise, in the early days of the evolution of leadership studies as an academic discipline when the knowledge base was narrow and drawn largely from related disciplines such as social psychology and sociology, quantitative research advanced the field in quantum leaps. Almost a century later, it has lost some of its luster as the field of leadership has matured and radical paradigm shift at this time can no longer come solely from the application of quantitative methods.

Qualitative leadership studies, when conducted with the same degree of rigor and concern for validity and quality, have several distinct advantages over quantitative approaches by offering more opportunities to explore leadership phenomena in significant depth, do so longitudinally, and answer "why" types of questions about leadership as opposed to "how" and "what" types of questions answered by quantitative research. Moreover, according to Steiner (2002), qualitative research has the potential to restore respect for ontological integrity and the capacity to replace esoterica with relevance.

Although quantitative research in leadership studies, as evidenced by articles published in top-tier journals such as the *Leadership Quarterly* (*LQ*), *Academy of Management Journal*, *Journal of Applied Psychology*, or *the Administrative Science Quarterly* (*ASQ*), will almost certainly retain the preoccupation with quantification, there is reason for optimism as there has been a surge in qualitative research on leadership. The upward trend in qualitative research began after the *ASQ* published a widely cited and influential special issue in 1979. In his editorial, Van Maanen (1979b), referring to the monopolistic grip that the quantitative paradigm has held on the production of knowledge in organizations, noted that

> There are however a number of organization theorists beginning to question the wisdom of allowing Gresham's Law to take its course. There is a growing concern about where quantitative techniques are carrying us. For example, questions have been raised about the extent to which our theories are guiding our research and concern has been expressed about the degree to which our procedures have become so ritualized that the necessary connection between measure and concept has been vanished (p. 521).

In this special issue, Van Maanen argued compellingly for the unrealized value of qualitative research and called on organizational scientists to utilize more qualitative techniques. This special issue of the *ASQ* was instrumental in facilitating the legitimacy of qualitative research and encouraged researchers to reconsider unflattering views of qualitative research. In the years following that influential call, organizational researchers, including leadership scholars, have responded favorable to Van Maanen's call. Since the publication of the *ASQ* special issue, qualitative research has experienced a boost in several leadership-related disciplines such as political science and sociology. Speaking for the field of leadership studies, Lowe and Gardner (2000) content analyzed the articles published in *LQ* from 1990 to 1999. The authors reported that qualitative studies, which made up 40 articles published during the nine-year period, were used with roughly half the frequency of quantitative studies with 78 quantitative articles published during the same period. The most frequent qualitative methods found in those 40 articles were content analysis ($n = 20$ or 53 percent), followed by case studies ($n = 17$ or 45 percent) and grounded theory ($n = 9$ or 24 percent). Between 1980 and the time of this writing, there has been a renewed interest in qualitative research readily indexed by the publication of numerous textbooks on qualitative methods (e.g., Creswell, 1994; 1998; Flick, 2002; Mason, 2002; Silverman, 2004), special journal issues on qualitative methods (e.g., *Management Decisions*, 2005(2)), review articles (e.g., Bryman, 2004; Lee, Mitchell, & Sablynski, 1999), and increased number of presentations on qualitative research at national and international conferences. Additionally, journals traditionally known for strong quantitative research, such as the *Journal of Applied Psychology* or *Organizational Research Methods*, now occasionally publish qualitative research (e.g., Bligh, Kohles, & Meindl, 2004a; Sandberg, 2005). Although there has been a shift toward the deployment of qualitative methods, the benefits of qualitative research on leadership have not been fully exploited.

WHAT IS QUALITATIVE RESEARCH?

What is qualitative research? Many people automatically assume that qualitative is simply defined as research that does not employ numbers or statistical procedures and use the omnibus term *qualitative research* to refer to approaches to research that rely on nonquantitative (or nonstatistical) modes of data collection and analysis (Prasad & Prasad, 2002). However, as will be seen later in this chapter and the chapters that follow, such a definition is overly simplistic and naïve when, in fact, qualitative research is far more complex and controversial than one might initially assume.

First, it is difficult to find an unambiguous, definitive statement as to what qualitative research is. This is, in part, because as Lancy (1993) points out to the fact that "... topic, theory, and methodology are usually closely interrelated in qualitative research" (p. 3). The qualitative paradigm embraces a diverse array of methodologies that can be mapped on a continuum ranging from purely qualitative to highly quantitative. For example, grounded theory (Chapter 7) and phenomenology (Chapter 8) are examples of qualitative methods almost purely anchored in the verbal tradition, whereas some forms of content analyses (Chapter 4), historiometry (Chapter 7), or mixed methods (Chapter 6) that triangulate qualitative and quantitative approaches rely heavily on traditional statistical analyses such as quantitative coding techniques or factor analyses.

Defining Qualitative Research

Denzin and Lincoln (1994) define qualitative research as follows:

> Qualitative research is multi-method in focus, involving and interpretive, naturalistic approach to its subject matter. This means that qualitative researchers study things in their natural settings, attempting to make sense of or interpret phenomena in terms of the meanings people bring to them. Qualitative research involves the studied use and collection of a variety of empirical materials—case study, personal experience, introspective, life story, interview, observational, historical, interactional, and visual texts that describe routine and problematic moments and meanings in individuals' lives (p. 1).

Creswell (1994) proposed the following definition:

> Qualitative research is an inquiry process of understanding based on distinct methodological traditions of inquiry that explore a social or human problem. The researcher build a complex, holistic picture, analyzes words, reports detailed views of informants, and conducts the study in a natural setting (pp. 1–2).

Definitions of "qualitative" often draw on specific epistemological positions, such as postmodernism, interpretivism, critical theory, and constructivism (Gebhart, 1999), which contribute to the many variations we find in definitions of qualitative research. In addition, there are geographical variations. For example, European scholars have long favored qualitative or ideographic methods over the nomothetic or quantitative approaches prevalent in the United States and embrace their own definitions. Therefore, the variety of epistemological positions and geographic variations in what "qualitative" means complicate the process of arriving at a widely agreed upon definition of qualitative research. Nevertheless, Holloway and Todres (2003) call our attention to the many elements of qualitative research shared between different approaches when they state

> such an overlap of epistemological, aesthetic, ethical, and procedural concerns can encourage a fairly generic view of qualitative research—a "family" approach in which the similarities are considered more important than the differences, and where the notion of flexibility becomes an important value and quest (p. 346).

Despite the coming of age of qualitative research, there are still numerous challenges qualitative researchers face when promoting their work (Prasad & Prasad, 2002). Cassell, Symon, Buehring, and Johnson (2006) in an empirical study based on 45 in-depth qualitative interviews with different stakeholder groups, including journal editors, practitioners, and academics involved in doctoral programs, identified five specific challenges:

1. Getting qualitative research past epistemological gatekeepers (journal editors, reviewers, and conferences committees). As Eisner (2001) pointed out, "there are still editorial boards and proposal review committees that look at all forms of qualitative research as reconnaissance efforts that precede 'real' research" (p. 137).

2. Conforming to journal editorial criteria and constraints generates pressures on researchers to justify their methods according to (sometimes) inappropriate (positivist) criteria such as objectivity, reliability, and validity.

3. The lack of exposure to alternatives in management (and leadership) publications.

4. Presently, there are no leadership or management journals solely dedicated to publishing qualitative research.

5. The lack of doctoral level qualitative research methods courses.

The authors also reported that for many interviewees in their study, credibility of qualitative research meant quantification, measurement, statistical analysis, rigor, and systematizations. One interviewee was quoted as saying, "but until some measures are in place, then all it is, is an interesting story" (p. 296). Explaining the poor representation of qualitative research in many social science journals, scholars typically refer to the inherent complexity and time-consuming nature of qualitative research, as well as the apparent incompatibility between the fundamental premises of qualitative research and the epistemological foundations of established social science journals (Pauwels & Mattyssens, 2004, p. 125).

Miller, Nelson, and Moore (1998) collected data over an eight-year period from over 300 expert and novice qualitative researchers—attendees at qualitative research conferences, doctoral students, authors of qualitative journal articles, members of dissertation committees—who were caught in the politics of epistemology and "strained against traditional positivistic assumptions embedded in the prevailing research language, customs, and processes of the contexts in which they worked" (p. 383). These researchers told stories from the trenches reflecting various types of disruption resulting from their attempts to conduct qualitative research. These disruptions ranged from the common scarcity of experienced qualitative advisors in doctoral programs and forced applications of positivist assumptions to qualitative research projects resulting in disruptions due to delays in the publication, funding, and tenure and promotion processes.

For example, respondents remarked that getting their research published was disrupted by excessive criticisms of lack of generalizability in the study submitted for publication. In such conflicted contexts, researchers at all career stages were often forced to make trade-offs, some of which affected the quality of their research. In contexts where resistance to qualitative research was active and deliberate, the stories suggested a deeply felt schism influencing both researchers and their work. Miller et al. (1998) noted that as researchers prepared for professional lives amidst paradigm clashes, they internalized time-intensive survival strategies and sometimes the conflicted epistemologies of their sociopolitical contexts (p. 398). They concluded that the quality, production, completion, and publication of qualitative research are affected by epistemological politics.

Finally, there is the challenge of synthesizing diverse bodies of qualitative leadership research into a coherent whole and accumulating a knowledge base that can serve both the academic and practitioner communities to overcome the current dislocation of research from practice. Effective synthesis of qualitative research on leadership can provide an effective means of producing an actionable knowledge base (Denyer & Tranfield, 2006). In quantitative research, techniques for synthesis exist in the form of meta-analytic techniques (Glass, 1976; Hunter & Schmidt, 1990; Lipsey & Wilson, 2001) which adhere to an explicit and reproducible methodology whereas qualitative research-comparable methods for systematic reviews are just beginning to be developed and have not been applied to leadership research. For example, Denyer and Tranfield (2006) discuss narrative synthesis, a systematic review technique that focuses on how studies addressing a different aspect of the same phenomenon can be narratively summarized and built up to provide a bigger picture of the phenomenon (p. 219). Applying this method to an aspect of leadership, for example, leadership failures, narrative analysis might look at personality variables, organizational context, and trigger events such as personal trauma to narratively build a composite of leadership failure. Rumrill and Fitzgerald (2001) argue that there are four potential objectives of a narrative analysis: to develop or advance theoretical models; to identify, explain, and provide perspectives on complicated or controversial issues; to provide information that can assist practitioners in advancing "best" practice; and to present new perspectives on important and emergent issues. These are critically important goals for leadership researchers. But when it comes to applying narrative synthesis to qualitative research on leadership, the proof will be in the pudding.

But whatever the specific definition, as Labuschagne (2003) notes, most methods under the qualitative umbrella imply an emphasis on processes and meanings that are rigorously examined but not measured in terms of quantity, amount, or frequency. Qualitative data provide depth and detail through direct quotation and careful, thick description of persons, situations (contexts), events, interactions, and observed behaviors. Unlike quantitative researchers who seek causal determination, prediction, and generalization of findings, qualitative researchers seek instead illumination, under-standing, and meaning making. Qualitative analysis seeks to capture the richness of people's experience in their own terms. It involves the nonnumerical organization of data to discover patterns, themes, and qualities found in field notes, interviews, tran-scripts, diaries, and cases. Qualitative research can refer methodologically to a set of techniques or philosophically to a paradigm.

CHARACTERISTICS OF QUALITATIVE RESEARCH

Qualitative research is characterized by a set of distinguishing features that sets this tradition apart from quantitative approaches. Often, qualitative research, which relies on interpretations and is admittedly value-bound, is considered to be subjective as opposed to the objective nature of quantitative research. In the eyes of quantita-tive researchers, subjectivity renders research unreliable, invalid, and nonreplicable. However, numerous researchers (e.g., Eisner, 1991; Lincoln & Guba, 1985) call into question the true objectivity of statistical measures and, indeed, the possibility of ever attaining pure objectivity. Patton (1990) argues that the terms objectivity and subjectivity have become "ideological ammunition in the paradigm debate." The author prefers to "avoid using either word and to stay out of the futile debates about objectivity versus subjectivity debate" (p. 55). In addition to the objectivity versus subjectivity dimension, a number salient features distinguish qualitative from qualitative research.

First, in contrast to the deductive research process embraced by quantitative research methods, qualitative research is predominantly inductive and conducted in natural settings. Second, strategies, logics, and purposes of sampling clearly differentiate qua-litative and quantitative methods. In qualitative research, sample size does matter but does not take on the same importance as in quantitative research where large sample sizes are the drivers of many statistical analyses such as factor analysis or linear structural equation modeling techniques and are needed to generalize from the sample to the underlying population. In quantitative studies, the effect of increasing sample sizes is to reduce sampling error. Qualitative research, on the other hand, is inappropri-ate for estimating quantities. Yet, the importance of sample size in qualitative research is not totally irrelevant. How many individual interviews or ethnographic observations are needed? Does a researcher miss something by only analyzing five organizational documents? How many bodies or segments of text have to be coded in a content analysis? How many respondents should be assembled into a focus group?

Instead of using random sampling as is the goal in quantitative research, qualitative research employs *purposive or theoretical sampling*, meaning the researcher intentionally selects participants who can contribute an in-depth, information-rich understanding of the phenomenon under investigation. Consequently, the samples used in qualitative research are often not inclusive, but this lack of inclusiveness should not be taken as detracting from the value of the research, especially as generalizability of research findings is often not a concern within the qualitative research tradition (Oberle, 2002). In many qualitative methods, the answer to the sample size question is found in the concept of saturation or the point in course of a study when adding another data element such as another interview, participant observation, or narrative story does not add new information. In other words, redundancy in participants' responses emerges and negates the need to collect additional data. The three application chapters (Chapters 10, 11, and 12) illustrate the concept of saturation as the decision-making rule for terminating data collection.

Third, qualitative data are derived from the participants' perspective. At the heart of qualitative research, the authentic voice of the informant must be represented. Participants and researchers collaborate in the design, data collection, and interpretation to arrive at a "story" that reflects the voice of participants. In collaborative inquiry, both researchers and research participants come to conceive an issue through shared perceptions. Research participants who have experienced a particular phenomenon report this experience in ways they find validating knowing that the researcher accepts and respects their reports as a valuable contribution to increased understanding of the phenomenon. Moreover, researchers, with all of their prejudices, bias, and professional baggage are the primary data collection instrument in a qualitative study.

Fourth, qualitative designs are flexible (i.e., reflexive) and can and should be changed to match the dynamics of the evolving research process. For example, after collecting semistructured interviews to elucidate dynamics involved in leadership failure, the researcher discovers that the interview protocol he or she has designed is missing an important question which is added and included in subsequent interviews. Therefore, interview protocols, observation techniques, and modes of analysis are rarely standardized and run counter to positivist notions of control, reliability, and replicability.

The role of the researcher in qualitative research is also considerably different from that of the quantitative investigator who serves in a role of authority and subject matter expert. As Redwood and Todres (2006) point out in a quantitative study, the boundaries between the researcher and the researched are fairly clear with the researcher following the research protocol and the participant being the recipient of the protocol. In a qualitative study, on the other hand, the participant is an active co-creator of the research process, is empowered to change the course of the research protocol, and is the owner of the knowledge that is co-constituted by the researcher and the participant. Finally, qualitative research reports are descriptive, incorporating expressive language and the "presence of voice in the text" (Eisner, 1991, p. 36).

Strengths of Qualitative Methods

Qualitative research methods add value to the study of leadership because they provide extensive, thick description of a phenomenon (Geertz, 1973). The ability of offering thick, detailed description of the leadership issue or problem under investigation helps us to capture multiple voices and perspectives. It also highlights the concern with the emic or insider view of a phenomenon and the flexibility to discern and detect unexpected insights during the research process (Lundberg, 1976). Qualitative methods bring the researcher closer to his or her informants instead of having to rely on more remote, inferential empirical materials (Denzin & Lincoln, 1994). Instead of treating the researcher as an invisible other, a neutral instrument whose personal characteristics do not significantly shape the responses of research participants, the qualitative researcher's individual standpoint and its impact on the research are an integral part of the qualitative research process. Qualitative methods focus on the lived experience of the research participants and their critical voices. They become a source of empowerment that can be seen as reflecting alternative scientific paradigms by acknowledging reality as being filtered through local, historical, contextual, and multiple lenses instead of emphasizing the importance of scientific objectivity and interpersonal detachment. They appreciate, emphasize, and promote the role of context. For example, Leavy and Wilson (1984) view leaders as tenants of time and context. Similarly, Pettigrew and Whipp (1991) insist that leadership is acutely context sensitive. Steiner (2002) notes that management researchers regularly reduce people to abstract "employees" by detaching them from their holistic contexts, making it difficult to re-integrate into the complex setting of a real organization populated by real people with lives beyond the organization and their jobs. Klenke (1996) stated that contexts shape the practice of leadership and determine what leaders can do in any given context. For example, in political systems, leaders are elected or appointed, whereas in grassroots, organizations leaders often emerge as a function of a crisis. Finally, qualitative methods provide researchers with conceptual road maps of previously uncharted territory and offer effective means to investigate symbolic dimensions (Morgan & Smircich, 1980), which are critical in leadership research.

QUALITATIVE RESEARCH AS PARADIGM

Paradigms occupy a central role in social science methodology. Thomas Kuhn, one of the most prominent historians and philosophers of science of the twentieth century, is commonly regarded as the progenitor of the concept of "paradigm" as it applies to the history and philosophy of science (Kuhn, 1962). Paradigm comes from the Greek, paradeigma, meaning a pattern, model, or plan. With the publication of Kuhn's *The Structure of Scientific Revolution*, the notion of a paradigm or worldview as an overarching framework that organizes our whole approach to being in the world has become commonplace. Reese (1996) in the *Dictionary of Philosophy and Religion* notes that

Kuhn holds that scientific theories are constructed around basis paradigms—for example, the solar system as a model of an atom—and that shifts in scientific theory require new paradigms. Kuhn used the term paradigm in a number of different ways but in the broadest way treated paradigms as worldviews or all-encompassing ways of experiencing and thinking about the world, including beliefs about morals, values, and aesthetics. The author observed that there is no paradigm-free way of looking at social phenomena. When our ways of looking are incommensurable, we can look at the same places, at the same things, and see them differently (Bochner, 2000).

Kuhn argued that one central characteristic of a paradigm is that it can attract an enduring group of adherents away from competing modes of scientific inquiry. Moreover, a paradigm, according to Kuhn, is not expected to result in a final answer shared by all members of a discipline, but instead it is "sufficiently open-ended to leave all sorts of problems for the redefined group of practitioners to solve" (1970, p. 10).

Denzin and Lincoln (1994), in the context of qualitative research, present a paradigm as

> A set of basic beliefs (or metaphysics) that deals with ultimates or first principles. It deals with a *worldview* that defines, for its holder, the nature of the "world," an individual's place in it and the range of possible relationships to that world and its parts, as, for example, cosmologies and theologies do. The beliefs are basic in the sense that they must be accepted simply on faith (however well argued); there is no way to establish their ultimate truthfulness. If there were, the philosophical debates reflected in these pages would have been resolved millennia ago (p. 107).

Creswell (1998) also endorses a definition of paradigms as worldviews when he states:

> Qualitative researchers approach their studies with a certain paradigm or worldview, a basic set of assumptions that guide their inquiries (p. 74).

Applying the concept of paradigm to leadership, in the history of the discipline, we have evidenced a number of paradigm shifts including trait (Kirkpatrick & Locke, 1991; Stogdill, 1974), behavior (e.g., Stogdill & Coons, 1957), and contingency theories (Fiedler, 1967). For the last 20 years, transactional/transformational theory (Bass, 1985) has been the poster child of leadership theory. Developed over two decades when organizations were significantly different from what they are today, I share with numerous other scholars the conviction the leadership studies as a field of scientific inquiry is on the cusp of a paradigm shift. Emerging models, but not radically new theories, include authentic leadership (e.g., Avolio & Gardner, 2005; Gardner, Avolio, Luthans, May, & Walumba, 2005, Klenke, 2005; 2007a), servant leadership (e.g., Greenleaf, 1977), stewardship (Block, 1993; Davis, Schoorman, & Donaldson, 1997), spiritual leadership (Fry, 2003; 2005), and zeitgeist leadership (Mayo & Nohira, 2005), are being discussed in the literature which, at least to some extent, reflect the search for a new paradigm that is congruent with twenty-first century organizational contexts and structures.

When viewed as paradigm, the specific research methods of qualitative inquiry reflect an underlying philosophy of science, one that eschews the traditional positivist belief in an objective reality that can only be understood through detached scientific inquiry. The posture of "not knowing" is a hallmark of the qualitative paradigm. According to this view, qualitative methods are consistent with and reflective of a social constructivist perspective, in which reality is best understood by studying the ways in which people perceive, experience, and make sense of the events of their lives. Consequently, scientific objectivity is regarded as an impossible stance as our values and biases permeate all aspects of the research process. Interpersonal detachment is seen as an obstacle to the sharing of personal beliefs; data are considered to be embedded separately from the specific contexts in which they are gathered; and the research process is ideally based on collaboration and mutual learning of the researcher and the researched (Banyard & Miller, 1998, p. 487). Qualitative research as paradigm presupposes that design choices, data collection, and analyses are inherently linked to paradigmatic assumptions.

Historically, there have been two major paradigms in the social and behavioral sciences: (1) logical positivism, which dominated the field from the 1950s through the early 1980s but continues to have a strong hold on certain disciplines including leadership studies, and (2) postpositivism or postmodernism, which may be used as a shorthand descriptor of qualitative paradigms such as constructivism, interpretivism, and critical theory. The hallmarks of the positivistic paradigm, as noted earlier, include objectivity, reliability, validity, generalizability, replicability, and falsifiability. The latter concept assumes that there are inaccuracies in the empirical content of theoretical propositions that can be detected only through contradictory observations—observations that disconfirm a prediction and thereby falsify the theory from which the prediction follows. The postpositivist paradigm, on the other hand, emphasizes the importance of reflectiveness about one's assumption. Postmodernism encourages attempts to deconstruct taken-for-granted meaning by exploring contradictions in the scientific literature and highlights the importance of historical, cultural, and political forces which influence the research process.

PHILOSOPHICAL ASSUMPTIONS UNDERLYING QUALITATIVE PARADIGMS

I suggest, as have many others, that it is not possible to conduct rigorous research without understanding its philosophical underpinnings. In qualitative and quantitative research, the researcher's philosophical assumptions about ontology, epistemology, methodology, and axiology are critical in framing the research process and require transparency. Each paradigm, positivist and postmodern, makes assumption about the nature of reality or ontology, how knowledge is constructed, or epistemology and assumes that the values (axiology) a researcher brings to selection of method, participants, data collection, analysis, and interpretation influence the research process. Thus, most discussions of research paradigms focus on the tripartite linkages between ontology, epistemology, and methodology. Others, such as pragmatism, also include the role of ethical and moral values in researchers' worldviews under the heading of axiology.

Many paradigm discussions incorporate the concept of "incommensurability" of paradigms or the claim that different research paradigms produce incommensurable kinds of knowledge arguing that the radically different assumptions about the nature of reality and truth made it impossible for researchers to operate under different paradigmatic assumptions. Thus, the belief in the incommensurability of paradigms means that accepting one paradigm such as positivism requires the rejection of other paradigms such as constructivism or interpretivism. Incompatibilities at the ontological level imply further incompatibilities regarding epistemological and methodological issues. Although the concept of incommensurability of paradigms is often attributed to Kuhn's (1962) original work, in postscripts to later editions of his work (Kuhn, 1996; 2000), he explicitly rejected the claim "that proponent of incommensurable theories cannot communicate with each other at all" (Kuhn, 1996, pp. 198–199).

Lincoln and Guba (1994) made important contributions pointing out differences between competing paradigms in qualitative inquiry and were instrumental in articulating alternatives to positivism. Their early comparisons (Lincoln & Guba, 1985; 1988), resting on the familiar trilogy of ontology, epistemology, and methodology, were between positivism and a competing paradigm called "naturalistic inquiry," which later became known as constructivism and occasionally interpretivism. Later, the authors later added critical theory, postpositivism, and participatory research as competing paradigms (Lincoln & Guba, 2000). Their later work does show some overlap between competing paradigms. The authors offer a compromise allowing for some permeability between paradigms as long as it does not involve key ontological assumptions. Although their work has been criticized because it privileged ontology over epistemology and methodology and the addition of other alternative paradigm such as realism and pragmatism (e.g., De Waal, 2005; Heron & Reason, 1997; Sayer, 2000; Wicks & Freeman, 1998), their work remains central to our understanding of qualitative paradigms.

Ontology

Ontology addresses the first paradigmatic question, "What is the nature of reality?" To ask "What is the nature of reality?" as a philosophic question about reality affects the way we do research or engage in other forms of inquiry. Qualitative researchers assume multiple and dynamic realities that are context-dependent and embrace an ontology that denies the existence of an external reality. According to Searle (1995), external reality means one that exists outside and independent of our interpretations of it. These individual interpretations are deeply embedded in a rich contextual web that cannot be readily generalized to other settings. Hence, qualitative researchers do not assume that there is a single unitary reality apart from our perceptions. Instead, they emphasize a relativistic ontology that posits that there is no objective reality but endorse multiple realities socially constructed by individuals from within their own contextual interpretation.

Epistemology

Our view of the nature of reality affects our beliefs about the nature of knowledge. Epistemology addresses the second paradigmatic question, "How do we know what we know?" What is the relationship between the knower and what is known? Epistemology is the branch of philosophy that deals with the origin, nature, and limits of human knowledge which focuses on the relationship between the knower and the known. Epistemology also deals with ways of knowing and the researcher's belief system about the nature of knowledge, such as beliefs about the certainty, structure, complexity, and sources of knowledge. When we are trying to understand the nature of knowledge and beliefs and the connections between beliefs and evidence, we are in the realm of philosophy. It is important to recognize that every researcher brings some set of epistemological assumptions into the research process (even if they are not aware of them) and that these assumptions influence how they understand and interpret their data. Schommer (1990) proposed that personal epistemology can be conceptualized as an epistemological belief system that includes beliefs about the nature of knowledge, namely beliefs about the structure of knowledge, the stability of knowledge, and the nature of learning including the speed of learning and the ability to learn. Moreover, it is possible for qualitative researchers to work in different epistemological traditions, such as pragmatism or constructivism, which may compete with one another. For example, a qualitative researcher who has adopted pragmatism as the defining paradigm and is investigating leadership failures is unlikely to ask theory-based questions. Instead, the researcher is interested in concrete and practical questions that resulted in executive derailment. A researcher working in the constructivism tradition, on the other hand, is interested in perceptions, "truth" explanations, beliefs, and worldviews of failed leaders. Finally, the researcher who believes that executive derailment is a leadership problem that has both theoretical and practical underpinning and consequences and who works in both paradigms is likely to experience the tensions generated by them.

Epistemological debates deal with issues of the possibility and desirability of objectivity, subjectivity, causality, validity, and generalizability (Patton, 2002, p. 134). Epistemology also deals with the relationship between the researcher and the researched. In addition, most epistemologies imply a moral stance toward the world and the researcher (Christians, 2005). Assumptions about the nature of reality (ontology) affect epistemology by placing the researcher either apart from what is researched (traditional scientific research which is usually quantitative) or interacting with what is researched (naturalistic, qualitative inquiry). According to Olson (1995), understanding the differences in epistemology among research designs begins primarily as a philosophical exercise, the question of whether there is one knowable reality or that there are multiple realities.

Finally, epistemology is intimately related to both ontology and methodology; ontology involves the philosophy of realty, epistemology addresses how we come to know that reality while methodology identifies the particular practices used to attain knowledge of it. Thus, ontological and epistemological assumptions are translated into specific methodological strategies.

Axiology

Axiology refers to the role of values and ethics in research. The traditional scientific approach seeks research that is value free and unbiased. However, all research is value laden and biased (Cederblom & Paulsen, 2001). Values are derived from disciplinary allegiances including predispositions toward disciplinary-related methodologies as "methodology is inevitably interwoven with and emerges from the nature of particular disciplines" (Lincoln & Guba, 2000, p. 164) as well as the personal history and research experiences of the investigator. The beliefs and values are made explicit by the researcher so that respondents and consumers of research know the context in which the research was conducted and have been exposed to critical examination.

Qualitative approaches recognize the impact of the researcher's values and through reflexivity seek to actively report the values and biases of the researcher as well as the value nature of data gathered (Creswell, 1994). The value system a researcher brings to his or her study informs the research methodology. Values are a part of the "basic beliefs" that undergird and affect the entire research process: choice of problems, guiding paradigm, rhetorical framework, data-gathering method, analysis strategy, and even the presentation format of the findings (Denzin & Lincoln, 2005). Even the philosophic roots of theory are value driven and shaped by the researcher's worldview (Cederblom & Paulsen, 2001).

The question of value was not included in Guba and Lincoln's (1994) definition of an inquiry paradigm. Other researchers, including this author, however, take the view that the value question is paramount in definitions of paradigms because the axiological question deals with values of being, about what human states are to be valued simply by virtue of what they are (Heron & Reason, 1997). Moreover, values play a significant role in the study of leadership especially as evidenced, for example, in values-based approaches to leadership.

Methodology

Epistemological and ontological assumptions are then translated into distinct meth-odologies. Methodology addresses the question "How should we study the world?" Methodological debates address issues of types of sampling, data, design, and analysis and the consequences that result from methodological choices. Methodology reflects the beliefs about the knowledge and values inherent in the paradigm within which the study is conducted and implies a concern and commitment to construct a particular type of knowledge.

Frequently, the terms methodology and method are used synonymously or are used in an inconsistent manner. For example, Woolcott (2002) asserts that participant obser-vation is at the core of all qualitative research approaches, whereas Morse and Field (1995) define it merely as a data collection technique. However, the distinction between methodology and method is important here because methodology is not a toolbox of different methods from which the researcher selects some on the basis of personal or

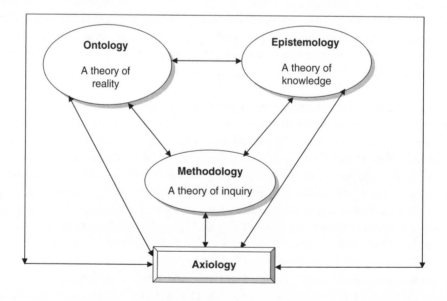

Figure 1-1   The research triangle

social preferences. Instead, methodology refers to philosophical issues related to epistemology, an integrated structure of epistemological processes concerning how we know what we know. Issues of research practice, on the other hand, are termed method (Bryman, 1984). Therefore, instead of an amalgamation of methods and techniques, qualitative leadership researchers need to develop epistemologically and methodologically congruent standards to frame their research.

Fig. 1-1 represents the four core elements of a research paradigm.

Major Research Paradigms in Qualitative Research

For decades, scholars have mapped paradigms, examining distinct sets of assumptions and their impact on researchers' worldview. Despite many variations, such maps polarize paradigms into seemingly incommensurable sets of ideologies, ontologies, and epistemologies. Some paradigms promote a selective focus because they are certain of their "truth" claims because such privileging is deemed a moral responsibility (e.g., critical theory as advocated by Parker, 1995). Others such as critical theory explicitly incorporate a political agenda into the research process as seen in feminist, Marxist, and critical race theory (e.g., Delgado, 1995; Pizarro, 1998; Tate, 1997). Under the umbrella of these latter approaches, research is conducted for the purpose of inducing radical change.

In this section, I discuss four major paradigms that underlie many qualitative research methods, which are presented in Table 1-1. I have added positivism for comparative purposes as many paradigm discussions are set up in opposition to their quantitative counterparts. There are a number of alternative paradigms discussed in the literature which have been intentionally excluded because they lack paradigmatic clarity or are closely aligned with positivism. For example, critical theory was excluded because this paradigm is often used as a blanket term denoting a set of alternative paradigms including feminism, materialism, and participatory inquiry (Denzin & Lincoln, 1994). Similarly, realism which assumes that we can study phenomena such as leadership so that our findings correspond as closely as possible to the real world is closely aligned with positivism. However, realism, as a philosophical paradigm, has elements of both positivism and constructivism and can serve as the "middle ground" between the poles of positivism and constructivism (Healy & Perry, 2000). Realist qualitative researchers adhere to positivist quality criteria such as objectivity, reliability, and validity (e.g., Ragin, 2000). However, realizing that absolute objectivity in the pure positivist tradition is impossible to attain, qualitative researchers working within this paradigm are prepared to admit and deal with imperfections in a phenomenologically messy and methodologically imperfect world. Yet they believe that objectivity is worth striving for (Patton, 2002).

Table 1-1 Comparisons of the major qualitative Paradigms and associated research methods

Paradigm	Ontology	Epistemology	Research methods
Constructivism	Relativistic—reality is socially and experientially based, local and specific in nature	Knowledge consists of mental constructions about which there is relative consensus	Case studies, interviews
Interpretivism	Researcher and reality are inseparable	Knowledge is based on abstract descriptions of meanings and constituted through a person's lived experience	Case studies, interviews phenomenology, ethnography, ethnomethodology
Symbolic interactionism	Researcher and reality are intertwined	Knowledge is created through social interactions and the meanings that arise from them	Grounded theory
Pragmatism	Reality is equivocal, but grounded in terms of language, history, culture	Knowledge is derived from experience; researcher as reconstructor of the subjectively intended and "objective" meaning of the actions of others	Interviews, cases, surveys
Positivism	Reality is objective and apprehendable	Knowledge acquisition is value-neural and stripped of moral content	Surveys, experiments, quasi-experiments

Source: Denzin, 1992; Denzin and Lincoln, 1994; Howe, 1988; Joas, 1993; Tashakkori & Teddlie, 2003a; Wicks & Freeman, 1998.

Although each of these paradigms embraces unique ontological and epistemological assumptions and use different methodologies, there are many similarities that undergird some of them, particularly constructivism and interpretivism. Despite the variety of approaches embedded in different qualitative paradigms, what unites them is their phenomenological base, which stipulates that social actors including researchers, their informants, and their worlds are inextricably coupled through the lived experience or what existential philosophers called "being in the world." Hence, most qualitative paradigms assume that reality is subjective and the knowledge is co-created by the researchers and their participants.

Constructivism

Constructivism or social constructionism begins with the premise that the human world is different from the natural, physical world and therefore must be studied differently (Guba & Lincoln, 1990). The authors are credited with the formulation of a "constructivist paradigm" which they originally discussed under the heading of "naturalistic inquiry" (Lincoln & Guba, 1985). Later, Guba and Lincoln (1989) introduced the term constructivism to refer to a paradigm that replaces the conventional, scientific, or positivist paradigm of inquiry (p. 10). The authors spelled out in detail the ontological, epistemological assumptions and methodologies associated with their approach. According to Guba and Lincoln, the constructivist philosophy is idealist, pluralistic, relativistic, and self-reflective. The social world cannot be described without investigating how people use language, symbols, and meaning to construct social practice. The authors set forth the following primary assumptions about constructivism:

- "Truth" is a matter of consensus among informed and sophisticated constructors, not of correspondence with objective reality.

- "Facts" have no meaning except within some value framework; hence there cannot be an "objective" assessment of any proposition.

- "Causes"and effects do not exist except by imputation.

- Phenomena can only be understood within the context within which they are studied; findings from one context cannot be generalized to another; neither problems nor solutions can be generalized from one setting to another.

- Data derived from constructivist inquiry have neither special status nor legitimation; they simply represent another construction to be taken into account in the move toward consensus (Guba & Lincoln, 1989, pp. 44–45).

Constructivist-qualitative inquiry is distinguished by its emphasis on a holistic treatment of phenomena (Stake, 1995). Accordingly, the constructivist approach sees the world as complex and interconnected. Constructivist researchers value context sensitivity and tend to place considerable emphasis on situational and structural facets of the context, that is, understanding a phenomenon in all its complexities and within its particular environment. This approach contrasts sharply with the positivistic-quantitative approach which may be multivariate but which eliminates all of the unique aspects of the context to apply the results to the largest number of research participants (Strauss, 1987).

Constructivism does not offer a unified paradigm but is made up of a variety of research approaches (Gergen, 1994; Schwandt, 1994) and may include critical theory (Habermas, 1972), ethnomethodology (Atkinson, 1988), symbolic interaction (Mead, 1934), theories of sense making (Weick, 1995), theories of truth (Kvale, 1995) as well as a range of other epistemologies that are in opposition to positivist assumptions. However, despite the great variety of approaches subsumed under constructionism, there are some common threads. Constructionists ascribe to a dualist ontology which implies a division of research objects into two main categories: a subject in itself and an object in itself (Giorgi, 1994). A leadership researcher, for instance, may identify leader and leadership as two separate entities.

Furthermore, constructivism assumes that truth is a particular belief system held in a particular context. Researching this constructed reality depends on interactions between the researcher and the researched, that is, the researcher has to be a "passionate participant" in the research process (Guba & Lincoln, 1994). Constructivists argue that knowledge and truth are created, not discovered. They emphasize the pluralistic and plastic character of reality—pluralistic in the sense that reality can be expressed in a variety of language and symbol systems; plastic in the sense that it can be stretched and shaped to fit the purposeful acts of social actors (Denzin & Lincoln, 1994). According to Bruner (1986), constructivists claim that "contrary to common sense, there is no unique 'real' world that preexists and is independent of human mental activity and human symbolic language" (p. 95). In place of a realistic view of theories and knowledge, constructivism emphasizes the instrumental and practical functions of theory construction and knowledge. Thus, developing theory is a central feature of constructivism (Creswell, 1994).

This paradigm, like most others in qualitative research, emphasizes the world of experience as it is lived and assessed by social actors. It uses inductive analysis and rejects a priori theory as a source of categories for deductive analysis. Guba and Lincoln (1989) note that one of the primary suppositions in constructivism is that phenomena are best understood in context. This means that statistical generalization is not the principal aim of socially constructed knowledge. Instead, the goal is analytical generalization that leads to theory building. It follows that leadership, as a socially constructed phenomenon (Conger, 1998), can be well informed by this paradigm.

Interpretivism

Interpretivism has been traced to the German intellectual tradition of hermeneutics and the "Verstehen" (understanding) tradition in sociology, the phenomenology of Alfred Schutz, and the critiques of scientism and positivism in the social sciences (Schwandt, 1994). The term interpretive is often used as a synonym for qualitative in general when, in fact, it should not. Interpretivists embrace the view that all knowledge, and therefore meaningful reality as such, is contingent upon human practices, being constructed in and out of interactions between human being and their world and developed and transmitted within a social context (Golfashani, 2003). Qualitative research may or may not be interpretive, depending upon the underlying philosophical assumptions of the researcher since classifying epistemologies into positivist, interpretive, and critical, qualitative research can be done with a positivistic, interpretive, or critical stance. What has been called the interpretive paradigm (Burrell & Morgan, 1979) is, in fact, a family of paradigms in which hermeneutics is a major philosophical underpinning.

Interpretivism holds the following views:

- Human beings are not mechanistic and embrace multiple realities which need to be understood in context.

- The social world cannot be described without investigating how people use language, symbols, and meaning to construct social practice.

- No social explanation is complete unless it adequately describes the role of meaning in human actions.

Interpretivists assume that knowledge and meaning are acts of interpretation, hence there is no objective knowledge which can be independent of thinking, reasoning human beings. Additionally, the interpretivist paradigm denies that there is an objective reality independent of the frame of reference of the observer; reality is mind-minded and influenced by the process of observation. It therefore, does not concern itself with the search for broadly applicable laws and rules but rather seeks to produce descriptive analyses that emphasize deep, interpretive understandings of social phenomena such as leadership.

Interpretive researchers assume that the meaning of human action is inherent in that action and that the task of the researcher is to discover meaning (Giddens, 1993). They refuse to play by the rules of positivism. According to Berger and Luckman (1967), interpretive research is committed to the broad philosophy of social construction, which sees reality as a constructed world built in and through meaningful interpretations. The goal of the researcher, therefore, is not to capture some pre-existing or predetermined reality but to understand the process of symbolic "worldmaking" (Schwandt, 1994) or constructing meaning from qualitative data. This ontological and epistemological commitment is the essence of interpretive paradigm.

Furthermore, interpretivists believe that value-free data cannot be obtained, as the researcher uses his or her preconceptions to guide the process of inquiry and interacts with participants. The perceptions of both parties may change and both parties are co-creators in the research process. From an interpretive perspective, there are no benefits in working with large random samples in qualitative studies as these encourage a positivist mentality toward analyzing the data. For example, it becomes all too easy to present very short decontextualized extracts from interviews, for example, rather than exploring how interviewees understand their activities in depth (Travers, 2001). Interpretivists wrestle with maintaining the opposition of subjectivity and objectivity, engagement and objectification (Denzin, 1992; Hammersley, 1989). They celebrate the permanence and priority of the real world of first-person subjective experience (Denzin & Lincoln, 1994). Within the interpretivist paradigm, rather than following the notion of causality as one variable preceding and causing another, interpretivism sees relationships as more complex and fluid with reciprocal rather than unidirectional directions of influence. Finally, interpretive researchers, like many other qualitative investigators, contextualize their studies by setting them into their social and historical context so that the reader can see how the current situation under investigation shapes the research process. As Parmenides observed, "you cannot swim the same river twice." As a consequence, interpretive research seeks to understand a moving target.

Some scholars (e.g., Denzin & Lincoln, 2005; Prasad & Prasad, 2002; Seale, 2003) argue that although interpretivism has produced new knowledge, it has also contributed to methodological and epistemological confusion, particularly the interpretive rejection of the so-called objective methodological procedures for generating knowledge. In other words, producing knowledge based on an objective ontology and epistemology is inconsistent with the qualitative paradigm. This confusion raises the question of how and to what extent knowledge produced within the interpretive paradigm can be justified (Sandberg, 2005). Furthermore, some of the confusion is linked to the fact that the various frames of inquiry—grounded theory, phenomenology, poststructuralism, hermeneutics, to name a few—are frequently identified as interpretive *and* qualitative. Such terminological imprecision, as Prasad and Prasad (2002) point out, does sometimes convey the impression that interpretive research is completely synonymous with qualitative research, broadly defined.

However, it is important to differentiate between the two and develop an understanding of how they differ from one another with respect to research questions raised, research directions pursued, and the research procedures employed. Therefore, it is necessary to recognize that although the different interpretive methods do share a common ground, each of these approaches is based on relatively unique methodological considerations that guide the conceptualization, design, and implementation of individual research projects (Denzin & Lincoln, 2000). At a minimum, interpretive researchers should identify what type of interpretivism (hermeneutics, deconstructionism, and critical theory) he or she prefers, specify its philosophical roots, and relate the particular strengths and weaknesses of the preferred philosophical stance to the purpose of the research.

Symbolic Interactionism

Symbolic interactionism is a paradigm that emerged during the 1930s and has its roots in American pragmatism. Symbolic interactionism is regarded as the continuation of certain parts of the work of a loosely knit interdisciplinary network of theoreticians, social researchers, and social reformers at the University of Chicago, which exercised a determining influence on American sociology between 1890 and 1940, during the disciplines phase of institutionalization (Joas, 1993). The dominance of the Chicago School began to wane in the 1940s and 50s, but the school's intellectual legacy was passed on through the influence pragmatism had on the development and elaboration of symbolic interactionism.

Simply put, symbolic interactionism addresses how meanings are produced by agents through their interactions with symbols. Blumer (1969), one of the prominent members of the Chicago School of sociology, who was influenced by philosopher and social theorist George Mead articulated the major premises of social interactionism as follows:

- Human beings act toward the environment on the basis of the meanings they ascribe to them.

- The meaning arises out of the social interactions people have with one another.

- The meanings of things are handled and modified through an interpretative process used by individuals as they encounter specific experiences.

More specifically, Blumer (1969) states that symbolic interactionism

> does not regard meaning as emanating from the intrinsic makeup of the thing that has meaning, nor does it see meaning as arising through a coalescence of psychological elements in the person. Instead, it sees meaning as arising in the process of interaction between people. The meaning of such a thing for a person grows out of the ways in which the other persons act toward the person with regard to the thing. Their actions operate to define the thing for the person. Thus, symbolic interactionism sees meanings as social products, as creations that are formed in and through the defining activities of people as they interact. This point of view gives symbolic interactionism a very distinctive position, with profound implications... (pp. 4–5).

Symbolic interactionism claims that the meanings an individual forms to interpret the world are instruments for guiding action. It seeks to determine what common sets of symbols and understandings emerge that give meaning to people's interactions which are shaped by the self-reflections individuals bring to their situations. Symbolic interactionism addresses the question of how shared meanings created through shared interactions become reality. Humans are seen as purposive agents who confront a world that must be interpreted rather than a world composed to a set of stimuli to which the individual must react. Symbolic interactionism posits that communication is symbolic because we communicate through language and other symbols and by communicating create meaning. Symbolic interactionism evinces a profound respect for the empirical world and asserts that the researcher can understand human action only by first entering the setting or situation of the people being studied to see their particular definition of the situation (Denzin, 1992; Plummer, 1996).

Pragmatism

Pragmatism, sometimes called the only unique American philosophy, is best known through the work of William James (1842–1910), George Herbert Mead (1863–1931), and John Dewey (1859–1952) for whom pragmatism was a form of social criticism. Pragmatism, central to the heritage of symbolic interactionism, is based on the premise that knowledge is an instrument for organizing experience, and it is deeply concerned with the union of theory and practice (Diggins, 1994; Joas, 1993). Pragmatism emphasizes the importance of experimenting with new ways of living, searching for alternative and more liberating vocabularies, and opening up an array of possibilities for human action (Rorty, 1989). Pragmatists share, with a wide array of anti-positivists, the view that there are multiple interpretations of events, and different concepts and classificatory schemes can be used to describe the phenomena we observe (Wicks & Freeman, 1998, p. 134). Furthermore, pragmatism supports the use of both qualitative and quantitative methods in the same study and thereby rejects the thesis that the two research traditions are incompatible. Pragmatics characteristically mix different kinds of methods because the complexity of the contexts in which they work demand multiple methods. Since the study of leadership is based on empirical and theoretical research that has applicability for practicing leaders, pragmatism is important in qualitative research on leadership but has been largely underutilized.

According to Datta (1997), to adopt a pragmatic stance means to believe that

> The essential criteria for making design decisions are practical, contextual, responsive, and consequential. Practical implies a basis in one's experience, of what does and does not work. "Contextually responsive" involves understanding the demand, opportunities and constraints of the situation in which the [inquiry] will take place. "Consequential" [means]... that the trust of a statement consists of its practical consequences, particularly the statement's agreement with subsequent experience (p. 24, emphasis in original).

Pragmatism presents a very practical and applied research philosophy that is oriented toward action. It emphasizes the importance of experimenting with new ways of living, searching for new and more liberating vocabularies, and opening up an array of possibilities for human action (Rorty, 1989). Pragmatists share, with other anti-positivists, the view that multiple interpretations of events and different concepts and classificatory schemes can be used to describe phenomena. While pragmatists reject an essential and fundamental distinction between objective and subjective, they can accept, for pragmatic reasons, that there are differences between facts and values and different methods of inquiry appropriate to each. The over-riding pragmatic criterion of value is usefulness, which reminds people that they can see different interpretations as having more or less value (i.e., better or worse), depending on their ability to serve given purposes and enable people to accomplish relevant goals (Wicks & Freeman, 1998). Researchers working within this paradigm do not assess their conclusions by their proximity to the truth per se but rather their utilitarian function and the ability to promote social action. Unlike constructivism and interpretivism which do not acknowledge the intrinsic value of practical know-ing, pragmatists place a premium on it. Finally, as noted earlier, the pragmatic research paradigm acknowledges that researchers' worldviews involve ethical and moral issues. Therefore, pragmatists go beyond the established trilogy of ontology, epistemology, and methodology and include axiology as a cornerstone in their paradigm.

In view of the increasing use of multiparadigm, multimethod research, it seems counter-productive to continue to regard all qualitative methodologies under a single "inter-pretive" or "constructivist" paradigm. Likewise, using a limited number of research methods such as case studies and interviews does not do the holistic, contextualized nature of qualitative research justice. Adding additional data collection techniques is one way of increasing the scope of the phenomenon being investigated. This is not to say that multiple or mixed method designs overcome the limitations afforded by a single method (Chapter 6). The use of interdisciplinary research teams, which join together researchers from different disciplines and with different types of methodolo-gical expertise, can also add to the richness of the design, analysis, and interpretation. Typically, these research teams are composed of members who are competent in either the qualitative or the quantitative tradition thereby overcoming the limitation of a researcher working within a single paradigm. Becoming increasingly versatile as qua-litative leadership researchers means deliberately building and diversifying our meth-odologies and making our ontological, epistemological assumptions as well as our values transparent.

Table 1-1 offers a comparison of the qualitative paradigms which are compared in terms of ontology, epistemology, and research methods associated with paradigms discussed in this section.

In research practice, it is sometimes difficult to discern the nuances of the differences between these paradigms in a qualitative study, which may be one of the reasons while in few published studies the paradigm is specified by the researcher. There are often more overlaps than clearly distinctive features because many times a paradigm is coupled with another tradition as in constructive realism or interpretive interactionism. Within each of the paradigm, we also find different intellectual orientations. For example, the interpretive research tradition includes hermeneutics, critical theory, and deconstructionist approaches. Moreover, many of the qualitative paradigms described here were formulated two or more decades ago when both the state-of-the art of social science and the research process were significantly different compared to contemporary approaches as well the political, social, and technological context in which we must place the research process. For example, Ladson-Billings (2003) examined how a single event, September 11, 2000, produced new epistemological challenges. The author notes three epistemological challenges that were made manifest as a result of the attacks: (1) the theme of defining humanity; (2) the theme of defining importance; and (3) the theme of determining the future. Using the theme of defining humanity as an example, Ladson-Billings argues that the us–them (normal people versus terrorists) that made sense in a cold war reality is inappropriate in post-9/11 realities where such binaries are useless. She also asserts that 9/11 highlights that all cultures are local—not universal; particularly, the Judeo–Christian culture of the West is a local culture, not a universal, transcendent, supraculture under which others must be subordinated (p. 6).

Thus, it is only recently that qualitative researchers are beginning to make explicit the paradigm that governs their research and even challenge the assumptions underlying the qualitative paradigm (e.g., Lincoln & Denzin, 2005; Sandburg, 2005). This is, however, not always the case as numerous qualitative researchers do not clearly articulate their philosophical stance although there is a considerable body of literature that speaks to need for ontological, epistemological, and axiological transparency.

New paradigms such as realism (Sayer, 2000), pragmatism (De Waal, 2005; Rorty, 1989), or more politically engaged ways of knowing such a feminism (Olesen, 2000) have appeared on the qualitative landscape that take into consideration the changing context of research, as organizations, the workforce and society are moving into different directions. As Greene and Caracelli (2003) suggest, a given set of assumptions about reality and knowledge is not sacrosanct; rather it can be modified, expanded, or constricted—altered to fit changing social needs and circumstances. Paradigms—both research and leadership—do need to change over time and place. In addition, a new generation of leadership scholars is trained in doctoral programs that are not as wedded to positivism and the superiority of quantitative approaches or the continuation of paradigm wars. Tashakkori and Teddlie (2003a) concluded that it is time to balance the philosophical, conceptual, practical, and political considerations so relevant to our inquiry (p. 108).

SUMMARY

In this foundational chapter, the role of qualitative research in the study of leadership was briefly reviewed. Despite a gradual increase of qualitative research in major leadership journals, the variety of qualitative studies available to the leadership researcher remains underutilized. Two ways of looking at qualitative research were presented, namely the treatment of qualitative research as a collection of paradigms which share a number of fundamental assumptions about the nature of qualitative research and a collection of methodologies that undergird the different paradigms. In this chapter, I introduced qualitative research as paradigm which rests on the tripartite concepts of ontology, epistemology, and methodology. Beginning with Kuhn (1962, 1996, 2000) who introduced the concept of paradigm or worldview as a fundamental concept in the philosophy of science, four major qualitative paradigms—constructivism, interpretivism, symbolic interactionism and pragmatism—were introduced and compared and contrasted with positivism, the still dominant paradigm in leadership research. The introduction of qualitative paradigms led to paradigm wars based on the assumption that different paradigms are incommensurable and researcher must design and conduct his or her research under the assumptions of a single paradigm.

However, qualitative research is not a single, unitary or generic endeavor. Multiple and contrasting epistemological perspectives now exist within the qualitative paradigm. It is important to recognize that every researcher brings some set of assumptions to the research process and that these influence his or her understanding and interpretation of qualitative data. In qualitative research, in epistemological terms, the knower and the known are interactive and inseparable. Unlike quantitative researchers who perform statistical tests of prediction and control, qualitative researchers strive for deep understanding of the phenomenon under investigation through thick description.

Krauss (2005) sums up the essence of qualitative analysis when he states:

> Through qualitative analysis, meaning is constructed in a variety of ways. Through construction, the researcher is not a blank state, rather he or she is an active participant in the process.... Epistemologically, the researcher is engaged in the setting, participating in the act of "being with" the respondents in their lives to generate meaning of them. Developing themes and storylines featuring the words and experiences of participants themselves is an important result of qualitative data analysis that adds richness to the findings and their meaning (p. 767).

Although qualitative research has endured many criticisms, more and more qualitative researchers in leadership studies team up with colleagues in other disciplines thereby not only expanding the multidisciplinary nature of the field but also exemplifying the dynamic, complex nature of leadership through multiparadigmatic, multimethod research.

2

QUALITATIVE RESEARCH AS METHOD

INTRODUCTION

In Chapter 1, I traced the role of qualitative research in leadership studies and introduced the philosophical foundation of qualitative research which rest on the tripartite concepts of ontology, epistemology, and methodology. Methodology was briefly introduced as a component of the trilogy but moves to center stage in this chapter. Before analyzing qualitative research as method, a few comments concerning the larger context in which qualitative research is conducted are in order.

In response to the prevailing climate of the 1980s and 1990s, organizational visions, missions, and cultural change toward more participatory, democratic leadership, and empowered workplaces became an essential part of the agenda of many leaders and a lucrative opportunity for the growing number of management gurus and leadership consultants (Turnbull, 2006). However, as we entered the postindustrial era, different economic, social, and cultural conditions dominated by turbulence and rapid environmental, technological, and social changes are prevailing now that are creating a different context for leadership research. As a result, the discipline of leadership studies is now at a juncture as new organizational designs—less vertical and hierarchical with more horizontal and fluid structures and global boundary spanning systems—are being created to support the transformation from an industrial to an information society populated by knowledge workers.

The early cohort of the millennial generation encompassing those born between 1982 and 2002 is the next source of leadership talent, a generation that has distinct characteristics that separates them from previous generations, which are bound to influence the way they approach, understand, and practice leadership. Highly educated millennials grew up during a time of instability in America. Members of this generation place priority on relationships with family and friends and therefore are sensitive to relational dynamics in leader–follower interactions. They are civic minded and feel personally responsible for making a difference in the world. As a group, they are optimistic about the future in general, and their own lives in particular, although events like 9/11 or the Iraqi war may have tempered their optimism somewhat. Millennials bring these generational attributes to leadership and are searching for a new paradigm that is congruent with the sociopolitical and economic context in which they will exercise their leadership.

In the postmillennial period we have entered, new leadership refrains or discourses such as distributed or dispersed leadership, authentic, and spiritual leadership are surfacing in response to today's sociopolitical and economic climate. Themes found in the literature portray images of leaders not as heroes or omnipotent individuals at the apex of the organization but as men and women characterized by adaptability, understanding of context, creativity, and tolerance for ambiguity and change. Bennis and Thomas (2002) describe these leaders as engaging others by creating voice and integrity who develop their leadership competencies through defining moments and crucibles instead of exercising authority through position power. Badaracco (2002) notes that this new generation of leaders, instead of being champions of high-profile causes or spearheading ethical crusades, leads quietly. These leaders move patiently, carefully, and incrementally. They are called quiet leaders because their modesty and restraint are in large measure responsible for their impressive achievements (p. 2). Among the metaphors which capture the new way of leading are the leader as artist, performer, gardener, or ordinary person who accomplishes extraordinary things implying that the "new" leadership must be radically different if it is to support the demands and constraints of postmillennial organizations.

In this chapter, the focus shifts to the third element of the ontology, epistemology, and methodology trilogy and presents a discussion of the major elements and assumptions that govern research methods in qualitative research, keeping in mind their ontological and epistemological underpinnings.

QUALITATIVE RESEARCH AS METHOD

In Chapter 1, we noted the growing dissatisfaction with the positivist paradigm which continues to rule the study of leadership. Osborne (1994) identified the early 1980s as a time when greater disenchantment with the limits of logical–empirical research methodologies, a defining characteristic of positivism, began to surface. Increasingly, questions emerged about the focus of inquiry, as well as exploration of methodologies that emphasized discovery, description, and meaning rather than prediction, control, and measurement. For example, Klein and Westcott (1994) stated that the last 25 years have been a time of growing crisis for mainstream positivistic psychology as both the philosophies and methodologies used in research came under scrutiny. Smith (1991) described this as a "crisis of value" that cannot be resolved simply by appealing to traditional forms of logic and authority. The precision, validity, and generalizability that define quantitative research are achieved at the expense of lesser attention to contextual factors and the multifaceted and rich dynamics that underlie leader–follower relationships in organizations.

Methodology refers to the specific research paradigm used by the researcher to investigate reality based on the assumption he or she makes about ontology and epistemology. Methods, on the other hand, are specific research strategies and techniques that undergird methodology as a philosophical foundation of qualitative research. Some qualitative researchers adopt a strictly methods-oriented view and define qualitative research as a set of specific research tools such as case studies, focus groups, life histories, structured interviews, observations, and content analysis of a variety of texts. Common to these diverse methods is the emphasis on process and shared meanings that are not measured in terms of quantity, amount, or frequency. Qualitative methods produce a wealth of detailed data about a small number of people and cases; they provide depth and detail through direct quotation and careful description of situations, events, interactions, and observed behaviors. Consequently, qualitative analysis involves the nonnumerical organization of data in order to discover patterns, themes, forms, and qualities found in field notes, transcripts, open-ended questionnaires, diaries, case studies, and so on (Labuschagne, 2003).

Qualitative researchers now can choose from a wide variety of research strategies (see Table 2-1). The range of qualitative methods found in published research reflects the disciplines from which such methods originate, preferences of journals for certain qualitative methods research, implicit or explicit editorial philosophies, and temporal factors that influence the popularity of certain methods over others. For example, computer technology has enabled the development virtual ethnography (e.g., Hine, 2000) and e-mail-facilitated reflective dialogue (McAuliffe, 2003) techniques, which did not exist when information technologies were less advanced. Likewise, advances in photography and video technologies are creating opportunities for nontext-based research in management that speak to the influence of temporality in research designs.

As shown in Table 2-1, qualitative methodologies have grown into a wide domain of techniques, each with its own underlying set of epistemological, ontological, and methodological assumptions. For some researchers, especially novices, such diversity can be a source of anxiety and consternation as there few road maps with detailed

Table 2-1   A sampling of qualitative methods: more than meets the eye

• Content analysis • Case studies—single, multiple, longitudinal • Interviewing • ethnography/autoethnography/virtual ethnography • Grounded theory • Participant observation • Focus groups • Hermeneutics • Semiotic analysis • Rhetorical analysis • Historiometry/historiography • Phenomenology	• biographical methods—autobiography, journals, life stories • Appreciative inquiry • Q-Methodology • Critical theory • Textual analysis • Document interpretation • Ethnomethodology • Naturalistic study • Ecological descriptive study • Literary criticism • Triangulation or mixed methods

Source: Klenke (2004).

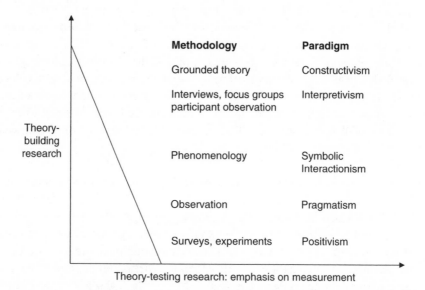

Figure 2-1   Paradigm method relationships. Theory-testing research: emphasis on measurement (Source: adapted from Healy & Perry 2000).

instructions to guide the researcher through this maze of available research methods. Fig. 2-1 shows the relationships between research paradigms and research methods by identifying some of the major qualitative methods employed under the auspices as the paradigms described in Chapter 1.

The practice of qualitative inquiry does not rest solely upon the adoption of particular research methods and techniques. Rather as depicted in Table 2-1, many different types of methodologies are available to researchers, each of which has its own theoretical perspective, its own approach to data collection and analysis. For example, as discussed in Chapter 7, grounded theory is used to describe social processes such as leader–follower relationships to generate descriptive theory while ethnography (Chapter 7) is aimed at uncovering cultural phenomena that undergird the practice of leadership. Thus, the epistemologies of the various types of qualitative research have implications for research questions, methods, and designs employed by qualitative researchers.

As in most disciplines, preferences for certain methods in study of leadership reflect the evolution of a field of inquiry as well as the Zeitgeist of an era. For example, in the early days of qualitative studies on leadership, interviewing was one of the preferred data collection techniques. Preoccupation with a specific research method (Koch, 1994), particularly at the expense of substantive issues (i.e., such as method instead of the research question driving the research process), has been referred to as methodolatry (Chamberlain, 1999; Janesick, 2000). Likewise, Danzinger (1990) argued that "preoccupations with the purity of method frequently deteriorate to a kind of method fetishism or methodolatry" (p. 5). Janesick (1994) defined methodolatry as

> A combination of method and idolatry, to describe a preoccupation with selecting and defending methods to the exclusion of the actual substance of the story being told. Methodolatry is the slavish attachment and devotion to method that so often overtakes the discourse (p. 215).

Chamberlain (1999) argues that methodolatry marks a carry-over from the predominance of positivist methodological assumptions which lead researchers to become preoccupied with the "correct" method at the expense of theoretical considerations. Instead of being constrained by a single method, qualitative researchers are increasingly encouraged to be flexible and utilize whatever methods necessary to explore the phenomenon under consideration. Chamberlain (1999) states:

> Deciding on the epistemology (e.g., constructionist) prior to selecting the theoretical perspective (e.g., critical theory or feminism) prior to choosing the methodology (e.g., grounded theory) and then the specific methods (e.g., focus groups) puts methodology and methods firmly in their place (p. 295).

Several problems result from methodolatry such as ignoring the philosophical position of the researcher or his or her stance on ontology and epistemology. As Chamberlain notes, methodolatry prevents us from looking at the assumptions behind our research. In addition, the dominance of method promotes obtaining and analyzing data but interferes with thinking theoretically. For example, content analysis often produces conceptual models depicted as variables in boxes connected by causal arrows, a practice Spicer and Chamberlain (1996) described as the pathology of flow-charting which also mitigate against theory construction. Thus, the point made here is that qualitative researchers should not be constrained within a "methodological straightjacket" and must be allowed to utilize whatever methods necessary to explore the social phenomenon under investigation. Although knowing about the different qualitative methods is important, we should not lose sight of the fact that methods are tools rather than ends themselves.

Treating qualitative approaches as method, according to Hammersley (1990), involves the following:

- Individual behavior is studied in everyday contexts rather than under experimental conditions created by the researcher.

- Data are gathered from a wide range of sources such as interviews or participant observations.

- The approach to data collection is "unstructured" in the sense that it does not involve proceeding according to a predefined data collection plan set up in advance nor are the categories for interpreting the data fixed.

- The focus of a qualitative study is usually a single setting or group on a relatively small scale. In case and life history research, the focus may be on a single individual.

- The analysis of the data involves interpretation of the meanings and functions of human action and mainly takes the form of verbal descriptions and explanations.

QUALITY STANDARDS IN QUALITATIVE RESEARCH

The issue of quality in qualitative research has concerned leadership scholars for at least a quarter of a century. As Sandelowski and Barroso (2002) have recently observed

> Scholars across the social disciplines have sought to define what a good, valid, and/or trustworthy qualitative study is, to chart the history of and to categorize efforts to accomplish such a definition, and to describe and codify techniques for both ensuring and recognizing good studies (p. 2).

However, they concluded that "after all this effort, we seem no closer to establishing consensus on quality criteria, or even whether it is appropriate to try to establish such a consensus" (p. 2).

The key issues in discussions about quality and rigor of qualitative research may be summarized by three distinct positions. First, there are qualitative researchers who openly adopt positivistic criteria for qualitative research. For example, Mays and Pope (1995) claim that reliability should be a benchmark of qualitative research. Others (e.g., Kirk & Miller, 1986) note that "issues of reliability have received little attention from qualitative researchers, who have instead focused on achieving greater validity in their work" (p. 42).

The second position calls for the establishment of distinct and separate criteria from those adopted in quantitative research. For example, Morse, Barrett, Mayan, Olson, and Spiers (2002) encouraged qualitative researchers to resist the urge to adopt the validity criteria used in quantitative research. Instead, they suggest that qualitative researchers devote their energy to challenging the notion of a universal set of quality criteria (whether qualitative or quantitative) rather than acquiescing to them. Likewise, the reconceptualization of traditional definitions of reliability and validity based on the work of Guba and Lincoln (1989) described below also reflects this second position. Sandelowski and Barrosa (2002) argued that the epistemological scope of qualitative methodologies is too broad to be represented by a single set of criteria. Instead, they advocate that qualitative research should be judged according to aesthetic and rhetorical considerations, pointing out that the "only site for evaluating studies—whether they are qualitative or quantitative—is the report itself" (p. 8). And finally, the third position advocates a complete rejection of all predetermined quality criteria. A theoretical resolution of these divergent positions is impossible as the core of their ontological and epistemological assumptions is so different. The following section briefly addresses these three different positions.

Understanding Reliability and Validity in Qualitative Research

In positivist research, there are objective criteria that allow researchers and reviewers of journals to judge the quality and rigor of a study. Reliability and validity are fundamental concerns in quantitative research but seem to have an uncertain place in the repertoire of the qualitative researcher. Traditionally, validity in qualitative research involves determining the degree to which researchers' claims about knowledge correspond to the reality (or research participants' constructions of reality) (Eisner & Peshkin, 1990). The two major quality criteria in quantitative research are external and internal validity. *Internal validity* in a quantitative study is achieved by the extent to which changes in a dependent variable such as leadership effectiveness can be attributed to controlled variation in an independent variable such as leader commitment to the organizational vision. Internal validity focuses on cause and effect relationships. It attempts to answer a question such as "Does a transformational leadership style cause follower motivation?" *External validity* or *generalizability* refers to the extent to which the findings based on the research sample apply to the population from which the sample was drawn or other populations and research settings. Replicating the original research is the means by which external validity is established.

Internal and external validity are criteria used for justifying knowledge production within the positivistic tradition. These criteria are based on an objectivist epistemology that refers to an objective, knowable reality beyond the human mind and that stipulates a correspondence criterion of truth (Salner, 1989). As Salner (1989) observed, the correspondence criterion of truth implies that "facts are out there to which our ideas and constructs, measuring tools, and theories must correspond" (p. 47). In qualitative research, however, except in studies that are intentionally quantitative in nature such as certain types of content analysis (Chapters 4), for which positivist criteria are appropriate, answering questions about quality and rigor is less likely to be based on clear, unambiguous criteria. Positivist criteria such as reliability and validity may be misleading in qualitative research and therefore have been redefined by various scholars. Although qualitative researchers working within positivist assumptions may not necessarily use the term "validity" to denote their methods of assessment, they nonetheless utilize terms parallel to those of quantitative research designs (Sparkes, 2001).

Some scholars (e.g., Healy & Perry, 2000) argue that the quality of a study in each paradigm should be judged in terms of its underlying paradigm. Strauss and Corbin (1990) suggest that the "usual canons of 'good science' require redefinition in order to fit the realities of qualitative research" (p. 250). For example, while the terms reliability and validity are essential criteria for quality in quantitative paradigms, the criteria in qualitative paradigms are the terms *credibility* (paralleling internal validity) or the extent to which the results are credible or believable from the standpoint of the participant, *transferability* (paralleling external validity) or the extent to which the results can be transferred to other contexts or settings, *dependability* (paralleling reliability) or the extent to which the same results can be obtained by independent investigators, and *confirmability* (paralleling objectivity) or the extent to which the results can be corroborated or confirmed by other (Lincoln & Guba, 1985). Confirmability means providing an audit trail consisting of (1) raw data, (2) analysis notes, (3) reconstruction and synthesis products, (4) process notes, (5) personal notes, and (6) preliminary developmental information (Lincoln & Guba, 1985, pp. 320–321). Together, credibility, transferability, dependability, and confirmability comprise the concept of trustworthiness or authenticity of qualitative research which Guba (1981) explicitly linked to the quantitative criteria of reliability and validity.

Drawing from the epistemological assumptions associated with constructivism, Lincoln and Guba (1985) put forth a theory of validity recast as trustworthiness. They purportedly draw from epistemological assumptions associated with social constructionism. According to the authors, the idea of discovering truth through measures of reliability and validity is replaced by the idea of trustworthiness. Seale (1999) states that the "trustworthiness of a research report lies at the heart of issues conventionally discussed as validity and reliability" (p. 266). Research reports aiming at credibility must address the following issues: (1) the theoretical positioning of the researchers which includes the ontological, epistemological assumptions as well as the values (axiology), motives, and personal history he or she brings to the study; (2) the congruence between method and methodology; (3) strategies employed to establish rigor and quality; and (4) the analytic lens through which the data are examined (Caelli, Ray, & Mill, 2003). Critics of reconceptualizing validity in terms of some other construct assert that these reconceptualizations function no different from their positivist incarnates. In other words, just as quantitative researchers judge a study on the basis of a binary opposition, that is, a study is either valid or invalid, qualitative researchers who judge a study as either trustworthy or untrustworthy are achieving the same ends—namely, policing social science research by de/legitimizing social knowledge, research practice, and experiential possibilities (Scheurich, 1996). Scheurich argues that even within these reconceptualizations of validity, "there must be a boundary line, a judgment criterion for deciding whose work is acceptable" (p. 51).

According to Guba and Lincoln (1989), authenticity as a quality criterion is consistent with the relativist view that research accounts do no more than represent a sophisticated but temporary consensus of views about what is considered to be true. Authenticity, according to the authors, demonstrated whether researchers can show that they have represented a range of different realities, also known as fairness defined as a balanced view that represents all constructions and the values that undergird them (p. 79). Research should also help members of the scholarly community to develop "more sophisticated" understandings of the phenomenon being studied (*ontological authenticity*), be shown to have helped members appreciate the viewpoints of others than themselves (*educative authenticity*) leading to improved understanding of constructions of others, to have stimulated some form of action (*catalytic authenticity*) providing value to practitioners and facilitating the practical use of research finding, and to have empowered members to act (*tactical authenticity*). An empowering research process never assumes a falsely dualistic stance where the research process (e.g., the means) is separate from the research findings (e.g., the ends) (Manning, 1997). Of course, as Seale (1999) points out, the view that fairness, sophistication, mutual understanding, and empowerment are generally desirable is itself a value-laden, culture-bound position (p. 469).

Table 2-2 compares the Lincoln and Guba (1985) criteria of reliability and validity with their quantitative counterparts.

Although there is a certain degree of parallelism between Guba and Lincoln's discussion of trustworthiness and positivist definitions of internal and external validity, it is

Table 2-2   Traditional and alternative criteria for judging qualitative research quality and rigor

Traditional criteria for judging quantitative research	Alternative criteria for judging qualitative research
Internal validity	Credibility
External validity	Transferability
Reliability	Dependability
Objectivity	Conformability

incomplete and does not represent a one-to-one correspondence between these concepts. Intended as guidelines rather than orthodoxy, certain aspects of the Guba and Lincoln criteria have been instrumental in the development of other standards used to evaluate qualitative research. While qualitative researchers continue to develop alternative criteria and search for new types of validity, it is unlikely that qualitative research will not require some type of "validation" for qualitative researchers to be accepted as serious scholars.

Table 2-3 depicts the relationships between research paradigms and the quality criteria favored by each paradigm. Again, it is important to re-emphasize that evaluating qualitative research (establishing "validity" and "reliability") is based on the paradigm from which qualitative methods are developed.

In addition, other criteria have been introduced that are more congruent with qualitative ontology and epistemology. For example, the positivist concept of reliability or consistency of measurement has been reformulated as interpretive awareness

Table 2-3   Quality criteria employed in major qualitative paradigms

Paradigm	Quality criteria
Constructivism	Trustworthiness and authenticity; commitment to canons of good science
Interpretivism	Reliability as interpretive awareness, validity as defensible knowledge claims, trustworthiness, authenticity
Symbolic interactionism	Authenticity, trustworthiness
Pragmatism	Accuracy, scope, simplicity, consistency, comprehensiveness

(Sandberg, 2005). The author suggests that while the main question of validity relates to the truthfulness of interpretation, the principal question of reliability concerns the procedure for achieving truthful interpretation (p. 58). Patton (2002) advocates a paradigm of choices that seeks methodological appropriateness as the primary criterion for judging methodological quality. Other researchers have developed their own concepts of validity as well and generated or adopted what they consider more appropriate terms that are congruent with the defining characteristics of qualitative research. This has lead to a plethora of terms and criteria resulting in confusion and a deteriorating ability to actually discern rigor (Morse et al., 2002) and the need to evaluate the validity and reliability of a qualitative study. When judging qualitative research, Strauss and Corbin (1990), as noted earlier, believe that "the usual canons of good science... require redefinition in order to fit the realities of qualitative research" (p. 250). Nevertheless, despite the introduction of these alternative criteria, the ghost of traditional reliability and validity continues to haunt qualitative researchers.

As qualitative research on leadership is slowly gaining breath and legitimacy, the application of rigorous research methods is no longer the exclusive foundation for a credible qualitative study. Notions of moral soundness, representation, and power differentials have entered debates of rigor and quality (Sandelowski, 1993; 2000). Yet, despite this proliferation of definitions and quality criteria, we continue to see some qualitative leadership researchers claim allegiance to a particular approach to rigor without acknowledging the historical context, incongruence, or potential datedness of their choices (Caelli et al., 2003).

STRATEGIES FOR ENHANCING QUALITY AND RIGOR IN QUALITATIVE RESEARCH

Rigor in qualitative data analysis is a requisite for maximizing the potential for meaning making (which is also an essential function of leadership). The question of what constitutes a rigorous qualitative study has been hotly debated for more than two decades. Qualitative rigor began with efforts to establish criteria that were equal in form and intent to those criteria held sacrosanct in quantitative research (Caelli et al., 2003). Although some researchers argue that the same reliability and validity criteria used in quantitative studies should also be employed in qualitative research, others have sought to identify criteria specific to qualitative research. The focus of this section is on the latter.

Researcher bias is one potential threat to validity that has to be controlled. Knowledge of prior theory, speaking from male voice (researcher's gender) or paradigmatic assumptions, can stand in the way of hearing and listening to the interpretive theories that operate in the minds of the respondents. Researcher bias can also be shaped by the ideological context in which the research is carried out, the investigator's knowledge of research techniques, familiarity with the power structure of the sponsoring organization, and its value system. Finally, a researcher's personality and personal attributes such as intuition, creativity, and problem-solving skills may determine that the selection of topics and institutional affiliation can be instrumental in gaining access to organizations willing to promote the study. For example, senior researchers from major research universities with external grants may find it easier to gain organizational access than their junior counterparts from less well-known or esteemed institutions. Additionally, the researcher's gender or race may close some avenues of access but clearly open up others (Martin, 1980). Controlling or bracketing researcher bias requires that investigators acknowledge that qualitative research, like quantitative research, is not value neutral. Hence, the qualitative researchers have to be able to "bracket" personal values and prior knowledge of a substantive field by identifying the positions from which they speak. Although all research is value driven, but few research approaches accord such significance to making values and assumptions transparent as does qualitative research.

> Investigators ... demonstrate ... their historical and geographical situatedness, their personal investment in the research, various biases they bring to the work, their surprises and "undoings" in the process of research ... and ... the ways in which they have avoided or suppressed certain points of view (Gergen & Gergen, 2003, p. 579).

It is this "self-exposure" and this "moment-to-moment" confrontation coupled with critical self-reflexivity that leads researchers to an in-depth exploration of the ways in which their personal histories saturate their inquiry. Reflexivity is conceptualized as a conscious act, is one that demands that the researcher situates himself/herself within the social and cultural context, and is willing to openly confront the self as the field work proceeds (Kacen & Chaitin, 2006).

A number of different strategies have been introduced to help qualitative researchers assess and verify the quality of their work. Verification is the process of checking, confirming, and making sure that data collection procedures, analyses, and interpretation are monitored, reflected upon, and constantly subjected to confirmation or disconfirmation. It refers to the mechanisms employed during the process of research to incrementally contribute to ensuring reliability and validity and thereby the rigor and quality of a study (Creswell, 1998; Kvale, 1989). Verification strategies to ensure both reliability and validity include activities such as ensuring methodological coherence, sampling sufficiency, developing a dynamic relationship between sampling, data collection and analysis, and thinking theoretically in order to develop theory (Morse et al., 2002). Although quality criteria within epistemological and methodological boundaries are available, they are not uniformly applied, and the search for a universal of criteria to evaluate quality and rigor has been proven futile. Qualitative research is iterative rather than linear. A conscientious qualitative researcher moves back and forth between design features, data collection, and interpretation to ensure congruence among question formulation, extant literature, selection of research participants, data collection strategies, and analysis. Data are systematically checked to achieve the best fit of data and the conceptual work of analysis through constant comparisons throughout the research process. Analysis and interpretation of the data are co-created with research participants through strategies such as respondent validation or member checking and negative case sampling. Using member-checking strategies, the researcher presents his or her informants with the results of the preliminary analyses and interpretations and solicits their consensus.

As noted earlier, Lincoln and Guba (1985) propagate trustworthiness comprised of credibility, dependability, transferability, and confirmability as quality criteria for qualitative research. In addition, a number of strategies for increasing the credibility and authenticity of qualitative research have been developed (Johnson, 1999; Manning, 1997; Morse et al., 2002):

- *Prolonged engagement* with participants to develop a trusting relationship with them and help them to obtain a deep understanding of the phenomenon under study.

- *Peer debriefing* based on regular meetings with other people who are not directly involved in the research such as colleagues in order to disclose blind spots and to discuss working hypotheses and results with them. Knowledgeable colleagues, peers, or mentors raise probing questions and play devil's advocate and facilitate the emergence of meaningful interpretations. The researcher may also ask peers to code a few transcripts to provide feedback on data analysis.

- *Member checking* also known as respondent validation is a technique that involves a process of continuous, informal testing of information by soliciting the reactions of respondents as a means of reassuring the credibility of constructions of the participants. It involves returning to research participants after data analysis to verify the interpretations. Member checking, including respondent review of the researcher's field notes, working hypotheses, and report drafts, means that the researcher is accountable to those sharing their words, lives, and experiences (Manning, 1997).

- *Negative case sampling* involves the identification and analysis of cases that disconfirm the researchers' expectations and tentative explanation. This procedure of looking for and analyzing deviant cases is applied after a preliminary interpretation of the data has been formulated. Learning from negative cases, being able to explain why this case, this person, is different from the others leads to more complex, dense and thick analysis.

- *Reflexivity* involves self-awareness and critical self-reflection by the researcher on his or her potential biases and predispositions as these may affect the research process and conclusions. Through reflexivity, researchers become aware of their potential biases and predispositions and monitor their attempts to control them.

Table 2-4   Summary of strategies for achieving trustworthiness in qualitative research

- Prolonged engagement with and observation of participants
- Peer debriefing (colleagues)
- Negative case analysis
- Bracketing
- Theoretical sampling
- Member checks
- Thick description
- Prevention of premature foreclosure on the data—achieving the point of saturation
- Triangulation—multiple methods of data collection, multiple investigators multiple contexts
- Maintaining a journal to enhance reflexivity

- *Triangulation* (Chapter 6) refers to verifying facts through multiple data sources. It addresses the issue of internal validity by using more than one method of data collection such as combining interviewing and participant observation to answer the research question. In addition to triangulating data, researchers also may also triangulate investigators by using multiple coders in a content analysis study or triangulate theories.

Theoretically, these efforts bolster reliability and validity. However, the absence of corroborate efforts through triangulation and the production of similar findings does provide grounds for refutation as different methods used in qualitative research furnish parallel data sets, each affording only a partial picture of the phenomenon under investigation (Table 2-4).

The Quantitative–Qualitative Debate: One More Time

According to Oakley (2000), the quantitative–qualitative debate, sometimes referred to as paradigm war between the adherents of quantitative and qualitative research because of the antagonism between proponents of qualitative and quantitative methods, started in the 1960s. In Oakley's words

> The warfare proceeds on a number of levels. Researchers presenting the results of their research often feel it necessary to claim their adherence to one or other camp as part of establishing their academic and political credentials (p. 27).

One main characteristic of this dispute seems to be the dichotomous way in which qualitative and quantitative research methods are presented as well as the resulting strict contraposition of the two (Bryman, 1992a).

Fundamentally, paradigm debates are driven by differing assumptions about ontology, epistemology, and methodology. Whereas, the qualitative, interpretive paradigm is based on the view that people socially and symbolically construct and sustain their own realities, the quantitative, positivist paradigm aims at an objective, verifiable account of the world to produce formal theory which can be tested. At the core of the debate are also differences regarding the nature of "truth" produced by scientific research. For quantitative researchers, truth is a matter of internal validity and the degree of isomorphism between the data and an independently existing reality that the data reflect (Guba, 1981). For qualitative researchers, on the other hand, truth is a matter of credibility, and reality is mind-constructed; it becomes realty only for a person at a given time and place. Debates over the relative merits of quantitative and qualitative research have been confounded by two problems: (1) lack of coherent paradigm definitions and (2) the focus of most discussion on methods instead of on the assumptions underlying the paradigm.

The qualitative–quantitative polarization is reminiscent of the many dichotomies found in leadership theory: autocratic versus democratic leadership, task-oriented leadership versus relationship-oriented leadership, and transactional versus transformational leadership. In both leadership studies and qualitative research, we need to move beyond the simple dualistic models that have dominated these fields for almost a century. In qualitative research, dichotomies are overly simplistic and misleading because they assume that the two approaches rest on two homogeneous traditions that are internally coherent and based upon opposing philosophical views. Yet, they fail to acknowledge that there is a range of paradigms and methods within each of these traditions that cannot be reduced to simple dichotomies without distortion. In reality, there is often a blurring of approaches. For example, Strauss (1987) in discussing grounded theory (Chapter 7) states that this particular qualitative method involves not only induction but also deduction and verification. Punch (1998) presents the following argument against dichotomization:

> Quantitative research has typically been more directed toward theory verification while qualitative research has typically been more concerned with theory generation. While that correlation is historically valid, it is by no means perfect, and there is no necessary connection between purpose and approach. That is, quantitative research can be used for theory generation (as well as verification) and qualitative research can be used for theory verification as well a generation (pp. 16–17).

Firestone (1987) identified two groups in the qualitative–quantitative camps called the "purists" and the "pragmatists." Purists in both camps believe that qualitative and quantitative research is incommensurable. The commensurability or compatibility of different paradigms has been hotly debated as has the requisite of binding philosophy to methodology and thereby to particular methods as, for example, in coupling positivism with experimentation or interpretivism with case studies (Howe, 1988). Lincoln and Guba (2000) also assert that the ontological foundations of positivist and interpretivist paradigms are fundamentally incompatible. Likewise, qualitative researchers, especially those who represent the purist approach that devalues and negates objectivity and generalizability, often believe that the two methods are incompatible because they are inextricably linked to paradigms that make different assumptions about the world and what constitutes valid research. Pragmatists, on the other hand, claim that methods are a collection of techniques that are not inherently linked to any paradigmatic assumptions.

As Hammersley (1992) notes:

> There are some serious problems with the paradigm view of the relationship between qualitative and quantitative approaches: for one thing, if we look at research today in the human sciences, we find that much of it does not fall neatly into one or the other "categories." There are multiple methodological dimensions on which research varies; these do not lie in parallel and each involves a range of positions, not just two (p. 160).

Moreover, Hammersley argues that the qualitative–quantitative divide is artificially polarized, disguising both methodological similarity and diversity. In an analysis that emphasizes the trade-offs and overlaps between experimental, survey, and quantitative research, the author concludes that no single approach is necessarily ideal and that selection of one over the other invariably involves losses as well as gains.

Along the low road of the debate, long-standing prejudices and animosities have pervaded the scene but have gone largely unmentioned in public forums as these "dirty secrets" are often glossed over or denied in quantitative–qualitative debates. As a result of the fundamental differences, some scholars (e.g., Smith & Hebius, 1986) have called for a moratorium and shutting down the debate. However, a more reasonable approach seems to be to redirect the debate to facilitate a constructive dialectic regarding the relative merits of each paradigm. If the link between epistemology and method is not axiomatic but rhetorical as McLaughlin (1991) asserts, then this rhetoric is not sufficient to constrain against the use of both methods within the same epistemological paradigm.

Nevertheless, the notion of qualitative *or* quantitative (the either/or position) remains well entrenched in the mind of many researchers. It has proven to be a dangerous distinction that has led to a confrontational debate with dysfunctional consequences. For example, many definitions of "qualitative" cite "quantitative," imply opposites, overlook the fact that the critical difference between the two perspectives lies in the research paradigm rather than the methods. This practice, at least implicitly, has led to an elevation of quantitative approaches treating them as superior, more scientific, and definitive compared to their qualitative counterparts. Hence, the debate has invoked the idea of the privileged position of quantitative methods (e.g., Smith & Hebius, 1986) due to their grounding in a paradigm that allows certitude regarding how the world "really" is. However, proponents of this view seem to overlook that "certitude" is often overplayed, especially when it comes to leadership because the complexity of leadership phenomena cannot be reduced to certain and definite answers that presumably constitute knowledge. At times, paradigm debates have also fostered the default conclusion that qualitative research must be unreliable, invalid, unscientific, and lacking in rigor. Moreover, the idea that only a certain type of analysis is appropriate for quantitative or qualitative data is unfortunate as it limits the extent to which new and innovative methods and findings can be realized.

Whereas Guba and Lincoln held to fundamental differences at the paradigmatic level, others (e.g., Miles & Huberman, 1984) recognize philosophical assumptions as important, but then "de-epistemologize" the debate as they move on to their principal concern of how to conduct qualitative research. Researchers in this camp have attempted to demonstrate that the distinction between qualitative and quantitative paradigms is not particularly helpful because many of the methodological problems associated with qualitative research are also encountered in quantitative research. For example, quantitative studies may lack generalizability as well when the findings in one study cannot be replicated in another setting. In many discussions of the empirical findings in quantitative studies, a common recommendation made by the researcher is the call for replication in a different context using different samples with the caveat that the findings are sample specific and without replication studies do not generalize to other settings. Similarly, quantitative approaches can also be susceptible to subjectivity. For example, the ways questionnaires are worded are open to interpretation; statistical data are often based on someone's definition of what to measure and how to measure it (Patton, 2002). It has also been shown again and again that quantitative research can also be affected by the bias of the researcher and the participants, samples can be manipulated, data can be tampered with or purposely excluded, surveys can be poorly constructed, and respondents can answer dishonestly (Patton & Appelbaum, 2003). Researchers who adopt the Miles and Huberman stance take the position that epistemological purity does not get research done and instead emphasize the need for developing a body of clearly defined methods for drawing valid conclusions from qualitative data (Miles & Huberman, 1994, p. 21).

More recently, the debate has included calls for finding ways of making the two perspectives more compatible and to encourage collaboration between quantitative and qualitative researchers. Efforts have been made to reconcile both paradigms, thus providing the opportunity to exploit the advantages of both approaches and opening the way for synergy effects. This can be seen most clearly in the proliferation of mixed methods studies (Chapter 6), in which quantitative and quantitative methods are combined by triangulating methods, theories, or researchers. Mixed method designs are, at least in part, a response to the decreased either/or approaches inherent in the paradigm wars. They are being replaced by the injunction to examine a phenomenon from multiple perspectives which may include multiple paradigms and methods. This is not to say that the boundaries between quantitative and qualitative research have been dissolved or that paradigmatic differences are no longer considered important. Instead, reliability and validly have been replaced by other criteria and standards for evaluation such as the overall significance, relevance, impact, and utility of a study as well a consideration of aesthetic and rhetorical concern (Morse et al., 2002; Sandelowski & Barroso, 2002), which can shed light on the quality of a qualitative study. Current trends in qualitative leadership studies reflect a growing understanding that qualitative research cannot be encapsulated a priori within a set of rigid rules as both leadership and quality are elusive constructs that cannot be prespecified by methodological rules. But again, this does not mean that quality criteria do not apply to the qualitative tradition. Recent guidelines are intended to improve the quality or credibility of qualitative research; however, their adoption does not automatically guarantee rigor. Seale (1999) posits a reconstitution of positivist orthodoxy regarding quality and rigor as a set of guidelines to be followed with intelligence and knowledge of a particular research context that may assist us in achieving good-quality work. Nevertheless tensions between the two paradigms continue to exist. For more than two decades, the call for integration of qualitative and quantitative methods, methodological eclectism, let alone synthesis of the two paradigms, has gone unheeded (Roberts, 2003). In leadership research, the methodological landscape may simply not be mature enough to respond to these calls.

New paradigms such as pragmatism (De Waal, 2005; Rorty, 1989) or more politically engaged ways of knowing such a feminism (Olesen, 2000) have appeared on the qualitative landscape that take into consideration the changing context of research as organizations, the workforce, and the society are moving into different directions. As Greene and Caracelli (2003) suggest, a given set of assumptions about reality and knowledge is not sacrosanct; rather it can be modified, expanded, or constricted— altered to fit changing social needs and circumstances. Paradigms—both research and leadership—change over time and place. In addition, a new generation of leadership scholars is trained in doctoral programs that are not as wedded to positivism and the superiority of quantitative approaches or the continuation of paradigm wars. Tashakkori and Teddlie (2003a) concluded that it is time to balance the philosophical, conceptual, practical, and political considerations so relevant to our inquiry (p. 108).

THE ROLE OF ETHICS IN QUALITATIVE RESEARCH

Qualitative researchers have documented the numerous ethical dilemmas that can arise during data collection and fieldwork, many of which revolve around issues of honesty and lying, power and privilege, and the overall quality of the relationship between researcher and researched. Additionally, there are ethical issues concerning the construction of knowledge as well as issues of advocacy (e.g., Doucet & Mauthner, 2002). Research on leadership (as well as research in other social sciences) is subject to approval by an institutional review board (IRB) charged with ensuring that the investigator adheres to ethical principles (usually the set of principles proposed by the American Psychological Association). Ethical guidelines are largely associated with gaining ethics approval from professional or academic bodies with approval premised on principles of informed consent, confidentiality and anonymity, and protection from harm. The major role of these ethics committees is to provide a bottom line safe environment and put into place accountability mechanisms that hold researchers responsible and accountable for ethical conduct and strictest adherence to ethical principles in research with human participants.

While ethics committees increasingly require researchers to produce consent forms for them to vet and for research participants to sign, the formality of such procedures certainly alienates some groups and individuals. Ethical codes have become more formalized over the past several decades, to the point where some say they unduly constrain the conduct of social research or protect the researcher more than the researched. Hammersley (1999), reflecting on an increasing concern with moving ethics to center stage, notes:

> ... a tendency to see research almost entirely in ethical terms, as if its aim were to achieve ethical goals or to exemplify ethical ideals... Whereas previously ethical considerations were believed to set the boundaries to what researchers could do in pursuit of knowledge, now ethical considerations are treated by some as constituting the very rationale of research. For example, its task becomes the promotion of social justice (p. 18).

Lincoln and Guba (1989) argue that ethics are part and parcel of the paradigm position held by the researcher. The authors believe that "much depends on the moral boiling point of the individual enquirer; different inquirers will make different decisions even when confronted with similar circumstances" (p. 226). Furthermore, they assert that nothing inherent in conventional modes of social science research either mandates or rewards ethical. For Lincoln and Guba, the naturalistic paradigm is more ethical than the quantitative paradigm although they acknowledge that "confidentiality and anonymity obviously cannot be guaranteed in naturalistic enquiry" (p. 233). However, as Shaw (2003) points out, no research methodology is ethically privileged, and formulations of ethical principles are no different for quantitative and qualitative methodologies. However, there are particular ethical questions presented by qualitative research. For example, ethnographers are often faced with the dilemma of being at once the snooping stranger and the good friend (Jatvie, 1982).

Among the most important ethical principles, the qualitative researcher has to adhere to are informed consent, voluntary participation, confidentiality, protection from harm, and maintenance of the well-being of the participants. *Informed consent*, from individuals capable of such consent, must be obtained in all forms of research. This requires informing participants about the overall purpose of the research and its procedures, as well as the risks and benefits of participation. Consent may be given in written format, verbally, and audio-taped or video-taped. Eisner (1991) argued that informed consent in qualitative research is often hazardous because "it implies that the researcher knows before the event...what the event will be and its possible effects" (p. 214). However, this is often not the case in qualitative research. *Voluntary participation* means that participants are not coerced to participate in the study and, at any time during the research, may withdraw their participation with penalties.

Confidentiality and *privacy* are also central issues in all forms of research. By ensuring confidentiality, the investigator agrees not to report private data that identify participants. One of the safest ways to ensure anonymity is not to record the names of participants by developing a coding scheme such as a system of random numbers that allows the investigator to connect individuals with their corresponding data sets. Unique identifying information must be removed or not gathered at all. In some types of qualitative research, such as focus groups or e-mail interviews, there can be no guarantee of confidentiality. Researchers who employ these methods are obligated to inform participants of the limits of confidentiality. Confidentiality issues are particularly salient when the results of a qualitative study with lengthy quotations from participant are published.

The *risk of harm* to participants must be minimal. For example, qualitative interviews on sensitive leadership topics such as leadership failures, abusive leader behaviors, or "bad" leadership may evoke powerful emotional responses from participants which obligate the researcher to protect the psychological well-being of the participants by, for example, making available appropriate referral sources for professional help should it be needed. Emotional reactions of the interviewer are also possible and need to be safeguarded against. Some scholars feel that traditional methods of in-depth qualitative interviewing are invasive and unethical because the techniques and tactics used are really ways of manipulating respondents. Types of sensitive topics that may produce harm to participants include those that delve into the personal experiences of participants, are concerned with social control, impinge on vested interests of powerful persons (political leaders, for instance), or deal with things sacred to the participants.

Table 2-5   Guiding ethical principles in qualitative research

- Respect for human dignity
- Respect for voluntary participation
- Respect for confidentiality and privacy
- Respect for justice and inclusiveness
- Balancing harm and benefits
- Minimizing harm
- Maximizing benefits

Expertise of the researcher and knowledge of the sensitive subject matter are factors that help balancing harm and benefits.

Table 2-5 summarizes the guiding ethical principles in qualitative research. In qualitative research, in addition to the ethical principles depicted in Table 2-5 issues such as sensitivity to others, difference and diversity may also become ethical issues.

Another important ethical issue concerns who has access to the data and who owns them. Ownership and dissemination of research findings must be negotiated so that they balance the rights, for example, of the interviewee (who owns the data), the interviewer, the sponsoring organization, and whatever other party may be in involved in the study. Furthermore, the interviewer needs to be able to offer the interviewee something in return for sharing their experiences, time, and insights. Will they or their communities benefit in some way form the results of the study? If promises are made, such as copies of the report, they must be kept. Ideally, there should be reciprocity in what participants give and what they receive from participation in a research project. The investigator is indebted to participants for sharing their experiences. Reciprocity may entail providing feedback on the results of the research, inviting participants to co-author publications that may emanate from the study.

Regarding ethics in qualitative research, Eisner (1991) concludes:

> We might like to ensure informed consent, but we know we can't always inform because we don't always know. We would like to protect personal privacy and guarantee confidentiality, but we know we cannot always fulfill such guarantees. We would like to be candid but sometimes candor is inappropriate. We do not like to think of ourselves as using others as a means to our own professional ends, but if we embark on a research study that we conceptualize, direct, and write, we virtually assure that we will use others for our purpose (pp. 225–226).

Ethical issues in qualitative research are often more subtle than issues in quantitative research. These issues are related to fundamental characteristics of qualitative research including prolonged and personal involvement between the researchers and the participants. Moreover, the researcher is the primary research instrument which creates different interactional dynamics between the researcher and the researched. However, there is a set of ethical issues shared by both qualitative and quantitative field methodologies that include informed consent, voluntary participation, protection of participants' privacy or confidentiality, and protection of the welfare of the participants. Moreover, the different qualitative methods such as content analysis or phenomenology embrace different epistemologies; therefore, we cannot separate epistemology from ethics as epistemology becomes an ethical issue.

Finally, most researchers are keenly aware that, to a greater or lesser extent, politics suffuses all social science research (Guba & Lincoln, 1989). As researchers, we make political decisions, consciously or unconsciously, when deciding what to study, whom to ask, what methods to employ. Power exists everywhere and is constantly negotiated during the research process between researchers, informants, and sponsoring organizations. Punch (1994) defines politics as everything from the micropolitics of personal relations to the cultures and resources of research units and universities, the powers and policies of government departments all of which influence the design, implementation, and outcomes of research. Van Maanen (1988b) discusses "tales of the field" where obstructionist gatekeepers, vacillating sponsors, and factionalism are subverting the research process and sexual shenanigans, disputes about publications, and veracity of findings impede the dissemination of the results. Likewise, Rabinowitz and Weseen (1997) reported on the negative effects created by the dynamics and varied political allegiances that influence how the qualitative–quantitative debate is approached. The authors showed that many research "allegiances" are the result of politics, peer group influence, and personal preference rather than being based on rational argument.

SUMMARY

Defining qualitative research and establishing criteria for judging the quality of qualitative research are complex and complicated issues and the validity of qualitative research, one critical quality criterion, continues to be hotly debated. Three different positions were identified, which involve applying quantitative quality standards to qualitative research, employing alternative criteria such as authenticity or trustworthiness congruent with qualitative ontology, and epistemology or the complete rejection of all predetermined quality standards. In the future, qualitative researchers must make their ontological, epistemological, and methodological commitments much more explicit when reporting their findings to facilitate assessment of quality in qualitative studies.

Qualitative research that offers rich, thick, context-sensitive descriptions can make significant contributions to the emergent discourse on leadership as the field moves into the postmillennial period. History has shown that leadership theory has constantly shifted paradigms from trait, behavioral, contingency to transactional/transformational theories, and now beyond. Quantitative researchers believe that while qualitative research can be a rich source of data, it remains unclear as to how qualitative researchers link data and interpretation and arrive at firm, valid, and legitimate conclusions. Quantitative research, on the other hand, involves precision yielding statistically significant effects but the meaning of the findings is open to question (Cupchik, 2001).

The alignment of quantitative research with positivism and qualitative research with interpretivism has led to a great deal of confusion in the debate over the relative merits of each paradigm. In fact, at times, the distinction between qualitative and quantitative research is amorphous as when qualitative researchers reach for traditional quantitative criteria such as reliability and reliability to establish and justify the quality and rigor of their study. Despite the many proposed differences between quantitative and qualitative epistemologies, ultimately the quantitative–qualitative debate is philosophical, not methodological. Because a paradigm is a worldview, spanning ontology, epistemology, and methodology, the quality of scientific research done within a paradigm has to be judged by its own paradigmatic terms. Tashakkori & Teedlie (2003) note that what best distinguishes research entities and researchers is not whether they are qualitative or quantitative but rather the overall attitude and interpretive treatment of the data collected in those studies. Methods do not by themselves signal much about the nature of the inquiry; rather it is the distinctive execution and representation of these methods that signal key differences in inquiry (p. 324).

Finally, I posited that the ethics of qualitative research place distinctive demands on the principles of informed consent, confidentiality, and privacy and freedom from risk and harm to the research participants. Ethical issues arise at all stages of the research process—from gaining access to research participants to the publications of the research findings. It is imperative that qualitative researchers engage in ongoing reflection on and responses to ethical issues throughout the research project. Ethical guidelines for qualitative research need to balance the need to do research against the need to protect individual rights. The knowledge that is gained from the research must be worth the risk that the research might cause to the participants.

Taken together, the two foundational chapters are intended to promote the understanding of the ontological and epistemological bases of qualitative research methodologies, their interrelationships, and linkages to research methods and the concomitant ethical issues that arise from qualitative research. Overall, the aim of qualitative research is to understand how the world is socially constructed by its participants and what meanings they ascribe to them. The notion of the world being socially constructed implies that individuals inhabit a social, personal, and relational world that is complex, layered, and can be construed from multiple perspectives (McLeod, 2001).

Part II

MAJOR QUALITATIVE TRADITIONS IN LEADERSHIP RESEARCH

3

CASE STUDIES IN LEADERSHIP RESEARCH

Case study research is remarkably hard, even though case studies traditionally have been considered to be "soft" research. Paradoxically, the "softer" a research technique, the harder it is to do.

(Yin, 1994, p. 26)

AN ILLUSTRATIVE LEADERSHIP CASE STUDY

Weed's (1993) study of Mothers' Against Drunk Drivers (MADD) is a representative of a single case study, which traces the development of MADD under the leadership of Candy Lightner whose daughter was killed in a DUI accident in California. Although traffic experts and alcohol researchers had already created the public image of a socially irresponsible drunk driver who injures or kills innocent people, what was missing from the public discourse was a person who personally identified with the issue. Candy Lightner was that individual who took on the role of victim-activist in the form of the angry, bereaved parent who made drunk driving a national political issue and whose energetic crusade led to the creation of MADD, a national, well-funded national organization. Victim status became the basis of legitimate authority for Candy Lightner and other local MADD chapter leaders. The case chronicles Lightner's leadership during her five years as president of MADD until she was replaced when she found herself embroiled in a conflict with the Board of Directors.

The data were collected through telephone interviews with chapter officers who were asked to reflect on their experiences with Lightner; additionally, the case study relied on published and unpublished documents and attendance of staff meetings by the researcher. The data were analyzed qualitatively to identify common themes represented in the quotes of interviewees.

The case provides an example of the conflict between the leadership qualities of a charismatic founder and the organizational demands placed on MADD as a nationally recognized reform movement. It examines the image of a parent victim-activist as a source of moral legitimacy for a charismatic leader, an image that was critical in focusing attention on the drunken driving problem in the United States and the development of MADD as a national organization. In 1981, MADD was recognized as a tax-exempt organization. Over the next three years, under Lightner's charismatic leadership, MADD accomplished a reform in California's drunk driving law, grew to over 90 chapters a cross the country, and by the time Lightner left the organization had about 360 local chapters and 600 000 members and donors. Successful fund raising put Lightner on the payroll. The use of money and the operations of MADD which was increasingly staffed by professionals with backgrounds in corporate law and finance some of whom also served as Board members led to a dispute which resulted in the appointment of a new Executive Director.

The case analysis focused on Lightner's leadership style which was centralized, partly because she identified with MADD to such an extent that the organization became an extension of herself. In 1985, the new Board members found her leadership style unusual and at odds with what they felt were sound management practices of a national organization. The change in policy that dealt with reducing the number of local chapter representatives on the board with professionals was the turning point in the history of the organization as Lightner then fell under the control of managers. Her salary package came under attack and she was critized for charging personal expense to the organization. Eventually, Lightner was relegated to a position as a consultant under a two-year contract with a reduced salary.

As Weber (1947, p. 363) put it, charisma "has a character specifically foreign to everyday routine structures." Consistent with this observation, Weed (1993) found that the rational administrative practices developed in the MADD organization conflicted with the charismatic leadership of its founder, who was eventually replaced. The author concluded that the history of MADD's charismatic founder reflects Max Weber's prediction that "in its pure form charismatic authority has a character especially foreign to everyday routine structure" (Weber, 1964, p. 363).

INTRODUCTION TO CASE STUDY RESEARCH

Case studies are widely used in organizational studies and across the social sciences. Stake (2005) suggests that case studies have become one of the most common ways to conduct qualitative inquiry. According to Yin (2003), using case studies remains one of the most challenging of all social science endeavors. It is driven by the desire to understand complex social phenomena because the case study method allows investigators to retain the holistic and meaningful characteristics of real-life events such as leadership processes.

My experience in conducting case research and working with doctoral students on dissertations in organizational leadership that use case study methods confirms Yin's view that case study research is indeed remarkably complex and hard. The demand of a case study researcher's intellect and affective capacity to process complex emotions involved in interactions with research participants and gatekeepers are considerate and often exceed those of other designs. Case study research requires clear research questions, a thorough understanding of the extant literature, a well-formulated research design resting on explicit paradigmatic assumptions, and the ability to synthesize large amounts of data from interviews, field notes and transcripts, documents, observations of meetings, and from all these data produce a theoretically informed and persuasively argued conclusion (Scapens, 2004). A good case researcher knows how to ask good questions; he or she is a good listener, minimally bound by his or her ideologies and preconceptions, and sensitive to contrary information.

In addition, the case researcher needs excellent interpersonal and communication skills to interact and negotiate effectively with research participants, gatekeepers, and consumers of the research as well as an understanding that he or she is not neutral bystander or operates independently of the case. In short, the demands case studies make on a researcher's cognitive, emotional, and motivational capacities are often greater than those imposed by other research strategies. Therefore, a well-trained and experienced researcher is needed to conduct a high-quality case study because of the multiple challenges and labor-intensive nature of case study research.

Case Study Defined

A case study investigates a leadership phenomenon within its real-life context especially when the boundaries between the phenomenon and context are not clearly defined. Stake (1995) defined case study as the exploration of a "bounded, integrated system" over time through detailed in-depth data collection involving multiple sources of information and rich context. The author distinguishes between intrinsic and instrumental cases. When the case itself is of interest, it is called an *intrinsic case*. Here, the interest is in a particular case such as leadership succession in a nonprofit agency. Alternatively, if the focus of the case is on the dynamics of the issue(s) and the need for a general understanding, it is called an *instrumental case*. Here, the case is used to understand more than what is obvious to the observer. For example, a leadership researcher may be interested in studying how different leadership education programs—skills training programs promoting the development of specific leadership skills such as conflict resolution or decision-making or academic programs focused on the cognitive understanding of leadership processes—enhance the effectiveness of business leaders participating in these programs. Here, the case study is instrumental in understanding something else, namely leadership effectiveness. Hartley (1994) defines a case study as a "detailed investigation, often with data collected over a period of time, of one or more organizations, or groups within organizations, with a view to providing an analysis of context and processes involved in the phenomenon under investigation" (pp. 208–9). Most definitions agree that case studies can accomplish a variety of purposes: to provide an in-depth description of a phenomenon, test theory or generate theory. However, according to Frederickson (1983), the ultimate aim of case study research is the construction of middle-range explanatory theory where the researcher disaggregates complex contexts into more discrete, carefully defined chunks, and then reintegrates these parts with an explicit analysis of their context (Peterson, 1998).

Role of Theory in Cases Studies

The extent to which existing leadership theories drive the design of a qualitative study is an issue in all qualitative research. However, it is particularly prominent in case studies because one of the explicit purposes of a case study is to build theory. As a result, we find case study researchers who have adopted divergent positions regarding the role of theory in their work. According to one point of view, which I refer to as the purist approach, we find scholars who argue that the case researcher should approach his of her study without being influenced by existing theory—in other words, as a tabula rasa or canvas which has not been painted on. The opposing view acknowledges that few of us, particularly seasoned researchers with strong paradigm convictions, can completely distance ourselves from existing theories. At the extreme, researchers adhering to this position use constructs from theories to frame their research questions and generate hypotheses. For example, Theus (1995) uses the case of the sudden resignation of the president of American University as a vehicle to illustrate a model that she deduced from the literature. In this case study, data were coded relating to key dimensions suggested in the literature such as sense making, uncertainty, power relations, and organizational structure during and subsequent to the crisis-induced departure of the organizational leader (Theus, 1995, p. 33). However, the researcher used theory in a different way than is common in positivist research. Instead of attempting to falsify theories on which the study was based, the author used theory as a sensitizing device to offer certain insights and interpretations.

Eisenhardt (1989), in the context of organizational research, identifies three distinct uses of theory: (1) as an initial guide to design and data collection; (2) as part of an iterative process of data collection and analysis; and (3) as the final product of the research. The motivation of the use of theory in the earlier stages of a case study is to create an initial theoretical framework which takes into account previous knowledge and which creates a theoretical basis to inform the topics and approach to the early empirical work. For example, Matteson (2006) suggested that some of the concepts discussed by positive psychologists such as humility, courage, resilience and other human strength to develop a model of self-sacrificial leadership.

Although theory can provide a valuable initial guide, it limits the researcher to focusing on the concepts embedded in the theory, which stifles potential new issues and avenues of exploration. The concept of constant comparison encourages qualitative researcher to preserve a considerable degree of openness to the field data and willingness to modify initial assumptions and theories. Finally, with respect to the third use of theory as the final product of the research, Eisenhardt (1989) notes that the output of a case may be concepts, a conceptual framework, propositions, or midrange theory. Recent work on authentic leadership (i.e., Avolio & Gardner, 2005; Gardner, Avolio, Luthans, May, & Walumba, 2005; Klenke, 2005) illustrates this third use of theory. Collectively this body of research has introduced several conceptual frameworks of authentic leadership as well as new concepts such as the eudemonic well-being of the leader (Ilies, Morgenson & Nahrgang, 2005).

There is a paradox quoting Eisenhardt here since the author explicitly states her epistemological position as positivism, and midrange theory is something to, according to her views, be tested formally using positivistic approaches. This position on the role of theory would not be acceptable to many qualitative researchers in leadership although the view of theory as a desirable final product of case research would be generally shared (Walsham, 1995, p. 76).

Whatever a researcher's positions between theory-derived and theory-free positions, case researchers, explicitly or implicitly, bring some kind of conceptual framework to the research process which acts as a filter for data collection and interpretations that are partially determined by this filter. It would be unrealistic to suggest that researchers could or should enter the field devoid of frameworks or ideas about relevant concepts in their areas of interest. As researchers, we all interpret the world through some sort of conceptual lenses formed by our beliefs, previous experience, existing knowledge, assumptions about the world, and theories about knowledge and how it is accrued (Cepeda & Martin, 2005).

Case studies can have implication for both theory developments and theory testing. The term theory development is typically reserved for case studies which add new variables, hypotheses, or causal mechanism to a theory. Theory development through case studies is primarily an inductive rather than deductive process. Theory testing involves confirming or disconfirming theories as well as identifying the conditions under which they are most and least likely to apply. It aims at strengthening or reducing support for a theory or narrow or extend the scope of a theory. Both theory development and theory testing through case studies are essential to constructing good theories.

Miles and Huberman (1994) argue that a researcher's conceptual framework "explains either graphically or in narrative form, the main things to be studied, the key factors, constructs or variables—and the presumed relationships between them" (p. 18). Thus, the conceptual framework is created from the research themes, existing knowledge about the phenomenon of interest which is gathered from personal experience and the literature, and filtered by a researcher's paradigmatic assumptions and theoretical foundations. Moreover, participants, just as the researcher, are seen as interpreters and analysts who contribute to the appropriation of theoretical concepts.

Overall, reliance on existing theory or complete rejection of existing theory represents the boundaries within which the role of theory in case studies can be approached. Existing theoretical constructs can be useful in informing design and analysis of some case studies. Openness and sensitivity to participants' verbalizations offer unique windows for theory formulation in others.

THE ARCHITECTURE OF A LEADERSHIP CASE STUDY

As noted earlier, case studies in leadership may involve single (e.g., Dyck, 1994; Weed, 1993), multiple (e.g., Waldman, et al., 1998), and longitudinal (e.g., Gersick, 1994; Gronn, 1999; Neuman, 1995) research. The earliest examples of qualitative research on leadership tended to be based on a single case study. Although this has continued to be a popular approach, single case studies have gradually given way to multiple case study and cross-sectional research designs (Bryman, 2004). Moreover, case studies can employ an embedded design using multiple levels of analysis within a single study. Case studies can be both qualitative and quantitative; many use method and/or data triangulation. Case studies have been combined using a variety of epistemological positions, from positivist to phenomenological (Klenke, 2004). Case studies can be analyzed using within and between case analyses. Yin (1994) distinguishes between *exploratory, explanatory*, and *descriptive* case studies. Each of these three approaches can be either single or multiple case studies, where multiple case studies are replicatory, not sampled cases. In exploratory case studies, fieldwork and data collection may be undertaken prior to definition of the research questions. This approach is particularly useful if little previous research exists on the phenomenon under investigation. Cases can also be exploratory in nature or intentionally designed to build theory using inductive methods to generate hypotheses about new research questions. Explanatory cases are suitable for conducting causal studies while descriptive cases are theory driven. Yin (1994) sees a single case study as analogous to a single experiment in terms of theory testing and development. Hence, his approach is an example of the positivist approach to case study research and illustrates that what is shared between qualitative and quantitative research may therefore be more real than apparent (Becker, 1996).

Case Study as Method of Choice

According to Yin (1994), case studies are the preferred approach when "how" and "why" questions are to be answered, when the researcher has little control over events and when the focus is on a current phenomenon in a real-life context. The author presents at least four applications for a case study model: (1) to explain complex causal links in real-life interventions; (2) to describe the real-life context in which the intervention has occurred; (3) to describe the intervention itself; and (4) to explore situations in which the intervention being evaluated has no clear set of outcomes. Eisenhardt (1989), in a seminal paper arguing for the use of case studies to build theory, states that case studies are

> Particularly well suited to new research areas or research areas for which existing theories seem inadequate. This type of work is highly complementary to incremental theory building from normal science research. The former is useful in the early stages of research on a topic or when a fresh perspective is needed, while the latter is useful in the later stages of knowledge development (pp. 548–549).

This approach, which adopts a positivist view of research (as does Yin), relies on past literature and empirical data as well as on insights of the researcher to build incrementally more powerful theories. The author acknowledges that in comparison with Strauss (1987) and Van Maanen (1988a), the process she describes adopts a positivist view of case study research meaning that, in part, the process is directed toward the development of testable hypotheses and theory which are generalizable across settings.

Other researchers believe that Eisenhardt's approach represents a useful way of positioning case study research within the repertoire of methods available to leadership research but favor designs exploratory and descriptive methods as Eisenhardt (1989) posits to include all kinds of research: exploratory, descriptive, or explanatory. In the study of leadership, there are too many "why" types of research questions that cannot be answered by quantitative studies and await answers. Researchers who are more concerned with a rich, complex description of the specific cases tend to be less concerned with the development of generalizable theory, as Eisenhardt herself points out.

In addition to its theory building potential, the contextuality of the case study method is a reason for its selection as the method of choice. Many leadership problems are defined and shaped by the context in which they manifest themselves. For example, to study leadership in Eastern Europe, the researcher needs to investigate the context, both the macroenvironmental setting as well as industry-specific factors that may shape the leadership style of Eastern European leaders. In the turbulent, global environment in which leaders operate, there is an abundance of concepts and variables that determine leadership style, leader–follower relationships, and so on that are difficult to quantify using experimental or survey methods but can be carefully assessed using case study research. In general, then, case studies are the preferred strategy when the investigator has little control over events and when the focus is on a contemporary phenomenon within some real-life context (Yin, 2003).

Selecting Cases: Single and Multiple Case Studies

Yin (2003) emphasizes the importance of case selection being consistent with the research question. In other words, as with all choices of method, the research question drives the selection of method and the selection of cases. Moreover, the selection of cases should be congruent with the epistemological assumptions a researcher makes about the phenomenon he or she is studying. An investigator working within the constructivism paradigm, for example, will select a different case or set of cases than a colleague who bases the choice of cases on assumptions governing pragmatism or realism.

Case selection relies on *theoretical or purposive sampling* strategies; in other words, cases are selected because they may contribute to the emergent theory the investigator is attempting to build, or as Eisenhardt (1989) notes, they may be chosen to fill theoretical categories and provide examples of polar types or extreme situations. In theoretical sampling, the investigator selects both typical (i.e., cases that strengthen the emergent theory) and atypical cases (i.e., cases that produce contrasting results but for predictable reasons). For case studies, random selection is neither necessary nor even preferable. Instead, it is the theoretical issues and the purpose of the research that guide the sampling procedures (Glaser & Strauss, 1967). Finally, case study selection is influenced by resources involved in contacting case participants, traveling to their locations, transcription of interview data, and other practical issues of importance.

The criteria for case selection should be specific. They should address how many cases should be researched. Single cases are often critical, revelatory, uncovering unusual phenomena.

Patton (2002) suggests that *single case studies* are also appropriate if they represent unique situations or extreme cases such as specific organizations which experienced unusual examples of leadership successes or failures as in the case of MADD described earlier. Single case studies may be used to confirm or challenge a theory, or to represent a unique or extreme case (Yin, 1994). Single case studies are also ideal for revelatory cases where the observer may have to access a phenomenon that was previously inaccessible. These studies can be holistic or embedded, the latter occurring when the same case study involves more than one unit of analysis. For example, in addition to using organizational leaders as informants, many leadership researchers also include a small number of their followers or the team. Finally, single case studies are useful in pilot studies or exploratory research where they serve as a first step to later, more comprehensive studies. Many have argued that the major problem with the case study approach is the lack of generalizability, especially from single cases. However, although single case studies are not as strong a base for generalizing to a population of cases as other research designs, we can learn much that is general from a single case.

In *multiple cases*, the research questions remains the same but data are collected in different organizations. Pauwels and Mattyssens (2004) describe four pillars of multiple case study research—theoretical sampling, triangulation, pattern matching logic, and analytical generalization—and cover possible architectures that span these pillars with a single superstructure or roof: validation through juxtaposition and iteration. The authors posit that the way these pillars and the roof are conceived allow for a flexible architecture of case study research—strong and stable to withstand many of the methodological criticisms fired at qualitative research, yet flexible enough to allow for a research design that meets the challenges of the actual research question, the phenomenon under investigation, and the context of the study (p. 126). Validation through juxtaposition and iteration refers to the juxtaposition of data, extant theory and emergent theory while iteration refers to the cycling between data analysis, interpretation, emergent and extant theory.

Multiple cases have distinct advantages compared to the single case design. They offer the prospect of producing results that are less likely to be deemed idiosyncratic or unscientific. The evidence from multiple cases is often considered more compelling, and the conclusions tend to be more robust. The product of a multiple case study can require extensive resources and time beyond the means of a single case researcher. Therefore, the decision to employ the multiple case approach should not be taken lightly. Each case selected should serve a specific purpose within the overall scope of the inquiry. For example, Matteson (2006) deliberately selected case from three different contexts, situating each case within a different setting (business, nonprofit, and military), each with its own structural, sociopolitical, and economic boundaries to build a theory of self-sacrificial leadership. The author used method triangulation combining content analysis and interviews of multiple cases and hypothesized that leaders who are optimistic, resilient, and hopeful, constructs associated with the positive psychology movement (i.e., Luthans, 2002; Seligman & Csikszsentmihalyi, 2000), are more likely to engage in self-sacrificing behaviors compared to leaders who are less optimistic, resilient, and hopeful. The results supported the positive psychology constructs within each of the three cases, illustrating literal replication. However, across the three cases, Matteson also illustrated theoretical replication as additional concepts emerged across cases such as moral courage, implicit leadership theory, and faith in humanity that contributed to the self-sacrificing behaviors demonstrated by the three leaders in three different cases. One of the primary reasons for conducting multiple case studies, according to Firestone and Herriott (1994), is to escape the "radical particularism" of many single case studies and hence to provide a firmer basis for generalizability.

Each type of case study design—single cases, multiple cases, and triangulated case studies—has design features that the researcher makes explicit. In the most general sense, the design of a case study is a logical sequence that connects empirical data to the study's initial research questions and, ultimately, to the conclusions. Colloquially, a research design is a logical plan for getting from here to there, where here may be defined the initial hunches that lead to the formulation of the research question(s) and there is some set of answer and conclusions about these questions through the application of a specific case study design.

DATA COLLECTION AND ANALYSIS IN CASE STUDY RESEARCH

Data Collection Methods

Yin (2003) recommends six types of data collection strategies: interviews, direct observations, participant observation, documentation, archival records, and physical artifact. Despite the choice of data collection techniques, many case study researchers treat interviews as one of the most important data sources. However, in recent years, triangulation has become a common feature in case studies referring to the collection of data through different methods as Yin recommends. Triangulation may also involve different kind of data on the same phenomenon. For example, a leadership case researcher may collect data not only from leaders but from followers and other constituencies as well.

Most case studies follow an established protocol, which typically consists of a design phase to include the recommended procedures, an overview of the case study project, field procedures, and the case study research questions; and the actual conduct of the study, analysis of case study evidence based on specific analytic strategies such as pattern making or constant comparisons and the development of conclusions, recommendations, and implications based on the evidence. The reporting aspect is perhaps the most important aspect of a case study, at least from the reader's perspective.

Data Analysis Techniques

Data analysis initially involves developing a detailed description of the case. Collecting and analyzing data in case study research are not separate phases of the research cycle but represent an iterative process by which data collection impacts on design features which may be modified to reflect greater insight the researcher has gained during data collection. Likewise, results from initial analyses may redirect data collection procedures. For example, it is not unusual for a researcher after interviewing two or three participants in a multiple case study to revise the interview protocol by adding or deleting questions to incorporate tentative findings revealed by the preliminary analysis. Miles and Huberman (1994) assert that interweaving data collection and data analysis is the best policy because it allows theory to develop alongside the growing volume of data. At each phase of this iterative process of collecting data, the formulation of new questions leading to subsequent analysis and additional data collection, the case researcher aims to achieve higher levels of abstraction that progresses from description to explanation.

Formal methods for qualitative data collection and analysis have been developed, particularly by Miles and Hubeman (1994), for observing events, conducting interviews, and coding qualitative data. Furthermore, the use of multiple data collection methods provides stronger substantiation of constructs and hypotheses (Eisenhardt, 1989). Stake (1995) highlights many triangulation methods used in case studies to increase validity. Analyzing data in different spaces, at different times, and in different contexts; having other researchers, perhaps from totally different backgrounds, review procedures and interpretations, respondent validation (member checking); and using different data sources are ways to achieve triangulation and thereby enhance the validity of a case study and increase confidence in the conclusions (Patton & Appelbaum, 2003).

Stake (1995) advocates four types of data analyses. In *categorical aggregation*, the researcher seeks a collection of incidents from the data from which he or she expects relevant issues to emerge. In direct interpretation, the researcher looks for a single instance and draws meaning from it without looking for corroborating instances. This is a process of pulling the data apart and putting them together in a more meaningful way. *Pattern matching* is a technique in which an empirically based pattern is compared to a predicted pattern. If the patterns match, the internal validity of the study is enhanced. Another analytic technique is *explanation building*, which may be considered a form of pattern matching in which the analysis of the case is carried out by building an explanation of the case. It is an iterative process that begins with a theoretical statement, refines it, revises the proposition, and then repeats this process from the beginning. This data analytic strategy is particularly useful in explanatory case studies where the iterative process begins with a theoretical statement, refines it, revises the propositions derived from that statement, and recycles this process to the point of saturation. Finally, in *analytic generalization*, the researcher arrives at a pattern that consists of events and relationships between these events. Analytic generalization raises the question of whether or not these relationships hold outside the informants and organization(s) that participated in the study. Through analytical generalization, an investigator aims at testing the validity of the research outcome (i.e., a theory) against the theoretical network that surrounds the phenomenon and the research questions (Yin, 1994).

Thus, data collection and analysis are interrelated, iterative tasks that may involve re-reading the transcripts, revisiting the extant literatures, mining the data to arrive at a deeper understanding of the data and the patterns and themes underlying them. Data analysis also involves intentional periods of critical reflection—reviewing the research process, interactions with participants, seeking disconfirming evidence for tentative findings, changing the conceptual framework to incorporate accumulated knowledge and build theory. Reflection also means searching for alternative explanations of the findings and approaching making meaning of the data from different perspectives. This iterative process is not only inductive but also tightly interrelated with practice: field-work leads to theory building, which leads to further research into practice (Markus, 1997).

Another approach to analyzing case study data is known as w*ithin and between case analyses*. In within case analysis, a single case is chosen because it is thought to be critical, extreme, unique, and instrumental in the development or elaboration of theory. In other words, single cases are not chosen for representativeness. Within case analysis often results in pure descriptions which are central to generating insights. Although there is no standard format for this analysis, within case analysis typically involves the development of a case study data base, which includes the raw materials of the case such as interview transcripts, researchers' field notes, or documents collected during data gathering as well as code data, coding schemes, and other analytic materials.

Between cases analysis is based on multiple cases permitting cross-case analysis and follows what Yin (1994) calls replication rather than sampling logic. Multiple case studies allow the application of replication logic as each case is treated as a separate entity that permits replication and testing emergent theory in subsequent cases. Repli-cation logic requires the careful selection of each case so that it either (1) predicts similar results (a *literal replication)* or (2) predicts contrasting results but for predict-able reasons (a *theoretical replication)* (Yin, 2003 p. 47). Replication logic should not be confused with sampling logic, where a selection is made out of a population, for inclusion in the study.

Glaser & Strauss (1967) and Glaser (1999) suggest that the addition of new cases ceases when the researcher reaches theoretical saturation, that is, when the contribution of a new case to emergent theory is minimal. Practical considerations, such as time con-straints or available funding, may determine the decision to cease additional data collection. If a "good enough" picture has been established, its current conceptual framework should be compared to a broad range of literature.

Coding is another data analytic technique often used in case study research. Details of coding procedures are discussed in Chapter 4 on content analysis. Suffice it to say here that the purpose of coding is to translate responses of participants into increasing higher levels of abstraction to develop broad constructs that reflect common themes and patterns that form the basis of developing theory.

INTERPRETING THE FINDINGS OF CASE STUDY RESEARCH

The goal of data interpretation is to make meaning of the case analysis. The case researcher interprets the meaning of the case, whether it comes from learning about the issue of the case (instrumental case) or learning about an unusual situation (intrinsic case). Eisenhardt (1989) proposes a road map for building theories from positivist case study research. This road map synthesizes previous work on qualitative research (Miles & Huberman, 1994), the design of case study research (Yin, 1994; 2003), and grounded theory building (Glaser & Strauss, 1967). Eisenhardt's propositions as well as Yin's (1994; 2003) approach extend that work in areas such as a priori specification of constructs, triangulation of multiple investigators, within and between case analyses, and the role of existing theory.

In the final interpretive phase, the researcher reports, as Lincoln and Guba (1994) suggest, the "lessons learned" from the case considering the following two aspects:

1. Agreement between the findings and the literature so that the theory is build replicating, consolidating, or extending existing literature. Similar findings in different contexts lead to stronger theory. The support of existing theory (in other fields or discipline) may lift the theory to a higher conceptual level (Eisenhardt, 1989); abstract theory may be applicable to a variety of contexts (Strauss & Corbin, 1990).

2. Conflict between the findings and the literature. The areas and nature of any conflict needs to be examined to provide persuasive explanations accounting for the differences. In interpretive research, such conflicts may arise through different interpretations of similar data or through the particularities of the individual situation; such situations need to be analyzed by the researcher. Additionally, conflicting literature may encourage the researcher to pursue further developments, re-examine the data with new insights, or isolate contextual factors to explain the differences (Cepeda & Martin, 2005, p. 862).

QUALITY ASSESSMENTS IN CASE STUDIES

Because there are a variety of approaches each with its own epistemology, there are numerous views regarding the requirements for sound interpretation of case study data (Guba & Lincoln, 1994; Lee, 1991; Strauss & Corbin, 1990). Classical quality criteria in positivistic research include evaluation of the reliability, internal validity, construct validity, and external validity. In case study research, rigorous control measures analogous to those followed in experimental studies where a range of strategies are employed including pre- or posttesting, randomization, equivalence of treatment, and control groups are usually absent. Systematically ruling out alternative explanations and hypotheses throughout the research process is not pursued in case study research because they contradict and conflict with the ontological and epistemological assumptions underlying qualitative research. Hence, case study researchers operate with lesser controls intentionally avoiding the artificial contrivance of experimental controls. However, while many case study researchers do not subscribe to the idea that a predetermined set of criteria can be applied in a mechanistic way, it does not follow that there are no standards at all by what case study research can be judged.

Often case study researchers are not interested in *internal validity* because the intent of a case study is not to establish cause and effect relationships through a tightly controlled design that allows causal inferences. There are several reasons for the lack of concern with generalizability in case studies. First, people and contexts examined in qualitative research are rarely sampled at random which is the most powerful way to generalize from a sample to an underlying population. Random sampling is an essential feature and key indicator of study's quality and rigor in quantitative research. Secondly, case study researchers are typically more interested in documenting particularistic findings as opposed to universal laws asserting that the research context is shaped by the values of the researcher and researchers that populate that space.

A critical issue for case researchers concerns the external validity or generalizations that can be made from the results of their work. Yin (2003) notes that:

> How can you generalize from a single case study?" is a frequently heard question ... The short answer is that case studies ... are generalizable to theoretical propositions (p. 10).

The ability to generalize deals with knowing whether the findings derived from a case study are generalizable beyond the immediate case study in which the data were collected. Critics of case studies are quick to point out that they offer a poor basis for generalization, noting that the only generalization from case studies is that there is no generalization. Such critiques are implicitly or explicitly contrasting external validity of case studies with quantitative studies which are aimed at statistical generalization from samples to populations. Case study researchers, on the other hand, attempt to generalize a particular set of results to some broader theory thereby establishing *analytic generalization*.

Similarly, Stake (1995) argued for an intuitive, empirically grounded approach to generalization he termed "naturalistic" generalization. His argument was based on the harmonious relationship between the reader's experience and the case study itself. The author expected that the data generated by case studies would often resonate experientially with a broad cross-section of readers, thereby facilitating a greater understanding of the phenomenon.

Finally, Walsham (1993) argues that the validity of the inferences drawn from one or more cases does not depend on the representativeness of the cases in a statistical sense, "but on the plausibility and cogency of the logical reasoning used in describing the results from the cases, and in drawing conclusions from them" (Lee, 1989; Walsham, 1993, p. 15). The author (Walsham, 1995) postulates four types of generalizations from case studies: the development of concepts, development of theory, the drawing of specific implications, and the contribution of rich insights. Case study researchers in leadership studies tend not to generalize to philosophically abstract categories but to leadership theories such as pragmatic (e.g., Mumford & Van Doorn, 2001) or collaborative

Table 3-1   Case study strategies for design quality

Criterion	Description	Sample strategies
Construct validity	Establishing correct operational measures for constructs being studied. Measures must be faithful (or valid) representations of constructs in order for valid inferences to be made	• multiple sources of evidence • Review of case study report by key informant • Mix of qualitative and quantitative methods
Internal validity	Establishing causal relationships by demonstrating covariation between variables under investigation	• Explanation-building strategy with logical chain of evidence • Review of case study report by key informants • Site analysis meeting • Tying propositions to existing literature
External validity	Establishing domain within which a study's findings can be generalized	• Analytic generalization • Tying propositions to existing literature
Reliability	Demonstrating that the operations of a study can be repeated, with the same results	• Validation of coding scheme • Case study data base • Case study protocol

Adapted from Parè (2002)

(e.g., Feyerherm, 1994) leadership theory. The author argues that consumers of case study research on leadership should not be misled into too narrow a view of the generalizations readers can gain from studying the case study reports and that the ability of case studies to provide rich insights into a wide range of leadership topics offers a broader approach to generalizations. Table 3-1 summarizes strategies that can enhance the quality of case studies.

SELECTED CASE STUDIES IN LEADERSHIP RESEARCH

The most researched leadership and management topics covered by the case studies listed in Table 3-2 include leadership theory (Eisenhardt & Bourgeois, 1988; Gronn, 1999; Mumford & Van Doorn, 2001), leadership and change, strategic change (e.g., Gersick, 1994; Greiner & Bhambri, 1998), leadership style (Mumford & Van Doorn, 2001), collaborative leadership (e.g., Denis, Langley, & Cazale, 1996; Feyerherm, 1994), and global leadership (Martin & Beaumont, 1999; Shin, 1998/1999; Välikangas & Okurama, 1997). The emphasis on change is especially prominent in case studies of leadership which are often longitudinal in nature. There is a recurring theme in these studies of the need for leaders who are leading a change effort to secure commitment to the change process, address multiple (internal and external) constituencies, convey a sense of the need for change, and instill a vision of how change should be implemented and/or what the future state of the organization will look like (Bryman, 2004).

I intentionally cast a wide net in selecting the case studies depicted in Table 3-2 to cover a period of almost two decades, include case studies conducted not only in the United States but also in Europe, Canada, and Asia, diverse contexts covering both private and public sector, profit and nonprofit organizations, published in a variety of journals, include single cases (e.g., Alevesson, 1992; Mumford & Van Doorn, 2001; Weed, 1993), multiple cases (e.g., Bryman, Bresnen, Beadsworth & Keil, 1988; Waldman et al., 1998), longitudinal cases (e.g., Gersick, 1994; Shin, 1998/1999), and were conducted through different disciplinary lenses ranging from management information systems (e.g., Lee, 1989) to political science (e.g., Eisenhardt & Bourgeois, 1988). Table 3-2 is not intended to provide a comprehensive summary of all qualitative leadership case studies published so far but offers a representative listing to give the reader a flair of the diversity of leadership problems and contexts investigated, the specific case study methods used, and a sampling of the methodological issues arising from the case. Purely descriptive cases that did not include formal data collection or analysis (e.g., Bania, Nirenberg & Menachem, 2000; Murray, 1999; Välikangas & Okurama, 1997) were excluded.

The most frequently researched topics dealt with the development and/or testing of leadership theory (Eisenhardt & Bourgeois, 1988; Gronn, 1999; Mouly & Sankaran, 1999; Mumford & Van Doorn, 2001, Sveningsson & Alvesson, 2003), leadership and

Table 3-2 Representative sampling of leadership case studies

Author(s)	Epistemology	Type of case	Method of data collection	Context	Reliability	Validity
Appelbaum et al. (2004)	NR[1]	Single case	Survey and descriptive interviews	Plastic manufacturing company	NR	NR
Sveningsson and Alvesson (2003)	NR	Single case studied at both level of manager and firm	Interviews with one female director of administration; annual reports	MNC high-tech company; result of merger of an American and Swedish organization	NR	NR
Alvesson and Sveningsson (2003)[1]	NR	Single case comprised of 6 mini-cases	40 interview with senior and middle managers	Intl. bio-tech Company; complex, ambiguous, knowledge-intensive	NR	NR
Mumford and Van Doorn (2001)	NR	Multiple cases drawn from Franklin's life	Analyses of documents including autobiography, speeches, assembly proposals; historical analyses	Different contexts including libraries, hospitals, police force, fire department	NR	Convergence of theory (pragmatic leadership) and study findings

(Continued)

Table 3-2 (Continued)

Author(s)	Epistemology	Type of case	Method of data collection	Context	Reliability	Validity
Greene, Black, and Ackers (2000)[2]	NR	Multiple (2) cases	Interviews with 20 shop floor employees at one plant, 19 at the other; documentary materials from union, management and local press	Unionized metal manufacturing plants in UK	NR	NR
Martin and Beaumont (1999)[2]	NR	Single case	Narrative story telling, semistructured interviews with 22 directors, senior, and middle managers	Multinational company (MNC)	NR	Analytic generalization
Gronn (1999)[3]	NR	Single case	Document and oral history study; open coding	Australian mountain school	NR	NR
Mouly and Sankaran (1999)[3]	NR	Single case	Direct observations of interim leader and colleagues	Indian R&D organization	NR	NR

Shin (1998/1999)[3]	NR	Multiple cases	Content analysis of cases collected over 10-year period	161 CEO of successful and 88 CEOs of unsuccessful Korean firms	NR	NR
Waldman et al. (1998)	NR	Multiple (3) cases	Observations interviews, tech reports	Manufacturing plant of MNC, hospital, police force, Canada	Interrater, ranging from 48–78%	NR
Kaarbo and Hermann (1998)	NR	Multiple (4) cases	Content analysis of interview responses of 4 European prime ministers	Parliamentary democracies of UK and Germany	NR	NR
Denis, et al. (1996)	NR	Single case	Documents retrospective interviews with 16 informants including managers, physician and Board members	Public hospital acquiring university affiliation	NR	Preliminary case and analysis presented to 4 informants for validation
Hunt and Ropo (1995)	NR	Single case	Interviews with CEO, Analysis of org. history	Automotive industry (GM)	NR	NR

(Continued)

Table 3-2   (Continued)

Author(s)	Epistemology	Type of case	Method of data collection	Context	Reliability	Validity
Dyck (1994)[3]	NR	Single case	Participant observation bio approach; survey of Shared Farming sharers and review of literature on Community Supported Agriculture (CSA)	Farming communities in Canadian prairies	NR	Analytic generalization through establishment of themes
Feyerherm (1994)	NR	Multiple (2) cases over 1-year period	Observations of steering committee members, interviews with 44 informants, document & field notes analysis	Pollution control companies	85% interrater reliability	NR
Gersick (1994)	NR	Single longitudinal case study	14 months of interviews with CEO and leading investors; code development	Venture capital backed start-up company	NR	NR

Selsky and Smith (1994)	Interpretivism	Multiple (2) cases	NR	Community energy development firm and nonprofit membership organization	NR	NR
Weed (1993)	NR	Single case	Interviews with chapter leaders, document analysis	Grassroots organization (MADD)	NR	NR
Alvesson (1992)[2]	NR	Single case	35 interviews with managers and consultants	Swedish computer consultancy, project organization, professional service adhocracy	NR	NR
Chen and Meindl (1991)	Interpretivism	Single case	Content analysis of newspaper and magazine articles about Donald Burr, founder and CEO of People Express; analysis of metaphors about Burr based on descriptive image data (written portrayals of CEO)	Airline industry	Coefficient kappa .89 between researchers and 5 independent judges; 91% average agreement for 5 individual coding categories	NR

(Continued)

Table 3-2   (Continued)

Author(s)	Epistemology	Type of case	Method of data collection	Context	Reliability	Validity
Bryman, Bresnen, Beardsworth and Keil (1988)[2]	NR	Three (3) construction projects	Semistructured interviews with supervisory/ management personnel	UK construction company	NR	NR
Eisenhardt and Bourgeois (1988)	NR	Multiple (8) cases, industry reports, internal documents, informal observations, questionnaire data	Interviews with CEOs, top management team	Microcomputer industry	NR	NR

[1] *N R, Not reported.*
[2] *European studies.*
[3] *Other international studies (Australian, Indian, and Korean).*

change, (e.g., Dyck, 1994; Gersick, 1994), global leadership (e.g., Martin & Beaumont, 1999; Shin, 1999), and longitudinal case studies (e.g., Feyerherm, 1994; Gersick, 1994). Because one of the major purposes of case study research is to develop theory, five theory building cases spanning a period of almost two decades are singled out for discussion.

Leadership Theory in Case Studies

Based on their study of eight firms in the microcomputer industry and analysis of a variety of data sources including interviews with CEOs and top management teams of the participating organizations, Eisenhardt and Bourgeois (1988) developed a model, which provided the rudiments of a midrange theory of political behavior among top managers of microcomputer firms operating in high-velocity environments. Following Yin's (1994) replication logic, each of the eight cases confirmed or disconfirmed inferences drawn from previous ones. A theoretical model was developed that suggests that politics arise from power centralization, lead to poor performance, and are organized around stable coalitions within a firm. The authors concluded that to the extent that the results obtained in their research are valid and can be supported by data from other research settings, a theory of power and politics in top management teams could inform a more general political theory of organization.

This study illustrates a number of methodological issues: this research exemplifies a multiple case study in which data collection methods were triangulated thereby producing a rich and detailed set of data that were context specific to the micro-computer industry. It also generated a set of propositions derived from the case data that framed the rudiments of a theory of power and politics in top management teams working in environments in which there is rapid and discontinuous change in demand, competitors, technology, or regulation so that information is often inaccurate, unavailable, or obsolete (p. 736). Although the propositions developed were essentially grounded in the data, the authors drew on concepts from the literature at various stages in the research to enrich and refine our understanding of the emergent theory.

Gronn's (1999) case study of the roles played by the founder and first headmaster of a well-known Australian mountain school and the partnership these two leaders developed during their tenure yielded the construct of the "leadership couple" to describe two members of a dyads in leadership roles whose temperaments contrasted sharply. The founder, a practical man, embodied traits seen as the hallmarks of the traditional Australian character: down-to-earth, laconic, stoical, and devoid of any hint of affection or pretense (Gronn, 1999, p. 47). The headmaster, on the other hand, was an upper-class Englishman, highly intelligent, erudite, cultured, urban, and intensely religious and moral individual (Gronn, 1999, p. 48). Although couples outside the context of marriage have been discussed in leadership and management (e.g., Bryman, 1993; Bryman, Gillingwater, & McGuiness, 1996), Gronn's research added important insight complimenting the existing literature. For example, Hodgson, Levinson, and Zaleski (1965) described a leadership couple as an executive role constellation or leadership arrangement marked by a division of role tasks and responsibilities along specialized and complimentary lines, and some type of negotiated understanding designed to maintain a requisite and robust understanding between its members (cited in Gronn, 1999, p. 44). Similarly, Bryman (1993) discussed a leadership couple consisting of siblings in a family business. Gronn's case study contributed to the existing knowledge of couples in the context of leadership and management by showing that successful and productive leadership coupling of the two leaders of the Australian school was related to the sharply contrasting personalities of the two leaders, an "odd couple" indeed. Instead of each members of duo being a clone or carbon copy of the other. The founder and headmaster also exchanged high levels of self-disclosure extending as far as revealing highly sensitive and personal vulnerabilities. Finally, Gronn's case study documented that existing leadership theory, particularly leadership substitute theory (e.g., Kerr & Jermier, 1978), could not readily account for the dynamics and mutual dependencies that characterized the relationship between the founder of the school and its first headmaster.

The third case study (Mumford & Van Doorn, 2001) was conducted to distinguish pragmatic leadership from other forms of outstanding leadership such as transactional/ transformational or charismatic leadership. In this single case study, also in keeping with Eisenhardt's recommendation for building theory from case studies, the authors created multiple cases from the life of Benjamin Franklin. Example of notable leadership acts during Franklin's presidency included the founding of subscription libraries, the formation of police and volunteer fire departments or improving the lightening of the streets in Philadelphia. Analysis of Franklin's autobiography, personal letters, editorial in the *Pennsylvania Gazette*, and speeches provided the raw data which were coded for manifestations of pragmatic leadership. These pragmatic leadership incidents were then examined with respect to an a priori theoretical model of pragmatic leadership derived from earlier work of Mumford and his colleagues (e.g., Mumford, Zaccaro, Harding, Jacobs, & Fleishman, 2000).

The image of Benjamin Franklin as a pragmatic leader depicted a US president known for identifying practical problems and arranging solutions to those problems. Franklin was a careful observer of people and social organizations, an attribute of the pragmatic leadership style. The authors also suggested that pragmatic leaders exercise influence through the use of elite social relationships, appeals to existing shared values, and effective communications of the merits of a project such as the founding of the police department or the Indian treated under Franklin's presidency.

Finally, in the discussion of their findings, Mumford and Van Doorn systematically ruled out other forms of outstanding leadership such as transactional/transformational and charismatic leadership. For example, the analyses of the cases clearly indicated that unlike transactional, transformational, and charismatic leaders, Franklin was successful not by virtue of a coherent, compelling vision, an integral element of charismatic leadership or intellectual stimulation, a key component of transformational leadership. Instead, Franklin often operated as a leader from behind the scenes using elites as intermediaries. Thus, the cases of outstanding (pragmatic) leadership demonstrated by Franklin did not seem to meet the criteria set forth for charismatic (e.g., House, 1977) and transformational leadership (e.g., Bass, 1985). Rather than exercising influence through articulation of a vision, Franklin exercised influence indirectly by structuring institutional and situational contingencies to set the stage for successful problem solution. As Mumford and Van Doorn (2001) point out, the vision involved may be less an instance of charismatic or transformational leadership and more of a case of unusually visionary problem solving (p. 297). Thus, Franklin's leadership style was pragmatic not charismatic at the time he led people in colonial Philadelphia. As a pragmatic leader, he founded hospitals, established a university, created fire and police departments, developed the institution of subscription libraries, and introduced paper currency. Each of these incidents represents a case of pragmatic leadership lending support to the authors' argument that "pragmatic leadership, as a functional, problem-based approach to leadership, may represent a distinct style of outstanding leadership" (Mumford & Van Doorn, 2001, p. 283).

The fourth case designed to develop theory (Mouly & Sankaran, 1999) was intended to capture of interim leadership by adopting the interim or acting leader as the unit of analysis. The authors, in a single case study, investigated the leadership of the acting director of an Indian R&D organization who had served in this capacity for 14 years prior to the investigation. Direct observation of the acting director, also the leading scientist, unstructured interviews with scientists and support staff, and annual reports provided the data which were coded to identify categories and concepts. Iteratively, the authors defined and re-defined concepts and categories vis-à-vis data collected constantly going back and forth between emergent theory and data. This process was discontinued when the point of theoretical saturation was reached. The interim leader was characterized by his passionate commitment to his calling as a scientist who downplayed his role and status of acting director, his selflessness (he was described as being a "saint"), and professional excellence. The director was an internationally renowned chemist in India, director of the most prestigious academic institution in the country with about 500 journal publications and recipient numerous awards and citations. The interim leader faced the challenge of stalling the organizational demise of a dying organization and was able to demonstrate that the company could remain productive as an R&D organization.

Although the authors linked their case with previous research on interim leaders, this case highlights the critical importance of context. It also calls our attention to the dangers of relying on one of the researcher as a source of determining what is theoretically significant in interim leadership since one of the authors previously conducted fieldwork in the organization. This study is an example of a highly ideographic case—an Indian federal agency that was already dying at the time of the exit of the last acting director 14 years before the study was conducted and an acting director who sought to avert any acceleration of that process following the departure of the incumbent (Mouly & Sankaran, 1999, p. 649). Thus, although this case yielded an interesting profile of an interim leader captured by the major themes that emerged from the analysis, it is primarily illustrative of case which only reports specific themes that were identified in a specific context but fails to take the research a step further to show what lies beyond the themes (Caelli et al., 2003).

The fifth case (Dyck, 1994) reported a case study of environmental and social change leadership using the key leader of the Canadian Shared Farming movement as the informant. The Shared Farming movement is an alternative agri-food system that is environmentally friendly, ecologically sound, and socially just. The case drew on various data sources including (1) participant observation; (2) biographical approach; (3) survey of Shared Farming sharers; and (4) review of literature on Community Supported Agriculture (CSA). Of the 220 surveys distributed, 140 were returned (64 percent). The researcher was an active member of the Shared Farming community, participating in community events, providing volunteer work on the farm, keeping regular contact with the key leader, and offering counsel. The leader was described as an entrepreneur with a strong sense of mission, "driven to solve world hunger and to be a farmer." He also emphasized the role of individuals in solving system problems. At the same time, he was somewhat naïve about his task, partly because he did not grow up on a farm. But he led by example, modeled integrity, empowered others, and listened to others to shape his ideas. Four major themes were identified: (1) eco-development leaders are driven by a sense of mission; (2) eco-developmental leaders empower others; (3) eco-developmental leaders listen and articulate well; and (4) eco-developmental have and facilitate integrity. These themes may be viewed as the rudimentary framework of a theory of eco-development leadership.

Finally, the last and most recent case (Sveningsson & Alvesson, 2003) was aimed at the development of identity theory and explored the construction of and struggle with various managerial and on-managerial identities of a single female participant. The study took place in a large R&D company. The authors assumed that identity and identity work, rather than being static, are dynamic and ongoing reflecting ongoing struggles around creating a sense of self. This approach focuses on identity emphasizing a sense of becoming instead of a sense of being. They suggest that individuals create several more or less contradictory and often changing managerial identities rather than one stable, continuous, and secure manager identity (p. 1165).

In this case study, the authors investigated identity at two levels; one was the senior manager and the other the organization in which she worked. Data were collected from six interviews with the manager as well as 40 middle managers who were familiar with the senior manager's situation. The authors also engaged in informal discussions with various members of the firm and observed managerial and employee meetings. The interviews were directed toward roles, expectations, coordinating efforts of the senior manager, globalization, and the managing of knowledge-intensive companies in general. Identity constructions of the senior manager were associated with the major work roles she occupied—administrator, ambassador, and cultural integrator. Her administrative work as manager of operations included managing technical facilities and administrative work in finance and human resource management. She had substantial difficulties in identifying herself with being a (traditional) manager of operations and saw this role as problematic for her identity, not because she regarded it as important but rather as something that was not her "thing." Instead, this manager wanted something more meaningful such as the role of chairperson of the management team, culture generator, or cell ambassador.

As a result, this senior manager struggled to avoid these "janitorial" aspects of her work and instead focused on her responsibilities in the areas of strategy and building culture.

The authors pointed to several contributions this case make to the organizational identity literature. For example, contrary to the commonly held assumption that identity work results in stable self-definition, the case of this senior manager illustrates identity as struggle. Another contribution concerns the idea of anti-identity the authors propose, the "not-me" position invoked by the informant when it came to work situations and role expectations relating the traditional ("janitorial") elements of her position as manager for operations. In this case, it was the "anti-janitor" and "culture creator" that were significant identity constructions for this leader.

Finally, this section concludes with some general observations regarding the cases listed in Table 3-2. Most noteworthy is the lack of information regarding paradigm assumptions and strategies to ensure reliability and validity using either traditional positivist criteria or alternative quality standards. Only two case studies (Chen & Meindl, 1991; Selsky & Smith, 1994) identified the paradigm within which the researchers were working. Although these case studies were conducted over 10 years ago when qualitative research on leadership was less frequent than today, the authors provided most of the information we are looking for in reported case studies today including paradigm, reliability, and validity. In the Chen and Meindl (1991) case, for example, the leadership of Donald Burr, founder and CEO of People Express, was examined through an interpretation of Burr's leadership successes and failure as reported by the media. Burr and his airline enjoyed prominent and extensive coverage in the popular journals and newspapers during the 1980s. In these accounts, Burr was often portrayed as an idealized representation of the American entrepreneurial spirit, a visionary, daring to dream, and daring to pursue the dream until it comes through (Chen & Meindl, 1991, p. 545). Burr was a self-made leader with People Express being the product of the Airline Deregulation Act which challenged the big monopolies in the industry. Yet, as People Express spun into decline, the media reconstructed Burr's image focusing on the "downside" of this idealism and motivation focusing on Burr's flaws in a way that accounted for his ultimate failure with People Express.

The empirical case studies review in this chapter highlight the growing concern over the number of case studies that have no guiding set of philosophical assumptions, do not denote the researcher's paradigmatic position, fail to distinguish method and methodology, or make explicit the approach to quality and rigor, and identify the researcher's analytic lens have been expressed by several researchers (e.g., Caelli et al., 2003). Quality criteria, as noted earlier on in this chapter, are available within methodological boundaries but are only sporadically applied. The authors posit that research reports aiming for credibility must address the following key issues:

- the theoretical positioning of the researcher—this refers to the identification of a particular paradigm shaped by the researchers' motives, assumptions about a phenomenon, disciplinary socialization, and personal history

- the congruence between methodology and methods—as discussed in Chapter 1, methodology reflects the beliefs about knowledge that arise from the values in the philosophic framework used; it represents a set of guidelines governing how the research should proceed Method, on the other hand, refers to the techniques used to collect and analyze the data which must be congruent with the epistemological and ontological inferences of the approach taken (Van Maanen, 1998b)

- strategies for establishing rigor and quality

To remedy these shortcomings, journal editors, manuscript reviewers, and faculty teaching qualitative methods courses need to encourage (and readers should well expect) more explicit accounts of ontological, epistemological, and methodological commitments in published studies.

SUMMARY

In this chapter, I have presented the fundamentals of the case study method to include design features, single and multiple case studies, the role of theory in case study research and a representative sampling of empirical studies that employed case study method to develop new concepts, theoretical frameworks, or midrange leadership theories. To illustrate the operation of these fundamental elements and principles of case study research, a number of leadership case studies were described to identify their epistemological assumptions and evaluate their quality. Techniques for improving case study methods by implementing and making explicit quality standards or criteria and recommendations for more rigorous reporting standards were presented. A number of researchers in the field of leadership studies have demonstrated that case studies, if carried out and written up carefully, can make valuable contributions to both leadership theory and practice.

Case studies have been criticized for their lack of rigor because they typically do not follow predetermined procedures and analytical techniques as the researcher is open to modifying data collection, analysis, and interpretation as new insights are gained in the research process. However, despite these methodological problems, conducting both single and multiple cases on leadership is desirable for many reasons such as theory development, observations, and descriptions of unusual events. Rather than lacking rigor, data collection in case studies is labor-intensive, can last for months or even years, and data overload seems almost inevitable. In the absence of statistical procedures or techniques for establishing causality, case study researchers have been accused of drawing conclusions from incomplete data, have to content with the limited capacity of human short-term memory, may pay more attention to influential informants, or discount disconfirming evidence.

Flyvberg (2006) notes a number of misunderstandings that contribute to the conventional view that case studies cannot be of value in and of themselves because they fail to be linked to hypotheses following the hypothetico-deductive model of explanation.

- *Misunderstanding 1*: General, theoretical (context-independent) knowledge is more valuable than concrete, practical (context-dependent) knowledge. Context-dependent knowledge and expertise lie at the center of the case study method and leadership research. The case study method acknowledges the limitations of analytical rationality along with need for the generation of both types of knowledge

- *Misunderstanding 2:* One cannot generalize on the basis of an individual case This view is one of the most devastating critiques leveraged against the case study method. However, the case study is a very effective way of generalizing using the type of test Karl Popper (1959) called falsification. Popper used the example by noting that all swans are white and proposed that just one observation of a single black swan would falsify this proposition. The case study method is well suited for identifying black swans because of its in-depth approach. Flyvberg (2006) concludes that we can generalize from a single case and that the case study may be central to scientific development through generalization as a supplement or alternative to other methods.

- Misunderstanding 3: Case studies are valuable only at certain stage of the inquiry process and least valuable in the theory testing stage This misunderstanding derives from the previous misunderstanding that one cannot generalize on the basis of individual cases. However, case studies are valuable at all stages of the theory building process. Eckstein (2002) points out that case studies are most valuable at the stage of theory building where least value is attached to them; the stage at which candidate theories are tested (p. 80).

- *Misunderstanding 4:* The case study method is biased toward verification, that is, the researcher's tendency to confirm his or her preconceived notions Experienced case researchers conduct their work in a way that is as rigorous as a quantitative scholar does.

- *Misunderstanding 5:* It is often difficult to summarize and develop general propositions and theories on the basis of specific case studies This final assumption, according to Flyvberg (2006), overlooks the fact that often it is not desirable in case study research to summarize large amounts of narrative data. But nevertheless, case study research on leadership phenomena contributes to the cumulative development of knowledge of the field.

Greater use of case studies on leadership and more frequent and concerted training in the case study method at the graduate level would remedy many of these misunderstandings.

4

CONTENT ANALYSIS IN LEADERSHIP RESEARCH

AN ILLUSTRATIVE LEADERSHIP CONTENT ANALYSIS STUDY

Through an examination of Bush's rhetoric and media coverage the authors, Bligh, Kohles, and Meindl, (2004b), before and after 9/11 the authors explored how elements in the President's speeches changed in response to the postcrisis environment. They argued that language is a fundamental aspect of the leadership process, shaped by both leaders and followers as they interact with each other in stable and turbulent environments. The authors employed a computerized dictionary-based content analysis. They drew on previous research which suggests a number of characteristics that might become more prevalent in a postcrisis environment, including optimism, bold and directive leadership, and collective support (Bligh et al., 2004b, p. 566). In a postcrisis environment, collective support of individuals who are both directly and indirectly affected by the crisis becomes critically important. Moreover, the authors speculated that the President's rhetoric in the wake of 9/11 would include more references to the American people and the patriotic and Judeo–Christian themes that have historically united them, resulting in more collective, patriotic, and faith-based language after the crisis.

Bligh et al. reported on three studies in this article and chose a program called DICTION, presumably the only software program that was explicitly designed to examine the linguistic elements of political leaders. DICTION uses 31 predefined dictionaries, containing over 10 000 words, to analyze a passage of text. The program generated eight composite variables from the 33 dictionaries included in DICTION. Among these eight composite variables were a collective focus observed in speeches of charismatic leaders, confidence in followers' worth, similarity to followers, and values and moral justification. Dictionary variables also included optimism, blame, hardship, denial, ambivalence, and faith to name a few. An example of a sample passage from one of Bush's speeches which was coded for patriotism stated

> *America was targeted for attack because we are the brightest beacon for freedom and opportunity in the world (September 11, 2001).*

Altogether, the corpus of text in the three combined studies consisted of 74 of the President's major speeches and radio addresses taken directly from the official web site of the White House. In addition to the speeches, the authors also analyzed media coverage using the major television networks and a variety of domestic newspapers.

Means, standard deviations, and intercorrelations were computed for each of the eight composite variables followed by MANCOVA to determine whether there were significant differences in Bush's speeches and whether this effect was also reflected in the media's response to the President's charismatic rhetoric before and after 9/11 in the variables of interest. In the third study, the sample comprised articles and transcripts from a variety of media outlets, television news programs. The authors then followed a similar procedure as in the first study utilizing DICTION to analyze each article.

For example, President Bush's postcrisis speeches were more aggressive when compared to those given in the first nine months of his administration. They were also more likely to reference the American people as collective and incorporate more patriotic and faith-based themes. Furthermore, in the post-9/11 environment, the President made increasing references to the hostility of the terrorist attacks and the despicable nature of terrorism. For example, the President's remarks on September 13, 2001, reflect his focus on condemning those responsible for the attacks: "Civilized people around the world denounce the evil doers who devised and executed these terrible attacks. Justice demands that those who helped or harbored the terrorists be punished—and punished severely. The enormity of their evil demands it" (Bush, 2001). The results from the President's speeches and the media coverage were very similar suggesting a good deal of correspondence between the content of the President's speeches and what the American media reported about those speeches.

Taken together, the results confirmed that the occurrence of the 9/11 crisis led to a change in Bush's rhetoric, resulting in language that has been theoretically linked to charismatic leadership. Moreover, and in parallel, the media's portrayal of the President after 9/11 also incorporated more charismatic language (Bligh et al., 2004b, p. 229).

This content analysis study illustrates one approach to this research method—a quantitative, computerized application. However, there are many different ways of conducting content analyses, some of which are illustrated in this chapter and later in Chapter 10.

INTRODUCTION

Defining Content Analysis

A wide range of theoretical frameworks, method, and analytical techniques have been labeled content analysis (Denzin & Lincoln, 2000; Miles & Huberman, 1994). Content analysis has been defined as a family of procedures for studying the contents and themes of written or transcribed texts (Insch, Moore, & Murphy, 1997). Shapiro and Markoff (1997), in view of the different approaches and contributing disciplines, offered a minimalist definition that defines content analysis as "any methodological measurement applied to text (or other symbolic materials) for social science purposes" (p. 14). As such, content analysis is a research tool used to determine the presence of certain concepts within texts. Texts can be defined broadly as books, articles, newspaper headlines, historical documents, advertising but also as nontext-based materials such as TV segments, photography, the performing and visual arts, or any communicative language.

Content analysis in leadership research highlights the importance of language as words, sentences and paragraphs form the unity of analysis. Language is a fundamental aspect of the leadership process, shaped by both leaders and followers as they interact. Content analysis, as Bligh et al. (2004a) note, focuses squarely on the linguistic map found in the relationship between leaders and followers but also the subsequent transformation of contextualized data into numeric output. The authors go on to say that as a research method, content analysis is ideally suited for researchers who seek to reliably study and systematically compare linguistically based elements of the leadership relationship. Content analysis is one of several types of textual analyses which include discourse, rhetorical analysis, narratology, and genre theory.

Content analysis is fundamentally concerned with readings of texts and the meaning of symbols (Krippendorff, 2004a). Text data may be in verbal, print, or electronic form and may be obtained from narrative responses, open-ended survey questions, interviews, focus groups, observations, or print media such as articles, books, or manuals (Kondracki & Wellman, 2002). The focus in this chapter is on textual materials and is illustrated in an empirical study reported in Chapter 10.

To conduct a content analysis, the text is coded or broken down into manageable categories on a word, phrase, sentence, or theme. According to Titscher, Meyer, Wodak, and Vetter (2000), content analysis is the "longest established method of text analysis among the set of empirical methods of social investigation" (p. 55). Content analysis has gained significance in the first half of the twentieth century with the dramatic expansion of mass communication (Mayring, 2000). But even before that, different approaches to analysis and comparison of texts in hermeneutic contexts (e.g., Bible interpretations), early newspaper analysis, and graphological procedures can be seen as early precursors of content analysis.

Content analysis covers a wide range of approaches and techniques ranging from purely qualitative to highly quantitative. Initially, researchers used content analysis as either a qualitative or quantitative method; later it was primarily used as a quantitative technique, with text data coded into implicit categories and then described using statistics. This approach is sometimes referred to as quantitative analysis of qualitative data (Morgan, 1993). Classical content analysis is essentially a quantitative method focused on the generations of codes, code clusters, categories, or families based on interrelated codes which are derived from word frequencies. However, content analysis can also be conducted qualitatively without generating word frequency codes. Mayring's (2002) qualitative content analysis tries to overcome the shortcomings of quantitative content analysis such as providing answers to how the categories were derived by applying a systematic, theory-guided approach to text analysis. Boyatzis (1998) also developed a set of procedures for qualitative content known as thematic coding in which the researchers proceeds from manifest to latent coding. Many content analysis studies include both quantitative and qualitative elements (Chapter 10).

DESIGNING A CONTENT ANALYSIS STUDY

Neuendorf (2002) and Insch et al. (1997) describe the process of conducting a content analysis study as a series of steps depicted in Fig. 4-1. As indicated in Fig. 4-1, the content analyst first researches the topic of interest, examines existing theory that has a bearing on the research question, and then goes through a series of design decision such as the use of manual coding versus computerized coding (or a combination of both). The next step involves the identification of the corpus of text (sampling), coder training, and establishing intercoder reliability which are described later in this chapter. Insch et al. (1997) add some additional components such as specifying the unit of analysis, data collection, and assessing construct validity. But regardless of the specific procedure employed, content analysis is typically presented as a series of well-defined steps that take the analyst from the initial identification of research questions and construct to the final interpretation of the data.

CONTENT ANALYSIS PROCEDURES

As content analysis is not unambiguously a qualitative or quantitative method, it is amenable to both qualitative (e.g., Boyatzis, 1998; Mayring, 2000; 2003) and quantitative analyses such as *t*-tests, correlations, and loglinear models (Krippendorff, 2004a;

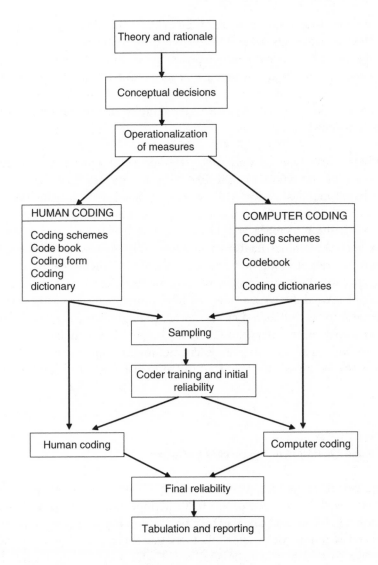

Figure 4-1 **The process of content analysis research** (*Source: adapted from Neuendorf (2002)*)

Neuendorf, 2002). Building a dictionary using a stop word list, selecting key words, subdividing a corpus of text into parts or phrases, collapsing codes into categories, and using one kind of software rather than another are examples of technical issues found in many content analysis approaches.

Data collection typically commences with the identification of the texts to be analyzed. As Sims and Manz (1984) note, the use of transcribed audio recordings or video tapes can expand upon the conventional use of textual data. In addition, the content analyst needs to decide whether an entire set of texts will be analyzed or whether a sampling strategy will be used to select fewer, representative items of text. The next decision before proceeding with the actual coding of a corpus of text concerns the determination of the unit of analysis or recording units, which is the basic unit of text to be analyzed. Units of analysis can be words, sentences, paragraphs, or entire documents where the entire text is assigned to a category.

Data analysis starts with reading all texts repeatedly to achieve immersion and obtain a sense of the whole (Tesch, 1990). Then data are read word by word to derive the initial manifest codes (Miles & Huberman, 1994; Morgan, 1993) by highlighting the exact words from the text that appear to capture key words and concepts. Next, the researcher approaches the text by taking notes of first impressions, thoughts, and initial analysis continuing this process until labels for codes emerge that are reflective of that one key thought. Content-bearing data must be converted into an acceptable format, such as numbers, categories, or codes. Coding is the heart of textual analysis. Codes initially come directly from the text and then are converted into the initial coding themes. A coding scheme is a translation device that organizes data into categories (Poole & Folger, 1981). It includes the process and rules of data analysis that are systematic, logical, and scientific. The development of a good coding scheme is central to trustworthiness in research using content analysis.

Qualitative and Quantitative Approaches to Coding

One of the key elements in content analysis is the systematic coding of text (Miles & Huberman, 1994; Strauss & Corbin, 1990). Krippendorff (2004a) defines coding as the transcribing, recording, categorizing, or interpreting of given units of analysis (words, speeches, book, web pages, photographic images, etc.) into the terms of a data language so that they can be analyzed. Codes are building blocks for theory and model building and the foundation on which the analyst's arguments rest. Implicitly or explicitly, they embody the assumptions underlying the analysis. As Bernard (1994) points out, a code can be used as an encryption, indexing, or measuring device. Codes add information to the text (rather than reproducing the text) through the process of interpretation that simultaneously breaks down the text into meaningful chunks or segments. Thus, the coding process must include specific guidelines for defining the boundaries of the text associated with a particular code. Data collection strategies generally fall along a continuum from minimally structured (e.g., transcribed interviews) to maximally structured (e.g., brief responses to open-ended survey questions) (Seidel & Kelle, 1995).

Types of Coding

In content analysis, there are five major types of coding: theoretical coding, open coding, axial coding, selective coding, and thematic coding. Regardless of the types of coding employed, researchers address the text regularly and repeatedly with the following basic questions (Strauss & Corbin, 1990, p. 77):

- What? Which phenomenon is mentioned.

- Who? Who are the persons involved? Which roles do they play? How do they interact?

- How? Which aspects of the phenomenon are mentioned (or not mentioned)?

- When? How long? Where? Time, course, and location.

- How much? How strong? Aspects of intensity.

- What for? With what intention, to which purpose?

- What are the means, tactics, and strategies for reaching the goals?

Theoretical coding is the procedure for analyzing data which have been collected in order to develop a grounded theory. This procedure was introduced by Glaser and Strauss (1967) and further elaborated by Strauss and Corbin (1990). Coding here is understood as "representing the operations by which data are broken down, conceptualized, and put back together in new ways. It is the central process by which theories are built from the data" (Strauss & Corbin, 1990, p. 57). Theoretical coding is based on the constant comparison method or a constant going back and forth between data to develop theory returning to the collection of additional data and refining the emergent theory. Starting from the data, the process of coding leads to the development of theory through progressive level of abstraction that combines into categories and eventually one or very few major themes. During the whole process, impressions, associations, questions are noted in code notes. This process is known as memoing, which is an integral process in most coding procedures (Flick, 2002).

Open coding is designed to express data in the form of concepts. For this purpose, data are segmented and expressions are classified by their units of meaning (single words, short sequences of words in order to attach concepts (codes) to them). Sometimes hundreds of codes result (Strauss & Corbin, 1990). The next step is to categorize these codes by grouping them around concepts and phenomena associated with the data which are particularly relevant to the research question. The resulting categories are then linked to codes which are now more abstract than those used in the first step. A text can be coded line by line, sentence by sentence, or paragraph by paragraph, or a code can be linked to whole texts (an interview protocol or a newspaper article). The result of open coding is a list of the codes and categories that were attached to the text. This should be complemented by memos the analyst writes to him or herself that are produced for explaining and defining the content of codes and categories (Flick, 1998).

Axial coding follows open coding as the next step to refine and differentiate the categories resulting from open coding. From the multitude of categories that were originated, those are selected that seem to be most promising for further elaboration. The axial categories are enriched by their fit with as many passages as possible. Most importantly, the relations between categories and their subcategories are clarified or established. Axial coding is summarized as follows:

Axial coding is the process of relating subcategories to a category. It is a complex process of inductive and deductive thinking involving several steps. These are accomplished, as with open coding, by making comparisons and asking questions. However, in axial coding, the use of these procedures is more focused and geared toward discovering and relating categories in terms of the paradigm model (Strauss & Corbin, 1990, p. 114).

Selective coding continues axial coding at a higher level of abstraction. The aim of this step is to elaborate the core category around which the other developed categories can be grouped and can be integrated. The result of this step is one single category or supercode.

Coding ends at the point of theoretical saturation when further coding, enrichment of categories, and so on no longer provides new knowledge. At that time, the procedure is flexible enough that the researcher can re-enter the same source text and same codes from open coding with a different research question and aim at developing and formulating a grounded theory of a different issue.

Thematic coding was initially developed by Strauss (1987) and elaborated on by Boyatzis (1998). According to Boyatzis (1998), thematic coding is a multistep procedure that can be performed inductively or deductively. Table 4-1 presents definitions of the major components of a thematic content analysis.

According to the author, a good code should have five elements:

1. A label.

2. A definition of what the theme concerns.

3. A description of how to know when the theme occurs (i.e., how to "flag" the theme).

4. A description of any qualifications or exclusions to the identification of the theme.

5. Examples, both positive and negative, to eliminate possible confusion when looking for the theme (Boyatzis, 1998, pp. x–xi).

Table 4-1   Thematic analysis definitions

Thematic analysis is a process for encoding qualitative information. The encoding requires an explicit "code"
A theme is a pattern found in the information that at a minimum describes and organizes the possible observations or at a maximum interprets aspects of the phenomenon. A theme may be identified at the manifest level (directly observable in the information) or at the latent level (categorizing issues underlying the phenomenon)
A code may be a list of themes; a complex model with themes, indicators, and qualifications that are causally related; or something in between these two forms
A codebook is the compilation or integration of a number of codes in a study

Source: Boyatzis, 1998 (p. 161).

These basic elements of a good thematic code are applied to authentic leadership as shown in Table 4-2.

Thematic coding makes distinction between manifest (themes directly observable in the information) and latent coding (themes underlying the phenomenon). In manifest coding, the visible or apparent content of a phenomenon is elucidated. In latent content analysis, on the other hand, the researcher is looking for the underlying aspects of the phenomenon under investigation that represent a higher level of abstraction (Boyatzis, 1998, p. 16). Potter and Levine-Donnerstein (1999) note that for latent content, coders must provide subjective interpretations based on their own mental schemata. This "only increases the importance of making the case that the judgments of the coders are intersubjective, that is, those judgments, while subjectively derived, are shared across coders, and the meaning therefore is likely to reach out to readers of the research" (p. 226). According to the authors, with manifest content, the coding task

Table 4-2   Coding example illustrating Boyatzis elements of a good code

What am I going to call (label) it? *Authentic leadership*
How am I going to define it? *Leaders who are true to themselves*
How am I going to recognize it in the data? *When respondents explicitly say they are authentic leaders who are deeply aware of how they think and behave and are perceived by others as being aware of their own and others' values/moral perspectives and of high moral character* (Avolio & Gardner, 2005)
What do I want to exclude? *Authenticity stems from self-awareness, knowing one-self, one's strength, and weaknesses. Attributions of authentic leadership to external forces or socialization agents does not qualify as authentic leadership*
What is an example? *Boards should choose authentic leaders for character, not charisma, for their values, and for their ability to motivate employees to create genuine value for customer*

Table 4-3   The Weber coding protocol

Definitions of coding units (e.g., word, phrase, sentence, and paragraph)
1. Defining the coding categories
2. Test of coding on a sample
3. Assessment of the accuracy and reliability of the coding sample
4. Revision of the coding rules
5. Return to Step 3 until sufficient reliability is achieved
6. Coding of all text
7. Assess the achieved reliability or accuracy

Source: Weber (1990).

is one of clerical recording and objectivity that can be achieved relatively easily. Objectivity is much more difficult to achieve with latent content. Thematic content analysis and code development enable the researcher to arrive at both manifest and latent codes at the same time. The compilation or integration of a number of codes is called a codebook. Though a codebook appears to have a simple and stable structure, the process of building a codebook is dynamic.

A content analysis coding scheme consists of categories, classification rules, and the words (or units) assigned to the categories (Insch et al., 1997). Codes are then sorted into categories based on how different codes are related and linked (Patton, 2002). The basic goal in the coding process is to organize a large body of text into much fewer content categories. As analysis proceeds, additional codes are developed, and the initial coding scheme is revised and refined. Categories may be defined based on the research question and/or underlying theories and constructs. For example, House, Spangler, and Woycke (1991), using House's (1977) theory of charismatic leadership, established categories of charismatic behaviors such as self-confidence and strong moral and ideological appeals to followers.

Regardless of the specific types of codes and procedures followed, Weber (1990) suggests an eight-step process for creating, testing, and implementing a coding scheme which is presented in Table 4-3, which is applicable to many coding tasks.

DATA COLLECTION AND ANALYSIS

Data collection and analytic procedures depend on whether the content analyst employs a quantitative or qualitative approach or a combination of both. At one end is an exclusively qualitative and verbally descriptive approach to the phenomenon under investigation; at the other end is a primarily quantitative approach of statistically analyzing the phenomenon under investigation. For quantitative approaches, data to be analyzed may be frequency counts and lists of categories to which a variety of statistical procedures including correlations, t-tests, and structural equation models can be applied. For example, Bligh et al. (2004b) in their content analysis of the rhetorical content of President George Bush's speeches before and after the terrorist attacks of 9/11 reported means, standard deviations, and intercorrelations between the categories the authors had identified and additionally conducted a one-way analysis of covariance (NCOVA) to examine whether there were significant differences in Bush's speeches before and after 9/11 on the variables of interest.

On the other hand, if the content analyst pursues a purely qualitative analytic strategy, he or she usually does not standardize the corpus of text and is more likely to weave quotes from the analyzed texts into the analysis and interpretation. For example, in the analysis of life stories of leaders, the content analyst may mark key activities, competencies, obstacles to success, thoughts, and emotions as potential themes in the outline of these life stories. However, descriptive or interpretive analyses does not preclude scoring or scaling of themes, and if the analyst has a sufficient sample size of text, thematic analysis allows him or her to translate the qualitative codes into numeric themes or empirically creating clusters of themes.

An example of a purely qualitative content analysis was conducted by Shamir, Arthur, and House (1994) who examined Jesse Jackson's speech to the National Convention of the Democratic part in July 1988. The speech drew remarkable attention from both convention delegates and television viewers. The authors first proposed five processes by which charismatic leaders have their motivational effects on followers. Example of such a process was the leader instilling faith in a better future or increasing followers' commitment to a common goal. Next, they presented speech characteristics of charismatic leaders such as more references to collective identity and fewer references to self-interests or more references to values and moral justifications and fewer references to tangible outcomes or instrumental justification. In their speeches, charismatic leaders interpret the present and the past, link presenting a vivid image of the future exemplifying certain values and identities, and present their vision of the future (Shamir et al., 1994, p. 29).

For the thematic content analysis, Shamir et al. examined Jackson's speech according to the content categories suggested by the propositions the authors developed. For example, one of the propositions presented earlier dealt with references charismatic leaders make to a shared identity. Here is an excerpt from Jackson's speech that the orator used to emphasize a shared identity which is reflected in his quilt metaphor:

> America's not a blanket woven from one thread, one color, one cloth. When I was a child growing up in Greensville, SC, and grandmother could not afford a blanket, she didn't complain and we did not freeze. Instead, she took pieces of

old cloth—patches, wool, silk, gabardine, crockersack on the patches—barely good enough to wipe off your shoes wit. But they didn't stay that way very long. With sturdy hands and strong cord, she sewed them into a quilt, a thing of beauty, power, and culture. Now, democrats, we must build such a quilt (Shamir et al., 1994, p. 33).

In this thematic content analysis, the reader would look in vain for numbers or statistics.

Bottlenecks in content analysis refer to aspects of the analytic work that take the most time for the least analytical payoff. Data coding is the most time- and effort-consuming stage of content analysis because it involves considerable effort on part of the researcher, that is, getting to know the data, identifying recurrent concepts, abstracting from the data, and building theoretical models. However, a number of qualitative software programs can greatly reduce that labor-intensive efforts required by hand coding.

Use of Software in Content Analysis

Computer programs have been developed over the last years to support content analysis and the interpretation of textual data and can serve a number of different functions (Fielding & Lee, 1998):

- Computer programs assist the content analyst by working through the material, underlining, writing marginal notes, defining category definitions and coding rules, and recording comments on the material. Most software programs offer helpful tools for handling text, searching, collecting, and editing passages.

- Computer programs function as documentation center, recording all steps of analysis of all interpreters thereby facilitating replication.

- Computer programs offer links to quantitative analyses by allowing data transfer to other programs such as SPSS.

In addition, the advent of computer-assisted text analysis has increased the scalability of the method to include quite ambitious projects (see Chapter 10) by enhancing access and automating some of the tasks and functions such as data storage, dictionaries, and word counts. Software program offers features for organizing, searching, retrieving, and linking text that render the process of handling a large project more manageable, especially as the complexity and interrelationships of concepts increases exponentially with the quantity of data (Kabanoff, 1997).

Software programs used in content analysis include Atlas.ti, NVivo, NUD*ST, and winMAX. Atlas.ti, for example, is a powerful software workbench for analysis of large bodies of textual, graphical, audio, and video data, whereas winMAX is a tool for textual analysis that enables the combination of both qualitative and quantitative analytical procedures. These programs are particularly useful in the initial stages of the analysis as most of them provide the so-called auto-code functionality, which is typically limited and only applicable to the level of words or basic patterns, not concepts. Qualitative analysis software also facilitates codebook development, the production of multiple versions of a codebook, the generation of reports that lists coding guidelines and changes the analyst made to them in the coding process, and the preparation of outputs in a variety of formats including ASCII text files, spreadsheets, and other database formats.

Computerized content analysis has both strengths and limitations. Morris (1994) points out a number of advantages, including (1) perfect stability of the coding scheme, (2) explicit coding rules yielding comparable results; (3) perfect reliability (freeing the researcher to focus on issues of validity, interpretation, and explanation); (4) easy manipulation of the text to create outputs such as frequency counts and key-word in-contexts listings; and (5) the ability to easily uncover co-occurrences of important concept.

However, despite its strength, a number of limitations of computerized content analysis have been described as well. They include (1) a lack of natural language processing capabilities, (2) an insensitivity to linguistic nuances such as negation, irony, and tone, (3) the inability of the program to provide a completely exhaustive listing of key words, (4) the inability of software to resolve references back and forth to words elsewhere in the text, and (5) the danger of word crunching or transforming rich meanings into meaningless numbers (Morris, 1994). The author concluded that computerized and human content analysis may be equally effective, but differences in results may occur at the higher levels of analysis (i.e., the paragraph or the whole document) in which humans are more sensitive to larger contextual cues. Even with the best content analysis software tools, the researcher is still faced with a considerable amount of manual labor. In addition, humans are more prone to errors than machines, especially when fatigue sets in. Finally, media content analysis including screen scraping of TV data, Internet-focused text research, and graphical visualization of analytical relationships encoded in the text are poorly served by existing software. Like the human content analyst, software applications are not neutral tools.

QUALITY CRITERIA AND VALIDATION ISSUES

Intercoder Agreement in Content Analysis

Intercoder reliability, and more specifically intercoder agreement, is a critical component of content analysis because if the coding is not reliable, the analysis cannot be trusted (Singletary, 1993). It shows to what extent different coders agree in the coding of the same text. Because of the problems of reliability, the coding of texts are usually assigned to multiple coders so that the researcher can determine whether the constructs being investigated are shared and whether multiple coders can reliably apply the same codes. As Neuendorf (2002) notes, "given that a goal of content analysis is to identify and record relatively objective (or at least intersubjective) characteristics of messages, reliability is paramount; without the establishment of reliability, content analysis measures are useless" (p. 141). Likewise, Kolbe and Burnett (1991) write that "interjudge reliability is often perceived as the standard measure of research quality. A high level of disagreement among judges suggests weakness in research methods, including the possibility of poor operational definitions, categories, and judge training" (p. 248). There are also important practical reasons to establish intercoder reliability. Neuendorf (2002) argues that, in addition to being a necessary (although not sufficient) step in validating a coding scheme, a high level of reliability also has the practical benefit of allowing the researcher to divide the coding work among different coders.

Measuring intercoder reliability

Intercoder reliability is assessed by having two or more coders categorize units (articles, stories, words, speeches, etc.) and then using the categorizations to calculate a numerical index agreement between or among the coders (Krippendorff, 2004a; Neuendorf, 2002; Patton, 2002). Coders are also referred to as scorers, unitizers, interpreters, or judges. Krippendorff (2004b) divides agreement indices into two broad classes: chance-corrected agreement and raw or percentage agreement. Among the many different agreement indices available, commonly three specific statistics are used to determine intercoder reliability in content analysis in leadership research: (1) percent agreement; (2) Scott's pi (π); (3) Cohen's kappa (κ); and (4) Krippendorff's alpha (α).

Percentage agreement is based on the percentage of all coding decisions made by a pair of coders on which the coders agree. Percentage agreement takes values ranging from .00 (no agreement) to 1.00 (perfect agreement). The obvious advantage of this statistic is that it is simple, intuitive, and easy to calculate. It can also accommodate any number of coder. The major weakness of percentage agreement is that this method fails to account for agreement that would simply occur by chance. For example, assume that two coders are given 100 news stories to code for making reference or not making reference to leadership success. Without any coder or training, even without knowing the concept they are to code, they will agree half of the time, and these random agreements will produce a percentage agreement value of .50. Characteristics of percentage agreement also allow researchers to artificially inflate reliability by adding categories they know will rarely be used or produce disagreement. Kolbe and Burnett (1991) note that, while this can be done with other agreement indices as well, it is a particular problem with percentage agreement. Another limitation is that percentage agreement only records agreements and disagreements and gives no credit for coders whose decisions are "close" (Cohen, 1960).

Scott's π is intended to control for the role of chance agreement and uses a joint distribution across two coders. As Neuendorf (2002) points out, this takes into account not just the number of categories but how these categories are used by the coders. The normal range of this statistic is from .00 (agreement at chance level) to 1.00 (perfect agreement). Scott's π assumes nominal level data, is only appropriate for two coders, and ignores differences in how the two coders distribute their evaluations across coding categories (Scott, 1955). In other words, this index does not account for the differences in how the individual coders distribute their values across the coding categories, a potential source of systematic bias. It assumes that coders have distributed their values across the categories identically, and if this is not the case, the formula fails to account for the reduced agreement (Craig, 1981; Neuendorf, 2002).

Cohen's κ (1960, 1968) index also accounts for chance agreement using the same conceptual formula as Scott's π. This statistic was intended as an improvement over Scott's π, taking into account the differences in coders' distributions by using a multiplicative term instead of an additive on (Cohen, 1960). More specifically, expected agreement by chance in this case is calculated based on the "multiplicative marginals" rather than additive ones, which has the effect of accounting for differences in the distribution of values across the categories of different coders. Cohen (1968) proposed a weighed κ to account for different types of disagreements. Like π, it assumes nominal level data and has a normal range from .00 (agreement at chance level) to 1.00 (perfect agreement). Both π and κ have been criticized as being overly conservative, giving credit only to agreement beyond chance, a tough challenge in the case of extreme distributions (Potter & Levine-Donnerstein, 1999).

Kriffendorff's α (Krippendorff, 1980) takes into account chance agreement and, in addition, the magnitude of the misses, adjusting for whether a variable is measured as nominal, ordinal, interval, or ratio. The author (Krippendorff, 2004a) claims that this index is the most general agreement measure for appropriate reliability interpretations in content analysis. It can be applied to a variety of data and any number of coders, is applicable to small and large sample sizes alike, and is using the same assumptions as Scott's π of equal marginal proportions for the coders. The biggest drawback to its use has been its complexity and the resulting difficulty of hand calculations, especially for interval and ration-level variables. However, recently "macros" or customized programming that can be used with existing software to automate calculations have become available in statistical programs such as SPSS as well as stand-alone software such as ProGAMMA (2002).

A number of rules of thumb for standards of intercoder reliability have been proposed. For example, in many textbooks on qualitative research methods (i.e., Patton, 2002), 75 to 80 percent agreement or intercoder correlations of .70–.80 and higher is suggested as indicative of high reliability. Krippendorff (1980), without specifying the type of reliability, proposes that as a rule of thumb, intercoder reliabilities above .80 are acceptable whereas reliabilities between .67 and .80 result in highly tentative and cautious conclusions about the reliability of codes. Neuendorf (2002) reviews rules of thumb set out by several methodologists and concludes that intercoder "coefficients of .90 or greater would be acceptable to all, .80 or greater would be acceptable in most situations, and below that, there exists great disagreement" (p. 145). Likewise, Riffe, Lacy, and Fico (1998) assert that "research with reliability assessments below .70 becomes hard to interpret and the method is of dubious value to replicate" (p. 131). The criterion of .70 is often used for exploratory research. Higher criteria should be used for indices known to be liberal (i.e., percent agreement), and lower criteria can be used for indices known to be more conservative (Cohen's κ, Scott's π, and Krippendorff's α).

Threats to reliability in content analysis may result from a number of conditions including (1) a poorly executed coding scheme; (2) inadequate coder training; and (3) coder fatigue. The following recommendations (Krippendorff 2004b; Neuendorf, 2002) to enhance reliability in content analysis have been offered:

- reliability data defined as the sample of data from which the trustworthiness of a population of data is to be inferred must be generated by coders who are widely available

- follow explicit and communicable instructions (a data language)

- work independently of each other

- for two coders, large sample sizes and nominal data, π is such a coefficient. Alpha (α) can handle multiple coders, all scales of measurement, missing data, and small sample sizes. An acceptable level of agreement below which data are to be rejected as too unreliable must be chosen depending on the costs of drawing invalid conclusions from these data.

- after data have been generated, reliability may be improved by removing unreliable distinctions from the data, recoding or lumping categories, or dropping variables that do not meet the required level of reliability.

- a preferred approach is to calculate and report two (or more) indices, establishing a decision rule that takes into account the assumptions and/or weaknesses of each (e.g., to be considered reliable, a variable may be at or above a moderate level for a conservative index or at or above a high level for a liberal index). In any case, the researcher should be prepared to justify the criterion or criteria used.

- Do NOT use only percent agreement to calculate reliability. Despite its simplicity and widespread use, there is consensus in the methodological literature that percentage agreement is a misleading and inappropriately liberal measure of intercoder agreement (at least for nominal-level variables); if it is reported at all, the researcher must justify its value in the context of the attributes of the data and analyses at hand.

Validity in Content Analysis

Just as here are several indices of reliability, there are also different measures of validity. *Semantic validity* relates to the meaning reconstruction of the material and is expressed in the appropriateness of the category definitions, the key examples, and the rules for coders. Evidence of semantic validity ascertains the extent to which the categories of an analysis of texts correspond to the meanings these texts have within the chosen context. *Sampling validity* refers to the usual criteria for precise sampling. Ideally, content analysts actively sample a population, using sampling plans to ensure representativeness. But in many practical situations, texts become available by their sources' choice and contain unintentional biases in representing the phenomena of their interest. *Correlative validity* refers to the degree to which the findings obtained by one method correlate with findings obtained by other methods such as observation.

Predictive validity establishes the degree to which the answers of a content analysis accurately anticipate events, identify properties, or describe states of affairs. It can only be used as a quality criterion if predictions can be reasonably be made from the material. *Construct validity* relates to previous success with similar constructs, established theories and models, and representative interpretations.

Stability refers to whether the same results are obtained in a renewed application of the same analytical tool to the same text, and reproducibility is the extent to which the analysis achieves the same results under different circumstances, for instance with different coders. It can be measured through intercoder reliability for which a range of indices have been developed. Finally, *accuracy* assumes stability and reproducibility and denotes the extent to which the analysis meets a particular standard. Riffe, Lacy, and Fico (1998) conclude, "The essence of the validity problem in content analysis as well as in other research ... is that research should speak as truthfully as possible to as many as possible" (p. 150).

The different types of validity are shown in Table 4-4.

Major sources of bias in content analysis that threaten the validity of a study are the researcher and the selection of texts to be analyzed. In addition, the development of

Table 4-4   **Quality criteria for content analysis based on different validity indices**

Validity	Reliability
Material-oriented Semantic validity Sampling validity	Accuracy
Results-oriented Correlative validity Predictive validity	Reproducibility
Process-oriented Construct validity	Stability

Source: *Krippendorffa, 2004, pp. 214–216, 318–338.*

categories is not a neutral or value-free phase of the research process. Instead, as Insch et al. (1997) note, category development involves the researcher biases that are also present in the development of questionnaires.

EXAMPLES OF CONTENT ANALYSIS IN LEADERSHIP RESEARCH

As in the case of choosing a representative sample of case studies on leadership, a wide net was cast in selecting the content analysis studies depicted in Table 4-5. Included in sample of content analysis in leadership research are diverse topics including charismatic leadership (e.g., House et al., 1991), leadership as a social contagion (Meindl, 1990), analysis of speeches of political leaders (e.g., Bligh et al., 2004), leader emergence during the polish solidarity movement (Biezenski, 1996), women's leadership styles (e.g., Stanford, Oates, & Flores, 1995), studies conducted in the United States as well as abroad, and diverse methodologies to include both quantitative and qualitative content analysis techniques, manual and computerized coding. In this section, the goal is to highlight both the uniqueness and versatility of content analysis in leadership research. For most of the studies listed in Table 4-5, there are additional studies addressing the same topics. For example, content analyses of presidential speeches were also conducted, for example, by Immelman (1998).

Table 4-5 reveals that analysis of speeches of political leaders is a major topical stream in content analysis research. For example, Winter (1998) selected four major Clinton speeches from the 1992 campaign and his first term as president and analyzed them for imagery of the achievement, affiliation, and power motives. The achievement motive involves concern for excellence which leads to restless activity. The affiliation motive

Table 4-5 Sampling of content analysis studies in leadership research

Author(s)	Purpose	Respondents	Data sources	Unit of analysis	Analyses	Reliability
Bligh et al. (2004)	To explore how elements of President Busch's speeches changes in response to 9/11		74 speeches and radio addresses	Speeches	Quantitative: descriptive statistics, intercorrelations, ANCOVA	Kendall's coefficient of concordance
Strange and Mumford (2002)	To test for a distinction in the behaviors of ideological (personalized) and charismatic (socialized) leaders	Visionary leaders	Biographies, historic outcome data	Word, phrase, sentence	Quantitative: multivariate, univariate analyses, discriminant analysis, correlation coefficients	Cohen's kappa
Tan and Wee (2002)	Examine the effect of the rhetorical behavior of a charismatic leader on frame alignment and trust	Singaporean leaders	Speech	Theme	Quantitative: longitudinal analysis	Cohen's kappa
Boulais (2002)	To examine leadership themes in children's literature using Posner and Kouzes framework	Children's textbook authors	Selected children's books	Metaphor, imagery	NR	NR

(*Continued*)

Table 4-5   (Continued)

Author(s)	Purpose	Respondents	Data sources	Unit of analysis	Analyses	Reliability
Kirkpatrick Wofford, and Baum (2002)	To demonstrate the feasibility of the motive coding methodology applied to vision statement	Wood working firms; federal engineering services agency	Vision statements		Qualitative: thematic coding of texts	Descriptive statistics, correlations regression
Brown and Barker (2001)	To identify components of the Hersey-Blanchard Situational Leadership Model framework	Managers of Fortune 500 financial services company	Responses to open-ended survey questions	Sentence, phrase	Quantitative: percentages	Cohen's kappa
Buttner (2001)	To determine female entrepreneurs' roles in organizations using relational theory	129 female entrepreneurs	Focus group transcripts	Sentence, phrase	Quantitative: computer-assisted analysis	Test–retest reliability (87.9%) with 5 months interval between coding procedures
Golan and Wanta (2001)	To determine how newspapers framed Bush and McCain during the New Hampshire Republican primary	Journalists	Articles from regional newspapers; gallup reports	Paragraph	Quantitative: frequencies chi-square tests, comparison to gallop data	NR

Bystrom, Robertson, and Banwart (2001)	To explore the media's portrayal of female candidates in comparison to male candidates in primary races for governor & US Senate offices	Journalists	Articles from major national and regional newspapers	Article	Quantitative: descriptive statistics, frequencies, squares, paired-sample *t*-tests	Holsti intercoder reliability
Awamleh and Gardner (1999)	To examine the effects of vision content, delivery, and organizational performance on perceptions of leader charisma	Actors	Video-taped speeches	Rhetorical theme	Quantitative: frequencies, factor analysis	NR
Winter (1998)	To analyze the content of Clinton's speeches from the 1992 campaign and first term for imagery of achievement, affiliation, and power motives	NA	*New York Times* analysis of four major Clinton speeches between 1995 and 1996	Words, images	Qualitative/ quantitative (motive scores)	NR
Stanford, et al. (1995)	To explore the leadership styles of females; to build a heuristic model of female leadership	Female business owners and managers	Transcripts of tape-recorded interviews	Word, statement, theme	Qualitative/ quantitative: Heuristic analysis, frequencies, rankings, ratings	NR

(Continued)

Table 4-5 (Continued)

Author(s)	Purpose	Respondents	Data sources	Unit of analysis	Analyses	Reliability
Shamir, et al. (1994)	To advance the study of the relationship between rhetorical behavior and charismatic leadership	Charismatic speakers	Speech	Speech	Qualitative: rhetorical analysis based on theoretical propositions	NR
Gibson, Fiedler, and Barrett (1993)	To determine under what conditions of stress leader intelligence and creativity correlate with group performance	Army and Navy ROTC cadets	Transcripts of group discussions generated in group creativity experiment	Phrase, sentence	Quantitative: regression	Pearson correlations
Barczak and Wilemon (1992)	To examine differences between more and less effective new product team leaders	10 leaders of new product development teams	Written responses	Sentence	Quantitative: Z-test, multiple discriminant analysis	Post hoc categories, reliability coefficients
House, et al. (1991)	To test personality and charismatic leadership theories	Past US presidents, cabinet members, biographers	Transcripts of inaugural addresses, letters, speeches, newspaper editorials	Word, phrase, document	Quantitative: structural equation modeling	NR

Howell and Higgins (1990b)	To investigate personality characteristics leadership behaviors, and influence tactics of champions of technological innovations; to test a theoretical model	Champions	Tape-recorded interview transcripts questionnaire	Phrase	Quantitative: paired t-tests, partial least squares discriminant analysis Kolmogorov–Smirnov tests	NR
Barczak and Wilemon (1989)	To examine the roles, functions and methods employed by leaders of operating and innovating new product development teams	10 leaders of new product development teams	Content analysis of transcribed semistructured interviews with team leaders	Phrase	Qualitative/ quantitative	Percentage reliability (85.5%) for two coders
Sims and Manz (1984)	To develop observational measures	College students	Transcripts of video-taped leader-follower interactions	Phrase, sentence	Quantitative: frequencies, ANOVA	Spearman–Brown interrater reliability
Yukl and Van Fleet (1982)	To explore effective patterns of leadership behavior across situations, using multiple methods	Military cadets Air Force	Written descriptions of critical incidents Interviews	Phrases, sentences	Quantitative: means, percentages, frequencies, t-test, Pearson product-moment correlation	NR

involves a concern for warm friendly relationships while the power motive involves concern for impact and prestige. It leads to inspiring, charismatic leadership and a cluster of variables such as verbal aggression, risk taking, and alcohol and substance abuse. Among politicians, power motivation is associated with war and violence but also with historians' ratings of greatness. Examples of past power-motivated presidents include Roosevelt, Truman, and Kennedy.

The author analyzed Clinton's motive profile based on Clinton's announcement of his candidacy for the 1992 presidential campaign and his first inaugural address using a motive scoring procedure developed by the author. In his announcement speech, Clinton scored a little above in achievement and affiliation, and a little below in power. In his inaugural address, Clinton showed elevated scores in all three motives, especially achievement and power. Still, the overall profile was similar to his campaign announcement speech. Among past American presidents, Clinton, the campaigner, most closely resembled Lyndon Johnson, but Clinton, the president, had become more like Jimmy Carter (Winter, 1998, p. 370). Based on Clinton's motive profiles, Winter made some predictions about his presidency and concluded:

> One central area of vulnerability for President Clinton is that the inherent frustrations of politics may in the end overwhelm his aspirations for change, improvement, and "re-inventing government" driving him down the bitter paths trod by Wilson, Johnson, Nixon and Carter. In other words, over the long run, the balance of Clinton's power and achievement motives—in everyday language, his capacity to derive pleasure from the office while at the same time pursuing his aspirations and so avoid frustrations, illegalities, and micromanagement—may turn out to be the defining feature for the Clinton presidency (Winter, 1995, p. 128).

Boulais (2002) examined leadership in children's literature based on the Kouzes and Posner (1995) leadership framework by analyzing various works of children's literature for leadership themes. Kouzes and Posner (1995) developed a framework which became very popular designed both to understand leadership and as a tool for the development of leaders. The model rests on five leadership practices: The first leadership practice is called Challenging the Process, which, according to Kouzes and Posner (1995), focuses on seeking out and accepting challenges as well as leaders who challenge the process by recognizing and supporting innovative ideas and taking risks to bring about change. A children's book containing strong images and metaphors and examples of Challenging the Process is *A Story, A Story* (Haley, 1970), a story based on African folklore. It retells the story of Ananse, the Spider man, who challenges the process by first taking the risk of approaching the Sky God and asking for the golden box of stories. The second leadership practice, known as Inspiring a Shared Vision, refers to a leadership practice based on the leader's ability to imagine the future and clearly articulate the vision to others. A children's book rich in imagery reflecting this leadership practice is Ringgold's (1991) *Tar Beach*. The heroine of the book is a young girl named Cassie who grew up as a minority in Harlem. Cassie spends many summer nights on the roof of her apartment building from where she sets out on a visionary journey flying over the city. Ringgold notes that the imagery of flying draws on traditional African-American folktales where flying is a metaphor of escaping slavery. In the end, the author portrays the importance of sharing a vision by showing how Cassie enlists her brother in the common vision of hope for a better life (Boulais, 2002, p. 58).

Enabling Others to Act, the third category in Kouzes and Posner's (1995) leadership framework is a shorthand description that includes leadership practices such as teamwork, building trust, and empowerment. A children's book containing strong imagery, metaphors, and examples of this leadership practice is Ransome's (1968) retelling of *The Fool of the World and the Flying Ship*. This book is based on a Russian folktale in which a young man builds a flying ship and sails off to win the hand of the Czar's daughter. On the journey, the young man encounters and befriends a variety of unusual individuals like the Swift-goer and Eater who enabled him to meet the challenges. The Czar demanded a series of seemingly impossible tasks to be completed before allowing him to marry the Princess. Modeling the Way, as defined by Kouzes and Posner (1995), describes the importance of leading by example. Buntings' (1984) *Smoky Night* provides an example of how an old man can learn from the young. The book tells the story of two families living during the Los Angeles riots. The prejudice and tension has been passed on to Daniel, a young boy, and is further exemplified through the conflict over the families' two cats. As the riots begin and fire breaks out in the apartment building, the families are forced to move into a common shelter. In the move, however, the cats were temporarily lost. Daniel models the way by pointing out to the elders the concept of harmony when the cats were discovered and were drinking from the same bowl. Finally, Encouraging the Heart captures a leadership practice based on small and large actions by a leader who encourages and supports the followers and helps the team to celebrate victories. Results of Boulais's (2002) content analysis identified several children's book in this category. Musgrove's (1976) book, *Ashanti to Zulu: African Traditions*, illustrated by Leo and Diane Dillon is an alphabet book which draws on the alphabet theme to describe 26 distinct aspects of African culture such as ceremonies, celebrations, and other customs. The authors are able to effectively utilize the format of this alphabet picture book to recognize and celebrate the individual contributions of multiple African tribes and cultures that together weave the tapestry of Africa (Boulais, 2002, p. 60).

Finally, Boulais, through content analysis, identified several other children's books that also exemplify each of the five leadership practices outlined by Kouzes and Posner (1995). Weisner's (1999) *Sector 7* is one example. In this story, a young boy on a class trip to the Empire State Building meets and is befriended by a small cloud. They travel together to Sector 7, which is the factory where all the clouds are created. In the story, the clouds have a vision of changing the old cloud designs into fun shapes. When the young boy arrives at Sector 7, the clouds share their vision with the young boy. Inspired to help the clouds achieve their goals, the young boy enables the clouds to act by creating blueprints from their ideas. With these new designs in hand, the clouds challenge the process and tradition of old cloud making by becoming the new and innovative shapes. Despite the boy's expulsion from Sector 7, the idea of innovation, uniqueness, and thinking outside the box is modeled for the adult cloud designers. Likewise, the boy's support of the clouds' desire for uniqueness encourages their heart and celebrates their self-expression.

Although from a methodological perspective, this study is lacking rigor as Boulais (2002) does not describe sampling procedures that led to the identification of the children's books that were content analyzed nor were the specific content analysis steps and procedures described in the article, it is an innovative and creative study that shows a unique application of content analysis by using the well-established leadership model developed by Kouzes and Posner (1995) and analyzing the five-model components in the context of children's literature. In addition, many of the books included in the sample were illustrated allowing not only for textual analysis but also exploring the five leadership practices for imagery themes and found in the illustrations.

Buttner (2001) conducted a content analysis of female entrepreneurs' leadership style using relational theory as the guiding conceptual framework. Numerous studies of female–male differences in leadership style (e.g., Eagly & Johnson, 1990; Helgeson, 1990; Rosner, 1990) reported that women leaders prefer a style that focuses on the quality of leader–follower interactions, emphasize information sharing, are more participative in decision making, and other "feminine" attributes that characterize women's leadership styles, The author described her study as exploratory, intended to capture womens' "voice." The women entrepreneurs participated in focus group interviews in which they discussed their experiences as business owner and the way they enacted their role as leaders in their organization. The interviews were video-taped and transcribed. A ethnographic software program, ETHNOGRAPH, was used for the content analysis of the focus group comments. All comments in the transcripts in which the entrepreneurs talked about relationships with or management of subordinates were assembled into a master file and then were sorted into four categories: (1) persevering characterized by a focus on task through nurturing, protecting, and safeguarding; (2) mutual empowering characterized by a focus on developing another person such as a subordinate or client; (3) achieving characterized by using relational skills to enhance the entrepreneur's own professional growth and effectiveness; and (4) creating team characterized by a focus on creating a sense of team. Each of these four categories had a number of subdimensions (Buttner, 2001, p. 259).

The results indicated that relational theory is a useful framework for examining the ways women entrepreneurs approach relationships in their business. Their management style was based on their values and beliefs about effective ways to relate to employees and clients outside a previously male-dominated culture or tradition (p. 263).

Finally, an early content analysis of a widely cited study conducted by Howell and Higgins (1990a) the authors content analyzed the interview transcripts of 25 matched champions and nonchampions of technological innovation. They hypothesized that champions exhibit charismatic leadership behaviors, that is, articulate ideological goals, display nonconventional behaviors, express confidence in their followers, communicate high expectations, and display individualized consideration to a greater extent than nonchampions (Howell & Higgins, 1990b, p. 251). They also hypothesized that champions use a wider variety of influence strategies, including friendliness, bargaining, sanctions, assertiveness, higher authority, and coalition than nonchampions (p. 252). Champions and nonchampions were identified through peer nomination, a procedure in which respondents were asked to identify key people associated with innovation. Champions and nonchampions were interviewed. Three independent raters coded the transcripts for presence/absence of leadership behaviors and influence tactics. The data were then analyzed statistically using discriminant analysis, a multivariate statistic to determine whether champions and nonchampions could be distinguished on the basis of their leadership behaviors and influence tactics. The first hypothesis which stated that champions display more charismatic behaviors than nonchampions was supported as the discriminant function for the leadership variables was statistically significant. The second hypothesis posited that champions utilize a greater variety of influence tactics was also supported suggesting that champions rely on coalition, reason, higher authority, and assertiveness to convince others to accept innovative ideas (Howell & Higgins, 1990b, p. 260).

The review of the content analysis studies cited in this section leads to two major observations. First, in terms of topics addressed in content analytic studies, charismatic and political leadership were the most frequently investigated topics. Charismatic leadership was the topic of numerous studies using content analyses (e.g., Den Hartog & Verburg, 1997; Howell & Higgins, 1990b; Shamir et al., 1994; Tan & Wee, 2002). To many people, charisma is a mystical and almost magical form of attraction between leaders and followers. Charismatic leaders have been defined as persons who "by the force of their personal abilities are capable of having profound and extraordinary effects on followers" (House & Baetz, 1979, p. 339). Often followers are mesmerized and captivated by charismatic leaders' rhetoric such as Martin Luther Kings' "I have a dream" and J. F. Kennedy's "Ask not what your country can do for you. Ask what you can do for your country." Frequently, charismatic leaders are spellbinding orators. Although leaders can be charismatic without being spellbinding orators, the ability to capture an audience through oratory plays an important part in the formation of charisma (Bryman, 1992b). In fact, several theories of charismatic leadership emphasize that the ability to articulate well is inherent in charismatic leadership (Conger & Kanungo, 1998; Shamir et al., 1994). The motivational theory of charismatic leadership postulated by Shamir et al. (1994) represent one theoretical framework that provides a basis to explore the relationship between speech content and charisma. Given the importance of the charismatic leader's rhetoric and the relationship between the content of the speeches and charismatic leadership, it is not surprising that charismatic leadership is a favored topic in content analysis. Moreover, Conger and Kanungo (1998) theorized that charismatic leaders assess environmental resources and constraints needed to bring about change in their organizations and engage in unconventional, countercultural, and innovative behaviors while leading their followers toward the realization of their vision. These attributes of charismatic leaders are often reflected in their speeches.

The second observation concerns the preponderance of quantitative (and combined quantitative/qualitative) content analyses which support the approach of Krippendorff (2004a) and Neuendorf (2002). It also reflects the lingering hegemony of positivism in the study of leadership. Quantitative content analyses are more likely published in top-tier journals, such as the *Journal of Applied Psychology*. Software programs facilitate the task of word crunching, and the results of the automated coding can easily be imported into statistical packages such as SPSS or SAS to perform univariate or multivariate analyses.

SUMMARY

This chapter introduced content analysis as a flexible and versatile qualitative research method frequently used in the study of leadership. It described fundamental procedures for conducting a content analysis and discussed the various approaches to content analysis to include qualitative, quantitative, and computerized methods. A key strength of content analysis is the analytical flexibility it allows. At one level, the manifest content can be captured and revealed in a number of text statistics. At this level, software programs greatly facilitate the word-crunching activities yet leave the final interpretive burden on the human content analyst. Despite the availability of a variety of software programs, for researchers who wish to examine more than simple frequency counts, content analysis remains a laborious process of devising reliable coding schemes and applying human judgments. These problems are only exacerbated by the ease with which software programs can collect thousands of documents and millions of words on a variety of topics. However, computer-based content analysis programs do not replace the human analyst who needs to find the deeper meaning behind the words and sentences that make up a body of text. It is at this second level where the researcher is interested in discovering the latent content and deeper meaning embodied in the texts, which requires the human interpreter. Content analysis provides a replicable methodology to access deep individual or collective structures such as values, attitudes, and cognitions (Carley, 1997) and offers a means to conduct both inductive and deductive research.

A number of empirical studies were reviewed in this chapter which addressed different leadership topics such as political and charismatic leadership. These published studies illustrate various aspects of content analysis such as the development of codebooks, intercoder reliability, and statistics that have been applied to codes to generate categories and themes and how issues of validity and rigor have been dealt with in these studies. Content analysis, because of the wide range of procedures that are subsumed under this umbrella, continues to be one of the more frequently employed methods in leadership studies.

5

QUALITATIVE INTERVIEWING IN LEADERSHIP RESEARCH

AN ILLUSTRATIVE QUALITATIVE INTERVIEWING LEADERSHIP STUDY

Given the recent ethical scandals in business, government, sports, nonprofits prominent, and religious organizations, people are asking, what is wrong with our leaders? Treviño, Brown, and Pincus Hartman (2003) conducted 40 semistructured interviews, 20 with corporate ethics/compliance officers and 20 with senior executives representing medium to large American corporations. To set the stage for the interviews, the authors asked interviewees to think about a specific executive from their experience whom they could use as a point of reference in answering the questions without having interviewees identify the leader. The authors began the study by conducting telephone interviews with the 20 ethics officers, 15 of whom were male and five were female. Of the 20 senior executive interviews, 10 were conducted over the phone and the other 10 in person. Each telephone interview lasted between one and two hours. The interview protocol included general questions about ethical leadership designed to generate spontaneous responses, followed by more specific probing questions. The general questions asked interviewees for their definition of executive, ethical leadership, the traits and behaviors associated with ethical leadership, and the ethical leader's motivation and vision for the future of the organization. Some of the questions were derived from the literature. In addition, the authors employed the "contrast principle" by asking interviewees to think about what unethical leadership entails.

Data from both sets of interviews were analyzed using Boyatzis (1998) thematic analysis consisting of both manifest content analysis and latent content analysis. For the manifest content analysis, the transcripts were read and divided into distinct "thought units" or concepts as suggested by Miles and Huberman (1994) and Strauss and Corbin (1990). A thought unit or concept could be a word, a phase, a sentence, or multiple sentences which were recorded on separate index cards. These cards were then organized into emergent categories and labeled. This process resulted in 33 categories that contained 10 or more entries of which one third was used to establish intercoder reliability. The p-statistic was used to compute intercoder agreement. For the ethics officer, the intercoder agreement was 92.1 percent, and for the executive interviews, it was 88.7 percent. The manifest content analysis was followed by latent content analysis to go beyond the obvious elements and probe the underlying meaning of the manifest codes.

For both groups of interviewees, the ethics officers and the senior executives, the results were fairly consistent. Both groups believed that ethical leaders as people serve as role models of ethical conduct by walking the ethics talk, were honest and trustworthy individuals who valued integrity, and modeled a high moral compass. Beyond that, they were credible, consistent, and predictable and believed in doing the right thing in the right way for the right reasons. Ethical leaders were seen as fair and principled decision makers who care about people and the broader society who behave ethically in their personal and professional lives. The researchers characterized this as the moral person aspect of ethical leadership, representing interviewees' perceptions of the leader's personal traits, character, and altruistic motivation.

Interviewees also indicated that ethical leaders set the ground rules for ethical behavior in the organization and hold people accountable relying on rewards and punishment to reinforce ethical conduct and avoid ethical lapses. Treviño et al. (2003) labeled this aspect of ethical leadership the moral manager dimension to capture a leader's proactive efforts to influence followers' ethical and unethical behavior. The authors stated that moral managers make ethics an explicit part of their leadership agenda by communicating an ethics and value agenda and by visibly and intentionally role modeling ethical behavior.

Finally, this in-depth qualitative interviewing study also highlighted the importance of context—the interviews took place in the midst of the Clinton–Monica Lewinsky scandals, and the interview protocol included an explicit question about whether personal morality was related to ethical leadership. The ethical climate in the White House at the time of the scandal reflected a context that supported unethical behavior allowing the unethical leader, Bill Clinton, to get ahead with his unethical leadership philosophy. Ample evidence exists showing that organization context affects leadership behaviors, effectiveness, and outcomes (Porter & McLaughlin, 2006; Shamir & Howell, 1999; Tosi, 1991). Tolerance for ethical lapses in the White House was mirrored in business organizations such as Enron and Tyco and religious organization such as the Catholic Church, which at times lacked a strong climate for ethical leadership.

INTRODUCTION

Defining Interviews

Interviews have become part of our daily lives. We read interviews in papers; we see people interviewed on television; we follow celebrity interviews. The number of television programs, daytime talk shows, and newspaper articles that provide us with results of interviews continue to proliferate. Silverman (1997), seeing the widespread use and impact of interviews on contemporary life, has suggested that we live in an "interview society" (p. 248) in which we are constantly bombarded with newspaper, radio, and television interviews claiming to enlighten us about the private lives of others. In the information society, researchers, the mass media, human service providers, educational institutions, and other types of constituencies increasingly generate data by interviewing. Interviewing is undoubtedly one of the most widely used technique for conducting systematic social inquiry, as psychologists, sociologists, anthropologists, administrators, politicians, and yes, leadership scholars treat interviews as their window on the world (Gumbrium & Holstein, 2002). Atkinson and Silverman (1997) concluded that interviewing is the central resource through which contemporary social science (and society) engages with issues that concern it. Indeed, Briggs (1986) claims that it is estimated that 90 of all social science investigations use interview data.

Because of their pervasiveness, most people are familiar with interviews: television interviews, job interviews, therapeutic interviews, exit interviews, forensic investigative interviews, cultural interviews, life history interviews, to name a few. One consequence of this familiarity is a tendency to simplify the interview process: an interviewer asks the interviewee questions—a question eliciting an answer (Gumbrium & Holstein, 2002). However, asking questions and getting answers is a much more difficult task than it may first appear (Fontana & Frey, 1994). The authors (Fontana & Frey, 2000) go on to say

> The spoken or written word has always a residue of ambiguity, no matter how carefully we word the questions and how carefully we report or code the answers. Yet the interview is one of the most common and most powerful ways in which we can understand our fellow human being (p. 645).

Empirically, this statement is buttressed by the extensive literature purporting how to teach interviewing, both quantitative and qualitative (Fielding, 2002). In view of the extensive body of literature on how to conduct interviews, interviewer qualifications, or how to train interviewers, a discussion of interviewing pragmatics is not included in this chapter. A cursory glance at texts devoted to qualitative research reveals that the hows of interviewing continue to be discussed in the scholarly literature (e.g., Arksey & Knight, 1999; Rubin & Rubin, 1995; 2005; Silverman, 2001; Wengraf, 2001) as well.

Still, there is no consensual definition of interviewing. Even if we accept minimal definitions—asking questions and getting answers or a conversation that is to be reported—there are complicating factors. Qualitative interviewing provides a way of generating empirical data about the social world of informants by asking them to talk about their lives. In this respect, interviews are special forms of conversation. Although these conversations may vary from highly structured, standardized, quantitatively oriented survey interviews to free-flowing informational exchanges, all interviews are interactional (Holstein & Gumbrium, 2004, p. 141). The interview in qualitative research is a critical method. Unlike the interview of the popular media with its rigid question and answer format, the interview in qualitative research comes in many guises. Social scientists have typically seen the face-to-face (FTF) encounter as the quintessence of qualitative research. The FTF interview is often seen as the optimal way to actively engage with the informant in a manner that narrows the gap between researcher and researched and maximizes the efficacy and equality of the data collection enterprise (Seymour, 2001). Qualitative interviewing goes beyond mere fact gathering and attempts to construct meaning and interpretation in the context of conversation (Kvale, 1996).

According to Silverman (2001), for interviewers in the interactionist tradition, interviewees not only construct narratives but their social world. For researchers in this tradition, "the primary issue is to generate data which give an authentic insight into people's experiences" (Silverman, 2001, p. 87). The strength of qualitative interviewing is the opportunity it provides to collect and rigorously examine narrative accounts of social worlds (Miller & Glassner, 2004, p. 137). Holloway and Jefferson (1997) argue that interviews that elicit narratives can be more meaningful than interviews based on a question and answer format because they turn questions about a given topic into storytelling invitations. It is often assumed that qualitative interviews may allow for descriptions of the life world of the interviewee to unfold and contribute intimate closeness to the field of research (Rubin & Rubin, 1995, p. 1). Interviewing provides access to the context of people's behaviors and affords researchers the opportunity to understand the meaning of that behavior (Seidman, 1998).

Holstein and Gubrium (2004) insist that interviewees are not so much repositories of knowledge as they are constructors of knowledge in collaboration with the interviewers. Hence, they coined the term "active interview." The authors argue against the notion that "those who are curious about another person's feelings, thoughts or experiences" merely need "to ask the right questions" and the other's "reality" will be theirs (p. 2). For these authors, interviewing is far too often seen as a search-and-discovery mission, in which the interviewer tries to find out what is inside the interviewee, and the challenge lies in extracting information as directly as possible. According to them, interviews are not pipelines for transmitting knowledge but reality-constructing, meaning-making occasions. Second, Holstein and Gumbrium ask researchers to turn their attention to the processes by which narrative competence is assigned to interviewees. Among all the potential meaning makers, researchers treat some as useful interviewees, that is, interesting and competent surveyors of thoughts and feelings, whereas others are classified as narratively irrelevant or incompetent. The question is "Do conceptions of interviewee competence lead us to unwittingly encourage some representations of experience and silence others, thus restricting our understanding of the phenomenon under study?" Third, the meaning-making processes in active interviewing is pursued with the help of patterned narrative linkages that Holstein and Gumbrium call horizons of meaning. There are always operative interpretive frameworks, whether the interviewer and interviewee are aware of them or not, and a primary objective of active interviewing is to promote the visibility of these horizons (Carspecken & Cordeiro, 1995).

Each party—interviewer or interviewee—is likely to grasp the exchange differently. Furthermore, meaningful conversation implies a need for action. The realization depends on the purpose of the interview with its discursive structure and the life trajectory of those who are doing the talking (Wengraf, 2001). When we implicate conversation in a scientific effort, the researcher's theoretical orientation, and ontological and epistemological assumptions determine the interpretation of the interview. Furthermore, interpreting the depth of experience captured by interviewing is complicated by issues such as the perception of the need for addressing traditional scientific criteria of validity and reliability.

Interviews are collaborative efforts, involving interviewers and interviewees in meaning-making work in the process (Alasuutari, 1995). Interviews are not one-way information-gathering situations. They are guided or dialogical conversations (Guba, 1981; Lincoln & Guba, 1994) between interviewer and interviewee and are conducted such that both parties view reality as a process, always becoming and characterized by openness and collaboration (Schwandt, 1994). Because of the nature of the inquiry, it is impossible to have a priori knowledge of the meanings that will emerge.

TYPES OF INTERVIEWS AND INTERVIEW QUESTIONS

Before the interviewer asks the first question, he or she has to establish rapport with the interviewee. Merely "fronting up" for an interview provides both the interviewer and the interviewee with an extensive amount of information. As Seymour (2001) notes, instant judgments are made on the basis of appearance, dress, and bearing. Perceived similarities in terms of gender, ethnicity, and other demographics influence the likelihood that significant insights will be revealed. Interviewer competence, trust, ability to move the interview forward toward a shared outcome, and interviewees' willingness to self-disclose and serve as an active co-creator of the experience are fundamental dynamics in shared meaning making. Through their cooperation in the research process which is dependent upon the quality of the rapport that is established between interviewer and interviewee, both parties act as co-creators of knowledge and meaning.

As part of developing rapport, qualitative interviews typically start with a few sentences describing the nature of the research, the upcoming interview, the interviewer's interest in the study, and offers additional information the interviewee wants or needs to know. The interview should be recorded after the researcher obtained permission from the interviewee to do so. Many interviewers begin the interview with questions about noncontroversial topics. They are neural in content and designed to establish rapport. A very useful opening question is to ask the interviewee to tell about him/herself. Establishing rapport with the interviewee not only eases the person into the interview situation but opens the door to more informed research.

Mutuality of trust is a critical component in building rapport. Mutual trust is facilitated by empathetic listening and egalitarian relationships between interviewer and interviewee. Establishing and maintaining rapport must be marked by respect, interest, attention, understanding, being nonjudgmental, and good manners on part of the interviewer (Arksey & Knight, 1999). There are numerous ways to establish trust as a basis for rapport such as making the interview schedule available before the interview, inviting clarifying questions, or informing interviewees fully about the time frame of the interaction. By providing an overview of the purpose of the study, the researcher's intended use of the data, measures taken to protect confidentiality and anonymity, and obtaining permission for tape recording or note-taking are instrumental in establishing a relaxed, comfortable climate which is essential in developing rapport with the interviewee.

A typical guideline on interviewing recommends that

> ... the interviewer starts with the most general possible question and hopes that this will be sufficient to enable the interviewee to talk about the subject. If the interviewee has difficulty ... then the interviewers can move to the prompt which is more specific. Hopefully this will be enough to get the participant talking ... It is likely that a successful interview will include questions and answers at both general and specific levels and will move between the two of them fairly seamlessly (Smith, 1991, p. 15).

Structured Interviewing

Structured interviewing refers to a situation in which the interviewer asks each interviewee a series of preestablished questions with a limited set of response categories. The backbone of the structured interview is the interview protocol, also referred to as the interview guide or interview schedule. An interview protocol lists the questions or issues that are to be explored in the course of the interview. It provides a framework within which the interviewer develops his or her questions, sequences those questions, and makes decisions about which to pursue in greater detail during the interview (Patton, 2002). The exact wording and sequence of questions are determined in advance. In structured interviews, the researcher reads previously developed questions from the interview protocol and the interviewee offers his or her response. Once the interviewer has worked out the formal interview protocol, discussed the issues he or she wishes to cover, made the introductions, and has set the scene and established rapport with the interviewee, the actual interview can begin.

All interviewees are asked the same questions in the same order. Other interactions between the researcher and the researched are kept to a minimum. Structured interviews assume that there is a common vocabulary for potential interviewees, question formats are meaningful to both parties, and the context of each question is obvious. As interviewees are asked the same questions, comparability of the responses is guaranteed. In reference to the structured, Converse and Schuman note

> The interviewer is charged with the responsibility of conducting inquiry in something in the manner of a conversation. The product of the encounter is supposed to be good "hard" data—the stuff of codes and computer analysis. The process is supposed to be at least somewhat "soft"—the stuff of a pleasant conversation (1974, p. 22, cited in Suchman & Jordan, 1990).

Structured interviewing typically relies on close-ended questions in which the interviewee is asked to choose between several predetermined answers. For example, the question "How satisfied are you with your group leader?" may be coded as (1) very satisfied; (2) satisfied; (3) neither satisfied or dissatisfied; (4) dissatisfied; and (5) very dissatisfied. Even more restricted are interview questions that elicit "Yes/No/Do not know" responses. The underlying assumption made by the interviewer using close-ended questions is that these questions are relevant to the area of inquiry. The primary criticism of close-ended questions is that they do not allow the interviewer to find out from the interviewee what is relevant to them or allow them to express different views.

An important factor in structured interviewing concerns the relationship between the interviewer and the interviewee and the respective roles they play. The general assumption is that the interviewer controls the flow of the verbal exchange by asking questions and recording the responses of the interviewee. In fact, the interviewee is often referred to as "subject" because the person is expected to respond to a set of questions rather than to inform through participation in a conversation. The interviewing situation is regarded as a one-way process in which the interviewer elicits and receives but does not provide information. In structured interviewing, detachment from the interviewee is seen as essential for the reliability of the data.

The structured interview protocol depicted in Table 5-1 comes from a study designed to examine leadership attributes, behaviors, and leadership success of three executive leaders in the highly regulated long-term healthcare industry (Crawford, 2005). In highly regulated industries such as health care or airline companies, prior research has suggested that leaders in these contexts often are highly constrained and have little discretion in decision making and strategy formulation. The informants in this study were three senior executives of nursing home corporations. The content of the structured interview was designed to elicit information about the health care industry in general, the three leaders who participated in the study as well as predictors of successful leadership the researcher had gleamed from leadership theories. The results revealed that common themes emerged from the interview data which included the similarities of personal characteristics, the entrepreneurial spirit, emphasis on goals and standards, importance of relationships (both internal and external to the organization), and perception of high performance that represented critical success factors of three outstanding executive leaders within the long-term healthcare industry.

Table 5-1   Sample interview protocol

What are the strengths of your organization that you can leverage in the future?
What do you see as future opportunities for your organization within the industry?
What are the major projects or initiatives that you are working on and when are they targeted for completion (start to finish)?
What direction or trends do you see for the industry over the next five years? How do you ground that prediction?
When bad things happen in your organization, what is typically the cause? Can you give an example (temporary/permanent; specific/pervasive; internal/external)?
Tell me one goal you would like to really obtain. What steps will you take to reach it (goal-setting)?
Tell me what you think are your greatest capabilities as a leader?
What things do you have control over in your job and what things don't you (control)? Can you give an example of things you have let go?
What do you value most about yourself (at work and outside of work; as a human being, friend, parent, spouse, leader, etc.)?
What do you think is the core life giving value of your organization? That is if it didn't exist it would make your organization totally different than it is today?
Is there anything else you would like to add to today's conversion? What question do you have for me?

Source: Adapted from Crawford (2005).

Table 5-2   Advantages and disadvantages of structured interviews

Advantages	Disadvantages
Attention focused on a given issue	A full understanding of the important issue is needed to direct the interview
Detailed information is gained on the issue discussed	Concepts not contained in the focus of the interview may not be found
Insight into declarative knowledge used is provided	It may provide weak insight into procedural knowledge
General rules and problem-solving strategies can be uncovered	

Among the advantages of structured interviewing are answers that are easy to code, the direction of the inquiry is clear, high reliability, the production of comparable data, and the reduction of interviewer bias. Structured interviews reduce interviewer effect and bias particularly when several interviewers are used. On the other hand, structured interviews offer little flexibility in relating the interview to particular interviews and circumstances. In addition, the standardized wording of the questions may limit naturalness and relevance of questions and answers (Patton, 2002, p. 349). There is generally little room for variation in responses except when an infrequent open-ended question is included. Because the number of possible responses is limited in structured interviews, interviewees may be forced into giving responses which do not reflect their true feelings, thereby raising validity problems (Table 5-2).

Unstructured Interviewing

Unstructured or open-ended interviewing is designed to elicit an authentic account of the interviewee's subjective experience. Unstructured interviews aim to delve deep beneath the surface of superficial responses to obtain true meanings that interviewees assign to their experiences and the complexities of their attitudes and behaviors. The interviewer uses open-ended questions that emerge from the immediate context and asks in the natural course of things instead of relying on a predetermined sequence. There are no predetermined question topics or wording. Using open-ended questions, the interviewer inquires about the interviewees' feelings about the topic under scrutiny, for example, "How do you feel (or, what do you think) about the ethical behavior of our political leaders?" The responses to open-ended often lead to further questions. Unstructured interviews dispense with formal interview schedules and rely on the social interactions between the interviewer and interviewee to elicit the information. Unstructured interviews are intended to increase the salience and relevance of the questions.

Table 5-3   Advantages and disadvantages of unstructured interviews

Advantages	Disadvantages
Probe complex issues	Time consuming
Genera understanding of the problem is provided when very little is known about the problem	Attention not focused on a given issue
Important issues are uncovered that eventually can guide future inquires	Very little factual information is provided
Insight into general problem-solving method is provided	Less detail is provided on general concepts

Although unstructured interviewing allows for greater social interaction between interviewer and interviewee, with few constraints on the interview schedule, interviewers need to minimize their own, potentially biasing role, limiting their interactions to encouraging nodes and expressions and nondirective, neutral probes. They must resist the urge to agree or disagree with interviewees and need to perfect the art of creating expectant, not embarrassing silences.

The advantages of unstructured interviews are that more complex issues can be probed, answers can be clarified, and a more relaxed research atmosphere may contribute to the elicitation of more in-depth as well as sensitive information. There are also weaknesses of unstructured interviews: (1) the outcome of the unstructured interview results in different types of information collected from different interviewees who are asked different questions thereby limiting the comparability of responses and (2) the outcome is a less systematic and comprehensive set of data which may make the organization and analysis of the data difficult (Patton, 2002, p. 349). Collecting data through unstructured interviewing is also very time consuming. There are greater opportunities for interviewer bias to intervene, and because it is a time-consuming method, the unstructured interview is expensive and only feasible with small samples. Although there is invariable potential for interviewer bias in qualitative interviews, it is offset, at least to some extent, by the greater participation and involvement of the interviewer in the interaction aimed at reaching greater depth, It is assumed that once the level of communication has reached this "depth," interviewees will reveal their "true" inner feelings. The strengths and weaknesses of unstructured interviews are summarized in Table 5-3.

Semistructured Interviewing

In semistructured interviewing, the researcher combines the use of close-ended and open-ended questions. Essentially, this process entails researchers using a broad topic such as leadership issues in the health care industry. An interview protocol is then developed around a list of topics without fixed wording or fixed ordering of questions. The content of the interview is focused on issues that are central to the research question, but this type of questioning and discussion allows for greater flexibility than the structured interview. Semistructured interviews are modeled more closely on the unstructured than the structured interview. This means that the topic area guides the questions asked, but the mode of asking follows the unstructured interviewing process. This leaves the interviewer free to rephrase the questions and add further inquiries such as "Who?" "Where?" "When?" "Why?" and "How?" based on the interviewee's answers and conversation flow. Parker (2005) states:

> An interview in qualitative research is always "semi-structured because it invariably carries the traces of power that holds things in place and it reveals an interviewee's, a co-researcher's creative ability to refuse and resist what the researcher wants to happen. The task of radical research, then, is to make the interview and encounter that reveals patterns of power and creative refusal of a set research agenda" (p. 41).

To do this kind of interviewing requires at least two things. According to Parker (2005), (1) we have to admit that interviewing is not a mere data collection technique but a methodology involving some analysis in the very process of collecting the material and (2) we have to focus on the interview process itself so that what the interviewer says is treated with as much attention as what the interviewee says. Parker argues that the account of the interviewee is not private and collected from his or her inner psyche but something spoken in context and spoken against. This will open up the contradictions between the respective agendas of the interviewer and the interviewee. The idea here is that the interview must express curiosity and openness toward contradictions and disagreements which may be at work during the interview process.

Collectively, unstructured and semistructured represent the essence of *in-depth qualitative interviewing*. In-depth interviews, according to Taylor and Bogdan's (1984) useful definition, are "repeated FTF encounters between the researcher and informants directed toward understanding informants' perspectives on their lives, experiences or situations as expressed in their own words" (1984, p. 77). In-depth interviewing implies an egalitarian relationship between the interviewer and interviewee which contrasts the imbalance of power in structured interviewing. Rather than focusing on the researcher's perspective as the valid view, it is the informant's account which is being sought and highly valued. The interviewer attempts to retrieve the interviewee's world by understanding their perspective in a language that is natural to them. This reduces the possible distorting effects of symbols and language (i.e., research related terminology) which are not part of the interviewee's everyday usage. As a result, in in-depth interviewing there is a significant move from the interrogative stance followed in a structured interview toward a more conversational exchange.

To achieve the level of depth and level of detail sought in in-depth interviewing, the researcher works out main questions, probing questions, and follow-up questions. Main questions focus on the phenomenon under investigation and ensure that the overall subject is covered. According to Rubin and Rubin (2005), main questions are the scaffolding of the interview, the skeleton of it. A main question translates the research topic into terms that the interviewee can relate to and discuss. This combination of producing a topic-initiating question, according to Rapley (2001), and following up the interviewee's answer with a follow-up question is the central way in which semistructured interviews come off. The author asserts that

> The topic initiating questions introduce topics of talk on which the interviewer would like the interviewee to focus; the follow-up questions provide the possibility to gain very detailed and comprehensive talk on those specific topics. They constantly seek "to unpack" the prior talk, and allow a multiple number of issue, or "mentionables", that the interviewee raises to be explored and/or followed up ... The methodological rational of semi-structured interviews—that they allow a rich, deep and textured picture—is locally produced in and through the "simple" method of producing topic-initiating and follow-up questions (p. 315).

Interviewers usually prepare a limited number of main questions. Although there are no fixed rules, in most in-depth interviews, they limit the number to about half a dozen and may actually ask only a subset of these questions. *Probing questions* are used to elicit information more fully than the original questions which introduced a topic. Many interviewees talk in generalities, so probes such as "Can you give me an example of that?" or "What did s/he say?" will move the interview forward and encourage the interviewer to elicit the language and specific meaning involved in the conversation. Sometimes silence is the best probe, keeping in mind that there are multiple meanings for both talk and silence (Poland & Peterson, 1998). The authors note that as the "apparent" opposite of speech, silence is often overlooked in qualitative research. Silences are profoundly meaningful; they may mean withholding or resistance, reflects a cultural mode of self-representation, or may represent the unthinkable (Poland & Peterson, 1998, p. 295). Remaining silent once interviewees pause can also encourage them to continue the conversation. Kvale (1996) points to the possible utility of silence as a strategic device to enhance data collection while others (e.g., Spradley, 1979) argue that silence represents a failure on part of the interviewer to "draw out" the requisite "data" from the interviewee. From this perspective, silence reflects either interviewer or interviewee inadequacy.

Probing is sanctioned as part of the research process that differentiates in-depth interviewing from everyday conversations. It is an indication that the researcher is aware that he or she cannot take for granted the common sense understanding that people share because these may be differently interpreted by interviewee and inter-viewer. The use of probing questions is a method of clarifying and gaining more detail, especially when the researcher is trying to understand the meaning that informants attach to the original question. Probes are also used when the informant's statements seem vague, incomplete, or give no answers. One strategy that serves as a probe involves asking the devil's advocate question. This question format provokes the interviewee into elaborating on previous comments, either to provide the interviewer with more detailed information or test the validity of the interviewer's interpretation of the interviewee's position on a particular issue.

Probing questions are intended to elicit greater detail. Probes are used to deepen the response, increase the richness and depths of responses; they give cues to the interviewee about the level of response the interviewer is seeking. They fill in the blanks and are usually when, who else, where, and what types of questions. Questions such as "Would you elaborate on that?" or "Could you say a little more about that?" are typical examples of probing questions. Probing questions can also be elicited through nonverbal language such as nodding and leaning forward toward the interviewee. To achieve richness and depth of understanding, those engaged in qualitative interviewing listen for and explore key words, ideas, and themes and use follow-up questions to encourage the interviewee to expand on what he or she has said that the researcher feels is important.

In in-depth interviewing, researchers are confronted with the possibility of nonanswering. An interviewee may at some point during the interview decide not to answer a question. There are many reasons an informant may decide not to answer a question. For example, he or she may be uncertain of the type of comment or detail the researcher is seeking. Or the interviewee may think that the question is too personal and constitute an infringe-ment of privacy. Or the interviewee may not understand the question and does not wish to appear foolish or stupid. Because of the complex dynamics involved in in-depth inter-viewing, this type of interview requires highly competent researchers who are fully cognizant of the aims of their study, are skilled at encouraging the interviewee to talk, and are good listeners. Interviewers must be sensitive to nonverbal messages, the effects of the setting on the interview, and nuances of the relationship. They must also be able to cope with alternating phases of openness, withdrawal, trust, distress, and embarrassment. While these subjective factors are sometimes considered threats to validity, they can also be strengths because a skilled interviewer can use flexibility and insight to ensure in-depth, detailed understanding of the interviewee's experience.

As the interviewer is the data collection instrument in in-depth interviewing, he or she must develop the level of skill appropriate for a human instrument or the vehicle with which the data are collected and interpreted. The skills needed in the in-depth inter-view—physical, social emotional, communicative—embody the act of interviewing, but those alone will not determine answers to research questions. For such determinations, aspiring qualitative interviewers must learn the skill of comprehension, the complex aptitude, and competence of reflection and representation which are perhaps unteachable by any other method than trial and error. As Seidman (1998) states:

> Researchers must ask themselves what they have learned from doing the interviews, studying transcripts, marking and labeling them, crafting profiles, and organizing categories of excerpts. What connective threads are there among the experiences of the participants they interviewed? How do they understand and explain these connections? What do they understand now that they did not understand before they began the interviews? What surprises have there been? What confirmations of previous instincts? How have their interviews been consistent with the literature? How inconsistent? How have they gone beyond (pp. 110–111)?

In-depth interviewing has the advantage of allowing participants to describe what is meaningful or important to them, using their own words rather than being restricted to predetermined response categories. It provides high credibility and face validity and allows investigators the flexibility of applying their knowledge, expertise, and interpersonal skills to explore interesting or unexpected ideas or themes raised by participants. There is consensus that in-depth interviews provide the opportunity to gain an account of the values and experiences of the respondent in terms meaningful to them. On the other hand, in-depth interviewing can be extensive and time consuming because it requires considerable skill and experience on part of the interviewer often necessitating interviewer training. Because of the more subjective nature of in-depth interviewing, analyzing and interpreting the data are more com-plex than analyzing and interpreting structured surveys. Moreover, in-depth inter-viewing may be more reactive to personalities, moods, and interpersonal dynamics between the interviewer and interviewee than more quantitatively oriented approaches to qualitative interviewing.

Role of the interviewer in in-depth interviewing

The qualitative interview is obviously and exclusively a social interaction between the interviewer and the interviewee in which both participants create and construct narra-tive versions of the social world in which they live. In analyses of interview data, it becomes apparent that interviewees are actively engaged in a collaborative process in which meanings are constantly being negotiated and agreed upon. The socially con-structed data are "created by the self-presentation of the interviewee and whatever interactional cues have been given off by the interviewer about the acceptability or otherwise of the accounts being presented" (Dingwall, 1997, p. 59). Through the use of questions, formulations, assessments, and acknowledgement tokens, a researcher shows his or her ongoing work in the process of data generation. Kvale (1996) discusses a craft-like approach to qualitative interviewing when he asserts:

> Craftsmanship here includes a shift from method to the person of the researcher, relating science to art, a skill model of transition from novice to expert, and the learning of research through apprenticeship (p. 105).

Interviewees respond to interviewers based on who they are—in their lives as well as social categories to which they belong such as age, gender, class, and race (Miller & Glassner, 2004, p. 127). This is a practical concern as well as an epistemological and theoretical one. The goals of both the interviewer and interviewee need to be clarified prior to the interview. The investigator specifies the purposes of the study to the best of his or her knowledge including the role of gatekeepers and shareholders. They must remain open and curious, casting the net widely (Geertz, 1973). Interviewees, on the other hand, as the "owner" of the data, can expect to be treated as equal participants in the research process and be entitled to negotiate and renegotiate their roles as the study progresses.

Glaser and Strauss (1967) and Strauss and Corbin (1990) argue that interviewers must have what the authors refer to as "theoretical sensitivity":

> Theoretical sensitivity refers to a personal quality of the researcher. It indicates an awareness of the subtleties of meaning of data . . . [It] refers to the attribute of having insight, the ability to give meaning to data, the capacity to understand, and the capacity to separate the pertinent from that which isn't (Strauss & Corbin, 1990, p. 42).

Strauss and Corbin believe that theoretical sensitivity comes from a number of sources, including professional literature, professional experience, and personal experience. The credibility of a qualitative research report relies heavily on the confidence readers have in the researcher's ability to be sensitive to the data and to make appropriate decisions in the field (Eisner, 1991; Patton, 2002) (Table 5-4).

Focus Group Interviews

The focus group is a research methodology that has gained popularity in a growing number of context over recent decades (Hydén & Bülow, 2003; Wilkonson, 1998). In this method, a small group of participants gather to discuss a particular issue under the guidance of a facilitator (the researcher) who often plays a detached role.

Table 5-4   Advantages and disadvantages of semistructured interviews

Advantages	Disadvantages
Positive rapport between interviewer and interviewee	Dependent on skill of the interviewer (ability to formulate questions during the interview) and ability of respondent to articulated answers
Result in high reliability	Not very reliable
Addresses and clarifies complex issues	Time consuming and expensive
Reduce pre-judgment on part of the interviewer (i.e., researcher predetermining what will or will not be discussed due to few predetermined questions)	Depth of information difficult to analyze
	Generalizability limited
	Lack of validity

Focus groups are unstructured or semistructured interviews with small groups of people who interact with each other and the group leader. They have the advantage of making use of group dynamics to stimulate discussion, to gain insights, and generate ideas in order to pursue a topic in greater depth. Focus groups are of particular value because of their ability to allow researchers to study how people engage in collective sense making, that is, "how views are constructed, expressed, defended, and (sometimes) modified in the context and discussion and debate with others" (Wilkonson, 1998, p. 186). They can be used, for example, to examine not only what group members think but also how they think and why they think in a given way, their understandings and priorities. The group processes can help people to explore their views and generate questions in ways that they would find more difficult in FTF interviews. The emphasis in focus group interviews is on interactions within the group based on topics that are supplied by the researcher who typically takes the role of the moderator. A focus group interview is, first and foremost, an interview. It is not a problem-solving session. It is not a decision-making group. According to Maykut and Morehouse (1994), a focus group interview brings several different people into contact through a process that is open and emergent. The object is to get high-quality data in a social context where people consider their own views in context of the views of others (Patton, 2002, p. 386).

Kruger (1994) identified six characteristics of the focus groups interview, the combination of which sets it apart from other group processes. The defining characteristics of focus group interviews are (1) they involve people; (2) they are conducted in a series; (3) participants are reasonably homogeneous yet unfamiliar with each other; (4) they are methods of data collection; (5) the data are qualitative; and (6) they constitute a focused discussion. The author suggests that "The focus group is beneficial for identification of major themes but not so much for the microanalysis of subtle difference" (Kruger, 1994). Focus groups have to be carefully composed and balanced in relation to the characteristics of the interviewees to prevent group members from feeling socially constrained.

Although there are no guidelines about the number of focus group members to aim for, groups are typically comprised of 5–50 people with similar backgrounds who participate in the interview for one or two hours but that is dependent on the complexity of the topic. In the focus group interviews, this author and some of her doctoral students have conducted, the groups typically consisted of about 6 to 12 participants and a group leader (e.g., the interviewer) who uses an unstructured interview guide to stimulate and guide the discussion. The groups are audio- or video-taped and then transcribed and analyzed. The methods of analysis are similar as for in-depth interviews.

Focus group interviews have several advantages including cost-effective data collection and the presence of group members who tend to provide checks and balances on each other, which weeds out false or extreme views (Kruger & Casey, 2000). However, focus groups like all forms of data collection techniques also have their limitations, such as a restricted number of questions that can be asked in a group setting, the limited time available for individual interviewees in order that all voices are heard, and considerable group process skills on part of the interviewer. Critics of focus groups as a research method (e.g., Agar & MacDonald, 1995; Kitzinger, 1994) point out that even though the interaction between participants is considered to be the hallmark of such research, the interaction itself has seldom been evaluated or analyzed.

Telephone Interviewing

Qualitative researchers generally rely on FTF interviewing when conducting semistructured and in-depth interviews. The three types of interviews described above are characterized by synchronous communication in time and place. The telephone interview, on the other hand, is synchronous communication of time and asynchronous communication of place. Using telephone interviews for collecting data is appropriate when the social cues of the interviewee such as gender or ethnicity are less or not important. They are also appropriate when standardization of the interview situation is not important or the interviewer cannot access interviewees at physical facilities such as military bases or prisons. Thus, telephone interviews are an alternative to access hard-to-reach participants (Sturges & Hanrahan, 2004). Telephone interviews are often used for short structured interviews in very specific situations as the telephone interview typically generates short-answer questions rather than in-depth descriptive and reflexive accounts produced by FTF interviews. Telephone interviews are usually cheaper and quicker to conduct as they remove geographical limitations. Moreover, researchers have reported that telephone interviews increase participants' perceptions of anonymity. A final consideration regarding the suitability of the telephone interview is cost saving. Using the telephone makes it possible to collect relatively inexpensive data as it eliminates the need for the interviewer to travel to the interviewees' location. Wasserman's (2000) work on eminent women scientists is an example of making use of telephone interviews.

Internet Interviews

Computers have long been employed by quantitative social researchers, but new information and communication technologies have recently opened up new opportunities for qualitative researchers as well. New software program constantly appear on the market, which facilitate electronic interviewing and the virtuality of the Internet offers unprecedented possibilities of extending the range of participants beyond those who are available for FTF interviewing. As a result, there has been a growth in the literature on the use of the web as a primary tool for conducting research. For example, approaches such as virtual focus groups, chat rooms, and conferences have been used to explore experiences, emotions identities of participants.

Internet or e-interviews are asynchronous communications of time and place. In relation to time, the interactions between interviewer and interviewee are likely to be asynchronous, with pauses of varying length between communication episodes. Furthermore, an asynchronous e-mail exchange encourages participants to explore and revisit their responses. Asynchronicity has the advantage that either the interviewer or the interviewee has to identify a mutually convenient time to conduct the interview. In terms of space, the relationship takes place at a distance through the medium of electronic, screen-based text. When the interviewer and interviewee are separated by different time zones, the e-interview offers a viable option.

Internet interviewing represents a cost-effective way of collecting data. Many of the financial difficulties (cost of travel and access to sponsoring organization) associated with organizing FTF venues disappear. A further consideration is that, with on-line interviews, interaction results in the immediate production of a text file. Unlike research using FTF interviews, the researcher has no need to budget for recording equipment, transcribing equipment, or transcription costs, and delays caused by translation are eliminated (Mann & Stewart, 2002). Using e-mail for collecting data is appropriate when social cues of the interviewee are not important sources of information and when the interviewer has a small budget and little time for traveling. E-interviews are also appropriate when standardization of the interview situation is not important but anonymity is requested. However, Internet interviewers need to be aware that access to and use of the Internet is a matter not only of economics (the haves versus the have-nots) but also of one's place in the world in terms of gender, culture, and ethnicity (Mann & Stewart, 2002).

The identities that virtual interviewees create on-line may differ from their other identities through the use of pseudonyms, as the lack visual communication allows one to create a practically new self. The move to electronic interviewing is perhaps most problematic for in-depth interviewing. Rather than the parties to the interview being FTF, interaction centers on "virtual" interviewees and "virtual" interviewers, all of whose empirical groundings are unclear. This lack of clarity leads to a melding together of everyday media realities, confounding the traditional boundaries of text and identity (Fontana, 2002, p. 169).

Among the advantages of using e-mail for interviews are that e-interviews allow the interviewee to respond whenever he or she wishes or when time permits. Interviews can be conducted between people living in different continents and in different time zones. E-interviews can be conducted without traveling. And there is no need to transcribe verbal data, because the response has already been written in e-mail. Online conversations allow interviewees to take back their words prior to posting them so that the evolving conversation can be accommodated. In addition, the absence of visual cues and the fixed nature of the printed word allow interviewees to stay focused on the task. Lastly, when asynchronous, interviewees have the time and access to resources to inform, revise, and reflect on their responses. On the other hand, because the e-mail interview takes place asynchronously, the effects of nonverbal cues, voice intonations, and elements of surprise are lost. Interruptions occur frequently, and there is no way for the interviewer to know when the interviewee is pausing for reflection or trying to continue typing a response. As the use of e-mail becomes almost universal in developing countries, the e-interview may take its place as an alternative option in the qualitative researcher's toolbox. In the future, web-cam will allow qualitative researchers to transform an artificial electronic situation into a more real-life situation.

Virtual Focus Groups Interviews

Social researchers have begun to recognize the opportunity the Internet provides to recruit participants or conduct research online. Online survey research has prolifer-ated. Likewise, developers of traditional FTF groups have turned their attention to virtual focus groups (Greenbaum, 2002). Recently, Adler and Zarchin (2002) intro-duced virtual focus groups as a tool for formal qualitative research. Applying Kruger's (1994) definitional criteria of focus group interviews to virtual group inter-views, Turney and Pocknee (2005) conducted virtual focus group interviews with

3 and 12 groups and concluded that virtual focus group interviews foster democratic participation, eliminate verbal, and visual cues that indicate and enable hierarchy and dominance of views prevalent in FTF settings, maintain anonymity, and facilitate collection of qualitative data by allowing interviewers to download interviewees' responses to questions and probes. Although at the time of this writing qualitative leadership researches have yet to avail themselves of virtual focus group interviews, new technologies continue to open up new possibilities for qualitative interviewing online. Additionally, with the increased shift to team-based organizations and dispersed, shared leadership which prevails in these organizations, we can expect an increase in the use of virtual focus interviews.

DATA COLLECTION AND ANALYSIS

Data analysis is an issue that should be considered very early in the process of designing a qualitative study. Bodgan and Biklen (1982) define qualitative data analysis as "working with data, organizing it, breaking it into manageable units, synthesizing it, searching for patterns, discovering what is important and what is to be learned, and deciding what you will tell others" (p. 145). In qualitative interviewing, the researcher is the primary data collection tool. The human-as-instrument is a concept coined by Lincoln and Guba (1985) to illustrate the unique position of qualitative researchers in the process of data collection. While this concept applies to many qualitative research methods including narrative analysis, ethnography, and phenomenology, it is probably nowhere more apparent than in the qualitative interview. As a person, the "human-as-instrument," is the only instrument flexible enough to capture the complexity, subtlety, and constantly changing situation which is the human experience. As Lincoln and Guba (1985) point out, there is no way to determine in advance the exact instrument we will use because "only the human instrument has the characteristics necessary to cope with an indeterminate situation (p. 193). Merriam (1998) adds:

> Certain characteristics differentiate the human researcher from other data collection instruments: the researcher is responsive to the context; he or she can adapt techniques to the circumstances; the total context can be considered; what is known about the situation can be expanded to nonverbal aspects . . . (p. 7).

Methods for analyzing data generated from interviews have been well documented (e.g., Huberman & Miles, 1994; Kvale, 1996; Patton, 2002) and vary widely. Kvale (1989) describes five methods of analysis that include (1) meaning condensation, (2) meaning categorization, (3) narrative structuring, (4) meaning interpretation, and (5) generating meaning through ad hoc methods. Patton (2002) also addresses a number of techniques for quantifying and analyzing qualitative interview data. According to

Rapley (2001), an awareness and analysis of the interviewers' talk in producing both the form and the content of the interview should become a central concern for researchers when analyzing interview data, whatever analytic stance they take on data (pp. 304–305). In other words, an analysis of interview data should be sensitive to how the conversation is produced as interviews are social interactions.

Qualitative interviews and their transcripts produce a large volume of material which must be condensed, categorized, and/or otherwise interpreted and made meaningful. In course of the analyses, comments made during an interview are broken down into data units, blocks of information that are examined together. Part of analysis involves combining data units on the same topic, both within single interviews and across multiple interviews. Researchers make permanent records of their interviews through either notes or recordings. Digital audio recording on mini-disc has many advantages over the traditional tape recording including increased fidelity, longer recording time, and the ability to index recordings. Although more expensive than traditional tape recorders, mini-disc recorders have many features that are useful for data analysis that make the benefits outweigh the higher cost of the equipment (Givens, 2004). Voice recognition software can also greatly facilitate the task and accuracy of transcription.

Although it is common practice for someone other than the interviewer to transcribe tapes recorded for purposes of data collection, Tilley (2003) argues the importance of interviewers taking seriously the ways in which the person transcribing tapes influences the data. Similarly, Poland (1995) explicitly addresses the work of hired transcribers in relation to data analysis and asserts that interviewers who have taken into account the interpretive nature of transcription have ignored issues arising from hiring out that work. Lapadat and Lindsay (1999) concluded:

> It is not just the transcription product—those verbatim words written down— that is important in the process; it is the process that is valuable. Analysis takes place and understandings are derived through the process of constructing a transcript by listening and re-listening, viewing and reviewing... Transcription facilitates the close attention and interpretive thinking that is needed to make sense of the data... Transcription as a theory-laden component of qualitative analysis warrants closer examination (p. 82).

The fact that individuals hired to do transcriptions may become emotionally involved in the work, connecting to characters they construct based on the tapes, contrasts with the commonly held notion that a transcript is a truthful replication of some objective reality (Kvale, 1996), and transcribing as an accurate, dispassionate process. Although audio tapes capture voices interacting, they miss out on other elements that constitute the interview experience. Moreover, when recorded on tape, the interview conversation is already once removed from the moment interactions were spoken, and then an additional distance is created when what is spoken is translated into text (Tilley, 2003). The author concludes:

> The degree of research rigor is open to question when accuracy of transcripts is left in doubt whether it is the researcher doing the transcription work or hired help. Rather than remaining silent about the transcription process, researchers can strengthen claims of trustworthiness of data by making visible the complexity of transcription work, acknowledging the interpretive reality of data constructed, and providing insights into the ways in which they specifically address issues of trustworthiness in their research practice (p. 771).

Once transcribed, data are organized by topics and themes coded into categories (Chapter 4). After all the data are organized in computer files, the researcher looks for individual concepts, themes, events, and topical markers that speak to the research question and places an appropriately chosen label next to each data unit to allow retrieval of the coded items. In order to analyze and present data from qualitative interviews, the researcher must be thoroughly familiar with the field notes, the tape recordings and their transcriptions, and any other data collected such as notes from observations. In addition to concepts derived from transcripts, field notes and ideas for themes relevant to the research question may also come from the literature. The concepts and themes identified by the researcher, in turn, may suggest new, related concepts and themes that can lead to the construction of a typology.

Computer software programs are available that can exist in categorizing interview statements or counting key words, which may allow for some forms of quantitative analysis. Although computer software represents a helpful method to classify and analyze qualitative interview data, it should be used subordinate to acquiring deeper knowledge of the phenomenon under investigation through analysis of language and meaning (Murphy & O'Brien, 2006). In the final analysis, the most appropriate method of analysis for a qualitative interview study will depend on the purpose of the research as well as the time and resources available.

RELIABILITY AND VALIDITY IN QUALITATIVE INTERVIEWS

As noted in the preceding chapters, data interpretation implies and is influenced by the extent by which the researcher in convincing ways establishes reliability and validity of the findings. Qualitative researchers, including those availing themselves of qualitative interviewing as the method of choice, have to deal with the paradox of how to develop an objective interpretive science of subjective human experience (Schwandt, 2000, p. 119). Seidman (1998) states:

> What are needed are not formulaic approaches to enhancing either validity or trustworthiness but understanding of and respect for the issues that underlie those terms. We must grapple e with them, doing our best to increase our ways of knowing and avoiding ignorance, realizing that our efforts are quite small in the larger scale of things (p. 20).

In general, compared to reliability and validity issues in content analysis, techniques for establishing rigor and quality in interview studies are much less prescriptive or in some case are negligible. For example, in contrast to content analysis studies in which inter-coder reliability is an important concern, especially in studies that approach content analysis quantitative, in qualitative interviewing reliability and validity are infrequently discussed. Interinterviewer reliability (i.e., having two interviewers recording a single interviewee on two occasions) is often not feasible. What is feasible, however, is to establish intercoder reliability once the interview has been transcribed and compare the interviewer's codes and themes with those produced by a second coder.

Similarly, validation strategies are rarely reported in empirical studies. One way of assessing validity is the interviewer sharing his or interpretations with the intervie-wees (see member checking in Chapter 1). The idea behind this way of increasing validity is to place the interviewee in a position to corroborate or disapprove the interviewer's interpretations. As noted earlier, the trustworthiness of the qualitative interview may be enhanced by making potential influences of transcription work on data analysis transparent and acknowledging the interpretive nature of the transcript.

APPLICATIONS OF QUALITATIVE INTERVIEWING STUDIES IN LEADERSHIP RESEARCH

Despite the intuitive appeal of qualitative interviewing as a primary research method in the study of leadership, the number of empirical studies that utilized this meth-odology is relatively small. Contrary to what might be expected, interviews with individual high-profile leaders are uncommon, primarily because these individuals are less accessible to researchers as opposed to the media. In fact, the Hartwell and Torbert (1999a) interview with Andy Wilson, founder and CEO of Boston Tuck Tours and Massachusetts Entrepreneur of the year, was the only study in this category included in Table 5-5.

Table 5-5   Sampling of qualitative interviewing studies in leadership research

Author(s)	Purpose	Interviewees	Data sources	Analyses
Galanes (2003)	To explore leadership effectiveness of small group leaders	23 excellent small group leaders from variety of industry sector	Unstructured interviews; 21 FTF interviews; 2 telephone interviews	Constant comparison method to identify themes and commonalities
Brown and Gioia (2002)	To conduct an in-depth study of top executives of a Fortune 500 company's online division	17 members of top management teams of Fortune 500 company's online division	Qualitative interviews, taped and transcribed	NUDIST for coding data to identify themes and concepts; constant comparison method; validation of findings by interviewees
Wepner, D'Onofrio, Willis, and Wilhite (2002)	To identify the characteristics of the moral dimension of leadership	3 education deans, 1 dean with 3 faculty and 3 students	Vignettes framing moral issues	Thematic coding; consensual validation to establish agreement on how to classify interview text; theoretical validation
Pescosolido (2002)	To examine the role of emergent group leaders as managers of group emotions	20 semiprofessional jazz groups and collegiate rowing teams	Critical incident group interviews transcribed; field notes	Qualitative analysis to develop concept of leader as manager of group emotions
Alexander, Comfort, Weiner, and Bogue (2001)	To examine key leadership issues in community mental health partnerships	115 participants of Community Care Networks demonstration program	Semistructured FTF interviews transcribed word for word	NUDIST; iterative Q-sort to develop conceptual map of partnership leadership construct

Cooke et al. (2001)	To investigate the career development of 20 notable Latinas	20 Latinas in U.S. recognized as distinguished Hispanic-American women	Semistructured interviews; brief demographic questionnaire transcribed; sent to interviews for approval and corrections	Grounded theory method
Kamisnki, Kaufman, Graubarth, and Robins (2000)	To examine how empowered workers reach their goals	14 worker-trainers holding production jobs	Interviews (type unspecified)	Coding of interviews, identification of patterns
Giacopassi, Nichols, and Stitt (1999)	To examine attitudes toward casino gambling	128 community leaders in 7 gambling communities	Structured interview consisting of 9 open-ended core questions	Percentages
Hartwell and Torbert (1999)	To examine strategic priorities	The 1997 Massachusetts Entrepreneur of the Year (A. Wilson)	Unstructured interviews conducted by members of a PhD consulting seminar; tape recorded	No analysis per se; interview and feedback; verbatim description of interview
Tandon, Azelton, and Kelly (1998)	To document the nature of community leadership	77 community leaders	Semistructured interviews	Data reduction through generation of 56 codes resulting in 5 dimensions of community leadership; data display of each of the 5 dimensions resulting in tree template; intercoder reliability coefficient (kappa)

(Continued)

Table 5-5   (Continued)

Author(s)	Purpose	Interviewees	Data sources	Analyses
Bresnen (1995)	To explore the subjective meanings placed upon the and leadership construct and examine the relationships between leadership and structural relations of management authority, power, and control	Managers in construction industry (sample size unspecified)	Semistructured interviews with open-ended questions; taped	Inductive*
Bensimon (1990)	To explore congruence between college presidents' self-descriptions as leaders and the portrayals given to them by campus leaders and locate presence (or absence) of four organizational frames	32 colleges and universities; 27 chief academic officers, 28 faculty leaders, 25 trustees	Semistructured interviews; transcribed	Coding for four organizational frames; percentage data for presidents' self-descriptions and campus leaders' descriptions of president
Isabella (1990)	To develop a model of how managers construe organizational change events as change unfolds	40 managers of financial services company	In-depth interviews; transcribed	Grounded theory; constant comparison method; coding of 25 excerpts by independent coder—96% level of agreement

*Inductive in this context means that no specific details describing the exact nature of the data analyses were provided by the authors of the articles (e.g., Bresnen, 1995).

As in previous chapters, a small subset of the qualitative interviewing studies depicted in Table 5-5 is reviewed to highlight the strength and weaknesses to include both individual FTF and group interviews. These studies were conducted in a variety of organizational contexts ranging from community organizations to semiconductor firms.

Hartwell and Torbert (1999a) in 1997 together with PhD students in Torbert's consulting seminar at Boston College interviewed Andy Wilson, founder and CEO of Boston Duck Tours, which since 1994 has provided narrative historic tours of Boston in authentic World War II amphibious vehicles. The interviewers approached the interview without an interview protocol or schedule. The authors' state:

> For the class members, the interview with Andy constituted an opportunity to practice (a) interviewing an executive; (b) creating a mutual, transformational environment with a stranger; (c) clinically apply developmental theory in real time; and (d) experimenting with one's own pattern of inquiry and self-disclosure, support and confrontation (p. 183).

Andy volunteered for this interview in the hope of receiving feedback from the professor and his students as he was navigating a difficult personal and professional transition. He invited the seminar members to share his struggle with some of the more challenging incongruities in his life and approached the interview as a frame-challenging inquiry (p. 189).

In the interview, Andy portrayed himself as a transformational leader whose charisma derives from a willingness to face his own transformational issues. He founded the company after five years in corporate America at age 30 and was able to start the business while he was still working for the corporation. On a visit to his aunt in Memphis, from his hotel room Andy saw as sightseeing bus outside his window using a World War amphibious truck known as a Duck Tour. He signed up for the tour and kept the brochure. Again, it is interesting to note the role of context. At that time Bill Clinton was running for president, campaigning across the country on a bus trip. Andy speculated that the Duck Tours idea would work in Boston and spent the next two years raising money and clearing red tape with various government agencies since tourism is a highly regulated industry.

Successful well beyond his dreams with 50 employees, the front-runner in the industry and a strong organizational culture based on core values relating to human dignity and freedom, Boston Duck Tours is in a worldwide expansion mode. In route to success, Andy became very political, which "led him into a platform of making a difference in the world, which is important to me" (p. 186). Although he recognized that hard work and profit are essential in making a visionary company grow, as Collins and Porras (1994) have shown, he was more passionate about the excitement of accomplishing his dreams.

Despite all of his successes, the CEO struggled with personal issues. He has been in a personal relationship for 15 years but building and running the business left little time for a personal life. His significant other was also in the business, in fact, she established her own franchise in a different city. Andy wanted to feel good about himself and struggled with the work/relationship balance (or lack thereof) issue on a daily basis. He sincerely wanted to balance his personal and professional life. He desired to be able to influence the world and still meet his obligations to himself, his investors, his employees, and his lover. Finding that balance was the biggest issue in the current life of this business leader.

In a follow-up article, Hartwell and Torbet (1999b) explained six developmental frames such as diplomat, achiever, and strategist that emerged in eight stages. In the interview with Andy Wilson, the CEO manifested several of the stages and frames discussed by the authors. For example, Wilson illustrated strategist-like qualities when he talked about considering expanding the business worldwide although it conflicted with the competing goal of achieving balance in his personal life. Like a strategist, Wilson was deeply committed to the principles of freedom and social responsibility and how they were interwoven with his personal life. Six months after the interview, the authors met again with Wilson after they had sent him a copy of the report for a feedback session. Values were at the center of Andy Wilson's leadership philosophy.

Cha and Edmondson (2006) conducted an in-depth interview study to shed light on the mechanisms through which charismatic leadership and values achieve their effects on followers. Values play a central role in charismatic leadership. Lord and Brown (2001), for example, argued that they influence follower affect, cognition, and behavior. According to Conger and Kanungo (1998), charismatic leaders often invoke values or higher ideals as part of their compelling vision for an organization. The authors suggested that it is the "idealized quality of the charismatic leader's goals—supported by an appealing rhetoric—that distinguishes him or her from other leaders" (p. 158). More specifically, Cha and Edmondson sought to develop theory of how charismatic leadership affects followers through the impact of values that are contained in the leader's vision. They speculated that the positive effects of charismatic leadership can be a double-edged sword that can heighten followers' experience of meaning at work but also increase the risk of subsequent disenchantment as they lose trust in the leader.

In-depth interviews were conducted in a small advertising firm with 12 full-time employees. They were conducted in two phases and extended over several years. In the first phase (October 1994–January 1995), the authors explored the organizational structure of the company and inquired about group dynamics and employee motivation by interviewing nine employees and observing meetings and the workplace in general. At the time of the second round of interviews three years later (April 1998–April 1999), the company had grown to 31 employees. The authors interviewed 27 employees in phase 2 (several employees were interviewed two or three times during this time).

The interview notes and transcripts were analyzed following the inductive process described by Glaser and Strauss (1967) to identify recurring themes in both the CEO's and employees' understanding of the company's values. The authors identified incongruence or the presence of two somewhat different sets of values, one described by the leader (sent values) and one described by the employees (expanded values) as one salient construct as shown in Table 5-6

Table 5-6   Value incongruence between values articulated by CEO and employees

CEO values (sent values)	CEO's description	Employee value (expanded values)	Employee description
Being different	"Coming out of my previous business, I knew we had to be different." Anybody who peeked under our tent at all had to instantly know that we were going about things differently than everybody else, for marketing reasons, for positioning reasons, for branding reasons.	Equality	"We are more conscious than other organizations that I have worked in about being egalitarian, fair, respectful of individuals. And we're conscious of trying to be less hierarchical. We try to eliminate privilege and rank."
Unpretentiousness	"[Our company shirts] were…the kind of shirts that the fellow who shows up to pump your septic tank would wear, a big logo on the back, working-class-looking logo, with your name stitched in over the pocket."	Openness	"[The CEO] wanted everything to be open communication, no titles. If you see people's business cards here, their titles aren't on them."

(Continued)

Table 5-6   (Continued)

CEO values (sent values)	CEO's description	Employee value (expanded values)	Employee description
Community	"We've done goofy shirts, with our names on them, jackets and stuff absolutely from the get-go, because it gave people a feel of belonging to something that I think is absolutely critical."	Family	"The center of [the values] is treating people right, with respect, embracing all kinds of different. . .[The CEO] founded a company based on those principles. . .trying to create an environment where people enjoy each other, get along, have a sense of self-worth"
Employee growth	"[I started this] company for me-and I hope for other people-[to have] a venue to be venue to be as good as you can be. To use. . .all of your God-given potential, to take a professional track as far as you can."	Employee synthesis and expansion	"I think right now is a real test of John and the principles. An people in the office are saying, Are you gonna walk the walk. You can talk the talk, but are you gonna walk the walk."
Diversity	"It's more of a me thing than anybody else, but as we have gotten bigger, I've been very protective of this concept of, let's get different types of people in here."	Love your neighbor	"We're working for this nation of 'non-hierarchical,' 'treat people right.' It's like working for a much higher cause than 'create advertising,' 'make money.'"

Source: Adapted from Cha and Edmondson (2006).

Despite the apparent differences in these two sets of values, there is some overlap. For example, the authors note that the expanded value (employees) of family combines all five of the sent values (CEO)—being a different type of company, unpretentiousness, employee growth, and diversity—but all encompassed the notion that the company should take care of employees' needs. The authors interpreted the employees expanded values as being more ideological.

A second theme was labeled leader hypocrisy attribution, a pattern in which employees attributed multiple CEO actions to hypocrisy or the deliberate violation of the ad agency's values without considering alternative, legitimate explanations for his actions (p. 65). The hypocrisy attribution emerged as a consistent explanation for the leader's negative actions such as slow completion of employees' reviews, unclear determinants of raises, or lack of information sharing.

Cha and Edmonton iteratively developed a model of antecedents and outcomes of hypocrisy attributions by combing their data, reviewing literatures on values, charismatic leadership, and social cognition using interview notes to guide them to relevant quotes illustrating this phenomenon. They also examined "negative cases" (Chapter 2) or exception to the initial model to develop a theory of possible moderators. For example, a few employees interviewed did not attribute any leader actions to hypocrisy. They continued this process of iterating among data, related literature until they believed that their emergent theory effectively explained the data and incorporated the relevant literature. The authors concluded that after incorporating the moderating conditions, the theoretical model seemed a sufficiently complete explanation of value-triggered disenchantment.

The advertising company was led by a strong charismatic leader with good intention who made strong efforts to promote positive outcomes. His vision contained the idea of a "new kind" of advertising agency that would differ substantially from traditional agencies. He communicated this component of the vision through the organizational value of being different or being a new breed of advertising agency that would immediate strike employees and clients as something new and fresh. The CEO's vision also promised employees, many of whom had been previously dissatisfied and alienated at traditional agencies, a better future through organizational values of employee and community growth.

In second phase of the interviews, employees indicated that the company's decision to grow substantially was a massive change that threatened the firm's value system. They found this growth upsetting and began to interpret the CEO's behavior as hypocrisy. Thus, despite a strong set of values espoused by the CEO, he was unable to prevent the emergence of employee disenchantment. The authors concluded that a strong emphasis on shared values in an organization thus may be a double-edged sword. Leaders can reap the benefits of strong organizational values, and at the same time their behavior may be perceived as hypocritical.

Pescosolido's (2002) research on leaders as managers of group emotions illustrates a group interview study. Coupled with observations, the author interviewed 20 different groups asking them to describe a recent critical incident in their group's life together. The interviewer employed a limited number of questions to obtain a more detailed description of the incident describing how the group had clicked. The transcripts of the interviews and field notes were analyzed to identify examples of a group leader acting as the manager of the group's collective experience of emotion. The author laid the ground work for future research by developing a set of propositions regarding hypothesized relationships between group dynamics, leader characteristics, and the management of the group's emotion. For example, one proposition states that leaders who exhibit both charisma and empathy are more likely to engage in the management of group emotion.

The Cooke, Fassinger, Prosser, Mejia, and Luna (2001) study of Hispanic-American women leaders was also designed to develop theory; in this case, a theory of career development based on contextual, cultural, and personal variables that facilitate or limit vocational development of 20 influential women in different occupational fields and professional organizations. The authors conducted in-depth, semistructured interviews. Coding of the interview transcripts proceeded at four levels including open coding, the creation of categories yielding 80 distinct categories, axial coding to create key categories representing a higher level of abstraction, and selective coding to generate the core category. Members of the research team discussed confirming and disconfirming incidents from the original transcripts, discussed and integrated their conceptualization of key and core categories, used negative case analysis in the process, and arrived at a theoretical framework consistent of 14 key categories. These 14 categories were then collapsed into four meta-categories or super codes which included (1) the self; (2) culture, family, and personal background; (3) immediate context such as social support and managing work and family; and (4) sociopolitical conditions such as Hispanic subgroup experiences. The core category which evolved from the interaction of the four meta-categories was labeled career-life path. To verify the credibility of data analysis, interviewees were sent a draft of the manuscript prepared for publication and asked to comment on the usefulness of the model in describing their career development.

The results suggested that the career path of the 20 notable Latinas tended to be nonlinear and unplanned with interviewees attributing their career trajectory to serendipity or a created, encountered, or offered opportunity (Cooke et al., 2001, p. 291). The authors concluded that their emergent theory highlights the importance of ethno-historical relationships between person and environment, the influence of immigration experience and sociopolitical movements, and the salience of culture in Latina career development.

Finally, in one of the earlier studies, Isabella (1990) interviewed 40 managers from different organizational levels—senior, middle, and lower level management—from a medium-sized urban financial services company representing different functional areas such as marketing, accounting, finance, and human resources. Each manager was asked to describe five key events that had occurred in the organization over the previous five years that they considered critical. Examples of key events included the selection of a new president from the outside, relocation of corporate headquarters, and the implementation of a company-wide quality improvement program. With each manager, the author conducted two semistructured interviews collecting data about managers' career histories, experiences, and perceptions of core organizational values during the first interview, whereas the second interview focused on the five key organizational events.

Using the constant comparison method iterating between data collection and theory formulation, the data were organized into preliminary categories. An independent coder, blind to the purpose of the research, coded 25 randomly chosen excerpts from the interview transcripts, yielding a 96 percent level of agreement. The data revealed that interpretation of the key events evolved through a series of stages the author labels anticipation, confirmation, culmination, and aftermath. During anticipation, managers assembled rumors and other tidbits of information into an in-progress frame of reference while during confirmation, their frame of reference drew on conventional explanations and comparisons of past events. During culmination, managers compared conditions before and after a salient event and looked for symbolic meaning. Finally, during aftermath, they reviewed the consequences of the event (Isabella, 1990, pp. 15–16). Thus, a different construed reality and predominant frame of reference characterized each stage.

It should also be noted that in many of these studies, qualitative interviewing was employed in tandem with content analysis with researcher coding the interview transcripts. The classification of the empirical studies as either content analysis or qualitative interviewing is somewhat arbitrary based on my assessment of whether the interview represented the primary research method of choice augmented by coding of the interview transcripts as opposed to those studies in which content analysis resulted in the major findings. Sometimes, the authors classified their research as an interview study. For example, the Cha and Edmondson (2006) study was described as a longitudinal single-case research design, but the interview was the most important data collection tool (augmented by observations).

ETHICAL CONSIDERATION IN QUALITATIVE INTERVIEWING

Ethical principles in qualitative research were discussed in Chapter 2. However, there are some ethical issues that are unique to qualitative interviews which will be briefly mentioned here. *Informed consent* must be obtained from interviewees after they have been carefully and truthfully informed about the nature of the research. Approval usually requires that prospective interviewees sign a consent form agreeing to participate, after being informed of potential risks and benefits. This gives the interviewee a chance to refuse to comply with the interview request. *Confidentiality* requires that the interviewer guarantees to keep the names and other identifying information associated with the interviewee anonymous. Because interviewees may be sharing highly personal information, it is important for the interviewer to assess how much confidentiality he or she can promise. When data are collected through FTF interviews, granting anonymity to interviewees is impossible as the two parties know each other. In telephone and electronic qualitative interviewing, on the other hand, the interviewer does not know the interviewee and can ensure confidentiality. Finally, *protection from harm* means that the interviewer protects the interviewee from physical, emotional, psychological, or any other kind of damage. Even though "just talking" may seem inherently harmless, people who participate in qualitative interviews may experience psychological stress, legal or political repercussions, or ostracism of peers or staff who believe that the participant has said unflattering things about them to the interviewer.

Although interviewers must adhere to these ethical principles, ethical considerations in qualitative research which focuses on the complexity of researching private lives cannot be solely addressed by the application of abstract rules principles or guidelines. For example, Miller and Bell (2002) argue that gaining "informed" consent in qualitative research is problematic because informants do not always know what they are consenting to. If the focus of the research, for example, is to explore a leadership transition, how can the outcome of the research be known? Researchers need to decide what they are expecting participants to consent to. Is consent just about participation in term of being interviewed or does it go further involving reading and commenting on transcript and the analysis of data (Miller & Bell, 2002, p. 65)? The authors prefer "consent" as an ongoing, constantly negotiated, and renegotiated process between interviewer and interviewee throughout the research process. They also call our attention to the fact that providing consent is presumed to be a voluntary in the absence of any coercion. However, this assumption ignores the potentially complex power dynamics that can operate around consent especially where issues of gender and/or ethnicity are manifest.

Summary

Among the different qualitative research methods used in leadership research, the interview occupies a privileged position as it involves a conversation and negotiation of meaning between interviewer and interviewee. Interviews are a common tool of qualitative inquiry. By their very nature, they represent a form of social interaction grounded in talk (DeVault, 1990). Qualitative interviewing is sensitive to and reflects the nature of the phenomenon under investigations, the context in which interviewer and interviewee interact and subject to ethical concerns. There are compelling reasons for the selection of qualitative interviews in leadership research, yet many leadership scholars remain unfamiliar with this particular qualitative method.

This chapter examined various types of qualitative interviewing including individual FTF interviews using structured, unstructured, and semistructured interviews as well as group focus and Internet interviews as well as focus groups and e-interviews. As we have seen, researchers who consider interviewing online have many factors to weigh in the balance. The excitement of working with an interviewing medium that is not constrained by boundaries of time and space and that offers digital data at one's fingertips is matched by the growing realization that the virtual venue makes practical, legal, ethical, and interpersonal demands that move beyond the knowledge and expertise that researchers may have acquired in conducting FTF interview (Mann & Stewart, 2002). In addition, as long as Internet interviewing remains a text-based interchange, there are factors—such as the nature of language used on-line and the implications of disembodiment for issues of identity and/or power relations in cyberspace—which many researchers need to consider before embarking on an online study (Mann & Stewart, 2002). Text-based Internet interviewing may eventually be seen as one of many ways to interview using this medium as new technologies develop. Clearly, different types of interviewing are needed to answer different research questions and the demands of different situations.

One of the issues I was grappling with in writing this chapter concerns the use of language in qualitative interviewing. Although the use of terms such as participants, respondents, or interviewees as in case of this chapter is used to denote the researched and terms such as investigator or interviewer are employed to capture the researcher represent an improvement over the use of the term "subject," the language remains awkward and stale. Language and meaning in the field of management and leadership have been studied in a number of ways (e.g., Isakson, 2000), but as Murphy and O'Brien (2006) point out, the number of qualitative works explicitly discussing multiple layers of meaning and language is extremely low in relation to the total number of studies. What are the multiple layers of meaning underlying terms such as informant, respondent, interviewer, and interviewee? What are the hidden or repressed meanings underlying these terms that may shape the outcome of the interview?

6

MIXED METHODS IN LEADERSHIP RESEARCH

AN ILLUSTRATIVE MIXED METHODS LEADERSHIP STUDY

Lauterbach and Weiner (1996) noted that according to popular opinion, male and female managers use different strategies to influence their superior. Male managers are supposed to be more direct in their approach and more concerned with getting what they want, whereas female managers are said to be more consensual in their approach and more concerned with maintaining a positive relationship with their superiors. However, empirical research on the effects of gender on the use of upward influence has yielded contradictory results.

In this mixed method studies, the authors drew on Chodrow's (1978) theory which predicts that gender identity is formed on the early relationships between infants and their mothers. Moreover, according to this theory, mother–child attachments differ for infant girls and boys with girls emerging from childhood with a feminine sense of identity that is characterized by emotional connectedness, whereas boys' sense of self-characterized by emotional distance or separateness. According to Chodrow, these enduring differences make up the core of adult gender identity and shape men's and women's relational capacities (p. 89). Based on this theory, Lauterbach and Weiner developed and tested a series of hypotheses embedded in a five-stage process model of upward influence. They selected a matched sample of 10 male and 11 female middle managers in a multinational Fortune 100 manufacturing company.

The first phase of this study involved semistructured interviews based on a protocol that was constructed to reflect the five-stage model of upward influence. More specifically, participants were asked to describe in detail one time during the past six months when they attempted to influence their superior specifically soliciting examples of upward influencing pertinent to each of the five stages. The interviews were recorded and transcribed verbatim. Following the interviews, the participants completed a 70-item survey that consisted of a series of questions reflecting the five stages of the influence process and thereby matching the interview protocol. The interviews were analyzed following the Miles and Huberman (1984) coding procedure which organizes the data into larger categories which include (1) kinds of opportunities for influence; (2) criteria for decision to act; (3) planning a strategy; (4) implementation of strategy; and (5) evaluation of the influence attempt. The codes were then compiled into a coding manual and given to two independent raters who read the interviews and coded them. The interrater reliability was 93.6 percent.

The analysis of the quantitative component of the study included factor analysis of the 70-item survey, reliability testing and hypothesis testing using analysis of covariance (ANCOVA). The factor analysis of the survey yielded 10 factors with scales measuring self-interest, directness, getting my way, and success to name a few. Interrater reliabilities using Cronbach α ranged from .54 to .97, with an average reliability of .74. Seven of the nine hypotheses tested provided either full or partial support for the notion that female managers' influence process displayed greater concerns for others (relatedness), while male managers' influence process showed greater concern for self (individuation). More specifically, female managers were more likely to act out of organizational interest, consider the thoughts and feelings of others about the influence attempt, involve others in planning, and focus on both task and interpersonal aspects during implementation and evaluation of the influence attempt. In contrast, male managers were more likely to act out of self-interest, show less consideration for how others might feel about the influence attempt, plan their strategy along, and focus primarily on the task during implementation and evaluation (p. 102).

For example, the finding that women managers are more likely to consider the viewpoints of others than their male counterparts is reflected in the following comments. A female manager described how she focused on others:

> *I considered not only the major impact on people that do the work, but also the impact on my customer. So I spent a fair amount of time talking with the customer about their perspective on why we should do this, and what is important to them, and what the alternatives might be if we didn't do it.*

Conversely, this male manager focused exclusively on the issue:

> *I was just trying to communicate the real story, the real need, and trying to make sure that he understood it. I was trying to explain it in a larger perspective that kind of pointed away from the bottom line dollars and cents and toward a larger, longer range vision, and trying to sell the leap of imagination to where in the hell we could be if we did something a little bit different (p. 95).*

This study illustrates several points which are elaborated on in this chapter; they include the use of theory to derive the research hypotheses which is uncommon in qualitative research but characteristic of quantitative research and the triangulation of interviews and surveys, one of the most frequently used combination of qualitative and quantitative components in a mixed method design and the frequent application of the Miles and Huberman (1984) coding procedures which we encountered in previous chapters.

INTRODUCTION

According to Johnson and Onwuegbuzie (2004), for more than decades, the advocates of quantitative and qualitative research paradigms have engaged in ardent disputes. From these debates, purists have emerged on both sides. Quantitative purists (e.g., Maxwell & Delaney, 2004) articulate assumptions that are consistent with positivism. That is, quantitative purists believe that social observations should be treated as entities in much the same way that physical scientists treat physical phenomena. Further, they content that the observer is separate from the observed and maintain that social science should be objective. Quantitative research values time- and context-free generalizations arguing that causes of scientific outcomes can be determined reliably and validly. According to this school of thought, leadership researchers should eliminate their biases, remain emotionally detached and uninvolved with research participants, and test and empirically justify their hypotheses. Qualitative purists (also called constructivists or interpretivists) reject positivism. Qualitative purists (e.g., Guba & Lincoln, 1989) argue for the superiority of constructivism, idealism, relativism, humanism, and hermeneutics. They believe that the knower and the known cannot be separated, that time- and context-free generalizations are neither desirable nor possible, that research is value-bound, and that it is impossible to differentiate fully between causes and effects. Qualitative purists also are characterized by a dislike for the detached and passive style of writing, preferring instead, detailed, rich, and thick description, written directly and some informally (p. 14).

Tashakkori and Teddlie (1998) dated the explicit emergence of mixed methods research to the 1960s as it became popular with the waning of the paradigm wars (Chapter 1). They also identified a subsequent integration of additional aspects of qualitative and quantitative approaches—not just methods—beginning during the 1990s, which they called "mixed models" studies (p. 16). Maxwell and Loomis propose an alternative way of thinking about mixed methods design as the combination of two or more methods. They view mixed methods as being comprised of more than just different qualitative and quantitative methods to include purpose of the research, conceptual framework, research questions, and validity strategies in addition to methods and the ways in which these different components are integrated (p. 242). The authors refer to their approach as the interactive model of design consisting of two essential properties: the components themselves and the ways in which these are related (Maxwell & Loomis, 2003). The Maxwell and Loomis model represents a more qualitative approach to mixed methods design, emphasizing particularly, context, holistic understanding, and the process by which a particular combination of quantitative and qualitative elements play out in practice, in contrast to a more quantitative approach based on categorization and comparison (p. 269).

Bryman (2006) searched the Social Science Citation Index for articles on mixed methods research using key words such as "quantitative," "qualitative," "mixed method," or "multi-method." Moreover, he restricted the search to articles published between 1994 and 2003. In this way, a total of 232 articles were generated and content analyzed. The major contributing disciplines were sociology (36 percent), social psychology (27 percent), organizational behavior (23 percent), geography (8 percent), and media and cultural studies (7 percent). Each article was coded in terms of the research methods that were employed. A striking finding was that a small number of methods accounted for the vast majority of all methods employed. More specifically, survey methods and qualitative interviews accounted for the majority of the methods used. Another interesting finding was that only in 10 articles was there a clear indication that quantitative and qualitative research had each been designed to answer specific and different research questions. The author made a case for encouraging researchers to be explicit about the grounds on which the multistrategy research was conducted.

Combining methods by mixing qualitative and quantitative methods is becoming increasingly popular in leadership research as well as in other disciplines as diverse as medicine and sociology, information systems, and psychotherapy. This chapter covers mixed methods that combine methods within the qualitative paradigm such as participant observation and qualitative interviews as well as studies that combine qualitative and quantitative methods such as case study and survey. These studies make up the bulk of the empirical studies in the leadership literature, in part, because of continued pressures on qualitative researcher to build objectivity, generalizability, and replicability into their research designs to provide greater legitimacy for a qualitative study. Again, as mentioned in Chapter 2, relics of the hegemony of quantitative paradigm and its underlying ontological and epistemological assumptions continue to linger in leadership research. In accordance with the convention established in this body of literature, I am using the abbreviations QUAL to refer to qualitative methodologies and QUANT to quantitative methodologies.

MIXED METHODS DESIGN CONSIDERATION

Defining Mixed Methods Research

Moran-Elis et al. (2006) define mixed methods as the use of two or more methods that draw on different meta-theoretical assumptions and can include standard positivistic-quantitative and interpretive-qualitative components or a mix of qualitative data (interpretive, phonological, and visual). Different methods reflect epistemological debates about the status of data produced by different methods. These have implications for the way researchers see the relationships among findings generated by methods situated within distinct theoretical perspectives (p.46). One of the definitions of triangulation define it as an epistemological stance concerning what more can be known about a phenomenon when the findings from data generated by two or more methods are brought together (for reviews of the concept of triangulations, see Bryman, 2004; Greene & Caracelli 2003; Kelle, 2001). Tashakkori and Teddlie's (2003a), in the glossary of the *Mixed Methods,* book define triangulation as "the combinations and comparison of multiple data sources, data collection and analysis procedures, research methods, and/or inferences that occur at the end of the study" (p. 717). Bryman (2004; 2006) offers several ways of combining qualitative and quantitative research to include

- *Triangulation*—which emphasizes the complementary nature of qualitative and quantitative data. An example is the Kan and Parry (2004) study of nurse leaders in New Zealand which demonstrates how the conflict between quantitative and qualitative data can be used as a springboard for theoretical development within a grounded theory approach rather than being a problem of reconciliation.

- *Preparation*—where qualitative research is conducted as exploratory to pave the way for quantitative research. This approach was illustrated by Mizrahi and Rosenthal (2001) that examined the complexities of building coalitions.

- *Complementarity*—seeks elaboration, enhancement, illustration, clarification of the results of one method with the results from another (Greene, Caracelli & Graham, 1989, p. 259). The potential complementarity of qualitative and quantitative research methods has been emphasized by Flick (1998) who concluded, "Triangulation is less a strategy for validating results and procedures than an alternative to validation (…) which increases scope, depth, and consistency of methodological proceedings" (p. 230).

- *Expansion*—quantitative and qualitative research are combined so that one data set can expand upon other sets. Voelck (2003) employed this technique to address different topics in relation to gender differences in management styles.

- *Initiation*—"seeks the discovery of paradox and contradiction, new perspectives of frameworks, the recasting of questions or results of one method with the results from another" (Greene et al., 1989, p. 259).

- *Development*—"seeks to use results from one method to develop or inform the other method, where development is broadly construed to include sampling and implementation, as well as measurement decisions" (Greene et al, 1989, p. 259).

Two meanings of triangulation have appeared in the literature: (1) triangulation as the process of cumulative validation or (2) triangulation as a means to produce a more complete picture of the investigated phenomena. Quantitative analyses show phenomena on an aggregate level and can thereby allow the description of macrosocial structures. Although qualitative analyses may also relate to phenomena on a macrosocial level, their specific strength lies in their ability to lift the veil on microsocial processes and to make visible hitherto unknown cultural phenomena (Kelle, 2001).

Mason (2006) argues that there is still limited engagement with the theoretical or methodological underpinnings of integrative research strategies (p. 10). The author presents a number of reasons for her basic premise that combining qualitative and quantitative methods can be a very good thing.

1. *Mixing methods encourages outside the box thinking.* Our way of seeing and of framing research questions are strongly influenced by the methods we have at our disposal, and researchers can fail to appreciate how method-driven are their questions. Mixing methods encourages researchers to see differently, or think "outside the box. For example, the use of nontext based methods that utilize visual, aesthetic, kinesthetic input as sources of data or consider bio-genetic methods reflect out of the box thinking" (p. 13).

2. *Mixing methods can enhance our capacity for theorizing beyond the micro and macro.* Macroscale theories tend to make claims about far-fetching, sometimes global phenomena. An example in the leadership literature is GLOBE (House, Hanges, Javidan, Dorfman, & Gupta, 2004) study which examines a large number of leadership, cultural, and organizational variables in 60 societies. The results of this research have been criticized for claiming too much cross-cultural ecological and construct validity and generalizability of their findings and recommendations (Graen, 2006). On the microside, Mason argues that qualitative researchers have engaged effectively with the micro/macroquestion, starting at the other end from the "big" theorists. Mixed method research has a major contribution to make in the micro/macrodebate beyond what I am rather unhelpful impasse (Mason, 2006, p. 15).

3. *Mixing methods can enhance and extend the logic of qualitative explanation.* Qualitative research has an edge in this regard because it is concerned with explanation (i.e., designed to answer "why" types leadership questions) in a wider sense than measurement and causation prevalent in quantitative analysis. In addition, another core element of qualitative research is the focus on context, explicating how different dimensions of context (i.e., climate, purpose, structure, time) weave together in relation to the research question.

4. *Mixed methods research provides stronger inferences* resulting from quantitatively derived experiences through standardized questionnaires and qualitative capture experiences derived from open-ended questions (Tashakkori & Teddlie, 2003a, p. 675).

5. Mixed methods research provides the opportunity for presenting a greater diversity of divergent views (Tashakkori & Teddlie, 2003a, p. 676).

Types of Multimethod Designs

The literature makes a distinction between mixed methods and mixed models designs (e.g., Johnson & Onwuegbuzie, 2004). The *mixed method approach* is a typology of different methods derived from the qualitative and quantitative paradigms. It only considers method which is but one stage in the research process. The *mixed model approach*, on the other hand, mixes qualitative and quantitative elements across the entire research process and include other elements such as the research questions, validity issues, and data interpretation. There are four types of designs: (1) concurrent mixed designs, (2) sequential mixed designs, (3) multimethod conversion designs, and (4) fully integrated models which prescribe procedures for combining qualitative and quantitative methods in a single study.

The *concurrent mixed design* typically has multiple research questions to be addressed by qualitative and quantitative designs. Here, each question is answered separately by collecting QAUL and QUAN data which are pulled together in the inferences made based on the findings. The inferences from one phase do not determine the questions or procedures of the other phase (Tashakkori & Teddlie, 2003b, pp. 686–690). In *sequential mixed designs*, one method (e.g., QUAL) emerges as a result of, or in response to, the finding of the QUANT phase or vice versa. Data using the two approaches are collected and analyzed sequentially. This design is mixed in its data collection and analysis phase only. Time ordering of the qualitative and quantitative dimensions is important when mixed methods research is carried out sequentially or concurrently.

The *fully integrated design*, which is considered to be the most advanced and most dynamic of mixed model designs, incorporates two or more of the previous designs. In this type of study, multiple questions are asked and answered through the collection and analysis of both QUAL and QUANT data. Inferences are made on the basis of the QUAL and QUANT results of data analyses and are combined together at the end to form a meta-inference (Tashakkori & Teddlie, 2003b, p. 689). This approach was also discussed by Caracelli and Greene (1997), who labeled it the *transformative design*. In such designs, value commitments of different traditions are integrated, giving voice to different ideologies and interests in the settings studied. An integrated study may also involve qualitative and quantitative methods embedded in experimental or quasi-experimental designs. An example of this type of integrated design is Milgram's (1974) experimental study of how people respond when they are ordered by authorities to inflict pain and possible serious harm on other. Although the author did not use the term "integrative design," this experimental study included participant observation, lengthy interviews with some participants after the experiment, and a follow-up questionnaire sent to all participants to collect information regarding their thoughts and feelings with respect to their participation and the experiment. The analysis of these data was primarily qualitative but closely integrated with the quantitative data.

Selection of Empirical Studies Employing Mixed Methods Design

Leadership research based on mixed methods studies has produced the largest number of empirical studies. For example, Bryman (2004), in his review of qualitative research in leadership studies, spanned a wide range of topics and methodologies. I wanted to achieve a similarly diverse representation of mixed methods design in this chapter but have also included studies that reflect a diversity of contexts in which research was conducted. For example, I examined mixed methods studies that combined different qualitative methods in contexts as diverse as the semiconductor industry (Beyer & Browning, 1999), family-run business (Kisfalvi, 2000; Kisfalvi & Pitcher, 2003), semiprofessional jazz ensembles, and collegiate rowing groups (Pescosolido, 2002), a cross-cultural study conducted in an R&D organization (Mouly & Sankaran, 1999), and gender, race/ethnicity, and role within the organization as context for leadership (Kezar, 2002). Excluded were studies that only tangentially related to leadership such as Mullen and Cochran (2000) study on organizational change. To avoid redundancies, this also led to the elimination of studies that were basically variations of the same research design. For example, of the two studies conducted Kisfalvi (Kisfalvi, 2000; Kisfalvi & Pitcher, 2003) on the influence of CEO character on top management team dynamics, only one study was included. Furthermore, I also wanted to include sample studies with unique features. For example, few qualitative studies use existing theory as the point of departure. Yet, Kezar (2002) framed her research question based on the tenets of propositionality theory. Finally, triangulated studies that illustrated similar problems and weaknesses discussed later in this section were also excluded.

Nevertheless, there is a certain degree of arbitrariness in defining a study as a mixed method design. For example, many of the studies discussed in Chapter 3 on case studies and content analysis in Chapter 4 employed additional methods such as document analysis; technically, they therefore qualify as mixed methods as well. The studies that appear in this chapter were selected because the authors clearly labeled them as mixed methods.

DATA COLLECTION AND ANALYSIS

A variety of data collection methods have been employed in studies that combine qualitative and quantitative methods. They include interviews, observations, document analysis on the qualitative side of the equation and surveys, questionnaires, and experiments on the quantitative side. Moreover, more so than in the methods discussed in the previous four chapters, many of the triangulated studies originated outside of the North American continent such as Israel, the United Kingdom, and Australia. Both probability and purposive (theoretical, nonprobability) sampling strategies are used with sample sizes varying greatly. The analyses cover both inductive and deductive techniques along with a variety of statistics including univariate and multivariate analyses.

Priority may be given to either the qualitative (e.g., Howell & Higgins, 1990a; Ruderman, Ohlott, Panzer, & King, 2002; Yukl & Van Fleet, 1982) or the quantitative component of a mixed method design (e.g., Hirst, Mann, Bain, Pirola-Merlo, & Richver, 2004; Rao, Hashimoto, & Rao, 1997; Tsui, Zhang, Wang, Xin & Wu, 2006) with data analyses either performed in chronological stages or concurrently. The question of how to integrate the results of a mixed methods study remains a critical issue in leadership research. Bryman (2004) discussed the difficulties combining qualitative and quantitative studies. Most difficult to integrate within the still dominant quantitative research paradigm are those qualitative investigations that problematize leadership by questioning the utility and application of qualitative research in the study of leadership. As the author notes, while qualitative researchers are not alone in questioning the concept of leadership, they have been particularly instrumental in probing its meaning and in conducting investigations that underline its problematic nature. For example, Alvesson and Sveningsson (2003) asked whether leadership really exists in the context of an international biotech firm. The authors combined 40 interviews with manager of different levels of the organization with observations of management meetings in six mini cases. They asked participants to discuss their experiences as managers in a knowledge-intensive context. Most managers talked about leadership and the extent to which they were able to practice it. In one of the cases, for instance, when asked how the manager provides leadership, the respondent said that

> ... you have to be "on message" all the time to decide what you vision, what are your values that you are working to, what's the direction that the group is going in; you personally as a manager have to live that vision.

She further went on to say that to live a vision means that

> It's well, things like, take every opportunity to say "You can do that," say to people that "you're just the person I like to talk to" so it's promoting a team and promoting can and should be doing, saying to people "have you thought about putting some work into this team" or conversely, "we ought to be doing that ..." so that you are constantly thinking of what we should be doing and could be doing, what we are best at, what we could do and try not to get diverted because quite often it could be that someone ends up doing something just because it helps but he may not be the best person... (Manager H, p. 369).

APPLICATIONS OF LEADERSHIP STUDIES COMBINING DIFFERENT QUALITATIVE METHODS (WITHIN QUALITATIVE MIXED METHODS STUDIES)

To facilitate the discussion, I divided the mixed methods studies reviewed here into two groups: (1) those that triangulated method by combining different qualitative methods, I refer to those as within qualitative mixed methods, and (2) those that combine qualitative and quantitative methods, I refer to those as between mixed methods designs. Research in the former categories includes studies that employ a combination of qualitative interviews, case studies, document analysis, participant observation, phenomenology, and content analysis to name a few. For example, Chapter 12 presents an application of this approach where cases are nested in a content analysis to develop a model of leadership in at-risk, distressed communities. The most common way of triangulating QUAL methods has been combining interviews and observations (Table 6-1).

Kezar (2002) draws on positionality theory to explore how gender, race/ethnicity, level of administrator, and the role of the leader within the organization affect the way the leader constructs images of leadership. The concept of positionality resists a static view and proposes that people have multiple overlapping identities. The author interviewed community college faculty and administrators to examine their beliefs and contextual conditions that foster diversity of perspectives. As Longino (1993) points out, people make meaning of their identities taken into consideration gender, social class, and professional identity. In addition, Kezar employed a positioned informant approach which assumes that people's role within an organization impacts their responses using a sequential sampling strategy. She combined interviews with observations, document analysis, and analysis of the physical environment. The interviews focused on partici-pants' personal leadership philosophy, their perceptions of campus leadership, and the influences on their beliefs about leadership. The basic research question this study was intended to answer was, "how does positionality (gender, race, position within an organization, field of study or disciplinary orientation, etc.) relate to constructions of leadership?"

The data analyses consisted of two phases: categorical analysis which emphasized the development of categories and patterns and componential analysis which searches for components of meaning associated with cultural meaning and in language (Spradley, 1979, p. 174) utilizing narrative analysis for understanding the particular details in participants' constructions of leadership. The results showed that race/ethnicity, gender role within the organization, and field of study (i.e., positionality theory) did influence participants' definitions of leadership. For example, the careers faculty of the college emphasized authority, individuality, influence, directives, and vision-centered leader-ship, whereas the liberal arts studies faculty focused on openness, collaboration, diversity, and collective leadership. The faculty in this group described leadership in terms of the defining characteristics of servant leadership.

Role within the institution was also related to the way individuals constructed leader-ship. The administrators' definitions were different in the content, structure, and language from those of the faculty which emphasized behaviors and characteristics of a leader or a process. The dominant model of leadership on the campus was

Table 6-1 Selected leadership studies combining different qualitative methods

Author(s)	Purpose	Informants	Data sources	Analyses
Kezar (2002)	To examine how positionality (e.g., race, gender, etc.) relate to the construction of leadership	36 community college administrators and faculty	Interviews, document analysis, accreditation reports, observation, analysis of physical environment	Interpretive
Pescosolido (2002)	To study the emotional dynamics in a semiprofessional jazz ensemble and a collegiate rowing team	Two groups with 20 members each	Observation, group interviews, critical incident interviews	NUD*IST generated codes, content analysis, code reduction to categories
Kisfalvi (2000)	To explore the role of CEO personal issues in the allocation of resources allocated to strategic activities	Founder of a small entrepreneurial firm	Interviews with multiple informants, direct observations, archival documents	Interpretive

(Continued)

Table 6-1   (Continued)

Author(s)	Purpose	Informants	Data sources	Analyses
Meyer and Browning (1999)	To trace the struggle of survival of a firm in the semiconductor industry trough cultural leadership of CEO and study the history of the organization	Study 1: 80 interviews with CEO, senior executives and staff over 2-year period Study 2: 60 interviews with individuals involved in founding and early days of the organization Study 3: Interviews with two supplier companies	Interviews, archival data, news articles, meeting observations	Successive rounds of coding following Strauss and Corbin (1990); collapsing codes into larger categories; selective coding for charisma, routinization, and cultural leadership themes
Fineman (1996)	To explore the emotional meanings managers attach to corporate greening	17 senior managers of 6 UK supermarkets	Semistructured interviews, meeting observations, company documents	Interpretive coding of emotional displays and clustering of major emotional subtexts following Miles and Huberman (1994)

associated with administrative work such as scheduling classes or dealing with student complaints. In terms of identity, administrators tended to provide a macroorganizational conceptualization of leadership that centered on a philosophy or the whole organization and a vivid picture through the use of metaphors which reflected their administrative role. The metaphors of the administrators included an orchestra, a musical group, a performing group or theater, living organisms, and a family. In contrast, among the faculty, only a few members could provide a metaphor of the organization.

Another positioning issue was the greater awareness of administrators of the way gender was related to their personal understanding of leadership. Women of color, for example, were more likely to define their personal leadership philosophy in terms of servant leadership characteristics emphasizing equal power relations, collaboration, empowerment, and team orientation compared to administrators who were mostly white males. Kezar (2002) discovered that multiple aspects of a person's identity were related to different knowledge of leadership reflecting overlapping, dynamic identities impacted by different influences resisting stereotyping, and open to change.

Pescosolido (2002) conducted a narrative analysis of emergent leaders as managers of group emotion. In contrast to this study, past research has focused more on the leader's individual attributes and behaviors than his or her role in the group. The author proposed that the role of a group leader, and more specifically an emergent group leader, is to interpret ambiguous situations and then to model an appropriate emotional response (p. 586). In ambiguous situations, group members turn to the group leader for a variety of reasons including the notion that he or she may have the greatest amount of knowledge and experience or has the most positive relationships with members of the group. Moreover, Pescosolido proposed that group leaders manage group emotional responses by first empathizing and identifying with the collective emotional state of group members. According to the author, group leaders then craft a response to the situation that is causing the emotional reaction and communicate their response to the group both verbally and by taking action.

This research involved group observations of 20 different groups followed by whole group critical incident interviews with each of those groups. Following Strauss and Corbin (1998), the author used a theoretical sampling procedure to access two types of groups: a semiprofessional jazz music group and a collegiate rowing crew. All of the jazz groups were observed during performances while the rowing groups were observed during practice sessions. The author took field notes describing which group members took initiative, which ones were treated with respect, how group members talked about incidents that might affect their task performance, how they expressed emotion within the group context, and they described a recent critical incident (Flanagan, 1954) describing an experience where they "all felt that the group clicked." The transcripts of the field interviews and the field notes were analyzed to identify excerpts of group leaders acting as managers of the group's collective experience of emotion.

Pescosolido postulated three propositions. First, he proposed that emergent leaders will be more likely to manage group emotion when the group receives ambiguous performance feedback from relevant stakeholders. For example, the jazz ensemble during a performance was confronted with a period of silence after the audience had demonstrated its appreciation of the performance earlier in the evening. Thus, the group was faced with an ambiguous response from the audience. The trumpet player emerged as the leader as he stepped forward for a solo. This display of confidence had an immediate effect of restoring an active audience. The groups in the collegiate rowing crews interpreted feedback entirely in the context of practice sessions when concrete feedback (i.e., winning or losing a race) is not available. The second proposition presented by the author stated that emergent leaders will be more likely to engage in management of group emotion when the group has developed norms that allow and encourage the expression of emotion within the group context suggesting that emergent leaders take advantage of particular group norms in order to establish and use their ability to manage group emotion. In the rowing crews, one captain of a boat resolved a crisis situation by redefining the group's goals and performance standards. The captain's ability to reshape the group's emotion by not feeling defeated when their boat placed sixth out of eight by emphasizing that her team had beaten its local rival. She cheered up her team members and everyone in the boat followed suit. In the interview following the race, the captain acknowledged that her actions were definitely shaped by the group's norms.

Finally, the third hypothesis postulated by Pescosolido was that emergent leaders who exhibit both charisma and empathy will be more likely to engage in the management of emotions. An example of an emergent leader using personal charisma and empathy to manage the group's emotion was found in another of the rowing crews. This crew was known as the "lightweight" team because all team members weighed less than 155 pounds. Sean, the informal leader of the lightweight rowers, led his teammates to think that they were a real competition for the opposing team, the "open weight" team composed of taller, stronger, and heavier young men. His conviction was such that for the light weights every practice session came to hold the same emotional intensity and importance of the race day, even though the coach explicitly discouraged competition between the two teams. By the end of the spring season, the light weight team had improved to the point of occasionally beating the open weight team in practice sessions. Each winning race was celebrated, a celebration that could be easily confused with the victory celebrations after an actual race (Pescosolido, 2002, p. 593). Several team members mentioned the optimism and enthusiasm expressed by the emergent leader as a critical factor in the crew's success.

During the group interviews, five of the jazz groups and eight of the rowing crews mentioned that the leader demonstrated empathy for his or her fellow group members.

In addition, 6 of the 10 jazz teams and all 10 of the rowing crews mentioned an emergent leader enacting charisma though personal commitment to the team and its goals. Pescosolido concluded that the management of a group's emotional state depends upon an emergent leader's ability to convince others of the validity of a particular emotional response as well as the demonstration of the leader's capacity to understand the team's goals and hopes. The major weakness of this study is the inability of the reader to link the data to the methods used to test the propositions.

Kisfalvi (2000) investigated the link between CEO character and its relationship to the firm's strategic orientation employing a longitudinal, interpretive approach in a small entrepreneurial firm. The author combined interviews with multiple informants, direct observation, and document analysis based on memos, reports, and meeting agendas. Interviews with the CEO were used to identify the company's strategic behavior. Both unstructured and semistructured interviews with CEO and his top management team were conducted. For the direct observation, the researcher positioned herself outside the CEO's office to observe his day-to-day activities. Transcripts of the interviews, field notes, and archival materials were entered into NUD*IST. Coded items were grouped into higher order categories which were subsequently content analyzed. The analysis based on the interviews with the CEO produced three distinct sets of categories: (1) one dealing with various aspects of the CEO's personal history and personal issues, (2) the CEO's strategic priorities, and (3) the company's strategic choices in the past and present.

The CEO, born in Poland, spent time in a concentration/labor camp during the 1940s, eventually moved back to his village and eventually settled in the United States where he founded his first business with a fellow inmate from the concentration camp. At the time of the study, the CEO ran a company which manufactured chemicals. He worked with a diverse management team which included his two sons. From the narratives the CEO provided, personal issues rooted in trauma provided the underpinnings for all of his activities. His strategic priorities were shaped by his personal issues which in his mind were interconnected. For example, one of his personal issues was survival. As the first-born son of a Jewish farming family, the CEO grew up in an era of growing anti-Semitism. The CEO's parents and one sister died in Auschwitz while he ended up in another concentration camp where he barely escaped death. His personal history reflected the hardship and trauma he endured during his childhood and youth. Other personal issues included recognition which was important to him throughout his life and career, product development, and succession planning. The CEO's personal issues laid the groundwork that made him susceptible to strategic persistence in core areas of the business. For example, he persisted in his commitment to one of the two divisions of the organization continuing to pursue the same product-market strategy that had been successful in the past. Kisfalvi concluded that the CEO's personal issues played a highly influential role which drove his strategy orientation. She notes that the very same persistence may be labeled intuition or vision if it leads to success, thereby vindicating the leader's persistence or escalation of commitment if it leads to failure.

Beyer and Browning (1999), in three separate studies published in the same article, examined cultural leadership and the charismatic leadership of the founding leader of a company in the semiconductor industry. In study 1, the first author conducted 80 interviews over a two-year period of time. In a separate longitudinal study, she conducted additional interviews with staff members and managers of the company as well as the Chief Administrative Officer as well as with two supplier firms. In addition, she observed a meeting of the regional quality council. The second author collected data on the history of the organization through 60 interviews which were conducted with employees who had been with the firm since the founding days. The second author additionally had access to the company's archives which included correspondences, speeches, press clippings, and video tapes and observed 15 company meetings. The interviews were analyzed using the Strauss and Corbin (1990) coding procedures. Another round of selected interviews were conducted which focused on the elements of charisma, routinization of charisma, and cultural leadership.

The search for a leader for the firm was the first of a series of crises for the proposed consortium. After repeatedly refusing the job and coming out of retirement, Bob Noyce finally accepted the position. He had co-founded and led two other companies including Intel in the semiconduct industry and had become the spokesman for the industry. Bob was described as extraordinarily gifted, a man of strong convictions and a magnetic personality. His sense of moral duty was one of the reasons he accepted the CEO position. He also served on many boards of private and public sector companies. Andy Grove who worked with Bob at Intel said the following of him:

> [Bob's lasting contribution] is not ultimately his opinions; it is not ultimately going to be that he started Intel and that he invented the semiconductor, but that he realized that we had to start working together as an industry and with the government and stop worrying about being so competitive. He said that before I ever thought about going to Washington. Bob was always the visionary—that was true in everything he did. He was always six or ten steps ahead of the rest of us (Beyer & Browning, 1999, p. 297).

Grove was able to observe many of Bob's visions while working with him at Intel. Beyer and Browning describe how Bob's charisma and visions were routinized through structures and policies he established and by incorporating a charismatic vision into the traditions of the organizations. The company used many rites and symbols to celebrate its culture based on a democratic and participative ethos. When Bob decided to retire, the company selected a successor whose management style was very different from Bob's and who also lacked his warmth and charisma.

Finally, Fineman (1996) conducted a within qualitative methods triangulated study aimed at exploring the emotional meanings 17 managers of six UK supermarkets ascribed to corporate greening which included environmental policies, recycling, energy, and the promotion of environmentally sensitive products. The participating supermarkets with individual stores ranging from 126 to 5000 individual stores were ranked from most green to least green. For example, the most green supermarket chain was characterized by a long tradition of socially responsible trading and the only market in the sample which had a department specifically dedicated to environmental affairs. The author used semistructured interviews in which managers were asked to describe their markets position on environmental issues, details of their personal involvement in setting environmental policies, and sources of environmental pressures their stores were facing. In addition, he observed meetings and analyzed internal company records documenting environmental initiatives, public relations materials, and trade association publications. The data were coded for emotional displays, both verbal and nonverbal, associated with corporate greening and then clustered according to their major subtexts following Miles and Huberman (1984).

Four clusters were identified. The first cluster was labeled enacting green commitment. In the more green markets, managers expressed a commitment to a cause, namely an ethical green culture and engaged in socially responsible action to protect the environment. In the less green companies, on the other hand, references to "responsibility" or "concern" were rarely expressed. The second cluster, contesting green boundaries, was displayed in one of the supermarkets where the manager had ceased to explicitly express his pro-environmental beliefs and sought environmental improvements on the back of less emotive changes in the organization. In the third clusters, emotional meanings were summarized as the "defence of autonomy" cluster (p. 489). In the United Kingdom, supermarkets are confronted by green pressure groups which scrutinize their policies, products, and equipment making it difficult for managers to control their environmental performance. According to Fineman, the emotional significance of this was a mix of defiance, wariness, threat, irritability, admiration, and faint praise (p. 489). The last cluster, labeled "avoiding embarrassment," was captured by managers' efforts to avoid the discomfort of embarrassment. As the author noted

> The supermarkets with the highest public profile on environmental protection had the most to fear from embarrassment. Once managers had invested their image and reputation in claims for environmental care, loss of face could be a blow to role identity, to professional status within the company and to corporate image (p. 491).

Fineman (1996) concluded that high-profile leadership, organizational structures, and roles dedicated to environmental protection are need to establish and maintain a green ethical culture. Implications for green organizational change call for leaders to shape an organizational climate and culture that supports pro-environmentalism.

In sum, the studies reviewed in this section combined qualitative methods in a number of ways including interviews, direct observations, documents, newspaper clippings, and video tapes. The contexts in which these studies were conducted ranged from small entrepreneurial firms (Kisfalvi, 2000) to extensive interviews in the semiconductor industry (Beyer & Browning, 1999). Likewise, methods of analysis include computerized coding, replications of Strauss and Corbin's (1990) coding procedures, and purely interpretive analysis in which the exact analytical techniques were not specified. The data for several studies were collected outside of the United States (e.g., Fineman, 1996; Kisfalvi, 2000).

APPLICATIONS OF LEADERSHIP STUDIES COMBINING QUALITATIVE METHODS AND QUANTITATIVE METHODS (BETWEEN MIXED METHODS DESIGNS)

In this category, we find the largest number of studies which combined surveys, questionnaires, and experimental designs with interviews, documents, and observations thereby triangulating qualitative and quantitative methods. Again, the review of these studies is intended to give the reader a sense of the variety of ways of triangulating quantitative and qualitative methods, contexts in which the data were collected, sample sizes, types of data collection methods, and the different journals in which the studies were published. In this section, over two decades of mixed methods research in leadership were examined. Decision rules which may reflect this author's biases were applied. For example, in the years 2000, 1997, and 1986 several studies were located but for each year, a single study was selected. As in the previous section, the review of the studies in this section is not meant to be exhaustive but represents a representative sampling of combining qualitative and quantitative methods. The most frequently used triangulation combined survey and interview data. It is also interesting to note that several studies depicted in Table 6-2 reported several investigation within the same published article.

Tsui et al. (2006) were interested in determining when and why decoupling of CEO behavior from organizational culture occurs in senior executives in the People's Republic of China (PRC) where despite economic reforms that state still appoints CEOs in state-owned firms who continue to have limited authority compared to their counterparts in privately owned firms. The authors conducted two survey studies and one interview. Based on a number of theoretical perspectives, they postulated a number of hypotheses specifying relationships between CEO behavior and organizational culture. For example, they predicted that decoupling of leadership and culture will occur more frequently in state-owned firms, next in foreign-invested firms, and least in private domestic firms which emerged as the result of China's economic reforms. In the first two studies, the authors employed the same procedures, instruments, and analysis but using two different samples, one consisting of MBA students from two different universities in Beijing and the second comprised of 1054 middle and senior managers

Table 6-2   Selected leadership studies combining qualitative and quantitative methods

Author(s)	Purpose	Informants	Data sources	Analyses
Tsui, et al. (2006)	To analyze the relationship between CEO leadership behavior and organizational culture	Study 1: 542 MBA students in two universities in Beijing holding managerial jobs Study 2: 1045 middle and senior managers in 152 Chinese firms	Surveys using Chinese CEO Leadership Measure; measure of organizational culture; firm performance measure	Exploratory factor analysis in sample 1; confirmatory factor analysis in sample 2; rwg; intraclass correlations; cluster analysis; multivariate discriminant analysis; ANOVA; grounded theory; content analysis of interview data
Hirst, et al. (2004)	To examine the impact of leader's learning on facilitative leadership and team performance	50 leaders of two public and two private Australian R&D companies	Questionnaire measuring amount of new knowledge leaders acquired from project work; measures of team performance and project quality; interviews with 36 project leaders	Confirmative factor analysis; moderated regression analyses; content analysis of interview data
Ruderman, et al. (2002)	To examine the relationships between multiple life roles, psychological; well-being; and managerial skills in two studies of female managers	Study 1: 61 female managers and executives enrolled in leadership development program Study 2: 276 female middle and upper middle managers enrolled in leadership development program	Study 1: Telephone interviews Study 2: Psychological well-being measure; multiple life role commitment scale; managerial effectiveness measure; performance data for subset of 177 respondents, biographical information	Boyatzis (1998) thematic coding procedure Study 2: Confirmatory factor analysis; hierarchical regression analysis

(Continued)

Table 6-2   (Continued)

Author(s)	Purpose	Informants	Data sources	Analyses
Meindl, et al. (1985)	To examine leadership as a romantic concept showing that individuals overestimate the degree to which leaders control organizational outcomes	Study 1: N/A (archival) Study 2: N/A (archival) Study 3: N/A (archival) Study 4: (experimental) 59 undergraduate students Study 5: (experimental) 116 undergraduate students Study 6: (experimental) 72 undergraduate students	Study 1: Wall Street Journal articles published from 1972 to 1982; business performance data Dissertation Abstracts International (DAI); American Doctoral Dissertations; Handbook of Basic Economic Statistics General business periodicals Vignettes Vignettes	Frequencies; coding dictionary; computation of "leadership quotient"; ANOVA; correlations Lagged partial correlations Lagged partial correlations Descriptive statistics; ANOVA Orthogonal polynomial regression analysis ANOVA; polynomial regression analysis
Yukl and Van Fleet (1982)	To advance understanding of military leader effectiveness	Corps of cadets in noncombat, academic situation US Air Force officers during Korean War Study 3: Corps of cadets in noncombat, academic situation 42 unit first sergeants 76 male platoon leaders in a combat exercise held during ROTC summer camp	Study 1: 3111 critical incidents of effective and ineffective leadership behaviors Study 2: Interviews collecting critical incidents Leadership questionnaire; structured interviews; composite rating of each units performance during march ceremonies Study 4: Leadership behavior questionnaire competed by cadets for unit leaders	Categorization of critical incidents into 19 behavioral categories; percentage scores; correlation between frequency scores of two judges = .91 Same as in study 1; correlation between behavior frequency scores between two judges = .92 Study 3 not subjected to formal analysis Classification of questionnaire items into 14 behavior categories

in 152 Chinese firms. With the MBA students, the authors asked them to not only complete the survey instruments themselves but also distribute them to 10 middle managers in their employing companies (snowball sampling). The instruments included a Chinese leadership questionnaire which tapped leader behaviors such as risk taking, relationship building, vision articulating, and an organizational culture measure. Statistical analyses were including ANOVAS and multiple discriminant analysis. The results of the QUANT part of this mixed method design supported the hypothesis that CEOs of state-owned enterprises in China have the most limited leadership discretion while in private firms, the owner-CEOs had the greatest discretion, resulting in the lowest occurrence of decoupling in employees' perceptions of the CEOs leadership behaviors and the cultural values of the firm.

In the QUAL part of this study, Tsui et al. developed a structured interview protocol with questions probing into issues of culture. In addition, they also analyzed documents in the form of company newsletters, advertising flyers, product brochures, and website information. The bodies of textual data were then content analyzed following Guba and Lincoln's (1994) coding procedures. The interview data pointed to the importance of internal institutionalization of cultural values suggesting an institutional perspective on the development on organizational culture. The QUAL data prompted the authors to redefine organizational culture as shared social knowledge about the prevalent rules, norms, and values that shape the preferences or actions of organizational members.

The QUANT component consisted of the use of the Chinese CEO Leadership measure which consists of 21 items measuring five types of leadership behavior including risk taking, relationship building, employee caring, vision articulation, and monitoring. Respondents rated their CEOs on each of these behaviors. They also completed a measure of organizational culture. The results of the quantitative portion of this study showed strong relationships between CEO behavior and organizational culture. Taken together, this research offered insights into both leadership behaviors of CEOs in different types of Chinese firm who varied in the amount of discretion they had and institutional factors that may account for the decoupling between CEO leadership behavior and organizational cultural values.

The Hirst, et al. (2004) mixed method study was included because it employed a longitudinal design to determine how leaders learn from their workplace experiences. Much of the research on leadership development is cross-sectional in nature not taking into consideration that the leadership development spans varying time horizons. For example, it may take as long as 20 years for an individual to develop himself or herself from a novice leader to an expert leader. Hirst et al. hypothesized that a leader's learning would be related to facilitative leadership, team reflexivity, and team performance. Additionally, they also predicted that new and experienced leader would also differ in the amount they learned from their experiences as project leaders. Four R&D

organizations representing two public and two private sector companies participated in this study yielding a sample of 50 leaders, 25 of whom were new and 25 who were experienced. Questionnaires measuring the amount of new knowledge acquired, facilitative leadership, team reflexivity, and team performance were completed. Moderated regression analyses were conducted on the questionnaire data. Of the 50 leaders comprising the sample, 36 were interviewed using structured protocols which were recorded, transcribed, and subsequently content analyzed. The results showed that the QUAL analyses extended those of the QUANT results indicating that leadership learning was translated into facilitative leadership behaviors, associated with team reflexivity, and customer ratings of team performance. Furthermore, new leaders reported that they were learning more than experienced leader.

Ruderman et al. (2002) triangulated QUAL and QUANT methods in two studies to examine the impact of multiple life roles on the effectiveness of female managers. Study 1 represented the QUAL component based on three-hour telephone interviews with 61 female managers enrolled in a leadership development program for women only. In addition, the authors conducted one-hour telephone interviews with the participants a few weeks after the completion of the program. Following Boyatzis' (1998) (Chapter 4) procedures of thematic coding and coding analysis, the authors developed a codebook. Intercoder agreement ranged between 67 and 91 percent. The results from the qualitative analysis showed that female managers who were engaged in multiple roles experienced beneficial effects on their performance as managers. More specifically, the most frequently used theme mentioned by 42 percent of the sample suggested that nonwork role experiences enhanced opportunities to enrich interpersonal skills which, in turn, positively affected work performance. Other themes included receiving emotional support and advice from family and friends, handling multiple tasks, and learning about leadership through personal experiences positively influenced the work roles of the managerial women.

In the QUANT portion of this study, the same issues that were examined qualitatively were also explored quantitatively. The sample and sample characteristics in study 2 were practically identical to those in study 1; 267 female managers attending a leadership development program for women only and performance data were available for 177 of the attendees. Standardized instruments measuring multiple role commitment as the dependent variable and psychological well-being and managerial skills as the independent variables replaced the interview protocol. The results showed that commitment to multiple life roles correlated positively with feelings of psychological well-being and women's effectiveness in two leadership domains.

Densten and Gray (1998) conducted a QUANT/QUAL analysis using one subscale of the Multiple Leadership Questionnaire (MLQ) (Bass, 1985), the Management-by-Exception subscale to clarify the concept of management by exception. Bass initially identified Management-by-Exception as a unidimensional construct but later research suggested a multidimensional construct consisting of two dimensions, Management-by-Exception, active and passive (Hater & Bass, 1988), that both represented the transactional leadership style. Four hundred and eighty Australian police officers completed the MLQ (Form 5R) including the 10-item Management-by-Exception subscale to which the authors added one open-ended question soliciting respondents' comments concerning the leadership style of their organization. LISREL analysis revealed that the one-factor model provided a good fit to the data. The QUAL part of the study analyzed the single item open-ended comments on the MLQ based on 260 responses using NUD*IST. Comments were classified as Transformational Leadership, Transactional Leadership, or Nonleadership. The comments categorized as Transactional Leadership were further subdivided into Contingent Reward and Management-by-Exception.

Management-by-Exception reported by 50 police officers is reflected in comments such as

> There is still a feeling of "us against them." The only time that subordinates normally see an officer is when they are being disciplined (Senior sergeant with chief executive as leader).

> or

> Most of the current leaders only report when things go wrong (Chief inspector with a superintendent as leaders) (Densten & Gray, 1998, p. 86).

The QUAL analysis validated the findings from QUANT analysis indicating that in both sets of results Management-by-Exception emerged as a single factor construct.

Rao et al. (1997) triangulated factor analysis and content analysis to examine universal and culturally specific aspects of managerial influence in Japanese managers. The authors mailed 150 copies of the Japanese version of the Profile of Organizational Influence–POIS/M—developed by Kipnis and Schmidt (1982) to the HR manager of a large international trading company headquartered in Tokyo who distributed copies of the instruments to the manager at the home office. The POIS measures 33 influence tactics. Additionally, managers were asked to list other influence tactics not observed in their company. One hundred and thirty-five usable questionnaires were returned including a total of 73 new influence tactics that the managers reported using with their subordinates. The POIS was factor analyzed and the 73 new tactics were content analyzed.

The factor analytic results revealed a six-factor solution of the Japanese POIS with reason being reported as the most frequently used influence strategy, followed by assertiveness and friendliness. These three factors were the same reported by Kipnis, Schmidt, and Wilkinson (1980) based on a sample of low-level North American managers. For the QUAL portion of the study, the 73 new influence tactics contributed by the managers were coded into influence categories appearing on the POIS and were subsequently categorized. While the Japanese managers used tactics such as assertiveness, sanctions, and appeals to higher authorities, they also employed culturally specific strategies such as coalition building, a strategy typical of collective societies such as Japan, personal development, and socializing after work in bars to influence subordinates. Rao et al. concluded that managers and subordinates in both the United States and Japan must understand specific culturally influence tactics in order to avoid misunderstandings in international interactions.

Howell and Higgins (1990b) investigated personality characteristics, leadership behaviors, and influence tactics of champions of technological innovations in a sample of twenty-five matched pairs of champions and nonchampions. The authors wanted to develop a model inductively that integrates the factors influencing how individuals assume the champion role drawing from the literature on entrepreneurship to identity personality dimensions of technological champions, leadership as many champions serve as informal leaders and influence because champions act as influence agents to promote their ideas. These relationships have been previously established (e.g., Dean, 1987; Maidique, 1980; Van de Van, 1986). These authors reported that champions are characterized by the capacity to inspire others with their vision of the potential of a technological innovation, show extraordinary confidence in themselves and their mission, and rally others behind their ideas. Based on this literature, Howell and Higgins (1990a) postulated three hypotheses: (1) champions will exhibit transformational leader behaviors, that is charisma, inspiration, intellectual stimulation, and individualized consideration to a greater extent than nonchampions (p. 321); (2) champions will exhibit higher achievement, persistence, persuasiveness, and risk taking than nonchampions; and (3) there will be a more positive relationship between personality dimensions and transformational leader behaviors for champions and nonchampions.

The authors mailed a survey to 350 CEOs of Canadian firms to identify organizations that had implemented innovations defined in this study as the adoption of a new product that reflected the application of information technology. Additional interviews with the CEOs led to the identification of 28 organizations that met the authors' criteria of a technology innovation who agreed to participate in the study. Identification of champions and nonchampions was accomplished through peer nomination, a process in which key people associated with the innovation are asked to describe their role in the innovation. Through peer nomination and snow ball sampling, 153 individuals in the participation firms were interviewed using a structured interview protocol. After the interviews were completed, recorded, and transcribed, the same 153 individuals completed a questionnaire composed of measures of personality and leadership behaviors with a response rate of 88 percent. The author also established a procedure for differentiating champions from nonchampions by identifying several criteria. For example, both champions and nonchampions were involved in the same innovation within the same organization; they had to be comparable in technical knowledge and had to be peers at the same organizational level.

To analyze the QUAL/QUANT data, the authors content analyzed the transcripts of champions and nonchampions for the presence of themes reflecting leadership behaviors and influence tactics. They developed descriptions of transformational leadership behaviors using the theories of Bass (1985) and Conger and Kanungo (1998). Descriptions of influence tactics were adapted from Kipnis and Schmidt (1982). The authors recruited university students and trained them as coders who were randomly assigned to code the interview transcripts for either leader behaviors or influence tactics. The data from the content analysis were then used to determine the frequency of transformational leadership behaviors displayed by champions and nonchampions using a paired *t*-test for differences between the two samples. A similar procedure was employed to test for differences in personality characteristics between champions and nonchampions. This portion of the study illustrates the use of content analysis with a strong quantitative component as described in Chapter 4.

For the remainder of the analyses, the authors entered the champions and nonchampions' scores from the personality characteristics instrument which included risk taking, innovation, and social adroitness, leadership behaviors which were measured by the MLQ and influence tactics into to a series of regression analyses. The results of these analyses indicated that champions scored significantly higher of achievement orientation, risk taking, persuasiveness, persistence, and innovativeness, exhibited more transformational leadership behaviors, and used a greater number and employed a greater variety of influence strategies than the nonchampions.

Wells Swede and Tetlock (1986) content analyzed Kissinger's *White House Years* to identity personal characteristics of world leaders described in the book. Reading the book paragraph (the unit of analysis) by paragraph, the authors extracted description of 229 leaders from 34 countries, the majority of which were from the United States (107), followed by the Soviet Union (21), and the Republic of China (12). The world leaders occupied 72 public roles including presidents, ambassadors, prime ministers, and cabinet secretaries. Of the initial 229 leaders, 38 who were described in 15 or more paragraphs were selected for further coding. After the authors established a set of rules for identifying trait descriptors, four trained judges extracted 3759 separate trait descriptions ascribed to the 38 leaders with a 76 percent agreement between the four judges. The trait descriptions were then categorized differentiating between negative trait categories such as suspicious or tormented and positive trait categories such as courageous and profound.

Following the QUAL analyses, the authors performed principal component analysis for data reduction purposes which produced a five-component solution. The first component included traits that described the emotional strain on and the political toughness of senior policy makers which Wells Swede labeled "professional anguish." Kissinger speculated that William Rogers and Indira Gandhi were likely to experience professional anguish. The second component, named "ambitious patriotism," included traits that captured a blend of suspicion, ambition, and patriotism that Kissinger felt characterized many national leaders such as Richard Nixon and Nguyen Van Thieu, President of South Vietnam. The third component, named "revolutionary greatness," included traits that described the ruthless, visionary, and often charismatic characteristics of revolutionary leaders. Examples of leaders with these characteristics in Kissinger's book were Anwar Sadat Mao Tse-tung and Leonid Breszhnev. The fourth component was comprised of traits that reflected the cognitive and social sophistication characteristic of highly skilled political leaders which was named "intellectual sophistication," which according to Kissinger were exemplified by John Connally and Le Duc Tho of Vietnam. Finally, the fifth component captured traits that described leaders' capacity for close friendship as well as unsentimental criticism and was labeled "realistic friendship," exhibited by Kissinger himself, Nelson Rockefeller, and Edward Heath of Great Britain.

Wells Swede and Tetlock (1986) performed a variety of other statistical analyses to construct scales for each of Kissinger's personality themes and developed personality profiles for each of the 38 world leaders. The authors concluded that the five organizing themes—professional anguish, ambitious patriotism, revolutionary greatness, intellectual sophistication, and realistic friendship—provide a potential key for understanding how Kissinger structured the extraordinarily complex political environment he faced in the first Nixon administration (p. 639).

Meindl, Ehrlich, and Dukerich (1985) triangulated archival studies of the popular, academic, and business literature (QUAL) with a series of experimental studies (QUANT) to explore and validate the "romance of leadership construct." This construct captures the notion that leadership is a romantic concept suggesting that the general public views leaders as heroic, larger-than-life individuals and tends to attribute the causes of organizational successes and failures to their leaders. More specifically, according to the author

> The romanticized conception of leadership results from a biased perception to understand important but causally indeterminant and ambiguous organizational events and occurrences in term of leadership. Accordingly, in the absence of direct, unambiguous information that would allow one rationally to infer the locus of causality, the romanticized conception of leadership permits us to be more comfortable in associating leaders—by ascribing to them control and responsibility—with events and outcomes to which they can be plausibly linked (p. 80).

The archival (QUAL) investigation included three separate studies. In the first one, popular press articles published between 1972 and 1982 in the *Wall Street Journal* were analyzed to find evidence for a romanticized conception of leadership. For performance data, the authors obtained secondary data from the *Value Line Investment Survey*. Thirty-four companies listed in the Fortune 500 compilation of large US corporations comprised the sample. An article was classified as leadership oriented if the title included words such as leadership, management, or senior executive. If the article did not include leadership-related key words, it was assigned to an "other" category. A total of 33 248 articles about the firms were located for the time period sampled. Meindl et al. found both significant negative and positive correlations between conceptions of leadership and organizational performance indicating that the poorer the performance of the companies, the more leadership was emphasized. The second of the archival studies examined dissertation research which suggested that there was an association between good or bad economic times and the interest in leadership. The third study was a replication of study 2 but focused on publications in business journals instead of dissertations. The authors were interested in examining whether or not the general business community's collective interest in leadership was also responsive to fluctuations in the national economy. However, unlike study 2 which revealed mixed results, in the third archival study, the relationship between conceptions of leadership and organizational performance was largely positive suggesting that the interest in leadership in the business community was the highest in times of upswings in the national economy.

The archival studies were followed by three experimental studies designed to quantitatively test causal relationships between conceptions of leadership and organizational performance. These studies used undergraduate students enrolled in business and organizational behavior classes as respondents who evaluated different vignettes of organizational performance, described as high, moderate, or low. After reading the vignettes, the students were asked to rate the extent to which they considered the leader to be an important determinant of organizational performance. The results supported the authors' hypothesis that high- or low-organizational performance was attributed to the leadership of the organization. The second experimental study was a replication of the first after revisions of the vignettes to increase the range of organizational performance. The findings in this study reinforced the results of the first experiment providing support for the hypothesis that the greater the organizational performance, whether positive or negative, the more likely respondents were to infer that the leader was responsible for performance outcomes. The purpose of the third experiment was to replicate the patterns of results obtained in the first two. Again, the results supported the findings of the previous experimental studies and indicated that extreme organizational performance led to a proportional increase in the preference to use the leader as a causal explanation (p. 96). Collectively, the archival and experimental studies showed that the romanticized conception of leadership which suggests that leaders have the ability to control and influence the destiny of their organizations was valid across a variety of organizational settings. In short, leadership made a difference when it came to organizational performance. However, this is not to say that organizational performance was not affected by environmental factors such as industry fluctuations or political and social pressures. Meindl and his associates concluded that "the romance and the mystery surrounding leadership concepts are critical for sustaining follower-ship and that they contribute significantly to the responsiveness of individuals to the needs and goals of the collective organization" (p. 100).

Finally, Yukl and Van Fleet (1982), in one of the early mixed methods studies, examined military leadership effectiveness using two survey and two content analysis studies. The two content analysis studies used the critical incident technique in which respondents were asked to write short descriptions of effective and ineffective leader-ship behaviors that they observed in drill and nondrill situations. In the first of these two studies, critical incidents were collected from cadets at Texas A & M University in a noncombat, academic context. The respondents provided a total of 3111 critical incidents; however, only positive critical incidents ($n = 1511$) were content analyzed according to Yukl's (1981) taxonomy of leader behaviors. A random sample of 100 drill and nondrill incidents, rather than the entire set of positive critical incidents, comprised the database for analysis. Two judges rated these critical incidents across Yukl's (1981) behavior categories with an interrater agreement of .91. In the second content analysis, the critical incidents were collected from US Air Force officers during the Korean War through interviews. The interviews allowed for longer and more detailed positive and negative critical interviews. A total of 129 critical incidents were content analyzed. Interrater agreement was assessed in the same way as in the first study resulting in an agreement index of .92 for behavior frequency scores.

The two survey studies were conducted in a noncombat, academic setting (Texas A & M University) and during a ROTC exercise at Fort Bragg. Participants in the noncombat setting completed Yukl's leadership questionnaire. The criterion for leadership effective-ness was a composite rating of cadet unit performance during the formal "march in" ceremonies (p. 95). The platoon leaders completed a short version of Stogdill's (1963) Leader Behavior Description Questionnaire (LBDQ). The results of these two correla-tional surveys essentially replicated the critical incident studies but did show some method effects. For example, consideration was important for the critical incident studies but not in the surveys. Nevertheless in all four studies, performance emphasis was related to leader effectiveness as were inspiration, role clarification, and discipline in both combat and noncombat situations. The discrepancies in the results were attributed to uncontrolled differences and situational differences in role requirements for leaders across the four studies.

Taken together, studies triangulating qualitative and quantitative methods were more likely to follow the positivistic paradigm than studies triangulating different qualitative methods. More specifically, in studies combining qualitative and quantitative methods, researchers were more likely to conduct a literature review and formulate propositions or hypotheses compared to investigators who combine different qualitative methods. In addition to method triangulation, triangulation of theories (i.e., Tsui et al., 2006) was also used. Finally, the majority of the studies were conducted by one or more investigators demonstrating researcher triangulation as well.

A desirable goal in leadership research is to move beyond combining qualitative and quantitative approaches toward an integrated methodology. According to Moran-Elis et al. (2006), "integration" denotes a specific relationship between two or more methods where the different methods retain their paradigmatic nature that are intermeshed with each other in the pursuit of the global goal of "knowing more." Integration, according to the authors, involves the generation of a tangible relationship among methods, data, and/or perspectives, retaining the integrity of each through a set of actions clearly specified by the researcher team and that allows them to "know more" about their research topic (p. 51). Similarly, Pawson (1995) is critical of multiple/method multiple data approaches which primarily generate more data about a phenomenon without addressing how the plurality of data is combined analytically (p. 10). Consequently, it is not surprising that most mixed methods designs defer integration to the point of analysis or to the point of theoretical integration. The authors propose that when data generated by different means are brought together at the level of analysis or theory, we may speak of analytic or interpretive integration (p. 56).

Determining a typology for mixed methods designs (i.e., identifying the basic procedures for using both QUAL and QUANT strands in a single study) is among the most complex and controversial issues in mixed methods studies. Tashakkori and Teddlie (2003b) identified more than 40 types of mixed designs in their book (p. 680). The authors also point out that the worst residue of the paradigm wars has been their impact on students. They note that many students suffer from "dual-lingualism," which represents a split personality in methods of study and ways of thinking (p. 699). This split is also evident in text books which usually have separate sections devoted to QUAL and QUAN methods. For the mixed method design as the third methodological movement to achieve its impact, courses on mixed methods need to be taught in graduate school, more journal space needs to be allocated to mixed methods research, and funding agencies need to consider mixed methods design on equal par with quantitative research in the evaluations of research proposals. The creation of the International Journal of Mixed Methods Research was one right step in this direction.

Summary

The leadership studies articles reviewed in this chapter demonstrated that the QUAL studies showed a variety of strategies for improving the validity of ideographic research including audit trails, peer debriefings, prolonged engagement, and thick description

(Chapter 2). A variety of types of data and methods of analysis are employed in triangulated designs qualitative which often correlate quantitative and qualitative responses. Onwuegbuzie and Teddlie (2003) recommend that in mixed methods designs, researchers should be cognizant of and should check the assumptions underlying each of their data analysis techniques (p. 369). In both qualitative and quantitative methods, data transformation is a shared characteristic. In qualitative studies, data are converted into narratives, whereas in quantitative studies data are translated into numbers. Potentially, mixed method designs have the ability to reduce some of the problems associated with single methods. By utilizing quantitative and qualitative methods within the same study, mixed methods research in leadership studies can incorporate the strength of both methodologies. On the other hand, mixed methods research makes considerable demands on the researcher who has to be skilled, competent, and experienced in both types of methods.

Part III

UNDERUTILIZED QUALITATIVE METHODS IN LEADERSHIP STUDIES

7

GROUNDED THEORY, ETHNOGRAPHY, AND HISTORIOMETRY

This chapter covers three distinctive qualitative methods: grounded theory (GT), ethnography, and historiometry which span the spectrum from highly qualitative (GT and ethnography) to highly quantitative (historiometry). Despite their intuitive appeal for the study of leadership, these qualitative methods are used less frequently than those presented in Chapters 3–5. Part of the reason is that with the exception of historiometry, the methods covered in this chapter truly require prolonged engagement with the research participants, and it is not unusual for a GT or ethnographic study to take several years to complete.

GROUNDED THEORY

An Illustrative Grounded Theory Leadership Study

Lakshman (2007) conducted a study that built a GT of the role of leadership in knowledge management firms by analyzing 37 in-depth interviews of CEOs who have managed information and knowledge to drive their companies to a position of competitive advantage. This study addressed the lack of emphasis in the leadership literature of the role of leaders in knowledge management given the fact that knowledge has become a key corporate resource and the necessity to manage that resource has become crucial. For the purpose of this study, the author conceptualized knowledge management as the "overall set of processes that are put into place for the purpose of identifying sources of relevant data and information in organizations, the eventual conversion of these data and information to knowledge, and their subsequent dissemination to different points in the organization where they are needed" (p. 55). Knowledge management, according to the author, can be operationalized through the existence of extensive networks, both social and technological, at multiple levels throughout the organization. The key constructs in this study were leadership and knowledge management which were drawn both deductively from the relevant literatures and inductively based on the data collected to generate a theory describing how leaders manage knowledge and information.

In-depth interviews are a key component of data collection in the GT approach. The interviews with the CEOs were sourced from articles published in the Harvard Business Review (HBR) over a long period of time (since 1989) and were conducted by different interviewers at different points in time. Using the method of comparative comparisons proposed by Glaser and Strauss (1967), Lakshman verified the data obtained from the interviews with the CEOs with other independent interviews and case studies. For example, information about Ford obtained from the HBR interview was corroborated by another independent interview and a Fortune magazine article that described aspects of the company's knowledge sharing practices (p. 58).

This GT study resulted in a model depicting the relationships between executives' different functions in the information management such as their use of sociocognitive and technological knowledge management networks, the importance of internal and external customers, and the personal participation of the CEOs in knowledge management activities on a day to day basis as well as specially organized events. For example, at Dell, CEO Michael Dell talked about the value of personal participation in the forums set up to ensure the free flow of information with customers on a constant basis such as the Platinum Councils, regional meetings of Dell's largest customers worldwide. This study highlights both deductive and inductive approaches in a little researched area, namely knowledge leadership of CEOs.

Introduction to Grounded Theory

GT is a research method in which theory emerges from the data and is grounded in it (Glaser & Strauss, 1967). It was introduced in 1967 with Glaser and Strauss' seminal work, "*The discovery of grounded theory*," as a qualitative method to "uncover and understand what lies behind phenomenon about which little is known" (Strauss & Corbin, 1990, p. 19). Glaser's (1992) definition of GT is "a general methodology of analysis linked with data collection to generate an inductive theory about a substantive area" (p. 19). The authors introduced GT as a general method of comparative analysis which would allow for the emergence of categories from the data as an alternative to the hypothetico-deductive approach in social research. Following the *Discovery* book, a crucial measure against the forcing of data into a Proccrustean bed would be to "literally to ignore the literature of theory and fact of on the area of study, in order to assure that the emergence of categories will not be contaminated . . ." (Glaser & Strauss, 1967, p. 37).

GT is a highly systematic general method used for data collection and analysis for the purpose of generating theory as opposed to verifying theory used in describing and explaining basic common patterns in social life by continuously comparing the data (Glaser, 1978; 1998; Glaser & Strauss, 1967). GT does not aim at an accurate perception of participants' voices but an abstraction of both their actions and their meanings, that is, a perspective and conceptualization of their behaviors and their voices. As a result, GT concepts are abstract with regard to time, place, and people. Because GT operates on an abstract and conceptual level, relating concept to concept, it can tap the latent structure that drives and organizes behavior (Glaser, 2001). GT represents a methodology which utilizes breadth and depth of data and generates theory instead of pursuing theory testing.

GT is described by Creswell (1998) as one of five research traditions in addition to biography, phenomenology, ethnography, and case study and distinguished in terms of reporting approaches, philosophical assumptions, data collection activities, the logic of sampling, data analysis strategies, representation, rhetorical structures, and terms about verification.

According to Sousa and Hendricks (2006), GT analysis generates theory from minimum prior knowledge. As an inductive method, it seeks to discover theoretically relevant issues from data rather than from existing theories, preconceived notions, and professional interests. Entering a research field with as few predetermined ideas as possible increases the theoretical sensitivity of the researcher (Glaser, 1978). Kelle (1995) points out that researchers need to cultivate an empty head in order to theorize the GT way, a head devoid of theoretical concepts that can possibly blur the unprejudiced observations toward the field of research (p. 41). This does not apply that researchers approach reality as a tabula rasa. If they have a perspective, it will help them to see relevant data and abstract significant categories from the scrutiny of the data (Glaser & Strauss, 1967, p. 3). Because no researcher can possibly obliterate all previously learned theories, the trick is to line up what one takes as theoretically plausible with what one finds in the substantive field through an emergent fit. However, the researcher using GTA must be aware that while preconception lends structure, it also derails relevance and fit, thus workability (Glaser, 2001).

Parry (1998) argues that GT is a valid method for researching the process of leadership because leadership is often defined as a social influence process. The author contends that mainstream leadership research methodologies have been partially unsuccessful in theorizing about the nature of these processes. He refers the reader to Glaser (1992) who noted that the contribution of GT to mature areas of research is not the generation of a new concept or pattern, since these are usually saturated, but a better understanding of basic social processes which might be missing. Leadership is a well-worked area of research, and GT may give a better conceptual grasp of the basic social processes associated with leadership (Parry, 1998, p. 90).

Data Collection and Analysis in Grounded Theory

A number of data collection and analysis procedures have been well documented in the methodological literature (e.g., Charmaz, 1990; Creswell, 1998; 2005; Harry, Sturges, & Klinger, 2005; Seale, 1999), particularly in terms of coding processes, to illustrate the validity of a GT study and the credibility of the findings. Charmaz (2003) describes the theoretical understanding of the interaction between data collection and analysis when she states:

> Essentially, grounded theory methods consist of systematic inductive guidelines for collecting and analyzing data to build middle-range theoretical frameworks that explain the collected data. Throughout the research process, grounded theorists develop analytical interpretations of their data to focus further data collection, which they use in turn to inform and refine their developing theoretical analyses (p. 250).

In GT, the researcher is advised to refrain from conducting a pre-research literature of the topic he or she wishes to study, since this will set the stage for preconceptions about what to find. To discover what is really going on is difficult, if we are desensitized by

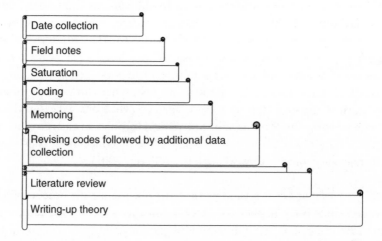

Figure 7-1   Summary steps in grounded theory (GT) data collection and analysis

borrowed concepts. Typically, the extant literature is reviewed in the discussion section of a GT study and comes at the end of a published article or in Chapter 5 of a GT dissertation for GT analysts who follow Glaser's procedure.

Initial data collection in GT is conducted through interviews or observations. Generally, GT favors the use of different data sources which give the analyst different views to understand a category and its properties. The researcher often uses audio or video-tapes the interaction with the participants which are subsequently transcribed. The unit of analysis (element of transcribed data) may be a sentence, a line from a transcript, a speech interaction, a one second sequence in a video, or a combination of elements such as these. It is important to clarify and choose the level exactly we intend to examine in the analysis and choose the level of granularity accordingly. For example, if the goal is to derive a theory of collective decision making, then analyzing parts of sentences that indicated an understanding, misunderstanding, agreement, disagreement, and so on may provide a relevant granularity, whereas analyzing a transcript by whole sentences may not. According to Lowe (1996), a useful way to start is to perform a line-by-line analysis of the transcribed data. Moreover, author recommends that the gerund forms of words (ending in -ing) should be used to label each identified theme "to sensitize the researcher to the processes and patterns which may be revealed at each stage" (p. 8). Strauss (1987) suggests that the researcher should differentiate between in vivo codes, which are derived from the language and terminology used by the participants and scientific constructs, which derive from the researcher's scholarly knowledge and the scientific understanding of the leadership literature.

Glaser (2002) reminds us that GT is the generation of emergent conceptualizations into integrated patterns, which are denoted by categories and their properties. This is accomplished by the many rigorous steps of GT woven together by the constant comparison process designed to generate concepts from all the data. The constant comparison method involves sorting data into coded categories by constant comparison among categories as a means of determining to determine that the data can be discriminated in a meaningful way. Glaser (2002) also points out that GT cuts across research methods (experiment, survey, content analysis, and all qualitative methods).

Category development in grounded theory

The three basic elements in GT are concepts, categories, and propositions. Concepts are the basic units of analysis from which the theory is developed. Categories are at a higher level of abstraction; they are generated through the same analytic process of making comparisons to highlight similarities and differences that are used to produce the lower level concepts. Categories are the cornerstones of developing theory and provide the means by which the theory can be integrated (Strauss & Corbin, 1990, p. 7). Finally, propositions, the third elements in GT, were originally called hypotheses by Glaser and

Strauss (1967) but were renamed since propositions involve conceptual relationships whereas hypotheses require measured relationships.

GT is an iterative process in which concepts, categories, and propositions are constantly refined by constantly comparing sampled data with emergent theory until conceptual saturation is achieved. Categories are generated from the data, and properties are generated concepts about categories. As the data are being categorized, relationships among categories are noted and compared to the theoretical codes which may integrate those categories into a cohesive theory (Glaser, 1978). This process continues until the relationships among categories produce a final theory. GT does not capture the voice of participants when naming categories; instead, it uncovers many patterns that the participant does not understand or is not aware of (Glaser, 1998). It is a method of successive abstractions that allows the researcher to develop a theory on a core variable, such as leadership talent, organizational chance, leaders' emotional labor, or authentic leadership.

The process of analyzing data in GT, according to Strauss and Corbin (1990; 1998), consists of open coding, axial coding (Chapter 4), and selective coding. It typically begins with the identification of *open coding* categories which refers to labeling codes as indicated by the data. The products of open coding are concepts. The authors suggest that 10 is a reasonable number of categories, but this number depends on the extent of the database and the complexity of the research topic. From open coding, the researcher proceeds to *axial coding* and the development of a coding paradigm. Axial coding involves establishing connections between categories and subcategories. This also entails the process of selecting a core category from the coding possibilities and positioning it at the center of the axial coding process (Locke, 2001). Core categories, according to Strauss and Corbin (1990), must be the sun which stands in an orderly relationship to its planets (p. 124). They represent the categories with the greatest explanatory power and should be saturated as completely as possible. Finally, in *selective coding*, the categories developed earlier to form an initial theoretical framework are integrated.

In the next phase of the analysis, the researcher returns to data collection or re-analyzes the data to identify several categories that relate to the core category. In the entire process, but particularly in the various coding phases, memoing (the researcher writing theoretical memos to him/herself) plays an important role with the researcher writing memos about the emerging theory. According to Glaser (1998), memoing is the core stage of GT methodology since memos are the theorizing write-ups of ideas of substantive codes and their theoretically coded relationships as they emerge during coding, collecting, and analyzing data. Likewise, Corbin and Strauss (1990) maintain that

> Writing theoretical memos is an integral part of doing grounded theory. Since the
> analyst cannot readily keep track of all the categories, properties, hypotheses, and

generative questions that evolve from the analytic process, there must be a system for doing so. The use of memos constitutes such a system. Memos are not merely "ideas." They are involved in the formulation and revision of theory during the research process (p. 6).

The three types of memos discussed by the authors include code memos, theoretical memos, and operational memos. Code memos relate to open coding and focus on conceptual labeling. For example, early memos might record notes of the researcher indicating that a specific leadership theory, transformational leadership, and complex organization may be possible categories. Another memo might query that leadership is important because it may lead to better practice. Theoretical memos relate to axial and selective coding and focus on paradigm features. Finally, operational memos keep track of the research process. In memos, the researcher depicts the relationship between concepts in two-by-two tables, in diagrams or figures, or whatever makes the ideas flow and generates comparative power.

Table 7-1 depicts a general model of the GT process. However, it should be noted again that GT is not a linear procedure despite the sequential delineation of steps in the table.

Inductive analysis plays a major role in GT studies. Strauss and Corbin (1998) recognize the role of inductive reasoning in GT and deal with it as follows:

> We are deducing what is going on based on data but also based on our reading of that data along with our assumptions about the nature of life, the literature we carry in our heads, and discussions we have with colleagues. (This is how science is born). In fact, there is an interplay between induction and deduction (as in all science) ... This is why we feel it is important that the analyst validates his or her interpretations through constantly comparing one piece of data to another (pp. 136–137).

It is important to note that there are significant differences between the analytical procedures developed by Glaser (1992) and Strauss (1987; Strauss & Corbin, 1998). At the core of the debate is the notion whether theory emerges from flexible, inductively employed data analysis or whether theory is derived as the result of applying structured analytical methods. According to Kelle (2005), one of the most crucial difference between Glaser's and Strauss' approaches to GT lies in the fact that Strauss and Corbin propose the utilization of a specified theoretical framework based on a certain understanding of human behavior, whereas Glaser emphasizes that coding as a process of combining "the analyst's scholarly knowledge and his research knowledge of the substantive field" (Glaser, 1978, p. 70) has to be realized ad hoc, which means it has often to be conducted on the basis of a more or less implicit theoretical background knowledge. The controversy between Glaser and Strauss boils down to the question whether the researcher uses a well-defined coding paradigm and always looks systematically for causal conditions, phenomena/context, intervening conditions, action strategies, and consequences in the data (the Strauss & Corbin position) or whether theoretical codes are employed as they emerge in the same way as substantive codes emerge, but drawing on a huge fund of coding families (Glaser's position). Substantive codes are developed ad hoc during open coding, the first stage of the coding process, and relate to the empirical substance of the research domain. Theoretical codes which researchers always have to have at their disposal "conceptualize how the substantive codes may relate to each other as hypothesizes to be integrated into a theory" (Glaser, 1978, p. 72).

Glaser (1992) argues that the generation of GT emerges from categories and patterns provided by the participants and by socially constructed realities. Strauss emphasizes the canons of good science to data analysis and coding while Glaser argues that the codes should emerge from the data. Glaser views Strauss's method of applying specific coding methods (the categorization of causal conditions, context, action/interaction strategies, and consequences) as forcing theoretical constructs and challenges the resulting theories as being more descriptive than processural or structural. Therefore, it is important for grounded theorists to identify which approach to GT they are following.

Quality and Rigor in Grounded Theory

A GT researcher is likely to ask, "Do all the parts of the theory fit with each other and do they appear to explain the data?" As a way of answering this question, the criteria of credibility and authenticity (Chapter 2) may be substituted for internal validity (Miles & Huberman, 1994). It is important to avoid falling into a hierarchical coding scheme by default as this approach is too often used to fit the data to a researcher's preconceived (Alexander, 1966). Silverman (1993) asserts that the constant comparison method, or analytic induction, is a source of validity. However, the mechanistic application of constant comparison will not remove the inductive bias (subjectivity) from the findings. The use of multiple data collection techniques such as observation or document analysis to supplement interviewing, for example, is a widely accepted method for enhancing validity. Likewise, the use of multiple observers and extensive field notes helps to maintain both reliability and validity. Parry (1998) adds that the use of theoretical sampling in GT ensures that sufficient internal variety in data sourcing is obtained to saturate the categories which emerge from the analysis. A theory is saturated when it is stable in the face of new data (i.e., no new categories emerge after additional data collection).

Sousa and Hendricks (2006) offer several other criteria for enhancing the quality of GT research. One of these is the theoretical sensitivity of the researcher. Glaser and Strauss (1967) coined the term to denote the researcher's ability to see relevant data that means to reflect upon empirical data material with the help of theoretical terms derived from the researcher's discipline and theoretical orientation and understanding. The authors believe that theoretical sensitivity has two characteristics: (1) the involvement of the researcher's personal and temperamental bent and (2) the researcher's ability to have theoretical insights. Sousa and Hendricks (2006) discuss the role of trust in GT and assert that fit, workability, relevance, and modifiability are the fundamental sources of trust in GT. The authors equate trust with validity. Like validity, fit is concerned with whether a concept expresses adequately the pattern in the data that it purports to denote. In other words, fit has to do with how closely concepts fit with the incidents they are representing, and this is related to how thoroughly the constant comparison of incidents to concepts was carried out. Workability addresses the issue of whether the set of integrated and conceptually plausible grounded hypotheses sufficiently accounts for how the main concern of the participants is continually resolved. Relevance derives from the importance of what is truly important to the participants. A relevant study is one that evokes "grab" and captures the attention. Modifiability points to the notion that theory generation is an ever modifying process based on an emergent fit (p. 335). A modifiable theory can be altered when new relevant data are compared to existing data.

Glaser (1998) puts these four concepts in simple language when he states that a theory that fits, that works, that is relevant, and that can be easily modified engenders trust in the method.

Applications of Grounded Theory in Leadership Research

Table 7-1 presents the major GT studies located in the leadership literature.

The first study in Table 7-2 (Komires, Mainella, Longerbeam, Osteen, & Owen, 2006) describes a stage-based model of identity leadership. The authors interviewed 13 diverse students—eight white students, three African-American students, one Asian student, and one African student who immigrated as a child. Student data were organized into one central category, developing a leadership identity and five categories which influence the development of leadership identity to include broadening view of leadership, developing self, group influences, developmental influences, and the changing view of self with others. The authors presented the Leadership Identity Development Model (LID) and argued that students progress through one stage before progressing to the next, thereby resembling the various stage model we find in psychology, such as cognitive development or moral development. Although stage models typically assume that development proceeds in a linear fashion, Komires et al. noted that the development of leadership identity can also be cyclical.

Douglas (2006) conducted a GT study designed to identify conceptual categories and their properties. The author obtained data from a manager/owner of a highly specialized

Table 7-1   Applications of grounded theory in leadership studies

Author(s)	Purpose	Informants	Data sources	Analyses
Komires et al. (2006)	To describe a stage-based theory of leadership identity development	13 students at a large mid-Atlantic university	Interviews	Open, axial, and selective coding; constant comparison; credibility and trustworthiness established through member checking and peer debriefing
Douglas (2006)	To examine inductively derived theory through application of GT To critically discuss two theoretical categories; To contribute to the qualitative and interpretive discussion	16 full-time staff	Semistructured interviews	Constant comparison; data explication; discussion of decision literature after data analysis
Komires et al. (2005)	To understand how identity develops	13 diverse students	Semistructured interviews	Open, axial, selective coding; constant comparison
Reichard (2005)	To develop a theory of leadership development for women military officers	Not reported	Unstructured interviews 2005	Open, axial, and selective coding; constant comparison
Parry (1999)	To use GT to theorize about social influence processes of leadership in a substantive setting	36 individual from three organizations	Observation; interviews	Theoretical coding; comparison; linking; and reduction of categories

engineering firm. At the time of the study, the company had the manager/owner, the leader, and a full-time staff of 10 which included four senior engineers, five individuals with general engineering skills, and an office administrator. Data were collected in the field, using semistructured, unstructured, and semistructured interviews. In addition, the manager met with his employees on several occasions and took field notes in situ or sometime after the visit. In the second phase of data collection, which lasted for three weeks, individual, in-depth interviews were carried out off-site. Again, they involved semistructured, open-ended interviews with all employees which were audio-taped and subsequently transcribed. Constant comparison method was employed with the researcher constantly seeking verification of the emergent theoretical categories and their properties.

Two categories emerged from the data which the author labeled (1) management decisions and consequences based on employees' perspectives and (2) self-as-manager which captured the manager's perceptions. The manager had recently moved to a new facility with large rental cost because he planned on expanding the business. Additionally, he had acquired another company. The manager also abolished the annual wage rise and the Christmas parties. One of the senior engineers who had been with the company for 26 years had the following to say:

> [I] tried everything for him to stop buying this company, and the lad knew that it was a bad buy. But that's the way he is, that's the way he wanted to take us. It all went wrong in a very big way (Douglas, 2006, p. 266).

Overall, the employees developed strong negative perceptions of the manager and described his decisions as demoralizing, undermining, and upsetting. The manager, on the other hand, on purchasing the company sought to make decisions that would result in changes that he believed would increase his wealth. To bring about these changes, he decided to manage organizational change from an individualistic approach and not seek or appear to encourage employees' involvement in decision making. He said:

> They are terrified about security and the fact that the company will do under if I continued to make these wild decisions and take it in areas it has never been before (p. 297).

Moreover, the manager believed that the principal engineers had adopted an oppositional stance against him as their manager of the business. Douglas concluded with the following statement:

> Self-as-manager grounds the analyses in original data. Like the employees' data, it creates a multidimensional account of the managers' meanings to him with regards to important (to him) issues that shape his individual perceptions, feelings, emotions, and behaviors, subsequently impacting on the business,

employees and him. What appears to have emerged from the manager's explanation is a range of defenses and rationales to challenges leveled at his decisions and managing the enterprise (pp. 269–270).

The Komires et al. (2005) was almost identical to the 2006 study and therefore is not described in detail here.

Reichard (2005) set out to develop a theory of leadership development for women. The author defined leadership as the level of the position in the organization, in this case the officer level. She did not postulate a prior theory to frame the study; instead a context-specific theory was discovered based on the data collected. Data collection involved interviews which were unstructured and open-ended focusing on women officers' leadership experiences. The interviews were followed by open coding, axial coding, and selective coding and the utilization of constant comparisons. Six categories emerged: family, relationships, watching, feedback, understanding, outcomes, and training and education. According to one participant

My father taught me how to be tough, stand up for myself, and set high goals and manage growing up with two brothers.

This female officer stressed the importance of family as the key to her military success. Reichard proposed that a model of female leadership development composed of four major themes: relationships, engaged experiences, incorporating feedback, and leadership strategies. From these themes, a number of propositions were developed which proposed relationships between the different model components. For example, one proposition stated that feedback mediates the relationship between relationships and the development of leadership strategies. Finally, the author drew parallels between her model of female leadership and authentic leadership development (Luthans & Avolio, 2003).

Two Australian leadership scholars (Kan & Parry, 2004) employed GT to examine resistance to change in a hospital setting in New Zealand. The data collection included the completion of the Multifactor Leadership Questionnaire (MLQ), 50 hours of nonparticipant observation over three wards, 30 hours of semistructured interviews, and 25 hours of informal and unstructured interviews, and document analysis. One hundred and ninety-six respondents rated the leadership of their 20 nurse managers. All respondents were fellow nurses or associated professionals. Categories were developed establishing coding families as described by Glaser (1978). Memos were generated using the software program NVivo. Early in the coding process, categories were generated that related to the family responsibilities of nurses, the role of nursing history in reinforcing their present professional culture, and the nature of the nursing profession itself. Identifying paradox emerged as the highest order category by which all similarities and variations in leadership behaviors and interactions could be explained.

Kan and Parry interpreted identifying paradox as referring to the implicit recognition that the situation and understanding of the respondents of the situation were paradoxical. For example, the nurses made paradoxical statements to enhance their own position through a time of perceived inequality and change. A recurring theme was that nurse leaders had the potential to achieve greater influence within the health care environment. However, an equally recurring theme was that the potential was repressed by cultural and societal forces factors and outside nursing.

Finally, Parry (1999) completed a GT study in three organizations, two of which were undergoing severe turbulence and change by being amalgamated and the third was in a relatively stable stage. The informants gathered observations about leadership at work. An initial set of 16 individuals was interviewed; the remaining 20 participants interviewed were assessed over time in accordance with the principles of theoretical sampling. A key informant who was a long-term member of one of the organizations assisted with the data collection. This study used a combination of theoretical and statistical sampling. The initial 16 interviewees were randomly selected and came from different levels and functional areas. Theoretical sampling was used to ensure that interviewees were selected according to the extent to which they would contribute rich information. The subject of the interviews was the nature of change occurring in the organizations which participated in the study. Theoretical sampling was discontinued when the categories became saturated. Several informants were interviewed more than once leading to a total of 43 interviews supplemented by observational data.

The constant comparison of existing categories with newly obtained data lead to the creation of new categories. The two explanatory categories were resolving uncertainty and enhancing adaptability. These two categories integrated the aggregated categories of leadership, following and change. It was also found that the strategies, behaviors, and activities of leaders had the effect of resolving uncertainty in the minds of followers as well as in the minds of the leaders. When the existing data were re-interrogated, enhancing adaptability emerged as another salient category. Leaders who are adaptable to the uncertainty of change have a clear perception of the leadership role they play. This enhanced adaptability, which in turn leads to increased manifestations of leadership and enables leaders to enhance the adaptability of followers to change.

Summary

The GT approach involves the generation of emergent theory from empirical data. The theory is based upon patterns found in empirical data, not from inferences or the association of ideas. A variety of data collection techniques have been employed, such as interviews, participant observation, and document analysis. There is constant comparison by the researcher between emergent theory (concepts and categories) and new data. The constant comparison method integral to GT is presented as a step-by-step qualitative data analysis: inductive category coding based on "units of meaning of textual (or visual) data, refinement of categories, exploration of patterns and relationships across categories leading to an integration of data or sense-making" (Maykut & Morehouse, 1994). Constant comparison confirms that theoretical constructs are found across and between data samples, driving the collection of additional data until the researcher feels that theoretical saturation has been reached.

Computer programs such as NUD*IST, NVivo, and ATLAS.ti have basic coding and retrieval functions culminating in complex theory-building capabilities. Data analysis is at once conceptual and organizational, interpretive as well as mechanical. Coding for expedient retrieval (of categories) and theory building (relationship among categories) involves the pragmatics of breaking down or dissecting the data into manageable and meaningful analytical units. Coding as such "is a theorizing process" (Richards & Richards, 1994, p. 148) where the ethical and practical exigencies of inclusion/exclusion are factored in.

GT is ideal for theory development, but it has been underutilized in leadership research. Parry (1998), arguing for the use of GT as a valid method for researching the process of leadership, stated that leadership is a social influence process and that mainstream leadership methodologies have been unsuccessful in theorizing about the nature of these processes. The author asserts that a rigorous GT study will help overcome the deficiencies in mainstream leadership research, in part because GT is a very time-consuming method that does not favor the novice researcher.

ETHNOGRAPHY

An Illustrative Ethnographic Leadership Study

Pratt (2000) conducted an ethnographic examining how Amway distributors manage their members by changing how members think and feel about themselves framing this research from an organizational identification theory perspective. Amway, one of the largest and financially most successful network marketing organizations (NMO), uses distributors to sell its products and services FTF. In addition, distributors sponsor new members. The more successful distributors spend considerable amount of time personally teaching new members how to build the business. In 2005, the company generated worldwide retail sales of US$6.4 billion. With operations in more than 80 countries and over 450 products and services, Amway has established itself as a leading multilevel organization offering business opportunities around the globe.

As an NMO, Amway differs from traditional organizations in a number of important ways: (1) members are often not co-located; (2) members typically pursue a career in Amway on a part-time basis; (3) they are required to pay a membership fee of about $100.00 as well as pay for training materials; and (4) they are not legally employees but act as independent franchises that must follow legal and ethical guidelines set forth by the parent organization (Pratt, 2000, p. 459). Amway is built on the principle of providing a business opportunity that empowers people to realize their dreams and live better lives.

Pratt employed three data collection techniques to include semiovert participant observation, open-ended interviews, and archival data. Semiovert participant observation means that the author joined Amway but informed his fellow distributors of his dual role as an employee and researcher. This data collection method allowed the author to gain the trust of his co-workers and offered the opportunity to ask questions that might otherwise seem unusual coming from a typical co-worker. Data collection took place over a two-year period with participant observation taking place mainly over a nine-month period. In the open-ended interviews, that author asked road questions such as "Can you tell me about what you do as a distributor?" or probing questions such as "Could you tell me by what you mean by the word of dream?" The interview protocol was intended to gain insights into the organizational experiences of the distributors. The author interviewed 17 current distributors and 16 former distributors who had left within a year of joining. Finally, company books and booklets, audio cassettes, success stories published in Amagram, the monthly newsletter, and Amway-related websites were the source of the archival data.

Data analysis consisted of iterating between the data and emergent themes which were organized into a coherent framework. Pratt found that the successes and failures in two organizational practices, "dream building" and "positive programming," seemed to account for different reactions to the organization. Dream building refers to helping distributors set personal and sales of goals while positive programming involves helping them to surround themselves with inspirational and organizationally supportive people. Building on theories of organizational identification, Pratt found that the combination of successful dream building and positive programming was associated with positive identification whereas successful dream building and unsuccessful positive programming led to disidentification. Financial success in the organization was not related to identification. Amway managed identification of its distributors by using two types of practices: sense breaking practices that break down meaning and sense giving practices that provide meaning. A primary sense breaking practice in Amway is dream building whereas positive programming is an example of a sense giving practice. When both were successful, distributors displayed positive identification with the organization. Pratt concluded that identification, which involved identity change among distributors, was itself a product of sense making.

Introduction to Ethnography

Among the qualitative methodologies currently in use, the ethnographic method has a long and distinguished history. Herodotus may have been the first Greek ethnographer who recorded the infinite variety and strangeness he saw in other cultures. According to Van Maanen (1979a), the ethnographic approach is that of anthropology and to a more limited extent, sociology under the stiff but precise tag of participant observation (p. 539). Extended participant observation means that at least a year is devoted to an ethnographic study. As currently practiced, ethnography involves a particular set of methodological and interpretive procedures that evolved primarily in the twentieth century. The writings of Ruth Benedict, Margaret Mead, and Bronislaw Malinowski are classics documenting the early days of ethnographic research at the beginning of the twentieth century which focused on first-hand collection of data in primitive cultures on the Pacific Islands.

Defining ethnography

Ethnography is a description and interpretation of a social group or system. It involves immersion in the social context being studied. The ethnographer examines the group's observable and learned patterns of behavior, and the way of life (Harris, 1968) and ground their research in ethnographic fieldwork. As a process, ethnography involves extended observation of the group typically through participant observation, in which the ethnographer is immersed in the day-to-day lives of the people, or through one-to-one interviews with members of the group. Ethnographers study the meanings of behaviors, language, and interactions of members of the culture sharing group by going "native" or living in a foreign locale for an extended period of time and adopting the interpretive view of the informants. As a qualitative method, ethnography cannot reasonably be defined as a single method or technique; rather it is a research discipline based upon culture as an organizing concept and a mix of both observational and interviewing techniques to record behavioral dynamics (Mariampolski, 1999). Ethnographic research questions usually concern the link between culture and behavior and how cultural processes develop over time.

Ethnography may also be defined as an end product, the written report, and an approach to research. It is holistic and looks for anthropological and local categories of meaning such as myths, rituals, and social structure. The goal of ethnography according to LeCompte and Preissle (1993) is "to create a vivid reconstruction of the culture studied" (p. 234). Ethnographers seek to gain an emic or the native's point of view without imposing their own conceptual frameworks as opposed to the etic or outsider's view of the cultural group they are studying. As practiced, ethnography allows a field worker to use the culture of a setting to account for the observed patterns of human activity. Procedurally, ethnography is described by Conklin (1968) as involving "a long period of intimate study and residence in a well-defined community employing a wide range of observational techniques including face-to-face contact with members of local groups, direct participation in some of the group's activities, and a greater emphasis on intensive work with informants than the use of documentary or survey data" (p. 172). The strategy most commonly employed by field workers is to explicitly examine the linguistic categories used by informants in the setting to describe various aspects of their routine and problematic situations (Van Maanen, 1979b, p. 541). Like other qualitative researchers, ethnographers must learn to use themselves as the principal instrument of observation and interpretation.

Types of ethnographic studies

There are four primary types of ethnographies: autoethnography, critical ethnography, collaborative ethnography, and virtual ethnography.

Autoethnography

Autoethnography can be defined as "research, writing and the method that connect the autobiographical and personal to the cultural and social. This form usually features concrete action, emotion, embodiment, self-conscious introspection [and] claims the conventions of literary writing" (Ellis, 2004, p. xix). It is a genre of writing and research that connects the personal to the cultural, placing the self within a social context (Reed-Danahay, 1997). The author explains that autoethnographers may vary in their emphasis on graphy (i.e., writing or the research process), ethnos (i.e., culture), or auto (i.e., self). But no matter how we define auto ethnography, Reed-Danahay asserts that one of the main characteristics is that the autoethnographer is a boundary-crosser.

Autoethongraphies are usually written in the first person and feature dialogue, emotion, and self-consciousness as relational and institutional stories affected by history, social structure, and culture (Ellis & Brochner, 2000). According to Denzin and Lincoln (2000), the introduction of the first person in research texts is a postmodern response to a crisis of representation and current angst about identity. This "authoring of self" into a research text blurs the boundaries between the self and other, subject and object, takes many forms, serves diverse functions, and generates varying responses to how researchers do and write ethnography. By writing themselves into their own work as major characters, autoethnographers have challenged accepted views about silent authorship, where the researcher's voice is not included in the presentation of the findings (Charmaz & Mitchell, 1997).

The use of the self as the only data source in autoethnography has been questioned by numerous qualitative researchers (e.g., Sparkes, 2001). The author suggests that auto-ethnography is at the boundaries of academic research because such accounts do not fit comfortably with traditional criteria used to judge qualitative inquiries. Hence, auto-ethnography is still quite vulnerable to the hegemonic pressures of more canonical, powerful discourses within mainstream methodologies and traditional epistemologies

(Holt, 2003). Others (e.g., Coffey, 1999) have criticized autoethnographies as being too self-indulgent and narcissistic. But, as Sparkes (2002) cautions, although autoethnographies can be self-indulgent, the universal charge of self-indulgence labeled against autoethnographies is a result of misapprehension of the genre due to a mistrust of the work of self (Sparkes, 2001).

Critical ethnography

Critical ethnography takes the conventional ethnography and incorporates tenets of critical theory in order to critique the culture (Thomas, 1993). It includes an advocacy perspective to ethnography (Carspecken, 1995; Carspecken & Apple, 1992). Critical ethnographers advocate for the emancipation of groups marginalized in society (Thomas, 1993). Likewise, Alvesson and Deetz (2000) argue that critical ethnography entails viewing cultural phenomena in more critical terms, "accentuating the repressive and circumscribing aspects of culture" (p. 199). According to Thomas (1993), critical ethnography attempts to answer the "so what" question for its audience by adding a political purpose.

Critical ethnographers are typically politically minded researchers who seek, through their work, to advocate against inequality and domination (Carspecken & Apple, 1992). Critical ethnography explicitly assumes that cultures are positioned unequally in power relations. Furthermore, critical ethnography sees descriptions of culture as shaped by the interests of the researcher, the sponsors of the project, the audience, and the dominant communities (Brewer, 2000).

Collaborative ethnography

Collaborative ethnography typically involves those studies in which two or more ethnographers coordinate their field efforts to gather data from a single setting. Collaborative ethnography presents special opportunities for expanding and improving the ways in which ethnographers present their work. For example, as Buford May and Pattillo-McCoy (2000) point out, in collaborative ethnography, at least two researchers view a particular setting and can compare their field notes, thereby highlighting more than one perspective of the complex social world of informants.

Virtual ethnography

Virtual ethnography is a new development in the field of ethnography which is now situated within a world saturated by multimedia technologies including recorded sound, still and moving images, and, of course, the Internet. Virtual ethnography attempts to maintain the values of traditional ethnography by providing a "thick" description through the immersion of the researcher in the lives of their informants. Virtual ethnography is not forwarded as a new method to replace the old; rather it is a way of bringing into focus both the assumptions on which ethnography is based and the features which are specific to the technologies involved. The key question for virtual ethnographers is "how can ethnography be pursued in technologically mediated settings?"

Mason (2001) describes virtual ethnography as follows:

> A virtual ethnography is one that fully immerses the ethnographer into the consensual reality experienced by groups of people who use computer-mediated communication as the primary, and often only, means of communication. As such, the online or virtual persona of the participants is the main focus of the ethnographer. Generally, researchers have wanted to focus on the person on the keyboard; a virtual ethnographer reverses this and works instead with the persona that has been projected into cyberspace by the typist. This is not the only way to do fieldwork via the Internet but it is useful and it helps to realize that when we do participant observation we usually do it in the same medium in which the culture we study is communicated (p. 63).

Hine (2000) argues that our understanding of the Internet and its denizens has been limited, in part, by a tendency of scholars to examine it either as a cultural context, in the sense that it is socially constructed and discursively performed, a cultural artifact, a technology shaped by the practices and products of users. It is, in fact, both, and failure to recognize the indeterminacy will obscure the "processes through which the [online/ off] boundary is itself constructed" (p. 39). In other words, the Internet is both a culture and also a cultural artifact. As Hine notes, the object of ethnographic inquiry can be usefully reshaped by concentrating on the flow and connectivity rather than location and boundary as the organizing principle.

Data Collection and Analytic Processes in Ethnography

Data collection

In ethnographic studies, as in GT, data drive theory. There is no way to determine in advance the exact instrumentation that will be used because only the human instrument has the characteristics necessary to cope with an indeterminate situation (Lincoln & Guba, 1985; 1994) characteristic of the ethnographic approach. Both the site and individuals and subgroups at a site must be selected. As noted earlier, participant observation is the primary data collection tool in ethnography; secondary forms of data collection include artifacts and physical trace evidence, archival materials and demographic data banks, and gathering stories, myths, and rituals.

Van Maanen (1979a) distinguishes between presentational and operational data. Operational data are derived from the running stream of conversations and activities engaged in and observed by the ethnographer while in the field. Presentational data, on the other hand, are assembled from appearances that informants strive to maintain (or enhance) in the eyes of the field worker, outsiders and strangers in general, work colleagues, close and intimate associates, and to varying degrees, themselves. Data in this category, as the author notes, are often ideological, normative, and abstract, dealing far more with a manufactured image of idealized doing rather than with routinized practical activities actually engaged in by members of the studied organization. In short, operational data deal with observed activity (behavior per se), and presentational data deal with the appearances put forth by informants as these activities are talked about and otherwise symbolically projected with in the research setting (p. 542).

To collect data, the ethnographer engages in extensive fieldwork, gathering information through observations, interviews, and other materials helpful in creating a portrait and the rules of the culture sharing group. Fieldwork includes gaining access to the group through gatekeepers, locating key informants, and dealing with reciprocity issues (between the ethnographer and the informants) and reactivity issues or the impact of the ethnographer on the site being studied and the informants.

Participant observation demands complete commitment to the task of understanding the world of the informants. The ethnographer becomes part of the setting being studied, a fact known as going native. In addition to the time required, participant observation saps the emotional energy of the researcher. According to Reeves Sanday (1979), the ethnographer who becomes immersed in other people's realities is never quite the same afterwards. The author speculates that total immersion creates a kind of disorientation—culture shock—arising from the need to identify with and at the same time remain distant from the process being studied (p. 527).

Besides participant observation and recorded interactions with informants, other data sources may be derived from life histories (Darnell, 2001), narrative analysis (Cortazzi, 2001), and photography and audio or video recordings (Nastasi, 1999).

Data analysis and interpretation

The first step after all the data have been collected is to create a description of the cultural group studied. During the analysis stage, analytic induction and constant comparison may be used. One of the most popular analytic procedures is the search for patterned regularities in the data which produces a detailed description of the informants and analysis of the culture sharing group by themes and patterns. Ethnographers look for patterns from which they construct a cultural narrative in an attempt to make sense of different cultural contexts. The interpretation stage is characterized by theoretical consolidation, theoretical application, the use of metaphors, similes and analogy, and synthesis. There are no formal rules for analyzing ethnographic data.

Strengths and weaknesses of the ethnographic method

Ethnographic research can result in science or fiction depending on how the ethnographer interprets or explains his or her experiences in the field. Using systematic data collection procedures and basing analysis on such collected data is a key aspect of quality assurance in the ethnographic study. High regard is also held for explaining behavior from the emic perspective although not necessarily exclusively from this point of view as the philosophical stance of the ethnographer(s) may also dictate certain criteria for judging the value of an ethnographic study.

Ethnographers have been criticized for producing fictional accounts which are neither valid nor reliable and in no way "scientific." The "so what" factor of ethnographic accounts leave consumers of ethnographic research searching for more scientifically rigorous research which often results from studies that are more nomothetic in nature. Numerous ethnographers argue that new means of judging ethnographic research are required. Consensus appears to favor the criteria of credibility (over validity), transferability (over generalizability), dependability (over reliability), and a fourth particularly related to knowledge claims in qualitative research—confirmability. The criteria for judging the descriptive adequacy of a completed ethnography are at once simple and complex. Wolcott (1999) suggests that the quality of ethnographic research is to be evaluated by the ability of a stranger to a culture (the ethnographer) to use ethnographic statements as instructions for appropriately anticipating the scenes of society. Richardson (2000) believes in holding all ethnography to high and difficult standards and proposes five criteria to evaluate ethnographic research: (1) substantive contribution; (2) aesthetic merit; (3) reflexivity; (4) intellectual and emotional impact; and (5) expresses a reality, that is, a credible cultural or social account or communal sense of the "real" (p. 254).

Applications of Ethnography in Leadership Research

Searching the extant leadership literature for ethnographic studies produced few studies, at least in the major leadership and closely related journals. Table 7-2 summarizes the few studies that were located in the published literature.

Maitlis and Lawrence (2007) classified their study of triggers and enablers of sense giving in organizations as a longitudinal ethnography which was conducted over a two-year period of time in three British orchestras. The authors argued that orchestras share many characteristics with other business organizations including products (concerts and recording) which must be marketed and sold and customers that need to be satisfied. Structurally, orchestras also resemble midsized firm in that they have an administrative

Table 7-2   Applications of ethnography in leadership research

Author(s)	Purpose	Participants	Data sources	Analyses
Maitlis and Lawrence (2007)	To investigate the conditions associated with sense giving by stakeholders and leaders and identify triggers and enablers of sense giving	Members of three British orchestras	Formal interviews, meeting observations, documents, rehearsals, orchestra tours	Development of narratives of sense making; identification of first- & second-order concepts associate with sense giving through constant comparison methods; document analysis
Holmberg and Akerblom (2001)	To explore images of outstanding leadership presented in the Swedish media	N/A	853 media statements about leadership	Content analysis of selected phrases and articles; categorization of key words resulting in 60 categories; identification of underlying leadership themes
Pielstick (1988)	To describe an analysis of the leadership literature to identify themes and patterns that describe transforming leadership	Community college leader as portrayed in data sources	Research and writings of senior contemporary leadership scholars and studies of transformational leadership in community colleges	Meta-ethnography; constant comparison; ETHNOGRAPH software; open, axial, and selective coding

Adler (1996)	To identify global women leaders who have led modern countries and government	25 global women leaders as portrayed in data sources	Database on global leaders from academic books, articles, newspaper, and magazine reports, archival documentary footage from BBC and U.S. television networks	Meta-ethnography; grounded theory
O'Connor, et al. (1995)	To test a model of personality constructs found to contribute to destructive behaviors of charismatic leaders	82 male historical leaders; 44 classified as socialized and 38 as personalized charismatic leaders	History texts, biographical listings; encyclopedias; responses to personality measures of fear; need for power; narcissism	Interrater reliabilities .70–85; descriptive statistics; *t*-tests; intercorrelations; MANCOVAs and ANCOVAS; LISREL V
Gioia and Chittipeddi (1991)	To examine the initiation of a strategic change effort in a large, public university to make the university a "Top 10" institution	President, Provost, and other senior executives	Multiple taped interviews, ethnographer's diary of events, internal memos, confidential reports	Search for patterns and themes; qualitative content analysis; analysis of data across informants for patterns of divergence and convergence; extracting theoretical dimensions; integrating patterns into theoretical framework

team consisting of finance, marketing, and human resources functions and are headed by a CEO who reports to the board. The authors agree with Allmendinger and Hackman (1996) that with numerous powerful and diverse stakeholders, orchestras offer a context wherein sense giving behaviors are important and visible.

Data were collected using semistructured interviews with the executive director and every member of the management teams, principal conductor, and all musicians who served as representatives on the board and committees for each of the three orchestras that participated in this study. In total, the first author conducted 120 interviews, of which 106 were recorded and transcribed. The early interviews focused on the orchestra members' organizational roles, the main issues they encountered, and descriptions of their own sense giving and that of others. In addition, the first author collected data in 107 meetings she observed including meetings of various groups within each orchestra (e.g., executive team and board) and meetings between orchestra leaders and external stakeholders (e.g., funding organizations). Finally, a variety of documents including reports, newsletter, meeting minutes, policy documents, and organizational appraisal documents were included.

The authors analyzed the large sets of data in three phases. In the first phase, they created narratives of the sense making process drawing from interview quotes, meetings, documents, and field notes, each chronicling sense making associated with an issue domain in an orchestra. An organizational issue was defined as a topic of discussion that involved a question or concern that was connected with the organization as a whole. Examples of domain issues include "appointment of second concert master" or "improving orchestra's stage presence" (Maitlis & Lawrence, 2007, p. 61). Following Strauss and Corbin (1998), data were reduced to categories broad enough to address issues that arose in all three orchestras. Principal conductor appointment was one such issue. In this first phase of the analysis, nine issue domains were identified and a narrative of 5–25 single-spaced pages that captured the sense making activities for each of these issue domains in each orchestra resulting in a total of 27 narratives.

In the second phase of the analyses, the authors identified stakeholders and leaders engaged in sense giving based on previous findings which showed that there are significant differences between leader and stakeholder responsibilities for sense giving. For each of the 27 issue domains, leaders and stakeholders were classified as sense giving or nonsense giving. Finally, in the third phase, the authors identified the conditions associated with leader and stakeholder sense giving by identifying first- and second-order concepts. In this phase, the Glaser and Straus (1967) method of constant comparison was used. Through this process, the authors produced two lists, one associated with stakeholder sense giving and the other with leader sense giving. In addition, they used axial coding to distill more abstract descriptions of the conditions associated with stakeholder and leader sense giving.

Among the results of this complex and intensive series of analyses were the following: (1) stakeholder sense giving was associated with their perceptions that an issue such as stakeholder compensation was important and (2) sense giving by stakeholders was associated with "perceptions of a lack of leader competence" (p. 67). Enabling conditions facilitating stakeholder sense giving included possession of relevant expertise based on professional training and opportunities for engaging in sense giving behaviors. Leader sense giving, on the other hand, was associated with leaders' perceptions of an issue as uncertain, ambiguous, or unpredictable. For example, the CEO of one orchestra described the ambiguity associated with assessing the strength and weaknesses of a conductor. Another condition that triggered leader sense giving was an association of an issue's association with complex stakeholder issues. For example, one of the orchestra leaders described programming in the orchestra to illustrate the theme of stakeholder complexity as programming involves a large number of different stakeholders ranging from members of the board to part-time artistic advisors and external consultants. Conditions enabling leader sense giving included the leader's expertise and credibility relating to the domain issue and performance of the organization in the issue domain such as achieving good financial returns and harvesting a surplus at the end of the season. The article concludes with a conceptual model of conditions associated with sense giving triggers and enablers for both stakeholder and leader groups.

Holmberg and Akerblom (2001) used an ethnographic semantics method to analyze descriptions of outstanding leadership in five major Swedish printed media to identify the culturally specific characteristics of a particular Swedish leadership style. According to Agar (1996), ethnographic semantics is "semantics" because it deals with words, and it is "ethnographic" because the aim is to create and resolve "rich points" or empirical observations that do not make sense from the researcher's point of view and that therefore suggest a gap between two worlds of knowledge. Central to this approach to ethnography is the idea that an understanding of a particular culture emerges from the exploration of concepts (relevant to leadership) that are tied together within a particular culture.

As we have seen in Chapter 4, the media plays an important role in shaping views of leadership and produce their own implicit theories of leadership (Chen & Meindl, 1991) that are an expression of the national culture at large. Hence, the central question in this study was whether or not a possibly unique Swedish leadership style was an expression of the Swedish culture. Several authors earlier identified distinguishing characteristics of the Swedish leadership style or Scandinavian management to include a preference for teamwork and cooperation, a strong focus on performance, the ability to create consensus, the acceptance of challenges and risk taking, and frequent and direct dialogue among organizational members. Edström and Jönsson (1998) described the Swedish leadership as follows:

> Swedish leadership is vague and imprecise [. . .] a typical Swedish order is "See what you can do about it!" What does this mean? Obviously it has to do with

delegation of authority. Managers who say "See what you can do about it!" are demonstrating trust in their co-workers. It is also a matter of the exercise of control by a common understanding of the problem rather than by giving direct orders. This must be regarded as strength of the egalitarian Swedish society (p. 167).

Ethnographic descriptions of the Swedish culture have noted the sharp differentiation between private and public life with Swedes being fundamentally individualist in the private sphere and collectivistic in the public sphere. In addition, Swedes have a preference for independence, solitude, and pragmatism.

The sample in the Holmberg and Akerblom (2001) consisted of five major Swedish newspapers examined over two two-week periods resulting in the identification of over 8000 articles. These articles were then scanned for key words and phrases pertaining to leadership. The 853 key words that emerged were categorized into 60 categories which included accountable, delegator, ethical, reasonable and pragmatic, and strategic and entrepreneurial. The five categories with the highest frequencies among the 60 categories which represented 20.5 percent of the key words were action-oriented, working for equality, communicative and verbal, and enthusiastic and inspiring. After an iterative process of framing, testing, and reframing the links between the 60 categories, the authors arrived at the following description of an outstanding Swedish leader:

> Performance and action oriented, charismatic and visible within and outside the organization, honest, modest, pragmatic, a good team builder, working for egalitarian consensus, entrepreneurial and procedural (p. 78).

However, a number of paradoxes were noted in this description of an outstanding Swedish leader. For example, how can a leader be both entrepreneurial, meaning being bold, audacious, and prone to taking considerable risks and procedural, meaning the opposite: being a careful planner and organizer who avoids taking any risks?

The authors then returned to the original data sources and conducted a new analysis by splitting the articles into two groups: a private business group and a political group. By grouping the data according to context, two implicit models of leadership emerged. Charisma was an aspect of leadership that was very much prevalent in the business context while action orientation, egalitarianism, consensus, modesty, and honesty described outstanding leadership in the political context. The distinguishing characteristics in business leadership were performance orientation, team-building, an entrepreneurial approach, and visibility. Thus, the institutional contexts, business, and politics provided significantly different implicit models of leadership within the same cultural framework (i.e., the Swedish welfare state), emphasizing that excellent leadership is exercised and enacted as an expression of socially constructed institutions and culturally grounded values (Holmberg & Akerblom, p. 83).

The next two entries in Table 7-2 (Adler, 1996; Pielstick, 1988) employed meta-ethnography, a research methodology that has its quantitative counterpart in meta-analysis. Meta-analyses are quantitative reviews of a body of literature on a specific topic; its counterpart, meta-ethnography synthesizes a body of existing qualitative research. As an interpretive methodology, meta-ethnography has been described as

> [our] meta-ethnographic approach enables a rigorous procedure for deriving substantive interpretations about any set of ethnographic or interpretive studies... A meta-ethnography can be considered a complete study in itself. [Meta-ethnography compares and analyzes texts, creating new interpretations in the process. It is much more than what we usually mean by a literature review] (Noblit & Hare, 1988, p. 9).

Adler's (1996) study of global leaders, for example, sampled 25 women who served as presidents and prime ministers of their countries around the globe in countries as diverse as Sri Lanka, Ireland, Turkey, India, Pakistan, and the former Yugoslavia. These women leaders came from heterogeneous family, economic and religious backgrounds, and were highly educated internationally. The majority were elected rather than appointed, and only one woman (Isabel Péron of Argentina) inherited her position. Although some women came to senior leadership positions of the countries because either by birth or marriage they came from highly prominent, political families (e.g., Corazon Aquino of the Philippines, Indira Gandhi of India, or Benazir Bhutto of Pakistan), most of the women leaders came to power without family connections. As Adler points out, contrary to popular belief, dynastic family ties, while extremely influential, are not strong enough to allow the widowed wife or daughter of a political leader to automatically inherit national leadership. All of the other women from dynastic families had to campaign, often for years, before they were personally elected. This meta-ethnography also showed that when examining the patter from a geographical perspective, it is evident that in Asian and Latin-American countries that have had women leaders, membership in a politically dynastic family is an extremely important, and perhaps even necessary, precondition for national leadership. With the exception of Isabel Péron, in all other cases, the women had to demonstrate leadership skills beyond family membership to gain sufficient popular and/or party support to be successfully elected (Adler, 1996, p. 144). Thus, synthesizing the literature from a variety of data sources including autobiographies and second-party results, the author was able to draw an interesting picture of the complexities of female global leadership over a period of more than 25 five years beginning with the first elections of national women leaders commencing with Sirimavo Bandarnaike (Sri Lanka in 1960), Indira Gandhi (1966), and Golda Meir (Israel in 1969) and following the emergence of global women leader to the mid-1990s.

Pielstick's meta-ethnography of the transforming leader employed a comprehensive analysis of the research and writings of senior contemporary leadership scholars including Bass (1985), Burns (1978; 2003), Bennis and Nanus (1985), and Kouzes and Pozner (1995) as well as studies of transformational leadership in community colleges and other educational organizations. The author created literature groups around each researcher or topic which were coded and analyzed using the software program ETHNOGRAPH. This software is designed to facilitate coding, sorting, and retrieving and the process of identifying patterns, themes, and categories across large volumes of data-based data. The analyses included many features of GT although no attempt was made to identify a single core category of transforming leadership. Instead, seven major themes emerged from the analysis to capture the composite profile of the transforming community college leader: (1) creating a shared vision; (2) communicating the visions; (3) building relationships; (4) developing a supporting organizational culture; (5) guiding implementation; (6) exhibiting character; and (7) achieving results. Taken together, these two studies illustrate how meta-ethnography can be used to conduct a synthesis of qualitative research and other secondary data sources.

In the studies reviewed in this section, it is also interesting to note that three of the studies (Gioia & Chittipeddi, 1991; Maitlis & Lawrence, 2007; Pratt, 2000) addressed sequential cycles of sense making and sense giving as explanatory constructs in very different contexts. According to Gioia and Chittipeddi, who studied the president of a large public university, sense giving involves "attempting to influence the sensemaking process . . . toward a preferred redefinition of organizational reality. It is the process of attempting to influence the sensemaking and meaning construction of others toward a preferred definition of organizational reality" (1991, p. 442). In this research, the sense giving agent was a new university president who used a range of sense giving tactics including holding meetings to espouse his vision and "disclosing intentions through hypothetical scenario presentations" in order to initiate and facilitate change (Gioia & Chittipeddi, 1991, pp. 442–443).

In the Pratt study, sense giving was facilitated for Amway distributors by practices such as forming cohesive groups or co-opting nonmembers. Both studies reveal the significant role that leader sense giving can play in effecting major change or serving as a trigger for major organizational change, a finding echoed in several other studies (e.g., Corley & Goia, 2004). Sense giving is not only an important activity of leaders but is also employed by stakeholders and board of directors who shape corporate strategy. Maitlis and Lawrence (2007) showed that routines, practices, and structures that give organizational leaders time and opportunity to engage in sense giving enable sense giving.

HISTORIOMETRY

An Illustrative Historiometric Leadership Study

Deluga (2001) studied the relationships among American presidential Machiavellianism measured by the Mach IV (Christie & Geis, 1970) scale, charismatic leadership both close and distant, and rated performance assessed by two archival measured of the constructs consensus of greatness and mean greatness. The author postulated two hypotheses: (1) American presidential Machiavellianism will be positively associated with close and distant charismatic leadership and (2) American presidential Machiavellianism will be positively associated with rated performance. Thirty-nine presidents from Washington to Regan made up the sample. To measure presidential Machiavellianism, Simonton's (1997; 1998) method of generating profiles was replicated. Simonton assembled profiles by using personality characterizations verbatim from various presidential fact sources and biographical materials. Three raters independently judged Machiavellianism (Cronbach $\alpha = .85$) for one of the 39 presidential profiles. The presidential charismatic and creative style scores also generated by Simonton (1988) were employed as measures of presidential leadership. The research hypotheses were tested using hierarchical regression analysis confirming the first hypothesis that presidential Machiavellianism was positively correlated with close and distant charismatic leadership. Additionally, the second hypothesis that Machiavellianism was positively correlated with rated performance was also supported. The author concluded that with American presidents, Machiavellianism appears to predict charismatic leadership and rated performance and that effective presidents may display a mixture of charismatic and Machiavellian leadership (p. 355).

Defining Historiometry

Historiometry examines biographical materials of prominent individuals by employing quantitative assessment without former theoretical commitment. A number of researchers have shown how psychologists can use biographical data to provide personality profiles of eminent leaders (e.g., Winter, 1987). Such profiles can then be compared with the existing literature concerning personality variables that moderate an individual's response to the trials and tribulations of living. Deluga (2001) has shown that historiometry includes the use of modified personality instruments along with biographical information and argues that historiometry strives to verify personality patterns from the specific (idiographic) to the general (nomothetic) across a sample of cases (Simonton, 1984a; 1986; 1999). In addition to developing personality profiles of leaders, historiometric methods can also be used to scrutinize more closely the dynamics of their character over the life span.

Data Collection and Analysis in Historiometry

The samples in most historiometric studies typically consist of historical figures such as American presidents, the first ladies of US presidents, or Olympic athletes, whose lives need some type of psychological interpretation (Elms, 1994). Simonton (1976) argued that the most eminent individuals in a domain are not only the most representative of the phenomenon of interest, but information about such individuals is likely to be more extensive and reliable.

According to Simonton (1990), there are two primary types of historical data, primary and secondary. The most commonly used primary source is the written document. Some of these documents may be public, such as campaign speeches, inaugural addresses, diplomatic communiqués, court decisions, poems, short stories, publication titles, and journal abstracts, whereas others may be private, such as correspondence and diaries. Secondary sources, in contrast, provide information by historians and other scholars. The most common sources are biographies, histories, biographical diction-aries, bibliographies, and obituaries (Simonton, 2003).

Increasingly, historical records appear in electronic forms, especially with the advent of the World Wide Web, thereby accelerating richness of the historical database. Data of historical records can be analyzed quantitatively or qualitatively although, as shown in the following section, most historiometric studies make ample use of univariate and multivariate statistics.

Applications of Historiometry in Leadership Research

Most of the applications of historiometric methods are found in the area of political leadership although some scholars (e.g., Simonton, 1984a) have also investigated composers, playwrights of acknowledged masterpieces such as Shakespeare, and other forms of artistic expressions such as operas and paintings (Simonton, 1998). For example, as early as in the nineteenth century, a Belgian mathematician, Adolphe Quetelet, studied the relationship between age and achievement by studying the careers of prominent French and English playwrights, work that is generally treated as the introduction of historiometry. Sir Francis Galton toward the end of the nineteenth century continued to popularize historiometry in his 1969 book, *Hereditary Genius*, in which he showed a correlation between reputation, intelligence, and heredity. Simonton (1989), one of the most prominent contemporary historiometry researchers, noted that historiometry often entails psychobiographical elements which are ideographic, quali-tative, and single case along with historiometry which is nomothetic, quantitative, and multiple cases. Simonton himself seems to emphasize the latter approach.

Table 7-3 presents a sampling of historiometric studies located in the leadership literature.

Table 7-3   Selected examples of historiometric studies in leadership research

Author(s)	Purpose	Research participants	Data sources	Analyses
Deluga (2001)	To study the relationships among American presidential Machiavellianism, charismatic leadership, and rated performance	39 American presidents (Washington to Regan)	Archival data; two measures of close charismatic leadership, two measures of distant charismatic leadership, 20-item Mach IV scale, and two measures of presidential rated performance; presidential fact sources and standard biographical volumes	Interrater reliability $r = .87$; hierarchical regression analysis
Deluga (1997a)	To examine the relationships of American presidential narcissistic behaviors with charismatic leadership and rated performance	39 American presidents from Washington to Regan	Biographical sources, presidential fact books, Narcissistic Personality Inventory (NPI), presidential charismatic and creative leadership style; 5 performance measures derived from archival data	Descriptive statistics; interrater agreement (eta coefficient) = .80; hierarchical regression analysis
Simonton (1991a)	To determine the career pattern of 120 classical composers	120 famous composers from Renaissance to twentieth century	Biographical information and career measures	Correlation and regression analyses

Deluga (2001), in a study very similar to Deluga (2003) presented at the opening of this section, examined the relationships of American presidential narcissistic behaviors and charismatic leadership and rated performance. The author hypothesized that narcissism will be positively related to both presidential charisma and performance. The sample consisting of the same 39 American presidents from Washington to Regan was used. Presidential profiles were prepared by abstracting personality descriptions verbatim from numerous standard biographical sources and presidential fact books. All profiles were rated for narcissism based on the Narcissistic Personality Inventory (NPI), and archival sources were used for two measures of charismatic leadership style (charisma and creative) and five performance measures including consensus of greatness, war avoidance, war entry, and great decisions cited. For each profile, three raters assessed presidential narcissism resulting in an interrater agreement of .80. The regression analyses showed that presidential narcissism explained a significant amount of variance in charisma (30 percent, $p < .01$), creativity (25 percent, $p < .01$), war avoidance (30 percent, $p < .01$), mean greatness (26 percent, $p < .01$), and consensus of greatness (32 percent) and great decisions cited (37 percent, $p < .01$). Using Roosevelt as an example, the author concluded that narcissism may be a key factor in presidential charismatic leadership and effective performance. Roosevelt's self-assurance, persuasive skills, and inflated favorable self-evaluation may have produced a personal magnetism necessary for the dramatic consequences of charismatic leadership. (p. 60).

The same author (Deluga, 1997) published another study following the same historio-metric procedures and sample to examine the relationship between American presidential proactivity, defined as a stable personality disposition to influence, charismatic leadership, and presidential performance. With the exception of the seventeen-item Proactive Person-ality Scale, the remaining variables were operationalized using the same measures employed in the other two historiometric studies conducted by the author. Again, pre-sidential proactivity explained significant amounts of incremental variance in four of the five performance measures (mean greatness, consensus of greatness, war avoidance, and great decisions cited) and both measures of charisma (charismatic and creative style).

O'Connor, Munford, Clifton, and Gessner (1995) tested a model of destructiveness based on differential personal characteristics to explain personalized versus socialized charis-matic leadership. Based on previous research, the authors identified seven personality constructs as predictors of destructive behaviors of the two types of charismatic leaders: (1) uncertainty outcome (or the degree to which the leader believed he or she would not get what was desired or valued because the world is uncertain and constantly changing); (2) need for power; (3) object beliefs (or viewing individuals as instruments to be used to achieve one's own goals; (4) negative life themes (or the extent to which the leader had a destructive view of the world; (5) narcissism (or the leader's propensity to exaggerate his or her achievements; extreme self-interest and selfishness on the part of the leader; (6) fear; and (7) self-regulation. The authors assembled a sample of 82 historical figures that were classified by independent judges as personalized or socialized charismatic leaders. All leaders were male and represented a variety of contexts including political, religious, business, and military. Of the 82 leaders, 44 were socialized (i.e., Charles De Gaulle, Andrew Carnegie, Winston Churchill, Dwight Eisenhower, Bishop Desmond Tutu, and Lech Walesa) and 38 were personalized (i.e., John DeLorean, Howard Hughes, Benito Mussolini, Jimmy Hoffa, Jim Bakker, and Fidel Castro) charismatic leaders. All leaders in the sample had to meet the criterion of having brought change or transformations to their organizations to qualify for inclusion.

In addition to evaluating leaders in terms of type of charisma, raters also classified them according to their ability to attribute destructive or constructive outcomes to each leader at the pinnacle of his career. A destructive leader was defined as an individual whose behaviors clearly harmed his or her organization or society, whereas constructive leader was defined as an individual whose actions clearly benefited the organization or society (O'Connor et al., 1995, p. 536). Five psychologists had to unanimously agree upon the assignment of each leader into these two categories. After these categorizations were made, independent judges read a single chapter in the leaders' biographies describing the individual's rise to power and a second chapter (labeled outcome chapter), which provided a summary of the leader's organizational and historical contributions.

The authors conducted a complex series of analysis including content-coding of destructive and constructive behaviors of charismatic leaders; interrater reliability for predictor variables from .70 to 85; means, standard deviations, t-tests, intercorrelations, MANOVA: discriminate function analysis, and LISREL, a linear structural equation modeling program. The path coefficients from these latter analyses indicated direct and indirect influences of the variables of interest. The results showed that a syndrome involving high need for power, object beliefs, negative life themes, outcome uncertainty, narcissism, and fear was found to be indicated of harm to the social system. Taken together, the results from these analyses lend considerable support to arguments for the model characteristics differentiating personalized leaders capable of considerable long-term harm to an organization from their more socialized counterparts (p. 549).

Simonton (1991a) analyzed the career course and success of 120 eminent composers from the renaissance to the twentieth century replicating a study the author conducted with eminent scientists (Simonton, 1991b) and based on a theoretical model developed to explain how creative productivity varies over the life span (Simonton, 1984b). This study was also an extension of earlier research (Simonton, 1977) in which the author studied 10 classical composers. As in the previous study, some of the composers like Mozart were child prodigies; others like Händel were late bloomers. As Simonton points out, because of the highly specialized expertise required for musical composition, composers tend to work solo compared to other creative artists and lead somewhat unusual lives.

To assess the composers on posthumous reputation, Simonton used a six-item composite measure of performance frequencies, age at which the composer produced the first successful melody (first hit), the age at which the last successful theme was produced (last hit), and total lifetime output. In addition, the author extracted information from the biographies of the composers which included complete catalogs of all major and minor works, levels of stress, and physical illnesses. Based on these measures, the results showed that the typical eminent composer obtained his first hit at age 31, his best hit at age 41, and last hit around 50. Maximum productivity was achieved around 37 when nearly four works appeared although there was quite a bit of variance among the composers sampled. Lifetime output correlated positively with maximum annual output and age at last hit and negatively with age at first hit. The ages at first lessons and first composition were also correlated indicating that creative musical output does not emerge as a result of a burst of inspiration but ensues after ample and arduous preparation. For example, the average age of first lessons was around 9 and compositions began around 17, but again with consider-able variation. Musical preparation was between 17 and 22 years, with a range of 0–48 years. Moreover, the data showed that a long period of musical and compositional preparation indicated an inferior prognosis for productivity and distinction once historical placement was controlled for (p. 873). The total productivity of a composer at the end of his career was a function of the age at first hit, the maximum annual output, and the age of last hit. These three variables demarcate the beginning, peak, and end of a composer's career course. In essence, the career pattern for composers was similar to that observed for eminent scientists and inventors (Simonton, 1991b).

Like any method in leadership research, historiometry and the analyses of historical data have both advantages and disadvantages. Simonton (2003) suggests the single most important reason for analyzing historical data is that such analyses permit the investiga-tion of research topics that cannot be addressed any other way. Historical records contain information about events and personalities of great practical importance. As a result, these data have great values for researchers wishing to deal with significant and important problems in the real world. Recent advances in statistical analysis such as latent variable models, time series analysis, and hierarchical linear models have made historical records a far more useful source of scientific data. On the negative side, quantitative analyses of historical data are typically correlational and have low internal validity. Historical data are also not always reliable and contain errors in information gaps that can contaminate the analysis, whether qualitative or quantitative. Finally, historical data have limited theoretical or substantive applicability.

Summary

In contrast to phenomenology and ethnography which fall on the more qualitative end of the continuum of qualitative methods, historiometric studies include a range of quantitative analyses. It is a highly specialized research method that has been most frequently been applied to the study of political leaders examining subjective personality traits ratings such as creativity, charisma, genius, and intelligence, a few studies have extended historiometry to the study of scientists and artists. Although it may be argued that historiometry basically falls into the mixed method design category because it includes statistical analyses and psychometrics as well as subjective assessments of, for example, the greatness of deceased politicians, it is included in this chapter to illustrate the lack of a clear typology of methods while also showing the contrast between highly qualitative methods such as phenomenology and ethnography and highly quantitative methods such as historiometry both of which are categorized as qualitative methods. It is interesting to note, however, how much this particular methodology is dominated by one or, at the most, two researchers (Simonton and Deluga).

8

PHENOMENOLOGY AND NARRATIVE ANALYSIS

AN ILLUSTRATIVE PHENOMENOLOGICAL LEADERSHIP STUDY

Wong and Slater (2002) reported a phenomenological study which examined the extent to which executive career development in the PRC corresponds to Western career patterns. This phenomenological study was designed to determine whether there are specific factors relating to Chinese executives' career paths. The authors briefly reviewed the sociopolitical context of China before and after the recent social reforms and the impact these reforms had on managerial careers. They noted that Chinese cultural traditions stemming from Confucian values attach considerable importance to hierarchical relationships. "Guanxi" or the direct and indirect personal relationships in organizations provide moral guidelines for the Chinese as to their behavior within family clans and in society at large. More pragmatically, as the authors stated, Chinese managers believe that making use of good personal guanxi relationship can help them to get things done more efficiently and effectively. Guanxi relationships are anchored culturally according to social class, seniority and age, and status or position in the family clan and in society. Before the Communists came to power, the classification of jobs and their importance in society were based on Confucian values. With the advent of communism, however, the traditional Chinese career paths were dismantled and along with lifelong employment.

As China transitioned from a socialist to an open market economy, many state-owned enterprises were restructured or closed. As a result, China's long established centrally planned employment system moved to a more market-oriented structure characterized by an extensive labor contract system. The new system affords managers greater mobility and also introduced reward systems which led to more competitive attitudes among managers as Chinese companies established links between performance and reward (Wong & Slater, p. 342). The authors hypothesized that the opening of labor markets in China is leading to a replication of Western style market allocation of labor and that Western career theories offer adequate explanations in the Chinese context. In addition, they proposed that guanxi, based upon Chinese traditions, is a critical factor driving successful promotions to increasingly more responsible managerial positions.

Wong and Slater (2002) conducted a pilot study to profile Chinese managers' careers and identify themes found in interviews with Chinese managers describing their career pathways. Forty-nine managers in Beijing and Shanghai, working for state-owned enterprises, privately owned companies, joint ventures, and foreign-owned firms, were selected using snowball sampling. Interviews were conducted with Chinese-born executives who had a track record in business management in China to ensure that relevant data tracking job progression to a managerial position could be extracted. Most of the informants in this study came from computer and engineering academic backgrounds.

Emergent themes form the pilot interviews were analyzed but because at the time of publication, the study was still ongoing and, therefore, interpretations are provisional in nature. One of the themes was the belief that most managers indicated that their talents and knowledge were underutilized by their companies. They also believed that maintaining good guanxi and flexibility in dealing with people were important compensations for their deficiencies in management education stating that good guanxi with subordinates and top management, besides enhancing team spirit could also facilitate career progress. From the preliminary results of the study, Wong and Slater (2002) concluded that Chinese managerial career progress seems very much influenced by changes in the social and political environments, along with personal factors such as education, personal values, family upbringing, and life experience (p. 253). Furthermore, changes from a closed to an open market system are forcing managers to reevaluate their belief systems and values as Chinese cultural traditions are continually undermined by current political and economic changes.

INTRODUCTION TO PHENOMENOLOGY

Defining Phenomenology

Broadly defined, phenomenology is defined as the study of phenomena: appearances of things, as they appear in our experience, or the way we experience things, and thus the meanings things have in our experiences. In essence, phenomenology studies various types of experiences derived from our perceptions, thoughts, memories, imagination, emotions, volition, embodied action, and social activity. All of these involve intentionality meaning that they are directed toward things in the world. Phenomenology concerns itself with the structure of our conscious experience as interpreted from the first-person point-of-view. It started as a philosophical movement of the structure of experience as it presents itself to consciousness, without recourse to theory, deduction, or assumptions from other disciplines such as the natural or social sciences. In the discussion of phenomenology as qualitative research method that follows, I have attempted to retain much of the language that evolved from the works of European philosophers on which this research tradition rests. The language of phenomenology is unique and clearly sets this approach apart from other qualitative research methods. But in this way, an attempt has been made to preserve the spirit of phenomenology.

As phenomenology is essentially the study of lived experience, it emphasizes the world as lived by a person, not the world or reality as something separate from the person (Valle, King, & Halling, 1989). Exploration of the inner world of experience by phenomenology enables researchers to reclaim that part of the human being that has been neglected by positivism or was inaccessible due to methodological constraint. The intent of phenomenological research is to understand the phenomena, in this case leadership phenomena, on their own terms to provide a credible description of human experience as it is experienced by the individual (Bentz & Shapiro, p. 96) and allowing the essence of that experience to emerge (Cameron, Schaffer, & Hyeon-Ae, 2001). The central structure of an experience is its intentionality or the way it is directed through its content or meaning toward a certain object in the world (Moran, 2000). Phenomenologists, in contrast to positivists, believe that researchers cannot be detached from their presuppositions and should not pretend otherwise (Hammersley, 2000).

A Brief History of Phenomenology: Husserl, Heidegger, and Gadamer

The practice of interpretation, or hermeneutics, dates to seventeenth century biblical and theological textual interpretations and has followed a changing course from rationalism to pragmatism to philosophy, and conservatism to radicalization (Grondin, 1994). However, phenomenology gained momentum as philosophical movement in the twentieth century when the three central figures, Husserl, Heidegger, and Gadamer, began publishing their works and engaging the public in philosophical discourse.

Edmund Husserl (1889–1928) is often called the father of phenomenology. Phenomenological philosophy, according to Husserl, was intended to be a science of consciousness. Husserl rejected the belief that objects in the external world exist independently and that information about these objects is reliable. Instead, to arrive at certainty, anything outside immediate experience must be ignored, and in this way, the external world is reduced to the contents of personal consciousness. He named his philosophical method "phenomenology," the science of pure phenomena (Eagleton, 1983, p. 55). Phenomenology came into being in the context of the ideological crises surrounding Europe at the end of World War I. Eagleton (1983) explains:

> The social order of capitalism had been shaken to its roots by the carnage of the war and its turbulent aftermath. The ideologies on which that order customarily depended, the cultural values by which it ruled, were also in deep turmoil. Science seemed to have dwindled to sterile positivism, a myopic obsession with the categorizing of facts; philosophy appeared torn between such a positivism on the one hand, and an indefensible subjectivism on the other; forms of relativism and irrationalism were rampant, and art reflected the bewildering loss of bearings (p. 54).

It is in this context, Husserl "sought to develop a new philosophical method which would lend absolute certainty to a disintegrating civilization" (Eagleton, 1983, p. 54). The attraction of phenomenology for Husserl (1970) was its promise as a new science of being. He purported that mind and object both occur within experience, thus eliminating mind–body dualism. Valle, et al. (1989) reported that Husserl viewed consciousness as a co-constituted dialogue between a person and the world.

Husserl introduced the notion of lifeworld, or Lebenswelt, a concept that characterizes our sense of a world that is present without our recognition or action (Smith, 1991). Strongly associated with the work of Husserl is the notion of intentionality which he understood as the movement of something beyond its point of initiation toward some intended meaning (Coltman, 1998). For Husserl, intentionality was an essential feature of consciousness. Because knowledge can only come through intentionality and because acts of cognition are conscious acts, the knower–known relationship is approached through intentionality (Giorgi, 1994, p. 203). Intentionality, therefore, refers to the fact that consciousness is always directed to an object that is not itself conscious. By intentionally directing one's focus, Husserl proposed, we could develop a description of specific realities (Edie, 1987). Furthermore, Husserl propositioned that all experience is shaped by the subjectivity of the interpreter (Husserl, 1952), an idea found in all phenomenological approaches. For example, Moustakas (1994) suggests that

> No position must be whatsoever must be taken…"nothing is determined in advance". The researcher remains present and focuses on his own consciousness by "returning to whatever is there in…memory, perception, judgment, feeling, whatever is actually there" (p. 94).

Martin Heidegger (1889–1976), a student of Husserl, created his own version of phenomenology known as existential phenomenology and introduced much of the language that sets phenomenology apart from other qualitative traditions. He articulated his views of our unsettled sense of *Dasein* or *being-in-the-world*, which fundamentally refers to how we make sense of the world, our place in it, and how we become aware of this place. Our being-in-the-world is a specific but holistic form of existence which emerges in reciprocal interdependence with other human beings. In other words, according to Heidegger (1962; 1998), we exist in a world where there is reciprocal interdependence between the self, others, and objects which slowly come to our awareness as the need arises. We interact with people in a transparent (or unaware) way without thinking much about what we are doing until we are stimulated by unusual thoughts, emotions, or events. At the point when we become aware, at some level, of what we are doing, we change our level of awareness and ways of interacting to fit the context. Understanding the world we inhabit is deeply entrenched in the profound ontological makeup of Dasein marked by care, existence, temporality, and being (Heidegger, 1962; 1996; 1998). Dasein is a thereness of being that is distinguished by the capacity for self-reflection on our existence. Heidegger maintained that human life is not given to us as a phenomenon which requires explication, but as a question, an address, something which is revealing and concealing, coming and going, present and absent.

Although Husserl was interested in acts of attending, perceiving, recalling, and thinking about the world and human beings were primarily understood as knowers, Heidegger viewed humans as being as individuals concerned with their fate in an alien world (Annells, 1996). Consciousness, according to Heidegger (1962/1927), is not separate from the world but is a formation of historically lived experience. He believed that understanding is a basic form of human existence in that understanding is not a way we know the world but rather the way we are (Polkinghorne, 1983). Through this understanding, one determines what is "real." Heidegger has been described as having a view of people and the world as indissolubly related in cultural, historical, and social contexts. In Heidegger's opinion, all understanding is connected to an individual's background as defined by his or her history. In fact, Heidegger went as far as to claim that nothing can be encountered without reference to a person's background, and meaning can only be constructed from our background and experiences.

Finally, Hans-Georg Gadamar (1900–2002) is a major figure in phenomenology based on his work on philosophical hermeneutics. Gadamer's work (1976; 1985; 1996) converged and diverged from Heidegger's work, reinforced and extended it, and showed areas of agreement as well as departure. Grondin (1995) argued that there is no question that contemporary hermeneutics received its most forceful and coherent exposition in the work of Hans-Georg Gadamer (p. xi), a student of both Husserl and Heidegger. Gadamer's (1989) extension of Heidegger's existential hermeneutic theory, for example, included the significance of the researcher, the importance of historical understanding of all interpretations, and a clarification of the fusion of horizons where horizon is seen as the range of vision which can be seen from a particular viewpoint. Understanding occurs when horizons of the other and ourselves fuse to extend the range of vision (Palmer, 1969). On the other hand, while Heidegger addressed time and temporality as an extension into the future, Gadamer embraced temporality as an extension of the past into the present (Coltman, 1998). However, Gadamer did not simply discard what he disliked of Heidegger's work; instead, he carried on in faith with many of Heidegger's concepts while also claiming an obligation to retrieve philosophy for use in the academic world. Given the centrality of the works of these writers, it is important for students of phenomenology to understand the basic tenets of his existential philosophy, preferably by reading the foundational works in the original language.

The writings of Husserl, Heidegger, and Gadamer and some others including Jean-Paul Sartre (1905–1980) and Maurice Merleau-Ponty (1908–1961), whose work extensively expanded the influence of Husserl and Heidegger (Vandenbeng, 1997) gave rise to distinctive branches within phenomenology including hermeneutic, existential, and transcendental phenomenology. These branches represent different philosophical approaches of conceptualizing experience and ways to organize and analyze phenomenological data. Moerer-Urdahl and Creswell (2004) note that these branches differ in their historical advocates (e.g., Heidegger or Husserl), methodological procedures (Laverty, 2003), and their current proponents (Van Maanen, 1990).

Data Collection, Analysis, and Interpretation

As in GT, the phenomenologist uses purposive or theoretical sampling in an effort to identify informants who can illuminate the phenomenon of interest and can communicate their experiences. The researcher begins with a full description of his or her experience with the phenomenon to be examined which is often documented in the form of field notes or memos. The data are usually collected through in-depth interviewing, sometimes augmented by participant observation. Sample size in a phenomenological study may vary from 2 to 25; however, there is no generally agreed upon consensus on the number of informants required. The researcher needs a solid grounding in the philosophical precepts of phenomenology, also known as the philosophy without presuppositions. The method of phenomenology is radical reflection intended to emulate the lived experience.

Phenomenology is a rigorous descriptive–analytic approach that is governed by three interrelated processes: phenomenological reduction, description, and search for essences (Giorgi, 1997). Moustakas (1994) introduced a set of systematic procedures for analyzing phenomenological data. Step 1 involves achieving epoche or phenomenological reduction. Husserl introduced phenomenological reduction as a methodological device to refer to setting aside prejudgments. However, this does not mean that the researcher empties himself or herself of all possible past knowledge and approaches a phenomenological study with a tabula rasa. Instead, the phenomenologist puts aside or renders noninfluential past knowledge so that the phenomenon under investigation has a chance to present itself in its fullness in a given situation (Giorgi, 1997).

Setting aside presuppositions is accomplished through *bracketing,* also known as phenomenological reduction (Caelli, 2001; Kruger, 1988; Kvale, 1996). There are two types of bracketing, one from the researcher's and the other from the informant's point of view. A researcher must bracket his or her own preconceptions to enter into the informant's lifeworld and use the self as an experiencing interpreter (Miller & Crabtree, 1992, p. 24). Bracketing is the process of continually identifying one's presuppositions about the nature of the phenomenon and attempting to set them aside (bracket them) in order to see the phenomenon as it is. Husserl proposed that the researcher needs to bracket out the outer world as well as individual biases (inner world) in order to successfully achieve contact with essences. The second form of bracketing involves the informants who may be asked to set aside their preconceptions and describe the lived experience in a language as free from the constructs of the intellect and society as possible (Bentz & Shapiro, 1998, p. 96). This is accomplished by asking respondents to think and feel about the experience in the most direct way. The epoche is the first step of the phenomenological data reduction process in which the researcher suspends all judgment.

How do we go about the process of bracketing? A number of different writers have described the phenomenological reductions as necessitating a threefold process including exemplary intuition, imaginative variation, and synthesis. In exemplary intuition, researchers choose a phenomenon and hold it in their imagination. The phenomenologist then develops examples of similar experiences through imaginative variation as suggested by Husserl to find the essence of the phenomenon being researched. Finally, integration of these variations is achieved through synthesis of the essences of interest. Giorgi (1997) summarizes phenomenological reduction when he states:

> To enter into the attitude of phenomenological reduction means (a) bracket past knowledge about a phenomenon, in order to encounter it freshly and describe it precisely as it is intuited (or experienced), and (b) to withhold the existential index, which means to consider what is given precisely as it is given, as presence, or phenomenon. No work can be considered phenomenological if some sense of reduction is not articulated and utilized (p. 240).

To date, phenomenologists continue to debate whether or not Husserl's epoche or reduction is useful, necessary, or even possible.

Hycner (1999) and Moustakas (1994) proposed the following five-step procedure for the analysis of phenomenological data:

1. Bracketing and phenomenological reduction.

2. Delineating units of meaning

3. Clustering of units of meaning to form themes.

4. Summarizing each interview, validating it and where necessary modifying it.

5. Extracting general and unique themes from all the interviews and making a composite summary.

Bracketing and phenomenological reduction

Bracketing out (or epoche) is the suspense of the researcher's presuppositions and not letting him or her allow meanings, interpretations, or theoretical concepts to enter the unique world of the informant (Creswell, 1998, p. 54; Moustakas, 1994, p. 90). Phenomenological reduction to pure subjectivity is a deliberate and purposeful opening by the researcher to the phenomenon in its own right with its own meaning (Fouche, 1993). The here and now of the personal experiences of the informants is what gives phenomena existential immediacy. The aim of reduction or epoche is to achieve direct contact with the world by suspending prejudgments, bracketing assumptions, deconstructing claims, and restoring openness. The method of reduction is intended to bring the aspects of meaning that belong to the phenomena of our lifeworld into nearness by focusing on the uniqueness of the particular phenomenon to which we are oriented.

Delineating units of meaning

This phase in the analysis is critical in the explication of the data in that those statements that illuminate the researched phenomenon are extracted (Creswell, 1998; Hycner, 1999). During this phase, the researcher is required to make a substantial amount of judgment calls while consciously bracketing his/her own presuppositions to avoid inappropriate conclusions incongruent with the data. In this process, the list of units of relevant meaning isolated from each interview is carefully scrutinized and redundant units are eliminated (Moustakas, 1994). In this step, the statements of the informants are also transformed by the researcher in accordance with his or her disciplinary orientation. Thus, a leadership researcher takes the statements provided by the informants in everyday language and dresses them into the language of leadership.

Clustering of units of meaning to form themes

Clusters of themes are formed by grouping units of meaning together. By examining the list of units of meaning, the researcher tries to elicit the essence of the meaning units within the holistic context. Again, this calls for judgment calls as the researcher is engaged in something that cannot be precisely delineated. As Hycner (1999) points out, it is imperative that the researcher returns to the recorded interview to search for nonredundant units of meaning to derive the appropriate clusters of meaning. This involves eliminating overlap between clusters to determine the central themes, which express the essence of these clusters (Hycner, 1999, p. 153). The experiences of different informants are then compared to identify, for example, the essence of a leadership phenomenon such as the lone ranger that many leaders who are operating at the apex of their organization (its lonely at the top) experience.

Summarizing, validating, and modifying each interview

Ellenberger captures this phase as follows:

Whatever the method used for phenomenological analysis the aim of the investigator is the reconstruction of the inner world of experience of the subject. Each individual has his own way of experiencing temporality, spatiality, materiality, but each of these coordinates must be understood in relation to the others and the total inner world" (as cited in Hycner, 1999, pp. 153–154).

The final structure is synthesized into a description which captures the essence of the phenomenon. At this point, the researcher conducts a "validity check" (Chapter 2) by returning to the informant to determine whether the essence of the experiences as related in the interview has been captured correctly. Modifications are made at this stage if called for.

General and unique themes for all interviews and composite summary

In the final phase of the analysis, the researcher looks for the themes common to most or all interviews as well as the individual variations paying attention and bringing out the unique or minority voices regarding the phenomenon researched (Hycner, 1999). The investigator concludes the analysis with a composite summary, which includes the context from which the themes emerged. According to Sadala and Adorno (2001), the researcher, at this point, "transforms participants' everyday verbalizations into expressions appropriate to the scientific discourse supporting the research" (p. 289). However, Coffey and Atkinson (1996) emphasize that "good research is not generated by rigorous data alone . . . [but] 'going beyond' the data to develop ideas" (p. 139). Initial theorizing must include the data which was latent in all participants' protocols but only noticed once by one person

(Osborne, 1994, p. 179). Data collection, analysis, and interpretation, as in GT, follow a re-spiralling pattern where interpretation of extant data may influence additional data collection and analysis (e.g., interpretation of extant data may prompt further investigation aimed at illuminating some ambiguities in the data, which, when resolved, may lead to new insights just as inconsistencies in the data might lead to uncovering an aspect of the phenomenon that was not considered earlier in the research process).

The phenomenological report is intended to help the reader to come to understand the essential, invariant structure or essence of the experience thereby recognizing that a single, unifying experience exists. This means that all experiences have an underlying structure. For example, the structure of the experience of grief, for example, is the same whether we are grieving for a lost child or puppy. Ultimately, phenomenological inquiry cannot be separated from the practice of writing. The intent of writing is to produce textural portrayals that resonate the meanings we recognize in our lived experiences (Van Maanen, 2000). The challenge of writing up a phenomenological study is to capture the richness of experience in a holistic sense. Metaphors, poetry, etymological tracings and more recently graphics, animations, and multimedia are available to assist the phenomenologist to meet this challenge.

Table 8-1 summarizes the five-step procedure for the analysis of phenomenological data.

Table 8-1   Summary of five-step procedure for analyzing phenomenological data developed by Moustakas (1994)

Step	Process
1. Achieving epoche	Research suspending predetermined judgments through bracketing
2. Horizontalization	Identifying specific statements identified from transcripts that provide information about participants' lived experiences
3. Establishing meaning units and themes	Searching for nonredundant, nonoverlapping clusters of meaning
4. Developing textural and structural descriptions	Describing "what" was experienced in textural descriptions and "how" it was experienced in structural descriptions
5. Essence of experience	Synthesizing textual and structural descriptions developed in step 4 into a composite description of the phenomenon through the research process; essences can range from individual to typical to universal.

Source: Adapted from Moerer-Urdahl & Creswell (2004)

In phenomenology, analysis becomes synonymous with interpretation which begins with reflection (Gadamer, 1989). The researcher identifies all themes distilled from the interview protocol and sorts them into thematic clusters which are then sorted into higher order clusters. Phenomenological analysis involves careful and detailed reading and rereading of all texts allowing to bring forth general impressions and searching for themes which can be validated by the reemergence and repetition of specific ideas. The process of interpretation involves entering the *hermeneutic cycle* which is the generative recycling between the whole and the part. It is a dynamic immersion with the data as a whole and the data in part, through extensive readings, re-readings, reflections, and writings (Hycner, 1999). The author cautions that "analysis" has dangerous connotations for phenomenology because the term analysis usually means "breaking into parts" and therefore often means the loss of the whole phenomenon...[whereas "explication" implies an]...investigation of the constituents of a phenomenon while keeping the context of the whole" (p. 161). Explication is a systematic procedure for transforming the data through interpretation.

Validity and Quality in Phenomenology

Gadamar (1989) suggested that there are many ways of interpreting phenomenological data, and though none are finite, there are some that offer a better account and ring truer. We already discussed qualitative criteria of rigor such as credibility, confirmability, dependability, and transferability. Koch (1994) suggests that a phenomenological study is credible not when the reader holds the same interpretations but when the reader can follow how researchers arrive at interpretations they present to their audience. Kuiken and Miall (2001) introduced a tripartite conception of quality including distinctiveness, coherence, and richness intended to enhance the quality and precision of phenomenological investigations. First, the authors speak of *distinctiveness* or the extent to which a phenomenon is discriminable from others. Distinctiveness fosters reliability. Second, *coherence* refers to the extent to which judgments about the attribute structure of the phenomenon are congruent; coherence is said to enhance validity. Third, *richness* entails the full differentiation of a phenomenon's attributes, identification of its structure, and appreciation of phenomenological research to address issues pertaining to the extent to which a category of experience is manifest in an experiential narrative.

Wertz (1986) describes reliability of phenomenological research as a multiperspective view of the phenomenon from which emerges the sameness of meaning even though there may not be sameness of fact or context. For purposes of validity, phenomenology relies primarily upon coherence of interpretations of the data. Findings are valid to the extent that they resonate with the experiences of others who have experienced the phenomenon in question. According to Gergen (1985), rhetoric is a critical factor in the presentation of a convincing case for the validity of a phenomenological study. Furthermore, the validity of the intuiting of general essences seems to be dependent on the capacities and skills of the researcher. For example, to quote Spiegelberg (1982), "careful intuiting and faithful description are not to be taken for granted, and they require a considerable degree of aptitude, training and conscientious self-criticism" (p. 689).

Rigor is demonstrated by bracketing, focusing on the insider (informants) perspective, faithfully recording and transcribing the interviews, and having informants validate the units of meaning and central themes. Another demonstration of rigor is showing that the research is consistent with the philosophical ground (i.e., existential, hermeneutic, or transcendental phenomenology) identified as the foundation undergirding the interpretation of the data. According to Madison (1988), a useful question for the researcher to ask is why some interpretations are more readily accepted by research participants and readers of published research than others. One explanation for why one interpretation is found to be more acceptable over another is because it seems more "fruitful, more promising ... it makes more and better sense of the text ... it opens up greater horizons of meaning" (Madison, 1988, p. 15).The author also proposed that "all interpretation works under the promise of truth ... when we opt for a given interpretations, we do not do so because we *know* it to be true ... but because we *believe* it to be the best" (p. 15). Additionally, rigor and quality of a phenomenological study can be enhanced when the researcher maintains a constantly questioning attitude in search for misunderstandings, incomplete understandings, deeper understanding (Benner, 1994) and makes explicit the shared world of understanding between the researcher and the researched.

Applications of Phenomenology in Leadership Research

As was the case with the qualitative methods discussed in Chapter 7, empirical studies using phenomenology and narrative analysis are also found infrequently in the leadership literature. In contrast, phenomenological approaches are reported with greater frequencies in fields such as health care, sociology and education. In Table 8-2, some representative studies illustrating key features of these methodologies are summarized which are reviewed in greater detail in this section.

Recently, Olivares, Peterson, and Hess (2007) conducted a study of leadership development experiences using phenomenology. The authors situated their research in the existential framework developed by Binswanger (1958), who suggests that experiences can be understood at three basic levels: Umwelt, Mitwelt, and Eigenwelt. Umwelt refers not only to our awareness of physical sensations, such as pleasure, pain, and hunger, but also to the biological and motivational makeup of the individual's lifeworld

Table 8-2   Selected phenomenological studies in leadership research

Author(s)	Purpose	Informants	Data sources	Analyses
Olivares et al. (2007)	To use an existential-phenomenological framework to better understand the features of experiences that facilitate leadership development	49 US Army officers	Verbal statements about leadership development experiences; demographic items; measure of self-efficacy	Rankings of leadership development experiences; percentages of beneficial and non-beneficial leadership development experiences; *t*-tests between beneficial and nonbeneficial elements of experience; cluster analysis, hierarchical linear regression to test for mediation
Moerer-Urdahl and Creswell (2004)	To explore the "ripple effect" in a leadership mentoring program	Nine individuals participating in a youth leadership mentoring program	Interviews	Moustakas' (1994) analytical procedure
de Sales Turner (2003)	To distill the essence of hope	Small number of Australian youth	Interviews, photographs	Explication of Gadamerian hermeneutic phenomenology

(Lebenswelt). Mitwelt is the sphere of existence that deals with our interactions and relationships with others or the social component of existence. Eigenwelt, according to Binswanger, can be classified as introspection or reflection. In order to understand our existence and experiences, we need to understand ourselves and others, and this is accomplished by reflecting on our behavior, values, and desires (Olivares et al., 2007, p. 78). Olivares et al. assert that leadership development experiences can be understood in the context of Binswanger's existential analysis. This study represents an important departure of a classical phenomenological approach in that it employed a nomothetic (quantitative) method of analysis.

The authors collected data from 49 US Army officers stationed at two US bases. Eighty-three percent of the informants were male and 17 percent female; all served in some type of leadership capacity and 25 percent had combat experience. In the first round of data collection, participants were asked to describe three experiences that they considered significant in their development as leaders. These descriptions were augmented by demographic questions tapping rank, occupational specialty, gender, Army tenure, and length of combat experience. In the second round of data collection, the officers were asked to think about experiences they thought would facilitate or be beneficial to their development as leaders but, in fact, were not. Participants were then asked to rate each beneficial and nonbeneficial experience on five elements of leadership experiences including self-efficacy, challenge, sociability, relevance, and reflexivity which have been identified in previous research as important for successful leadership development.

The findings produced 60 different experiences described as beneficial. The analysis focused on aggregate analysis instead of unique experiences of individual participants as typical in phenomenological research. The 11 experiences identified by three or more officers include experiences as Platoon Leader and Company Commander, Combat, and serving in a foreign country. Similarly, of the 66 experiences identified by two or more officers as nonbeneficial, only the officer basic course (OBC), which marks the onset of an officer's formal military development following commissioning, was identified by 14 officers as nonbeneficial. In addition, nine experiences were described as beneficial and nonbeneficial, but only one of these overlapping experiences was identified by more than two officers—the OBC.

The authors then performed a series of quantitative analyses including descriptive and inferential statistics such a t-tests between beneficial and nonbeneficial of leadership development experiences to test the hypothesis that experiences identified as beneficial to leadership development will be rated higher on the five essential elements than those identified as nonbeneficial. This hypothesis was supported as beneficial experiences were characterized as being more challenging, relevant, social in nature, and more likely to enhance self-efficacy compared to nonbeneficial leadership development experiences. The authors concluded that their findings from the current study are consistent with other approaches to leadership development such as competency approaches (e.g., Day, 2001).

Moerer-Urdahl and Creswell's (2004) study was grounded in Husserl's transcendental phenomenology to explore the "ripple effect" in a leadership mentoring program. The ripple effect refers to reinvesting in others as a result of a mentoring experience. In other words, individuals who have been protégés in a mentoring relationship and gained from the experience wish to pass on learning experiences to others in need of mentoring. According to Clifton and Nelson (1996), investing and reinvesting in others is the process of doing good for another person without consideration for self-reward. Moerer-Urdahl and Creswell selected nine former mentors who were participants of a prestigious leadership award offered by the Nebraska Human Resource Institute (NHRI) to college students to serve as mentors to younger children in elementary, middle, and high schools. The central research questions addressed in this phenomenological study was "What were the participants' experiences with the ripple effect?" and "In what contexts or situations did they experience it?" The researchers asked the participants why they became mentors, what was unique about their experiences as mentors, and what leadership skills they developed as a function of the mentoring program. The former mentors defined the ripple effect not only as the human investment made in helping their mentees, but also a long-term, multiplying investment that they and their mentees would continue to make in others throughout their lives (Moerer-Urdahl & Creswell, 2004).

While participating in the NHRI program, the mentors were trained in interpersonal and communication skills and then had to invest in a younger mentee for up to five years. The basic approach in the NHRI project was for mentors and mentees to assess their personal strength, learn how to invest in others, and later reinvest what they have learned (Moerer-Uhrdal & Creswell, 2004). The verbal descriptions of the ripple effect were analyzed using the procedures for organizing and analyzing phenomenological data according to Moustakas (1994) described earlier. The first author recalled her own experiences with the phenomenon and through bracketing cleared her mind of presuppositions. Transcripts from the audio-taped interviews were analyzed for statements indicative or suggestive of the ripple effect. The authors extracted 52 statements from the interviews. Table 8-3 presents a sampling of some of the verbatim statements offered by the participants.

After phenomenological reduction (epoche) and gathering significant statements that represented nonoverlapping, nonredundant statements describing the ripple effect (or horizontalization in the Moustakas procedure), the statements were assembled into meaning units or themes. Four meaning units emerged: (1) investing and reinvesting in others (sample statement: "As months went on, another ring would form and you could see people investing in other people"); (2) influencing others positively (sample statement, "You have incredible influence on how you can make a difference because it is not just you, it's the people you touch and people they touch. So you are working through other people to make a difference"); (3) giving and receiving (sample statement, "Gives you a chance to experience what it is like to have someone interested in what you are doing and develop these . . . like empathy or compassion or some enthusiasm for someone else's life and experiences"); and (4) interconnecting (sample statement, "How we affect those interconnections are a form of the ripple effect").

Table 8-3   Selective participant statements describing the "ripple effect" experience

> - Whatever good you build with one individual carries on to many more as each of you goes out and forms new relationships
>
> - The ripple effect is giving back what you have been given and passing it on. Reinvestment. Helping others to experience what you have experienced so they can pass it on
>
> - The biggest motivator ... investing in something that is going to outlive them, and that they are going to pass it on. And, I would say the ripple effect for me ... is what keeps my fire lit
>
> - It can be very powerful when you can return on that investment in a subjective way and qualitative way but also in a quantitative way, in terms of what you are doing for a living today
>
> - People that are not able to reinvest are bankrupt
>
> - As a mentor, you may be mentoring one person, but you do not know the thousands of people you may be impacting because you have made a positive impact on that individual and they, in return, have made a positive impact on another person. So, you affect many people, thousands of communities of people who are touched by the investment of one person

Source: Moerer-Urdahl and Creswell (2004)

The next step in Moustakas' analytical procedure involves textural and structural descriptions employing imaginative imagination to bring forth the essential structure of the phenomenon. Here, Moerer-Urdahl and Creswell probed into what the mentors experienced through the ripple effect (textural description) and in what context did they have the ripple effect experience (structural description). For example, many mentors talked how others such as parents, teachers, and peers influenced them when they were small children; others talked about parental values such as education which they internalized. Finally, the textural and structural experiences were synthesized into a composite description of the phenomenon. The essence of the rippling effect in this study was giving, and more specifically, giving that has the potential to be a multiplier.

The last study depicted in Table 8-2 (de Sales Turner, 2003) employed Gadamerian hermeneutic phenomenology to examine hope as seen through a small number of Australian youth (de Sales Turner, 2003). Hope theory has recently found its way into the leadership literature (Snyder, 1994; 2000; 2002). Napoleon once said that leaders are dealers in hope while Luthans and Avolio (2003) noted that "the force multiplier throughout history has often been attributed to the leader's ability to generate hope" (p. 253). Hope plays an important role in several leadership theories including authentic and servant leadership. Snyder and Shorey (2005) proposed that high-hope leaders are effective when they conceptualize goals or pathways (strategies or action plans) for their followers through which high-hope leaders are able to facilitate the attainment of overarching or superordinate goals.

de Sales Turner (2003) cites literature that reports that many Australian youth are facing severe challenges to their physical, emotional, social, psychological, and cultural integrity. Statistics on substance abuse, depressive disorders, homelessness, suicide, and youth crime capture the context in which young Australians grow up describing situations in which hope may be in high demand. The author began this research by applying Gadamer's concept of Bildung or openness to meaning by compiling a journal in which she chronicled her ideas, attitudes, and understanding of hope. She collected the data using open-ended interviews (number of participants interviewed not reported) which were transcribed. In addition, the author used photography as a means of prompting participants to reveal their understanding of hope. More specifically, de Sales Turner supplied each participant with a disposable color film camera and asked them to imagine that they were being paid to mount a photographic exhibition of hope. In other words, participants were asked to take pictures that in their view showed hope. After the photographs were developed at de Sales Turner's expense, the researcher brought them to the interview to stimulate discussions about hope. After the introduction of the photographs, the audio tapes revealed a marked difference to the tone, tempo, and animation of speech. In essence, the author found the photographs to be conversation enhancers enabling deeper and more reflective responses of participants' conceptualizations and understanding of hope.

Throughout data collection, the author constantly interacted with the text keeping track of biases that may have been shaped by her own understanding of hope. For example, de Sales Turner notes that she believed that some participants would probably be without hope, in other words, they would be hopeless. Yet participants' descriptions caused her to redefine her concepts of hope and hopelessness reaching the conclusion that the opposite of hope is not hopelessness but despair. By revealing her own assumptions and prejudices about hope, the author applied Gadamer's (1976/1989) interpretation of understanding as he states, "All understanding inevitably involves some prejudice" (p. 270). Furthermore, Gadamer asserts that understanding involves discriminating among prejudices, not eliminating them.

de Sales Turner herself completed verbatim transcription of each interview thereby creating the text for the analysis. She followed the iterative process of reading and rereading the text and the audio tapes while adopting an attitude toward openness to meaning. Early ideas, or fore-projections in Gadamerian terms, emerged about the whole of each participant's story of hope as well as their constituent parts as the researcher circled back and forth from the original texts to the data sets. Salient items and the author's margin notes in the texts were transferred onto computer spreadsheets. Throughout this analytic process, the researcher became increasingly more cognizant of her own prejudices as well as the prejudices of the participants revealed in the texts and acknowledged them as conditions of understanding. For example, the researcher's belief that hope passively existed was challenged by participants who described hope as something they had to struggle to hold onto, which enabled them to fight for what they believed in.

In the final stage of data analysis, the researcher grouped and regrouped the prejudices of the participants and explicated hope as a fusion of horizons (a distinctively Gadamerian term) between her understanding and prejudices of hope and those of the participants. Through this process, de Sales Turner reports that four dominant horizons of hope were apparent (but did not identify them) which, when taken together, provided an understanding of the phenomenon of hope as experienced by the participants and provided a platform for discussing horizons of hope with them. The author concluded that these horizons were used to develop a definition of hope (the definition was also not included in the article) that reflected the complexity of the phenomenon of hope.

Although this study omits much important information such as sample size, a description of the participants, the four horizons of hope that emerged from the analysis or the resulting definition of hope, it does bring to life some of Gadamer's basic principles such as openness to meaning, fore-projections and prejudice as a mean of understanding the phenomenon and using his philosophical orientation to analyze textural and pictorial (photographs) data.

Despite the scarcity of phenomenological studies in leadership research, I believe the few studies reviewed here do illustrate the basic philosophical assumptions, procedures, data collection and analytical methods used in phenomenology. They represent fairly recent studies suggesting that scholars may become more interested in applying phenomenology to leadership phenomena. But they also lead to the conclusion that the description of data collection, analysis, and interpretation in phenomenological studies can be weak and lack clarity.

Summary

From a historical perspective, there are two branches of twentieth century phenomenology. The primary branch is represented by Husserl's transcendental phenomenology; the second branch was derived from Heidegger's hermeneutic or existential phenomenology. While it is beyond the scope of this chapter to discuss the philosophical differences between them in detail, it is noteworthy to point out that hermeneutic or existential philosophy makes an interpretive leap beyond Husserlian phenomenology in order to elucidate concealed meanings (Spiegelberg, 1982, p. 712). As a philosophical movement and qualitative research method, phenomenology thematizes the phenomenon of consciousness and in its most comprehensive sense, refers to the totality of lived experiences that belong to a single person (Giorgi, 1997). Husserl developed phenomenology as a philosophical method which has to be understood first before it can be treated as a research method.

As a research method, the task of phenomenology is to describe the intentional objects of consciousness starting with phenomenological reduction. In order to discover meaning in the data, the phenomenologist brackets his or her subjectivity, biases and presuppositions, and maintains an open attitude to let unexpected meanings emerge. The search for essence or the most invariant meaning of a phenomenon in a specific context is the goal of phenomenological research. As such, phenomenology provides a systematic approach with procedures clearly identified by Moustakas (1994). Phenomenology employs a unique language that sets it apart from other qualitative methods. Words such as epoch, horizontalization, imaginative variation, and textural and structural description require an understanding of the philosophical tenets that undergird this method. Several authors (e.g., Giorgi, 1997; Moerer-Urdahl & Creswell, 2004) argue that phenomenologist continue fail to account for the historical, cultural, and social context in which individuals read and interpret text.

NARRATIVE ANALYSIS

An Illustrative Narrative Analysis in the Study of Leadership

Shamir, Dayan-Horesh, and Adler (2005) argued that a leader's biography is an important source of information from which followers learn about the leader's traits and behaviors, self-concept, commitment to collective values, and the level of trust engendered by the leader. From a life story followers also learn about leadership successes and failures. The authors conducted 16 in-depth interviews with a group of male managers in their 30s who participated in a leadership development course which were taped and transcribed. In addition, the authors read 10 autobiographies of political, military and business leaders including Benazir Bhutto, Ben Gurion, Anwar Sadat, Nelson Mandela, and Norman Schwarzkopf. These 10 autobiographies represented leaders in different contexts, gender, and cultural origin.

Instead of reconstructing or interpreting individual stories, the authors set out to distil as many central leadership development themes as possible. The autobiographies were read and re-read in an iterative process until the point of saturation was reached. The results of this inductive analysis revealed four major leadership development themes: (1) leadership development as a natural process; (2) leadership development as struggling and coping with difficulties; (3) leadership development as self-improvement through learning; and

*(4) leadership development as finding a cause. The first two themes, leadership develop-
ment as a natural process and leadership development as a result of struggling and coping
with difficulties, stand in sharp contrast to each other. The leadership development as a
natural process seems to support the "leaders-are-born" school of thought which implies
that leaders have special gifts and talents which manifest themselves early in life. This was
the case for most of the then leaders whose autobiographies were read. The second theme,
on the other hand, suggested that personal tragedies, trauma, and adversity propelled the
individual into the leadership role. Struggle stories were clearly indicated in the autobiographies of Mandela, Gandhi, and Golda Meir.*

*The third theme, leadership development as self-improvement through learning, reflects
the importance of role models including family, mentors, superiors, and teachers in
leaders' lives. As Shamir et al. (2005) note, in telling their stories, leaders present
themselves as role models to their followers. The authors note that "the special emphasis
on learning from role models reinforces followership presenting the leader as someone
who was, and sometimes still is, a follower, and by demonstrating the benefits of
followership" (p. 22). The final theme, leadership development as finding a cause, was
only found in political leaders. Stories reflecting this theme tied leadership development
to political or grassroots movements or ideologies. In addition to promoting the general
values of devotion to an idea or cause, development as finding cause stories also
legitimize the role of the leader as the representative symbol of the movement (Shamir
et al., 2005, p. 23). The authors concluded that telling the leader's biography is an
important leadership behavior that conveys critical messages about their identities,
values, traits, and beliefs.*

Introduction To Narrative Analysis

Myths, folk tales, legends, histories, epics, and sagas are part of oral and written
traditions in cultures around the world that are part of narrative structures. The classic
image of the storyteller depicts the narrator as someone who can make something out
of nothing, who can engage our imagination with a fascinating celebration of detail that
is entertaining, amusing, and emotionally rewarding. Credibility is rarely an issue here
since tall tales, myths, and outright lies carry the day (Labov & Waletzky, 1967). While
the role of narrative and storytelling in human affairs has been highlighted in many
disciplines for decades, writers on management and leadership have only recently
caught on. In the extensive literature on leadership, there are surprisingly few articles
on storytelling and narrative inquiry (Denning, 2007). But slowly narrative, as a
method of qualitative inquiry, is edging its way into the social sciences including
leadership studies. Chamberlayne, Bornat, and Wengraf (2000) speak of the "biographical turn in social science" which suggests a paradigm shift (Kuhn, 1962) within a
wide range of social science disciplines. This is, of course, a huge claim that is clearly

open to debate. But this claim seems to resonate in the qualitative research community. For example, Bochner (2001) uses the term narrative turn to attest to an increased use of narrative, also known as narratology, which honors people's life stories as data that can stand on their own as pure description of experience, worthy as narrative documentary of experience (p. 116). Day Sclater (2003) asserts:

> The narrative turn, manifested in such diverse activities as medicine, psychotherapy, and social scientific research, as well as visual and performing art, and in popular culture, seems set to confront the traditional boundaries that traditionally separated the Arts, Humanities, and the Sciences. In those "boundary crossings," I think, lie the possibilities for some truly innovative work in the theory and practice of qualitative research... What we are witnessing is an opening up of a new space for creative endeavor in the research process (p. 622).

Thus, although narrative and the broader field of storytelling have become the focus of attention in many academic and literary disciplines, the number of narrative analyses published in leadership and management journals studies remains relatively small. The narrative turn, despite its intuitive appeal for the study of leadership, has yet to manifest itself.

For most people, storytelling is a natural way of recounting experience, a practical solution to a fundamental problem in life, or creating reasonable order out of experience. Not only are we continually producing narratives to order and structure our life experiences, we are also constantly being bombarded with narratives from the social world we inhabit (Moen, 2006). Not only do we create narrative descriptions of our experiences for ourselves and others, we also develop narratives to make sense of the behavior of others (Zellmeyer, 1997). According to Polkinghorne (1988), people without narratives do not exist. Hence, life itself may be considered a narrative inside which we find a number of stories. In telling, listening, and relating to stories in action or decisions, individuals aim to understand and interpret practices in the organization of which they are part (Boyce, 1997; Czarniawska, 1997; 2000; Elliott, 2005). Stories can also be powerful tools for management that can be used to design, change, or refocus the organizations' culture (e.g., Denning, 2004). Creating a narrative implies a process whereby an accurate account of a story that unfolds in the collaborative interaction between the researcher and the participant becomes fixed in a written text. As Moen (2006) points out, by fixing the narrative in a text, it becomes detached from the moment in which it occurred and assumes consequences of its own. The story has been liberated from its origin and can enter into new interpretive frames. The narrative that is fixed in text can be considered an "open work" where the meaning is addressed to those who read and hear about it. Looking at narrative as an open text makes it possible to engage in a wide range of interpretations (Moen, 2006).

In the process of creating a narrative, the researcher raises questions such as, "How much voice do we accord participants, and in what form?" "Who chooses the stories to tell (and the ones to omit)?" "Who frames the quotes, and who challenges the researcher's conclusions?" "Given some telling of a story, what is the true pattern of the underlying events?" One important contextual issue in narrative inquiry concerns the background knowledge that both the storyteller and the listener bring to the narrative, how each interprets the background knowledge of the other, and how this background knowledge affects the narration and interpretation of the story. In producing the story, the researcher draws on disciplinary expertise to interpret and make sense of responses and actions of the participants. Because the story is offered as a scholarly explanation and realistic depiction of a human episode, the researcher needs to include evidence and argument in support of the plausibility of the offered story. Manicas and Secord (1983) state:

> It [the narrative inquiry] is engaged in understanding the concrete person and his or her life history and particular pattern of behavior, including as reflexively applied, self-understanding . . . As a scientific effort it requires also that the inquirer uses whatever special knowledge is available regarding implicated psychological structures and mechanism as these operate in the individual biography. And since the person is born and matures in a social world, this understanding inevitably also includes references to what is known about social structures pertinent to that biography (p. 407).

What is Narrative?

In Latin, the noun narrario means narrative or story and the verb narrare to tell or narrate. A narrative is a story that tells a sequence of events that is significant for the narrator or his or her audience. A wide range of definitions of narrative and narrative analysis can be found in the literature reflecting the different traditions ranging from contemporary biographies to ancient epics that fall under the umbrella of narrative. According to Polkinghorne (1995), narrative inquiry refers to a subset of qualitative research designs in which stories are used to describe action. In the context of narrative inquiry, narrative refers to a discourse form in which events and happenings are configured into a temporal unity by means of a plot. A plot is a type of conceptual scheme by which a contextual meaning of individual events can be displayed (p. 7). It has also been described by some analysts as being formed from a combination of temporal succession and causality. However, as Chatman (1978) noted, even without an explicit causal link being made between the events in a narrative, the audience will tend to read causality into a sequence of events recounted as a narrative.

William Labov, a prominent student of narrative, focused on narratives of personal experience which he defined as a report of a sequence of events that have entered into the biography of the speaker by a sequence of clauses that correspond to the original order of the events. Labov and Waletzky (1967) define narrative as the choice of a particular linguistic technique to report past events. The authors provided a linguistic account of narrative structures in terms of two components: what happened and why it is worth telling. Their framework, developed for oral narratives of personal experience, proved to be useful in approaching a wide variety of narrative situations and types, including memoirs, traditional folk tales, avant-garde novels, therapeutic interviews, and most importantly, the banal narratives of every-day life. Labov and Waletzky's definition separates narrative from other means of telling a story or recounting the past. By specifying that the experience must have entered into the biography of the speaker, the authors distinguish narrative from simple recounting of observations like the events of a leadership rally by a witness leaning out of the window. The events that have entered into the speaker's biography are emotionally and socially evaluated and so transformed from raw experience. Furthermore, Labov regards the temporal sequence as essential to narrative, but he locates this temporality in the meaning-preserving clauses in narrative discourse itself.

Alternatively, Freeman (1984) proposes narrative as a way of ordering the "landscape of events" (p. 7). The fact that particular forms of knowledge derive from retrospection, from an essentially backward look over the terrain of experience, is an irreducible "peculiarity of the human being" (1984, p. 9). For Polkinghorne (1995), "a storied narrative is the linguistic form that preserves the complexity of human action with its interrelationships of temporal sequence, human motivations, chance happenings, and changing interpersonal and environmental contexts" (p. 7). Finally, Tierney's (1987) narrative analysis looks at the intersection of the interpreted purpose of the text, the constructed and interpreted truth of a text, and the persona of the author in text creation, all of which are called into interpretive question. Harré (1997) concludes:

> It is an essential characteristic of narrative to be a highly sensitive guide to the variable and fleeting nature of human reality because it is, in part, constitutive of it. This makes it such an important subject of inquiry for human sciences in general... Narratives are both models of threshold and models of the self. It is through our stories that we construct ourselves as part of our world (pp. 278–279).

In the literature on narrative research, we find three basic underpinnings or claims. The first claim is that human beings organize their experience of the world into narratives. The narrative is regarded as "the primary scheme by which human existence is rendered meaningful" (Polkinghorne, 1988, p. 1). Following this line of thought, human experience is always narrated. Narrative research, consequently, is focused on how individuals assign meanings to their experiences through the stories they tell. Second, narrative researchers maintain that the stories that are told depend on the individual's past and present experiences, values, the people the stories are being told to, and when and where they are being told. The third claim, connected to the second, concerns the multiple voices that play an important role in narratives. Central to the construction of a narrative are time, place, and character (Clandinin & Connelly, 1994, p. 416). Participants not only make sense of their world through narrative but they proactively plan and enact narratives that are consistent with their expectations and values. People do not just tell stories, they enact stories, and these stories provide legitimacy and accountability for their actions (Czarniawska, 1997).

Thus, stories are at the center of narrative analysis. From an interpretive perspective, stories told by actors or local experts do not merely represent facts or information. Rather, they provide insights into the emotional and symbolic ascriptions and hence into the meanings that narrators ascribe to events in relation to their cultural background. Weick (1995) argues that stories can be understood as the result of ongoing accomplishments to make sense of what is happening in social entities such as groups, organizations, or even nations. Bruner (1991) asserts that stories provide an eminent medium to explore the construction of social life. For Soin and Scheytt (2006), stories are the fabrics of our lives. If we explain our actions to other or to ourselves, we tell stories. Stories help us make sense of what we are, where we come from, and what we want to be.

The story is the report about an event or situation as seen through the eyes of the storyteller who reports about his relations with an object or objects in that world. In stories, there has to be some kind of a plot that links diverse, more rational aspects of organizations with the feelings, events, and emotions of organizational members. However, not all narratives do so. This forms the basic difference between narratives and stories, in that stories are a specific type of narrative. Czarniawska (2000, p. 17) defines narratives as "spoken or written text given an account of an event/action or series of events/actions, chronologically connected, whereas stories need to be emplotted in that they are more complicated, imbued by emotions, descriptions of tensions, and/or moral conclusions." Similarly, Gabriel (2000) argued that "not all narratives are stories; in particular, factual and descriptive accounts of events that aspire at objectivity rather than emotional effect must not be treated as stories" (p. 5). For example, a formal description of how an organization works, guidelines for behavior, a chronicle of events, or an annual report do not constitute a story. Gabriel (1998) states that

> In telling a story, the requirements of accuracy and veracity are relaxed in the interest of making a point. Poetic license is the prerogative of storytelling. At the same time, by shrouding a point in symbolic terms, stories are able to evade censors, both internal and external, and express views and feelings, which may be unacceptable in straight talk (p. 136).

In a story, events and actions are drawn together into an organized whole by means of a plot defined as a thematic thread that links different elements of the story. The

Table 8-4 Levels of structure in narrative analysis

Level	Definition	Example
Text	Particular telling of a story by a particular narrator	Actual text of his or her story: "When I showed up at the interview … "
Story	Version of a fabula from a specific point of view	A new employee's own version of how he or she was hired
Fabula	Generic description of a particular set of events and their relationships	How a particular person was hired: what happened, who did what?
Generating mechanisms	Underlying structures that enable or constrain the fabula	Overall recruiting process: how people in general are hired
Participants' stories		**Researchers' stories**

Source: Pentland, 1999, p. 719

integrating function of the plot is known as emplotment. When happenings in narratives are configured or emplotted, they take on narrative meaning. Pentland (1999) offered a useful model that describes levels of narrative structures as they present themselves in the stories of the participant and the researcher. As indicated in Table 8-4, at the surface we have the specific text of the narrative as told. This is the level where people account and make sense of their own actions and those of others. This is also the level at which usually data are collected. At the next level, the story level, the story is told and narrated from a particular point of view—or localization (Bal, 1985). For example, Table 8-4 depicts a story of a new employee's version of how he or she was hired. Moving to a deeper level into the narrative structure, we have the fabula. The fabula refers to a specific set of events, actors, and their relationships (e.g., who does what, in what sequence, and so on). A fabula encodes an objective version of the basic events and characters required to uniquely identify a particular story. For example, a fabula may describe the process by which a person was hired. Finally, at the deepest level, generating mechanisms drive the narrative structure. According to Pentland, a generating mechanism might be a routine process, like recruiting or budgeting that repeats periodically.

Data Collection and Analysis in Narrative Inquiry

The field of narrative analysis within qualitative research is broad-based. There is no definitive approach comparable, for example, to Moustakas' (1994) procedures for analyzing phenomenological data. The types of analysis most explored are linguistic, psychological, and biographic as demonstrated in the illustrative narrative leadership study at the beginning of this section. A number of data collection strategies in narrative analysis are structured around basic research questions, such as "What are the participants' life histories?" and "What is their understanding of the world and their place in it?" Patton (2002) raised the following foundational questions, "What does this narrative or story reveal about the person and the world from which I came?" and "How can this narrative be interpreted so that it provides an understanding of and illuminates the life and culture that created it?"

A number of data collection methods are used in narrative analyses. They can take the form of field notes, journal records, interview transcripts, one's own and others, story-telling letter writing, autobiographical writing, organizational documents, newsletters and other texts, and picture (Connelly & Clandinin, 1990). To that list, I would add video recording which also can be very useful in narrative research.

QUALITY CRITERIA

Polkinghorne (1995) argues that in judging the credibility of a story, a distinction can be made between the accuracy of the data and the plausibility of the plot. It is the researcher's responsibility to assure that the reported events and happenings actually occurred. The use of triangulation in which several independent reports of an event are collected can help in producing confidence that the event occurred. The author also points out that the question of the accuracy of the configurative plots is of greater complexity. According to Polkinghorne, the storied narrative form is not an imposition on data of an alien type but a tightening and ordering of experience by explicating an intrinsically meaningful form (p. 20). Because of the gap between experienced actions and the emplotted explication of them, it is possible that the same data elements can be configured into more than one plot (Stake, 1988). Because configurative analysis is the researcher's construction, it is inappropriate to ask whether it is the "real" or "true" story (p. 20).

Hummel (1991) argues that the reference points for any questions of validity applying to a story told do not originally lie in the facts of the story; rather, they are constituted by its structure. Each structural element of the story must stand up to scrutiny: subject, object, and relationships between subject and object. Ultimately, the question is raised whether all of these together constitute a coherent and therefore plausible field of action

(p. 37). The validity the listener seeks is structural validity. Its key question is, "Are there those structures in the story told that the listener needs to orient himself or herself in the new world the story announces?" (p. 38). The validity standards applied to a story are relevance standards first and factual standards second. Relevance standards are epistemological standards because they ask the question: "Does this ring true?" Beyond ringing true, a story well and properly told opens up the possibilities for action—it broadens the world of the storyteller and the listener.

Several authors (Blumenfeld-Jones, 1995; Grummet, 1988; Moss 2004) have discussed fidelity as a measure of quality in narrative inquiry, a concept that resembles trust-worthiness (credibility, transferability, dependability, and confirmability) (Guba & Lincoln, 1989) as an alternative to validity in qualitative research (Chapter 2). Moss (2004) defines provisions of trustworthiness as acts of integrity that researchers take to ensure they seek the truth by contextualizing their studies and disclosing all relevant procedures. Grumet (1988), for example, states that in autobiographical research that "fidelity rather than truth is the measure of these tales" (p. 66). According to Blumen-feld-Jones, fidelity as a set of emerging criteria for evaluating the quality of a piece of narrative inquiry has a twofold character. First, the inquiry should address a sense of betweenness, acknowledging, and making explicit the bond between the inquirer and the participant and between the story and the story's context. Second, there should be a "believability" of the work in the story as both a reasonable portrayal of the specific story and as the story resonates with the audience's experiences. Blumenfeld-Jones takes truth to be "what happened in a situation" (the truth of the matter) and fidelity to be "what it means to the teller of the tale (fidelity to what happened for that person)" (p. 26). Thus, one of the pressing issue in narrative analysis is that of authenticity and, ultimately, of truth value. Narratives are re-fashioned in the light of present life experiences and are often judged by coherence and plausibility rather than "truth." Further, whether the teller believes the story is true does not prove its veracity (Phillips, 1997). The author asserts that in some cases "such as when policy or future weighty actions hang on an acceptance of the narrative," it is important for the narrative to be true (p. 102).

APPLICATIONS OF NARRATIVE ANALYSIS IN LEADERSHIP RESEARCH

Table 8-5 depicts a few representative leadership studies that utilized narrative analysis. The first study shown in Table 8-5 (Bryant, 2006) reported that voice was used in an attempt to make the workplace better after the implementation of a change initiative, with specific emphasis on making individuals' jobs better. More specifically, the author was interested in exploring how employee responses such as voice as used in different ways and justified by participants. Zhou and George (2001) define voice as an active attempt to "improve conditions, actively searching for and coming up with new ways of

Table 8-5   Selected examples of narrative analysis in leadership research

Author(s)	Purpose	Informants	Data sources	Analyses
Bryant (2006)	To study employee responses such as voice to organizational change	22 employees from Australian companies	Open-ended interviews	Inductive theme analysis of 14 narratives
Boudens (2005)	To understand workplace emotions	N/A	442 narratives drawn from published in two books on work	Intercoder reliability based on percent agreement
Sims (2003)	To understand life of middle managers by examining stories they tell to superiors, peers, and subordinates	Middle managers and vice presidents	Interviews	Interpretive
Beech (2000)	To identify narrative styles of managers and workers based on their stories	150 senior managers, middle managers, team leaders, and shop-floor workers; members of three Scottish organizations	33 focus group interviews; 23 one-to-one interviews	Grounded theory approach; NUD*IST for development of theoretical categories
Gabriel (1997)	To illuminate followers' dominant fantasies about their leaders	Three undergraduate students	Stories told by students 3 months after completion of internship	Interpretive

doing things and advocating changes to make things better" (p. 683). In the context of organizational change, voice may be used as a strategy to signal dissatisfaction about working conditions to management.

A total of 22 Australian participants were recruited by Bryant using snowball sampling techniques and qualitative interviewing. The article is based on the analysis of 14 narratives. During the interviews, participants talked about their experience with organizational change. Bryant states that she organized the stories into a clear structure with a clear beginning, middle, and ending known as narrative plots. The stories were analyzed using narrative theme analysis, which investigated inductive themes embedded within participants' stories and produced narrative types. As Frank (1995) pointed out, narrative types are different from narrative plots in that they are simply a way of "naming the most general storyline that can be recognized underlying the plot and [themes] of particular stories" (p. 75).

The use of voice was a primary theme embedded within the stories. Specifically, each participant reported a common experience of using voice in response to organizational change (Bryant, 2006, p. 250). One participant stated

> If I had a concern about organisational change I would take it directly to my manager and tell him exactly what I thought the problem was. I felt he was the best person to know about the effects of change on staff as he really was the only one that could probably do anything (p. 251).

The narratives were first analyzed by creating plots followed by narrative theme analysis. According to Boje (2001), whose procedures Bryant followed, adding narrative theme analysis, in addition to the plot analyses, enables the themes to be further investigated according to how participants interpret and sort their stories and according to themes that may not emerge in the process of analyzing plots. Voice was the major theme used by participants to produce the narratives. Further analyses revealed three subthemes of how voice was used to signal concerns about organizational change to management. Participants' narratives reflected the belief that organizational change altered their jobs and work conditions in a way that removed control or power from employees. Voice was used "as an honest attempt to tell managers that there were some problems and that we had valid suggestions as to how we could improve" (p. 252). Moreover, of the 14 participants whose narratives were analyzed, five participants specifically reported that they were not provided with many details about organizational change, which suggests that they may not have had a thorough understanding of the rationale for change or the way it was implemented, and voice was used as a way of seeking basic information. For example,

> We were sort of kept in the dark like little mushrooms. Management wouldn't volunteer any information so we had to constantly harp on and on, asking them how this would affect us and what was going to happen to us. This was probably not all that productive as I think they saw us as a pain in the butt after a while (p. 252).

Taken together, the narratives suggest a gap between employee intentions of using voice as a response to organizational change and managerial perceptions of voice and resistance. The primary rationale for using voice was out of concern for ownership and control of jobs, as well as to seek information about job security. Exploring the individual voices of employees from a critical perspective adds depths to the organizational change literature in which the dominant narratives are typically constructed at managerial levels of the organization (Boje, 1995).

In an earlier study, Bryant (2003) used the same participants and methodology to demonstrate that voice can be a constructive and destructive response to organizational change. In this earlier study, the author found that participants constructed conversion stories, indicating that the organizational change initiative was a turning point in their careers and embraced the new management practices resulting from the change effort because it lead to better job opportunities and promotions. At the same time, other participants constructed what the author referred to as "atrocity tales" in which change was associated with stories of workplace bullying, isolation, removal or denial of career opportunities, and workplace violence. Atrocity tales focus on the dark side of organizational change in an attempt to reflect the trauma and tragedy that individuals experience during different transformation processes. Moreover, this study reported that silence was an effective response to change. Participants who reported using voice as a response to change tended to construct atrocity tales, whereas those who remained silent were likely to construct conversion narratives. Thus, as an alternative to voice (usually used to indicate discontent and dissatisfaction but was not always supported in this research), silence is a response to change often adopted by individuals in the event that they have no means to change the situation (Perrewe & Zellars, 1999, p. 747).

Although Boudens' (2005) narrative analysis of workplace emotion does not deal explicitly with leadership, it is included because of the increasing attention that has recently been paid to in leadership: the role of emotion in leader behavior and leader–follower relationships (e.g., Ashforth & Humphrey, 1995; Ashkanasy & Tse, 2000; Barling, Slater, & Kelloway, 2000). Emotional intelligence (Goleman, 1995), for example, has been positively correlated with transformational leadership (e.g., Gardner & Stough, 2002) and is a strong requisite for effective leadership (e.g., Higgs & Aiken, 2003). Bouden's narrative analysis is based on interviews published in two books dealing with workplace behavior. The first source was *Working* by Terkel (1972), which contains a collection of interviews conducted over a three-year period of time with working class people, such as waitresses, letter carriers, miners and policemen. Terkel made it clear in the introduction to the book that his intent was to give voice to working class people. The second source *Gig*, edited by Bowe, Bowe, and Sabin (2000), also contains a collection of approximately 40 interviews conducted almost 30 years after the Terkel interviews. In contrast to Terkel whose book does reflect a political agenda (giving voice to franchised workers), the editors of *Gig* did not have a political agenda. The authors conducted unstructured interviews, sampling a wider range of occupations than Terkel and also included representatives of newer occupations which emerged during the intervening 30 year period since the Terkel interviews.

Boudens applied four criteria in her analysis of the narratives published in the two books. Each narrative must contain (1) a specific incident or connected series of incidents with a clearly identifiable beginning and end; (2) a temporal ordering of events or occurrences within the incident; (3) an indication by the teller that the events described are causally related; and (4) a change in the situation or at least one of the characters over the course of the story (p. 1289). Boudens then adapted Labov's (Labov & Waletzky, 1976) approach to narrative analysis focuses on the extraction of core stories from interviews for the purpose of simplifying the narrative. The purpose of this approach is to raise narratives to a level of abstraction that would show that the same plot or theme occurred across a number of contexts (Polkinghorne, 1988). In the next step of the analysis, the author sorted core stories into groups or themes following Lincoln and Guba's (1981) guidelines for categorizing qualitative data. The final step in analyzing the data involved the identification of the emotions associated with each story category.

The author analyzed the data separately for the two books. A total of 252 narratives were isolated from *Working* and condensed into 13 categories beyond which no further reductions were possible. Intercoder reliability was established based on percentage of agreement between two coders. The second coder placed 223 (88.8 percent) of the stories into the same categories as the authors. Disagreements were resolved by discussion. Category examples for *Working* include equity, power, trust, and support and solidarity. For example, in the equity category, stories were about discrimination, especially discrimination that occurred in the context of private interactions where there were no witnesses. The analysis of the interviews published in *Gig* based on 201 stories yielded an intercoder index of agreement of 87.5 percent. The most prominent categories culled from the *Gig* interviews included conflict, progress and promise, frustration, crime, ethics, and moral, and death, danger, and disgust. The *Gig* core stories covered a wide range of emotions, many of them positive, such as joy, satisfaction, pride, excitement, and feelings of accomplishment. This is not to say that there were no stories expressing negative emotions as well. In the frustration stories, the narrators talked about workplace situations in which they felt powerless or ineffective or expressed a sense of hopelessness or resignation.

Boudens (2005) concluded that three overarching themes which appeared in both books represent enduring aspects of the emotional life of the workplace. They were (1) the establishment and maintenance of balance relative to status and power; (2) the theme of silence which suggests that a sizable portion of organizational life plays itself out quietly; this theme was particularly evident in the equity and frustration stories in which the narrators chose to do and say nothing about the ways they felt; and (3) the final theme of boundaries. Many narrators of the stories found in both books talked about their struggles to maintain the boundary between self and work, made explicit statements about who they were as individuals, what their values and limits were, and what they wanted to stand for. Finally, as acknowledged by Boudens, the primary drawback of using narratives of this type is that the stories are based on secondary data. Hence, the researcher does not know the extent to which the stories were faithfully recorded, the manner in which they were edited, and why they were chosen for inclusion in the source books at all (p. 1303). Full-length interviews with real-life narrators would be a logical extension of this study.

Sims (2003) study sought "to illuminate our understanding of the lives of middle managers by considering the special pressures on them to tell stories about their organizations that make sense to three different audiences: their supervisors, their subordinates, and themselves" (p. 10). The central premise of this research was that middle managers' stories are vulnerable because many of them do not wish to live the life of a middle manager. The middle managers have to satisfy two constituencies: they have to construct a convincing story about their accomplishments that contribute to the success of the organization in the eyes of their superiors and another, often conflicting story that earns their respect in the eyes of their subordinate and peers. For example, one of the middle managers interviewed ran a department that contributed 12 percent of the revenue of his organization. When he was trying to fill a managerial position directly below him, his input was completely discarded by his superiors although they agreed that the middle manager had identified a suitable candidate who felt embarrassed and belittled. He was embarrassed in front of his subordinates because the event clearly diminished his power and authority. Sims (2003) concluded that it is at the middle management stage of their career that people have least control over the plot of their stories that they tell and the stories they live. Finally, Sims argues in favor of the narrative truth of the stories described by Spence (1984) as truth that, although it might be only a screen of memory or even a fiction, was still close enough to the real thing to start a reconstructive process.

Beech (2000) conducted his narrative analysis in three organizations that were implementing culture change as part of a performance improvement effort. The researcher was interested in examining the stories told by managers and workers about their experiences to identify underlying narrative styles. The three participating organizations included an international drink company, the commercial division of a local government organization, and a major health care organization, all located in the same geographic area of Scotland. Research participants included senior managers, middle managers, team leaders, and shop-floor workers. The author conducted 33 focus group and 23 one-to-one interviews with a total of 150 participants of the three organizations. The interviews were tape-recorded and transcribed and first read for recurrent themes which yielded the initial list of in vivo category headings.

This initial list of themes or meaning units was reduced using NUD*IST for theoretical category refinement. By eliminating duplications and overlapping categories, and applying the principles of iterating between data and emergent theories, the author arrived at 20 factors which represented plot summaries and more general descriptors of the narrative styles in practice. These factors were further reduced after the elimination of duplicate or overlapping categories resulting in six narrative factors. The six factors, according to Beech (2000), reflected participants' narrative style that captured their understanding of their experiences with organizational change. For example, one of the six factors was labeled "causal attribution" and represented the cognitions of the participants regarding the whys and hows of their organizational experiences. It focused on how participants attributed praise, blame, cause, and agency to their experiences in an attempt to make sense of them. Other factors that merged from this phase of the analysis dealt with temporal orientation and the behavioral style of the central character (Beech, 2000, p. 214).

In the search for underlying narrative styles, Beech reported four distinctive styles. Again, one of these styles is described here to illustrate the findings. It was referred to as the "Ironic Response to HRM." It was taken from a number of focus and individual interviews conducted with hospital employees. The hospital had implemented a change strategy that included training and development and communication initiatives and management by walking around (MBWA). Employee reactions to these efforts were largely negative. They believed that the reasons for such changes were that someone in a "high-up office" just dreamed them up and that their implementation was a "feather in the ward manager's cap." Communications with the ward manager were poor because she was "only interested in solutions," not problems. Similarly, nurses and general managers were not listening because "we're just auxiliaries, we don't know what we are talking about" (p. 220).

The other three styles were called the "Heroic Director," "Romantic Ward Manager," and "Tragic Skilled Worker" which portrayed the narrative style associated with the central actor in the narrative. Beech (2000) cautions readers not to routinely characterize people as heroic, tragic, and so on. Rather, the author argued that they can and do act in styles, but that, as individuals, they can be dynamic by embracing more than one narrative style. He cites the example of a group of surgeons in the health care organization that demonstrated both ironic detachment from the system and a heroic self-perception of their ability to make a difference and exercise power (p. 222). He pointed out that although this research does not support the notion that specific groups are invariably associated with particular styles, there were recognizable patterns. For example, managers in the three participating organizations were more likely to express the heroic style than any other. In contrast, workers were more likely to express the tragic style. In the drink company, a senior manager had a heroic style, a middle manager reporting to the senior manager embraced the romantic style, and workers reporting to the middle manager exemplified the status quo.

In the last article, Gabriel (1997) gathered the stories of three undergraduates that were compiled six months after the students satisfied their internship requirements to explore the fantasies students entertained when they met with top leaders of the companies sponsoring their internships. The three fantasies that emerged included: (1) the leader as reincarnation of the primal mother; (2) uncaring leaders; and (3) the leader as reincarnation of the omnipotent primal father. The account of one of the students illustrates the fantasy of the uncaring leader. The student describes the meeting with her boss, the Managing Director of a branch of a retail organization, as disappointing, leaving a bitter taste in her mouth. The student's faith in the leader fell apart after the meeting and destroyed her image of the organization. She used words such as "lesser mortal," "time wasted," and "not bothered" to indicate how hurt she was by her boss's lack of caring. As Gabriel (p. 327) notes, the student was not only hurt, but she was angry as well; her anger was the product of injured pride and self-respect. In her own words, the student wrote:

> I went to work without few preconceived ideas and no experience. Although, the organization turned out to be run like a military camp and was a complete shock to me socially and culturally, I just about managed to keep my head above water. As far as I was concerned, my placement had been a success that is until I had the parting chat with the Managing Director of the branch. Much of my confidence in management and the organization collapsed when I went to see the "Boss." The event that discoloured my opinion appears to sum up a classic syndrome afflicting many senior managers: "Time need not be wasted on lesser mortals" (Gabriel, 1997, p. 325).

Gabriel argues that the fantasies of top leaders of organizations embraced by the three students whose narratives he analyzed revolved around two configurations of fantasy: messianic and charismatic. In addition to these two focal fantasy configurations, the narratives of the students also included the discovery that leaders themselves are only human and fallible, a theme spawning myths, legends, and stories in many different cultures.

SUMMARY

Narrative inquiry and analysis cover a wide variety of approaches designed for the analysis of textual materials, and more recently, images and other nontext-based sources of data such as photographs or works of art (Chapter 9). They include autobiographies and biographies, life stories, recorded interviews of ordinary experiences, and a variety of literary genres. Despite its intuitive appeal for the study of leadership as illustrated in the sample narrative study at the opening of the second part of this chapter, narrative analysis was infrequently found in leadership. Boudens (2005) suggests that narratives offer a way of viewing organizational life from the ground up, building theories and developing ideas that are based on human experience. They represent unique challenges for the qualitative researcher as they require considerable skills in the collection of the narratives in their unaltered, unfiltered form and diligence to record and analyze them. As a result, the field of narrative analysis is extremely broad as seen in the broad description of the specific analyses that were used in a given study. In Chapter 2, I mapped a spectrum of qualitative methods ranging from purely qualitative to highly quantitative. For the most part, narrative analysis falls close to the purely qualitative pole. Narrative researchers sometimes adopt what might be called a common-sense approach to validity leaving it to the reader to make up his or her mind as to the extent to which the evidence collected meets quality standards. Working with narrative often requires considerable interpretive work, and based on the articles reviewed in this section, often insufficient information is provided to replicate the analyses. Finally, although much of the work on narratives has focused on the research participants who produced the stories, it is important to note the researcher or narrator, the way he or she critically reflects on the informants account of the events and delivers an analytic discussion of how their own theoretical and biographical perspective might impact their relationships with the participants, their interpretation of the research evidence, and the form in which the research is presented (Elliott, 2005, p. 155).

9

BEYOND WORDS: SIGHTS AND SOUNDS IN QUALITATIVE RESEARCH

A painter takes the sun and makes it into a yellow spot. An artist takes a yellow spot and makes it into the sun.

(Pablo Picasso)

INTRODUCTION

Artists, like leaders, have the power to inspire, transform, and connect us to something larger than ourselves (Klein & Diket, 1999). For many people, the great works of art, such as Leonardo's Mona Lisa, Michelangelo's David, indigenous drawings found all over the world, Martha Graham's choreography, Le Corbusier's architectural designs and icon buildings, and Beethoven's Fifth Symphony, evoke powerful responses that transcend reality and ordinary states of consciousness. Likewise, images found in film, documentaries, sculpture, music, and dance appeal to our intellect, emotions, and spiritual yearnings, and they do so in ways that are different from the written word. Lipsett (2007), speaking of the power of paintings, points out that by opening the door to color and form of an experience, it can be deeply felt, completely embodied while time is stilled forever, to be relived at will, each time offering a deeper understanding of the painting. Tung (2006) reminds us that art can be used to express people's innermost feelings, even among those whose verbal skills may be lacking. Therefore, it is not surprising that in a variety of disciplines, visual materials have found their way into the repertoire of qualitative researchers.

The past 25 years have seen slow but gradual growth in the use of qualitative research methods in leadership studies. Interests in new approaches to research in leadership continue to be motivated by dissatisfaction with the limitations of positivism and operationalism and the desire to secure more authentic information about leaders, followers, and the contexts in which they are studied. As Eisner (1997) notes, when everyone is quantifying the world, it looks as though there are no other options. The author argues that the public as a major consumer of research findings continues to be goaded into a horse race view of research, and for horse races, digits are much more effective and attractive than narratives or works of art. However, the growth and increasing legitimacy of qualitative research in leadership studies has opened the door for other nonquantitative methods to emerge. One of them is image or arts-based leadership research which at this time is very much of an unchartered terrain. In many ways, image-based leadership research today, like qualitative text-based research 20 years ago, is in its infancy, controversial, and often labeled nonscientific.

However, the use of images has a long history in social science research. Images are used in literature and art therapy. Fields such as sociology, anthropology, and education have developed subdisciplines such as arts-based education, visual anthropology, and visual sociology in which both researchers and artists for decades have been exploring the space where aesthetics and social meaning overlap in ways that are both artistic and scientific. For example, in anthropology, one field of specialization is known as visual anthropology which focuses on the study of visual forms and visual systems in their cultural context (Banks & Murphy, 1997). As the authors note, while the subject matter encompasses a wide range of visual forms—film, photography, "tribal" or "primitive" art, television and cinema, computer media—all are united by their material presence in the physical world. Likewise, cultural studies as an academic field has created a specified field, visual cultural studies, based on the argument that everyday life has become a visual culture. There has been an explosion of interest in visual culture coming largely from work in sociology, anthropology, and cultural and media studies. This new visuality of culture, according to Mirzoeff (1998), calls for its own field of study concerned with different kinds of visual information, their meanings, pleasures, and consumptions, including the study of all visual technologies, from oil paintings to the Internet (p. 3).

Visual sociology and anthropology in particular have long made use of photography, film, and documentaries. For example, anthropologists Bateson and Mead (1942) turned to photography after having studied the Balinese culture for a decade. They took more than 25 000 photographs of different aspects of the Balinese culture such as rites of passage or ceremonies. The images were catalogued, studied, and sorted into themes that derived from the cultural knowledge of the anthropologists (Harper, 1994). Bateson and Mead noted

We are attempting a new method of stating the intangible relationships among different types of culturally standardized behavior by placing side by side mutually relevant photographs...By the use of photographs, the wholeness of each piece of behavior can be preserved, while the special cross-referencing desired can be obtained by placing the series of photographs on the same page (p. xii).

In their book, Bateson and Mead's (1942) photographic sequences are accompanied by a textual narrative based on the researchers' field notes and observations from the pictures. Each photograph is referenced describing date, place, location, and theoretical points that the images are intended to substantiate. In her methodological discussion, Mead describes how the theoretical points were established prior to the selection of the images selected to illustrate them. Another pioneering study was conducted by the social psychologist Kracauer (1947) of German cinema from 1918 to 1933, who pointed to themes and images that gave insights into ideas of fate and destiny, leaders and followers and included an analysis of the Nazi propaganda film that became a model for subsequent film content analyses. Mullen (2003) notes that cultural politics play a conscious role in arts-based research with researchers/artists offering a critique of sociopolitical issues through artistic production.

New frontiers emerge from discontent with older paradigms, coupled with a growing interest in cognitive pluralism and sophisticated technologies (digitization, satellite imaging, virtual reality, etc.) that call for new ways of thinking about leadership using nonlinear thinking and nontext-based approaches. One such approach takes place at the interface of leadership and the arts. Numerous scholars from diverse disciplines, such as nursing and organizational behavior, are opining that visual research should be taken more seriously because many social sciences have marginalized the visual. After all, we live in a world where the visual is of tremendous importance. We are, as Welsch (1997) notes, without doubt experiencing a visual boom. We are bombarded with visual representations of all kinds—the media, music (MTV), road signs and billboards, restrooms, and personal adornments. From product advertisement to annual reports, internal newsletters to recruitment brochures, and mission statements to web sites, visuals are everywhere. In organizations, we see a similar proliferation of the visual, from corporate branding through logos, the display of artifacts as representations of organizational culture, beautification of corporate offices with works of art and photographs, maps, sketches, and cartoons. These images communicate a collective identity of the organization. In contemporary life, increasing emphasis is being placed on taking the opportunity to "get across the right image" and "look good" in order to achieve even the slightest of market advantages (Hancock, 2003). Dickinson and Svensen (2000) evoke a world in which corporate activity should constitute style, beauty, a positive attitude, and pleasing experiences (p. 3), not only for its members but for society as a whole. In a world dominated by multimedia, it is therefore not surprising that scholars increasingly recognize visual representations as valid sources of data (Richards, 2006).

In leadership studies, image-based research is a relatively unknown approach to collecting, analyzing, and interpreting data. However, there are four distinct bodies of literatures that can inform leadership researchers interested in image-based research: (1) visual sociology, visual anthropology, and visual ethnography which maintain that every image tells a story and thus opens opportunities for new visually inspired research (Denzin & Lincoln, 2005; Harper, 1994); (2) multiple literacies, which consider visual representations (e.g., works of art, photographs, cartoons, graffiti, film) as legitimate text that communicates meaning (e.g., Hobbs, 1997); (3) visual semiotics, the science of signs and meanings, which assumes that culturally agreed upon symbols, drawings, and other type of images represent reality (e.g., Rose, 2001; Van Leeuwen & Jewitt, 2001); and (4) dual coding theory, which connects the symbolic system of cognition with written language and imagery (e.g., Sadoski & Paivio, 2001). Although leadership researches have for the most part ignored visual approaches to gathering data, images in the form of works of art, film, documentaries, the performing arts, freehand sketches of informants, photography, and computer-generated graphics potentially represent rich sources of data for leadership researchers. This chapter explores approaches that have been pursued in other disciplines using images from different artistic media. The generic terms image- or arts-based research are used throughout this chapter to refer to data and interpretations derived from various forms of visual representation.

Visual data often complement narrative as the dominant mode of research. However, in this chapter, the emphasis is on image-based research as the primary mode of inquiry agreeing with Pink (2001) that visual representations can be more important than the written word. When seen in this manner, visual communication is perceived as a legitimate literacy (Richards & Anderson, 2003).

Defining Image-Based Research

The answer to the question of "What is image-based research?" can be located in the traditions of Socrates and the ancient Greeks that maintained the tension between image and word, imagination and thought. In *The Republic*, Socrates bans the poets from the just city, because, in his view, their images distort reality and stir the passions, thereby creating public disorder. Most of Plato's dialogues have an aesthetic dimension which after the Greeks was lost in the Western concept of knowledge for centuries.

Image-based research is not easily defined because the artistic process by nature is often ambiguous and uncertain. Drawing on McNiff's (1998, p. 13) definition, image-based research in the context of leadership studies is defined here as a method of inquiry that uses elements of the creative art expressions reflecting the various languages of the arts such as paintings, theater, dance, film to shape a new vision of what leadership can be, when the arts rather than positional language or numbers are used as the basis for in-depth investigation. The aim of arts-based research is to use the arts as a method, a form of analysis, a subject, and as such, image-based research falls under the heading of alternative forms of research. Mullen (2003) concludes that arts-based research is focused on the process of expressing the context of lived situations rather than final products disconnected from the context of its creation (p. 170).

On the one hand, image-based research is akin to text-based qualitative methods in a number of ways. Stewart (1999), for example, discusses how image-based research is like other forms of qualitative and, in some respects, also quantitative research methods. Visual art echoes the interests of other forms of research, in "originality, being primarily investigative, and having the potential to produce results sufficiently general so that the human stock of knowledge, theoretical and practical, is recognizably increased" (p. 2). The author goes on to say that "visual research models can be described as processes of reflective, critical inquiry which are concerned with the advancement or extension of knowledge, discoveries, solutions to problems and conceptual progress" (p. 3). Similarly, Watrin (1999) emphasizes that arts-based research is, at times, like text-based qualitative research in that it "seizes the fullness of the lived experience by describing, interpreting, creating, reconstituting, and revealing meaning" (p. 93). The author describes similarities between qualitative research and studio art practice. Art making, like qualitative research, is a combination of intuition, subjectivity, and objectivity, which leads to insight and understanding. The analysis of image-based data is similar to the artistic process in that it involves divergent thinking, inductive reasoning, making connections, and communicating meanings.

On the other hand, although there are similarities between image- and text-based qualitative research, there are also considerable differences in the two modes of inquiry. Images are seen, understood, and interpreted using both visual, usually the primary channel, and auditory perception. The uniqueness of image-based research lies in its artistic intent and process. The arts-based paradigm assumes that by handing over creativity (the content of research) to the research participant, the participant is empowered and the relationship between the researcher and the participant is intensified since interpretation of images is more culturally exact and explicit, drawing on multiple sensory modalities and using cognitive, emotional, and spiritual ways of knowing (Huss & Cwikel, 2005).

Leadership, Aesthetics, and Art

Many commentators have suggested that we have entered a new historical era, one in which the visual has become most important as a pivotal aspect of social life. Rose

(2001) asserts that we now live in a world where knowledge is visually constructed. Metaphors such as the leader as artist or conductor or the organization as an orchestra have become popular with several celebrity conductors of famous philharmonic orchestras offering leadership development books and workshops (e.g., Zander & Zander, 2000). In addition to the use of artistic metaphors, which are beginning to replace the pervasive use of sports metaphors of leadership, the interest in the role of the arts in leadership is manifesting itself in a number of different ways. For example, a number of major corporations have invited the poet David Whyte (1994; 2001) to address their senior executives. Across corporate America, artists are invited to the table to help empower managers and employees at a time when creativity, imagination, passion, seeing the big picture, and commitment to a cause are much sought-after leadership attributes, characteristics which are frequently found among artists. Likewise, companies in many industries experiment with arts-based workshops to enhance employee creativity, improvisational skills, spontaneity, and intercultural competencies capitalizing on artists' knowledge of the creative process. Some companies have created yet another "C" executive position along with Chief Learning Officers, Chief Ethical Officers known as the Chief Inspiration Officer to solve their business problems creatively.

Arts education has found its way into business school curricula of leading business schools both in the United States (e.g., MIT, Wharton) and Europe (e.g., Oxford) offering arts-based courses. According to Pink (2004), the Master of Fine Arts (MFA) is now perhaps the hottest credential in the business world (p. 21) with corporate recruiters searching for leadership and managerial talent at top art and design schools. Harvey Seifter (2004), Executive Director of Orpheus, the world's only leaderless musical ensemble, offers this assertion:

> Clearly many business leaders have concluded that there are viable lessons to be learned from the experiences and insights of artists, lessons that can help their companies stay profitable in these changing times...This represents a dramatic shift in the boundaries that traditionally defined experiences relevant to the business world, a shift triggered by profound technological and social changes that has transformed the culture of business over the past decade.

Similarly, David Whyte (2001) explains that

> There is good practical reason for encouraging our artistic powers within organizations that up to now have been unwelcoming or afraid of these qualities...The artist must paint or sculpt or write, not only for the resent generation but for those who have yet to be born. Good artists, it is often said, are fifty to a hundred years ahead of their time; they describe what lies ahead over the horizon in our future world...The artist...must...depict this new

world before all the evidence is in. They must rely on the embracing abilities of their imagination to intuit and describe what is as a yet germinating seed in their present time, something that will only flower after they have written the line or painted the canvas. The present manager must learn the same artistic discipline, they must learn to respond to something that will move in the same direction the world is moving, without waiting for all the evidence to appear on their desks (pp. 241–242).

However, not many leaders or managers are trained in the use of artistic media and may not appreciate what the arts have to offer to leadership.

International management scholar Adler (2006) argues that three distinct trends— discontinuous change, networked teams, and simultaneity of listening and observing while doing as opposed to sequential planning—account for business' appropriation of more image-based approaches (p. 490). The author goes on to say that world leaders increasingly turn to artists because the old ways no longer work as they used to and business leaders have been among the first to realize this. Thus, many different voices— researchers, strategists, futurists, and economists—are advocating the cross-fertilization of leadership and the arts. However, at the time of this writing, it seems that leadership researchers have yet to draw on new insights from art theory and works of art. Finley (2003) suggests that arts-based approaches might not yet have reached the point of acceptance as serious (i.e., "rigorous") inquiry because, "the research community [is] already biased against the intellectual viability of the arts as a conceptual framework for research" (p. 289).

IMAGE-BASED LEADERSHIP RESEARCH

Like other qualitative methodologies, image-based research in leadership can uniquely capture the richness of context that works of art offer the leadership researcher. Qualitative research, instead of decontextualizing research participants and settings, intentionally embeds context in the research design. Since leadership itself is embedded in social and cultural beliefs and values and cannot be fully understood apart from the context in which it exists, image-based leadership research offers a unique lens for examining contextual factors. Image-based inquiry looks to expressions in the context of lived situations rather than to final productions. As Becker (1996) points out, qualitative work including image-based inquiry allows for, indeed insists on, highly contextualized individual judgments in the attempt to produce a more or less coherent representation, carried by word or image, of an authentically claimed reality. For Becker (1998), the context in which images are viewed needs to be understood by the researcher when employing images since different people have different understandings which they bring to the viewing and interpreting of images.

The Aesthetics of Leadership

Aesthetics, introduced as an area of philosophy concerned with art and beauty, was developed in Germany in the eighteenth century. The word itself comes from the Greek, esthesis, and refers broadly to any kind of sensory experience, regardless of whether it is sensory or artistic. The aesthetic perspective to organizations and management originated in the mid-1980s, mainly as a protest to the positivist and rational paradigm that dominated organization and management thinking, as well as leadership theory. Aesthetics provided a philosophical point to develop an alternative to the mainstream paradigm that emphasized the logical, rational, and linear nature of organizational practices such as management and leadership. Management and leadership theories are explicitly more familiar with the discourse of control, profit, and effectiveness than with aesthetics. Nevertheless, an aesthetics dimension is always present in leadership practices as long as human beings are involved in social processes to accomplish something and open to discussions of aesthetics in leadership that goes beyond the metaphorical reference to leaders as artists.

The idea and practice of a philosophy of aesthetics goes back to antiquity (Hancock & Tyler, 2000). Plato asserted that beauty is itself a "form" and as such remains timeless, immutable, and therefore objective. Nevertheless, the notion that the appreciation of beauty is inevitably a subjective experience, which cannot be evaluated by objective criteria and as such, is immune to most forms of rational assessment prevailed. Kant's (1911) *Critique of Aesthetic Judgment* countered that while the appreciation of a beautiful object is in essence a subjective pleasure, its beauty is something, which could and should be universally appreciable through the human faculty of judgment. Alternatively, Hegel's philosophy of aesthetics viewed beauty as expressed through art, as the materialization of the unfolding of the absolute spirit through human consciousness and action. Beautiful art, therefore, for Hegel at least, is defined as that which most closely represents the unity of "nature and spirit" (Weiss, 1974, p. 318).

More recently, Strati (1992; 1996; 1999) and Gagliardi (1990; 1996) have addressed organizational aesthetics as a means of developing greater insight into how meanings are constructed and promoted within the cultural environment of the organization. For example, Gagliardi posits that organizational artifacts play a unique role in structuring and shaping members' beliefs and values. The author argues that through managerial strategies of cultural manipulation, which more or less rely on aesthetic qualities of objects and practices, corporate identity is shaped. Likewise, Carr (2003) posits that organizational artifacts are strategically deployed as a means of underpinning or reinforcing various managerial attempts to improve organizational efficiency and productivity. Aesthetics as rational tool of management, then, seeks to appropriate aesthetics for their own purposes of controlling staff and increasing productivity.

Schmitt and Simonson (1997) proposed a framework termed Corporate Aesthetics Management (CAM) that captures the drive to establish a systematic approach to the planning and design of an aesthetically oriented organizational environment. While the authors acknowledge that managers have tended to sidestep discussions of aesthetics due to the somewhat esoteric and generally subjective nature of the topic, the solution to this problem is simply to reduce the language of the aesthetic to a style more familiar to managers, thus allowing aesthetics to be more easily comprehended and deployed as the basis for a comprehensive and strategic approach to managing a corporation's aesthetic image. In the words of the authors, the subjective dimension of the aesthetic experience is carefully excluded, reducing potential obstacles to the construction of a systematic framework within which the aesthetic may be reduced to a set of variables subject to manipulation over both time and space. (Hancock, 2003, p. 53). As we share common goals and expectations as members of the qualitative research community, we can call upon the arts to help us express our vision, hopes, and dreams for the future.

Leadership aesthetics is concerned with developing, understanding, and representing leadership knowledge through sensory experience. It manifests itself pragmatically in the increasing display of works of art in executive offices, the promotion of art festivals by organizations, and the inclusion of art workshops at management and economic conferences. A growing body of research is beginning to emerge that suggests that it recognizes the value of the aesthetic dimension by those wishing to redefine their conceptualizations of organizational life. Mahon (2002) argues that the esthetic product is always part of broader social contexts around which there is a power struggle over different meanings. At the same time, the author claims that art includes elements and esthetic languages that are specific to it and that cannot be translated into action research or communication. Denzin (2000) challenged us to engage in a new movement of qualitative inquiry, a postinterpretive paradigm in which we move from the personal (the reflexive rational) into the political (reflexive activist), not in a disconnected way but by employing emotional critique to political action. This movement is described as a "radical ethical aesthetics" (Denzin, 2000, p. 261). According to Denzin

Aesthetics, art, performance, history, culture, politics [and leadership, parenthesis added] are intertwined for in the artful interpretive production, cultural heroes, heroines, mystical paths, and senses of moral community are created (p. 260).

Leadership, I would add, can make unique contribution to this developing movement, especially by forging into arts-based research as an alternative to text-based qualitative research. Aesthetics represents an alternative epistemological position in the acquisition of knowledge about leadership and leaders that needs to be explicated and experimented with. Like other epistemological positions—positivism, interpretivism, and constructionism—aesthetics is historically and culturally conditioned and contextually defined as are moral or political judgments. Within the larger domain of qualitative leadership research, image-based research holds the promise of creating new databases derived from works of art, music, film, video, and the performing arts and thereby extracting new knowledge that cannot be distilled from textual materials alone.

IMAGE-BASED RESEARCH AS AN EMERGENT METHODOLOGY

Image-based research is one of the newer developments in the research community. Historically, the arts have often challenged dominant political, religious, and aesthetic conversations while serving as a lightning rod for social change (e.g., Slattery, 2003; Spehler & Slattery, 1999). The postmodern era is marked by a proliferation of styles and narratives that cannot be contained and offers the opportunity to understand leadership and society from a multitude of perspectives. Broadly defined image-based research considers music, dance, drama, works of art video, pictures, photographs, computer-generated graphics, documentaries, and architecture that can be utilized as sources of data to create new leadership knowledge. Arts-based research asks questions such as what is awakened or evoked in the spectator when viewing an image, how it creates meanings, how it can heal, and what it can teach, incite, inspire, or provoke that is typically outside the boundaries of traditional perspectives and the canons of traditional methodologies.

Taylor and Hansen (2005) describe at least three ways that the arts can inform leadership. The first is through using art as a metaphor for leadership. Examples cited earlier include the leader as an artist, leadership as an orchestra, and management as a theater ensemble. Second, specific artistic methods can be employed to support leadership practices. For example, a business leader with some education in the visual arts could ask his or her team to paint a picture of their team. Third, arts-based methods may be used to generate artistic content. A leader with some knowledge and understanding of architectural design, for instance, may use this knowledge to create work spaces that reflect organizational values such as beauty, openness, balance, vision, creativity, and a holistic approach to leadership. Dune and Martin (2006) note that the design of products and services is a critical component of business and competitiveness to the extent that major companies such as Proctor and Gamble have committed themselves to become major design leaders (p. 512). Space, one element of design, is also a construct of social, political, intellectual, and life-sustaining activities. Artists create spaces that may be psychological, illusionary, theatrical, metaphorical, or sacred. Like O'Keefe's (2000) paintings, leadership can offer an archway to spaces where individuals and organizations can experience new horizons. According to Palmer (1983/1993), leaders can create spaces that are open, hospitable to ideas, and possibilities of truth where, like an artist's studio, there is ample light and quiet and a window to the world. Dune and Martin (2006) concluded that incorporating design thinking into management and approaching management problems as designers is beginning to gain recognition in both the academic literature and the business press.

Several qualitative researchers conducting image-based research (i.e., Finley, 2003; Mullen, 2003; Sclater, 2003) have argued that in arts-based research, elitism is replaced by art as communication, whereby the reactions to the art work are more important than the quality of the art in term of external esthetic criteria. Within this paradigm, according to these authors, the criteria of communication and social responsibility predominate over craftsmanship.

Image-based research offers a mode of inquiry that allows for exciting and innovative intersections among three major discourse traditions—art, leadership, and research. According to Levine (2000)

> To base research in the arts means to engage the imagination in the forming of our concepts and in the carrying out of the project itself. Not only may the initial inspiration come in the encounter with the image...but the conduct of the research itself must be imaginative. We must have faith that the imagination can inform us, that art is non-cognitive but that it binds together both feeling and form in a way that can reveal truth (p. 91).

Working within such generative space, however, also carries a risk for potential mis-understandings. Labaree (1998), in both analyzing and challenging the hierarchical classification of knowledge within the academy, sounded a cautionary note for those whose work pushes the contours of commonly accepted notions of research. She points out that the attack on the validity of the hard sciences has led to the position that softness is not a problem to be dealt with but a virtue to be celebrated. Frequently, the result is that qualitative methods are treated less as a cluster of alternative methodologies than as a license to say what one wants without regard to rules of evidence or forms of validation (p. 11).

Just as artists make a host of decisions as they craft a particular piece of art, image-based leadership researchers make numerous decisions as they design a particular arts-based study, beginning with the research question. What is the purpose of the study and what role(s) will art play in accomplishing this purpose? Art informs through its evocative power—to surprise, delight, mystify, disturb, and shock. Based on their sense of identity and the talents they bring to their work, some investigators may reasonably claim the stance of "artist as researcher" or "researcher as artist," claim their work is art, and prefer that it be judged primarily on its esthetic merits. But as a leadership discourse community, we need to be prepared to have our work judged as much on its esthetic as well as its scholarly merit. The arts and images are important as inquiry methodologies, not merely as innovations in forms of representation or interpretations. Promoting an esthetic analysis to challenge the dominant positivist paradigm as well as encouraging an understanding of how images may be appropriated for a diverse range of purposes in leadership research implies that different researchers are likely to employ artistic modes of inquiry differently. For example, as noted earlier, visual imagery may be deployed as a management device for creating and sustaining the commitment and support of employees to the corporate objectives. Likewise, leaders can sustain commitment of followers by using various types of visual information capitalizing, for example, on the ambiguity of the messages carried by images. However, mere existence or recognition of aesthetic, ethical, or emotional responses to leadership and organizational images found in various forms of artistic representation is no guarantee that linear logic and positivistic rationality that characterizes much of leadership research will be readily eclipsed.

IMAGE-BASED SOURCES OF DATA

Images of leaders and leadership can be located in sources as diverse as Egyptian hieroglyphs, sculptures of contemporary leaders and historical statues, tributes to leaders found in musical notes, or leaders self-presentation in films. They are found in plays, poetry, music, dance, graffiti, cartoons, films, photography, documentaries, and quilts. Speaking for the performing arts, Saldaña (2003) discusses ethnodrama which employs traditional craft and artistic techniques of formal theater production of research participants' experiences and/or researchers' interpretations of data for an audience. Characters in an ethnodrama are generally the research participants portrayed by actors, but the researchers and participants themselves may also be cast members (p. 218). Ethnotheater, according to Bagley and Cancienne (2002), represents a fairly recent movement in qualitative inquiry to experiment with artistic modes of research representation.

Barone (2003), a member of the arts-based research community, discusses the usefulness of film as a source of data and explores the artistic substance or educational value of a film's theme and esthetic form or the technical and formal qualities of themes in films. The author notes that the production of documentary projects includes many strategies that resemble those employed by social science-based qualitative researchers: interviewing, observation, participant observation, document analysis, and member checking. Barbash and Taylor (1997) characterize the process of film-making as

> The act of filming is often likened ... to the documentation or demonstration of research that precedes and determines it. It is seen to provide a record of intellectual work that, in essence, exists apart from it. The assumption misconceives the kind of interventions that take place when you film ... Film images have an inextricable relationship to their object, and, while shooting,

you're selecting and editorializing in ways that will be intrinsic to your final film. Once you recognize this, it's difficult to see research and filming as altogether separate stages (p. 70).

Dance and choreography are other artistic expressions that have found their way into arts-based research. For example, Bagley and Cancienne (2002) represented their educational research through dance, theater, poetry, music, collage, and photography. Cancienne and Snowber (2003), dancers, choreographers, and arts-based researchers, suggest that choreography, the art of dance, and everyday movement provide a rhythmic pattern, a system of meaningful motions of the body that can communicate an interpretation of the world we live in (p. 239). Dance is not only an expression of their research but a form of inquiry into the research process. The authors combine dance, a kinesthetic form, and writing, a cognitive form, to establish relationships between body and mind, cognitive and affective knowing, and the intellect with physical vigor. They draw on phenomenological research describing the body from lived experience and autobiographical and narrative inquiry as modes for integrating dance within the research process. As arts-based researchers, Cancienne and Snowber explore how individuals are socially constructed through their bodies and how physicality of technique and experience moves people beyond their social constructions (p. 239). Because the body is socially constructed, according to Desmond (1997), it communicates social practices and cultural meaning through voice, gesture, and movement. Cancienne and Snowber assert that dance is a corporeal way of knowing, a different way of seeing, questioning, and challenging.

ANALYZING VISUAL DATA

The analysis of visual data, like the analyses of all other qualitative research, should be guided by the research question. Since qualitative researchers often connect photographs, videos, drawings, paintings, and film with narrative description, the use of verbal and visual elements can be seen as a triangulation of data. Emmison and Smith (2000) argued that visual analyses should be approached as both data driven and theory dependent. They are data driven in the sense that since image-based researchers intend to capture the phenomenal features of the leader's essence in visual materials they use in their investigations and make them the objects of the analyses. They are theory dependent in the sense that is only through a conceptual framework that a given "object" can become data (p. 4). Van Leeuwen and Jewitt (2001) distinguish the image as reality versus the image as construct and note that different types of visual analyses flow from that distinction. In the first case, image as reality, the work of art is regarded as a reliable source of factual evidence much as the written word is. In the second, image as construct, the search is for underlying conceptual themes that capture the construct of interest. In a way, this distinction is analogous to the differences between manifest and latent coding introduced in Chapter 4. The challenge for image-based leadership researchers is to determine how to incorporate image or sound-based data at any stage of data collection, analysis, and presentation.

Watrin (1999) argues that analysis of textual and image-based data are similar in that hermeneutic phenomenologists and artists are both engaged in processes that synthesize knowledge, as well as describe and interpret lived experience in search for meaning (p. 98). In other cases, images are analyzed, not as evidence of the who, where, and what of reality but as evidence of how their maker(s) have (re-)constructed reality. From this perspective, the image is more unreliable and slippery as a source of factual information. As the authors point out, the issue of "record" versus "construct" exists because many images have an element of both and therefore require a mode of analysis which is sensitive to both. For example, advertising images are in the first place constructs and their analysis must reveal the nature of these constructs.

Visual analysis may be based on what is visible within a single image or a collection of images and then looks beyond the surface to explore symbolism and meaning behind the physical representation It may draw on contextual information, whether gleamed from video-taped interviews used in the field of visual anthropology or from archival research and background reading, as in the case of iconography. Most types of visual analyses also include narrative analysis as the image is translated into text or a story. The choice of method depends on the nature of the material to be analyzed and the goals of the analysis. Methods of visual analysis vary in terms of the extent to which the procedures are specified. In visual content analysis, for example, the procedures are fairly precise. Other forms of analysis provide less precise rules, offer a great degree of latitude for creativity based on the notion that the analyses of images cannot be conceptualized as a "step-by-step" procedure. For Colliers (2001), visual analysis is a complex process, which alternates between stages that require intuitive grasp of the whole and stages that require the hard work of structured analysis, of careful and methodological checking and double-checking. According to the author, it is necessary to "observe data as whole," to look at, and listen to "its overtones and subtleties," to "trust your feelings and impressions," and go through the evidence with specific questions (p. 39). Colliers sees visual analysis as both art and science:

> It is both necessary and legitimate to allow ourselves to respond artistically or intuitively to visual images ... However, while creative processes are essential to discovery, artistic processes may produce only fictitious statement if not combined with systematic and detailed analysis (p. 59).

I will briefly describe two specific methods of visual analyses to illustrate the range from quantitative, procedurally oriented approaches to more interpretive, intuitively oriented methods of analysis. The development of a more rigorous typology of image-based methods is work that remains to be done.

Content Analysis of Visual Data

According to Ball and Smith (1992), content analysis, following the tenets of content analysis outlined in Chapter 3, is considered the most appropriate technique for analyzing visual data. The objectivity of content analysis resides in the design of precisely defined categories applied to the materials—be they text or images—to be analyzed in accordance with explicitly formulated procedures. Content analysis of visual materials as well as content analyses of narratives follows established procedures which typically include (1) determining the research problem; (2) identifying the relevant visual materials; (3) devising a set of categories into which the content is to be coded; (4) formulating an explicit set of coding rules; and (5) analyzing the categories (i.e., frequency counts, cross-tabulation, etc.).

In visual content analysis, very much akin to content analysis used in text-based research, content analysis is an empirical (observational) and objective procedure for quantifying recorded visual (sometimes including verbal) representations using reliable, explicitly defined categories. A category may be a construct or dimension of artistic form such as size, color, material, or utilization of space. The first decision involves determining the corpus of images (analog to the selection of a corpus of text), sample size (how many images), and identifying the salient features of the artistic work such as context and art form. Based on these decisions, the images are classified into distinctive categories. Content analysis of visual data also includes quality measures to insure the consistency of coding categories using different indices of intercoder reliability.

Bell (2001) points out that to conduct a visual content analysis is to try to describe salient aspects of an image or a group of images as representations of some type of people, objects processes, events, and/or relationships between them. All systematic methods of visual analysis postulate some features of the image (and not others) as semantically significant, within the image's context. To make inferences from the findings of a content analysis that does go beyond the data means making a prediction about the salience or ideological importance and the visual significance of one's findings.

Content analysis of images requires that the researcher is able to offer a detailed description of the images and understands the context in which the images were produced. In preparing visual data for analysis, work sheets, much like field notes in text-based qualitative research that describe what the researcher sees in the image, what techniques have been used, how the image or art work has been designed recording format, tone, shape, texture color, spatial relations, and so on, the context in which the image was created, influences on the artist, meaning or purpose of the image of and in case critical discussions of the work and the artist are helpful in creating the narrative that often accompanies images.

Eisner (1997) also discusses specific skills image-based researchers need. With respect to film as the artistic medium, the author points out that those who want to use film (or any other form of art for that matter) as a major vehicle for conducting leadership research not only need to access a camera or be in command of other artistic techniques, they also need to understand how films and other forms of art are produced and how medium specific techniques such as painting, drawing, or making documentaries are applied. Furthermore, unless the university is sympathetic to image-based research as a legitimate way to promote one's contributions to the discipline, the arts-based researcher needs to be able to procure the resources necessary to carry out the project. Seale (1999), who attempted to move new paradigm research from the foundations of philosophy and resituate it within practice, advocates a studio apprenticeship model for learning a wide variety of research skills that an individual incorporates into his/her own repertoire of skills, "in much the same way as artists learn to paint, draw or sculpt in a number of different styles" (p. 476). The arts-based researcher needs visualization skills as well as the dualistic ability of mediating between image and the languages of text—an art literate individual with aesthetic reflexivity.

Iconography

Iconography can be a confusing term. Its original meaning refers to the study of icons, which still remains in some religious contexts, particularly in the Greek and Russian Orthodox Church. Unlike Barthian (Barthes, 1967) visual semiotics, iconography is based on visual, textual, and contextual analysis which is particularly appropriate for the corpus of sculptures selected for this research because it allows the researcher to employ intertextual comparisons and documentary research to support the interpretations (Van Leeuwen & Jewitt, 2001).

As a method of visual analysis, iconography refers to the discovery and identification of the deeper meaning in a work of art or image by distinguishing three layers of pictorial meaning: *representational meaning, iconographical symbolism*, and *iconological symbolism* (Panofsky, 1970). Panofsky, one of the founders of iconography as a method of visual analysis, used the term representational to mean the "primary or natural subject matter" (p. 33) describing it as the recognition of what is presented. Representational meaning (much like manifest coding in text-based content analysis), according to Panofsky, refers to the recognition of what is presented taking into account the stylistic conventions and the technical transformations involved in the representation—for example, the fact that in medieval paintings "human beings, animals, and inanimate objects seem to hang loose in space in violation of the law of gravity, without thereby pretending to be apparitions" (p. 60). While the analysis of the representational meaning of a contemporary image may seem an unnecessary step, in works of art from the past it is essential. Van Leeuwen and Jewitt (2001) point out that in historical works of art, however, faces may no longer be recognized, objects, gestures and activities may have become obsolete and establishing which of the people, places and things in a picture are iconographically significant (or, rather, were at the time of its production) may require a bit of research.

The second level, which focuses on *iconographical symbolism*, according to Panofsky, the persons, things, or places represented in an image are not only analyzed at the descriptive level but also for ideas or concepts attached to them. Panofsky describes this level of analysis as follows:

> [iconographical symbolism] is apprehended by realising that a male figure with a knife represents St. Bartholomew, that a female figure with a peach in her hand is a personification of veracity ... or that two figures fighting each other in a certain way represent the Combat of Vice and Virtue. In doing this we connect artistic motifs and combinations of artistic motifs (compositions) with themes or concepts (p. 54).

Finally, discovering the *iconological symbolism* in an image refers to isolating the ideological meaning of the image. To analyze it is, in Panofsky's word, to "ascertain those underlying principles which reveal the basic attitudes of a nation, a period, a class, a religious or philosophical persuasion" (Panofsky, 1970, p. 55). The third level of interpretation according to Van Leeuwen and Jewitt (2001) is the most contentious. Iconology draws together the iconographical symbols and stylistic features of an image or a representational tradition into a coherent interpretation, which provides the "why" behind the image analyzed. Panofsky understood iconology to be more than a search for symptoms but an exhaustive interpretation of art production.

Think of one of your favorite pieces of art and apply the three levels of analysis. For example, when we try to understand DaVinci's Last Supper using iconography, we begin with a description of the representational meaning of the painting or creating a detailed word picture to capture the characters, the content, and the content. Iconographical symbolism may focus on the Last Supper as a portrait of Leonardo's personality while iconological symbolism may suggest that the Last Supper documents the civilization of the Italian Renaissance. Panofsky argued that the symbolic values which the arts-based researchers tries to identify using at the third level of iconography which may be unknown to the artist himself and may even differ emphatically from what they intended to express is the object of iconology as opposed to iconography (p. 56). Artists often draw on unconscious inspiration rather than on consciously known symbolic traditions (Van Leeuwen & Jewitt, 2001).

In iconography, the analysis of art objects and other images is systematized into these three levels moving the iconographer from simple identification of familiar persons and objects to the second level where the researcher uncovers themes and concepts beyond conventional meanings to point out that works of art must be understood as carrying more-than-visual meaning. In iconography as a method of analyzing visual data, there is a clear progression from identifying generally accepted conventions to interpretations which may not be generally accepted, but which nevertheless are an indispensable part of the analysis. The first two levels of meaning, the natural and iconographical, according to Panofsky are phenomenal, while the third, intrinsic meaning is beyond the sphere of conscious volition. The separation of levels was only intended as an explanation of a process, which Panofsky understood would be fully integrated through intuition. It is sometimes argued that iconography favors the original meaning of art works from the past when these might mean something different today. Van Leeuwen and Jewitt (2001) concur when they point out that today's viewers of work of art get something different out of, for example, medieval and Renaissance paintings than the artists' contemporaries did (p. 102).

Regardless of the methods of visual analysis used, arts-based researchers who employ images as sources of data are encouraged to keep track of their ideas and insights as they contemplate each image in a journal or log if using computer software for the analyses. Field notes are an integral component in the analysis of most qualitative methods including content analysis, interviewing, and ethnography. This includes keeping a detailed account of the context that surrounds the image—where the people or objects came from, relationships between them, spatial organization, and so on. Recording thoughts about for whom the images were intended, how they were created, by whom and under what circumstances, what stories the images tell, how is power distributed, what knowledge is required to interpret them, and what are the researcher's emotional reaction to them are helpful in the analytic process. If the images consist, for example, of photographs or drawings, laying them out in different ways and thereby constructing different grouping are helpful in interpreting the images, especially if the investigator examines whether the groupings make sense in light of the research topic.

QUALITY ISSUES IN IMAGE-BASED

Because the culture of science-based research is so well ingrained in the field of leadership, the hallmarks of quality within this culture (e.g., validity, reliability, replicability, and generalizability) are taken as given and considered standard for all research methodologies. Individual research studies, including qualitative works, are often judged by the extent to which accepted procedures for meeting these hallmarks are followed. On the other hand, a culture of arts-based research has not yet evolved, and any consensus on the hallmarks for judging such studies has yet to emerge. Yet within the communities of artists, criteria for judging the merits of artistic products and performances exist.

According to Finley (2003) in order to develop an understanding for the potential of image-based research as a legitimate mode of inquiry, researchers should continue and expand their explorations of media other than verbal texts. Arts-based researchers include painters, sculptors, dancers, musicians, and other image-based researchers from various disciplines including leadership studies that create nonverbal performance texts (p. 290). Examples of discussions of image-based inquiries include, as noted earlier, explorations of the viability of dance as a representational mode (e.g., Bagley & Cancienne, 2001; Blumenfeld-Jones, 1995), motion pictures (Barone, 2003), and visual arts (Scott-Hoy, 2003).

The inclusion of images in qualitative research imposes many difficulties. According to Prosser (1998b), the problem with image-based research is this:

> The general message, perhaps unwittingly, is that: [films, videos and photographs] are acceptable only as means to record data or as illustration and subservient to that of the central narrative; they are unacceptable as a way of "knowing" because they distort that which they claim to illuminate; and images being socially created and mediated are skewed by the sociocontext of "making," "taking," and "reading;" and summatively images are so complex that analysis is untenable (p. 99).

For many quantitatively trained and oriented leadership researchers, image-based research is seen as undisciplined, soft, and lacking rigor. Finley (2003) argues that qualitative researchers who are engaged in image-based research often cross the boundaries between art and theory and model the creative process of discovery and invention employed by arts-based researchers who use the methodologies of the arts to define new practices of social inquiry. Eisner (1997) allows for the possibility that arts-based research might not be a conventional paradigm within the arts and, therefore, might also not be subjected to its categorical evaluations. Arts-based research may simply be among one of many systemic studies of phenomena undertaken to advance human understanding, not exactly art and not exactly science.

Loizos (2000) points out that one of the fallacies about visual data is the notion that images do not lie. Moreover, the author argues that the manipulation of images can be more subtle and cover, but distinctly ideological. For example, Moeller (1989) discusses how many famous war photographs have come to represent particular political perceptions of the conduct of war. Likewise, Loizos asserts that in film and video, there is no reason to introduce these media into the research situation unless it is the best or only way to record the data as making film or video is likely to distract informants, at least until they become comfortable and learn to act naturally in front of the recording system.

Lincoln (1995) began the discussion about quality criteria for qualitative research by identifying three interconnected commitments by qualitative researchers: first, to deepen participant and researcher interactions and involvements; second, to professional, personal, and political actions that might improve participants lives; and third, to future-oriented work that is based in a visionary perspective that encompasses social justice, community, diversity, civic discourse, and caring. As image-based approaches are far from having reached a point of recognition or minimal acceptance as a serious mode of inquiry in the study of leadership, discussions of quality standards may be premature. However, I believe they need also to be taken into consideration if image-based research is to attain credibility and parity with text-based methods.

Developing criteria for judging the merits not only of empirical–qualitative research but also interpretive image-based research is not possible without discussion of the epistemological, ontological underpinnings of image-based research. According to Prosser (1998a), in image-based research, contextual validity—the "context" of making and "interpreting" images—supersedes other types of validities considered in qualitative research making it difficult for orthodox researchers to attach credence in nontext. Criteria for judging image-based research are still developing (Finley, 2003). To avoid comparison with scientific inquiry or evaluations by the standards of science, image-based researchers must undergo a radical break from science as a standpoint for understanding. Whereas Lincoln (1995) asserts that new paradigm inquiry is not second rate inquiry, but is scientific inquiry in its own right.

Prosser (1998b) argued that representation and trustworthiness of data analysis are central to all qualitative methods including image-based research. How can we distinguish between "good" image-based and "bad" image-based? What are the criteria for quality when conducting arts-based inquiry that exhibits a "radical, ethical aesthetic," asks Denzin (2000, p. 261)? On what grounds, asks Slattery (2003), can image-based researchers claim legitimacy for their work? For example, it has been said that Delacroix's painting "Liberty Leading the People" has truly captured the essence of the French revolution, namely, the ultimate triumph of liberty over despotism (Tung, 2006, p. 506)? How does a leadership scholar who uses Delacroix's painting as the source of data validate such a claim? How can image-based leadership researchers address questions of quality in the scientifically oriented leadership research community? Or, "Who qualifies for membership in the image-based research discourse community?"

Alternatives to Validity and Quality Standards in Image-Based Research

As we have seen throughout this book, it has been asserted that validity is problematic in qualitative research. It is particularly problematic for mainstream researchers who apply traditional approaches to image-based research. Seale (1999) emphasized that the debate over quality has shifted from an exclusive focus on validity and reliability that was imported from positivism to other possibilities more befitting qualitative research.

Obviously, additional criteria will have to be developed for arts-based research. However, validity in image-based research is not a matter of satisfying a set of criteria, and measures of validity adapted from the quantitative or text-based paradigms are not appropriate because they do not adequately fit the axioms of image-based research.

Bamford (2007), for example, proposed that notions of form may provide some new axioms by which image-based methodologies can be assessed. The author argues that in image-based research, notions of form provide a more accurate way of determining the merit and value of research than traditional notions of validity. The term form is used in artistic and literary language to imply the manifestations that result from the fashioning of particular parts into a whole, creative shape. Form is the shape of things. It implies the creation of expressive frames that are visually, audibly, and/or imagina- tively perceivable. Form as opposed to traditional tenets of validity allows many individually conceived things and properties to be related to each other to produce a holistic picture. If a piece of arts-based research is valid in terms of form, then that form will convey the consciousness of the researcher as well as the consciousness of the participants. Moreover, form resonates with the researcher's biases. Using form as an alternative conception of validity means accepting the axiom that every researcher will see something different in the study. There will be multiple ways to interpret form, many of them specific to a particular art form and a range of techniques. Form is also ultimately born in the imaginings of individual researchers and viewers of the work. The researcher is a collagist or bricoleur who tries to pull pieces out from a form that already exists and then reconstructs it into a representation of the world reflecting his or her worldview. Through critical interpretation, the viewer experiences the interplay between form and context. The conceptual framework of the researcher, the partici- pants, and the audience mediate the understanding of form. To understand form, all stakeholders must learn to listen and look. Aesthetic form, as a determinant of the research merit and worth, Bamford (2007) notes, requires immersion, sympathy, openness, and awareness.

Herman (2005) proposes that validity of arts-based research is determined by how the audience stays engaged with the findings and allows them to affect them. Polkinghorne (1983) suggests that findings of image-based research should fulfill the esthetic criteria for validity—vividness, accuracy, richness, and elegance (p. 46). Simco and Warin (1997) proposed a different set of criteria to include (1) completeness; (2) accuracy of interpretation; (3) transparency; (4) self-reflection; and (5) aggregation of conflicting interpretations. Likewise, Richardson (2000), based on her ethnographic work, devel- oped a set of criteria that include substantive contribution, aesthetic merit, reflexivity, impact, and the reality in image-based research. As Mullen (2003) points out, new terms and criteria continue to proliferate, quality appears to be elusive phenomenon. Slattery (2003) appears to agree stating that if quality is elusive, then it becomes a futile exercise to pin it down.

According to Denzin and Lincoln (2000), the truth of artful findings "is determined pragmatically by their truth effects; by the critical, moral discourse, they produce; by the empathy they generate, the exchange of experience they enable, and the social bonds they mediate" (p. 1055). There can be no doubt that many examples of the representative arts—painting, sculpture, novel, and drama—are praised for their truth. We demand truth of coloring or line in painting, of form in sculpture, or character or social relation in the drama or novel, just as we seek for truth in normative science research.

Piantanida, McMahon, and Garman (2003) ask on what grounds can image-based researchers claim legitimacy for their work? What are the hallmarks of well-crafted image-based studies? Despite the rise of qualitative research and the recognition that artists and writers have much to contribute to the study of leadership, the positivist paradigm prevails and the continued conviction that as much as possible leadership research should adhere to the percepts of science and conform to the norms of a culture of science. As compelling as Piantanida et al. argument for adopting standard definitions of quality, such efforts are not likely to be persuasive when they are presented within a research community already biased against the intellectual viability of the arts as the conceptual framework for research (Finley, (2003). The author raised a number of questions, the answers to which may lead to the development of different quality standards for image-based research. Among them were

- Are researchers performing a useful, local, community service by conducting the research? Could the research be harmful in a way to the community of the participants?

- How does form of representation (regardless of whether it is, for instance, painting, dance, or narrative) create an open space for dialogue between readers/perceivers and research participants? Are research documents openly written or painterly?

- Does the research (practice and representation) allow a heuristic, "open" text, in which there are spaces for multiple meaning to be constructed? Does the research provoke questions rather than draw conclusions?

- Is the practice and representation passionate and visceral? Does it involve activity that creates opportunities for communion among participants, researchers, and the various research communities who might be audiences (and participants with) the research text?

- Does the representation, both through its form and its content, have the capacity to connect its local, community service with purposes of its audience? Is the reader/viewer, or participant, likely to be moved to some kind of action (p 294)?

Finally, the author acknowledges that craftsmanship, artistry, and expertise are not among the qualities she seeks in image-based research. Instead, the author is far more concerned with, and finds greater artistry in, experiences of passion, communion, and social responsibility. Locating quality criteria within a particular context and community rather than establishing rules for evaluation offers one way of assessing the quality of image-based research. Finley suggests moving away from standards in image-based research—especially as they apply to art. Likewise, the author cautions to be careful of following too closely the detailed guidelines for good writing as measures of good research narrative as a standard in image-based research.

Bochner (2000) also observed that standards and rules invite elitism, separatism, and a closed community. The author argues that when we converse about criteria and standards, our positions harden, conflicts escalate, and alienation increases. Image-based inquiry (like other qualitative inquiry) should embrace a set of communities that are, as Lincoln (1995) said, relational: first, to community—to dialogical, nurturing, caring, and democratic relationships between researchers and participants who share their commitment to understanding social life; second, to action within community—to engage research work that is locally usable and responsive to cultural and political issues and that takes a stance against social injustice (Denzin, 2000); and finally, to visionary critical discourses—to research efforts that examine how things are but also imagine how they could be otherwise. Eisner (1997) contends that image-based research might not be a conventional paradigm and, therefore, might not be subjected to its categorical evaluations. Image-based research may simply be one among many systemic studies of phenomena undertaken to advance human understanding, not exactly art and certainly not science.

Given its current status, image-based is in its infancy and very much marginalized. Fyfe and Law (1988) have provided one of the most comprehensive accounts of the marginalization of the visual in the social science including economic (cost of reproduction, copyrighting, and paper quality), philosophical, and methodological considerations as being responsible for the neglect of visual evidence. For example, the quality of a journal such as *Nature* depends on graphics—maps, sketches, and photographs. As the authors point out, the science that *Nature* reproduces would not be possible without depictions, which are constitutive of scientific production (p. 3). In addition, the legitimacy of art as a basis for inquiry—a means for producing knowledge and contributing to human understanding—has been questioned (e.g., Bochner & Ellis, 2003). For many, art as inquiry falls outside the realm of conventional research since what is important about art is what is awakened or evoked in the spectator, how it created meanings, how it could heal, and what it can teach, incite, inspire, or provoke (p. 507). Clearly, these sorts of questions do not fit snugly with the traditional cannon of research. Instead, they are calling for a shift of the boundaries of traditional perspectives on inquiry and knowledge and crossing the borders of research orthodoxy.

If image-based serves as a mode of constructing/generating knowledge, we need to ask what the epistemological, ontological, axiological, and methodological assumptions of this approach to research are. Does image-based research take us beyond an epistemological position to embrace a set of interpretive practices that encapsulates and interconnects aesthetics, art, epistemology, ontology, ethics, leadership, and political praxis? Piantanida et al. (2003, p. 186) assert that what gives the image-based community a distinctive identity is a commitment to exploring the intricacies of engaging in esthetic modes of inquiry into compelling phenomena. The purpose of these explorations is not to generate a narrow, hegemonic view of what constitutes image-based research. Rather, it is a call for conversations through which the contours of this landscape can be sculpted within a discourse community (p. 189).

EXAMPLES OF ARTS-BASED RESEARCH

In this section, I present several examples of image-based research to illustrate how different artistic media can be used in empirical research. Although no arts-based studies were located in the leadership literature that apply image-based methods to a particular leadership issue or problem, the examples presented in this section are intended to illustrate how leadership researchers may design an arts-based study. Moreover, they shed light on leadership processes established in the literature such as empowerment and the dark side of leadership.

Cancienne and Snowber (2003), defining themselves as moving researchers, describe a dance choreographed entitled "Women's Work" which involved three women performing movements associated with domestic activities which highlighted themes of gender in the dance. They present the body as the site of knowledge and the self as a place of discovery. Dance, according to the authors is

> Not only an expression of our research but a form of inquiry into the research process. The choreographer/performer has long known that the choreography process is one of sorting, sifting, editing, forming, making, and remaking; It's essentially an act of discovery. Combing dance, a kinesthetic form, and writing, a cognitive form, can forge relationships between body and mind, cognitive and affective learning, and the intellect with physical vigor. Fundamental to integrating dance as part of the research process is the premise that the body is the site of knowledge (pp. 23–238).

"Women's Work" is a dance choreographed by the first author (Cancienne) in which she enacted social constructions of gender. The three women performing the dance to the sound of water drums ranged in age from 32 to 50. They entered one at a time wearing black pants and multicolored shirts. After all three women entered the stage, the "work" phase begins, that is, the circle of washing and cooking begins. The substance for "Women's Work" consists of daily domestic chores. By moving separately and "in the round," the dancers enacted simultaneously a sense of independence and community (Cancienne & Snowber, 2003, p. 242). The authors claim that dancing bodies become the place that allows people to cultivate a sense of embodiment in an age in which analysis and fragmentation often thwart them from recognizing and exploring the meaning of the ordinary acts of their lives (p 239). They further suggest that movement methods such as dance, although represented in journal articles, should use other forms such as multimedia as legitimate representations of arts-based research methods.

The second author Snowber choreographed a dance to inquire into the relationships between mathematics and dance entitled "Beyond the Span of My Limbs." Snowber notes that as math has forms, rules, and patterns, so does choreography in its use of composition, design, pattern, repetition, shape, space, and quality of movement (p. 246). Central to the dance is exploring the limits of the body. The author concluded that the dance affected her writing both in its form and the emergent theme of paradox as central to embodiment. Both researchers/dancers argue that "writing from the body becomes an interaction between knowing and being, ontology and epistemology and the ordinary and extraordinary" (p. 248).

Huss and Cwikel (2005) studied the drawings of Bedouin women in the Negev by combining theories of art therapy and arts-based research as a means of giving voice to research participants in a non-Western culture who may not be responsive to expressing their views in verbal interviews or completing questionnaires. The authors noted that for many female Western researchers understanding the diverse concerns of Arab women, which are significantly different from their Western counterparts, is almost impossible. In this research, the authors, a Jewish Israeli Western-oriented art therapist and researcher and his co-authors, Director for the Center of Women's Health at Ben Gurion University of the Negev, were interested in exploring how arts-based research and art therapy can jointly contribute to the understanding of Bedouin women's concerns who live in a culture in which they are doubly expressed both by their patriarchal society and by the Israeli political regime.

Three groups of poor Bedouin women living in a township in the Negev participated in this study, including a group of single mothers meeting as a support group, a group of women undergoing vocational training to open early childhood centers within their homes for extra income, and a group of women without writing skills who wanted to learn arts and crafts for personal enrichment as well as being able to make products to sell. The first stage of the study focused on art making. Participants were asked to draw a symbol of themselves as an introduction, which is a common practice in art therapy sessions. However, they all drew a wish, something they wanted to be. Then they were introduced to art activities and asked to draw a picture in oil pastels or make a clay statue of a subject the researchers and participants had agreed on. The researchers reasoned that while the oil pastels include the elements of color and line that may encourage a "story" to be told, clay may be a more familiar medium for Bedouin women because they often fashion household goods of clay.

The art-making phase revealed some interesting products and insights. For example, the older Bedouin women responded immediately to clay. One of them did not draw at all but when the researchers offered clay as an option, she immediately made a clay ashtray before bursting into tears. She explained that the ashtray was like an older women, an empty, discarded container. A woman in the single mother support group also made an ashtray and broke it in many pieces creating a physical embodiment of the stress and pain she experienced raising her children without a husband or money. When the other women in the group offered advice and solutions, the single mother started putting the pieces of the ashtray back together. Another example involved an older woman who was silent in meetings but fashioned a cow, saying that a woman is like a cow: When she has no milk left, she is discarded.

In the second stage which followed the completion of the art works, the oil and clay products were laid out in a circle on the floor before each woman who had created it. In a group discussion, the women asked each other questions about their pieces allowing them to interact with each other and the researchers. During the third stage, according to Huss and Cwikel, the art works of the three groups were treated as a unified exhibition or group statement. For example, the authors noticed that when all pictures dealing with what a child needs were put together, the children played outside and were depicted in rich color. The caretakers, on the other hand, were depicted inside, without color in minimal pencil lines outlining their shapes. The authors concluded the collected representation of what a child needs illustrated that art work can become embodied with meaning that hold symbolic significance for the whole group. Finally, in the fourth stage of this study, in view of the group discussion and group exhibition, individual oil drawing and clay forms were re-examined through additional words or drawings. The authors suggested that this last stage, in terms of arts-based research, serves as a type of validating effort in that the group exhibition gives a chance for the themes to be discussed and verified on the spot through multiple voices or comments of the group. Expressing their concerns through art works empowered the participants to express themselves and the research contexts offered the researchers new insights to learn from lower income women in a different culture while at the same time benefitting and enriching the lives of the participants.

Herman (2005) describes an arts-based methodology to research images of evil events using the construct of liminal space. According to Herman, in academia

> Liminal space has become a cross-disciplinary trope that means a disordered place of engagement with the unexpected and surprising, outside the norms of one's culture...In this space, consciousness is altered, and we break the

normative rules that have limited our perceptions. In this luminal space, we access images that were previously outside our capacities to know them, and we are able to see new patterns in the chaos (p. 471).

This means that

> The presentation of such research should produce a moment(s) of disturbance in time and place—an experience of the luminal—where things do not make sense in the way they are normally known, where perceptions are changed. The text should be performative, meaning that whether it is typed or danced or sung, it produces an embodied affective response in readers/spectators who have been transported to a luminal state and later propelled to a coherent plan of action as their new knowledge is incorporated (p. 473).

Herman selected images, and more specifically images of evil as found in visual representations of Auschwitz as the worst evil event she could imagine. She recorded her encounters with the images and transcribed what happened to her as poems, dances, or songs arguing that researchers who use an arts-based methodology in luminal space to engage the images of evil events are compelled to make art. They cannot truthfully record the physical experience of their engagement with the image other than artfully (p. 275). The intense suffering, pain, and rage found in images of Auschwitz create visceral reactions and force viewers to suspend disbelief and enter realities other than their own. According to Herman, moving into luminal space creates understandings that are outside the margins of our personal and cultural experience and include a symbolic realm shared by humanity.

Self-portraits of leaders are another source of visual data which can be collected in a variety of context. As a leadership consultant, in a leadership succession project, I have asked members of the organization's top management team to draw portraits of their current CEO which I am analyzing for characteristics and particular attributes the senior executives assigned to their CEO. As a leadership educator, I have asked students to draw self-portraits at different times in course of a semester—before the beginning of the course, at various intervals during the course, and upon completion of the course. The self-portraits were analyzed for changes over time as they changed from images that portrayed anxiety and lack of preparedness to increasing levels of self-confidence and comfort with the materials they learned during the semester.

I am also conducting an arts-based study that uses sculpture as the art form and is intended to develop a power-related construct, namely the ontological power of the leader. Sculpture, particular for the purpose of this research, has several advantages over other forms of artistic expression. Because it preserves the full-dimensional presence of the body, sculpture is, next to drama, one of the most realistic art forms.

Characteristics of the material, in this study primarily marble and bronze, combine the power of undulating lines, proportions of length, and the power of angles making dramatic statements about form and the leader's physique. Within the contours, the statue stands alone; the space of the statue is the space it fills. The corpus of sculptures selected for this research are major sculptures of the 5th BC Greek sculptor Phidias who gave us the Parthenon and the statue of Zeus in the temple dedicated to him in Olympia, one of the seven wonders of the ancient world.

The sheer physical power of Phidias' work as well as the great symbolism embedded in the statues selected for analysis, the symbolism of dimensions, angles, and the dynamic power of confrontation not only with the sculptures and the divine but with the artist himself open the window for a new conceptualizations beyond those found in the leadership literature (e.g., French & Raven, 1959; Pfeffer, 1981). Methodologically, the work of Phidias lends itself to a two-tiered analysis using visual content analysis and iconography. Phidias sculptures offer many comparative dimensions through which the ontological power of the leader may be explored: gods versus humans, males versus females, full body versus torso sculptures, and single sculptures versus groups of sculptures found on the friezes of the Parthenon.

Many controversies surround image-based research in a science-based discipline such as leadership studies although many have argued that leadership is both an art and a science. There are theoretical problems because leadership research is very much theory driven. We have encountered this problem in text-based qualitative research such as grounded theory or phenomenology where some researchers are quite reluctant to provide an analytical or theoretical framework to situate the research question. In image-based research for frame, the research question based on theory but let the data drive theory development. It has been argued that works of art stand alone; after all, the author of a play does not provide a theoretical explication of the meaning of the play to the audience who beholds it (Eisner, 1997).

Then there are methodological problem which raise questions about the scientific merit of arts-based research. The shift from science to art as a source of research premises, principles, and procedures, as Barone (2003) notes, is repudiated by many researchers and especially those who lack familiarity with the arts or art theory. Replicability of research findings is a key premise in quantitative and many text-based qualitative research methods. In arts-based research, on the other hand, the replication of the research setting and conditions is often impossible. Visual techniques present some unique validity threats and potential sources of bias. In order to conduct image-based research, the investigator needs some artistic aptitude in the chosen visual medium. The search for alternative criteria of validity produced some options such as form, completeness, and the role of arts-based research as service to the local community. The arts-based research community is clearly divided between those who insist on quality standards comparable to those used in other scientific methods and those who are prepared to abandon those standards all together. However, there seems to be an emerging consensus that standards of quality adapted from the positivistic or even from some qualitative paradigms do not adequately fit the axioms of image-based and more creative forms of research. A new aesthetic epistemology of leadership will not emerge as long as researchers maintain that the scientific approach to validity and quality are the only options for image-based researcher.

Still another concern relates to what might be called "indefensible relativism" referring to the attitude taken by some researchers that since interpretations of images and works of art are always personal, and therefore, any interpretation is as defensible as any other. The logical implication of this view is that there is no basis whatsoever for making judgments about either the quality of the work or its meaning. Hancock (2003) calls attention to the consequences of seeking to re-integrate the aesthetic into the realm of calculable knowledge and practical reality. The author points out that in doing so, we not only debase the aesthetic, depriving it of that that which is genuinely identical to it, but also potentially render its useless in its own cause as well a depriving humanity of its radical potential, its potential to allow us to experience things other than they are. Reduced to yet another tool of the organizational technocrat, the neutralization of the aesthetic risks becomes absolute, rendering it indistinguishable in a world where aesthetic experience is reduced to nothing more than the deadened apprehension of a sterile landscape of society, and judgment the association of a contrived meaning with a fashionable corporate livery (p. 193).

SUMMARY

This chapter opened a new vista for qualitative leadership research through cross-fertilization with the arts. As a theory, and as a method, image interpretation offers an alternative to researchers who wish to study phenomena in new ways. Recent research has shown that aesthetic knowledge which can be generated through a variety of artistic media, from architecture to drawing and music to dance, plays an important part in organizational practice. Ewenstein and Whyte (2007) found that aesthetic knowledge not only provided a symbolic context for work but was an integral part of the work people do. The images that constitute the data base in arts-based inquiries enables researchers to escape purely linguistic protocols, constituting inquiry as a multimode process. According to Eisner (1997), art is not in competition with scientific traditions; rather it is a unique mode of making sense of the world.

Although at the time of this writing, no empirical work has been published that uses artistic expressions—music, poetry, painting, film, dance, architecture as sources of data in journals that publish leadership research because they favor the printed word over other forms of expression—the possibilities of image-based studies are intriguing and consequential for leadership theory, leadership education, and development and leadership practice. Arts-informed leadership has much to contribute to the advancement of qualitative research in leadership studies by providing opportunities and spaces for access to alternative forms of research. New forms of inquiry such as image-based research require new criteria to evaluate the quality and meaning of interpretations derived from such research. Denzin (2000) expressed the hope that image-based research can be the catalyst for movement into radical, ethical aesthetics.

In this chapter, I reviewed a number of studies from different disciplines to give the reader an idea of how arts-based research is conducted and how leadership researchers can learn from other disciplines. I included examples of studies that analyzed data derived from dance performances, drawings of Bedouin women, photograph, and film. I also offered examples of my own work which is based on visual analysis of sculpture to develop and explicate the construct of the ontological power of the leader. Ways of analyzing visual data were described and the issue of validity and standards of image-based research was discussed. The utility of traditional criteria for quality such as reliability and validity was examined along with several sets of alternative sets of standards that arguably are congruent with the axioms of art-based research. Quality criteria for image-based research are just developing. Many questions remain such as, "What are the distinctive forms of leadership knowledge that are best explored through the arts?" "Is there an artistic dimension to all image-based leadership research?" "What are the unique skills leadership scholars interested in conducting image-based need to acquire and in what context can they be learned?" "Is developing an arts-based research program a risky proposition for a newly minted Ph.D. in leadership studies in a tenure track position given the current criteria for promotion and tenure?" Clearly, as Mason (2005) pointed out, for image-based research both media and research skills are needed. Although the development of digital stills and video has made the technology more accessible (Ball & Smith, 1992; Pink, 2001), to fully utilize the opportunities provided by the technology, specialist skills are required or leadership researchers need to team up with technologists with expertise in image-based media.

In sum, although presently arts-based research is undervalued and underutilized in the academic community of leadership scholar, image-based leadership research hold many promises and possibilities: the possibility of exploiting the power of images based on the assumptions that leaders and followers possess more complex cognitive maps of leadership processes than they can verbalize, the promise of discovering new constructs and developing new theories, the opportunity of expanding the multidisciplinary nature of leadership by integrating the arts, and the possibility of creating a new community of leadership scholars where science and the arts are given equal voice with the goal of integrating the aesthetic into the realm of knowledge and practical reality when it comes to creative and innovative leadership research.

Part IV

EMPIRICAL QUALITATIVE LEADERSHIP STUDIES

10

CONTENT ANALYSIS OF THE WRITINGS OF MARY PARKER FOLLETT

Suzanne Martin

OVERVIEW OF THE STUDY

This study is the first computer-assisted content analysis of the writings of Mary Parker Follett, a political scientist and social worker with a substantial following among business leaders over 80 years ago. Her ideas are echoed in quality circles, empowerment, horizontal structures, and social networks as they are discussed in leadership theory and practice today. Ahead of her time, Drucker (1995) dubbed Follett the "prophet of management" (p. 1) for her forward thinking. The purpose of this research was to discover the major constructs and their relationships to one another in the published writings of Mary Parker Follett content analysis and to identify the relevance of these concepts to contemporary leadership theory and practice.

The corpus of text in this study consisted of seven of Follett's published texts. The total sample included over 1450 pages of Follett's writings from her earliest publication to her final publication and included her three major works, *The Speaker of the House of Representatives* (1896), *The New State: Group Organization, the Solution for Popular Government* (1918), and *Creative Experience* (1924). The sample also included two collections of papers and lectures, *Dynamic Administration* (1941) and *Freedom & Co-ordination: Lectures in Business Organisation* (1949), and two articles, "Community is a Process" (1919) and "The Teacher-Student Relation" (1928/1970). Over 1450 pages of text and 16 000 different words were reduced to 45 codes and 5 code families. The text was analyzed three ways: word frequencies, coding, and tracing the development of the words *leader, leaders, and leadership*.

The resulting comprehensive analysis of the writings of Follett establishes cohesive patterns in her work, identifies her as *the* mother of contemporary leadership theory and practice and pays tribute to Follett's legacy—a platform of ideas for new models and theories of leadership. The findings from this study provide the core constructs for a multilevel, postheroic model of leadership.

APPROACH TO THE TEXT

One assumption held by the author is that texts are produced to be read and are written with others in mind. The meaning of the text is conveyed through more than the physical qualities and must include how the text is used and by whom. Trying to read the text through the perspective of the potential reader contributes to the meaning of the text (Krippendorff, 2004). The author assumed that Follett was trying to communicate particular ideas to particular audiences. This researcher approached the text with a desire to discover Follett's voice and intended meanings and thus sought ways to let the content drive the process of inquiry.

Krippendorff's (2004) six basic assumptions guided the approach to the text. They are

1. Texts have no objectives outside of being read. They do not possess any "reader-independent qualities."

2. Texts do not have single meanings.

3. The meanings invoked by texts need not be shared by all readers.

4. Meanings (content) speak to something other than the given texts.

5. Texts have meanings relative to particular contexts, discourses, or purposes.

6. The nature of text demands that content analysis draw specific inferences from a body of texts to their chosen content (pp. 22–24).

In addition, the text is organic, always in process. The printed aspects do not change but the meaning can. Krippendorff's fourth assumption resonated with the axiological aspirations of this researcher—the content of Follett's texts can create new knowledge, feelings, and actions in the lives of readers. Follett attempted to do more than inform in her writings, she tried to provoke and equip individuals and groups to act in ways that created a better society.

Initial Questions

The initial three questions used in this study are paraphrases of three of Patton's (2002) "truth and reality-oriented" (p. 91) foundational questions:

1. What is really going on in the text?

2. What can be established with some degree of certainty about the text as a whole?

3. How do the findings of this study correspond to the real world?

These broad questions allowed the text to drive the research process. Questions were refined in an iterative process between the text and the literature. Additional research questions emerged during the process which led the researcher to a purer interpretation of Follett's writing than using an inflexible set of questions extracted exclusively from the leadership literature. This iterative process prevented the researcher from imposing predetermined constructs on the data and reduced the degree of researcher bias.

COLLECTING, EXPLORING, AND ANALYZING THE DATA

Data Collection Process

Locating seven texts for an adequate sample was the first hurdle. Follett's texts are hard to secure, even her published works. Most of her writings are out-of-print and others simply obscure. She wrote a number of unpublished documents which she requested to be burned upon her death. Some of her unpublished works are in the possession of individuals and remain inaccessible. This sample adequately covers Follett's major contributions at different stages of her professional life.

The Seven Text Sample/Hermeneutic Unit

A key to understanding this study is the ATLAS/ti concept of the Hermeneutic Unit (HU). The underlying premise is that all data and every step of the process are relevant to the whole. The project or HU is treated as one entity in which there is a hierarchy of objects. The *primary document* (PD) forms the base of the hierarchy. Other layers include quotes or segments of relevant text, codes, super codes, and code families. The network is the most sophisticated level in the Atlas/ti HU hierarchy and is a visual display of linkages between codes. Networks provide a way to "express meaningful 'semantic' relationships between elements" (Muhr, 1997, p. 12), one of the stated objectives for this study. All of the PDs, quotes, codes, super codes, families, networks, related memos, and notes are part of a single project, the HU.

Three of the PDs were books published during Follett's lifetime, *The Speaker of the House of Representatives* (1896), *The New State: Group Organisation, the Solution for Popular Government* (1918), and *Creative Experience* (1924). *The Speaker of the House* established Follett as a serious writer and scholar and contains the seeds of future core concepts such as integration, conflict, and power.

In *The New State: Group Organisation, the Solution for Popular Government* (1918), Follett argued that the group process was the answer to reinvigorating democracy. In *Creative Experience*, Follett (1924) described a "method whereby the full integrity of an individual, including personal desires, could be united with social progress in such a way that one's daily experiences would produce larger and larger spiritual values" (p. xvi). "Community is a Process" (Follett, 1919) is the only article in the sample published during Follett's lifetime. The other article in the sample, "The Teacher-Student Relation" (Follett, 1928/1970) was delivered during her lifetime and published much later.

Two books in the HU, *Dynamic Administration: The Collected Papers of Mary Parker Follett* (Metcalf & Urwick, 1941) and *Freedom & Co-ordination: Lectures in Business Organisation* (Follett, 1949), were published after Follett's death. *Dynamic Administration* is a collection of lectures included in early business management literature (Fox, 1970). *Freedom & Co-ordination* (1949) is a collection of Follett's final lectures given at the London School of Economics in 1933 as well as a lecture delivered to the Taylor Society in 1926. Lyndal Urwick (1935) described this book as the culmination of Follett's thought and stated that she intended to begin giving more order and structure to her body of work (Table 10-1).

Table 10-1   The hermeneutic unit

Title	Publication date	Description of primary document (PD)
The Speaker of the House of Representatives	1896	First publication (undergraduate thesis). Root concepts of power, conflict, and leadership emerge from analysis of archival data and in-depth interviews. 329 pages
The New State: Group Organisation, the Solution to Popular Government	1918	Critique of representative government. Focus on group process. Reprinted 5 times. 385 pages
"Community is a Process"	1919	Article in *Philosophical Review* critiquing popular pluralist and monist philosophies. 15 pages

Table 10-1   (Continued)

Title	Publication date	Description of primary document (PD)
Creative Experience	1924	Seminal work outlining theory of creative experience. Social critique. Offers new solutions to modern problems. 303 pages
"The Teacher-Student Relation"	1928/1970	Lecture delivered at Boston University in 1928, first published in *The Administrative Quarterly* in 1970. Discusses leadership in context of the student-teacher relation. 18 pages
Dynamic Administration: The collected papers of Mary Parker Follett	1941	Collection of lectures delivered between 1925–1932 to business managers through Follett's association with Metcalf and the Bureau of Personnel Administration in New York City. Metcalf and Urwick edited this collection published after Follett's death in 1933. 320 pages
Freedom & Co-ordination: Lectures in Business Organisation	1949	A collection of six lectures. One delivered in 1926 at a meeting of the Taylor Society in New York City and the others in 1933 to the newly formed Department of Business Administration at the London School of Economics. 89 pages

Locating and Securing the Texts

Data collection began with locating the texts as either hard copies and scanning them into electronic documents, cleaning and saving them, or finding them in electronic form. "Community is a Process" (Follett, 1919), "The Teacher-Student Relation" (Follett, 1928/1970), and the first three chapters of *Creative Experience* (Follett, 1924) were available from the Mary Parker Follett Foundation website, www.follettfoundation.org, in electronic formats. These documents had been scanned, cleaned, and saved as Word documents. The author retrieved an edited and cleaned electronic version of *The New State: Group Organization, the Solution for Popular Government* (Follett, 1918) from http://sunsite.utk.edu/FINS/Mary_Parker_Follett/Fins-MPF-01.html. Matthew Shapiro, President of the Mary Parker Follett Foundation, shared electronic versions of chapters 4–18 of *Creative Experience* (1924). These chapters required editing and cleaning that took approximately two weeks to complete.

Hard copies of *The Speaker of the House of Representatives* (Follett, 1896) and *Freedom & Co-ordination: Lectures in Business Organisation* (1949) were obtained through interlibrary loan and Samford University. A hard copy of *Dynamic Administration* (1941) was found serendipitously from a man giving away books in Maryland. A Samford University student scanned and cleaned *The Speaker of the House of Representatives* and *Dynamic Administration*. The author scanned and cleaned *Freedom & Co-ordination*. All three texts were saved as Word documents. The scanning and cleaning of these texts took 200 hours.

The author loaded each PD into the HU according to publication date. The seven texts or PDs comprise the HU or sample for this study. The HU contains over 1450 pages of text of Follett's writings from her earliest publication to her final publication.

New Questions That Shaped Approach to Text

After loading the documents into the HU, questions emerged that were more concrete and specific to ATLAST/ti than the three foundational questions cited earlier in this chapter. These eleven questions represent the starting point for working with the text.

1. What is the best way to approach 1450 pages of text?

2. Is there a way to approach dense text using a lean philosophy?

3. How might the Word Cruncher tool in ATLAS/ti be used to calculate and make meaning out of frequency data?

4. Can the Word Cruncher reduce the data without losing the meaning of the data?

5. What are the strengths and weakness of autocoding using both high- and low-frequency words from the Word Cruncher output files?

6. Are there drawbacks to using autocoding and line-by-line coding?

7. How does one move between open coding and autocoding?

8. When the researcher senses that the saturation point has been reached in the coding process, is it time to do autocoding?

9. How does one avoid getting bogged down in the data to the point of no longer being able to see the forest for the trees?

10. Are there number limits for memos, codes, and quotes per HU in ATLAS/ti?

11. What should one pay attention to when coding such a large HU?

Coding over 1450 pages of text is daunting and seeking answers to these questions before beginning was invaluable. As predicted by Ray Maietta, an expert on qualitative research and President of ResearchTalk, it took six months of four to five hours a day to code and to analyze the entire HU.

Mining for Gold

"Mining for gold" is an apt description of the analytical approach to the data. When analyzing 1450 pages of text, one cannot fixate on every word and each juxtaposition of words. Therefore, the researcher developed a strategy for systematically and efficiently sifting and retrieving the valuable data points using different tools within Atlas/ti, as well as a noncomputer-aided phase of coding. The analytic strategy evolved into a seven phase process that included word crunching, autocoding, line-by-line coding (some "by hand" or without computer software), creating code families, and networking. Table 10-2 lists the seven phases of coding.

Table 10-2   Seven phase coding process

Phase	Description of phase
Phase one	Word crunching , an ATLAS/ti tool
Phase two	Autocoding, an ATLAS/ti tool
Phase three	Line-by-line coding using ATLAS/ti
Phase four	Necessary pause to create leaner set of codes
Phase five	Hand coding, coding without ATLAS/ti
Phase six	Comparing ATLAS/ti code list with hand coded code list
Phase seven	Returning to ATLAS/ti to complete coding

Phase One: Word Crunching

Before coding any of the data, the author used the Word Cruncher tool to see all of the words that she would encounter within the HU. Word crunching is a purely quantitative function within Atlas/ti. It counts and tallies the number of occurrences of all words in either a single PD or the entire HU. The output of the Word Cruncher is an Excel table displaying an alpha list of the frequencies of all words in the entire HU. The first report contained over 16 000 cells. A second report displayed the words in descending order from highest to lowest frequency for the entire HU. This report included totals for the entire HU, as well as subtotals for each PD for comparison. The author created similar Excel reports for each PD. At the conclusion of this step within the word crunching phase, the author had a visual display of the most common words in the entire HU as well as in each PD. Within this report, it was possible to compare high-frequency and low-frequency words across PDs.

Analyzing the content of the 16 000 + cells took five weeks and resulted in two tables: Word Families and Concepts and Significant and Unique Terms. Word Families and Concepts is a list of 271 high-frequency word families. A word family includes all variations of one root word and in some cases synonyms and alternate spellings of the root word. This table represents a list of common concepts or ideas within the entire HU. The Significant and Unique Terms table includes 332 words that are significant or unique to one or more PDs. Many of the 332 words in this list are also high-frequency words, but not all of them. Some words appear in both tables. Table 10-3 and 10-4 are samples from the Word Families and Concepts and Significant and Unique Terms tables.

The first step involved analyzing the output reports for the entire HU, looking for nouns, adjectives, and verbs that reflected one or more of Follett's primary themes or words found in contemporary leadership literature. This textual mining for key words and concepts was informed by the author's knowledge of leadership literature, Follett's primary texts, and over a dozen dissertations and scholarly commentary on Follett. The author marked high-frequency words other than prepositions, adverbs, conjunctions as well as words with unusual spellings and words that appeared to have been created by

Table 10-3   Excerpt from word families and concepts table

Ranking	Word	Occurrences
1	We	4872
2	I	3286
3	With	2239
4	Our	2185
5	Think	1603
6	Will	1488
7	Man	1484
8	Us	1227
9	Group	1216
10	Power	1193
11	Individual	942

Table 10-3   (Continued)

Ranking	Word	Occurrences
12	Business	927
13	Organization	908
14	Relation	900
15	Life	852
16	Difference	827
17	Whole	825
18	Order	785
19	Process	774
20	Political	759

Table 10-4   Excerpt from significant and unique terms table

Word (s)	PD 1	PD 2	PD 3	PD 4	PD 5	PD 6	PD 7
Anarchy		12					
Annals	27						
Antislavery	8						
Appendix	44	1					
Aristocracy	1	10					
Behavior	4	2	4	128	1	31	2
Bok				12		1	
Bond (s)	3	39	1	5	0	4	1
Calculus				4			
Chair	268				1	5	2
Chauvinists		1					
Circular				63		20	
Citizenship		46		3			

(Continued)

Table 10-4   (Continued)

Word (s)	PD 1	PD 2	PD 3	PD 4	PD 5	PD 6	PD 7
Club(s)		70		1		1	
Commodity				1		10	
Compound(ing)		18		8			
Concept(s)		2	2	67		4	2
Conceptual		1		35			
Conciliation		4				48	1
Conciliator(s)						13	
Concrete		11	2	55		2	

PD1, *The Speaker of the House of Representatives*; PD2, *The New State: Group Organisation, the Solution to Popular Government*; PD3, "Community is a Process"; PD4, *Creative Experience*; PD5, "The Teacher-Student Relation"; PD6, *Dynamic Administration: The Collected Papers of Mary Parker Follett*; PD7, *Freedom & Co-ordination: Lectures in Business Organisation.*

Follett. One factor that added weight to a particular word was the number of iterations of a root word, that is, evolve, evolving, and evolution. The author created lists of words with prefixes that typically do not appear with prefixes or hyphens in other English texts. Among Follett's common prefixes were co-, inter-, and re-.

At the midpoint of this coding phase, the author moved to the bottom of the list and worked up from the lowest frequency words back to the midpoint. Lower frequency words deserved more study than the words in the middle because they had they were likely to be unique words and outliers. Many of the words identified at bottom appear in the Significant and Unique Terms table. This table included words exclusive to one or two particular texts and rare yet weighty words such as *gestalt, depersonalize, plusvalue, or followership*. Follett had a reputation for being meticulous and painstaking in her writing and selection of words (Hart, 1896; Urwick, 1935) and occasionally created words for specific contexts and lectures. For example, the word *repersonalise* occurred twice and only in two of her publications but when it appeared it was a deliberate play on words for Follett's critique of the scientific management practice of *depersonalising* orders. To overlook a word because it was infrequent would have been an analytic oversight.

The entire process of analyzing from top to middle and bottom to middle was repeated in order to identify words that may have been overlooked or overemphasized during the first examination. This was tedious and time intensive; however, in the absence of a second coder, the author concluded that it was necessary. Phase one equipped the author with a clearer and broader grasp of Follett's language which ultimately expedited the coding process. The frequency data provided an objective and quantitative resource for cross-checking the reliability of the codes and other findings throughout the research process. This phase also provided the author with a helicopter view of the whole HU and Follett's lexicon before examining separate texts. This phase strengthened the coding process and the identification of common thematic threads across texts.

Phase Two: Autocoding

Autocoding is tool in Atlas/ti that electronically marks occurrences of a particular word or phrase in a text. The author autocoded *The Speaker of the House of Representatives* (1896), Follett's first publication instead of coding line-by-line. The decision was based on the document's primary purpose and content. The purpose of this book was to describe the inner workings of the House and the role of the Speaker. It includes a large quantity of historical and legislative details that were not pertinent to this study. Autocoding allowed the author to code specific words from the frequency data tables that reflected major themes and emphases in the text as a whole, as well as with other texts in the HU.

The author autocoded 163 words from a list of the 350 highest frequency words in *The Speaker of the House of Representatives* (1896). This was the only PD autocoded instead of being coded line-by-line. The autocode function was used with other PDs but not as a substitute for line-by-line coding.

Phase Three: Coding Line-by-Line

Line-by-line coding is the electronic process of marking and assigning codes to sections of text. It is the basic function of Atlas/ti software. Codes within Atlas/ti are electronic locators for ideas with sources and consequences.

The author chose to code the 1450 pages of text as a tortoise and not a hare, resisting the temptation to rush. A hare approach could have resulted in sloppiness, inaccuracy, and confusion down the road, which, as in the fable, resulted in a loss for the hare. Coding slowly provides sufficient time and space to establish habits, to see patterns, and to identify significant meanings in the text. As familiarity with the text grew and when the text was repetitive, the author coded swiftly.

The author used open coding with the second PD, *The New State: Group Organisation, the Solution for Popular Government* (1918). Open coding allows the text to speak freely without the constraints and bias of a predetermined and predefined set of codes. Open coding during this phase was optimal for developing the purest reflection of Follett's ideas and her language for the code list. Although the author referred to the list of high-frequency words for this PD during coding, it was for comparison rather than code development.

Coding text segments is only the beginning of coding. If coding stopped at the coding of text segments, the data would not be reduced and generalizing would be highly problematic. Coding that creates leaner more manageable data is an ongoing process of seeing relationships between codes and concepts, combining codes with other codes, and creating families of codes. Within ATLAS/ti, the researcher can link codes and groups of codes. Codes are linked during coding as patterns emerge, not as an afterthought. Linking is a seamless part of coding within ATLAS/ti which helps the researcher to capture insights in the moment rather than relying on memory or disconnected notes. Linkages add *weight* to the significance of single codes. Therefore, within ATLAS/ti the researcher can evaluate the importance of a code based on both frequency and weight.

Code worthiness

Determining what is and is not code worthy is a fluid process throughout the analysis. Assigning a code to a data segment is subjective and prone to bias because the researcher is assigning value and meaning to words, phrases, and paragraphs within the texts. This author tried to control for the natural effect of bias by moving slowly through the data, writing memos on various codes and code decisions, and by establishing criteria for code worthiness. Three key questions shaped coding decisions in this study. They are

1. Would the reader care about this code?

2. What happens with this code within the text? So what?

3. How does this code move the topic of leadership forward or in a new direction?

The overall goal of looking for *inspiring movement* within the text was central to the coding process, sifting for pure, valuable, meaningful, nuggets of data. Part of the process involved looking, without forcing, for ideas about leadership that were original to Follett and ideas she discussed that can be found in contemporary leadership literature. Some of these constructs included leadership as a process, organizational level leadership, contextual factors, role of followers, role of the group, and transformational leadership at levels other than the individual or microlevel. Decisions about code worthiness were theoretically informed by the collective vocabulary of many contemporary leadership writers including Bass (1985); Burns (1978; 2003); Drucker (1995); Greenleaf (1977); Heifetz (1994); Heifetz and Linsky (2002); Senge (1990; 1994); and Wheatley (1992; 1999).

In coding, the author cast as wide a net as she could manage for this study. The author coded every word or idea associated with leadership in the text. She coded every occurrence of the root word leader and its iterations. She also coded text segments that reflected contemporary leadership constructs such as change, learning, community, understanding and working with others, conflict, difference, and followership. In addition, she coded segments that included Follett's social critique and statements concerning the nature of reality, the universe, humanity, and hope because these constructs undergird all of her writings. Lastly, the author coded Follett's practical suggestions for improving organizations, community, and the world as a whole.

Follett provided clues in her texts that assisted the author with coding. One clue was repetition, sometimes verbatim, of an idea within the same PD or in another PD. Follett often presented a slightly different angle, a new illustration, or a new word for the same concept. Many codes evolved. An example of an evolving code is the leadership code that evolved from a microlevel construct in *The Speaker of the House of Representatives* (1896) and *Creative Experience* to a more macroconcept of leadership as a process.

Follett's writing was peppered with dramatic statements like "the most important truth in the world," "the hope of the world lies in," "the reason I am writing this is," and "we must study this more." These personal and parenthetical statements provided clues to code worthy material. Follett's unanswered questions, suggestions, and the purposes for her writings were code worthy and broadened the author's perspective on Follett's motivations and ultimate concerns. Her sweeping statements also helped the author to develop a picture of the context and the realities within which Follett lived and wrote. In order to increase the accuracy of codes assigned to this kind of text, the author consulted Tonn's (2003) comprehensive biographical data on Follett.

Phase Four: A Necessary Pause

After several weeks of coding *The New State: Group Organisation, the Solution for Popular Government* (1918), the researcher made the decision to step away from the data and computer-assisted coding in order to regain freshness, accuracy, and clarity. Full time coding had resulted in saturation, fatigue, and over 150 codes. During this phase, the author engaged in exercises designed to help one look at the data differently. The exercises included creating a Table of Contents that would encapsulate the emerging themes; free writing all ideas discovered up to that point; reading some of Follett's texts like a novel rather than the object of study; summarizing the process thus far; and creating a leaner, more powerful code list.

Creating a leaner set of codes. Creating a leaner set of codes was more than an exercise. It is a necessary step in content analysis (Krippendorff, 2004; Neuendorf, 2002). This process involves refining code definitions, combining codes, creating code families, and reducing the number of codes. During this phase, 161 codes were reduced to 43 codes and 5 code families. Table 10-5 displays the leaner code list.

Phase Five: Hand Coding

Hand coding refers to coding without computer assistance. The essence of hand coding is the same as computer-aided coding. The difference is in the mechanics. The coder marks text with a pen, writes notes, and compiles results manually rather than with the click of the mouse. Two PDs, "Community is a Process" (1919) and *Creative Experience* (1924), were coded by hand.

Table 10-5   Five code families and 43 related codes

Code or code families	Related codes
Defining reality	Difference
	Environment
	Finding meaning
	Freedom
	God
	Life as evolving
	Purpose
	Society as psychic process
	Truth
	Unifying
	Unity
	Wholeness: life is relation
Framing Questions	
Group Principle	Applications of the group process
	Compounding consciousness
	Evolving social process
	Group (the)
	Interpenetration
	Promoting the group principle
	Unity of social process

Table 10-5   (Continued)

Code or code families	Related codes
Ideal Society	Creative Citizenship
	Neighborhood group
	Social progress
	True community
	True democracy
Individual (the)	
Influential ideas and thinkers	Biology
	Law-dynamic
	Philosophy
	Political Philosophy
	Psychology (new, social, group)
Leadership behaviors	
Morality and conscience	
Multilevel leadership	
Power	
Purpose of politics	
Purpose of publication	
Relating individual, group, and state	
Social Critique	Crowd mentality
	Describing the crisis
	Diagnosing: ineffective thinking and processes
	Identifying: signs of hope
	Prescribing: solutions and secrets

Computer-assisted coding can become cumbersome and confining. The researcher is also vulnerable to allowing the software and the "drop down" code list to drive the process rather than allowing new codes to emerge. After a code list has been refined and reduced, the researcher is reluctant to make changes. Another risk inherent in qualitative content analysis is losing a sense of the whole. This researcher was so engrossed with the details, that she became stuck at the data level and found it increasingly difficult to grasp the overall conceptual messages within the data. Hand coding allowed the researcher to stay close to the text, stay fresh without the fatigue associated with staring at a screen, and most importantly, allowed the text rather than the method or software to drive the process. In addition, hand coding two PDs enhanced the validity of the final results and constructs.

Coding *Creative Experience* was particularly useful in identifying *latent* codes, codes that underlie leadership, as opposed to the more easily identified *manifest* codes in which the theme is directly observable (Boyatzis, 1998). Latent codes in *Creative Experience* were codes related to the nature of reality and humanity, as well as several technical, scientific, and philosophical concepts embedded in Follett's more obvious themes, such as the functions of leaders or the concept of power.

During hand coding, the author did not consult the newly revised code list which allowed codes to emerge from the two PDs. If a code from the original list fit, it was applied, but from memory only which meant that it had to be an obvious match. The goal of this phase was to impose as little as possible on the coding process. After coding "Community is a Process," a code list specific to this PD was created, and the same was done for *Creative Experience* at the end of coding.

Coding by hand forced the researcher to become physically involved with the data, touching pages, sorting sheets of notes, grouping notes, counting pages dedicated to various concepts, and connecting ideas with scotch tape. The handling of text and making choices on how to physically group the data helped the researcher to begin to think *after* Follett more than she had been doing. The author saw new connections and overlap between ideas because she had to make choices about where to tape a quote or when to clip together a set of ideas that overlapped.

Phase Six: Code Comparisons Between Atlas/ti and Hand Coding

Phase six was a stage of code refinement that included combining definitions and condensing various codes. The researcher compared the two new code lists with the code list from phase four, seeking equivalent codes among the lists. The goal was to identify similarities between codes without losing the particular emphasis of each PD. The original code lists were saved and available to the researcher throughout data

Table 10-6   Sample from high-frequency words—PD comparison table

The Speaker of the House (SOH)	The New State (TNS)	Community as Process (CAP)	Creative Experience (CE)	The Teacher-Student Relation (TSR)	Dynamic Administration (DA)	Freedom & Co-ordination (FC)
House	We	We	We	We	I	I
Speaker	Our	Process	I	I	We	We
With	Group	I	Our	Our	Be	Be
Committee	With	Will	With	Be	With	One
I	Will	Group	Experience	With	One	With
Congress	All	Us	Us	Teacher	Business	They
One	One	With	One	All	Should	You
Vote	Life	Community	Social	Life	They	Business
Chair	I	They	Will	Should	You	Control
Members	State	Individual	Law	One	Our	All
Speakers	Us	Our	They	Their	All	Authority

(Continued)

Table 10-6   (Continued)

The Speaker of the House (SOH)	The New State (TNS)	Community as Process (CAP)	Creative Experience (CE)	The Teacher-Student Relation (TSR)	Dynamic Administration (DA)	Freedom & Co-ordination (FC)
Power	They	State	All	Relation	Do	Should
Party	Individual	Pluralists	Do	Think	Power	Think
Rules	Their	One	Process	Students	Think	Do
Committees	Do	Purpose	Power	Student	Their	Situation
All	New	Psychology	Their	They	Will	Our
Member	Social	See	See	Experience	Management	Their
Should	People	Study	Activity	How	Me	Coordination
They	Man	Political	You	Do	Us	Will
Order	Every	You	Situation	Part	See	Department

analysis. Although the codes and emphases varied within each PD, a clear thread of similarity and predictability was evident within the entire HU.

When possible, the researcher used the same code across PDs to capture commonalities. Each PD code list contains codes unique to that PD. The author compared the individual PD code lists to a table of high-frequency word comparisons across PDs (Table 10-6) for another validity check. Table 10-6 is a comparison of the 20 most common words across PDs, presented in descending order. Table 10-6 is a subset of a much larger table that contains 1514 words with an average of 216 words per column.

Phase Seven: Returning to Atlas/ti

The remaining three PDs, "The Teacher-Student Relation," *Dynamic Administration* (1941), and *Freedom & Co-ordination* (1949), were coded using ATLAS/ti and the codes from all prior documents including *Creative Experience* (1924) and "Community is a Process" (1919). The newly developed code comparison table was particularly helpful at this stage. After having the break from the computer coding, the author began to see more in the data and to experience more profound "aha" moments. This phase was the most comfortable and efficient phase of analysis.

At the midpoint of coding the last PD, *Freedom & Co-ordination* (1949), the author began to reach a point of saturation. There were no new ideas or codes emerging in the data. There were no new words for old ideas. There were multiple thematic similarities between *Freedom & Co-ordination* and *Dynamic Administration* (1941). These two PDs complemented one another. All codes that were needed were in place, a click away. Memos were becoming repetitive and duplicate quotes were being copied into code notes. After coding *Freedom & Co-ordination* (1949), the author was confident that she had coded all of Follett's ideas. The researcher had gained a broad knowledge of Follett's major themes and ideas that were applicable across time and contexts.

The greatest effect of the researcher was on the coding process. Although establishing intercoder reliability is one way to control for this effect, it was not feasible. Finding and paying for a second coder willing and equipped to work on this project for six months was not possible. In light of this reality, specific steps were taken by the researcher to control for bias in coding and to strengthen the reliability and validity of the results.

One effort to control for researcher bias was the choice to begin with frequency data and autocoding before open coding. When coding, the researcher honored Follett's context and voice by incorporating verbatim quotes and metaphors in the code definitions and notes. The author also tried to bracket twenty first century leadership scholarship by paying close attention to the context of her writings and the chronological development of her constructs. Close readings of Follett's original texts as well as a thorough reading of Tonn's (2003) 623-page biography which included extensive contextual, personal, and professional information enabled the researcher to immerse herself in the historical context and life of Follett and to bracket twenty first century scholarship during coding.

A FOLLETIAN FRAMEWORK FOR UNDERSTANDING LEADERSHIP

This study resulted in a Folletian framework for understanding leadership that integrates data from the frequency output, the Reality, Humanity, and Hope/Optimism code families, and the meaning and development of the words *leader, leaders,* and *leadership* across the seven PDs. Tracing these three words became the heart of the analysis. In the purest sense, the text took over. Allowing the text to guide the research, these three words became the thread used by the author to navigate the HU. Following the leadership word family led the researcher to a variety of related constructs, some more surprising than others. Two questions shaped this analytic path—"What was Follett saying about leadership?" and "How do Follett's constructs fit together?" At the end of the path, the author discovered that leadership was the unifying thread in Follett's writings. Although this was not her original intent, Follett discussed leadership from *The Speaker of the House of Representatives* (1896) to *Freedom & Co-ordination* (1949). The best lens for understanding the codes and the constructs within Follett's corpus of published texts is the construct of leadership.

Tracing Leader, Leaders, Leadership Across PDs

The purest way to extract Follett's ideas about leadership from the HU was to isolate and analyze the words *leader, leaders,* and *leadership* from the first PD to the last. Ten questions guided the tracing that ran the gamut from frequency of word, context, literal definition, essence, consistency of use across PDs, development of concept across PDs, progression or regression of interest in topic, comparison to contemporary thought, and Follett's legacy.

Each PD was analyzed in the same manner, and the results were presented using the same structure, beginning with the frequency and density data for *leader, leaders,* and *leadership.* The frequency number represented the number of times a word occurred in the text. The density data number represented the percentage of the PD dedicated to that word. The PDs varied in size, thus the density percentage was useful in comparing the amount of text dedicated to *leader, leaders,* and *leadership* between PDs.

Table 10-7 displays the density and frequency of *leader, leaders,* and *leadership* across PDs. A relatively low frequency number can still be a high-density percentage. For

Table 10-7   Leader, leaders, and leadership frequency and density data

Word	SOH	TNS	CAP	CE	DA	TSR	FC
Leadership	35 (.03)	25 (.02)	0	18 (.02)	175 (.18)	21 (.26)	83 (.24)
Leader	66 (.08)	17 (.01)	0	10 (.01)	113 (.12)	8 (.08)	36 (.10)
Executive					96 (.19)		
Administrative head					70 (.07)		67 (.19)
Teacher						70 (.70)	
Leaders	39 (.05)	29 (.03)	0	14 (.01)		3 (.03)	12 (.03)
Executives					63 (.06)		
Administrative heads					38 (.04)		37 (.10)
Teachers						18 (.23)	
Leader–follower	0	0	0	0	1	3 (.03)	0
Teacher–student						12 (.15)	

CAP, "Community is a Process"; CE, *Creative Experience*; DA, *Dynamic Administration*; FC, *Freedom & Co-ordination*; SOH, *Speaker of the House*; TNS, *The New State*; TSR, "Teacher-Student Relation."

example, in "*The Teacher-Student Relation,*" leader–follower occurred three times but has a .03 density which is the same density as 29 occurrences of *leaders* in *The New State*. Most frequency percentages for leadership were less than 1 percent, which was also true for most words in the HU. For example, the most common word in the HU, *of*, occurred 5242 times in *The New State*, which is .48 percent of the text. *We* occurred 1708 times in *The New State* and represented 1.78 percent of the text.

After examining frequency and density data in a single PD, the researcher compared the PD with others to identify trends, if any, in the amount of text dedicated to the subject of leadership. After comparing the numerical data, the author summarized the content, format, and purpose of the PD followed by an interpretation of the terms. Overlap in meanings between words often complicated the interpretation. Although it was problematic to isolate *leader* from *leadership*, the author attempted to, particularly when Follett made a distinction herself. The analysis of single PDs concluded with a summary of the findings.

The frequencies and densities of *leader, leaders*, and *leadership* steadily increased across PDs. Follett's definitions expanded as her interest in leadership intensified. In later publications, Follett expressed that she was barely scratching the surface of the subject of leaders and leadership. Her scholarly interest in leadership grew in relation to her conviction that the world's greatest need was a wide and diffused leadership. Follett's two shortest as well as her final published documents, "The Teacher-Student Relation" and *Freedom & Co-ordination*, had the highest densities of *leader, leaders*, and *leadership* compared to the other five PDs.

Leader and leaders

In all of the PDs, the word leader referred to a person with influence. Variables such as title, position, and status contributed to the power of a leader. In later writings, Follett asserted that everyone had the potential to lead. In *The New State* (1918) the lines between the leader and the group were beginning to blur and the leader was portrayed as a part of the group. The concept of the leader as a single person or as a hero faded steadily across texts. Leaders were central participants in leadership but were not the dominant force. Although traits of leaders were addressed in the HU, the emphasis on traits diminished across PDs and there was a noticeable change in the *kinds* of traits discussed. There was a shift from an emphasis on the personality, charisma, and force of a leader to more altruistic and analytical abilities like foresight, discernment, interest in people, moral reasoning, and being an active learner. Follett acknowledged the importance of the individual leader at the top of the organization. She discussed the executive leader as one of many distinct and necessary roles in the leadership process rather than as the "real" or only leader in the situation. The situation demanded more than a single leader. In addition, leaders engaged in followership and modeled what it meant to follow the invisible leader [common purpose]. Follett also identified undesirable leaders as those who may hold an office or position but whose methods include coercion, manipulation, and a type of persuasion bent on compliance from followers. Follett noted that many of the best leaders were "grown" in neighborhoods, community clubs, civic groups, and in progressive businesses.

Follett identified function as the most significant variable in determining the effectiveness of a leader, more so than the leader's personality, traits, or abilities. She also asserted that many leader qualities, such as self-control, discernment, and a variety of analytical skills, were learnable. In several texts, Follett stated that traditional ascendancy traits (e.g., dominance, charisma, aggression, and pugnacity) often had a negative effect on leader effectiveness. The most prevalent leadership ability across PDs was foresight, the ability to see and to understand the total situation. Foresight enabled a leader to perform key leadership functions such as defining purpose, anticipating the next situation, adapting to change, and creating new purposes or developing visions.

The concept of leader developed into an overseer of four social processes of control within an organization: evoking, interacting, integrating, and emerging. Follett described these leadership processes as ongoing, universal, and occurring at all levels of the organization. The leader was neither the cause of nor the primary trigger of these processes. Instead the leader valued and supported these processes through three major power-generating functions: coordination, articulation of purpose, and anticipation. These three functions enabled the leader to facilitate the four social processes and thus grew power within the organization or community. The organizational structure and the appropriate function as opposed to personality and position determined who would lead.

Leadership

The ultimate purpose of all types of leadership was to create organizational control (or functional unity) and to generate power throughout the organization to ensure relevancy and survival. The four basic leadership processes—evoking, interacting, integrating, and emerging—were group-oriented and interdependent. These social processes created unity for the organization without sacrificing the integrity of the individuals involved. Leaders and followers were active partners in the process. Follett depicted the essence of leadership as the creation of a partnership of following between leaders and followers who shared joint responsibility around a common task.

The concept of leadership developed from a microconstruct of leadership to an organizational or macrolevel construct across PDs. Microlevel leadership was the traditional, heroic understanding of leadership as a capacity possessed by a leader to influence others using one's position, personality, and traits. It was also a responsibility to serve. As an organizational level construct, leadership was a reciprocal influence between leaders, followers, and the context which Follett called the total evolving situation. Leadership was a collective process that created networks for communication and action and ultimately, organizational control. The power of leadership resided in the organization's ability to integrate all of the demands, abilities, needs, and desires of the situation. Effective leadership created unity, coherence, individual freedom and efficacy, organizational growth, leaders out of followers, and ultimately social progress.

Three categories of leadership functions emerged within the data—creating integrative unities, anticipation, and empowerment. Each concept represents multiple codes, applications, and elements. Creating integrative unities involved organizing and coordinating all of the conflicting diverse forces or powers within an organization. This leadership function located a unifying thread in the competing demands, created organizational control, and generated power for the leader and the organization as a whole. Anticipation, or "making the next moment," involved developing foresight and communicating a vision that enabled the organization to adapt to the evolving situation which included the common purpose. It also resulted in the creation of new values and new purposes.

IMPLICATIONS FOR CONTEMPORARY LEADERSHIP THEORY

Follett left an indelible yet essentially invisible mark on leadership theory. Her ideas are echoed in virtually every major leadership theory in the last 80 years including trait, behavioral, charismatic, situational, contingency, TQM, servant, and transformational theories. She was the first to challenge the "great man" paradigm, to link organizational structure to leadership effectiveness, to describe the essence of leadership as a reciprocal relationship, to frame diversity and conflict as necessary to effective leadership, and to include dialogue as an essential integrative leadership process. The paper does not discuss all of the results (see Martin, 2005). The discussion involves five of Follett's original scholarly contributions and their contemporary counterparts: hope and optimism, shared leadership, power and empowerment, followership, and invisible leader.

Hope and Optimism

Hope and optimism were unexpected codes that emerged in this study. Follett infused every text with a word of hope and concrete reasons for her optimism. Follett used hopeful language and described signs from the real world to inspire readers to respond to the call to leadership by acting on behalf of others. For example, Follett described the world as "growing more spiritual" (Follett, 1918, p. 161) after the Great War. Follett (1924) was hopeful because she observed a growing appreciation for "collective creativeness" (p. 94) among co-operatives, the League of Nations, and in business organizations.

Faith in humanity emerged alongside hope and optimism as a code family to contain Follett's beliefs about human freedom, individuality, human potential, finding meaning, and the nature of human relationships. This code family was linked to leadership threads across texts. Human beings possessed "vast" powers and potential to contribute to the progress of the world. Individuals found meaning in groups and by following purposes larger than themselves. The pinnacle of human activity was living the "consciously creative life" every day and helping others do the same. Far from being a Pollyanna, Follett acknowledged human darkness and frailty. The proper response was to help individuals find their callings within the whole. To do this was to engage in education and leadership (Follett, 1918).

The connection between constructs of hope, optimism, empathy, dispositional resilience, and human strength collectively known as positive psychology (Cameron, Dutton, & Quinn, 2003; Chang, 2000; Seligman, 1990; Seligman & Csikszentmihalyi, 2000; Seligman & Gillham, 2000; Simonton & Baumeister, 2005; Snyder & Lopez, 2002) and leadership have found their way into literature in the last decade. Hope is included as a dynamic and powerful leadership process in several emerging leadership models including organizational leadership (e.g., Shorey & Snyder, 2004). Authentic leadership offers a comprehensive and well-developed set of constructs that link leadership to hope, optimism, and human strengths (Avolio & Gardner, 2005; Avolio, Gardner, Walumbwa, Luthans, & May, 2004; Gardner, Avolio, Luthans, May & Walumbwa, 2005; Klenke, 2005; Luthans & Avolio, 2003).

Shared Leadership/Team Leadership

In all texts, Follett discussed the need for multiple leaders at all levels of the organization and the key role that group process played in both organizational and social progress. She described group process as the hope for the world. Within the group process, there were multiple leaders who varied in type, function, level, and responsibilities. The combined capacities of multiple leaders created more power for the organization or community and also diminished the need for a single leader. Multiple leaders shared the responsibility for facilitating the group process at varying levels of an organization. The group process unified diverse members into a single and powerful consciousness without extinguishing the individual. Working together, a team of leaders contributed more to overall organizational viability than a single leader at the top ever could. Follett's emphasis on collaborative or shared leadership is echoed in the work of Chrislip and Larson (1994), Cronin (1987), Hackman (1990), Hickman (1998), Hollander (1978), and Rost (1991).

Follett's (1896) recommendations regarding team training (again among the first), the creation of networks, and shared decision making are reflected in the literature on self-directed work teams (Fisher & Miller, 1993; Hackman, 1990; Nygren & Levine, 1996; Zawacki & Norman, 1994). Follett called on scholars in various disciplines to engage in research to determine the most effective ways to combine the capacities of multiple leaders through collaboration and networking. If she were alive, Follett would applaud the growing scholarly interest in team leadership and specific processes that contribute to effective outcomes (Komaki & Minnich, 2002; Manz & Sims, 1993; Sivasubramaniam, Murry, Avolio & Jung, 2002; Zaccaro & Klimosky, 2002; Zaccaro, Rittman, & Marks, 2001). Zaccaro et al.'s (2001) discussion of functional leadership within teams echoes Follett's discussion of leadership as a set of functions and processes shaped by the demands of the context rather than the preferred behaviors and traits of the leaders.

We-Power and Empowerment

We-power or "power with" as distinct from a more traditional "power over" was a theme across texts and embedded within Follett's discussion of leadership. As the highest frequency pronoun, *we* occurred more than *I*. *Power* was the fourth highest frequency noun in the entire HU, and together they created a construct of *we-power* which is reflected in Follett's construct of "power-with." Creating we-power was an outcome of the group process (see above) and the key to social progress. All of Follett's major constructs including leadership link back in some way to power-with or we-power in the data. Leadership was essentially about we-leadership rather than I-leadership, an essentially heroic construct. Leadership was about we-power, the power of the group together, diverse, conflicting yet integrating, generating new values, solutions, and power for social progress. We-power leadership was a meta-theme that shaped the core of the analysis in this study—tracing the occurrences of *leader, leaders,* and *leadership.*

Follett portrayed the primary function of a leader as that of helping others to contribute to the collective purpose of, and growing power within, the organization. These ideas are reflected in the contemporary construct of empowerment (Conger & Kanungo, 1998; Offerman, 1995; Spreitzer, 1995; 1996; Spreitzer, De Janasz, & Quinn, 1999; Spreitzer & Quinn, 1996; Thomas & Velthouse, 1990). The word *empowerment* was neither common nor associated with leadership in Follett's era, yet she identified training and development of leaders as "essence" of leadership. Two of the four leadership processes, evoking and integrating, are processes that create power and empower individuals. Evoking was a process that freed the creative energies of individuals, and integrating was a process that wove together the diverse contributions (energies) of people so that each person was contributing to the whole.

A pioneer in promoting employee training, Follett also emphasized the need to teach people how to think for themselves, to solve their own problems, and to exercise control over their environments. Follett's empowerment practices included connecting resources to people, creating appropriate structures and networks that fit the needs of the situation, and providing information to many people at varying levels of the organization. Today, these concepts are more prevalent and supported by the research of the aforementioned scholars.

Followership

Followership appears once in the entire HU; however, it is a highly significant finding. After researching the origins of the word *followership,* the author has concluded that Follett was the first to use the word and most likely coined it. If not, Follett is a pioneer in discussing the key role of active followers in leadership at least 50 years before followership was discussed in the literature (Crainer, 2000). Followers were active participants in the four leadership processes that provided organizational control. Followers joined leaders in a partnership of following the common purpose [invisible leader]. Followers were doing leadership by virtue of the fact that they were acting on their belief in the common purpose. A follower sometimes functioned as a leader or took on a more directive role when his or her experience, knowledge, and abilities fit the needs of the moment and context. Follett also redefined the leader–follower paradigm as something that was bidirectional rather than unidirectional. Seeking to erase what she deemed as a false dichotomy between leaders and followers, Follett proposed that leaders and followers shared equally in the leadership process, as partners following the invisible leader, the common purpose.

Followership is not in most modern dictionaries but is part of the current leadership lexicon (Ehrhart & Klein, 2001; Hollander, 1978; 1992a; 1992b; 1995; Hughes, Ginnett & Curphy, 1993; Kelley, 1988; 1992; Rost, 1991.) In 1955, Hollander and Webb posited that leaders and followers were interdependent, and the boundaries between the two were fluid and sometimes, depending on system demands, roles were reversible. Kelly (1992) depicted followers as valued partners or co-creators in the leadership process with very similar qualities and competencies. Both Burns (1978) and Greenleaf (1970; 1977) elevate the role of followers in leadership and reflect Follett's initial call to train followers to be leaders. Follett initiated the idea that followers were critical, but it has taken years for the scholarly community to catch up.

Invisible Leader

Follett developed and introduced the construct of invisible leader. The invisible leader was not a person but rather the common purpose of the group or organization that generated loyalty and power. This nonhuman construct began as a moral principle in *The New State* (1918). It was a moral purpose embodied by a group that also held the group together and focused the activities of all citizens. In later texts, the idea of the moral state morphed into the common purpose as the invisible leader. The common purpose held the group together, generated power, and guided the efforts of the whole. The common purpose emerged from the group process of interpenetration that unified all of the conflicting ideas and desires within an evolving situation. Thus, the common purpose was an organic leader and as it changed, so did the actions of the individuals and the organization as a whole. The invisible leader is a complex construct, more so than the standard organizational mission or purpose statements written post facto the establishment of the organization to satisfy external stakeholders rather than reflect the true power that holds the organization together. The invisible leader is similar to the contemporary construct of strange attractor of meaning in chaos theory (Burns, 2002, Marion & Uhl-Bien, 2001; Regine & Lewin, 2000; Schneider & Somers, 2006; Uhl-Bien, Marion, & McKelvey, 2007) in that it draws people to the group and at the same time generates the power and loyalty necessary for prolonged action. Follett argued that the charisma generated from the common purpose was more magnetic and enduring than the charisma of a person. Only Follett's words can do justice to this original idea.

> Leaders and followers are both following the invisible leader—the common purpose. The best executives put this common purpose clearly before their group. While leadership depends on the depth of conviction and the power coming there from, there must also be the ability to share that conviction with others, the ability to make purpose articulate. And then that common purpose becomes the leader. And I believe that we are coming more and more to act, whatever our theories, on our faith in the power of this invisible leader. Loyalty to the invisible leader gives us the strongest possible bond of union, establishes a sympathy which is not a sentimental but a dynamic sympathy (Follett, 1941, p. 287).

The concept of invisible leader was Follett's most progressive concept and remains unmatched today although several contemporary scholars (e.g., Badaracco, 2001; 2002; Collins & Porras, 1994/1997; 1995) are currently discussing leaders who lead quietly behind the scenes and combine humility with a professional will.

SUMMARY

This study sought to organize Mary Parker Follett's body of thought and to reduce the confusion and redundancy of her language (Fox, 1970; Lawson, 1999; Urwick, 1935). To date, this kind of contribution has not been made. The significance of the research is the degree to which the results provide a clear, comprehensive, and succinct presentation of Follett's theories.

For six months, the researcher mined the texts of Mary Parker Follett. HU included seven texts or PDs, totaling over 1450 pages of Follett's published writings. Similar to the process of mining for gold which involves sorting, crushing, and extracting, this study was executed in stages. First, the author collected, scanned, and loaded the data into a single HU followed by word crunching that resulted in word frequency totals for the entire HU, as well as sorted by PD. The most lengthy phase involved autocoding and line-by-line coding using ATLAS/ti computer software, as well as an interlude phase of hand coding two of the seven PDs. The act of coding was much like sifting gold from sand and gravel, sorting, naming the heaviest or the key concepts from the entire text. In the final phases, the researcher analyzed the HU in its entirety and extracted the most precious and timeless nuggets of insight, practical wisdom, and hope for meeting the leadership challenges of the twenty first century.

Leadership emerged as the unifying thread of Follett's body of work. The results of this comprehensive content analysis showed that Mary Parker Follett was a trailblazer and original thinker whose ideas and concepts expressed or anticipated many contemporary leadership constructs such as followership, conflict management, authority, control, and power and leadership theories including contingency theory, transformational leadership, the positive psychology movement, and complexity theory. Follett's ideas provide a platform for the next level of theory development that is multilevel and postheroic. According to Fletcher (2004, Fletcher & Kaeufer, 2003), postheroic leadership has three characteristics that distinguish it from more traditionally individualistic models: (1) leadership as practice: shared and distributed; (2) leadership as social process: interactions; and (3) leadership as learning: outcomes (Fletcher, 2004, pp. 648–649). These ideas were clearly evident in Follett's writing. After all, Follett was a pragmatist par excellence who described leadership as dispersed practice. She believed that leadership embraced a variety of social processes such as the concept of we-power and emphasized learning as an integral element of leadership in several of the PDs on which this research is based.

11

CALLING AND LEADER IDENTITY: UTILIZING NARRATIVE ANALYSIS TO CONSTRUCT A STAGE MODEL OF CALLING DEVELOPMENT

Frank A. Markow

INTRODUCTION AND THEORETICAL BACKGROUND

Calling is currently an emerging area of interest within positive organizational scholarship (Cameron, Dutton, & Quinn, 2003; Weiss, Skelley, Haughley, Hall, 2004) and spirituality and leadership (Fry, 2003; Fry, Vitucci, & Cedillo; 2005; Hicks, 2002; Krishnakumar & Neck, 2002). Yet, little empirical research has been done which supports the construct of calling. The purpose of this research is to utilize the research methodology of narrative analysis to illuminate the phenomenon of calling as it functions in relationship to leader identity so that we can more fully understand calling as a construct seen to be of importance within emerging and extant theories leadership.

The idea of call and vocation are notions that the Christian tradition has long used to address issues about one's place and purpose in the world. Central to this interpretation of vocation is "the idea that there is something—my vocation or calling—God has called me to do with my life, and my life has meaning and purpose at least in part because I am fulfilling my purpose" (Plachard, 2005, p. 2). A call can be viewed as one's perception that he or she has been set apart or marked for a specific vocation (from the Latin *vocare*, meaning *voice*) or otherwise. Professionals often have a sense of calling to their field, a dedication to their work, and a strong commitment to their careers (Filley, House, & Kerr, 1976). Calling has been held to be a primary source of purpose and vision in pastoral leadership (McNeal, 2000) and typically sets the course of one's life as a minister. However, calling can go beyond a sense of professional commitment to a certain line of work. It is the experience of transcendence or how one makes a difference through service to others and, in doing so, derives meaning and purpose in life (Fry, 2003).

The Development of Calling in the Management Literature

Calling was initially described as a divine inspiration to do morally responsible work (Weber, 1958). It moved away from this initial religious conception toward a broader secular view, characterized by doing good work out of a sense of inner direction that would contribute to a better world (Davidson & Caddell, 1994; Lips-Wiersman, 2002b; Wrzesniewski, McCauly, & Rozin, Schwartz, 1997). This view reflects calling as coming from an internal motivation that is not driven by instrumental goal seeking but rather reflects a generalized form of psychological engagement with the meaning of one's work (Dobrow, 2004; Kahn, 1990; Lips-Wiersman, 2002b; Wrzesniewski, 1997). The criteria for determining career success reflect personal standards, preferences, and rewards that are self-referent (Gattiker & Larwood, 1988). Subjective career success has been most commonly operationalized as either job or career satisfaction (Heslin, 2005). Career calling was also framed by Levinson (1978) in the concept of the career dream, the individual's vision of an ideal career state that is central to early adulthood. Shepard (1984) referred to a "path with a heart" (p. 34) to describe career success which was measured in terms of one's unique vision and central values in life. Table 11-1 illustrates the differing perspectives and language used to describe calling, both secular and religious.

Empirical Research on Calling and Related Constructs

Attempts to define and operationalize calling and related constructs have varied over the past. As noted, having a sense of calling is a highly individualistic and subjective

Table 11-1   Two views of calling (Hall & Chandler, 2005)

	Religious view	Secular view
Source of calling	From God or a higher being	Within the individual
Who is served?	Calling serves community	Serves individual and/or community
Method of identifying a calling	Discernment (e.g., prayer, listening)	Introspection, reflection, meditation, relational activities
The meaning	Enacting God's larger plan for an individual's life	Enacting an individual's purpose for personal fulfillment

experience (Hall & Chandler, 2005) which allows for a "self-relevant view of meaning" (Dobrow, 2004, p. 3). Therefore, as a highly subjective construct, there have been few attempts to operationalize and measure calling. Hall was an innovator in understanding and measuring calling and created a sense of calling scale which has not been widely used (Wrzesniewski et al., 1997). Some of the empirical research on calling as it relates to other known constructs have shown that people with a high sense of calling report a high sense of job satisfaction and low absenteeism when compared to those with other (e.g., job or career) conceptions of their work (Wrzesniewski et al.). In another empirical study of the notion of calling, job, and career, Davidson and Caddell (1994) showed that, for some people who internalized their religion, work itself was not seen as just a job but as having some sacred significance similar to a calling—the Protestant work ethic in action. Calling has been empirically shown to relate to a sense of personal meaning that is derived from a sense of self-transcendence and mediates the relationship between personal meaning and organizational commitment (Markow & Klenke, 2005).

Various writers have identified dimensions of calling. Dobrow (2004), Weiss et al. (2004), Novak (1996), and McNeal (2000) have described the following as aspects of a personal sense of calling. Dimensions include

1. It is a passion for one's work that energizes and sustains.

2. One's identity centers on their sense of calling.

3. A calling sustains over the life of the individual.

4. A calling consumes the ambitions and goals of one's life.

5. A calling gives meaning to work, and this meaning is self-relevant.

6. A calling "fits" one's skills and abilities.

7. A calling is for service of the community.

8. Each calling is unique to the individual.

9. A calling is discovered through reflection, prayer, feedback from others, and trial activities.

Relating Calling to Identity

Theory and research also has shown a connection between identity and concepts related to calling. Early related ideas include Strauss (1959) as well as others' (e.g., Denzin, 1994; Polkinghorne, 1988) idea of epiphanies; turning point experiences which are often accompanied by special encounters, a vision, or a sense of divine manifestation. Denzin (1989) discussed epiphany experiences with the potential to create lasting transformation in a person's life. Similarly, Loder (1989) described the "logic of transformation" which refers to the process by which one moves beyond rational and inductive ways of knowing and, through seminal moments and encounters, is able to generate from hidden resources new and powerful insights which transform ones thinking and being. Lips-Wiersman (2002a) sought to show how spirituality is one of the determinants of career behavior and influences career purposes, sense making, and coherence in a way that supports calling and self-identity. Individual spirituality allowed individuals to align their careers with perceived spiritual orderings outside of themselves. These findings are consistent with Markow and Klenke's (2005) who also found that calling was most salient among those whose sense of personal meaning was anchored in transcendent values.

Narrative Theories of Identity Development

Narrative psychology is based on the premise that "human experience and behavior are meaningful and that, in order to understand ourselves and others, we need to explore the 'meaning systems' and the 'structures' of meaning that make up our minds and our worlds" (Polkinghorne, 1988, p. 1). As human beings, we are essentially interpretive creatures; constantly evaluating events and activities, interpreting as we go along, creating their meaning and our selves in the process. Sarbin (1986) proposed what he called the narratory principle; the idea that human beings think, perceive, imagine, interact, and make moral choices according to narrative structures. Ricoeur (1992) argued that the self only comes into being in the process of telling a life story. Carr (1986) referred to the role of narration as that which organizes time and gives shape and coherence to the sequences of experiences we have as we are in the process of having them. We are constantly attempting to "surmount time in exactly the way a storyteller does...to dominate the flow of events by gathering them together in the forward-backward grasp of the narrative act..." (p. 62). Some have even suggested that there is something fundamentally religious about narrative structure, the attempt to order time, and give meaning to events and sequences of events (Roof, 1993).

Personal narrative is a story created, told, revised, and retold throughout life (Pallus, Nasby, & Easton, 1991). They represent people's identities because the life story represents an internal model of "who I was, who I am, and who I might become" (Bruner, 1991; Gergen & Gergen, 1986; McAdams, 1993). McAdams called this creating the "personal myth" (p. 102), the fashioning of a history of the self which is an account of the past that seeks to explain how and why events transpired as they actually did and how our past came to be and gave birth to the present. Seen in this way, one's calling may be a nuclear episode (McAdams) or series of events that are particularly salient and which have assumed especially prominent positions in one's understanding of who he or she was and who he or she is, the pivot point of one's personal myth.

In these views of the self, identity is not a static reality to be discovered but rather an ongoing process of interpretation (Ricoeur, 1992). Individuals understand themselves through the medium of language, through talking and writing. Through these, they are constantly engaged in the process of creating themselves (Crossley, 2000) as they perform their identity through the telling of narratives about themselves (Langellier, 1989; Mishler, 1999). Each retelling of the life story is an "intent to present themselves in a particular way and give a sensible account of their experience" (Mishler, 1999, p. 23).

Further, while narrative identity is personal and individualistic, it is not entirely so. Meaning is not the product of just the individual, it is formulated and mediated through cultural meaning systems such as language and larger cultural narratives, both of which connect our meaning systems across generations. The construction of narrative identity is dialogical and occurs within a social context (Murray, 2003) and are "socially situated actions" (Mishler, 1999, p.19), incorporating facets of personal relationships as well as larger cultural plot lines. Individuals draw on and redo culturally available plots in the process of creating their own unique stories (Mishler, 1999).

Narrative Identity and Leadership

Identity is a key construct in the understanding and development of leadership ability (Lord & Hall, 2005) as well as a central theme in the role of followership and leader effectiveness (van Knippenberg, van Knippenberg, De Cremer, & Hogg, 2004). Because self-identity strongly informs one's feelings, beliefs, attitudes, and goals (Leary & Tangney, 2003), effective and mature leaders are those who are aware of and growing in their own self-concept as leaders. Further, leader effectiveness is contingent upon the leader's ability to influence follower's attitudes and behaviors through their self-concept (van Knippenberg et al., 2004).

Self-concept and the relationship between self-concept and action is a defining characteristic of authentic leadership (Shamir & Eilam, 2005). Authentic leaders are seen as those who see their leadership role as a central component of their self-concept and have high levels of self-resolution and self-concept clarity, defined as the extent to which one's self-beliefs are clearly and confidently defined and internally consistent (Turner, 1976). Shamir and Eilam posited that authentic leaders achieve such self-knowledge through the development of a life story or narrative. This life story gives leaders self-identity and answers the question, "who am I?" Their identity is a story created, told, and revisited throughout their life (Pallus et al., 1991). The life story provides the leader with a meaning system from which to feel, think, and act and enables him or her to analyze and interpret reality in a way that gives life a personal meaning (Kegan, 1982).

RESEARCH DESIGN

Dobrow (2004) suggested that calling research should initially focus on exemplars and that the nonprofit sector and other untraditional types of occupations could be interesting and fruitful populations in which to study calling. Pastors with a proven record of leadership ability demonstrated through years of ministry service who indicate that they have been called, were deliberately selected from among leaders of a large Pentecostal denomination. The data were collected in communities in the western part of the United States. I met most participants in their church offices, though a couple came to my office.

Interview Protocol

Here are the main components of my research interview protocol. Question 1 referred to life chapters/ministry career history. In this first stage, the participant was asked to consider his or her ministry career as a book which can be divided into chapters, giving no more than seven or eight chapters. Each chapter was given a name and a brief description. Because the focus of my research was not on the entirety of the participant's life story, I focused primarily on the chapters relating to the participants' ministry career history which began at any point chosen by the participant. Interestingly, all participants chose to begin in their childhood; some gave family background in great detail with a few starting with their grandparents.

Question 2 focused on key events. The participants were asked to describe critical or significant episodes from each chapter of their stories including the accompanying characters, actions, thoughts, and feelings. Details about where they were, who was with them, what they did, and what they were thinking and feeling during the event were solicited along with any sense of personal meaning and impact on identity that these events held. Specific events considered included peak experiences (a high point in their story, a wonderful moment), nadir experiences (a low point in their story, a worst moment), and turning points (an episode where they underwent a significant change in their self-understanding vis-a-vis their ministry). These often seemed to illuminate the crux of the research questions, namely their experience of being called.

Question 3 focused on significant people. Though these often came out from the previous questions, the participants were asked specifically to describe several of the most important people in their life stories, particularly people who intersect with their sense of calling. A larger social context and network of ministry-related relationships were also solicited to discover relationship(s) to various people in their organizations as well as official organizational members who may have promoted or hindered their sense of calling.

Question 4 referred to future script. This portion of the interview protocol addressed plans, goals, aspirations, hopes, and dreams for the future. More specifically, future plans that relate to one's ministry were the focus.

Question 5 dealt with life theme. The final question asked participants to give a central theme, message, or idea that they felt ran throughout the entirety of their narrative as previously described. While some of the participants genuinely reflected back on the story as just told, most gave a picture of themselves that bore no resemblance to their account. The global life theme was often a biblical passage that participants felt somehow reflected their life, but I seldom saw a connection between it and what they had just recounted. Table 11-2 summarizes the research questions.

Table 11-2   Summary of interview questions

	Question	Description
Question 1	Life chapters/ ministry career history	Ask participant to divide life into a series of chapters, with a title for each chapter. This could begin at any point they like.
Question 2	Key events	Ask participant to describe critical or significant episodes from each chapter of their stories including the accompanying characters, actions, thoughts, feelings, peak experiences, nadir experiences and turning points.
Question 3	Significant people	Ask participant to specifically describe several of the most important people in their life stories, particularly people who intersect with their sense of calling.
Question 4	Future script	Ask participant to address plans, goals, aspirations, hopes, and dreams for the future. More specifically, future plans that relate to one's ministry were the focus.
Question 5	Life theme	Ask participant to give a central theme, message, or idea that they felt ran throughout the entirety of their narrative as previously described.

FINDINGS

The following section describes the results of my research. In the first part, individual level themes (themes within each narrative) will be described. Then, universal level themes (those that ran across all or most participants narratives) will be described and shown to cluster into a five-stage developmental model of calling. Next will be a description of three types of calling narratives, modeled after the suffering–crisis–transformation plot. Finally, a general psychological structure of calling and leader identity formation is given, which abstracts from the previous narratives a conceptual approach to understanding how one comes to identify a sense of call, as well as the consequences of having perceived a calling.

Table 11-3   Individual level themes

Participant	Main theme	Secondary theme
David	Reconciliation with father	
Isaac	Finding someone to trust	Letting go of career aspirations
Franz	Strong women figures	Getting out of poverty
Ken	Separating from a controlling mother	Am I am musician or pastor?
Edward	Mexican family culture influence	The good Boy Scout and obedient son
Carl	The outcast with no friends	Role ambivalence
Heath	It was bad, but I'm okay now	Being an entrepreneur/wrestling with going into business
Luke	Finding a father figure who would give me approval	Struggle to be mature/difficulty confronting elders/fears
Bernard	Making money/breaking away from business	Education plans being thwarted
Jacob	The Word becomes real, and so I must now show you this	
Gerard	Changing "gangs"/from the old drug gang to the new Christian gang	Destroyed by Arthur
Abraham	Breaking away from the control of mother and pastor	Being embraced by the denomination

Themes—Individual Level

While each story had unique circumstances, characters, plot developments, resolutions, and so forth, it was typical that, in each individual case, a specific issue presented itself and recurred throughout the story in a theme and variation pattern. The individual themes were usually presented early on in the interview, though it took some practice to be able to spot these. After several interviews, I realized the idiosyncratic nature of these themes and began to probe around these themes instead of assuming that the theme I heard from previous participants would also relate to the subsequent stories. Table 11-3 lists all unique themes found in the particular stories along with secondary/ subthemes.

Themes—Universal

I was able to cluster themes (Boyatzis, 1998) into five fairly consistent developmental stages. This is a descriptive model based solely on the data from my interviews. The following section describes the five stages including a title for the stage, a general description of the stage, subthemes in each stage, and the criterion variables.

Stage 1: precall antecedents—awaiting

This first stage consists of the participants' early years from birth through the teen or early adult years. Each participant was allowed to begin their story at any point, and all began at childhood. While several participants included evidence of a nascent call even in childhood, most felt that childhood was important because it often set the stage for latter events which were germane to their call. For example, one participant recalled from his childhood both victimization and abuse at the hands of his father along with the positive role model of a dedicated and caring Roman Catholic priest. These two issues carried on throughout his story: his inability to trust other leaders was admittedly a result of his early trauma, while his own compassion and care for others was something that he saw modeled at an impressionable age.

There were two, often competing, phenomena described by the participants in their early years which I describe as a congruous environment and rebellion. A congruous environment was one which, generally speaking, supported their faith, values, and beliefs; either those held as a child or those later adopted as an adult. The good Christian home or church-going family is typical of this stage. Participants had values taught to them at church or at home and saw parents who were devout and involved in ministry themselves. This naturally would lend to the family being supportive of their later sense of calling to ministry.

The other phenomena described by the participants was a sense of rebellion from their families values. These participants described a time when they left home, became involved in drug use, other religions, or no religion at all. This was often accompanied by tumultuous or hostile home environments. Several participants indicated a supportive Christian home environment and also a time of rebellion and departure form the family's values, though this was the exception in this sample.

A third theme in this stage was that of leadership opportunities. More than half of the sample indicated that they were involved as a leader in their early years, some even beginning at grade school. They experienced opportunities to lead others, stand for a cause, organize events or activities, hold office in a student body, or attain a higher status/role in their work. Some indicted that they always felt like leaders or were at least never aware of a specific time when they became a leader. It was just something they naturally did.

Stage 2: Recognition of the call through spiritual awakening and involvement—awakening

This second stage covers the years during which the participants typically became aware of the fact that they had a call. This stage has a very clear delineation between two categories or types of calling awareness, either calling as an epiphany or special event or calling as a by product (or gradual awareness). In the first category (calling as epiphany), the individual was able to recount a specific time and place in which they were called. It was often in a spiritual environment (at a church youth camp, a time of prayer or reflection, etc.), was accompanied by a spiritual or supernatural experience (a vision, the voice of God speaking to the soul, etc.), and was reinforced subsequently by other phenomena (i.e., a special prophetic statement spoken by another person which confirmed the initial epiphany).

The second type of calling experiences came in a less dramatic and/or supernatural means, the gradual awareness that came over time that was predicated by or the result of ministry service (e.g., working as a volunteer in a local church). There was no specific epiphany but rather a sense that, over time, this was what he was supposed to do with his life.

Stage 3: Realization of the call through experience, mentoring, and/or preparation for vocational service—actualizing

In this stage, the participants describe a series of events, experiences, people, or preparation activities that supported the fulfillment of their calling. These subthemes are having a personal mentor, being mentored from afar, going to college to prepare for ministry, going to college for self-discovery or personal enrichment (which led to confirmation or their calling), finding a passion for ministry service, experiencing success in ministry seen in expanded responsibility and/or establishing followers, and recognizing spiritual/supernatural indicators that supported or confirmed that they were called.

Stage 4: Struggle to separate from previous roles and identities/dealing with precall stage issues-anguishing

This next stage is characterized by two phenomena: a personal conflict with a significant character in their story (a parent, another leader, a pastor, etc.) and a struggle to release a previous role or identity. Both of these phenomena seem to serve as truly decisive moments in the calling accounts; as if somehow confronting and overcoming these nemeses was a liberating and transforming moment, one in which they could now be authentic to their true selves and aspirations. Though described as a stage, this struggle did not necessarily happen after the previous stage chronologically. In fact, it may have occurred during the previous stage. I felt that it deserved its own stage category because of the importance that these events seemed to serve in the participant's lives and because of the nature of the phenomena (conflict, tension, struggle, and resolution) which seem categorically different than passion, preparation, and the other issues involved in stage 3.

Personal conflict and release
The vast majority of the participants (all but two) recounted an incident in which they had to confront an important person in their lives; come to some sort of resolution to the conflict; and, as a result, felt a new sense of individuality or liberty to move ahead with their life and calling. For example, one individual recalled a time when he had to stand against the wishes of his controlling mother, recalling the event as "a very decisive moment . . . probably the biggest stand that I had ever taken in my life . . . it was also just a little after that that the call came." The ability to stand up to a controlling mother meant maturity, individuation, and the ability to make decisions on his own.

Identity conflict
In addition to these interpersonal conflicts and resolution accounts, a vast majority (all but one) of the participants recounted struggling with previous roles and identities, those that stood in contrast or somehow prevented them from embracing their sense of calling. For example, one participant discovered early in his life an entrepreneurial tendency, one which allowed him to successfully begin new businesses and make money. For many years, he wrestled with the decision to either follow this or to let go and to follow his call to enter the ministry. He eventually left behind his businesses and found that this entrepreneurial tendency was now an asset in ministry, the ability to develop new and important ministry strategies. One participant had a gift for music, one which he had developed and nurtured from childhood. In fact, he even entered

college to study music. Receiving his calling in an epiphany event, he questioned how he was to carry this out since he was a musician not a preacher. His initial inclination was to see his calling as one that would involve music. Incidentally, but not insignificantly, this struggle with previous roles and identities seems to be pervasive and hard to overcome. Many, even those with a strong confidence in their call to ministry, seem to struggle with separating from (or perhaps integrating) roles and identities developed prior to their sense of calling to ministry.

Stage 5: Identity integration and role merger of faith and work/subsequent wrestling with preferred roles/possible selves—acceptance

A final stage was identified, containing only two dichotomous criterion variables. This stage came primarily from the portion of the narrative describing hopes and plans for the future, the next chapter of their life stories. A minority of individuals expressed contentment with their current roles, that what they were currently doing was a good expression of their calling and that they had no desire or intent to change roles. The only consistent theme among these content individuals was to expand their role of teaching within their current ministry. Many seemed to express generative concerns for their followers, that they pass the torch to them effectively, and so forth.

Interestingly, the majority expressed a desire for or anticipation of a change in role. While role and identity are not necessarily synonymous, it seems that their desire to change had much to do with their self-perceptions and how their current role did not allow for the simultaneous employment and expression of their preferred self (Kahn, 1990). Often, the individual would harken back to a previous role, as if wondering aloud if they should reengage in this role. This is seen clearly in the example of one pastor who previously saw his identity as a musician:

> I struggle ... because I didn't stay true to who I was and I tried to become a preacher as apposed to letting God do what he wanted to do. I have lost a lot of time, and my music desires have probably not been where they could have been because I tried to jump to the other side.

Another, who had always struggled to integrate his entrepreneurial desires with his commitment to ministry, felt that eventually he would be moving on. Others did not see the reason for the discontentment quite as clearly. One expressed a general ennui about his current role: "I feel like a lost soul who is being faithful to my current assignment ... I don't feel incredibly effective, and I am probably more effective than I feel. I feel just kind of like a person floating in the fog ... " Table 11-4 lists these stages and universal themes.

Table 11-4 Stages and universal themes

Stage	Title	Themes
Stage 1	Precall antecedents/family/life circumstances *Awaiting*	Theme 1a. Congruous early environment Theme 1b. Rebellion Theme 1c. Early leadership opportunities
Stage 2	Recognition of the call through spiritual awakening or involvement *Awakening*	Theme 2a. Calling as an epiphany Theme 2b. Calling as a by-product of serving
Stage 3	Realization of the call through experience, mentoring, and/or preparation for vocational service *Actualizing*	Theme 3a. Has a personal mentor Theme 3b. Mentored from afar Theme 3c. College to prepare Theme 3d. College to discover Theme 3e. Newfound passion for serving Theme 3f. Success in ministry. Theme 3g. Supernatural or Spiritual indicators
Stage 4	Struggle to separate from previous roles and identities/dealing with precall stage issues *Anguishing*	Theme 4a. Personal conflict and release Theme 4b. Identity conflict and release
Stage 5	Identity integration and role merger of faith and work/subsequent wrestling with preferred roles/possible selves *Acceptance*	Theme 5a. Satisfaction with current role Theme 5b. Dissatisfaction with current role

Calling Narratives—Three Prototypes

Based on the thematic analysis of the interviews, three types of calling narratives can be seen. In keeping with the employed narrative methodology, these will be organized according to Plummer (1995) who described basic plot forms such as taking a journey, engaging in a contest, enduring suffering, pursuing consummation, and establishing a home. The common elements of all these plots are suffering that gives tension to the story, a crisis or turning point or epiphany, and a transformation. The following narratives are an extrapolation of the above stages and themes, framed in the suffering–crisis–transformation plot form, and can be considered prototypical calling narratives. They are put into first person so as to capture the sense of those who gave the stories. See Table 11-5 for a list of these prototypical calling narratives.

Table 11-5   Types of calling narratives

Type	Overview	Unique features of type	Participants this describes
Type I	I had a supportive, Christian environment. I did not rebel against my family. I was called to ministry (either epiphany or progressive). While certain people influenced me, there was no particular person that was a very close personal mentor. I went to college to prepare for ministry. I am satisfied in my current role	Supportive, Christian family and no rebellion described Satisfied with current role	Bernard, Jacob, Edward, Franz
Type II	I rebelled against my family, left, and did my own thing. I discovered through a progressive awareness that I was called to ministry. I went to college to help me discover my role in life and discern if I was called to ministry. There was a particular person in my life who mentored me. I am dissatisfied in my current role.	Rebellion from family described	Gerard, Isaac, Abraham, Luke
Type III	I had a supportive, Christian family; but, as I grew up, I departed from what they believed and left to do my own thing. I was called to ministry (either epiphany or progressive). I had a personal mentor (though I may not have). I went to Bible college. I am dissatisfied in my current role.	Supportive, Christian family. Rebellion described	Ken, Carl, Heath

Type I calling narrative

Suffering

My parents were not perfect, but they were wonderful role models for me growing up. I saw them serve in ministry, and they encouraged me from an early age in my faith. I had many opportunities to exercise leadership at an early age, and was often looked up to as a leader by my peers. But, I struggled to find my place in the world. Should I go in to ministry? business? music? I was not sure of my life's direction.

Crisis

Once I made a deeper commitment to my faith, things began to change. I was reenergized by a sense of calling and began serving in ministry. My calling was confirmed by others, and I experienced great success in ministry which served to further confirm that I had been called. Some very spiritual and even supernatural encounters also helped to confirm my sense of calling. I had others who guided me but mostly those I only knew from afar but who influenced me nevertheless. Gaining an education was something that helped me to prepare for my calling in ministry.

During this time of preparation, a crisis hit. I was confronted by the fact that someone I knew and respected was now a road block to my emerging sense of calling. This strained relationship seemingly prevented me from moving ahead with my calling. To further complicate things, I was struggling to let go of my previous identity. For years, I had developed and nurtured an image of myself; and, now, the calling in my life was challenging that image. It was so hard to let go of this person who I always thought I was.

Transformation

Eventually, I was able to overcome these crises. When I finally confronted this person who was the road block, I felt liberated and free to fully pursue my calling. I stood up to them, confronted my own fears about them, and was able to move forward confidently in my calling. Further, I was able to deal with my previous identity conflict and accept the new identity that my calling has placed on me. I now stand confident in my calling, my current role, and look forward to the future as I teach the next generation and other leaders.

Type II and type III calling narratives

Types I and II calling narratives are similar enough in their initial setting and in their final status as to be conflated into one narrative.

Suffering

My parents did the best they could, but their best was not good enough for me. My parents were not that affirming; and they sought to control our family life in general, me in particular. I had many opportunities to exercise leadership at an early age and was often looked up to as a leader by my peers. My early adult years were fraught with rebellion; and I went my own way, away from my family. This caused me and my family pain, and I was unsure of my life's direction.

Crisis

Once I made a commitment to my faith, things began to change. I was reenergized by a new sense of calling, which I became aware of in both natural and supernatural ways. I developed a passion to serve in ministry. My calling was confirmed by others, and I experienced great success in ministry which served to further confirm that I had been called. Some very spiritual and even supernatural encounters also helped to confirm my sense of calling. I had others who guided me and taught me, both those I grew to personally know and love and those I only knew from afar but who influenced me nevertheless. Gaining an education was something that helped me to both learn more about ministry and confirm that I had been called.

Then the crisis hit. I was confronted by the fact that someone I knew and respected was now a road block to my emerging sense of calling. This strained relationship seemingly prevented me from moving ahead fully with my calling. To further complicate things, I was struggling to let go of my previous identity. For years, I had developed and nurtured an image of myself; and, now, the calling in my life was challenging that image. It was so hard to let go of this person who I always thought I was.

Transformation

Eventually, I was able to overcome these crises. When I finally confronted this person who was the road block, I felt liberated and free to fully pursue my calling. I stood up to them, confronted my own fears about them, and was able to move forward confidently in my calling. Further, I was able to deal with, at least temporarily, my previous identity conflict and accept the new identity that my calling has placed on me. I still struggle though with this previous identity; it seems to keep creeping back into my life, seemingly wanting to propel me in a new direction, and often causes me to feel discontent in my current role. Yet, I still stand confident in my calling. Table 11-5 summarizes the types of calling narratives.

A GENERAL PSYCHOLOGICAL STRUCTURE OF CALLING AND LEADER IDENTITY FORMATION

The Impact of the Childhood and Early Adult Years

The early years of those called as ministry leaders impacts their later identities in several ways. If they perceive their childhood and teen years positively, then these years seem to have been nurturing and safe places for them to develop or consider the possibility of being called. Those whose parents were pastors or committed lay leaders in a local church saw ministry modeled for them regularly; and, to them, doing ministry was normal. The idea that their calling comes to them unbeknownst can occur to those in a home that embraces and models those beliefs that are later congruent with their faith values. Interestingly, those who experience an affirming home environment are more likely to express contentment with their current identity and roles with no intention of seeking other roles.

There were also those who did not grow up in a home that models faith values. In these homes, parents may be unconcerned with faith values at best, unaffirming or abusive at worst. This environment also impacts the leader's later identity in that he or she may have an important emotional or relational hurdle to overcome; by doing so, they are forced to take a stand for independence and control over their lives. In this sense, calling becomes a decisive affirmation of one's own self-identity, one that was not affirmed or supported by their family, as if to defiantly assert, "I am *now* someone, Dad!" In contradistinction, to those who had supportive and faith modeling homes, those who rebel in their early years are more likely to be dissatisfied with their current identity and appear to still be searching for a better identity/role merger.

Awakening to the Call

The awareness of having a call can come in two distinct ways. The first and less prevalent way is to have a singular event, typically in the context of a spiritual activity, which seemingly reveals through divine means that the person is called. Visions, prophetic messages spoken by others, an epiphany while meditating on Scripture, or a subjective impression that God has personally spoken to them are all means of receiving a call. The other means in which one comes to an awareness of a calling comes in a much less spiritual way and is gradually discerned over time in the context of heavy ministry involvement. This calling is propelled by a strong desire to be involved in ministry, an eagerness to do anything or everything their hands find to do that is related to ministry. Those who perceive a call in this manner are more likely to feel that the purpose of going to college is for self-discovery or to confirm whether or not they have been called. They will also feel successful in ministry and receive supernatural confirmations of their call but are less likely to develop a close mentoring relationship with another as were those described in the epiphany means of calling awareness.

Interpersonal and Identity Conflict

A recurring issue for those with a calling is in confronting chronic conflicted relationships with someone close to them and their own previous identities that challenged their emerging sense of identity as one called.

Interpersonal Conflict and Resolution

In the course of their lives, those with a calling seem to have someone (a parent, a pastor, a boss, etc.) who serves as a sort of nemesis. This person serves to foil their plans to reach their goal of fulfilling a calling. Examples include a controlling mother, a controlling or manipulative pastor, or an abusive or neglectful father. In all personal narratives, one person stands out in this sort of role. Further, only when this person (or their impact upon the individual) is finally confronted can the called individual move confidently into assuming their emerging identity.

Identity Conflict and Resolution

Those with a sense of calling are like everyone else in that, from early in life, they begin to form an identity often based on their culture, skills and abilities, physical traits, occupational role, and so forth. For those with an emerging sense of calling, this previous identity presents a formidable obstacle. Because their previous identity is deeply embedded in their psyche (one could argue it *is* their psyche), when confronted with a new and spiritually and religiously motivated identity, tension inevitably occurs. Those with a sense of calling will try, at least initially, to merge their former identity with their identity as one called. Though they seek to relinquish this former identity and completely assume the new, it may be the case that a failure to do so causes ongoing identity conflict, unmet expectations, unfulfilled aspirations, and a general sense that they are not doing what they are supposed to be doing.

Identity Integration and Role Merger of Faith

The final stage of calling development is the current era of the individual and their sense of either satisfaction or dissatisfaction with their current role. For some, there is expressed satisfaction with their role; it is a good fit for their sense of calling; it is them, and they have no intention of changing. They seem to have achieved engagement, that simultaneous expression of their preferred self and their work role (Kahn, 1990).

Conversely, there are those who, while asserting that they have a sense of calling on their lives, seem discontent with their current role. These are not those who are at the bottom of their chosen profession; in fact, some have achieved considerable success. Nevertheless, they express dissatisfaction with their current role; feeling that there is still something else, something better still out there for them to obtain. These individuals often wrestle with another side of their identity that is not given full expression in their current role. This other identity may be one that they have not fully jettisoned in their previous awakening or actualization stages. Former identities seemingly haunt these individuals with regrets of what should or could have been had they only pursued things differently. For others, this lack of contentment seems to be from the possibility of unexplored possible selves (Markus & Nurius, 1986). There is an identity that is still seeking release (the teacher, the missionary, the community activist, etc.). These are perhaps identities that have been nurtured over the past years of ministry service but have not been given full expression in the past or current roles. This lack of satisfaction could also be akin to Staw, Bell, Clausen (1986) and Staw and Ross' (1985) conclusions on the dispositional nature of work satisfaction or the lack thereof. Interestingly, this state of dissatisfaction seems more prevalent than the above state of satisfaction which appears more allusive even for those with a calling on their lives. These individuals also seem more likely to have experienced a young adulthood period of rebellion from their family value and belief systems than those who express current role satisfaction.

DISCUSSION

Existing definitions infuse calling with many positive and noble ideals such as meaning, purpose, passion, work with special value, commitment to career, uncovered personal destinies, true understanding of self, and metacompetencies (e.g., Fleischman, 1994; Fry, 2003; Hall, Zhu, Yan, 2002; Novak, 1996). Yet, throughout the process of investigating the lives of those who expressed a calling in their lives, these ideals were only tangentially mentioned if at all. Instead, individuals typically lamented over stories of conflict, struggled to relinquish previous hopes and dreams, battled personal demons, and questioned where they were going in life. Without sounding overly pessimistic, I would argue that most of the previous definitions and connotations of calling largely ignore the difficulties, the messiness that having a calling engenders. A calling, while alluded to as that which sustains, motivates, and guides, is often expressed as a source of ongoing challenge to overcome, persist in the face of obstacles, breach the personal or social conventions that one has come to know, accept an identity that challenges and re-configures previous self-conceptions, and find contentment in one's role. It is a hard-fought battle, the stake of which is one's very identity and sense of personal satisfaction. A more sober definition of calling in light of the evidence uncovered would suggest that a calling is an ongoing process by which one comes to terms with and overcomes both interpersonal conflicts with significant others and intrapersonal conflicts with the self over competing identities, the result of which is the removal of barriers which would otherwise prevent one from realizing their personal sense of destiny and purpose in life.

The following section will discuss how the current study relates to, expands, and challenges the career and leadership literature. Specifically, extant notions of calling and contextual identity variables, developmental stage models, and concepts of the preferred self will be explored and contrasted with the current study.

Various authors, including Dobrow (2004), Weiss et al. (2004), Novak (1996), and McNeal (2000) describe the following as aspects of a personal sense of calling: incorporates a passion for one's work that energizes and sustains; is sustained over the life of the individual; consumes the ambitions and goals of one's life; gives self-relevant meaning to work; fits one's skills and abilities; acts in service to the community; is unique to the individual; is discovered through listening, reflection, prayer, dialogue with others, trial activities, and persistence; determines one's identity. While the current research did not specifically seek to confirm these predefined characteristics of calling, there is some evidence throughout the participants' narratives that these hold true. However, the current research challenges ideas such as that one's identity centers on their sense of calling. While this may be true, my findings augment and provide a *process* by which this can be more fully understood. Because of its developmental and evolving nature, calling can be ambiguous and changing, and finding one's calling does not necessarily equal having arrived in the search for one's identity. Those with a sense of calling often describe deep interpersonal and intrapersonal conflicts which prevent them from realizing and maintaining a stable identity, even with a supra-identity imposed by their calling.

Further, the notion that calling is discovered only through reflection, prayer, feedback from others, and trial activities is somewhat limited. The current research suggests that calling is discovered through not just prayer and trial activities but through the trials of life itself. The discovery of a calling is inextricably linked to the sum and substance of one's life experiences, spiritual or otherwise. The early environment, relational conflicts, the ongoing parade of role models and influencers, and the conflict with other possible selves all bear upon the discovery and fulfillment of one's calling.

Hall and Chandler (2005) have proposed a calling model of psychological success and posited a relationship between calling, self-confidence, goals/effort, objective and subjective career success, and identity change as well as noting the contextual factors (socioeconomic, demographic, economic, and/or sociopolitical trends) which can either facilitate or hinder individual career agency and thus the enactment of one's calling. This research supports these notions and the iterative nature of coming to discover, confirm, and evolve in one's calling. Further, many contextual factors did indeed either hinder or facilitate the discovery and enactment of one's calling. This current research identifies these contextual factors more specifically and shows how different sets of factors can lead to different calling experiences. These contexts exist at several levels. The macrosocial context includes such events and movements as the Vietnam war, the Jesus movement of the early 1970s, the civil rights movement, and the Watts riots. The microsocial context includes family, bosses, pastors, and so forth. The religious context and environment (Roof, 1993; Spilka & Schmidt, 1983) was also evident in the values, beliefs, and worldviews as well as the circumstances which serve to drive and interpret and give meaning to the above factors. These all served as the social, relational, experiential, and ideological fabric from which individuals fashioned their calling narratives and identities found therein. This research gives clarity to the dialogical nature of narrative identity development which occurs within a social context (Mishler, 1999; Murray, 2003). My results find that personal relationships both define and constrict to a large extent one's "called-ness" or freedom to experience the call. Parents, pastors, spouses, and so forth all intersect with the calling narratives described, as posited by Mead and Cooley's early theories of identity development (Crossley, 2000). One could argue that the apprehension or tension individuals experience while attempting to discover or fulfill their callings comes as a result of the breach in relational and social conventions. While it is true that one's sense of calling appears to be a subjective merging between one's spiritual identity and the larger religious community to which he or she belongs, it is not without its struggles to make this merging come about.

The current research also suggests that, while epiphanies or trigger events occurred as a sign of a call, those with a sense of calling typically go through discernable periods of growth, transition, stability, reappraisal, and so forth, making calling a much more complex and long-term process as previously conceptualized. Calling in this research and the stage model developed therein helped articulate the major stages by which this development takes place, the challenges involved, and the types of calling experiences. Various theorists have discussed the developmental nature of faith (Fowler, 1981), morality (Kohlberg, 1969b) and career development specifically (McCauley, Drath, Palus, O'Conner, & Baker, 2006). For example, Levinson (1978) suggested a punctuated equilibrium model of life development based on chronological age in which careers were seen to consist of periods of stability and growth along with periods of transition and reappraisal. Identity is dynamic and fluid and can change due to changing contexts and life changes that come with developmental stages of one's life (McAdams, 1993). While Sullivan (1999) challenged previous stage models as being inadequate for understanding the increasingly complex career environment, it is apparent that those with a calling go through what could be generally referred to as distinct stages of identity development that allow their nascent sense of calling to emerge and solidify. This would support Weiss et al. (2004) who stated that "calling is a part of the development process of realizing one's identity—it doesn't begin or focus on finding the right 'career' or 'job' choice" (p. 197). These findings also support the admonition of McCauley et al. (2006) who have urged the development of more robust research and the linkage with ongoing streams of leadership research with constructive-developmental theories.

A practical implication is the use of the stage model construct for assisting emerging leaders in clinical settings to understand and cope with their present circumstances which may be perceived as threatening to or challenging the existence of their call. Many emerging leaders go through seasons of discouragement and disappointment which can cause them to question their calling. The current research would suggest that this is typical of those with a calling and that having a calling does not necessarily mean the absence of problems or struggles with identity. In fact, if the current sample is in any way representative, struggles may in fact be the evidence of a calling. This model can help leaders understand that the called go through various stages of calledness and, in all likelihood, will experience relational and identity conflicts and that these will serve to further validate and strengthen their call.

McAdams' (1993) concept of the imago, a personalized and idealized concept of the self which each of us consciously and unconsciously fashions, is also validated and expanded by this research. While one may have one dominant imago or many, the calling challenges one's previous imago. Fully embracing one's calling often comes at the sacrifice of an imago that is seen as inconsistent. Even though one may have a calling, the allure of a better imago or possible self (Markus & Nurius, 1986) may still loom on the horizon, causing identity conflict or tension within one's imago set.

CONCLUSION

The current research contributed to both the qualitative research methods literature and narrative theory and analysis applied to leadership. Qualitative research methods have been advocated to explore emerging and important areas in leadership research such as spiritual and authentic leadership (Arthur, Khapova, Wilderom, 2005; Cooper, Scandura, Schriesheim, 2005; Heslin, 2005; Shamir & Eilam, 2005; Sparrowe, 2005). I have demonstrated how one of these methods, narrative analysis (Chapter 8), can be applied to open up new levels of understanding and theory development. Further, this research impacts the field of leadership studies by framing an empirical and inductively grounded constructive-developmental model of calling as implored by McCauley et al. (2006). The frameworks of Kegan (1982), Torbert (1987), and Kohlberg (1969a) have previously been used with varying degrees of success in the leadership and management literature. This present research seeks to explicitly link extant theories of calling with a new and provocative way of viewing the heretofore little investigated aspects of calling.

This research challenges extant theories of calling by exploring the conflict, tensions, dilemmas, and ambiguity one faces when called. Contrary to many of these theories, calling is not an exclusively positive experience. It comes at the high price of personal identity crises, relational struggle, and great sacrifice. Calling does of course have its positive attribute: the ability to provide meaning, passion, purpose, confidence, and so forth. Yet, this is only one side of the calling coin. Through a better understanding of the developmental process and struggle one deals with in enacting a calling, theorists and practitioners can temper the often sought after panacea for satisfaction or career success. While an organization replete with those called to the mission seems like an ideal, this may only be an illusion; those with a calling are not necessarily anymore prone to be content, satisfied, or likely to persist in the organization. If this were true, churches would rarely experience leadership changes, and being a pastor would be among the most satisfying roles one could hope to find. This research highlights that this is not the case as evident in the amount of turnover, disappointment, and career challenges that this sample of pastors reveals.

The leader's life story is seen as an essential component of self-identity; by studying such life stories, one can come to know and appreciate the experiences which constitute the sum and substance of a leader along with the attendant passions, perspectives, and idiosyncrasies. While quantitative methods provide solid empirical support for the testing of leadership theories, they are limited in giving leadership scholars new and fresh perspectives on some of the abovementioned trends. This present research has chosen a particular area of current interest in the field of leadership studies (spirituality and calling) and has given us considerably more depth in our understanding of the process by which these phenomena develop by using a research technique that delves deeply into the intrapsychic processes of identity development. We now have a new way of approaching the phenomenon of calling that moves beyond the previous and largely positive descriptive approaches, one that reveals the complexity of calling emergence and development that is holistic and considers the totality of one's life and experiences. While these previous approaches as described in both the leadership literature and the Christian ministry development have been quite beneficial and important to our current understanding of calling, the present research serves to augment these ideas by showing what is essentially a longitudinal perspective on calling. This perspective spans a leader's entire life span and considers all salient aspects of his or her life including, among other things, one's family of origin, individuation processes, significant social relationships, vocational engagement and their related successes and failures, education, and role satisfaction. We now have a new way of speaking about calling, one that includes concepts such as process, conflict, and individuation, that is empirically grounded. Hopefully, these concepts can become an increasing part of the greater vocabulary of leadership studies and will challenge the static and largely positive extant notions currently associated with calling and leader identity clarification.

12

LEADERSHIP IN AT-RISK COMMUNITIES

J. Randall Wallace

INTRODUCTION

Rarely have the poor, impoverished, marginalized, and disadvantaged been a focus of leadership study. Burns (2003), in his most recent book, revisits the transforming leadership theory he formulated in 1978 and examines how leaders ultimately facilitate life, liberty, and the pursuit of happiness. "Nothing offers so clear and urgent a challenge to leadership, nothing tests it so decisively, as human wants and needs" (2003, p. 146). He identifies how leadership has failed in this regard when human need is addressed in nonorganizational terms. He states that

> ...the tests of applicability are even harder for transforming leadership, particularly when the biggest, boldest kind of leadership confronts the largest, most intractable problem facing humanity in the twenty-first century: the basic wants of the world's poor (2003, p. 231).

Burns argues that alleviating poverty and empowering the poor is the greatest challenge to leadership and should be our greatest concern. For him, the central problem is a lack of leadership that takes a hard view of the misconceptions of those "helpers" of the poor and learns to draw close to the poor, to see their problems as they see them. Burns finishes by stating that strategic leadership is the vital link in empowering the dispossessed and poses the question, can leadership develop from the bottom up (Burns, 2003, p. 236)?

This research focused on Myles Horton (1905–1990), who through his work at Highlander Folk School, later Highlander Research and Education Center, developed leaders in at-risk communities over a span of 50 years. He had a proven track record of empowering the poor to develop their own models and practices of strategic leadership and address their own problems. The purpose of the study was to look at Horton's success as a community leader and gain insight into (1) the leadership principles that contribute to successfully developing leaders in at-risk communities and (2) the emotional, psychological, cognitive states and traits leaders experience who work in at-risk communities.

MYLES HORTON: AN EXEMPLARY LEADER IN AT-RISK COMMUNITIES

Horton was born in Appalachia and determined at an early age to live according to the principles of radical democracy and honoring human dignity. His life in poverty and working among the poor while in college forged within him a commitment to helping the poor lift themselves out of poverty. Horton spent his college years searching for a model which would help him return to the mountains and empower the poor. His quest led him to Union Theological Seminary where he was able to study with, among others, Dietrich Bonhoffer and Reinhold Neibhur. His quest for a workable model led him to Denmark to look at the Danish Folk School movement. The values of: (1) students learning and living together, (2) peer learning and teaching, (3) nonvocational education, (4) freedom from examinations, (5) highly motivating purpose, and (6) group singing became the foundation for what he would later found in Tennessee, The Highlander Folk School.

Highlander became instrumental in training leaders for the American Labor Movement, the Civil Rights Movement, organizing Appalachian people to address economic and social problems, and training the poor in developing countries in how to organize themselves to address issues of poverty. In keeping with his principles, Horton sought to lead in such a way that the people themselves would be the source of goals and vision, the key architects of the work to be done, and the key leaders. He sought to shift the focus from external or expert leaders to the followers in such a manner that when the task is completed, the followers feel that they have accomplished the task themselves. Despite his remarkable success, few today know of him or the vital roles he played in two of the major social movements of the twentieth century.

Horton's commitment to human dignity was so strong that from its creation in 1932, Highlander was racially integrated. His demands for integration helped the labor movement move from a Jim Crow mentality which was crippling its ability to effectively organize various plants in the South. Because of his early commitment and track record of racial equality, he was approached to train leaders for the Civil Rights Movement. This commitment to the poor and to integration came with a cost. Highlander was burned to the ground, confiscated by the State of Tennessee and its tax-exempt status revoked. Horton suffered death threats, contracts on his life, numerous beatings, slander, and attacks on his family.

Horton used methods in training adults which were unheard of in his day. He opened new avenues of understanding in adult education, specifically in nonformal settings. He also practiced a form of leadership, emphasizing a bottom-up approach as identified within this study, which was uniquely suited to the challenging context of at-risk communities. His understanding of the differing leadership demands associated with context was also before its time.

THE ROLE OF CONTEXT IN LEADERSHIP

Traditionally, leadership studies have focused on leadership as residing within the leader, and hence have been leader-centric. This preoccupation with individual leaders has come under scrutiny as researchers recognize that leadership styles or approaches cannot be universally applied (Osborn, Hunt, & Jauch, 2002; Shamir & Howell, 1999). It is now recognized that leadership is embedded within the environment or context (Osborn et al., 2002) and factors such as organizational culture, the environment in which the organization exists, technology, and the structure of the organization have an effect on leadership. Within the realm of contextual influences reside a number of factors which possibly shed light upon at-risk settings such as the effect of crisis on an organization (Pascale, 1999; Youngblood, 1997) and edge of chaos situations (Osborn et al., 2002) in which everything is in disarray.

Two particular contextual situations mentioned by Osborn et al. (2002) have bearing on this study: crisis situations, and edge of chaos situations. Crisis within an organization is often viewed as stress on middle managers in a dynamic system. The authors found that in a crisis situation, the distinction between context and leadership fades. Unlike a stable environment where leaders tend to tell followers what is important, crisis situations force leaders to shift from telling to focusing on how individuals fit into the organization as a whole. Leaders are required to listen more closely to followers and their recommendations for change. Edge of chaos situations refer to situations in which everything is in disarray but not to the point where the organization disintegrates, which would be chaos. This context brings with it a high degree of change that requires a different focus for leaders. More specifically, leaders shift their focus from obtaining goals to developing fitness and the ability to survive in the turbulent setting. Rather than a top-down declaration of structure or order, the middle or bottom may determine what the focus should be as they are closest to where change is necessitated. Consequently, in edge of chaos situations, the leader is concerned with the development of distributed intelligence and human assets in order to multiply requisite variety and enable the organization to "learn" and adapt at the most basic levels. Organizations in an edge of chaos mode must be sensitive to inputs from below due to the need for more complex strategies and requisite variety. This is especially needed in at-risk communities, as some of the key contextual characteristics relate to issues of low social and human capital, low self-efficacy, and means efficacy fostered by leader-centered approaches in the past.

At-risk communities not only provide a specific context for the practice of leadership but they may also be viewed as representing a particular cultural perspective. Leadership demands are different in stable as opposed to crisis situations. Leadership expectations are different among followers from culture to culture and situation to situation. Thus, as Klenke (1996) argued, context determines to a large extent what leaders must and can do, and sets the boundaries within which leaders and followers interact. Just as different times call for different leaders and different styles of leadership, so do different contexts (p. 18).

All of these features support the premise that leadership requirements in at-risk or distressed communities may differ greatly from those in other organizational settings. At-risk or distressed communities are characterized by a host of political, social, and economic factors which are described below.

AT-RISK COMMUNITIES AS A CONTEXT FOR LEADERSHIP

The Appalachian Regional Commission defines at-risk communities within the United States as having an unemployment rate of 1.25 times the national average, a per capita market income that is two-thirds the national average and a poverty rate of 1.25 times the national rate. At-risk communities also show a trend toward becoming distressed (ARC, 2006). Distressed communities have a three-year unemployment rate at least 1.5 times the national average and a poverty rate that is two times the national average.

The following characteristics have been associated with distressed or at-risk communities not only in Appalachia but in other parts of the United States. These communities tend to have (1) higher rates of crime, (2) resources that are controlled by outside interests, (3) regional economic and political exploitation, (4) a lack of municipal or county services, (5) a large dependent population, (6) a large ratio of female-headed households, (7) a low percentage of college educated, (8) high levels of welfare dependency, (9) racism, (10) conflict, (11) weak social support networks, (12) dilapidated housing, (13) strained social institutions, (14) insufficient jobs, (15) gangs, (16) inadequate schools, (17) highly transient population, (18) high teen pregnancy rates, (19) social isolation, (20) geographic isolation, (21) poor health, (22) victimization, (23) severe population loss, (24) job flight, (25) high concentrations of poverty, and (26) a preponderance of negative versus positive role models (Fried, 1968; Glasmeier & Farrigan, 2003; Harrington, 1986).

At-risk communities exhibit an array of other social and psychological context-specific features often referred to as the culture of poverty. The components include (1) long periods of unemployment or intermittent employment leading to public assistance as the main source of income, (2) participation in jobs that are at the lowest of skill levels such as domestic service or unskilled labor, (3) high rates of marital instability resulting in high rates of female-headed households, and (4) unstable and superficial relationships with others (Lewis, 1968). Lewis identified over 70 separate characteristics associated with what he called the culture of poverty. One of the key characteristics relates to the reality that the poor tend not to be integrated into major institutions or voluntary associations in society. The poor tend not to join labor unions, banks, political parties, or social institutions. They may have a sense of community but it is at the individual level. Lewis goes on to say,

> Any movement, be it religious, pacifist, or revolutionary—that organizes and gives hope to the poor and effectively promotes solidarity and a sense of identity with larger groups destroys the psychological and social core of the culture of poverty (Lewis, 1968, p. 193).

This reality has profound implications for leadership as leaders seek to involve people in organized activity to accomplish goals. However, individuals in lower socioeconomic strata often do not have opportunity to participate in decision making in their communities and when they do attend meetings, they tend to participate less in discussion (Bell, 1961; Strodtbeck, Simon, & Hawkins, 1965). There is, therefore, a high need to foster participation in voluntary organizations that provide opportunity for the poor to exercise leadership.

The reasons for their nonparticipation are many. Members of these communities tend to have feelings of helplessness, victimization, weak ego structure, low impulse control, fatalism, a present orientation with little ability to defer gratification, lowered aspirations, strong feelings of powerlessness, and a lowered sense of self-efficacy (Bandura, 1995; Jarrett, 1995; Latz, 1989). Researchers point out that it is essential for the poor to gain a sense of entitlement that enables them to shape their own destinies, overcome shame and a sense of despair, and regain the power that is rightfully theirs (Borda, 1985; Freire, 1990; Gaventa, 1982).

Field (2003) focuses on social capital which is comprised of the network of interactions in which power, resources, values, and trust are shared and cultivated. When social capital is plentiful, communities tend to be healthy. High social capital has been associated with lower levels of crime in communities and greater resilience to crime. In an at-risk community, social capital is typically a scarce resource.

Giddens (1991) points out that modernity has placed added stressors on individuals resulting in a perpetual state of perceived risk which taxes individuals physically, socially, mentally, and psychologically. These perceptions are internalized by individuals creating feelings of powerlessness, fatalism, and lack of motivation. This is important when considering how these stresses affect the poor who have few resources acting as a buffer to the stressors.

The combination of volatile social relationships and stressful environment create high levels of internal stress that often serves to diminish motivation, leading to self-destructive coping mechanisms, malaise, and lack of trust (May, 1972; Warren, 1998). In a study of native Americans, it was discovered that the distressed environment led to a struggle with ethnic identity which led to more intense positive and negative emotional experiences leading to depression, anxiety, lowered self-esteem, and a higher level of conformist behavior (Newman, 2005).

This is not just an Anglo centric or developing world problem. The United Nations states that over 1 billion people live on less than one dollar a day and that over 2 billion live on less than two dollars a day (UNDP, 1995). These numbers represent the poorest of the poor who are for the most part people of color. These people often live in countries struggling to develop economically and politically. Often these countries have oppressive or unstable governments and civil unrest.

RESEARCH DESIGN

Data Sources for the Study

Having identified Myles Horton as a suitable candidate for exploring leadership in at-risk communities, it became necessary to obtain appropriate materials for use in the study. Horton passed away in 1990. Consequently, the first author visited the Highlander Research and Education Center in New Market, Tennessee, in order to explore their archives. Highlander's library contains over 19 boxes of documents, articles, interviews, speeches, a video interview, and books spanning Horton's life, work, and history in addition to the regular library holdings.

Using a purposive sampling method, only specific documents, passages, or portions of documents were selected for analysis. The criterion for selecting materials required that the texts be the actual words of Horton, either through transcribed interview or in writing. After careful reading of all documents, a total of 588 pages of potential material was selected. Each was read a minimum of five times. During the fifth reading, passages were marked which seemed most applicable to the study. The texts selected related to leadership, leadership development, distressed communities, at-risk communities, human needs, or education. Passages related to the early life of Horton, the history of Highlander, or anecdotal stories were not used unless they related directly to the topics mentioned above or provided unique perspective on context or Horton's life or the formulation of Horton's theories. Care was taken that the materials selected accurately reflected Horton's ideas without relying on another's summarization. The documents selected spanned a number of decades in dates of publication and consisted of 265 pages of quotations.

The corpus of text that represents the database for this study included (1) *The long haul: An autobiography of Myles Horton* (Horton, Kohl, & Kohl 1990); (2) Building democracy in the mountains: The legacy of the Highlander Center, an interview with Myles (Collum, 1986); (3) Myles Horton of the Highlander Research and Education Center: An interview (Olson, 1977); (4) Study the power structure, a presentation by Myles (Horton, 1968c); (5) Myles Horton's talk with Friends World Institute (Horton, 1968a); (6) On building a social movement, a Highlander workshop (Horton, 1968b); (7) It's a miracle, I still don't believe it: An interview with Myles Horton ("It's a miracle, I still don't believe it.," 1966); (8) The adventures of a radical hillbilly: An interview with Myles Horton by Bill Moyers (Moyers, 1981); and (9) *We make the road by walking: Conversations on social change, a spoken book between Myles Horton and Paulo Freire* (Horton & Freire, 1990).

Collectively, these data represent a body of text that has not been previously analyzed in relation to leadership studies. It is important to note that all but two of these texts were used in the content analysis phase. The two texts used in the case study phase include The adventures of a radical hillbilly: An interview with Myles Horton by Bill Moyers and *We make the road by walking: Conversations on social change*, a spoken book between Myles Horton and Paulo Freire. I selected these texts for two reasons. First, both were the results of interviews of Horton and second, both took place in the latter years of his life. I felt that during these interviews, the most significant or powerful images and examples from Horton's life would dominate his thinking as he sought to provide insight into his life's work.

RESULTS OF CONTENT ANALYSIS AND CASE STUDY

The analysis proceeded through two phases. First, content analysis texts and the case studies were coded, progressing through five levels of abstraction. The second phase involved analysis of the codes, following constant comparative analysis, in order to isolate a grounded theory, using the process outlined by Glaser and Strauss (1999).

Phase 1—Content Analysis Coding

The process for coding the content analysis involved first hand coding a document and then proceeding with computer-assisted coding through all the documents. The text,

The Long Haul, was selected for hand coding. The hand coding helped draw me into the text, making me familiar not only with the coding process but the nuances of how Horton expressed himself. The document was read and coded a minimum of five times, until saturation was reached. Whenever a code was identified, it was described in the coding dictionary. The coding dictionary contained definitions of each code, an example of where the code was used, an example of what the code was not as well as how it differed from other similar codes. This insured discriminant validity and provided guidance for researchers interested in replicating the coding procedure. This procedure was followed throughout each level of coding for both content analysis and case study methods. The codes generated in this hand coding procedure became the basis for initial codes to be used in the computer coding phase.

The second step in content analysis coding progressed to coding with Atlas.ti. All content analysis documents proceeded through five levels of coding involving over eight iterations to insure theoretical saturation. The initial code total from the first pass at level one coding was 285, too many codes. By eliminating codes with too few quotations (two or less) or codes which were too close in meaning and failed to provide adequate differentiation in nuance, the code total was reduced to 235. This was still far too many codes for theory building.

This led to Level 2 coding in which Level 1 codes were grouped into naturally occurring families of codes which dealt with the same topics or themes. These code themes produced 30 separate potential constructs for exploration. However, because the code families were merely compilations of Level 1 codes, these failed to produce adequate insight or significant patterns associated with the research questions posed. They also tended to reflect typical subjects currently examined in leadership literature such as change, leader traits, or learning. According to Glaser (1999), these would not be suitable for a grounded theory of leadership in at-risk communities due to their common use in leadership literature.

At Level 3, the previous two levels of codes were examined for new topics or themes arising from latent content. New categories of codes related to the effect of context on the community or its members; specific leadership practices or traits, either positive or negative, which shed light on the effects of leadership in at-risk communities; or codes which would provide insight into the internal struggles of leaders in at-risk settings were identified. This produced 19 S-codes (super codes). These S-codes were (1) grass roots focused, (2) leader restraint, (3) leader and conflict, (4) leader as communicator, (5) leader and community, (6) leader as educator, (7) leader character, (8) leader optimism, (9) leader knowledge of self, (10) leader people focused, (11) leader master of political/social context, (12) leader struggles, (13) contextual problems created by leadership, (14) contextual stressors impacting communities, (15) hope, (16) empowerment, (17) community or people characteristics, (18) leader as learner, and (19) leader roles.

Beginning at the third level of coding, significant insight into the phenomena of at-risk leadership began to emerge. A typical example of the richness of data associated with and insight within the S-code quotes is illustrated by Horton's explanation of how leaders must restrain themselves from providing answers, goals, or solutions to problems, allowing the people to come up with solutions or answers themselves. How far Horton would go in living out this belief is presented in the case study documented in a funny story that must have been pretty scary at the time it actually happened.

> That was very educational for me. I was trying to get those people to make a decision. The big thing is for the people to have confidence and make decisions. And I was doing pretty well, so they made all the plans and encouraged themselves but it got pretty rough. It looked like they were about to lose the strike. And the strike committee got pretty desperate and they weren't so sure of themselves. So they came up to my room one time and says, "We got to talk about plans." They talked it over and they said, "Myles you got to tell us what to do, we gone as far as we can." And I said, "You gotta' run this union so you might as well learn, learn when it's easy, you learn when it's rough. If you don't learn to make tough decisions, then I learn how to make the tough decisions and you don't. I get the learning experience, you don't. I need it less than you do. You need the learning experience. I can get along without it. So you got to make the decision." They said, "There's 2000 people involved in this decision." "Sure," I said, "That's why it's an important decision and you gotta make it." And one guy he said, "You make this decision." And I said, "No, no." And he said, "You're not at Highlander runnin' the school you're runnin' a strike. With these people here it's serious business and you just can't say we gotta' learn to do this." And I said, "No. You gotta make the decision." So he reached in his pocket and pulled out a gun and said, "You son of a bitch you make this decision right now." I came near going back on my principles of education than I ever did in my life. I said well, you can win this round but you still won't have made decisions after you get through. I admit I was scared (Moyers, 1981, p. 20).

Although these Level 3 S-codes provided a more manageable number of codes, they still failed to capture the essential aspects which would define adequately the general principles associated with leadership in at-risk settings. Another level of abstraction was added in the hope that it would isolate the defining features.

This fourth level of coding (P-codes or principle codes) focused on key principles forming the basis of a theory of leadership in at-risk settings. Level 4 coding produced seven specific P-codes whose code labels were (1) communal residence, (2) radical subordination, (3) responsibility, (4) reframing, (5) reconciliation, (6) restoration of people or community, and (7) replacement. These codes were constructed by arranging lower level codes into new combinations. Care was taken that no overlap or duplication existed between any of the codes used to construct the P-codes.

Each of the codes identified a specific principle essential to leadership in at-risk settings. These codes seemed to resonate with my experience of living and working in an at-risk community. Whether or not these codes accurately captured the phenomena would be tested in the case study phase of the research. The first code, communal residence, is illustrated in the following quote from Horton.

> We were learning fast that the way to find out where people are was to get with them. A little later on, we had some hosiery workers in a place called Sky, Tennessee not far from Chattanooga, in a sit down strike for a while, and they came to us and asked us if we would give them help. Well, we didn't know enough to help them. So what we decided to do instead of saying, "Yeah, we know the answers", was to move the school down there. And so I took the whole student body, everybody we had, about 30 or 40 people, the whole staff, mimeograph machine, the typewriters—loaded up and went down. We had a friend there, a preacher named Dejarnet, he'd been fired because of his interest in unions, and he had a big house, in a vacant community building. He just let us move in, so Highlander moved into the situation, we didn't bring people to us, we went there (Horton, 1968b, p. 3).

The remainder of the P-codes, their description, and quotes associated with them are explained in the analysis section in which content analysis and case study codes converge to form a grounded theory of leadership in at-risk communities.

Level 5 coding isolated three main themes which were expressed at each and every level of Horton's work, in every method and in every goal or purpose. These themes shaped his personal values and life's work. Consequently, these themes are his worldview (WV). The three themes were (1) love, (2) kenosis (self-emptying), and (3) justice. This completed the coding process. Two more passes through the documents failed to generate any new codes or reveal any new topics, manifest or latent, for consideration.

Fig. 12-1 illustrates how the coding process in content analysis moved from manifest codes at Level 1 to the most abstract latent codes at Level 5. Each level of codes built upon the previous levels. Each level of coding stood on its own and the codes included in that level were distinct from one another.

As the coding progressed through higher levels of abstraction, new combinations of codes and code families were created based upon Horton's approach to working with

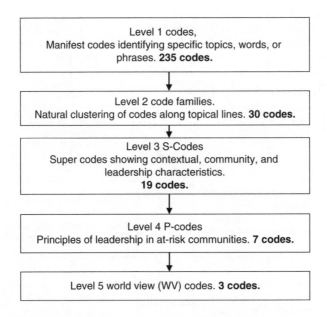

Figure 12-1   Progression of codes

those in at-risk settings. Each higher level more completely explained the dynamics of leadership in such a challenging setting.

Having reached theoretical saturation in the content analysis phase, it was now necessary to move on to the case study to discover whether the themes discovered in content analysis would be confirmed, expanded upon, or contradicted.

Phase 2—Case Study Coding

As mentioned earlier, two key texts were kept separate for the case study phase of the coding. The texts were entered into Atlas.ti for coding using the same method used in the content analysis phase. Both documents were triple checked for accuracy. Coding proceeded, in much the same manner as in content analysis through five levels of coding. Constant comparative analysis insured that codes were consistent in their definitions and application, distinct from other codes already in use, anchored to the data, and reflective of what Horton actually said or did. How this phase unfolded as a process is demonstrated in Fig. 12-2.

Coding, from the first through the fifth levels, utilized codes generated from the content analysis phase as a starting point in thematic coding. The coding progressed quickly and codes were added when necessary. After eight iterations, theoretical saturation was reached in the case study material. The five levels of coding were complete and a cursory

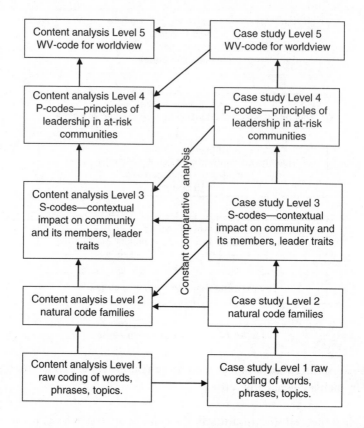

*Figure 12-2   Comparison of codes from content analysis and case study.
Phase 1 coding process for content analysis and case study*

examination revealed them to be very compatible with the conclusions of the content analysis findings. In order to more completely determine whether or not case study findings indeed supported content analysis findings, further analysis was required.

Content Analysis and Case Study Convergence of Findings

In analyzing the codes generated from content analysis and case study, a significant code confirmation between the methods became apparent. Of the top 50 codes (as measured by frequency of use) used in the two methods, nearly 49 percent are identical. In looking at the top 17 codes for both methods, 11 of the 17 codes are identical though differing in frequency.

There were differences in code labels between the two methods. Content analysis exhibited 54 codes unique to it with case study having seven unique codes. The content analysis code differences could be traced to the greater volume of material and the nature of the material used for the texts. Content analysis documents had four times as many pages and included workshops, a major portion of an autobiography, and more technical materials. The case study, while being smaller in size, was more informal as it was comprised of a video interview and a taped conversation with another major social leader, Paulo Freire. The overlap between codes in the two methods and the relative small number of unique codes for each method suggested a high level of agreement in the findings.

An analysis of Level 2, 30 code families generated in content analysis and case study revealed that 15 of the code families were affected by either having case study or content analysis codes that were exclusive to either method. Of those 15 codes affected, only two involved codes exclusive to case study, and in both cases, it involved a single code. Case study codes that were identical to content analysis codes were included within each of the two code families ensuring that the general findings were nearly identical.

The codes exclusive to content analysis affecting Level 2 coding also shared other identical codes with case study in the same code family. If the codes exclusive to content analysis were removed at the Level 2 code family grouping, the integrity of the Level 2 code families and the findings would not be significantly affected.

This shows a high level of convergence in the findings which proved to be consistent with the final three levels of code. Every code from Level 3 and above in both content analysis and case study are in complete agreement with no codes being unique to either method. Fig. 12-3 shows how the analysis progressed and how, after Level 2 codes, a strong convergence in findings was manifest.

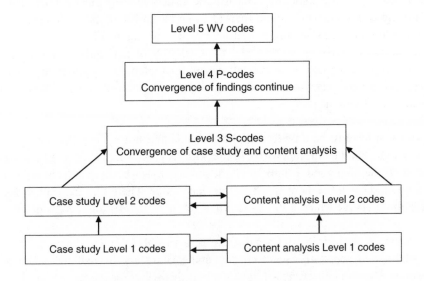

Figure 12-3   Convergence of findings in analysis phase

DISCUSSION

Level 3 S-Codes

Level 3 in the coding process provided insights into areas which are generally covered in leadership studies although not in reference to at-risk communities. The data revealed specific attributes associated with contextual stressors and realities in at-risk communities as well as leadership traits and practices which can be detrimental or beneficial to at-risk communities. Horton explains that top-down leadership approaches ultimately have at their foundation a paternalism which perpetuates dependency and a victim mentality within a community as the leaders have no expectation that the people have any skill, knowledge, or ability which may contribute to problem solution.

The code *contextual stressors* captured the natural environment of at-risk communities and the obstacles they must overcome. Poverty, economic challenge, class conflict, racism, absence of social justice, and the oppressive control of the status quo are pernicious and pervasive. Horton isolates a contextual stressor by pointing out, "Agriculture was pretty much like it is today in the sense that farmers were barely hanging on. This was about 1927: the Depression hit the rural south a long time before it was felt in New York" (Horton et al., 1990, p. 21).

These daunting problems are often magnified by toxic leadership practices as evidenced through the Level 3 S-code (super code), *contextual problems caused by leadership*. These toxic leaders are sometimes charismatic leaders looking out for themselves and their positions, leaders who impose their ideas and agendas on the community, leaders who sanction or promote discrimination, leaders acting in oblivion to context or community characteristics, leaders who use exploitive or manipulative power, leaders who are more concerned with institutions or their plans as opposed to developing people, or leaders who treat people as objects (Lipman-Blumen, 2005). Horton illustrates this by saying:

> And you have to be unsentimental about this and not assume that any poor struggling child from somewhere in the north is great, simply because he wants to do something good. I think of all the missionaries who have gone over to do good, and of all the damage which they have done. There's no reason for this, for those people who act like I did when I first came (Horton, 1968c, p. 7)

These activities, along with contextual stressors, act as abrasives, eroding a community's sense of hope, a people's sense of efficacy and positive esteem, and the willingness of community members to think of anyone but themselves as evidenced in the code, community, or people characteristics. People in the community internalize these pathologies. They begin to believe that they are powerless, they are unable to solve their own problems, they are dumb, and they are victims who must be saved by some outside force or person. People and communities become dependent, apathetic, or resigned to the fate they feel they deserve based upon the assessment of those who are above them. Horton explained in this manner:

> Most were victimized by the system, unaware of how badly they were exploited, and consequently they felt no rage. Until people feel exploited and able to do something about it, they're not going to make structural changes. The number of people who are angry is not big enough to bring about social change. So, I said to myself, "I got to find a way to work with people who should be angry but aren't" (Horton et al. 1990, p. 79).

The findings also show that there are leadership practices which are beneficial to communities and help reduce contextual stressors while building confidence and hope. Fifteen separate codes at this level related to leader practice, struggles, and focus. Leaders who want to help communities address poverty, powerlessness, personal, and community identity issues will generally have to keep the following in mind.

First, leaders will have to be committed to being grass roots and people focused. The leader's goals must come from people on the bottom, and methods must involve educating and developing community members. The leader approaches this education with a commitment to structure it along the needs, interests, and goals of the people served. If at all possible, the people must participate in the design and delivery of the education, removing them from passive to active agents.

Next, the leader should not only understand the role of conflict but be committed to utilizing it to reach goals as any focus on structural change which will inevitably lead to conflict with the status quo. The near inevitability of conflict requires the leader to be somewhat politically and socially savvy. For safety and success, there must be understanding of the potential forms of violence or coercion that may be brought to bear in any given situation as well as how to navigate the power structure.

Third, the leader must have positive character traits with humility being in the forefront. The best leaders in at-risk settings are learners. Their humility opens them to learning from the people and consequently allowing the people to "drive" the change initiatives and take the credit. This will involve significant reflexivity on the part of the leader as well as self-knowledge. Fourth, leaders should restrain themselves from overpowering people in the community with their gifts and abilities.

The Level 3 S-codes hint at the theory associated with leadership in at-risk communities. Although informative in their own right, they still fall short of providing the scope of how the leadership theory associated with at-risk communities operates. Level 4 analysis provides the essential components of a theory for leadership in at-risk settings.

Level 4 P-Codes: a Grounded Theory of Leadership in At-Risk Communities

Level 4 P-codes (principle codes) outline seven principles associated with leadership in at-risk communities. These seven principles embody the most salient issues from the lower three levels of codes while are remaining broad enough in scope to accommodate tailoring to specific situations. In some of the P-codes, nearly whole code families from levels two or three are included in the P-code. However, there are significant additions or deletions from those families which make the codes at this level more robust and discriminant.

Each of these P-codes is important and to some degree, they are interdependent. As an example, radical subordination arises from the need to foster responsibility within people in the community as well as to restore within them a sense of efficacy. For this to happen, individuals in the community must undergo a change of mind about whether or not to take responsibility because of a new recognition of their sense of efficacy or a new realization of an oppressive sociopolitical situation that requires reconciliation. All of this activity resides within Horton's emphasis. Leaders take up communal residence and become a part of the community in which they lead, identifying as closely as possible with the community's residents. The level 4 P-codes which describe the principles needed to lead in at-risk communities were (1) communal residence, (2) radical subordination, (3) responsibility, (4) reconciliation, (5) reframing, (6) restoration of people or community, and (7) replacement.

Communal residence

The idea that leaders need to become members, on more than just a residential level, of communities they lead is not new, just not easy and popular. Horton found this immersion and solidarity with people in at-risk communities so important that he often refused to provide any suggestions or guidance to people outside his cultural milieu and warned them about taking principles developed at Highlander and using them in another setting. He emphasized the need to get with the poorest people and learn from them, live with them, and let them teach you how to go about addressing their needs and contextual realities. At one point, as noted earlier, he forced the entire staff of Highlander to relocate to where people were having a strike in order to more fully understand them.

A number of theoretical constructs support and help illuminate the concept of communal residence. Social identity theory explains how people classify themselves and others into social categories based upon various forms of criteria including age, gender, class, and race, to name a few categories (Tajfel, 1978; Turner, 1978). Social identity affects individuals classifying themselves, even in terms of forming an internal concept of identity, based upon the characteristics of the group to which they perceive themselves belonging (Ashforth & Mael, 1989). Strong identification with the people also increases the degree to which at-risk community members perceive leaders to be prototypical and as a result, the potential degree of acceptance and effectiveness of their leadership (Hogg, Hains, & Mason, 1998). Strong identification and solidarity with people accelerates leader acceptance. Self-efficacy theory states that the self-efficacy of people is raised when they see others like themselves succeed in difficult circumstances or projects (Bandura, 1994). Strong leader identification accelerates this.

Radical subordination

Radical subordination involves the leader voluntarily subordinating his or her gifts, skills, abilities, goals, vision for the community, or timetable for change to the needs, desires, and aspirations of the people in the community. Radical subordination reduces the overt influence of the leader and makes room for the expression of the gifts, abilities, and dreams of those within the community. Horton explains that the leader's practice of radical subordination is constrained by two factors. First, the leader must identify with people in the community in a manner that accelerates his or her acceptance. Second, the leader must make room for the skills and abilities of community members whose often-fragile self-esteem and self-efficacy may cause them to avoid using their skills and abilities. Horton found out early that mountain people would gladly sit back and let him and his staff make decisions and do the work. It wasn't until he and his staff willingly and intentionally restrained themselves, refused to use their skills and abilities, force their time frames, and formulate visions or goals, that the people themselves felt comfortable stepping forward and making decisions.

The theoretical constructs of learned helplessness (Peterson, Maier, & Seligman, 1994), learned optimism (Seligman, 1998), and self-efficacy (Bandura, 1994) provide the theoretical underpinning for radical subordination. Through numerous personal failures, fear related to the fragility of life and survival, intimidation by authorities, and memes instilled by oppressive leaders, community members in at-risk communities often demonstrate traits outlined by Petersen and Seligman in their study of learned helplessness (1998). This helplessness is often manifest as apathy, deference to experts, dependency on outside leaders or experts, or the desire to have a knight in shining armor ride in and save them. All these manifestations of dependency exemplify what Bandura would refer to as low self-efficacy (1994).

In order for community members to attain the new skills necessary while building their sense of efficacy and optimism, leaders must create a supportive and safe environment in which community members can experiment, test, and try new ideas and build their sense of confidence in their personal and their community's ability to tackle problems. This is in keeping with the bottom-up versus top-down mentality leaders must possess in at-risk communities. It is crucial that leaders subordinate their personal skills, abilities, goals, and aspirations in order to not intimidate or supplant the goals, skills, abilities, or aspirations of those in the community. The practice of radical subordination forces those who have learned to be helpless to step up and take responsibility for their actions and future. This was illustrated earlier in Horton's story regarding the strike and the need for the workers to make decisions.

Radical subordination does not mean that the leader acts as though he or she has no skills or abilities. This robs the community of the leader's expertise and communicates to the community members that the leader is less than transparent. Horton's approach was to hold his knowledge and skill in abeyance until asked to share by the community members and even then, given the context, problem, and place in the development process of community members, he demonstrated he may not make his skills or knowledge available. Ultimately, the focus was on community members rising up and taking responsibility for their lives and futures. Any hindrance to that required restraint on the part of the leader.

Responsibility

Horton emphasizes the need for people to take responsibility for their own lives and communities. Failure to do this promotes a victim mentality and paternalism. Horton saw the lack of taking responsibility as a lack of hope.

> The people who are hopeless are grist for the fascist mill. Because they have no hope, they have nothing to build on. If people are in trouble, if people are suffering and exploited and want to get out from under the heel of oppression, if they have hope that it can be done, if they can see the path leads to a solution, a path that makes sense to them and is consistent with their beliefs and their experience, then they'll move. But it must be a path that they've started clearing. They've got to know the direction in which they are going and the general idea of the kind of society they'd like to have. If they don't have hope, they don't even look for a path. They look for somebody else to do it for them (Horton et al., 1990, p. 44).

Theorists have understood the impact of participation in decision making by people in organizations for some time (Bartlem & Locke, 1981; Gardner, 1977; Lewin, 1947). As positive as this is within the framework of an organization where people are brought together to accomplish specific tasks and are paid based upon their expertise and ability to contribute, the necessity is even more crucial in a community environment where people have been convinced that others should make decisions for them because they haven't the skill, knowledge, or ability to make their own decisions. Rather than emphasize mere participation, leaders in at-risk communities must place community members in the driver's seat when it comes to decision making and planning.

Again the research of Petersen, Maier, and Seligman (1994), as well as Bandura (1995) is brought to bear on this factor as it relates to the development of confidence, optimism, and efficacy of a community and its members. Both individuals and at-risk communities must replace helplessness with a sense of efficacy. It has already been shown that increased self-efficacy has profound effect on life trajectories in turbulent times (Elder, 1995), overcoming stressful life transitions (Jerusalem & Mittag, 1995), healthy educational development (Zimmerman, 1995), and overcoming risk behaviors (Schwarzer & Fuchs, 1995). Developing a strong sense of efficacy involves mastering experiences (Bandura, 1995, p. 3).

Another theory area related to responsibility is hope. Hope involves the belief that there is a course of action that can be successfully followed to attain desirable goals and that the person or group has the agency to accomplish it (Snyder, 2000, p. 31). This combines the concept of self-efficacy with means-efficacy, the wherewithal to obtain a goal. By allowing community members to plan and execute strategies, the leader allows them to build psychological capital, confidence, which in turn becomes a bank on which they draw when they encounter resistance. The embarking upon a course of action and the taking up of responsibility for one's future and well-being reveal a level of hope within the individual or community. Horton learned early that only those communities in which hope was alive were ready for any change activity.

Reconciliation

Horton saw poverty and hopelessness as partially being the result of fractured social and economic relationships. The conflict necessary to ensure true reconciliation comprised a great deal of Horton's work. Whether it is radical individualism, racial prejudice, or competition for scarce resources, these fractured relationships erode and weaken a community's ability to address and solve problems. While people are fighting each other, they cannot focus their energy and harness their anger in addressing specific causes for their plight. To work together requires reconciliation.

Two key areas of theoretical examination may prove useful in relation to reconciliation. One is from positive psychology and is the psychology of forgiveness (King, 1981; McCullough & Witvliet, 2005). Central to the ability for reconciliation to happen is the ability for forgiveness to take place. Before the grace of forgiveness can be extended, the old wounds and current slights and injustices must be brought to light and given a hearing. For this reason, the second theoretical area shedding light on reconciliation will be conflict.

Conflict needs to be examined in terms of political and economic democracy and class conflict. With globalization of business accelerating, corporate leaders wield tremendous power beyond the walls of their corporations and often, unknowingly, feed conflict between classes. Their negotiations and requests for policy changes are generally carried on with those who comprise the elite of the societies they enter (Faux, 2006; Lasch, 1995). Often these policies, either intentionally or unintentionally, work against those in the lowest levels of the society (Stiglitz, 2003). This is unjust. Justice, therefore, becomes another theoretical construct which supports the concept of reconciliation. Whether looking at justice as fairness (Rawls, 2001) or justice as anchored in virtue (MacIntyre, 1984; 1988; 1990), reconciliation is ultimately an expression of social justice and a high view of human rights and dignity.

Reframing

Nearly every form of leadership style addresses some level of reframing, whether it is defined as vision casting or paradigm shifting in its emphasis. People in at-risk communities can become stuck in how they perceive the world, how they understand the forces they encounter daily, and how they interpret causal relationships. Leaders help people look at the same stimuli and circumstances in new ways, often freeing them from paralysis and enabling them to move to higher levels of understanding and action.

One key element of reframing is the development of critical consciousness. Critical consciousness involves a critical analysis of everyday life in terms of political, economic, class, racial, or ethnic forces that shape and sometimes control actions. Critical consciousness involves changing the way the oppressed see the world (Freire, 1990, p. 38). The development of critical consciousness manifested in praxis, the ability to act and then reflect or analyze action, was a key means, identified by Myles Horton, for those in at-risk settings to learn and consequently reframe their perceptions of the world.

The concept of reframing is related to several theoretical constructs. The theoretical arenas of change and change readiness are of particular interest. The whole process of moving a community to a point where it "tips" and begins the radical process of paradigm shift is a key area of inquiry (Armenakis, Harris, & Mossholder, 1993; Gladwell, 2000; Kuhn, 1970).

Because reframing involves creative and applied problem solving, these two areas of theory are also key to the concept (Reiter-Palmon & Illies, 2004). In addition, creative thinking is another area which supports reframing as a key activity in at-risk communities (Basadur, 2004; Umiker, 1988).

Horton most often explained the activity of the leader engaged in reframing, within an at-risk community, in terms of adult learning. For this reason, there may be significant insights and techniques within the framework of informal adult education that will prove useful in understanding the reframing process (Bandura, 1977; Brookfield, 1986). This is particularly true when considering that learning by doing or experiential learning was a significant technique employed by Horton. Therefore, how to utilize experiential techniques would also be a key area of investigation (Ayas & Zeniuk, 2001).

Restoration of people and community

Restoration of people and community encompasses not only a process but also a goal. It views the means of community transformation as ultimately being its end. Leaders involved in at-risk communities are interested in both individual and community empowerment. The manifestations of this empowerment will include (1) willingness to struggle to attain goals, (2) greater democratic involvement in economics and decision making, (3) a renewed sense of purpose or meaning, (4) an ability and willingness to take risks, (5) critical consciousness, (6) greater interdependence within the community when it comes to problem solution, (7) just and caring community structures and climate, (8) redistribution of wealth and expertise, (9) existence of a reflective and learning approach to life, (10) increased competence or confidence among community members, (11) increased community and individual aspirations, (12) a commitment to human rights and justice, and (13) a strong sense of hope.

Theoretical constructs which lend support or shed light on restoration of individuals or community focus on a wide range of issues. First, justice as fairness addresses issues of redistribution of wealth or expertise (Rawls, 2001), a concept which, depending upon political orientation, can be a controversial topic. For communities to be transformed, structural change that affects how wealth is concentrated and distributed is essential. Empowerment is linked to redistribution. As Martin Luther King, Jr. stated, "...it isn't enough that we're able to eat a hamburger with white people, you have to have the money to buy it" (Moyers, 1981, p. 15). Empowerment therefore addresses not only the acquisition of new skills, but the development of critical consciousness, the means for economic transformation, and alternative development strategies (Freidman, 1992; Freire, 1990; Quinn & Spreitzer, 1997).

Another theoretical framework which provides insight into the restoration of people or community is the study of risk as it relates to its effect on society (Beck, 1992; Giddens, 1991). The greater fluidity of culture and the rapidity of change have brought new risk factors to bear upon individuals and communities. How the people react to these new stressors and the coping mechanisms they use provides insight into how to restore individuals and communities. One of the problems encountered in at-risk communities is the tendency for its members to begin to have a type of tunnel vision in relation to the range of responses available to confront various challenges brought on by change. Often leaders perceive the way to address this is through carefully calculated activity which, through a series of steps, take people from very small to ever larger challenges. Horton strongly disagrees with this approach. First, Horton states it communicates to the people that they are weak or somehow deficient. He states that people know when they are given "childish" goals. He advocates taking on greater risk, for in embracing and engaging large challenges, community members are not only energized by the loftiness of the goals, goals which call to the human spirit, they gain confidence that they can tackle large tasks.

Replacement

Replacement is the construct which lurks in the background throughout Horton's experience and writing. Horton understood that if leadership is to be developed within the community, at some point the leader must relinquish control and even possibly leave, so that grassroots leadership can step forward and assume control. The leader in an at-risk community seeks to work him or herself out of a job. As the leader restrains him or herself in order for community members to express their gifts and abilities, so also the leader must prepare to remove him or herself so the community members may exercise their own leadership.

Level 5 Worldview—Horton's Foundational Concepts

Throughout the documents examined, Horton continually refers to three key overarching values. These are love, justice, and kenosis. I have used the term love in the sense of agapáo, the Greek term meaning moral love. It is love which seeks to do what is right socially or morally. Horton traces it back to his mother teaching him to love God and to love other people. He not only spoke of the need to love people in terms of a brotherly love, he characterized that love as including a respect for human dignity and worth. This value encompasses Level 4 principles of communal residence, reconciliation, restoration of people or community, and responsibility. This helps round out his second emphasis, justice.

Justice embraces all five aspects of justice: distributive, meaning equitable distribution of goods or resources; commutative, meaning fair exchange of goods and business; retributive, appropriate punishment for wrong doing; restorative, meaning fair ways to correct injustice and restore socioeconomic wholeness for persons and communities; and procedural justice, meaning fair legal process for both the rich and the poor. Horton speaks often of the need for justice and equality. Horton's life and work can be seen as a quest for justice on behalf of the poor in every aspect of how the term is defined. Level 4 principles associated with justice include reframing, responsibility, reconciliation, and restoration of people or community. These are expressed in a complex interaction beginning with reframing, the development of critical consciousness which recognizes political and economic exploitation and exposes the need for conflict to bring about reconciliation. Horton explains that people need to feel the need, on an emotional level, for correcting injustice before they will take responsibility to act and restore justice to their communities. Empowerment never really takes place until the level of control over resources, influence, and decision making is anchored in the people rather than leaders at the top.

The final term, kenosis, is a Greek term which embraces the dual practices of communal residence and radical subordination which are outlined in Level 4 P-codes. Kenosis is a self-emptying or laying aside of privilege, skill, abilities or traits and a complete identification with those one hopes to help.

These three components of WV serve as a fountainhead from which the principles outlined in Level 4 gain their meaning and power. Love and justice are forceful elements which are in turn partially constrained and given direction by kenosis. Each of the components operates in conjunction with the other. Love constrains justice so that it is not without mercy. Justice tempers love so that it is not reduced to a naïve romanticism. Kenosis helps provide the insight and understanding of context necessary to determine what is just and what course of action will most embody moral love. The consequence, as evidenced in the life of Horton, is an approach to leadership which is both forceful but restrained; demanding but gentle and just; and uniquely tailored to the particular needs, contextual realities and individual differences associated with the at-risk community.

A MODEL OF LEADERSHIP IN AT-RISK COMMUNITIES

How these components interact together is illustrated in Fig. 12-4. Communal residence enables the leader to understand and adapt to the contextual milieu. It exists as the framework from which the other constructs emerge and are expressed. Radical sub-ordination, responsibility, reframing, and reconciliation interact within the context, each becoming a temporary focal point or receding into the background as needed. All of the constructs exist in order to ensure the restoration of the people or community and its sense of efficacy, esteem, and power. As the leader embraces these constructs in developing new leaders and organizing a community to address its own problems, a time comes when the leader must step aside (replacement), allowing the community members to rise to the challenge of being champions of their own destiny.

The seven components of leadership in at-risk communities find support from a broad range of theories. These theoretical underpinnings included but are not necessarily limited to (1) social identity, (2) prototypicality, (3) self-efficacy, (4) diffusion of innovations, (5) learned helplessness, (6) optimism, (7) hope, (8) psychology of forgiveness, (9) conflict

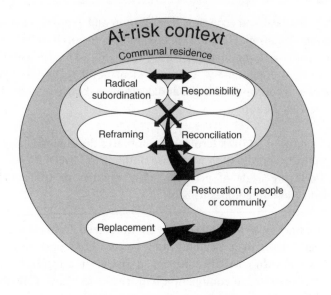

Figure 12-4   The model of leadership in at-risk communities

theory, (10) justice, (11) critical consciousness, (12) change and tipping points, (13) creative and applied problem solving, (14) creative thinking, (15) social learning theory, (16) empowerment, and (17) the study of risk as it relates to society. The theory of leadership in at-risk communities itself seems to act as a meta-theory, that is, an overarching framework in which a variety of leadership styles may find expression as long as they do not conflict with the overarching principles outlined as the core elements of the theory.

Summary

In exploring a previously unexplored topic in the study of leadership, nesting a case study within content analysis, coding patterns, and themes identified in the corpus of text that comprise the database for this research proved to be fruitful. Valuable insight was gained in not only leadership in at-risk communities but contextual, community and leadership-specific challenges and practices in these settings. Each of these areas is worthy of further research.

Confirmation of codes from content analysis was reinforced through the analysis of the case studies. By combining methods, a clearer picture of context, leadership style, and challenges impacting at-risk settings emerged. The complex interaction of environment, psychological frames, and leadership activity helped explain the necessity for the key principles associated with how to practice leadership in a manner which affirms the dignity and self-respect of the poor.

The lower two phases of coding generated an array of topics spanning over 235 different codes and 30 code families. These manifest codes provided a foundation for the codes at Levels 3, 4, and 5 which revealed a combination of latent and manifest topics. However, these early patterns were insufficient for identification of a specific approach to leadership in at-risk settings.

The third level of coding unearthed valuable information of how at-risk communities view themselves, the effect of good and toxic leadership on the mindset of community members and community self-evaluation, and how stressors arising from the environment affect a community's perception of itself in terms of efficacy and esteem. However, these codes also seemed to echo topics already discussed within leadership studies and failed to isolate key principles unique to at-risk settings. An understanding of how to lead in an at-risk setting required another level of abstraction in which lower codes were combined into new categories.

The fourth level of coding identified seven specific aspects of leadership in at-risk communities. These seven principles; communal residence, radical subordination, responsibility, reconciliation, reframing, restoration of community or people, and replacement, were defined and explained. Each component was examined in terms of how it positively contributed to leadership in at-risk settings as well as its indispensability. The model proposed in Fig. 12-4 showed how the seven components interacted with each other and their mutual dependence. These seven constructs were then examined in view of the contemporary leadership literature to garner support for this emergent theory.

The fifth level of coding, WV, was presented and its components were defined. How these elements interacted with one another and their association with Level 4 principles were demonstrated as well. Horton made reference to overarching or guiding values numerous times. Love was a central theme. He said, "I think you to have to love people to do this. If I don't love people I can't help people learn to love their neighbor" (as cited in Moyers, 1981). He also spoke of justice and equality as an overarching concept which fueled his action.

> I realized that what's good for me, if I just want to live my own life, I've got to think everyone should have the same rights. You know, the universality of rights, if it's right for me I have to work for it to be right for everybody else (as cited in Moyers, 1981).

Over 150 separate quotations helped explain the need for leaders to deeply identify with the community and its members to the point where they become experts about context, restrain themselves so that community members have room to express their gifts and abilities, and relinquish power, notoriety, and resources. These served as the basis for kenosis, completing the triad of WV guiding principles.

The convergence of codes at Levels 3, 4, and 5 helped anchor a grounded theory in the data and led to recommendations for future research. A first step has been taken in response to Burns (2003) and Bennis (2001) who called for research on leadership among the poor. This opens the door for those who follow and provides a point of reference which will hopefully launch a concerted effort to understand leadership from the bottom up within impoverished settings.

13

EPILOGUE

Qualitative research has gradually come into its own and is now recognized for its significant contributions to the development of knowledge and insight into the field of leadership studies. An proliferation of textbooks, guidebooks, and handbooks (e.g., Denzin & Lincoln, 2005; Patton, 2002; Silverman 1997; 2001; Strauss & Corbin, 1990) define and describe the different philosophical foundations underlying qualitative research, the specific methods used, and criteria to judge the quality of qualitative research. In this book, I reviewed, analyzed, and discussed conceptual/theoretical and empirical articles describing both frequently and infrequently used research methods in the study of leadership. For some of these methods, such as phenomenology (Chapter 8), for example, there is a considerable imbalance between theoretical and empirical studies. Similarly, in narrative analysis, theoretical papers outweigh the empirical studies. In other instances, there is a more balanced presentation of theoretical and empirical works. For instance, mixed methods leadership studies (Chapter 6), which yielded the largest number of published articles, theoretical discussions of triangulating qualitative and quantitative methods, are mirrored by a critical mass of empirical studies which illustrate the various ways of combining different techniques falling into the qualitative and quantitative camps.

In this final chapter, I revisit some of the major themes running through this book including the contributions of qualitative research to the study of leadership, the paradigm wars, the underutilization of a considerable number of qualitative techniques, and briefly discuss the emergence of new models of leadership which lend themselves to qualitative analyses.

Cassell, Symon, Buehring, and Johnson, (2006) in their investigation of the role and status of qualitative research in business and management research identified a number of barriers that account for the lack of visibility of qualitative research to include (1) getting research past epistemological gatekeepers such as journal editors and conference review committees; (2) having to conform to journal editorial criteria which have been set up with quantitative studies in mind; (3) pressures to justify research methods according to (sometimes) inappropriate (positivist) criteria; and (4) the lack of exposure to alternative management publications and on management courses (pp. 291–292). The authors argue that these factors in combination can undermine the potential contributions of qualitative research and discourage researchers from conducting qualitative studies. One of the stakeholders, a journal editor, interviewed by Cassell et al. offered the following opinion:

> …my own philosophical inclination is I have somewhat more confidence in them [statistical studies using large data sets] than I would in studies which depended upon, you know, the richness of language or the understanding of one's interviewee where, you know, how well he or she understands the question, the lack of facility with the language, a lack of intelligence perhaps and all of these things seem to me to run the risk of in a way of dirtying the data and making it, from my point of view, less reliable (p. 296).

CONTRIBUTIONS TO THE STUDY OF LEADERSHIP

Qualitative research, although still trailing behind the dominant quantitative, positivistic paradigm, makes significant and unique contributions to the study of leadership. In championing qualitative methods, Bryman (1984) epitomizes the beliefs that underpin this position. He posits that qualitative research is committed to contextual under-standing: behavior which is understood in the context of meaning systems used by a particular group of people in society. Qualitative research is flexible and fluid; it is reflexive. Finley (2003) defined reflexivity in qualitative research as researchers enga-ging in explicit self-aware meta-analysis. Through critical reflection, the author asserts, researchers use reflexivity to continually monitor, or even audit, the research process (p. 220). According to Van Maanen (1988b), critical reflexivity is a confessional tale and a transparent account of the research which is a defining, if not the defining characteristic of qualitative research.

Qualitative research in the study of leadership captures the subjective experiences of leaders and followers, its slippery nature, and the local context in which leadership takes place. In leadership research, several calls have been issued for increased atten-tion to the context in which leadership plays itself out (e.g., Osborn, Hunt, & Jauch, 2002). Paradoxically, in qualitative research, which by its very nature is context rich and context dependent, calls for such increased attention to context have not fallen on fertile ground as measured by published articles that paid attention to context (Porter & McLaughlin, 2006). Examples of contextual characteristics relevant to the study of leadership include climate/culture, structure, organizational life cycles, CEO succession history, time, degree of formalization and centralization, task ambiguity, and demographic variability within the organizations. As Alvesson (1992) notes, understanding leadership calls for the consideration of social, relational processes and cultural context. Qualitative methodologies are able to shed light on the complexities, ambiguities, and multifarious nature of leadership in context. Consequently, Bryman (2004) argues for a greater development of qualitative explorations of leadership, suggesting that their significance is underplayed when, in fact, the results of qualitative studies can facilitate new ways of thinking about the complex, shifting dynamics of leadership.

THE DEBATE OVER METHODS

Paradigm wars have been a frequently discussed topic throughout the chapters of this book. According to Oakley (2000), the qualitative–quantitative debate started in the early 1960s. At the center of paradigm debate is what is the nature of qualitative evidence in research? How does it exactly configure into qualitative analysis? Are textual data evidence? Is evidence restricted to numbers and statistics? Does auditing increase the validity of qualitative findings? Qualitative and quantitative approaches have been distinguished and defined on the basis of the type of data used (textual or numeric; structured or unstructured), the logic employed (inductive or deductive), the type of investigation (exploratory or confirmatory), the method of analysis (interpretive or statistical), and on the underlying paradigm (positivistic or interpretive) (Bazeley, 2004). For example, Huberman and Miles (1984, p. 1) contend that qualitative data consists of words rather than numbers. However, this distinction is questionable as most quantitative data are ultimately accounted for by words. Likewise, qualitative researchers often code their data (Chapters 4, 5, and 12).

Throughout the various chapters, the differences between the qualitative and quantitative paradigms and corresponding methodologies have been addressed. In qualitative research, the emphasis is upon discovery, description, and meaning as opposed to quantitative criteria of prediction, control, and measurement. Furthermore, traditional notions of random sampling, reliability, validity, replicability, and so on are not appropriate in many qualitative contexts. Although the techniques used by qualitative researchers to ensure the reliability and validity of their findings (Chapter 2) are different from those used by quantitative investigators, they do in fact exist, and they are as rigorous (Kirk & Miller, 1986). However, it is important to remember that erroneous assumptions, invalid measures, insufficient power, and other limitations in quantitative research may render the findings of such research invalid as well. Bavelas (1995), for example, contends that quantitative methods are not value-free and doubts whether there are any inherently objective methods and data.

The qualitative–quantitative debate produced a dialectic that resulted in many dichoto-mies and dualities such as realist versus idealist, subjective versus objective, inductive versus deductive, and positivistic versus anti-positivistic. As Roberts (2003) and others (i.e., Bavelas, 1995; Oakley, 2000) have noted, this kind of dichotomous frame of reference has exaggerated what differences exist between qualitative and quantitative methods. The debate also resulted in two distinctive camps of researchers: the purists and the pragmatists (Tashakkori & Teddlie, 2003b). The purists believe that the two methods are incompatible because they are inextricably linked to paradigms that make different assumptions about the world and what constitutes valid research. They claim that there is a logical relationship between the principles inherent in the paradigm and the methods chosen and that epistemology informs method. The pragmatists challenge purists and argue that methods are a collection of techniques that are not inherently linked to paradigmatic assumptions (Firestone, 1987). Hammersley (1992) also refers to purist and pragmatist approaches. However, he also notes that

> ... there are some serious problems with the paradigm view of the relationship between qualitative and quantitative approaches: for one thing, if we look at research today in the human sciences, we find that much does not neatly fall into one or the other "categories." There are multiple methodological dimensions in which research varies: these do not lie in parallel and each involves a range of positions, not just two (p. 160).

Quantitative and qualitative methods do have contrasting strength and weaknesses. The very fact that the quantitative approach emphasizes causality, variables, and heavily prestructured approach while qualitative research is concerned more with the elucidation of respondents' perspectives, process, and contextual detail (Bryman, 1992a) means that the resulting data may not be as comparable as advocates of triangulation sometimes argue.

In Chapter 1, we discussed the nature of paradigm wars, the lingering hegemony of the positivist paradigm, and the dominant perception in the field that high-quality research is associated with quantification. The popularity of mixed methods designs (Chapter 6) seems to reinforce this perception. After a period in the paradigmatic wilderness, mixed methods research has not only gained acceptability but also popularity (Bazeley, 2004). There are different postures toward the integration of qualitative and quantitative methods, only one of which is triangulation, either within qualitative methods or between qualitative and quantitative techniques. The broad idea in triangulation is that if diverse kinds of data support the same conclusion, confidence in the conclusion is increased. The question of whether qualitative and quantitative methods can, or should, be combined has been answered by noting that the differences between quali-tative and quantitative methods are reconcilable although the purists in both camps who argue against such a marriage stress that the two paradigms are based on completely different philosophical assumptions and values. Those who argue for a combination, on the other hand, see the methods used in qualitative and quantitative research as different tools, suited for different tasks. The latter viewpoint (combination) has gained in popularity evidenced, for example, by the formation of the *International Journal of Mixed Methods Research*. This is not to say that qualitative and quantitative techniques are necessarily equal partners in this marriage as a qualitative study is often used in an exploratory manner to precede a presumably more rigorous quantitative study. However, as noted in Chapter 6, both the qualitative and quantitative components of a mixed method design can be executed simultaneously instead of sequentially so that each can inform the other as the research unfolds and the findings from both methods complement each other. Thus, the competition between qualitative and quantitative research has been increasingly resolved into complementarity. However, Popay (2003) points out that researchers continue to run the risk of seeing qualitative research as playing a complimentary but "unequal handmaiden" role to quantitative research. Some scholars have argued that qualitative research does not deliver on its promise, because many qualitative studies, at least in the social sciences, are still seen as being under the covert influence of positivism, while its rules and rationality are overtly rejected.

New ways of conceptualizing validity have been proposed (e.g., Lincoln & Guba, 1985; Sparkes, 2001), and discussion of qualitative methodologies have grown exponentially. Of particularly interest are attempts to reconceptualize validity within the social constructionist/poststructural epistemologies that postulate a radical divergence from their positivistic predecessors. Lincoln and Guba (1985), for example, purported to draw from epistemological assumptions associated with social constructivism and put forth a version of validity recast as "trustworthiness" (Chapter 2). However, Scheurich (1996) suggests that even within these reconceptualizations, "there must be a boundary line, a judgment criterion for deciding whose work is acceptable" (p. 51) and whose work is not. Constructed in this way, according to Scheurich, validity, in whatever epistemological disguise it is clad, is assessed within an either/or framework (e.g., trustworthy/untrustworthy; valid/invalid). Thus, these reconceptualizations function no differently from their positivist incarnates and similarly serve to police social science projects by de/legitimizing social knowledge, research practice, and experiential possibilities (Scheurich, 1996).

Bochner (2000) argues that qualitative researchers often argue behind the terminology of the academic language games we have learned to play, gaining some advantage by knowing when and how to say "validity," "reliability," "grounded," and the like (p. 267). The author notes that quality criteria always have a restrictive, limiting, regressive, thwarting, halting quality to them, and they can never be completely separated from the structures of power in which they are situated. He concludes that discussions "focusing on criteria have as their subtext a tacit desire to authorize or legislate a preexisting or static set of standards that will thwart subjectivity and ensure rationality" (p. 269).

UNDERUTILIZATION OF METHODS

There is a need for greater awareness among leadership researchers of the rich diversity of methods that are subsumed under qualitative research (see Table 2-1 in Chapter 2). Methods that have been underutilized in the study of leadership include critical theory, rhetorical, semiotic, and discourse analysis and life narratives. Speaking for critical theory, Alvesson and Wilctt (1992) note that the use of this particular qualitative method is virtually nonexistent in management research. Likewise, nowhere in the leadership literature have nontext sources of data found in film, works of art, choreography, cartoons, and music been considered (Chapter 8).

I will briefly touch upon two methods that beg for the attention of leadership researchers.

Participant observation involves the researcher observing the phenomenon under study in the naturalistic setting and in real time. Participant observation has a long history, first among ethnographers and later in sociology, and has its theoretical roots in the symbolic interaction perspective (Chapter 1). It has been defined as the "process of learning through exposure to or involvement in the day-to-day or routine activities of participants in the researcher setting" (Schenul, Schenul, & LeCompte, 1999, p. 92). Participant observers study people in their natural environment in order to gain depth of insight into the thoughts and feelings of the research participants.

Goering and Streiner (1996) point out that the balance between participation and observation is variable, ranging from the researcher actively taking part in the group that is being observed through being defined as a member of the group, but not being a participant in all of its activities, to being seen as an observer who is not part of the group. Thus, there is a spectrum ranging from full participant observation to partial observation to observation as an outsider looking in. As with most research decisions, trade-offs are involved. The more the researcher is seen as an active member, the more the group members will trust him or her and be open about their thoughts and feelings (p. 493).

Participant observation usually involves a range of research methods: informal interviews, direct observation, participation in the life of a group, collective discussions, document, and self-analyses and life histories and, therefore, often can be classified as mixed methods. Participant observation is particularly appropriate to studies of interpersonal group and team processes. The participant observer attempts immersion in the local culture when collecting and analyzing the data. This may require the researcher to acquire the language of the group or culture that is being studied, live in the setting, or defer to the local culture. To conduct participant observation, the researcher ideally lives in the context to facilitate prolonged engagement, one of the activities listed by Lincoln and Guba (1985) necessary to establish trustworthiness.

Data collection, mostly collected in situ in the form of field observations and field notes, is often supplemented by video recording which can add to the depth and breadth of in-person observations. For example, Harel (1991) used a video camera on a tripod as a "silent observer" (p. 449) to supplement her handwritten field notes of children's behaviors in a classroom. Because we tend to ascribe lack of bias to the authoritative record that is provided by video technology, video-recorded data are often presumed to and precise than what is observed by the human researcher. According to Atkinson and Hammersley (1995), the use of technology allows the researcher to assume a privileged gaze in which the importance of relationships with participants becomes less relevant to the collection of data. Observational data collection continues when the researchers achieve theoretical saturation, that is, when the generic features of new findings consistently replicate earlier ones. Depending on the observers' style of data analysis, they may engage in more casual theoretization or more formal theory building (Adler & Adler, 1994).

Kutsche (1998) states that researchers who are analyzing data from observation, field notes and/or interviews should develop a model that helps them to make sense out of what participants do. The author points out that the researcher is constructing model of culture, not telling the truth about the data, as there are numerous truths, particularly when presented from several participants' viewpoint. He further suggests that researchers organize the collected data into a narrative in which they tell a story of a day or a week in the lives of the informants.

The general advantages of participant observation include flexibility, the quality and depth of research it produces, and the opportunity for understanding it encourages. Participant observation provides the opportunity to collect data where it is important to capture human behavior in its broad natural context at several times and from multiple perspectives (Glaser, 1996). Other arguments in favor of this qualitative method include reliance on first-hand observation, high-face validity of data, and the use of relatively simple and inexpensive data collection techniques. Like any research method, participant observation also has its limitations. It is not the most reliable technique. Nor is it one of the most objective qualitative methods because it relies heavily on the integrity and intellectual honesty of the researcher. Studies employing participant observation are, by their very nature, impossible to replicate as the data they produce are often the opinion of a single observer. Other related negative features include threat to the objectivity of the researcher, unsystematic gathering of data, reliance on subjective measurement (the human observer), and possible observer effects such as observations distorting the observed behaviors.

An example of a leadership-related study that employed participant observation was conducted by Waddington (1986) who observed a 20-week strike at a brewery in the United Kingdom. The study was based on five-month participant observation augmented by unstructured interviews with the strikers. The strike, which involved 1000 workers, began in opposition to the implementation of a four-day working week and culminated in the permanent closure of the brewery. The workers believed that management behaved exploitatively and moral and trust were low in the organization.

After an initial growth period, the brewery, founded in 1875, experienced deteriorating relationships between management and workers, and questions of productivity and redundancy became recurrent themes in conflict between the two parties. The chairman and managing director informed his employees that their wages were too high and that the brewery was overstaffed. Between 1975 and 1980, the workforce at the brewery became increasingly militant as evidenced in a series of well-publicized disputes with management. The chronic conflicts taught the brewery workers to appreciate the worth of strongly defiant unionism. In 1980, the company demanded greater job mobility, the elimination of some weekend overtime, and the introduction of cleaning and engineering contractors. Management then delivered an ultimatum that, unless certain categories of workers returned to work by a given deadline, employees would be served with dismissal notices for breach of contract and the brewery would be closed. In February 1981, the union declared the strike official and assembled pickets at the entrance of the brewery. For several months thereafter, a large scale picketing operation was carried out.

Waddington (1986) accounted for the development of the strike not as an event perpetuated by management-labor conflict but analyzed the events based on social-cognitive theory, psychological imagery, beliefs, and values underlying the employees' behavior. For example, the brewery had an informal recruitment policy that gave preference to friends and relatives of existing employees which encouraged homogeneity of values. Likewise, in the past, disputes with management followed a script whereby strike action (or, sometimes the mere threat of it) produced a satisfactory settlement for the workers. The brewery never reopened.

The second method that holds promise for the study of leadership is *appreciative inquiry* (AI) introduced by David Cooperrider and his associates (e.g., Cooperrider, 1990; Cooperrider & Whitney, 2005; 2000; Whitney & Trosten-Bloom, 2003). Unlike participant observation with its long-standing history, AI arrived on the research landscape in 1987 when Cooperrider and Srivastva published their seminal article on AI. Like many postmodernists, the authors argued that logical positivistic assumptions trap us in a rear-view world and methods based on these assumptions tend to (re)create the social realities they purport to be studying (Bushe, 1999). AI has been described as a radically affirmative approach to change, and organizational development intervention, and an approach to leadership. Cooperrider and Whitney (1999) define AI as

> The cooperative search for the best in people, their organizations, and the world around them. It involves systematic discovery what gives a system "life" when it is

most effective and capable in economic, ecological, and human terms. Appreciative inquiry involves the art and practice of asking questions that strengthen the system's capacity to positive potential. It mobilizes inquiry through crafting and "unconditional positive question" often involving hundreds or sometimes thousands of people. In appreciative inquiry intervention gives way to imagination and innovation; instead of negation, criticisms and spiraling diagnosis, there is discovery, dream and design. Appreciative inquiry assumes that every living system has untapped, rich, and inspiring accounts of the positive. Link this "positive change core" directly to any change agenda and changes never thought possible are suddenly and democratically mobilized (p. 10).

In the words of its primary originator, AI asks managers, leaders, and their constituencies to pay special attention to the best of the past and the present in order to ignite the collective imagination of what might be. AI assumes that human organizing and change is a relational process of inquiry, grounded in affirmation and appreciation. It works by focusing the attention of an organization on its positive core—people's collective wisdom about the organization, tangible and intangible strengths, capabilities, resources, potentials, and assets. Johnson and Leavitt (2001) describe AI as an approach "uniquely suited to organizations that seek to be collaborative, inclusive, and genuinely caring for both the people within the organization and those they serve" (p. 129). White, President of GTE, asks, "In the long run, what is likely to be more useful? Demoralizing a successful workforce by concentrating on their failures or helping them over their last few hurdles by building a bridge with their successes?" (Lord, 2007). Smethurst (2002) describes the benefits of AI as liberating leadership within everybody.

Proponents of the AI movement contend that the foundation for affirmative change is fostering conversation that inquires into life-generating experiences, core values, and moments of excellence in organizational life (Cooperrider & Whitney, 1999; Cooperrider, Sorensen, Whitney, & Yaeger, 2000). Barge and Olicer (2002) note that AI connects to the emotional life of organizational members by tapping into their passions and strong feelings of what constitutes excellence in their work context. They also state the emphasis of AI on valuing what works well within organizational life and argue that certain forms of emotional and spiritual expressions are required to foster learning and change (p. 125).

At the center of the 4-D cycle is *Affirmative Topic Choice,* topics that cover strategically important areas that are chosen to guide 4-D process. For example, in the AI project implemented by British Airways, workers and managers arrived at the following topics: happiness at work, harmony among work groups, continuous people development, and exceptional arrival experience (Whitney & Trosten-Bloom, 2003). The appreciative interview is at the core of this process. As in other qualitative methods, themes and common threads begin to emerge as group members tell stories which are later shared with a larger group.

AI is based on the 4-D cycle of inquiry, depicted in Fig. 13-1, which begins with an in-depth identification of what is to be studied. This phase is known as *Discovery* of affirmative topics. The topics that are selected provide a framework for collecting stories, discovering and sharing the best practices, and creating a knowledge-rich environment. The most often used data collection tool is the interview but may also include the use focus groups. The discovery phase typically begins with the collaborative act of crafting appreciative interview questions and developing an appreciative interview protocol. In this phase, participants share their stories and write down answers to the interview protocol; they affirm past and present strength and successes. The discovery phase represents an extensive search to understand the "best of what is" and "what has been" and focuses on problem solving and need identification. This phase results in a rich description or mapping of the organizations positive core.

The second D, *Dream*, involves envisioning the future of the organization; it is an energizing exploration of "what might be." It is a time for participants to think big, out of the box, and out of the boundaries of what has been in the past. The purpose of the dream phase is to identify and spread generative, affirmative, and hopeful images about the future. Typically, this is accomplished in a group of different stakeholders who arrive at "provocative

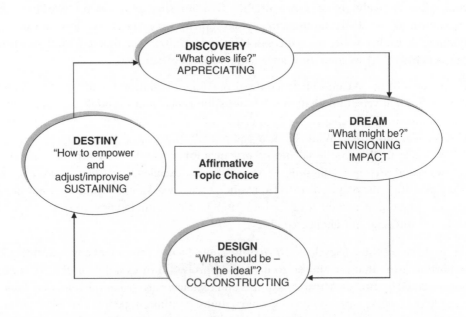

Figure 13-1   The appreciative inquiry 4-D cycle (Source: Cooperrider & Srivastva, (1987))

propositions" which reflect their sense of purpose and strategic vision. Provocative propositions are statements of organizational aspirations and intent, based on the analysis of the organization at its very best. By coming to agreement on a set of provocative propositions, people have a compelling vision of the organization at its best which serves as a motivator for new behaviors. The sessions of the dream stage are conducted to emphasize the positive core, create positive dreams of the organization's strategic visions, and to develop a higher sense of purpose (Whitney & Troste-Bloom, 2003).

The *Design* phase takes the products of the first two stages and transfers them into an architecture of change. This phase involves making choices about "what should be." It is a transformative stage during which organizational structures, processes, policies, and systems are aligned with the organizations positive past (Discovery) and highest potential (Dream) to facilitate the replication of the peak performance and the implementation of the new dream. Design takes the form of creating positive affirmations by writing provocative propositions describing the organization's image of itself in the ideal; it focuses on encouraging all employees to contribute to the service of the organization.

The final phase, *Destiny*, brings the 4-D cycle to closure by focusing on implementation of and experimentation with the actions identified in the Dream phase. It focuses specifically on personal and organizational commitments to change in major systems within the organization such as human resources, customer service systems, measurement systems, and work processes and structures. The destiny phase invites action inspired by the outcomes of the discovery, dream, and design phases.

AI has been successfully employed in organizations as diverse as the airline industry and the Catholic Church. Proponents of AI assert that the great promise of this qualitative method is that it generates self-sustaining momentum within the organization toward actualizing the values that lead to superior performance. AI can produce significant breakthroughs in our understanding of leadership and change processes. Underutilized and often criticized by those unfamiliar with the assumptions underlying AI and how to conduct an AI leadership study, AI offers the opportunity to approach leadership and organizations with a view of possibilities rather than past failures. AI, in many ways, and the positive psychology movement (Chapters 10 and 13) share similar views about human nature and leadership effectiveness emphasizing strengths, successes, and the positive core of individuals and organizations.

Rainey (1996) conducted an AI study into the factors of culture continuity during leadership transitions in a Canadian company, LeadShare, which consisted of a partnership of 350 accountants and management consultants. Within the past 25 years, the firm expanded its spectrum of client services and reshaped itself for double-digit growths and now ranks among the top accounting firms in Canada. In anticipation of transitions in two key executive positions over the next 3 years, the company had implemented a leadership succession plan to ensure minimum disruption and continuity of culture which valued innovation, human capital, and professional development for all employees. The organization launched the "Roundtable" initiative to discuss leadership without hierarchy, shared resources, and cross-functional networks. A desired outcome for Roundtable participants was to develop a group of agents of culture to sustain the company's traditions, practices, and behaviors while multiplying the factors of success. At the same time, LeadShare realized that it must find ways to articulate the implicit aspects of its culture if it expects to grow in new directions.

The primary objective of AI in the Roundtable program, a multiyear organizational intervention, was to assist the organization in envisioning a collectively desired future and put that vision for the future into practice. The work included the design of the AI protocol, data collection, thematic analysis of the data, data feedback, and identification of future direction. Forty partners who were elected to participate in the Roundtable conducted open-ended formal interviews with the entire population of partners in the firms. Historical documents consisting of reports, speeches, newsletters, and memoranda were reviewed and content analyzed. In addition, observational data were collected in meetings, office visits, and during company retreats. Finally, a survey was included during the second phase of this AI project at the annual meeting of the partners to provide convergent validation to the interview data.

The data were analyzed by two independent researchers in addition to the author. Word counts and interpretations were consistent among but no reliability indices were reported. The following themes emerged from the analyses: (1) feeling of unity which was exemplified by shared decision making, partner support, working, and playing together; (2) respected, responsible, inspirational leadership evidence by partners confidence in the courageous and responsible leadership of the firm; (3) justice and equality seen in the company's consensus building process, the compensation system, a commitment to diversity and autonomy; and (4) people development and professional competence with LeaderShare considering constant learning and partner development as high priorities. Although the 4-D cycle of AI was not evident in this study, Rainey (2001) claims that AI built culture, mobilized maximum commitment, and facilitated adaptability to the changing environment.

THE FUTURE OF QUALITATIVE RESEARCH IN THE STUDY OF LEADERSHIP: CHALLENGES AND OPPORTUNITIES

Around the globe, qualitative research in many disciplines is flourishing in countries such as Germany, Japan, and Mexico. The Internet has added a new dimension to data collection and analysis in qualitative research. Journals such as the *Academy of*

Management Journal, known as a bastion of quantitative research, have issued open invitations encouraging scholars to submit their qualitative research to this journal (Gephart, 2004). In leadership research, we have seen a significant increase in qualitative research over the past two decades (Lowe & Gardner, 2000). Qualitative research, in the study of leadership that is rigorously and systematically conducted, is flexible and contextual, demonstrates critical self-scrutiny by the researcher or active flexibility, and produces explanations or arguments rather than offering mere description is said to meet the criteria rigor and quality. Qualitative research of this type continues to be important for leadership scholarship because it provides thick, detailed, context-rich data that enrich the study of leadership. Qualitative research often advances the field by providing unique, memorable, socially important and theoretically meaningful contributions to scholarly discourse and the study of leadership (Gephart, 2004, p. 461). Creswell and Maietta (2002) offer an important caveat when they state:

> Qualitative methods are not alternatives to quantitative methods. They are not another way to answer the same research question. Instead, they constitute a relatively new way to answer a different type of question, one characterized by a unique approach with a different set of underlying assumptions reflecting a different worldview of how individual and group behavior can best be studied (p. 143).

In this final section, I will focus on opportunities and challenges facing the qualitative leadership researcher beginning with an assessment of the state-of-the-art of leadership as scientific field of interest that has reached a stage of evolution that may be particularly conducive to qualitative research. I conclude with a brief discussions of areas of research within the qualitative paradigm that, when improved upon, will enhance the credibility of qualitative research.

The future of qualitative leadership research is closely linked with the future of the study of leadership which appears to be positioned for a paradigm shift. Some scholars point to the vast amount of money and effort expended on understanding leadership with little return on the investment. For example, leadership development is a multibillion dollar annual business, yet we still know very little about how to develop and educate effective leaders. Established leadership theories such as transactional/transformational leadership (Bass, 1985; Burns, 1978; 2003), which generated a large body of theory and research, were formulated over two decades ago when organizations and the environments in which they function were significantly different from contemporary organizations that are being challenged. Most leadership theories, including transactional/transformational leadership, have remained two-dimensional models (autocratic versus democratic leadership, task-oriented versus relationship-oriented leadership, and management versus leadership) at a time when the world is no longer two-dimensional. As Kuhn (1970) noted, data empirically derived from the reigning paradigm are bound temporally and spatially and are subject to decay as new theories and methodologies challenge the validity and utility of the prevailing paradigm (Klenke, 2007a).

Partly in response to these criticisms and partly because of a Zeitgeist that is responsive to a paradigm shift that seems to permeate the field of leadership studies, a wave of new perspectives have emerged that were introduced in Chapter 1. They included spiritual leadership (e.g., Fry, 2003; 2005), contextual leadership (e.g., Osborn et al., 2002), paradoxical leadership (e.g., Kark, Shamir, & Chen, 2003; Klenke, 2003), stewardship (e.g., Block, 1993), connective leadership (e.g., Lipman-Blmen, 1996), self-sacrificial leadership (e.g., Choi & Mai-Dalton, 1999), chaos and complexity theory (e.g., Marion & Uhl-Bien, 2001; Schneider & Somers, 2006), shared leadership (e.g., Klenke, 1997; Pearce & Conger, 2003), ethical leadership (e.g., Brown & Treviño, 2006), and authentic leadership (e.g., Gardner & Avolio, 2005; Klenke, 2005).

Although there are important differences in terminology and foci among these emergent perspectives, they converge on the premise that leadership effectiveness depends less on the heroic actions of an omnipotent leader at the apex of the organization but is produced through collaborative efforts sustained by a network of leaders and followers engaged in collective achievement, teamwork, and shared accountability. These models conceptualize leadership as a shared, relational process distributed across different organizational levels and dependent on social influence and networks of influence. Fletcher (2004) argued that it is this focus on fluidity, mutuality, and two-directional influence processes that serve as the connected tissue that provides the common denominator for the emergent perspectives that have recently evolved. Many of these emergent theories are in the early stages of development and/or lack a strong theoretical infrastructure as well as reliable and valid measure of the foundational concepts. For example, Cooper, Scandura, and Schriesheim (2005) took a critical look at the relatively new leadership construct of authentic leadership. After identifying shortcomings of current construct definition of authentic leadership which lack conceptual clarity, the authors outline a research program that may lead not only to an improved construct definition but also to a measure of authentic leadership. Most of their recommendations are based on qualitative approaches.

For example, case studies of leaders who meet the current criteria of authentic leadership can be employed to identify the specific behaviors, key attributes, and values of leaders such as Bill George, the former chairman of Medtronic and author of *Authentic Leadership: Rediscovering the Secrets to Creating Lasting Value* (George, 2003), or Warren Buffet, Mandela, and Eleanor Roosevelt who have been cited as examples of authentic leaders. Case studies can be supplement with interviews and grounded theory methodology to map the dimensions of authentic leadership. Another qualitative approach would include the life story approach (Shamir, Dayan-Horesh & Adler, 2005) analyzing both biographies of authentic leaders coupled with the collection of life stories collected from individuals close to authentic leaders such as family members, associates, and followers that then can be compared to the leaders' stories (Shamir & Eilam, 2005). Qualitative text-based methods can be extended into image-based approaches. Qualitative research of this type should help to advance existing knowledge of authentic leadership. Many of the emergent perspectives are gold mines for qualitative research waiting to be mined.

Qualitative leadership research remains a contested terrain. More qualitative studies are being published in leadership and management journals. New journals are being created and new methods such as AI have been developed. Established methods such as case studies are being revised and reconceptualized. For example, VanWynsberghe and Khan (2007) pointed out that case study has been variously defined as a method, methodology, or research design and as a result is used as a catch-all category for a variety of research methods. The authors argue that defining case study as a method implies that it is a research technique like content analysis or phenomenology. They content that case study is not a method because case study researchers employ various techniques such as interviewing, document analysis, and content analysis. Moreover, there are different types of case studies including exploratory, explanatory, intrinsic, and instrumental. Case study is also not methodology. Methodology, as discussed in Chapters 1 and 2, is one of the elements of most tripartite definitions of paradigm which include ontology, epistemology, and methodology. We noted in Chapter 1 that all methodologies must be situated in the context of a particular paradigm. Stake (2005) severed case study from methodology by stating, "Case study is not a methodological choice but a choice of what is to be studied" (p. 438).

VanWynsberghe and Khan (2007) reviewed the prototype of a case study by identifying the necessary elements for a study to be classified as case study which were described in Chapter 4. After reviewing existing definitions of case study and based on their analysis, the authors then propose what they argue is a more precise and encompassing definition that reconciles various definitions of case study:

> Case study is a transparadigmatic and transdiciplinary heuristic that involves the careful delineation of the phenomena for which the evidence is being collected.

Taking a closer look at the fundamental elements of this definition, transparadigmatic means that case study is relevant regardless of the researchers' paradigm that undergird their study. Thus, case studies can be conducted within a number of different paradigms such as constructivism, interpretivism, or pragmatism. Transdisciplinary calls our attention to the fact that no single discipline has the monopoly on case study and consequently we find case studies in the social sciences which include leadership studies, business, and the humanities. With regard to heuristic, VanWynsberghe and Khan (2007) assert that heuristic at its most general level is an approach that focuses the case study researcher's attention on learning, discovery, construction, and problem solving. The authors cite earlier research by Eckstein (2002), who used the term heuristic to describe a special type of case study that employs analytic induction (Chapter 4) to discover or find out the essence of the case.

From the perspective of a leadership scholar, the proposed definition is congruent with the directions the study of leadership is taking. As a field of inquiry, leadership studies since its inception has been multidisciplinary or transdisciplinary as there is hardly an academic discipline that has not contributed to the study of leadership. Increasingly, the study of leadership is also becoming multiparadigmatic as it moves out of the major paradigm, namely, the social sciences. For example, complexity and chaos theory (e.g., Marion & Uhl-Bien, 2001; Schneider & Somers, 2006) is drawing from the natural science, particularly quantum physics, when complexity theorists introduce concepts such as artificial neural networks and nonlinear systems dynamics. As more qualitative leadership studies appear in the literature, many definitions of established research methods such as case study will need to be re-evaluated and redefined vis-à-vis new findings.

Qualitative research has gone into cyberspace. Virtual ethnography, virtual focus groups, and e-interviews are just three examples of research methods that have migrated to the Internet. Technologies are creating new opportunities for qualitative leadership researchers, but they also bring new problems. Bazeley (2004) pointed out that with the computerization of qualitative analysis and the increasing use of qualitative analysis software, there is a tendency for researchers to include much larger volumes of unstructured data than have been traditionally used in qualitative studies. Murphy and O'Brien (2006) note that although qualitative data analysis has never been easier in terms of the availability of software programs but warn that we must collectively ensure that technology is not restricted to the role of quantifying qualitative research for the sake of perceived legitimacy.

One of the consequences of the increased use of the Internet is the need to reexamine and perhaps redefine the traditional ethical guidelines (Chapter 2). Standard ethical requirements including informed consent, anonymity, confidentiality, and protection from harm become more difficult to enforce when research is conducted online. For example, is consent required when investigating postings in a public forum such as chat rooms or listservers? If consent is required, who should provide it? The list owner, the participants, or both? Who owns the data? There are many leadership-related listservers which engage participants in ongoing discussions about substantive and often controversial discussions of various leadership topics. Content analyses of these posting would make for interesting research but raises a host of ethical problems. For example, one important issue concerns copyright. If we treat Internet communications as written material, then, as with other published materials, quoting without citing the source is a violation of copyright laws. However, as Mann and Stewart (2002) pointed out, there is also an implied license that mitigates absolute copyright. According to the authors, this implied license refers to reading and archiving materials posted on the Internet. If copyright laws were to be followed in the literal sense, then no one could read or download a message without explicit permission from the copyright owner, normally the author. However, as Kitchin (2002) notes the issue of ownership is further complicated since perhaps the server administrator, the owner of the server system or the moderator of a discussion group might also have ownership rights.

Haggerty (2004) discusses an ethical phenomenon which he labeled "ethical creep" which the author defined as "a dual process whereby the regulatory structure of the ethics bureaucracy [i.e., institutional review boards] is expanding outward, colonizing new groups, practices, and institutions, while at the same time intensifying the regulation of practices deemed to fall within its official ambit" (p. 392). The author fears that litigation and rule following as opposed to critical evaluation of research proposals are becoming the key components that determine what kinds of research can be conducted. This ethical creep narrows what kind of research is approved and has real implications for primary researchers whose primary space for gathering information is the Internet (Whitman, 2007). The Internet as a research environment is a medium that is not well understood and defined which makes the enforcement of traditional ethical guidelines that govern its use difficult to enforce. Thus, while cyberspace offers new platforms for qualitative leadership studies, with these new possibilities also come new problems. Moreover, Klenke (2007b) argued that the online environment represents a unique cultural context in its own right defined, in part, by the characteristics of the technologies such as speed and media richness.

The future of qualitative leadership research also hinges on greater availability of graduate level courses on qualitative research methods. As leadership educators, we need to ensure that courses in qualitative methodologies are adequately represented in doctoral programs in organizational leadership. Many of these program offer three or four quantitative courses such as a course in multivariate analysis, factor analysis, and linear structural equation modeling but not a single course on qualitative methods. Quantitative courses typically progress to more and more complex levels analysis. A doctoral program should offer at least two courses in quantitative methodologies, covering the more frequently used methods such as content analysis, case studies, and qualitative interviewing in one course and presenting the more advanced methods such as grounded theory, phenomenology, and narrative analysis in the second course. Programs that have added qualitative methods course to their offerings are likely to have a leading scholar in qualitative methodology on the faculty. We also need to ensure that continued training in qualitative is available for faculty who wish to broaden their research skills. Many qualitative conferences offer workshops in various qualitative methods, and there are independent research organizations that provide a smorgasbord of short courses on a variety of qualitative methods.

Reporting practices of empirical finding is another area that can be improved upon. Throughout this book, I have noted examples of inadequate reporting including failure to discuss the relationship between theory and methodology, missing information regarding the exact procedures used, inadequate and incomplete presentation of data, faulty explanations describing how the author(s) connected data with interpretations, and lack of argumentative persuasiveness. Van Maanen (1988b) assesses the situation as follows:

> There are probably rules for writing the persuasive, memorable, and publishable qualitative research article but, rest assured, no one knows what they are (p. xxv).

As qualitative leadership researchers, we need to model good reporting practices. A number of calls have been issued that call for improved accuracy and more detailed description of the methods, results, and interpretations. These calls stress the need for greater communication and transparency of qualitative research reports. Better reporting begins with the identification of the paradigm undergirding the study. However, in many of the studies reviewed in this book, paradigms are rarely mentioned; instead the focus is typically on the actual methods used and the results obtained. A research report that claims to be scientific must have argumentative defensibility, which requires argumentative quality in the eyes of the reading public.

As in the case of ethical guidelines for online research which require a re-assessment of the applicability of traditional ethical guidelines which may have to be redefined, guidelines for writing up qualitative studies also need to be re-evaluated. According to Noris (1997), new quality criteria for qualitative reports are needed. We also need more discussions in the methodological qualitative literature that address writing up qualitative research which is a topic inadequately discussed (Golden-Biddle & Locke, 1997). Developing criteria for quality qualitative scientific reports would go a long way to remediate the current situation.

SUMMARY

In this epilogue, I looked a little bit into the crystal ball to provide the reader with a sense of where qualitative research in the study of leadership may be going. As we noted, there are a number of predictors that encourage increased qualitative research. They include the greater credibility and legitimacy qualitative leadership has achieved, the willingness of gatekeepers such as journal editors to entertain qualitative submission, the addition of qualitative research method courses in doctoral programs in organizational leadership, and the migration of some qualitative research methods to the Internet. Technologies that enhance the rigor of qualitative research have helped legitimation. However, with improvements in the legitimacy of the qualitative paradigm come new responsibilities.

While maintaining the strengths of qualitative methods, we need to address the traditional weaknesses of qualitative methods such as data quality and validity and credibility issues, in whatever they are translated. Making quality concerns a fertile obsession (Lather, 1993) will render empirical research more plausible and convincing. Better typologies of qualitative methods are needed. While virtually all qualitative studies employ more than one method, published method discussion usually positions the research more in one method than others. Rather than using the current compilation of methods which is simply a listing of existing methods, qualitative methods can be categorized as a function of how meaning is constructed under the umbrella of the existing methods or according to values they embrace. Leadership scholars need to apply underutilized methods such as critical theory or AI. Ethical guidelines and quality standards for writing up qualitative research need to be improved.

In sum, qualitative methods have a lot to offer to the study of leadership including a wide range of techniques, emerging theories, and life stories of leaders and followers and cross-cultural concepts that lend themselves to the creation of new knowledge through qualitative research in a discipline that is dynamic and constantly evolving.

REFERENCES

Adler, N. (1996). Global women leaders: An invisible history, an increasingly important future. *The Leadership Quarterly, 7(1)*, 133–161.

Adler, N. (2006). The arts & leadership: Now that we can do anything, what will we do? *Academy of Management Learning and Education, 5(4)*, 486–499.

Adler, P., & Adler, P. (1994). Observation techniques. In N. Denzin, & Y. Lincoln (Eds.). *Handbook of qualitative research* (pp. 377–392). Thousand Oaks, CA: Sage.

Adler, C. L., & Zarchin, Y. R. (2002). The "virtual focus group": Using the internet to reach pregnant women on home bed rest. *Journal of Obstetric, Gynecologic, and Neonatal Nursing, 31(4)*, 418–427.

Agar, C. (1996). *Professional stranger: An informal introduction to ethnography.* New York: Academic Press.

Agar, M., & MacDonald, J. (1995). Focus groups and ethnography. *Human Organization, 54(1)*, 78–86.

Alasuutari, P. (1995). *Qualitative methods and analysis.* London: Sage.

Alexander, C. (1966). A city is not a tree. *Design, 206*, 46–55.

Alexander, J., Comfort, M., Weiner, B., & Bogue, M. (2001). Leadership in collaborative community health partnerships. *Nonprofit Management & Leadership, 12(2)*, 159–175.

Allmendinger, J., & Hackman, J. (1996). Organizations in changing environments: The case of East German symphony orchestras. *Administrative Science Quarterly, 41*, 337–369.

Alvesson, M. (1992). Leadership as social integrative action: A study of a computer consultancy company. *Organization Studies, 13(2)*, 185–209.

Alvesson, M. (1996). Leadership studies: From procedure and abstraction to reflexivity and situation. *The Leadership Quarterly, 7(4)*, 455–485.

Alvesson, M., & Deetz, S. (2000). *Doing critical management research.* London: Sage.

Alvesson, M., & Sveningsson, S. (2003). The great disappearing act: Difficulties in doing leadership. *The Leadership Quarterly, 14(3)*, 359–381.

Alvesson, M., & Wilctt, H. (1992). *Critical management studies*. London: Sage.

Appalachian Regional Commission (ARC) (2005). ARC-designated distressed counties, FY 2005. Retrieved June 2005 from www.arc.gov/index.so?nodeI = 2322.

Appalachian Regional Commission County Economic Status Designations in the Appalachian Region, Fiscal Year. Retrieved January 15, 2007 from http://www.arc.gov/index.do?nodeId = 2934.

Appelbaum, S., Bartolomucci, N., Boulanger, J., Corrigon, R., Doré, I., Girard, C., & Serroni, C. (2004). Organizational citizenship behavior: A case study of culture, leadership and trust. *Management Decision, 42(1)*, 13–40.

Arksey, H., & Knight, P. (1999). *Interviewing in the social sciences*. London: Sage.

Armenakis, A. A., Harris, S. G., & Mossholder, K. W. (1993). Creating readiness for organizational change. *Human Relations, 46(6)*, 681.

Arthur, M. B., Khapova, S. N., & Wilderom, C. P. M. (2005). Career success in a boundaryless career world. *Journal of Organizational Behavior, 26(2)*, 177–202.

Ashforth, B., & Humphrey, R. (1995). Emotions in the workplace: A reappraisal. *Human Relations, 48*, 97–125.

Ashforth, B., & Mael, F. (1989). Social identity theory and the organization. *The Academy of Management Review, 14(1)*, 20–39.

Ashkanasy, N., & Tse, B. (2000). Transformational leadership as management of emotions: A conceptual review. In N. Ashkanasy, C. Härtel, & W. Zerbe (Eds.). *Emotions in working life: Theory, research, and practice* (pp. 221–235). Westport, CT: Quorum.

Atkinson, P. (1988). Ethnomethodology: A critical review. *Annual Review of Sociology, 14*, 441–465.

Atkinson, P., & Silverman, D. (1997). Kundera's immortality: The interview society and the invention of the self. *Qualitative Inquiry, 3(3)*, 304–325.

Avolio, B. J., & Gardner, W. L. (2005). Authentic leadership development: Getting to the root of positive forms of leadership. *The Leadership Quarterly, 16(3)*, 315–338.

Avolio, B. J., Gardner, W. L., Walumbwa, F. O., Luthans, F., & May, D. R. (2004). Unlocking the mask: A look at the process by which authentic leaders impact follower attitudes and behaviors. *The Leadership Quarterly, 15(6)*, 801–823.

Awamleh, R., & Gardner, W. (1999). Perceptions of leader charisma and effectiveness: The effects of vision content, delivery, and organizational performance. *The Leadership Quarterly, 1(3)*, 345–373.

Ayas, K., & Zeniuk, N. (2001). Project-based learning: Building communities of reflective practice. *Management Learning, 32(1)*, 61–76.

Badaracco, J. L. (2001). We don't need another hero. *Harvard Business Review, 79(8)*, 121–127.

Badaracco, J. L. (2002). *Leading quietly: An unorthodox guide to doing the right thing.* Boston, MA: Harvard University School Press.

Bagley, C., & Cancienne, M. (2001). Educational research and intertextual forms of (re)presentation: The case for dancing the data. *Qualitative Inquiry, 7(2)*, 221–237.

Bagley, C., & Cancienne, M. (2002). *Dancing the data.* New York: Peter Lang.

Bal, M. (1985). *Narratology: Introduction to the theory of narrative.* Toronto: University of Toronto Press.

Ball, B., & Smith, G. (1992). *Analyzing visual data.* Newbury Park, CA: Sage.

Bamford, A. (2007). Form: An alternative to validity in qualitative, arts-based researched. Retrieved June 15, 2007 from http://www.aare.edu.au/00pap/bam00016.htm.

Bampton, R., & Cowden, C. (2002). The e-interview. *Forum: Qualitative Social Research, 3(2)*. Retrieved December 16, 2006 from http://www.qualitative-reserach.net/fqs-texte/2-02/2-02bamptoncowton-e.htm.

Bandura, A. (1977). *Social learning theory.* Englewood Cliffs, NJ: Prentice Hall.

Bandura, A. (1994). Self-efficacy. In V. S. Ramachaudran (Ed.). *Encyclopedia of human behavior* (Vol. 4, pp. 77–81). New York: Academic Press.

Bandura, A. (Ed.) (1995). *Self-efficacy in changing societies.* New York: Cambridge University Press.

Bania, M., Nirenberg, J., & Menachem, M. (2000). Leadership in self-managing organizations: Orpheus and a date plantation. *Journal of Leadership Studies, 7(3)*, 3–17.

Banks, M., & Murphy, H. (Eds.) (1997). *Rethinking visual anthropology.* New Haven, CT: Yale University Press.

Banyard, V., & Miller, K. (1998). The powerful potential of qualitative research for community psychology. *American Journal of Community Psychology, 2(4)*, 485–505.

Barbash, I., & Taylor, L. (1997). *Cross-cultural filmmaking.* Berkeley, CA: University of California Press.

Barczak, G., & Wilemon, D. (1992). Successful new product team leaders. *Industrial Marketing Management, 21(1)*, 61–68.

Barge, K., & Olicer, C. (2002). Working with appreciation in managerial practice. *Academy of Management Review, 26(1)*, 124–142.

Barker, R. (1997). How can we train leaders if we do not know what leadership is? *Human Relations, 50(4)*, 343–362.

Barling, J., Slater, F., & Kelloway, E. (2000). Transformational leadership and emotional intelligence: An exploratory study. *Leadership & Organization Development Journal, 21(3)*, 57–161.

Barone, T. (2003). Challenging the educational imagery: Issues of form, substance, and quality in film-based research. *Qualitative Inquiry, 9(2)*, 202–217.

Barthes, R. (1967). *Elements of semiology*. New York: Hill and Wang, The Noonday Press.

Bartlem, C. S., & Locke, E. A. (1981). The Coch and French study: A critique and reinterpretation. *Human Relations, 34(7)*, 555–566.

Basadur, M. (2004). Leading others to think innovatively together: Creative leadership. *The Leadership Quarterly, 15(1)*, 103–121.

Bass, B. (1985). *Performance beyond expectations*. New York: Harper & Row.

Bateson, G. & Mead, M. (1942). *Balinese character: A photographic analysis*. New York: New York Academy of Sciences.

Bavelas, J. (1995). Quantitative versus qualitative? In W. Leeds-Hurwitz (Ed.), *Social approaches to communication* (pp. 49–62). New York: Guilford.

Bazeley, P. (2004). Issues in mixing qualitative and quantitative approaches to research. In R. Buber, J. Gadner, & L. Richards (Eds.). *Applying qualitative methods to marketing management research* (pp. 141–156). Houndsmills, UK: Palgrave Macmillan.

Beck, U. (1992). *Risk society. Towards a new modernity*. Thousand Oaks, CA: Sage.

Becker, H. (1996). The epistemology of qualitative research. In R. Jessor, A. Colby, & R. Schweder (Eds.). *Essays on ethnography and human development* (pp. 53–72). Chicago, IL: Chicago University Press.

Becker, H. (1998). Visual sociology, documentary photography, and photojournalism: It's (almost) all a matter of contexts. In J. Prosser (Ed.). *Image-based research: A sourcebook for qualitative researchers* (pp. 84–96). London: Falmer Press.

Beech, N. (2000). Narrative styles of managers and workers: A tale of star-crossed lovers. *Journal of Applied Behavioral Science, 3(2)*, 210–228.

Bell, W. (1961). *Public leadership*. San Francisco, CA: Chandler.

Bell, P. (2001). Content analysis of visual images. In T. Van Leeuwen, & C. Jewitt (Eds.). *Handbook of visual analysis* (pp. 12–34). Thousand Oaks, CA: Sage.

Benner, P. (Ed.) (1994). *Interpretive phenomenology: Embodiment, caring, and ethics in health and illness*. Thousand Oaks, CA: Sage.

Bennis, W. (2001). The future has no shelf life. In G. S. Warren Bennis, & Thomas G. Cummings (Ed.). The Future of Leadership. Today's top leadership thinkers speak to tomorrow's leaders. San Francisco, CA: Jossey-Bass.

Bennis, W., & Nanus, B. (1985). *Leaders: Strategies for taking charge*. New York: Harper & Row.

Bennis, W., & Thomas, R. (2002). *Geeks and geezers: How era, values, and defining moments shape leaders*. Boston, MA: Harvard University School Press.

Bensimon, E. (1990). Viewing the presidency: Perceptual congruence between presidents and leaders on their campuses. *The Leadership Quarterly, 1(2)*, 71–90.

Bentz, V., & Shapiro, J. (1998). *Mindful enquiry in social research*. Thousand Oaks, CA: Sage.

Berger, P., & Luckman, T. (1967). *The social construction of reality*. Garden City, NY: Anchor.

Bernard, H. (1994). *Research methods in anthropology: Qualitative and quantitative approaches* (2nd edn). Walnut Creek, CA: AltaMira Press.

Beyer, J., & Browning, L. (1999). Transforming an industry in crisis: Charisma, routinization, and supportive cultural leadership. *The Leadership Quarterly, 10(3)*, 483–520.

Biezenski, R. (1996). The struggle for solidarity, 1980–1981: Two waves of leadership in Conflict. *Europe-Asia Studies, 48(2)*, 261–285.

Binswanger, L. (1958). The case of Ellen West (Trans: W. Mendel, & J. Lyons). In R. May, E. Angel, & F. Ellenberger (Eds.).*Existence: A new dimension in psychiatry and psychology* (pp. 237–264). New York: Simon & Schuster.

Bligh, M., Kohles, J., & Meindl, J. (2004a). Charting the language of leadership: A methodological investigation of President Bush and the crisis of 9/11. *Journal of Applied Psychology, 89(3)*, 562–574.

Bligh, M., Kohles, J., & Meindl, J. (2004b). Charisma under crisis: Presidential leadership, rhetoric, and media responses before and after the September 11 terrorist attacks. *The Leadership Quarterly, 15(2)*, 211–239.

Block, P. (1993). *Stewardship: Choosing service over self-interest*. San Francisco, CA: Berrett-Koehler.

Blumenfeld-Jones, D. (1995). Fidelity as a criterion for practicing and evaluating narrative inquiry. In J. Hatch, & R. Wisniewski (Eds.). *Life history and narrative* (pp. 42–65). London: The Palmer Press.

Blumer, H. (1969). *Symbolic interactionism.* Englewood Cliffs, NJ: Prentice Hall.

Bochner, A. (2000). Criteria against ourselves. *Qualitative Inquiry, 6(2)*, 266–272.

Bochner, A. (2001). Narrative's virtues. *Qualitative Inquiry, 7(2)*, 131–157.

Bochner, A., & Ellis, C. (2003). An introduction to the arts and narrative research: Art as inquiry. *Qualitative Inquiry, 9(4)*, 506–514.

Bodgan, R., & Biklen, S. (1982). *Qualitative research for education: An introduction to theory and methods.* Boston, MA: Allyn and Bacon, Inc.

Boje, D. (1995). Stories of the storytelling organization: A postmodern analysis of Disney as "Tamara-Land." *Academy of Management Journal, 38(4)*, 997–1035.

Boje, D. (2001). *Narrative methods for organizational and communication research.* London: Sage.

Borda, O. F. (1985). *Knowledge and people's power. Lessons with peasants in Nicaragua, Mexico and Colombia.* New Delhi, India: Indian Social Institute.

Boudens, C. (2005). The story of work: A narrative analysis of workplace emotion. *Organization Studies, 26(9)*, 1285–1306.

Boulais, A. (2002). Leadership in children's literature: Qualitative analysis from a study based on the Kouzes and Posner leadership framework. *The Journal of Leadership Studies, 8(4)*, 55–63.

Bowe, J., Bowe, M., & Sabin, S. (Eds.) (2000). *Gig.* New York: Crown.

Boyatzis, R. E. (1998). *Transforming qualitative information: Thematic analysis and code development.* Thousand Oaks, CA: Sage.

Boyce, M. (1997). Organizational story and storytelling: A critical review. *Journal of Organizational Change Management, 9(5)*, 5–26.

Brookfield, S. D. (1986). *Understanding and facilitating adult learning.* San Francisco, CA: Jossey-Bass.

Bresnen, M. (1995). All things to all people? Perceptions, attributions, and constructions of leadership. *The Leadership Quarterly, 6(4)*, 495–513.

Brewer, J. (2000). *Ethnography.* Buckingham, England: Open University Press.

Briggs, C. (1986). *Learning how to ask: A sociolinguistic appraisal of the role of the interview in social science research.* Cambridge, UK: Cambridge University Press.

Brown, N., & Barker, R. (2001). Analysis of the communication components found within the situational leadership model: Toward integration of communication and the model. *Journal of Technical Writing and Communication, 31(2)*, 135–157.

Brown, M., & Gioia, D. (2002). Making things click: Distributive leadership in an online division of an offline organization. *The Leadership Quarterly, 13(3)*, 397–419.

Brown, M., & Treviño, L. (2006). Ethical leadership: A review and future directions. *The Leadership Quarterly, 17(6)*, 595–616.

Bruner, J. (1986). *Actual minds, possible worlds.* Cambridge, MA: Harvard University Press.

Bruner, J. (1991). The narrative construction of reality. *Critical Inquiry, 18(1)*, 1–21.

Bryant, M. (2003). Persistence and silence: A narrative analysis to employee responses to organizational change. Retrieved April 29, 2007 from http://socresonline.org.uk/8/4/bryant.html.

Bryant, M. (2006). Talking about change: Understanding employee responses through qualitative research. *Management Decision, 44(2)*, 246–258.

Bryman, A. (1984). The debate about quantitative and qualitative research: A question of method or epistemology. *British Journal of Sociology, 35*, 75–92.

Bryman, A. (1988). *Quality and quantity in social research.* London: Unwin Hyman.

Bryman, A. (1992a). Quantitative and qualitative research: Further reflection on their integration. In J. Brannen (Ed.). *Mixing methods: Qualitative and quantitative research* (pp. 57–78). Brookfield: Avebury.

Bryman, A. (1992b). *Charisma and leadership in organizations.* London: Sage.

Bryman, A. (1993). Charismatic leadership in business organizations: Some neglected issues. *The Leadership Quarterly, 4(3–4)*, 289–304.

Bryman, A. (2004). Qualitative research on leadership: A critical but appreciative review. *The Leadership Quarterly, 15(6)*, 729–769.

Bryman, A. (2006). Integrating qualitative and quantitative research: How is it done? *Qualitative Research, 6(1)*, 97–113.

Bryman, A., Bresnen, M., Beadsworth, A., & Keil, T. (1988). Qualitative research and the Study of leadership. *Human Relations, 41*, 13–30.

Bryman, A., Stephens, M., & Campo, C. (1996). The importance of context: Qualitative research and the study of leadership. *The Leadership Quarterly, 7(3)*, 353–370.

Buford May, R., & Pattillo-McCoy, M. (2000). Do you see what I see? Examining collaborative ethnography. *Qualitative Inquiry, 6(1)*, 65–87.

Bunting, E. (1984). *Smoky night*. New York: Harcourt.

Burns, J. M. (1978). *Leadership*. New York: Harper & Row and The Free Press.

Burns, J. S. (2002). Chaos theory and leadership studies: Exploring unchartered seas. *Journal of Organizational and Leadership Studies, 9(2)*, 42–57.

Burns, J. M. (2003). *Transforming leadership: The new pursuit of happiness*. New York: Atlantic Monthly Press.

Burrell, G., & Morgan. G. (1979). *Sociological paradigms and organizational analysis*. London: Heineman.

Bush, G. (2001). Address to a joint session of Congress and the American people. Retrieved January 10, 2007 from http://www.whitehouse.gov/news/releases/2001/09.

Bushe, G. (1999). Advances in appreciative inquiry as an organizational development intervention. *Organizational Development Journal, 17(2)*, 61–68.

Buttner, H. (2001). Examining female entrepreneurs' management style: An application of a relational frame. *Journal of Business Ethics, 29*, 253–269.

Bystrom, D., Robertson, T., & Banwart, M. (2001). Framing the fight. *American Behavioral Scientist, 44(12)*, 1999–2013.

Caelli, K. (2001). Engaging with phenomenology: Is it more of a challenge than it needs to be? *Qualitative Health Research, 11*, 273–282.

Caelli, K., Ray, L., & Mill, J. (2003). "Clear as mud": Toward greater clarity in generic qualitative research. *International Journal of Qualitative Research Methods, 2(2)*. Article 1. Retrieved October 25, 2006 from http://www.ualberta.ca/~ijqm/backissues/pdf.caellietal.pdf.

Cameron, K. S., Dutton, J. E., & Quinn, R. E. (2003). *Positive organizational scholarship: Foundations of a new discipline*. San Francisco, CA: Berrett-Koehler.

Cameron, M., Schaffer, M., & Hyeon-Ae, P. (2001). Nursing students' experience of ethical problems and use of ethical decision-making. *Nursing Ethics, 8*, 432–448.

Cancienne, M., & Snowber, C. (2003). Writing rhythm: Movement as method. *Qualitative Inquiry, 9(2)*, 237–253.

Caracelli, V., & Greene, J. (1997). Crafting mixed methods valuation designs. In J. Greene, & V. Caracelli (Eds.). *Advances in mixed-methods evaluation: The challenges and benefits of integrating diverse paradigms* (New Directions for Evaluation, No. 74), (pp. 19–32). San Francisco, CA: Jossey-Bass.

Carley, K. (1997). Extracting team mental models through textual analysis. *Journal of Organizational Behavior, 18*, 533–558.

Carr, D. (1986). *Time, narrative and history*. Bloomington, IN: Indiana University Press.

Carr, A. (2003). Art as a form of knowledge: Implications for critical management. In A. Carr, & P. Hancock (Eds.). *Arts and aesthetics at work* (pp. 7–37). Hampshire, UK: Palgrave.

Carspecken, P. (1995). *Critical ethnography in educational research: A theoretical and Practical guide*. London: Routledge.

Carspecken, P., & Apple, M. (1992). Critical qualitative research: Theory, methodology, and practice. In M. LeCompte, W. Millroy, & J. Preissle (Eds.). *The handbook of qualitative research in education* (pp. 507–553). San Diego: Academic Press.

Carspecken, P., & Cordeiro, P. (1995). Being, doing, and becoming: Textual interpretations of social identity and a case study. *Qualitative Inquiry, 1(1)*, 87–109.

Cassell, C., Symon, G., Buehring, A., & Johnson, P. (2006). The role and status of Qualitative methods in management research: An empirical account. *Management Decision, 44(2)*, 290–303.

Cederblom, J., & Paulsen, D. W. (2001). *Critical reasoning*. Belmont, CA: Wadsworth Thompson Learning.

Cepeda, G., & Martin, D. (2005). A review of case studies publishing in management decision 2003–2004. *Management Decision, 43(6)*, 851–876.

Cha, S., & Edmondson, A. (2006). When values backfire: Leadership, attribution, and disenchantment in a values-driven organization. *The Leadership Quarterly, 17(1)*, 57–78.

Chamberlain, K. (1999). Methodolatry and qualitative health research. *Journal of Health Psychology, 5(3)*, 285–296.

Chamberlayne, P., Bornat, J., & Wengraf, T. (2000). *The turn to biographical methods in social science*. London: Routledge.

Chang, E. C. (2000). *Optimism & pessimism*. Washington, DC: American Psychological Association.

Charmaz, K. (1990). Discovering chronic illness: Using grounded theory. *Social Science & Medicine, 30*, 1161–1172.

Charmaz, K. (2003). Grounded theory: Objectivist and constructivist methods. In N. Denzin, & Y. Lincoln (Eds.). *Strategies of qualitative inquiry* (pp. 249–291). Thousand Oaks, CA: Sage.

Charmaz, K., & Mitchell, R. (1997). The myth of silent authorship: Self, substance, and style in ethnographic writing. In R. Hertz (Ed.). *Reflexivity and voice* (pp. 193–215). London: Sage.

Chatman, S. (1978). *Story and discourse; narrative structure in fiction and film*. Ithaca, NY: Cornell University Press.

Chen, C., & Meindl, J. (1991). The construction of leadership images in the popular press: The case of Donald Burr and People express. *Administrative Science Quarterly, 36*, 521–551.

Choi, Y., & Mai-Dalton, R. (1999). The model of follower responses to self-sacrificial leadership: An empirical test. *The Leadership Quarterly, 9(4)*, 475–501.

Chodrow, N. (1978). *The reproduction of mothering: Psychoanalysis and the sociology of gender*. Berkeley, CA: University of California Press.

Chrislip, D. D., & Larson, C. E. (1994).*Collaborative leadership: How citizens and civic leaders can make a difference*. San Francisco, CA: Jossey-Bass.

Christians, C. (2005). Ethics and politics in qualitative research. In N. Denzin, & Y. Lincoln (Eds.). *The SAGE handbook of qualitative research* (3rd edn) (pp. 139–164). Thousand Oaks, CA: Sage.

Christie, R., & Geis, F. (1970). *Studies in Machiavellianism*. New York: Academic Press.

Clandinin, D., & Connelly, F. (1994). Personal experience methods. In N. Denzin, & Y. Lincoln (Eds.). *Handbook of qualitative research* (pp. 413–427). Thousand Oaks, CA: Sage.

Clifton, D., & Nelson, R. (1996). *Soar with your strengths*. New York: Dell Publishing.

Coffey, P. (1999). *The ethnographic self*. London: Sage.

Coffey, A., & Atkinson, P. (1996). *Making sense of qualitative data: Complementary research strategies*. Thousand Oaks, CA: Sage.

Cohen, J. (1960). A coefficient for agreement for nominal scales. *Educational and Psychological Measurement, 20*, 37–46.

Cohen, J. (1968). Weighted kappa: Nominal scale agreement with provision for scaled disagreement for partial credit. *Psychological Bulletin, 70*, 213–220.

Colliers, M. (2001). Approaches to analysis in visual anthropology. In T. Van Leeuwen, & C. Jewitt (Eds.). *Handbook of visual analysis* (pp. 35–60). Thousand Oaks, CA: Sage.

Collins, M., & Porras, J. (1994). *Built to last*. New York: Harper Collins.

Collins, J. C., & Porras, J. I. (1995). Organizational vision and visionary organizations. *California Management Review, 34(1)*, 30–52.

Collum, D. (1986). Building democracy in the mountains: The legacy of the Highlander center. *Sojourners: An Independent Christian Monthly, 15(4)*, 26–31.

Coltman, R. (1998). *The language of hermeneutics: Gadamer and Heidegger in dialogue.* Albany, NY: SUNY.

Conger, J. (1998). Qualitative research as the cornerstone methodology for understanding leadership. *The Leadership Quarterly, 10(3),* 107–121.

Conger, J. A., & Kanungo, R. N. (1988). The empowerment process: Integrating theory and practice. *Academy of Management Review, 13(3),* 471–482.

Conger, J., & Kanungo, R. (1998). *Charismatic leadership in organizations.* Thousand Oaks, CA: Sage.

Conklin, H. (1968). Ethnography. In D. Sills (Ed.). *International encyclopedia of the Social Sciences, 5,* (pp. 115–205). New York: Free Press.

Connelly, M., & Clandinin, J. (1990). Stories of experience and narrative inquiry. *Educational Researcher, 19(5),* 2–14.

Cooke, K., Fassinger, R., Prosser, J., Mejia, B., & Luna, J. (2001). Voces abriendo Caminons (Voices forging paths): A qualitative study of the career development of notable Latinas. *Journal of Counseling Psychology, 48(3),* 286–300.

Cooper, C., Scandura, T., & Schriesheim, C. (2005). Looking forward but learning from our past: Potential challenges to developing authentic leadership theory and authentic leaders. *The Leadership Quarterly, 16(3),* 475–493.

Cooperrider, D. (1990). Positive image, positive action: The affirmative basis of organizing. In S. Srivastva, & D. Cooperrider (Eds.). *Appreciative management and leadership* (pp. 91–125). San Francisco, CA: Jossey-Bass.

Cooperrider, D., & Srivastva, S. (1987). Appreciative inquiry in organizational life. In W. Pasmore, & R. Woodman (Eds.). *Research in organizational change and development, 1,* (pp. 129–169). Greenwich, CT: JAI Press.

Cooperrider, D., & Whitney, D. (1999). *Appreciative inquiry.* San Francisco, CA: Koehler-Berrett.

Cooperrider, D., & Whitney, D. (2000). *Collaborating for change: Appreciative inquiry.* San Francisco, CA: Berrett-Koehler.

Cooperrider, D., & Whitney, D. (2005). *Appreciative inquiry: A positive revolution in change.* San Francisco, CA: Berrett-Koehler.

Cooperrider, D., Sorensen, P., Whitney, D., & Yaeger, T. (Eds.) (2000). *Appreciative inquiry: Rethinking human organization toward a positive theory of change.* Champaign, IL: Stipes.

Cooperrider, D., Sorensen, P., Yaeger, T., & Whitney, D. (Eds.) (2001). *Appreciative inquiry: An emerging direction for organizational development.* Champaign, IL: Stipes.

Corbin, J., & Strauss, A. (1990). Grounded theory research: Procedures, canons, and evaluative criteria. *Qualitative Sociology, 13*, 3–21.

Corley, K., & Goia, D. (2004). Identity ambiguity and change in the wake of a corporate spin-off. *Administrative Science Quarterly, 49*, 173–208.

Cortazzi, M. (2001). Narrative analysis in ethnography. In P. Atkinson, A. Coffey, S. Delamont, J. Lofland, & L. Lofland (Eds.). *Handbook of ethnography* (pp. 384–394). London: Sage.

Craig, R. (1981). Generalization of Scott's index of intercoder agreement. *Public Opinion Quarterly, 45*, 260–264.

Crainer, S. (2000).*The management century: A critical review of 20th century thought and practice*. San Francisco, CA: Jossey-Bass.

Crawford, D. (2005). The bases for executive action: A multiple case study of leadership in the highly regulated long-term healthcare industry. Unpublished doctoral dissertation. Regent University, Virginia Beach, VA.

Creswell, J. (1994). *Research design: Qualitative & qualitative approaches*. Thousand Oaks, CA: Sage.

Creswell, J. (1998). *Qualitative inquiry and research design: Choosing among five traditions*. Thousand Oaks, CA: Sage.

Creswell, J. (2005). *Educational research: Planning, conducting, and evaluating qualitative research*. Upper Saddle River, NJ: Merrill Prentice Hall Pearson Education.

Creswell, J., & Maietta, J. (2002). Qualitative research. In D. Miller, & N. Salkind (Eds.). *Handbook of research design and social science measurement* (pp. 143–183). Thousand Oaks, CA: Sage.

Cronin, T. E. (1987). Leadership and democracy. *Liberal Education, 73(2)*, 35–38.

Crossley, M. L. (2000). *Introducing narrative psychology: Self, trauma and the construction of meaning*. Philadelphia, PA: Open University Press.

Cupchik, G. (2001). Constructivist realisms: An ontology that encompasses positivist and constructivist approaches to the social sciences. Retrieved October 21, 2006 from http://qualitative-research.net/fqs-eng.htm.

Czarniawska, B. (1997). *A narrative approach to organization studies*. Thousand Oaks, CA: Sage.

Czarniawska, B. (2000). *Narratives in social science research.* London: Sage.

Danzinger, K. (1990). *Constructing the subject: The history of psychological research*. Cambridge, UK: Cambridge University Press.

Darnell, R. (2001). *Invisible genealogies: A history of Americanist anthropology.* Lincoln, NB: University of Nebraska Press.

Datta, L. (1997). A pragmatic basis for mixed methods designs. In J. Greene, & V. Caracelli (Eds.). *Advances in mixed methods evaluations: The challenges and benefits of integrating diverse paradigm (New Directions for Evaluation, No. 74,* pp. 33–46). San Francisco, CA: Jossey-Bass.

Davidson, J. C., & Caddell, D. P. (1994). Religion and the meaning of work. *Journal for the Scientific Study of Religion, 33,* 135–147.

Davis, J., Schoorman, F., & Donaldson, L. (1997). Toward a stewardship theory of management. *Academy of Management Review, 22(1),* 20–47.

Day, D. (2001). Leadership development: A review in context. *The Leadership Quarterly, 10(4),* 581–613.

Day Sclater, S. (2003). The arts and narrative research—Art as inquiry: An epilogue. *Qualitative Inquiry, 9(4),* 621–624.

Dean, J. (1987). Building the future: The justification process for new technology. In J. Pennings, & A. Buitendam (Eds.). *New technology as organizational intervention* (pp. 35–58). Cambridge, MA: Ballinger.

Delgado, R. (Ed.) (1995). *Critical race theory: The cutting edge.* Philadelphia: Temple University Press.

Deluga, R. (1997). Relationship among American presidential charismatic leadership, narcissism, and rated performance. *The Leadership Quarterly, 8(1),* 49–65.

Deluga, R. (1998). American presidential proactivity, charismatic leadership, and rated performance. *The Leadership Quarterly, 9(3),* 265–291.

Deluga, R. (2001). American presidential Machiavellianism: Implications for charismatic leadership and rated performance. *The Leadership Quarterly, 12,* 339–363.

Den Hartog, D., & Verburg, R. (1997). Charisma and rhetoric: Communicative techniques for international business leaders. *The Leadership Quarterly, 8(4),* 355–391.

Denis, J., Langley, A., & Cazale, L. (1996). Leadership and strategic change under ambiguity. *Organization Studies, 17(4),* 673–699.

Denning, S. (2004). Telling tales. *Harvard Business Review, 82(5),* 122–127.

Denning, S. (2007). *The leader's guide to storytelling: Mastering the art and discipline of business narrative.* International Leadership Association Member Connector, 5–10.

Densten, I., & Gray, J. (1998). The case for using both latent and manifest variables to investigate management-by-exception. *Journal of Leadership Studies, 5(3),* 80–92.

Denyer, D., & Tranfield, D. (2006). Using qualitative research synthesis to build an actionable knowledge base. *Management Decision, 44(2)*, 213–227.

Denzin, N. (1989). *Interpretive biography*. London: Sage.

Denzin, N. (1992). *Symbolic interactionism and cultural studies*. Cambridge, UK: Basil Blackwell.

Denzin, N. K. (1994). The art and politics of interpretation. In N. Denzin & Y. Lincoln (Eds.). *Handbook of qualitative research* (pp. 500–515). Thousand Oaks, CA: Sage.

Denzin, N. (2000). Aesthetics and the practice of qualitative inquiry, *Qualitative Inquiry, 6(2)*, 256–265.

Denzin, N., & Lincoln, Y. (1994). Introduction: Entering the field of qualitative research. In N. Denzin, & Y. Lincoln (Eds.). *Handbook of qualitative research* (pp. 105–117). Thousand Oaks, CA: Sage.

Denzin, N., & Lincoln, Y. (Eds.) (2000). *Handbook of qualitative research* (2nd edn). Thousand Oaks, CA: Sage.

Denzin, N., & Lincoln, Y. (Eds.) (2005). *Handbook of qualitative research* (3rd edn). Thousand Oaks, CA: Sage.

de Sales Turner (2003). Horizons revealed: From methodology to method. *International Journal of Qualitative Methods, 2(1)*. Article 1. Retrieved February 15, 2007 from http://www.ualberta.ca/~iiqm/backissues/2_1/html/turner.htm.

Desmond, J. (1997). Embodying difference: Issues in dance and cultural studies. In J. Desmond (Ed.). *Meaning in motion: New cultural studies of dance* (pp. 29–54). Durham, NC: Duke University Press.

DeVault, M. (1990). Talking and listening from women's standpoint: Feminist strategies for interviewing and analysis. *Social Problems, 37*, 96–116.

De Waal, P. (2005). *On pragmatism*. Belmont, NJ: Wadsworth.

Dickinson, P., & Svensen, N. (2000). *Beautiful corporations: Corporate style in action*. London: Prentice Hall.

Diggins, J. (1994). *The promise of pragmatism: Modernism and the crisis of knowledge and authority*. Chicago, IL: University of Chicago Press.

Dingwall, R. (1997). Accounts, interviews, and observations. In G. Miller, & R. Dingwall (Eds.). *Context and method of qualitative research* (pp. 51–65). London: Sage.

Dobrow, S. R. (2004). *Extreme subjective career success: A new integrated view of having a calling*. Academy of Management. Conference Best Paper Proceedings.

Doucet, A., & Mauthner, N. (2002). Knowing responsibly: Linking ethics, research practice and epistemology. In M. Mauthner, M. Birch, J. Jessop, & T. Miller (Eds.). *Ethics in qualitative research* (pp. 123–145). Thousand Oak, CA: Sage.

Douglas, D. (2006). Intransitivities to managerial decisions: A grounded theory case. *Management Decision, 44(2)*, 259–275.

Drucker, P. F. (1995). Mary Parker Follett: Prophet of management. In P. Graham (Ed.).*Mary Parker Follett-Prophet of management: A celebration of writings from the 1920s* (pp. 1–10). Boston, MA: Harvard Business Press.

Dune, D., & Martin, R. (2006). Design thinking and how it will change management: An interview and discussion. *Academy of Management Learning and Education, 5(4)*, 512–523.

Dyck, B. (1994). From airy-fairy ideas to concrete realities: The case of shared farming. *The Leadership Quarterly, 5(3–4)*, 227–246.

Eagleton, T. (1983). *Literary theory: An introduction.* Oxford: Basil Blackwell.

Eagly, A., & Johnson, B. (1990). Gender and leadership style: A meta-analysis. *Psychological Bulletin, 108*, 233–256.

Eckstein, H. (2002). Case study and theory in political science. In R. Gomm, M. Hammersley, & P. Foster (Eds.). *Case study method: Key issues, key texts* (pp. 119–163). London: Sage.

Edie, J. (1987). *Edmund Husserl's phenomenology: A critical commentary.* Bloomington: Indiana University Press.

Edström, A., & Jönsson, S. (1998). Sventskt ledarskap. In B. Czarniawska (Ed). *Organisiationsteori på svenska.* Malmö: Liber Ekonomi.

Ehrhart, M. G., & Klein, K. J. (2001). Predicting followers' preferences for charismatic leadership: The influence of follower values and personality. *The Leadership Quarterly, 12(2)*, 153–180.

Eisenhardt, K. (1989). Building theories from case study research. *Academy of Management Review, 14(4)*, 532–550.

Eisenhardt, K., & Bourgeois, L. (1988). Politics of strategic decision making in high-velocity environments: Toward a midrange theory. *Academy of Management Journal, 31(4)*, 737–770.

Eisner, E. (1991). *The enlightened eye: Qualitative inquiry and the enhancement of educational practice.* New York: Macmillan Publishing Company.

Eisner, E. (1997). The promises and perils of alternative forms of data representation. *Educational Researcher, 26(6)*, 4–20.

Eisner, E. (2001). Concerns and aspirations for qualitative research in the new millennium. *Qualitative Research, 1(2)*, 135–145.

Eisner, E., & Peshkin, A. (Eds.) (1990). *Qualitative inquiry in education: The continuing debate*. New York: Teachers College Press.

Elder, G. (1995). Life trajectories in changing societies. In A. Bandura (Ed.). *Self-efficacy in changing societies* (pp. 46–68). Cambridge, UK: Cambridge University Press.

Elliott, J. (2005). *Using narrative in social research: Qualitative and quantitative approaches*. Thousand Oaks, CA: Sage.

Ellis, C. (2004). *The ethnographic I: A methodological novel about teaching and doing ethnography*. Walnut Creek, CA: AltaMira.

Ellis, C., & Brochner, A. (2000). Autoethnography, personal narrative, reflexivity: Researcher as subject. In N. Denzin, & Y. Lincolns (Eds.). *Handbook of qualitative research* (2nd edn) (pp. 773–768). Thousand Oaks, CA: Sage.

Elms, A. (1994). *Uncovering lives: The uneasy alliance of biography and psychology*. New York: Oxford University Press.

Emmison, M., & Smith, P. (2000). *Researching the visual*. Thousand Oaks, CA: Sage.

Ewenstein, B., & Whyte, J. (2007). Beyond words: Aesthetic knowledge and knowing in organizations. *Organization Studies, 28(5)*, 689–708.

Faux, J. (2006). *The global class war*. Hoboken, NJ: John Wiley and Sons.

Feyerherm, A. (1994). Leadership in collaboration: A longitudinal study of two interorganizational rule making groups. *The Leadership Quarterly, 5(3–4)*, 253–270.

Fiedler, F. (1967). *A theory of leadership effectiveness*. New York: McGraw-Hill.

Field, J. (2003). *Social capital*. New York: Routledge.

Fielding, N. (Ed.) (2002). *Interviewing*. Thousand Oaks, CA: Sage Benchmarks in Social Research.

Fielding, N., & Lee, R. (1998). *Computer analysis and qualitative research*. London: Sage.

Filley, A. C., House, R. J., & Kerr, S. (1976). *Managerial processes and organizational behavior*. Glenview, IL: Scott, Foresman and Company.

Fineman, S. (1996). Emotional subtexts in corporate greening. *Organization Studies, 17(2)*, 479–500.

Finley, S. (2003). Arts-based inquiry in QI: Seven years from crisis to guerilla warfare. *Qualitative Inquiry, 9(2)*, 281–296.

Firestone, W. (1987). Meaning in method: The rhetoric of quantitative and qualitative research. *Educational Researcher, 16,* 16–21.

Firestone, W., & Herriott, R. (1994). Multisite qualitative policy research; some design and implementation issues. In D. Fetterman (Ed.). *Ethnography in educational evaluation* (pp. 67–93). Beverly Hills, CA: Sage.

Fisher, K., & Miller, A. (1993). Leading self-directed work teams. New York: McGraw-Hill.

Flanagan, J. (1954). The critical incident technique. *Psychological Bulletin, 51,* 327–358.

Fleischman, P. R. (1994). *The healing spirit: Explorations in religion and psychotherapy.* Cleveland, OH: Bonne Chance Press.

Fletcher, J. (2004). The paradox of postheroic leadership: An essay on gender, power, and transformational change. *The Leadership Quarterly, 15(5),* 647–661.

Fletcher, J., & Kaeufer K. (2003). Paradox and possibility. In C. Pearce & J. Conger (Eds.). Reframing the hows and whys of leadership. London: Sage.

Flick, U. (1998). *An introduction to qualitative research.* Thousand Oaks, CA: Sage.

Flick, U. (2002). *An introduction to qualitative research.* Thousand Oaks, CA: Sage.

Flyvberg, B. (2006). Five misunderstandings about case study research. *Qualitative Inquiry, 12(2),* 219–245.

Follett, M. P. (1896). *The Speaker of the House of Representatives.* New York: Longmans, Green.

Follett, M. P. (1918). *The new state: Group organization, the solution of popular government.* New York: Longmans, Green.

Follett, M. P. (1919). Community is a process. *Philosophical Review, 28,* 576–588.

Follett, M. P. (1924). *Creative experience.* New York: Longmans, Green and Co.

Follett, M. P. (1928/1970). The teacher-student relation. *Administrative Science Quarterly, 15(2),* 137–148.

Follett, M. P. (1941). Leadership theory and practice. In H. C. Metcalf & L. Urwick (Eds.). *Dynamic administration: The collected papers of Mary Parker Follett* (pp. 281–294). New York: Harper.

Follett, M. P. (1949). *Freedom & co-ordination: Lectures in business organization* (L. Urwick, ed.). London: Management Publications Trust, Ltd.

Fontana, A. (2002). Postmodern trends in interviewing. In J. Gubrium, & J. Holstein (Eds.). *Handbook of interview research* (pp. 161–180). Thousand Oaks, CA: Sage.

Fontana, A., & Frey, J. (1994). Interviewing: The art of science. In N. Denzin, & Y. Lincoln (Eds.). *Handbook of qualitative research* (pp. 361–376). Thousand Oaks, CA: Sage.

Fontana, A., & Frey, J. (2000). The interview: From structured questions to negotiated text. In N. Denzin, & Y. Lincolns (Eds.).*Handbook of qualitative research* (2nd edn) (pp. 645–670). London: Sage.

Fouche, F. (1993). Phenomenological theory of human science. In J. Snyman (Ed.). *Conceptions of social inquiry* (pp. 87–112). Johannesburg, South Africa: Heineman.

Fowler, J. W. (1981). *Stages of faith*. New York: Harper & Row.

Fox, E. M. (1970). The dynamics of constructive change in the thought of Mary Parker Follett. Dissertation Abstracts International, 31*(06), 2549 (UMI No. 7023437)*.

Frank, A. (1995). *The wounded storyteller: Body, illness and ethics*. Chicago, IL: Chicago University Press.

Frederickson, J. (1983). Strategic process research: Questions and recommendations. *Academy of Management Review, 8(4)*, 565–575.

Freeman, M. (1984). History, narrative, and life-span developmental knowledge. *Human Development, 27*, 1–19.

Freidman, J. (1992). *Empowerment: The politics of alternative development*. Cambridge, MA: Blackwell.

Freire, P. (1990). *Pedagogy of the oppressed* (32nd edn). New York: Continuum.

French, J., & Raven, B. (1959). The bases of social power. In D. Cartwright (Ed.). *Studies in social power* (pp. 150–167). Ann Arbor: University of Michigan, Institute of Social Research.

Fried, M. (1968). Deprivation and migration: Dilemmas of causal interpretation. In D. P. Moynihan (Ed.). *On understanding poverty. Perspectives from the social sciences* (pp. 111–159). New York: Basic Books.

Fry, L. W. (2003). Toward a theory of spiritual leadership. *The Leadership Quarterly, 14(6)*, 693–727.

Fry, L. (2005). Toward a theory of ethical and spiritual well-being and corporate social responsibility through spiritual leadership. In R. Giacalone, C. Jurkiewicz, & C. Dunn (Eds.). *Positive psychology in business ethics and corporate social responsibility* (pp. 47–840). Greenwich, CT: Information Age Publishing.

Fry, L. W., Vitucci, S., & Cedillo, M. (2005). Spiritual leadership and army transformation: Theory, measurement and establishing a baseline. *Leadership Quarterly, 16*, 835–862.

Fyfe, G., & Law, J. (1988). Introduction: On the invisibility of the visible. In G. Fyfe, & J. Law (Eds.). *Picturing power: Visual depiction and social relations* (pp. 1–14). London: Routledge.

Gabriel, Y. (1997). Meeting God: When organizational members come face to face with the supreme leader. *Human Relations, 50,* 315–343.

Gabriel, Y. (1998). The use of stories. In G. Symon, & C. Cassell (Eds.). *Qualitative methods and analysis in organizational research* (pp. 135–160). London: Sage.

Gadamer, H. (1976). *Philosophical hermeneutics* (Trans: D. Linge). Berkeley, CA: University of California Press.

Gadamer, H. (1985). The origins of philosophical hermeneutics. In H. Gadamer (Ed.). *Philosophical apprenticeships* (Trans: R. Sullivan) (pp. 177–193). Cambridge, MA: MIT Press.

Gadamer, H. (1989). *Truth and method* (2nd edn) (Trans: J. Weisnheimer & D. Marshall). New York: Continuum (Original work published in 1972).

Gadamer, H. (1996). *The enigma of health: The art of healing in a scientific age* (Trans: J. Gaiger & N. Walker). Stanford, CA: Stanford University Press.

Gagliardi, P. (1990). Artifacts as pathways and remains of organizational life. In P. Gagliardi (Ed.). *Symbols and artifacts: Views of the corporate landscape* (pp. 3–38). New York: de Gruyter.

Gagliardi, P. (1996). Exploring the aesthetic side of organizational life. In S. Clegg, C. Hardy, & W. Nord (Eds.). *Handbook of organization studies* (pp. 565–580). London: Sage.

Galanes, G. (2003). In their own words: An exploratory study of bona fide group leaders. *Small Group Research, 34(6),* 741–770.

Gardner, G. (1977). Workers' participation: A critical evaluation of Coch and French. *Human Relations, 30(12),* 1071–1078.

Gardner, W., & Stough, C. (2002). Examining the relationship between leadership and emotional intelligence in senior level managers. *Leadership & Organization Development Journal, 23(1),* 68–78.

Gardner, W., Avolio, B., Luthans, F., May, D., & Walumba, F. (2005). "Can you see the real me?" A self-based model of authentic leader and follower development. *The Leadership Quarterly, 16(3),* 343–372.

Gattiker, U. E., & Larwood, L. (1988). Predictors for managers' career mobility, success and satisfaction. *Human Relations, 41,* 569–591.

Gaventa, J. (1982). *Power and powerlessness: Quiescence and rebellion in an Appalachian valley.* Chicago, IL: University of Illinois Press.

Geertz, C. (1973). *The interpretation of cultures.* New York: Basic Books.

George, B. (2003). *Authentic leadership: Rediscovering the secrets to creating lasting value.* San Francisco, CA: Jossey-Bass.

Gephart, R. (1999). Paradigms and research methods. *Research Forum, 4(Summer).* Retrieved August 24, 2006 from http://aom.pace.edu/rmd/1999_RMD_Forum_Paradigms_and Research_Methods.htm.

Gephart, R. (2004). Qualitative research and the academy of management journal. *Academy of Management Journal 47(4)*, 454–462.

Gergen, K. (1985). The social constructionist movement in modern psychology. *American Psychologist, 40(3)*, 266–275.

Gergen, K. (1994). *Realities and relationships: Soundings in social constructivism.* Cambridge, MA: Harvard University Press.

Gergen, K. J., & Gergen, M. M. (1986). Narrative form and the construction of psychological science. In T. R. Sarbin (Ed.). *Narrative psychology: The storied nature of human conduct* (pp. 22–44). New York: Praeger.

Gergen, M., & Gergen, K. (2003). Qualitative inquiry: Tensions and transformations. In N. Denzin, & Y. Lincoln (Eds.). *The landscape of qualitative research* (2nd edn) (pp. 167–207). Thousand Oaks, CA: Sage.

Gersick, C. (1994). Pacing strategic change: The case of a new venture. *Academy of Management Journal, 37(1)*, 9–45.

Giacopassi, D., Nicholas, D., & Stitt, G. (1999). Attitudes toward community leaders in new casino jurisdictions regarding casino gambling's effects on crime and quality of life. *Journal of Gambling Studies, 15(2)*, 123–147.

Gibson, F., Fiedler, F., & Barrett, K. (1993). Stress, babble, and the utilization of the leader's intellectual abilities. *The Leadership Quarterly, 4(2)*, 189–208.

Giddens, A. (1991). *Modernity and self-identity. Self and society in the late modern age.* Stanford, CA: Stanford University Press.

Giddens, A. (1993). *New rules of sociological mind* (2nd edn.). Stanford, CA: Stanford University Press.

Gioia, D., & Chittipeddi, K. (1991). Sensemaking and sensegiving in strategic change initiation. *Strategic Management Journal, 12*, 433–448.

Giorgi, A. (1994). A phenomenological perspective on certain qualitative research methods. *Journal of Phenomenological Psychology, 25*, 191–220.

Giorgi, A. (1997). The theory, practice, and evaluation of the phenomenological method as a qualitative procedure. *Journal of Phenomenological Psychology, 28*, 235–260.

Givens, L. (2004). Mini-disc recorder: A new approach for qualitative interviewing. *International Journal of Qualitative Methods,3(2)*. Article 5. Retrieved February 2, 2007 from http://www.ualberta.ca/~iiqm/backissues/3_2/pdf/given.pdf

Gladwell, M. (2000). *The tipping point.* New York: Little, Brown and Company.

Glaser, B. (1978). *Theoretical sensitivity.* Mill Valley, CA: Sociology Press.

Glaser, B. (1992). *Emergence vs. forcing: Basics of grounded theory analysis.* Mill Valley, CA: Sociology Press.

Glaser, B. (1996). The challenge of campaign watching: Seven lessons from participant observations. *Political Science and Politics, 29*, 533–557.

Glaser, B. (1998). *Doing grounded theory: Issues and discussions.* Mill Valley, CA: Sociology Press.

Glaser, B. (1999). The future of grounded theory. *Qualitative Health Research, 6*, 836–845.

Glaser, B. (2001). *The grounded theory: Conceptualizations contrasted with description.* Mill Valley, CA: Sociology Press.

Glaser, B. (2002). Conceptualization: On theory and theorizing using grounded theory. *International Journal of Qualitative Methods, 1(2)*. Article 3. Retrieved March 26, 2007 from http://www.ualberta.ca/~ijqm/.

Glaser, B., & Strauss, A. (1967). *The discovery of grounded theory.* Chicago, IL: Aldine.

Glasmeier, A. K., & Farrigan, T. L. (2003). Poverty, sustainability, the culture of despair: Can sustainable development strategies support poverty alleviation in America's most environmentally challenged communities? *Annals, AAPSS, 590 (November)*, 56–70.

Glass, G. (1976). Primary, secondary, and meta-analysis of research. *Educational Researcher, 5*, 3–8.

Goering, P., & Streiner, D. (1996). Reconcilable differences: The marriage of qualitative and quantitative methods. *Canadian Journal of Psychiatry, 41(October)*, 491–497.

Golan, G., & Wanta, W. (2001). Second-level agenda setting in the New Hampshire Primary: A comparison of coverage of three primary newspapers and public perceptions of candidates. *Journalism and Mass Communication Quarterly, 78(2)*, 247–259.

Golden-Biddle, K., & Locke, K. (1997). *Composing qualitative research*. Thousand Oaks, CA: Sage.

Goleman, D. (1995). *Emotional intelligence*. New York: Bantam Books.

Golfashani, N. (2003). Understanding reliability and validity in qualitative research. *The Qualitative Report, 8(3)*, 597–606.

Graen, G. (2006). In the eye of the beholder: Cross-cultural lessons in leadership from the project GLOBE. *Academy of Management Perspectives, 20(4)*, 95–101.

Greenbaum, T. (2002). The case against internet focus groups. *MRA Alert Newsletter, 40(4)*. Retrieved January 12, 2007 from http://www.groupsplus.com/pages/case2.htm.

Greene, A., Black, J., & Ackers, P. (2000). The union makes us strong? A study of the dynamics of workplace union leadership at two UK manufacturing plants. *British Journal of Industrial Relations, 38(1)*, 75–93.

Greene, J., & Caracelli, V. (2003). Making paradigm sense of mixed method practice. In A. Tashakkori, & C. Teddlie (Eds.). *Handbook of mixed methods in social and behavioral research* (pp. 91–110). Thousand Oaks, CA: Sage.

Greene, J., Caracelli, V., & Graham, W. (1989). Toward a conceptual framework for mixed-methods evaluation designs. *Educational Evaluation and Policy Analysis, 11(3)*, 255–274.

Greenleaf, R. K. (1970). *The servant as leader*. Indianapolis, IN: K. The Robert Greenleaf Center.

Greenleaf, R. (1977). *Servant leadership: A journey into the nature of legitimate power and greatness*. New York: Paulist Press and San Francisco, CA: Jossey-Bass.

Greiner, L., & Bhambri, A. (1998). CEO intervention and dynamics of deliberate strategic change. *Strategic Management Journal, 10*, 67–86.

Grondin, J. (1994). *Introduction to philosophical hermeneutics* (Trans: J. Weinsheimer). New Haven, CT: Yale University Press.

Grondin, J. (1995). *Sources of hermeneutics*. Albany, NY: SUNY

Gronn, P. (1999). Substituting for leadership: The neglected role of the leadership couple. *The Leadership Quarterly, 10(1)*, 41–62.

Grummet, M. (1988). *Bitter milk: Women and teaching*. Amherst: University of Massachusetts Press.

Guba, E. (1981). Criteria for assessing trustworthiness in naturalistic inquiry. *Educational Communication and Technology, 29*, 79–92.

Guba, E., & Lincoln, Y. (1989). *Fourth generation evaluation.* Newbury Park, CA: Sage.

Guba, E., & Lincoln, Y. (1990). Can there be a human science? *Person-Centered Review, 5(3)*, 130–154.

Guba, E., & Lincoln, Y. (1994). Competing paradigms in qualitative research. In N. Denzin, & Y. Lincoln (Eds.). *Handbook of qualitative research* (pp. 1–17). Thousand Oaks, CA: Sage.

Gumbrium, J., & Holstein, J. (2002). From the individual interview to the interview society. In J. Gumbrium, & J. Holstein (Eds.). *Handbook of interview research: Context & method* (pp. 3–32). London: Sage.

Habermas, J. (1972). *Knowledge and human interest.* London: Heinemann.

Hackman, J. R. (1990). Work teams in organizations: An orienting framework. In J. R. Hackman (Ed.). *Groups that work (and those that don't): Creating conditions for effective teamwork* (pp. 1–4). San Francisco, CA: Jossey-Bass.

Haggerty, K. (2004). Ethics creep: Governing social science research in the name of ethics. *Qualitative Sociology, 27(4)*, 391–414.

Haley, E. (1970). *A story, a story.* New York: Atheneum.

Hall, D. T., & Chandler, D. E. (2005). Psychological success: When the career is a calling. *Journal of Organizational Behavior, 26(2)*, 155–176.

Hall, D. T., Zhu, G., & Yan, A. (2002). Career creativity as protean identity transformation. In M. Peiperl, M. B. Arthur, & R. Goffee (Eds.). *Career creativity: Explorations in the remaking of work* (pp. 159–179). London: Oxford University Press.

Hammersley, M. (1989). *The dilemma of the qualitative method: Herbert Blumer and the Chicago tradition.* London: Routledge.

Hammersley, M. (1990). *Reading ethnographic research: A critical guide.* Melbourne: Longman.

Hammersley, M. (1992). *What's wrong with ethnography? Methodological explorations.* London: Routledge.

Hammersley, M. (1999). Some reflections on the current state of qualitative research. *Research Intelligence, 70*, 16–18.

Hammersley, M. (2000). *Taking sides in social research.* London: Routledge.

Hammersley, M., & Atkinson, P. (1995). *Ethnography: Principles and practice.* London: Routledge.

Hancock, P. (2003). Aestheticizing the world of organizations—Creating beautiful untrue things. In A. Carr, & P. Hancock (Eds.). *Art and aesthetics at work* (pp. 42–64). Houndsmill, UK: Palgrave Macmillan.

Hancock, P., & Tyler, M. (2000). "The look of love": Gender and the organization of aesthetics. In J. Hassard, R. Holloday, & H. Willmott (Eds.). *Body and organization* (pp. 108–129). London: Sage.

Harel, I. (1991). The silent observer and holistic note taker. In I. Harel, & S. Pupert (Eds.). *Constructionism* (pp. 449–464). Norwood, NJ: Alex.

Harper, D. (1994). On the authority of image: Visual methods at crossroads. In N. Denzin, & Y. Lincoln (Eds.). *Handbook of qualitative research* (pp. 403–412). Thousand Oaks, CA: Sage.

Harré, R. (1997). He lived to tell the tale. *Journal of Narrative and Life History, 7(1–4)*, 331–334.

Harrington, M. (1986). *The new American poverty*. New York: Penguin Books.

Harris, M. (1968). *The rise of anthropological theory: A history of theories of culture*. New York: T. Y. Crowell.

Harry, B., Sturges, K., & Klinger, J. (2005). Mapping the process: An exemplar of process and challenge in grounded theory. *Educational Researcher, 34(2)*, 3–13.

Hart, A. B. (1896). Introduction. In M. P. Follett (Ed.). *The speaker of the house of representatives* (pp. xiii–xvi). New York: Longmans Green.

Hartley, J. (1994). Case studies in organizational research. In C. Cassell, & G. Symon (Eds.). *Qualitative methods in organizational research: A practical guide* (pp. 208–229). London: Sage.

Hartwell, J., & Torbert, W. (1999a). A group interview with Andy Wilson, founder and CEO of Boston Duck Tours and Massachusetts Entrepreneur of the Year. *Journal of Management Inquiry, 8(2)*, 183–190.

Hartwell, J., & Torbet, W. (1999b). Analysis of the group interview with Andy Wilson. *Journal of Management Inquiry, 8(2)*, 191–204.

Hater, J., & Bass, B. (1988). Superiors' evaluation of subordinates' perceptions of transformational and transactional leadership. *Journal of Applied Psychology, 73*, 695–702.

Healy, M., & Perry, C. (2000). Comprehensive criteria to judge validity and reliability of qualitative research within the realism paradigm. *Qualitative Market Research—An International Journal, 3(3)*, 118–126.

Heidegger, M. (1962). *Being in time*. New York: Harper (Original work published in 1927).

Heidegger, M. (1996). *Being in time* (Trans: J. Stambaugh). Albany, NY: SUNY (1st published in 1927).

Heidegger, M. (1998). On the essence of BEING. In W. McNeill (Ed.). *Pathways* (pp. 291–322). Cambridge, UK: Cambridge University Press (Original work published in 1967).

Heifetz, R. A. (1994). *Leadership without easy answers.* Cambridge, MA: Belknap Press of Harvard University.

Heifetz, R. A., & Linsky, M. (2002). *Leadership on the line: Staying alive through the dangers of leading.* Boston, MA: Harvard Business School Press.

Helgeson, S. (1990). *The female advantage: Women's way of leading.* New York: Doubleday.

Herman, L. (2005). Researching the images of evil events: An arts-based methodology in luminal space. *Qualitative Inquiry, 11(3)*, 468–480.

Heron, J., & Reason, P. (1997). A participatory inquiry paradigm. *Qualitative Inquiry, 3(3)*, 274–295.

Heslin, P. A. (2005). Conceptualizing and evaluating career success. *Journal of Organizational Behavior, 26(2)*, 113–136.

Hesse, E. (1980). *Revolutions and reconstructions in the philosophy of science.* Bloomington, IN: Indiana University Press.

Hickman, G. R. (1998). Leadership and the social imperative of organizations in the 21st century. In G. R. Hickman (Ed.). *Leading Organizations* (pp. 559–571). Thousand Oaks, CA: Sage.

Hicks, D. A. (2002). Spiritual and religious diversity in the workplace: Implications for leadership. *Leadership Quarterly, 13*, 379–396.

Higgs, M., & Aiken, P. (2003). An exploration of the relationship between emotional intelligence and leadership potential. *Journal of Managerial Psychology, 18*, 814–823.

Hine, C. (2000). *Virtual ethnography.* Thousand Oaks, CA: Sage.

Hirst, G., Mann, L., Bain, P., Pirola-Merlo, A., & Richver, A. (2004). Learning to lead: The development and testing of a model of leadership learning. *The Leadership Quarterly, 15(3)*, 311–327.

Hobbs, R. (1997). Literacy for the information age. In J. Flood, S. Heath, & D. Lapp (Eds.). *Research on teaching through the visual and communicative arts* (pp. 7–14). New York: Simon & Schuster.

Hodgson, R., Levinson, D., & Zaleski, A. (1965). *The executive role constellation: An analysis of personality and role relations in management*. Boston, MA: Graduate School of Business Administration, Harvard University.

Hogg, M., Hains, S., & Mason, I. (1998). Identification and leadership in small groups: Salience, frame of reference, leader stereotypicality effects on leader evaluations. *Journal of Personality and Social Psychology, 75(5)*, 1248–1263.

Hollander, E. P. (1978). *Leadership dynamics*. New York: Free Press.

Hollander, E. P. (1992a). The essential interdependence of leadership and followership. *Current Directions in Psychological Science, 1(2)*, 71–75.

Hollander, E. P. (1992b). Leadership, followership, self, and others. *The Leadership Quarterly, 3(1)*, 43–54.

Hollander, E. P. (1995). Ethical challenges in the leader-follower relationship. *Business Ethics Quarterly, 5(1)*, 55–65.

Hollander, E. P., & Webb, W. B. (1955). Leadership, followership, and friendship: An analysis of peer nominations. *Journal of Abnormal and Social Psychology, 50*, 163–167.

Holloway, W., & Jefferson, T. (1997). Eliciting narrative through in-depth interview. *Qualitative Inquiry, 3(1)*, 53–71.

Holloway, I., & Todres, L. (2003). The status of method: Flexibility, consistency, and coherence. *Qualitative Research, 3(3)*, 345–358.

Holmberg, I., & Akerblom, S. (2001). The production of outstanding leadership—an analysis of leadership images in the Swedish media. *Scandinavian Journal of Management, 17*, 67–85.

Holstein, J., & Gubrium, J. (2004). The active interview. In B. Silverman (Ed.). *Qualitative research: Theory, method, and practice* (pp. 140–161). Thousand Oaks, CA: Sage.

Holt, N. (2003). Representation, legitimation, and autoethnography: An autoethnographic writing story. *International Journal of Qualitative Methods, 2(1)*. Article 2. Retrieved February 28, 2007 from http://alberta.ca/~iiqm/backissues/2_1/html/holt.html.

Horton, M. (1968a). Myles Horton's talk with the Friends World Institute. In A. Meyer (Ed.). *Friends World Institute*: Record Group 2, Box 7, File folder 103–120, Highlander Research and Education Library.

Horton, M. (1968b). *On building a social movement*. Unpublished manuscript, Highlander Folk School, TN.

Horton, M. (1968c). Study the power structure. Paper presented at the Consultation on Appalachia-Rural Poverty in North America, Berea College, Berea, KY.

Horton, M., & Freire, P. (1990). *We make the road by walking. Conversations on education and social change*. Philadelphia, PA: Temple University Press.

Horton, M., Kohl, J., & Kohl, H. (1990). *The long haul: An autobiography*. New York: Teacher's College Columbia University.

House, R. (1977). A 1976 theory of charismatic leadership. In J. Hunt, & L. Larson, (Eds.). *Leadership: The cutting edge* (pp. 189–207). Carbondale, IL: Southern Illinois University Press.

House, R., & Baetz, M. (1979). Leadership: Some generalizations and new research directions. In B. Staw (Ed.). *Research in organizational behavior* (Vol. 1, pp. 341–423). Greenwich, CT: JAI Press.

House, R., Hanges, P., Javidan, M., Dorfman, P., & Gupta, V. (2004). *Culture, leadership, and organizations: The GLOBE study of 62 societies*. Thousand Oaks, CA: Sage.

House, R., Spangler, W., & Woycke, J. (1991). Personality and charisma in the U.S. Presidency: A psychological theory of leader effectiveness. *Administrative Science Quarterly, 36*, 364–396.

Howe, R. (1988). Against the quantitative-qualitative incompatibility thesis or dogmas die hard. *Educational Researcher, 17(8)*, 10–16.

Howell, J., & Higgins, C. (1990a). Leadership behaviors, influence tactics, and career experiences of champions of technological innovation. *The Leadership Quarterly, 1(4)*, 249–264.

Howell, J., & Higgins, C. (1990b). Champions of technological innovation. *Administrative Science Quarterly, 35*, 317–341.

Huberman, A., & Miles, M. (1994). Data management and analysis methods. In N. Denzin, & Y. Lincoln (Eds.). *Handbook of qualitative research* (pp. 428–444). Thousand Oaks, CA: Sage.

Hughes, R. L., Ginnett, R. C., & Curphy, G. J. (1993). *Leadership: Enhancing the lessons of experience*. Homewood, IL: Richard D. Erwin, Inc.

Hummel, R. (1991). Stories managers tell: Why they are valid as science. *Public Administration Review, 51(1)*, 31–41.

Hunt, J., & Ropo, A. (1995). Multilevel leadership: Grounded theory and mainstream theory applied to the case of general motors. *The Leadership Quarterly, 6(3)*, 379–412.

Hunter, J., & Schmidt, F. (1990). *Methods of meta-analysis*. Newbury Park, CA: Sage.

Huss, E., & J. Cwikel (2005). Researching creations: Applying arts-based research to Bedouin women's drawings. *International Journal of Qualitative Methods, 4(4)*. Article 4. Retrieved June 17, 2007 from http://www.ualberta.ca/~iiqm/backissues/4_4/pdf/ Huss.pdf.

Husserl, E. (1952). *Ideas: General introduction to pure phenomenology* (Trans: W. Boyce Gibson). London: Allen & Unwin.

Husserl, E. (1970). *The idea of phenomenology*. The Hague, The Netherlands: Nijhoff.

Hycner, R. (1999). Some guidelines for phenomenological analysis of interview data. In R. Bryman, & R. Burgess (Eds.). *Qualitative research* (Vol. 3, pp. 143–163). London: Sage.

Hydén, L., & Bülow, P. (2003). Who's talking: Drawing conclusions from focus groups. Some methodological consideration. *International Journal of Social Research Methodology, 6(4)*, 305–321.

Ilies, R., Morgenson, F., & Nahrgang, J. (2005). Authentic leadership and eudaemonic well-being: Understanding leader-follower outcomes. *The Leadership Quarterly, 16(3)*, 373–394.

Immelman, A. (1998). The political personalities of 1996 U.S. presidential candidates Bill Clinton and Bob Dole. *The Leadership Quarterly, 9(3)*, 335–366.

Insch, G., Moore, J., & Murphy, L. (1997). Content analysis in leadership research: Examples, procedures, and suggestions for the future. *The Leadership Quarterly, 8(1)*, 1–25.

Isabella, L. (1990). Evolving interpretations as change unfolds: How managers construe key organizational events.*Academy of Management Journal, 33(1)*, 7–41.

Isakson, J. (2000). Constructing meaning despite the drudgery of repetitive work. *Journal of Humanistic Psychology, 40*, 84–107.

It's a miracle, I still don't believe it. (1966). *Phi Beta Kappan, 490*–497 (Available from Highlander Research and Education Center, 1959 Highlander Way, New Market, TN).

Janesick, V. (1994). The dance of qualitative research design. In N. Denzin, & Y. Lincoln. *Qualitative research methods* (pp. 209–219). Thousand Oaks, CA: Sage.

Janesick, V. (2000). The choreography of qualitative research. In N. Denzin, & Y. Lincoln (Eds.). *Handbook of qualitative research* (pp. 379–399). Thousand Oaks, CA: Sage.

Jarrett, R. L. (1995). Growing up poor: The family experiences of socially mobile youth in low-income African-American neighborhoods. *Journal of Adolescence Research, 10(1)*, 111–135.

Jerusalem, M., & Mittag, W. (1995). Self-efficacy in stressful life transitions. In A. Bandura (Ed.). *Self-efficacy in changing societies* (pp. 177–201). Cambridge, UK: Cambridge University Press.

Joas, H. (1993). *Pragmatism and social theory*. Chicago, IL: University of Chicago Press.

Johnson, B. (1999). Examining the quality structure of qualitative research. *Education, 18(2)*, 282–292.

Johnson, G., & Leavitt, W. (2001). Building on success: Transforming organizations through appreciative inquiry. *Public Personnel Management, 30(1)*, 129–137.

Johnson, B., & Onwuegbuzie, A. (2004). Mixed methods research: A paradigm whose time has come. *Educational Researcher, 33(7)*, 14–26.

Jöreskog, K., & Sörbom, D. (1989). *LISREL 7: A guide to the program and applications*. Chicago, IL: SPSS Inc.

Kaarbo, J., & Hermann, M. (1998). Leadership style of prime ministers: How individual differences affect the foreign policy making process. *The Leadership Quarterly, 9(3)*, 243–263.

Kabanoff, B. (1997). Computers can read as well as count: Computer-aided text analysis in organizational research. *Journal of Organizational Behavior, 18*, 507–511.

Kacen, L., & Chaitin, J. (2006). "The times they are changing": Undertaking qualitative research in ambiguous, conflictual, and changing context. *The Qualitative Report, 11(2)*, 209–228.

Kahn, W. (1990). Psychological conditions of personal engagement and disengagement at work. *Academy of Management Journal, 33*, 692–724.

Kaminski, M., Kaufman, J., Graubarth, R., & Robins, T. (2000). How people become empowered? A study of union activists. *Human Relations, 53(10)*, 1357–1383.

Kan, M., & Parry, K. (2004). Identifying paradox: A grounded theory of leadership in overcoming resistance to change. *The Leadership Quarterly, 15(4)*, 467–491.

Kant, I. (1911). *Critique of aesthetic judgments* (Trans: J. Meredith). Oxford: Clarendon Press.

Kark, R., Shamir, B., & Chen, G. (2003). The two faces of transformational leadership: Empowerment and dependency. *Journal of Applied Psychology, 88(2)*, 246–256.

Kegan, R. (1982). *The evolving self*. Cambridge, MA: Harvard University Press.

Kelle, U. (1995). Theories as heuristic tools in qualitative research. In I. Maso, P. Atkinson, S. Delamont, & J. Veerhoeven (Eds.). *Openness is research: The tension between self and other* (pp. 30–50). Assen: Van Gorcum.

Kelle, U. (2001). Sociological explanations between micro and macro and the integration of qualitative and quantitative methods. *Forum: Qualitative Social Research, 2(1)*. Retrieved May 14, 2007 from http://www.qualitative-research.net/fqs/fqs-eng.htm.

Kelle, U. (2005). Emergence vs. forcing of empirical data? A crucial problem of grounded theory reconsidered. *Forum: Qualitative Social Research, 6(2)*. Article 27. Retrieved July 20, 2007 from http://www.qualitative-research.net/fqs/texte/2-05/05-2-27.e.htm.

Kelley, R. E. (1988). In praise of followers. *Harvard Business Review, 66(6)*, 321–341.

Kelley, R. E. (1992). *The power of followership: How to create leaders people want to follow, and followers who lead themselves.* New York: Doubleday.

Kerr, S., & Jermier, J. (1978). Substitutes for leadership: Their meaning and measurement. *Organizational Behavior and Human Performance, 22*, 374–403.

Kets de Vries, M. (1999). High performance teams: Lessons from the Pygmies. *Organizational Dynamics, Winter*, 66–77.

Kezar, A. (2002). Reconstructing static images of leadership: An application of positionality theory. *Journal of Leadership Studies, 8(3)*, 94–110.

King, M. L. (1981). *Strength to love.* Philadelphia, PA: Fortress Press.

Kipnis, D., & Schmidt, S. (1982). An influence perspective of bargaining within organizations. In M. Bazerman, & R. Lewicki (Eds.). *Negotiating in organizations* (pp. 303– 319). Beverly Hills, CA: Sage.

Kipnis, D., Schmidt, S., & Wilkinson, I. (1980). Intraorganizational influence tactics: Explorations in getting one's way. *Journal of Applied Psychology, 65(4)*, 440–452.

Kirk, J., & Miller, M. (1986). *Reliability and validity in qualitative research.* Beverly Hills, CA: Sage.

Kirkpatrick, S., & Locke, E. (1991). Leadership: Do traits matter? *The Academy of Management Executive, 5(2)*, 48–61.

Kirkpatrick, S., Wofford, J., & Baum, R. (2002). Measuring motive imagery contained in vision statements. *The Leadership Quarterly, 13(2)*, 139–150.

Kisfalvi, V. (2000). The threat of failure, the perils of success and CEO character: Sources of strategic persistence. *Organization Studies, 21(3)*, 611–639.

Kisfalvi, V., & Pitcher, P. (2003). Doing what is right: The influence of CEO character and emotions on top management team dynamics. *Journal of Management Inquiry, 12(1)*, 42–66.

Kitchin, H. (2002). The tri-council in cyberspace: Insights, oversights and extrapolations. In S. Jones (Ed.). *Doing internet research: Critical issue and methods for examining the net* (pp. 160–174). Thousand Oaks, CA: Sage.

Kitzinger, J. (1994). The methodology of focus groups: The importance of interaction between research participants. *Sociology of Health and Illness, 16(1)*, 103–121.

Klein, S., & Diket, R. (1999). Creating artful leadership. *International Journal of Leadership in Education, 2(1)*, 23–30.

Klein, P., & Westcott, M. (1994). The changing character of phenomenological psychology. *Canadian Psychology, 35(2)*, 133–157.

Klenke, K. (1996). *Women and leadership: A contextual perspective*. New York: Springer.

Klenke, K. (1997). Leadership dispersion as a function of performance in information systems teams. *The Journal of High Technology Management Research, 8(1)*, 149–169.

Klenke, K. (2003). The leader's new work: Living with paradox. Paper presented at the Annual Conference of the International Leadership Association, Guadalajara, Mexico, November 1–5.

Klenke, K. (2004). Qualitative research methods in leadership: Paradigm shift or paradigm analysis. Paper presented at the 5th International Interdisciplinary Annual Conference on Advances in Qualitative Methods, Edmonton, Alberta, Canada, January 29–February 1.

Klenke, K. (2005). The internal theater of the authentic leader: Integrating cognitive, affective, conative and spiritual facets of authentic leadership. In W. Gardner, B. Avolio, & F. Walumba (Eds.). *Authentic leadership theory and practice: Origins, effects and development* (pp. 155–182). New York: Elsevier Science.

Klenke, K. (2007a). Authentic leadership: A self, leader, and spiritual identity perspective. *International Journal of Leadership Studies, 3(1)*, 68–97.

Klenke, K. (2007b). E-spirituality: Spirituality at the confluence of affect and technology. *Journal of Management, Religion and Spirituality*, in press.

Koch, T, (1994). Establishing rigor in qualitative research: The decision trail. *Journal of Advanced Nursing, 19*, 829–836.

Kohlberg, L. (1969a). *Stages in the development of moral thought and action*. New York: Holt, Rinehart & Winston.

Kohlberg, L. (1969b). Stage and sequence: The cognitive development approach to socialization. In D. Goslin (Ed.). *Handbook of socialization: Theory and research* (pp. 347–380). New York: Rand McNally.

Kolbe, R., & Burnett, M. (1991). Content analysis research: An examination of applications with directives for improving research reliability and objectivity. *Journal of Consumer Research, 18*, 243–250.

Komaki, J. L., & Minnich, M. R. (2002). Crosscurrents at sea: The ebb and flow of leadership in response to the shifting demands of racing sailboats. *Group & Organization Management. 27(1)*, 113–142.

Komires, S., Mainella, F., Longerbeam, S., Osteen, L., & Owen, J. (2005). *Journal of College Student Development, 46(6)*, 593–619.

Komires, S., Mainella, F., Longerbeam, S., Osteen, L., & Owen, J. (2006). A leadership identity model: Applications from a grounded theory. *Journal of College Student Development, 47(4)*, 401–419.

Kondracki, N., & Wellman, N. (2002). Content analysis: Review of methods and their applications in nutrition education. *Journal of Nutrition Education and Behavior, 34*, 224–230.

Kouzes, J., & Posner, B. (1995). *The leadership challenge: How to keep getting extraordinary things done in organizations* (2nd edn). San Francisco, CA: Jossey-Bass.

Kracauer, S. (1947). *From Calgary to Hitler*. Princeton: Princeton University Press.

Krauss, S. (2005). Research paradigms an meaning making: A primer. *The Qualitative Report, 10(4)*, 758–770.

Krippendorff, K. (1980). *Content analysis: An introduction to its methodology*. Beverly Hills, CA: Sage.

Krippendorff, K. (2004a). *Content analysis: An introduction to its methodology* (2nd edn). Thousand Oaks, CA: Sage.

Krippendorff, K. (2004b). Reliability in content analysis: Some common misconceptions and recommendations. *Human Communication Research, 30(3)*, 411–433.

Krishnakumar, S., & Neck, C. P. (2002). The "what," "why" and "how" of spirituality in the workplace. *Journal of Managerial Psychology, 17(3)*, 153–164.

Kruger, D. (1988). *An introduction to phenomenological psychology* (2nd edn). Cape Town, South Africa.

Kruger, R. (1994). *Focus group interviews: A practical guide for applied research*. Thousand Oaks, CA: Sage.

Kruger, R., & Casey, M. (2000). *Focus group interviews: A practical guide for applied research* (3rd edn). Thousand Oaks, CA: Sage.

Kuhn, T. (1962). *The structure of scientific revolutions*. Chicago, IL: University of Chicago Press.

Kuhn, T. (1970). Postscript—1969. *The structure of scientific revolutions* (2nd edn). Chicago, IL: University of Chicago Press.

Kuhn, T. (1996). *The structure of scientific revolutions* (3rd edn). Chicago, IL: University of Chicago Press.

Kuhn, T. (2000). *The road since structure*. Chicago, IL: University of Chicago Press.

Kuiken, D., & Miall, D. (2001). Numerically aided phenomenology: Procedures for investigating categories of experience. *Forum: Qualitative Sozialforschung/Forum: Qualitative Social Research, 2(1)*. Retrieved March 21, 2007 from http://www.qualitative-research.net/fqs/texte/1-01/1-01kuikenmiall-e.htm.

Kutsche, P. (1998). *Field ethnography: A manual for doing cultural anthropology*. Upper Saddle River: Prentice Hall.

Kvale, S. (1989). *Issues of validity in qualitative research*. Lund, Sweden: Chartwell Bratt.

Kvale, S. (1995). The social construction of validity. *Qualitative Inquiry, 1(1)*, 19–40.

Kvale, S. (1996). *Inter Views: An introduction to qualitative interviewing*. Thousand Oaks, CA: Sage.

Labaree, D. (1998). Educational researchers: Living with a lesser form of knowledge. *Educational Researcher, 27(8)*, 4–12.

Labov, W., & Waletzky, J. (1967). Narrative analysis: Oral versions of personal experience. In J. Helm (Ed.). *Essays on verbal and visual arts* (pp. 12–44). Seattle, WA: University of Washington Press.

Labuschagne, A. (2003). Qualitative research: Airy fairy or fundamental. *The Qualitative Report, 8(1)*, 6–10.

Ladson-Billings, G. (2003). It's our world, I'm just trying to explain it: Understanding our epistemological and methodological challenges. *Qualitative Inquiry, 9(1)*, 5–12.

Lakshman, C. (2007). Organizational knowledge leadership: A grounded theory approach. *Leadership & Organization Development, 28(1)*, 51–75.

Lancy, D. (1993). *Qualitative research in education: An introduction to the major traditions*. New York: Longman.

Langellier, K. (1989). Personal narratives: Perspectives on theory and research. *Text and Performance Quarterly, 9*, 243–246.

Lapadat, J., & Lindsay, A. (1999). Transcription in research and practice: From standardization of technique to interpretive positionings. *Qualitative Inquiry, 5(1)*, 64–86.

Lasch, C. (1995). *The revolt of the elites and the betrayal of democracy.* New York: W. W. Norton and Company.

Lather, P. (1993). Fertile obsession: Validity after poststructuralism. *Qualitative Sociology, 34(4)*, 673–693.

Latz, M. B. (1989). *The undeserving poor: From the war on poverty to the war on welfare.* New York: Pantheon Books.

Lauterbach, K., & Weiner, B. (1996). Dynamics of upward influence: How male and female managers get their way. *The Leadership Quarterly, 7(1)*, 87–107.

Laverty, S. (2003). Hermeneutic phenomenology and phenomenology: A comparison of historical and methodological consideration. *International Journal of Qualitative Methods, 2(3)*. Article 3. Retrieved March 4, 2007 from http://www.ualberta.ca/~iiqm/backisssues/2_3final/pdf/lavety.pdf.

Lawson, R. G. (1999). *Mary Parker Follett: An analysis of her explorations in reform.* Dissertation Abstracts International, *61(03), 1156 (UMI No. 9965367)*.

Leary, M. R., & Tangney, J. P. (Eds.) (2003). *Handbook of self and identity.* New York: Guilford Press.

Leavy, B., & Wilson, D. (1984). *Strategy and leadership.* London: Routledge.

LeCompte, M., & Preissle, J. (1993). *Ethnography and qualitative design in educational Research* (2nd edn). San Diego: Academic Press.

Lee, A. (1989). A scientific methodology for MIS case studies. *MIS Quarterly, 13(1)*, 33–52.

Lee, A. (1991). Integrating positivistic and interpretive research: Approaches to organizational research. *Organization Science, 2(4)*, 342–365.

Lee, T., Mitchell, T., & Sablynski, J. (1999). Qualitative research in organizational and vocational psychology, *Journal of Vocational Behavior, 55*, 161–187.

Levine, S. (2000). Researching imagination—Imagining research. *Poesis: A Journal of the Arts & Communication, 2*, 88–93.

Levinson, D. J. (1978). *The seasons of a man's life.* New York: Knopf.

Lewin, K. (1947). Frontiers in group dynamics. *Human Relations, 1*, 5–41.

Lewis, O. (1968). The culture of poverty. In D. P. Moynihan (Ed.). *On understanding poverty: Perspectives from the social sciences* (pp. 187–200). New York: Basic Books.

Lincoln, Y. (1995). Emerging criteria for quality in qualitative and interpretive research. *Qualitative Inquiry, 1(3)*, 275–289.

Lincoln, Y., & Guba, E. (1985). *Naturalistic inquiry.* Newbury Park, CA: Sage.

Lincoln, Y., & Guba, E. (1988). Do inquiry paradigms imply inquiry methodologies? In D. Fetterman (Ed.). *Qualitative approaches to evaluation in educational research* (pp. 89–115). Newbury Park, CA: Sage.

Lincoln, Y., & Guba, E. (1989). Ethics: The failure of positivistic science. *Review of Higher Education, 12(3)*, 221–240.

Lincoln, Y., & Guba, E. (1994). *Naturalistic inquiry* (2nd edn). Thousand Oaks, CA: Sage.

Lincoln, Y., & Guba, E. (2000). Paradigmatic controversies, contradictions, and emerging confluences. In N. Denzin, & Y. Lincoln (Eds.). *The handbook of qualitative research* (2nd edn) (pp. 191–216). London: Sage.

Lipman-Blmen, J. (1996). *The connective edge.* San Francisco, CA: Jossey-Bass.

Lipman-Blumen, J. (2005). Toxic leadership: When grand illusions masquerade as noble visions. *Leader to Leader, 36(Spring)*, 29.

Lipsett, L. (2007). Images of September 11. Retrieved June 6, 2007 from http:// home.oise.utoronto.ca/~aresearch/completed.html.

Lips-Wiersman, M. (2002a). Analyzing the career concerns of spiritually oriented people: Lessons for contemporary organizations. *Career Development International, 7*, 385–397.

Lips-Wiersman, M. (2002b). The influence of spiritual "meaning making" on career behavior. *Journal of Management Development, 21(7)*, 497–520.

Lipsey, M., & Wilson, D. (2001). *Practical meta-analysis.* Thousand Oaks, CA: Sage.

Locke, K. (2001). *Grounded theory in management research.* Thousand Oaks, CA: Sage.

Loder, J. E. (1989). *The transforming moment* (2nd edn). Colorado Springs, CO: Helmers and Howard.

Loizos, P. (2000). Video, film and photographs as research documents. In M. Bauer, & G. Gaskell (Eds.). *Qualitative researching with text, image and sound* (pp. 93–107). Thousand Oaks, CA: Sage.

Longino, H. (1993). Feminist standpoint theory and the problems of knowledge. *Signs, 19(1)*, 201–212.

Lord, J. (2007). The quote center. Retrieved July 10, 2007 from www.apprciative-inquiry.org/AI-Quotes.htm.

Lord, R., & Brown, D. (2001). Leadership, values, and subordinate self-concepts. *The Leadership Quarterly, 12(1)*, 133–152.

Lord, R. G., & Hall, R. J. (2005). Identity, deep structure and the development of leadership skills. *Leadership Quarterly, 16*, 591–615.

Lowe, A. (1996). *An explanation of grounded theory (Working Paper)*. Glasgow, Scotland: University of Strathclyde, Department of Marketing.

Lowe, K., & Gardner, W. (2000). Ten years of the leadership quarterly: Contributions and challenges for the future. *The Leadership Quarterly, 11(4)*, 459–514.

Lundberg, C. (1976). Hypothesis creation in organizational behavior research. *Academy of Management Review, 1(1)*, 5–12.

Luthans, F. (2002). The need for and meaning of positive organizational behavior. *Journal of Organizational Behavior, 23*, 695–706.

Luthans, F., & Avolio, B. J. (2003). Authentic leadership: A positive developmental approach. In K. S. Cameron, J. E. Dutton, & R. E. Quinn (Eds.). *Positive organizational scholarship* (pp. 241–261). San Francisco, CA: Berrett-Koehler.

MacIntyre, A. (1984). *After virtue: A study in moral theory*. Notre Dame, IA: University of Notre Dame Press.

MacIntyre, A. (1988). *Whose justice? Which rationality?* Notre Dame, IN: University of Notre Dame Press.

MacIntyre, A. (1990). *Three rival versions of moral enquiry: Encyclopedia, genealogy and tradition*. Notre Dame, IA: University of Notre Dame Press.

Madison, G. (1988). *The hermeneutics of postmodernity: Figures and themes*. Bloomington, IN: Indiana University Press.

Mahon, M. (2002). The visible evidence of cultural procedures. *Annual Review of Anthropology, 29*, 467–492.

Maidique, M. (1980). Entrepreneurs, champions, and technological innovation. *Sloan Management Review, 21(2)*, 59–76.

Maitlis, S., & Lawrence, T. (2007). Triggers and enablers of sensegiving in organizations. *Academy of Management Journal, 50(1)*, 57–84.

Manicas, P., & Secord, P. (1983). Implications for psychology of the new philosophy of science. *American Psychologist, 33*, 399–413.

Mann, C., & Stewart, F. (2000). *Internet communication and qualitative research: A handbook for researching online*. London: Sage.

Manning, K. (1997). Authenticity in constructivist inquiry: Methodological considerations. *Qualitative Inquiry, 3(1)*, 93–116.

Manz, C. C., & Sims, H. P., Jr. (1993). *Businesses without bosses*. San Francisco, CA: Jossey-Bass.

Mariampolski, H. (1999). The power of ethnography. *Journal of the Market Research Society, 41(1)*, 75.

Marion, R., & Uhl-Bien, M. (2001). Leadership in complex organization. *The Leadership Quarterly, 12 (4)*, 389–418.

Markow, F., & Klenke, K. (2005). Personal meaning, calling and organizational commitment: An empirical investigation. *International Journal of Organizational Advancement, 13(1)*, 8–27.

Markus, M. (1997). The qualitative difference in IS research and practice. In A. Lee, J. Liebenau, & J. deGross (Eds.). *Information systems and qualitative research* (pp. 2–27). London: Chapman and Hall.

Markus, H., & Nurius, P. (1986). Possible selves. *American Psychologist, 41(9)*, 954–969.

Martin, S. (1980). *Breaking and entering: Policewomen on patrol*. Berkeley, CA: University of California Press.

Martin, S. S. (2005). *Toward a theory of invisible leadership: A content analysis of the writings of Mary Parker Follett*. Dissertation Abstracts International, *66(12A)*, 4552 *(UMI No. 3202607)*.

Martin, G., & Beaumont, P. (1999). Co-ordination and control of human resource management in multinational firms: The case of CASHCO. *The International Journal of Human Resource Management, 10(1)*, 21–42.

Mason, B. (2001). Issues in virtual ethnography. In K. Buckner (Ed.). *Ethnographic studies in real and virtual environments: Inhabited information spaces and connected communities* (pp. 61–69). Proceedings of Esprit i3 Workshop on Ethnographic Studies. Edinburg: Queen Margaret College, January, 1999.

Mason, J. (2002). *Qualitative researching* (2nd edn). Thousand Oaks, CA: Sage.

Mason, P. (2005). Visual data in applied qualitative research: Lessons from experience. *Qualitative Research, 5(3)*, 125–146.

Mason, J. (2006). Mixing methods in a qualitatively driven way. *Qualitative Research, 6(1)*, 9–25.

Matteson, J. (2006). The emergence of self-sacrificial leadership: An exploration of the theoretical boundaries from the perspective of the leader. Unpublished doctoral dissertation. Regent University. Virginia Beach, VA.

Maxwell, J., & Loomis, D. (2003). Mixed methods: An alternative approach. In A. Tashakkori, & C. Teddlie (Eds.). *Handbook of mixed methods in social & behavioral research* (pp. 241–271). Thousand Oaks, CA: Sage.

May, R. (1972). *Power and innocence. A search for the sources of violence.* New York: A Delta Book.

Maykut, P., & Morehouse, R. (1994). *Beginning qualitative research: A philosophic and practical guide.* London: Falmer.

Mayo, A., & Nohira, N. (2005, October). Zeitgeist leadership. *Harvard Business Review*, 45–60.

Mayring, P. (2000). Qualitative content analysis. *Forum: Qualitative Social Research, 2(1).* Article 20. Retrieved December 24, 2006 from http://www.qualitative-research. net/fqs-texte/2-00/2-00mayring-e.htm.

Mayring, P. (2003). *Einführung in die qualitative Sozialforschung: Eine Anleitung zum Qualitativen Denken* (5th edn). Weinheim: Beltz.

Mays, N., & Pope, C. (1995). Rigour and qualitative research. *British Medical Journal, 311,* 109–112.

McAdams, D. P. (1993). *The stories we live by: Personal myths and the making of the self.* New York: Guilford Press.

McAuliffe, D. (2003). Challenging methodological traditions: research by e-mail. *The Qualitative Report, 8(1).* Retrieved March 7, 2003 from http://www.nova.edu/QR/ QR8-1/mcaulliffe.html.

McCauley, C. D., Drath, W. H., Palus, C. J., O'Conner, P. M. G., & Baker, B. A. (2006). The use of constructive-developmental theory to advance the understanding of leadership. *Leadership Quarterly, 17,* 634–653.

McCullough, M., & Witvliet, C. v. (2005). The psychology of forgiveness. In C. R. Snyder & S. J. Lopez (Eds.). *Handbook of positive psychology* (pp. 446–458). New York: Oxford University Press.

McLaughlin, E. (1991). Oppositional poverty: The quantitative/quality divide and other dichotomies. *Sociological Review, 39,* 292–308.

McLeod, J. (2001). *Qualitative research in counseling and psychotherapy.* London: Sage.

McNeal, R. (2000). *A work of heart: Understanding how God shapes spiritual leaders.* San Francisco, CA: Jossey-Bass.

McNiff, S. (1998). *Arts-based research.* London: Jessica Kingsley.

Mead, G. (1934). *Mind. Self, and society from the standpoint of social behaviorist.* Chicago, IL: Chicago University Press.

Meindl, J. (1990). On leadership: An alternative to the conventional wisdom. In B. Staw, & L. Cummings (Eds.). *Research in organizational behavior* (Vol. 12, pp. 159–203). London: JAI Press.

Meindl, J., Ehrlich, S., & Dukerich, J. (1985). The romance of leadership. *Administrative Science Quarterly, 30,* 78–103.

Merriam, S. (1998). *Qualitative research and case study applications in education.* San Francisco, CA: Jossey-Bass.

Metcalf, H. C., & Urwick, L. (Eds.) (1941). *Dynamic administration: The collected papers of Mary Parker Follett.* New York: Harper.

Meyer, J., & Browning, L. (1999). Transforming an industry in crisis: Charisma, routinization, and supportive cultural leadership. *The Leadership Quarterly, 10(3),* 483–520.

Miles, M., & Huberman, A. (1984). Drawing valid meaning from qualitative data: Toward a shared craft. *Educational Researcher, 13,* 20–30.

Miles, M., & Huberman, A. (1994). *Qualitative data analysis: An expanded sourcebook* (2nd edn). Thousand Oaks, CA: Sage.

Milgram, S. (1974). *Obedience to authority: An experimental view.* New York: Harper & Row.

Miller, T., & Bell, L. (2002). Consenting to what? Issues of access, gate-keeping, and Informed consent. In M. Mauthner, M. Birch, J. Jessop, & T. Miller (Eds.). *Ethics in qualitative research* (pp. 53–69). Thousand Oak, CA: Sage.

Miller, W., & Crabtree, B. (1992). Primary care research: A multimethod typology and qualitative roadmap. In B. Crabtree, & W. Miller (Eds.). *Doing qualitative research: Research methods for primary care* (Vol. 3, pp. 37–55). Newbury Park, CA: Sage.

Miller, J., & Glassner, B. (2004). The "inside" and the "outside": Finding realities in interviews. In B. Silverman (Ed.). *Qualitative research: Theory, method, and practice* (pp. 125–139). Thousand Oaks, CA: Sage.

Miller, S., Nelson, M. W., & Moore, M. (1998). Caught in the paradigm gap: Qualitative researchers' lived experience and the politics of epistemology. *American Educational Research Journal, 35(3),* 377–416.

Mirzoeff, N. (1998) (Ed.). *The visual culture reader.* London: Routledge.

Mishler, E. G. (1999). *Storylines: Craftartist's narratives of identity.* Cambridge, MA: Harvard University Press.

Mizrahi, T., & Rosenthal, B. (2001). Complexities of coalition building: Leaders' successes, strategies, struggles, and solutions. *Social Work, 56*, 63–78.

Moeller, S. (1989). *Shooting war: Photography and the American experience of combat.* New York: Basic Books.

Moen, T. (2006). Reflections on the narrative research approach. *International Journal of Qualitative Methodology, 5(4)*. Article 5. Retrieved April 11, 2007 from http://www.ualberta.ca/~iiqm/bckissies/5_4/htlm/moen.htm.

Moerer-Urdahl, T., & Creswell, J. (2004). Using transcendental phenomenology to explore the "Ripple Effect" in a leadership mentoring program. *International Journal of Qualitative Methods, 3(2)*. Article 2. Retrieved March 4, 2007 from http://www.ulaberta.ca/~ijqm/3_2/pdf/moerercreswell.pdf.

Moran, D. (2000). *Introduction to phenomenology.* London: Routledge.

Moran-Elis, J., Alexander, V., Cronin, A., Dickinson, M., Fielding, J., Sleney, J., & Thomas, H. (2006). Triangulation and integration: Process, claims and implications. *Qualitative Methods, 6(1)*, 45–59.

Morgan, D. (1993). Qualitative content analysis: A guide to paths not taken. *Qualitative Health Research, 3*, 112–121.

Morgan, G., & Smircich, L. (1980). The case for qualitative research. *Academy of Management Review, 5(4)*, 491–500.

Morris, R. (1994). Computerized content analysis in management research. *Journal of Management, 20*, 903–931.

Morrow, R. (1994). *Critical theory and methodology.* Thousand Oaks, CA: Sage.

Morse, J., & Field, P. (1995). *Qualitative research methods for health professionals.* Thousand Oaks, CA: Sage.

Morse, J., Barrett, M., Mayan, M., Olson, K., & Spiers, J. (2002). Verification strategies for establishing reliability and validity in qualitative research. *International Journal of Qualitative Methods, 1(2)*, Article 2. Retrieved October 25, 2006 from http://www.ualberta.ca/~ijqm.

Moss, G. (2004). Provisions of trustworthiness in critical narrative research: Bridging intersubjectivity and fidelity. *The Qualitative Report, 9(2)*, 359–374.

Mouly, S., & Sankaran, J. (1999). The "permanent" acting leader: Insights from a dying Indian R&D organization. *The Leadership Quarterly, 10(4)*, 637–651.

Moustakas, C. (1994). *Phenomenological research methods.* Thousand Oaks, CA: Sage.

Moyers, B. (Writer) (1981). *The adventures of a radical hillbilly: An interview with Myles Horton [Video Tape]*. New Market, TN: Highlander Research and Education Center.

Muhr, T. (1997). *ATLAS/ti: Short user's manual*. Berlin: Scientific Software Development.

Mullen, C. (2003). A self-fashioned gallery of aesthetic practice. *Qualitative Inquiry, 9(2)*, 165–182.

Mullen, C., & Cochran, F. (2000). Creating a collaborative leadership network: An organic view of change. *International Journal of Leadership Education, 3(3)*, 183–200.

Mumford, M., & Van Doorn, J. (2001). The leadership of pragmatism: Reconsidering Franklin in the age of charisma. *The Leadership Quarterly, 12*, 279–309.

Mumford, M., Zaccaro, S., Harding, F., Jacobs, T., & Fleishman, A. (2000). Leadership skills for a changing world: Solving complex social problems. *The Leadership Quarterly, 11(1)*, 20–28.

Murphy, S., & O'Brien, A. (2006). Listening above the Din: The potential of language in organizational research. *International Journal of Qualitative Methods, 5(2)*. Article 10. Retrieved February 3, 2007 from http://www.ualberta.ca/~ijqm/backissues/5_2/pdf/murphy.pdf.

Murray, G. (1999). Courage to create and courage to lead: A case study of the artistic leader Toni Morrison. *Journal of Leadership Studies, 6(1–2)*, 134–149.

Murray, M. (2003). Narrative psychology and narrative analysis. In P. M. Camic, J. E. Rhodes, & L. Yardley (Eds.). *Qualitative research in psychology: Expanding perspectives in methodology and design* (pp. 95–112). Washington, DC: American Psychological Association.

Musgrove, M. (1976). *Ashanti to Zulu: African traditions*. New York: Dial/Penguin Group.

Nastasi, B. (1999). Audiovisual methods in ethnography. In J. Schensul, M. LeCompte, B. Nastasi, & S. Borgatti (Eds.). *Enhanced ethnographic methods: Audiovisual techniques, focused group interviews, and elicitation techniques* (pp. 1–50). Walnut Creek, CA: AltaMira Press.

Neuendorf, K. A. (2002). *The content analysis guidebook*. Thousand Oaks, CA: Sage.

Neuman, A. (1995). Context, cognition, and culture: A case analysis of collegiate leadership and cultural change.*American Educational Journal, 32(2)*, 251–279.

Newman, D. L. (2005). Ego development and ethnic identity formation in rural American Indian adolescents. *Child Development, 76(3)*, 734–746.

Noblit, G., & Hare, R. (1988). *Meta-ethnography: Synthesizing qualitative studies*. Newbury Park, CA: Sage.

Noris, J. (1997). Meaning through form: Alternative modes of knowledge representation. In J. Morse (Ed.), *Completing a qualitative project: Details and dialogue* (pp. 87–116). London: Sage.

Novak, M. (1996). *Business as calling: Work and the examined life.* New York: Free Press.

Nygren, R., & Levine, E. L. (1996). Leadership of work teams: Factors influencing team outcomes. In M. M. Beyerlein, D. Johnson, & S. T. Beyerlein (Eds.). *Interdisciplinary studies of work teams: Team leadership* (Vol. pp. 67–104). Greenwich, CT: JAI Press.

Oakley, A. (2000). *Experiments in knowing: Gender and method in the social sciences.* New York: The New Press.

Oberle, K. (2002). *Ethics in qualitative health research. Annals RCPSC, 38(8)*, 563–566.

O'Connor, J., Mumford, M., Clifton, T., & Gessner, T. (1995). Charismatic leaders and destructiveness. *The Leadership Quarterly, 6(4)*, 529–555.

Offerman, L. R. (1995). Leading and empowering diverse followers. In G. R. Hickman (Ed.).*Leading organizations: Perspectives for a new era* (pp. 397–403). Thousand Oaks, CA: Sage.

Olivares, O., Peterson, G., & Hess, K. (2007). An existential-phenomenological framework for understanding leadership development experiences. *Leadership & Organization Development Journal, 28(1)*, 76–91.

Olson, H. (1995). Quantitative "versus"qualitative research: The wrong question. Retrieved October 10, 2006 from www.ualberta.c/dept/slis/cais/olson.htm.

Olson, B. (1977). Myles Horton of the Highlander Research and Education Center. *Ryegrass School Working Papers, September 1977* (Available from Highlander Research and Education Center, 1959 Highlander Way, New Market, TN).

O'Keefe, G. (2000). *Museum gallery display.* Santa Fee, NM: The Georgia O'Keefe Museum.

Olesen, V. (2000). Feminism and qualitative research at and into the millennium. In N. Denzin, & Y. Lincoln (Eds.). *Handbook of qualitative research* (2nd edn) (pp. 215–255). Thousand Oaks, CA: Sage.

Onwuegbuzie, A., & Teddlie, C. (2003). A framework for analyzing data in mixed methods research. In A. Tashkkori, & C. Teddlie (Eds.). *Handbook of mixed methods in social & behavioral research* (pp. 351–384). Thousand Oaks, CA: Sage.

Osborne, J. (1994). Some similarities and differences among phenomenological and other methods of psychological qualitative research. *Canadian Psychology, 35(2)*, 167–189.

Osborn, R., Hunt., & Jauch, L. (2002). Toward a contextual theory of leadership. *The Leadership Quarterly, 13(6)*, 797–837.

Pallus, C. J., Nasby, W., & Easton, R. D. (1991). *Understanding executive performance: A life-story approach.* Greensboro, NC: Center for Creative Leadership (Report Number 148).

Palmer, R. (1969). *Hermeneutics: Interpretation theory in Schleiermacher, Dilthey, Heidegger, and Gadamer.* Evanson, IL: Northwestern University Press.

Palmer, P. (1983/1993). To know as we are known: Education as spiritual journey. San Francisco, CA: Harper.

Panofsky, E. (1970). *Meaning in the visual arts.* Harmondsworth: Penguin.

Pare, G. (2002). Enhancing rigor of qualitative research: Application of a case methodology to build theories of IT implementations. *The Qualitative Reporter*, Retrieved October 15, 2006 from http://nova.edu/ssss/OR/QR7-4/pare.html.

Parker, M. (1995). Critique in the name of what? Postmodernism and critical approaches to organization. *Organization Studies, 16(4)*, 553–565.

Parker, I. (2005). *Qualitative psychology—Introducing radical research.* Buckingham, UK: Thousand Oaks, CA: Sage.

Parry, K. (1998). Grounded theory and social process: A new direction for leadership research. *The Leadership Quarterly, 9(1)*, 85–106.

Parry, K. (1999). Enhancing adaptability: Leadership strategies to accommodate change in local government settings. *Journal of Organizational Change Management, 12(2)*, 134–156.

Pascale, R. (1999). Surfing the edge of chaos. *Sloan Management Review, 40(3)*, 83.

Patton, M. (1990). *Qualitative evaluation and research methods* (2nd edn). Newbury Park, CA: Sage.

Patton, M. Q. (2002). *Qualitative research and evaluation methods* (3rd edn). Thousand Oaks, CA: Sage.

Patton, E., & Appelbaum, S. (2003). The case for case studies in management research. *Management Research News, 26(5)*, 60–71.

Pauwels, P., & Mattyssens, P. (2004). The architecture of multiple case studies in International business. In R. Marshan-Piekkari, & C. Welch (Eds.). *Handbook for qualitative research methods for international business* (pp. 124–143). Cheltenham, UK: Edward Elgar.

Pawson, R. (1995). Quality and quantity, agency and structure, mechanism and context, dos and don'ts. *BMS, Bulletin de Methodologie Sociologique, 47*, 5–48.

Pearce, C., & Conger, J. (2003). *Shared leadership: Reframing the hows and whys of leadership*. Thousand Oaks, CA: Sage.

Pentland, B. (1999). Building process theory with narrative: From description to explanation. *Academy of Management Review, 24(4)*, 711–724.

Perrewe, P., & Zellars, K. (1999). An examination of attributions and emotions in the transactional approach to the organizational stress project. *Journal of Organizational Behavior, 20(5)*, 739–752.

Pescosolido, A. (2002). Emergent leaders as managers of group emotion. *The Leadership Quarterly, 13(5)*, 583–599.

Peterson, M. (1998). Embedded organizational events: The units of process in organization science. *Organization Science, 9(1)*, 16–33.

Peterson, C., Maier, S. F., & Seligman, M. E. P. (1994). *Learned helplessness. A theory for the age of personal control*. New York: Oxford University Press.

Pettigrew, A., & Whipp, R. (1991). *Managing change for competitive success*. Oxford: Blackwell.

Pfeffer, J. (1981). *Power in organizations*. Boston: Pitman.

Phillips, D. (1997). Telling the truth about stories. *Teaching and Teacher Education, 13(1)*, 101–109.

Piantanida, M., McMahon, P., & Garman, N. (2003). Sculpting the contours of arts-based educational research within a discourse community. *Qualitative Inquiry, 9(2)*, 182–191.

Pielstick, D. (1988). The transforming leader: A meta-ethnographic analysis. *Community College Review, 26(3)*, 15–34.

Pink, S. (2001). *Doing visual ethnography: Images, media, and representation in research*. London: Sage.

Pink, D. (2004, February). Breakthrough ideas for 2004. *Harvard Business Review, 84*, 21–22.

Pizarro, M. (1998). "Chicana/o power!" Epistemology and methodology for social justice and empowerment in chicana/o communities. *Qualitative Studies in Education, 11(1)*, 57–80.

Plachard, W. C. (Ed.). (2005). *Callings: Twenty centuries of Christian wisdom on vocation*. Grand Rapids, MI: William B. Eerdmans.

Plummer, K. (1995). *Telling sexual stories: Power and change and social worlds*. London: Routledge.

Plummer, K. (1996). Symbolic interactionism in the twentieth century: The rise of empirical social theory. In B. Turner (Ed.). *The Blackwell companion to social theory.* Oxford, UK: Blackwell.

Poland, B. (1995). Transcription quality as an aspect of rigor in qualitative research. *Qualitative Inquiry, 4(3)*, 290–310.

Poland, B., & Peterson, A. (1998). Reading between the lines: Interpreting silences in interviews. *Qualitative Inquiry, 4(2)*, 293–313.

Polkinghorne, D. (1983). *Methodology for the human sciences.* Albany: State University of New York Press.

Polkinghorne, D. (1988). *Narrative knowing and the human sciences.* Albany, NY: State University of New York Press.

Polkinghorne, D. (1995). Narrative configuration in qualitative analysis. In J. Hatch, & R. Wisniewski (Eds.). *Life history and narrative* (pp. 5–23). Bristol, PA: Palmer.

Poole, M., & Folger, J. (1981). Modes of observation and validation of interaction Analysis schemes. *Small Group Behavior, 12*, 477–493.

Popay, J. (2003). Quaitative research and epistemological imagination: A vital relationship. *Gaceta Sanitaria, 17(3)*, 58–63.

Popper, K. (1959). *The logic of scientific discovery.* New York: Basic Books.

Porter, L., & McLaughlin, G. (2006). Leadership and the organizational context: Like the weather? *The Leadership Quarterly, 17(6)*, 559–576.

Potter, W., & Levine-Donnerstein, D. (1999). Rethinking validity and reliability in content analysis. *Journal of Applied Communication Research, 27*, 258–284.

Prasad, A., & Prasad, P. (2002). The coming of age of interpretive organizational research. *Organizational Research Methods, 5(1)*, 4–11.

Pratt, M. (2000). The good, the bad, and the ambivalent: Managing identification among Amway distributors. *Administrative Science Quarterly, 45*, 456–493.

ProGAMMA (2002). AGREE [Computer software]. Retrieved from http://www.gamma.rug.nl/.

Prosser, J. (1998a). *Image-based research: A sourcebook for qualitative researchers.* London: Routledge/Falmer.

Prosser, J. (1998b). The status of image-based research. In J. Prosser (Ed.). *Image-based research: A sourcebook for qualitative researchers* (pp. 97–112). London: Routledge/Falmer.

Punch, M. (1994). Politics and ethics in qualitative research. In N. Denzin, & Y. Lincoln (Eds.). *Handbook of qualitative research.* Thousand Oaks, CA: Sage.

Punch, M. (1998). *Introduction to social research: Quantitative and qualitative approaches.* Thousand Oaks, CA: Sage.

Quinn, R. E., & Spreitzer, G. M. (1997). The road to empowerment: Seven questions every leader should consider. *Organizational Dynamics, 26(2)*, 37–49.

Rabinowitz, V., & Weseen, S. (1997). Elu(ci)d(at)ing epistemological impasses: Reviewing the qualitative/quantitative debates in psychology. *Journal of Social Issues, 53(4)*, 605–631.

Ragin, C. (2000). *Fuzzy-set social science.* Chicago, IL: University of Chicago Press.

Rainey, M. (1996). An appreciative inquiry into the factors of culture continuity during leadership transitions: A case study of LeadShare, Canada. *OD Practitioner, 28(1–2)*, 34–41.

Ransome, A. (1968). *The fool of the world and the flying ship.* New York: Farrar.

Rao, A., Hashimoto, K., & Rao, A. (1997). Universal and cultural specific aspects of managerial influence: A study of Japanese managers. *The Leadership Quarterly, 8(3)*, 295–312.

Rapley, T. (2001). The art(fullness) of open-ended interviewing: Some considerations on analyzing interviews. *Qualitative Research, 1(3)*, 303–323.

Rawls, J. (2001). *Justice as fairness: A restatement.* Cambridge, MA: Harvard University Press.

Redwood, S., & Todres, L. (2006). Exploring ethical imagination: Conversation as practice versus committee as gatekeeper. *Forum: Qualitative Social Research, 7(2).* Article 34. Retrieved July 1, 2007 from http://www.qyalitative-rsearch.net/fqs-texte/ 2-06/06-2-34-e.htm.

Reed-Danahay, D. (1997). *Auto/Ethnograph rewriting the self and the social.* Oxford: Berg.

Reese, W. (1996). *Dictionary of philosophy and religion.* Amherst, NY: Humanities Books.

Reeves Sanday, P. (1979). The ethnographic paradigm(s). *Administrative Science Quarterly, 24*, 527–538.

Regine, B., & Lewin, R. (2000). Leading at the edge: How leaders influence complex systems. *Emergence, 2(2)*, 5–23.

Reichard, B. (2005). Toward a grounded theory of female leadership development. Unpublished manuscript. University of Nebraska, Lincoln.

Reiter-Palmon, R., & Illies, J. J. (2004). Leadership and creativity: Understanding leadership from a creative problem solving perspective. *The Leadership Quarterly, 15(1)*, 55–77.

Richards, J. (2006). Post-modern image based research: An innovative data collection method for illuminating preservice teachers' developing perceptions in field-based courses. *The Qualitative Report, 11(1)*, 37–54.

Richards, J., & Anderson, N. (2003). What do I see? What do I think? What do I wonder (STW): A visual literacy to help emergent readers focus attention on storybook illustrations. *The Reading Teacher, 65*, 442–444.

Richards, L., & Richards, T. (1994). From filing cabinet to computer. In A. Bryman, & R. Burgess (Eds.). *Analyzing qualitative data* (pp. 146–172). London/New York: Routledge.

Richardson, L. (2000). Evaluating ethnography. *Qualitative Inquiry, 6(2)*, 253–256.

Ricoeur, P. (1992). *Oneself as another* (Trans. K. Blamey). Chicago, IL: University of Chicago Press.

Riffe, D., Lacy, S., & Fico, F. (1998). *Analyzing media messages: Using quantitative content analysis in research*. Mahwah, NJ: Lawrence Erlbaum.

Ringgold, F. (1991). *Tar beach*. New York: Crown Publishers, Inc., Random House.

Roberts, A. (2003). A principled complementarity of method: In defense of methodological eclecticism of the qualitative-quantitative debate. *The Qualitative Report, 7(3)*. Retrieved October 10, 2006 from http://www.nova.edu/ssss/QR/QR7-3/roberts.html.

Roof, W. C. (1993). Religion and narrative. *Review of religious research, 34(4)*, 297–310.

Rorty, R. (1989). *Contingency, irony, and solidarity*. New York: Cambridge University Press.

Rose, G. (2001). *Visual methodologies*. Thousand Oaks, CA: Sage.

Rosner, J. (1990, November–December), Ways women lead. *Harvard Business Review, 68*, 119–125.

Rost, J. (1991).*Leadership for the 21st century*. Westport, CT: Praeger.

Rubin, H., & Rubin, I. (1995). *Qualitative interviewing—The art of hearing data* (2nd edn). Thousand Oaks, CA: Sage.

Rubin, H., & Rubin, I. (2005). *Qualitative interviewing—The art of hearing data*. Thousand Oaks, CA: Sage.

Ruderman, M., Ohlott, P., Panzer, K., & King, S. (2002). Benefits of multiple roles for women. *Academy of Management Journal, 45(2)*, 369–386.

Rumrill, P., & Fitzgerald, S. (2001). Using narrative reviews to build a scientific knowledge base. *Work, 16*, 165–170.

Sadala, M., & Adorno, R. (2001). Phenomenology as a method to investigate the experiences lived: A perspective from Husserl and Merlau-Ponty's thought. *Journal of Advanced Nursing, 37(3)*, 282–293.

Sadoski, M., & Paivio, A. (2001). *Imagery and text: A dual coding theory of reading and writing.* Mahwah, NJ: Lawrence Erlbaum.

Saldaña, J. (2003). Dramatizing data: A primer. *Qualitative Inquiry, 9(2)*, 218–236.

Salner, M. (1989). Validity in human science research. In S. Kvale (Ed.). *Issues of validity in qualitative research* (pp. 47–72). Lund, Sweden: Studentliteratur.

Sandberg, J. (2005). How do we justify knowledge produced within interpretive approaches? *Organizational Research Methods, 8(1)*, 41–68.

Sandelowski, M. (1993). Rigor or rigor mortis: The problem of rigor in qualitative research revisited. *Advances in Nursing Science, 16(2)*, 1–8.

Sandelowski, M. (2000). Focus on research methods: Whatever happened to qualitative description? *Research in Nursing and Health, 23*, 246–255.

Sandelowski, M., & Barroso, J. (2002). Reading qualitative studies. *International Journal of Qualitative Methods, 1(1)*. Article 5. Retrieved October 25, 2006 from http://www.ualberta.ca/~ijqm.

Sarbin, T. R. (Ed.). (1986). *Narrative psychology: The storied nature of human conduct.* New York: Praeger.

Sayer, A. (2000). *Realism and social science.* Thousand Oaks, CA: Sage.

Sayles, L., & Stewart, A. (1995). Belated recognition for work-flow entrepreneurs: A case for selective perception and amnesia in management thought. *Entrepreneurship, Theory and Practice, 19(3)*, 7–24.

Scapens, R. (2004). Vignette: The many skills of the qualitative case research. In R. Marshan-Piekkari, & C. Welch (Eds.). *Handbook for qualitative research methods for international business* (107–108). Cheltenham, UK: Edward Elgar.

Schenul, S., Schenul, J., & LeCompte, M. (1999). *Essential ethnographic methods: Observations, interviews, and questionnaires* (Book 2 in the Ethnographer's Toolkit). Walnut Creek, CA: AltaMira Press.

Scheurich, J. (1996). The masks of validity: A deconstructive investigation. *Qualitative Studies in Education, 9(1)*, 49–60.

Schmitt, B., & Simonson, A. (1997). *Marketing aesthetics*. New York: Simon & Schuster.

Schneider, M., & Somers, M. (2006). Organizations as complex adaptive systems: Implications of complexity theory for leadership research. *The Leadership Quarterly, 17(4)*, 351–365.

Schommer, M. (1990). The effects of belief about the nature of knowledge on comprehension. *Journal of Educational Psychology, 82*, 498–504.

Schwandt, T. (1994). Constructivist, interpretivist approaches to human inquiry. In N. Denzin, & Y. Lincoln (Eds.). *Handbook of qualitative research* (pp. 118–137). Thousand Oaks, CA: Sage.

Schwandt, T. (2000). Constructivist, interpretivist approaches to human inquiry. In N. Denzin, & Y. Lincoln (Eds.). *Handbook of qualitative research* (2nd edn) (pp. 286–305). Thousand Oaks, CA: Sage.

Schwarzer, R., & Fuchs, R. (1995). Changing risk behaviors and adopting health behaviors: The role of self-efficacy beliefs. In A. Bandura (Ed.). *Self-efficacy in changing societies* (pp. 259–289). Cambridge, UK: Cambridge University Press.

Sclater, D. (2003). The arts and narrative research. *Qualitative Inquiry, 9(4)*, 621–625.

Scott, W. (1955). Reliability of content analysis: The case of nominal scale coding. *Public Opinion Quarterly, 19*, 321–325.

Scott-Hoy, K. (2003). Form carries experience: A story of the art and form of knowledge. *Qualitative Inquiry, 9(2)*, 268–280.

Seale, C. (1999). Quality in qualitative research. *Qualitative Inquiry, 5(4)*, 465–478.

Seale, C. (2003). Quality in qualitative research. In Y. Lincoln, & N. Denzin (Eds.). *Turning points in qualitative research: Tying the knots in a handkerchief.* (pp. 465–478). Walnut Creek, CA: AltaMira Press.

Searle, J. (1995). *The construction of social reality*. New York: The Free Press.

Sechrest, L. (1992). Roots: Back to our first generations. *Evaluation Practice, 13*, 1–8.

Seidel, J., & Kelle, U. (1995). Different functions of coding in the analysis of textual data. In U. Kelle (Ed.). *Computer-aided qualitative data analysis: Theory, methods, and practice*. Thousand Oaks, CA: Sage.

Seidman, I. (1998). *Interviewing as qualitative research: A guide for researchers in education and the social sciences* (2nd edn). New York: Teachers College Press.

Seifter, H. (2004). Artists help empower corporate America. *Arts and Business Quarterly Newletter, Spring*. Retrieved June 6, 2007 from http:/www.artusa/ private_sector_affairs/arts_and_business_council/about_us/newsletter/2004/ spring.asp.

Seligman, M. E. P. (1990). *Learned optimism*. New York: Pocket Books.

Seligman, M. E. P. (1998). *Learned optimism*. New York: Pocket Books.

Seligman, M., & Csikszsentmihalyi, M. (2000). Positive psychology. *American Psychologist, 54*, 5–14.

Seligman, M. E. P., & Gillham, J. (2000). *The science of optimism and hope*. Philadelphia, PA: Templeton Foundation Press.

Selsky, J., & Smith, A. (1994). Community entrepreneurship: A framework for social change leadership. *The Leadership Quarterly, 5(3–4)*, 277–296.

Senge, P. (1990). *The fifth discipline: The art and practice of the learning organization*. New York: Doubleday/Currency.

Senge, P. (1994). *Fifth discipline fieldbook: Strategies and tools for building the learning organization*. New York: Doubleday/Currency.

Seymour, W. (2001). In the flesh or online? Exploring qualitative research methodologies. *Qualitative Research, 1(2)*, 147–168.

Shamir, B., & Eilam, G. (2005). What's your story?: A life-stories approach to authentic leadership development. *The Leadership Quarterly, 16(3)*, 395–417.

Shamir, B., & Howell, J. (1999). Organizational and contextual influences on the emergence and effectiveness of charismatic leadership. *The Leadership Quarterly, 10(2)*, 257–270.

Shamir, B., Arthur, M., & House, R. (1994). The rhetoric of charismatic leadership: A Theoretical extension, a case study, and implications for research. *The Leadership Quarterly, 5(1)*, 25–42.

Shamir, B., Dayan-Horesh, H., & Adler, D. (2005). Leading by biography: Towards a life-story approach to the study of leadership. *The Leadership Quarterly, 1(1)*, 13–29.

Shapiro, G., & Markoff, G. (1997). In C. Roberts (Ed.). *Text analysis for the social sciences: Methods for drawing statistical inferences from texts and transcripts* (pp. 9–31). Mahwah, NJ: Erlbaum.

Shaw, I. (2003). Ethics in qualitative research and evaluation. *Journal of Social Work, 3(1)*, 9–29.

Shepard, H. A. (1984). On the realization of human potential: A path with a heart. In M. B. Arthur, L. Bailyn, D. J. Levinson, & H. A. Shepard (Eds.). *Working with careers* (pp. 25–46). New York: Columbia University Graduate School of Business.

Shin, Y. (1998/1999). The traits and leadership styles of CEOs in Korean companies. *International Studies of Management & Organizations, 4,* 40–48.

Shorey, H. S., & Snyder, C. R. (2004). Hope as a common process in effective leadership. Paper presented at the UNL Gallup Leadership Summer Institute, June 10–12.

Sieber, S. (1973). The integration of fieldwork and survey methods. *American Journal of Sociology, 78(6),* 1335–1359.

Silverman, D. (1993). *Interpreting qualitative data: Methods for analyzing talk, text, and interaction.* London: Sage.

Silverman, D. (1997). *Qualitative research: Theory, method, and practice.* London: Sage.

Silverman, D. (2001). *Interpreting qualitative data: Methods for analyzing talk, text, and interaction.* Thousand Oaks, CA: Sage.

Silverman, D. (2004). *Qualitative research: Theory, method and practice.* Thousand Oaks, CA: Sage.

Simco, N., & Warin, J. (1997). Validity in image-based research: An elaborated illustration of the issues. *British Educational Research Journal, 23(5),* 661–673.

Simonton, D. (1976). Biographical determination of achieved eminence: A multivariate approach to the Cox data. *Journal of Personality and Social Psychology, 33(2),* 218–226.

Simonton, D. (1977). Creative productivity, age, and stress: A biographical time-series analysis of 10 classical composers. *Journal of Personality and Social Psychology, 35(11),* 791–804.

Simonton, D. (1984a). *Genius, creativity, and leadership.* Cambridge, MA: Harvard University Press.

Simonton, D. (1984b). Leaders as eponyms: Individual and situational determinants of monarchal eminence. *Journal of Personality, 51,* 149–160.

Simonton, K. D. (1986). Presidential personality: Biographical use of the Gough Adjective Check List. *Journal of Personality and Social Psychology, 51(2),* 149–160.

Simonton, D. (1988). Presidential style: Personality, biography, and performance. *Journal of Personality and Social Psychology, 55(10),* 928–936.

Simonton, D. (1989). Shakespeare's sonnets. A case of and for single-case historiometry. *Journal of Personality, 53,* 695–721.

Simonton, D. (1990). *Psychology, science, and history: An introduction to historiometry.* New Haven, CT: Yale University Press.

Simonton, D. (1991a). Emergence and realization of genius: The lives and works of 120 classical composers. *Journal of Personality and Social Psychology, 61(5),* 829–840.

Simonton, D. (1991b). Career landmarks in science: Individual differences and interdisciplinary contrasts. *Developmental Psychology, 27,* 119–130.

Simonton, D. (1998). Arnheim award address to division 10 of the American Psychological Association. *Creativity Research Journal, 11(2),* 103–110.

Simonton, D. (1999). Significant samples: The psychological study of eminent personalities. *Psychological Methods, 4,* 425–451.

Simonton, D. (2003). Quantitative and qualitative analyses of historical data. *Annual Review of Psychology, 54,* 617–640.

Simonton, D. K., & Baumeister, R. F. (2005). Positive Psychology at the Summit. *Review of General Psychology, 9(2),* 99–102.

Sims, D. (2003). Between millstones: A narrative account of the vulnerability of middle managers' storying. *Human Relations, 56,* 1195–1205.

Sims, H., & Manz, C. (1984). Observing leader behavior: Toward reciprocal determinism in leadership theory. *Journal of Applied Psychology, 64,* 222–232.

Singletary, M. (1993). *Mass communication research: Contemporary methods and applications.* Boston, MA: Addison-Wesley.

Sivasubramaniam, N., Murry, W. D., Avolio, B. J., & Jung, D. I. (2002). A longitudinal model of the effects of team leadership and group potency on group performance. *Group & Organization Management, 27(1),* 66–96.

Slattery, P. (2003). Troubling the contours of arts-based educational research. *Qualitative Inquiry, 9(3),* 192–197.

Smethurst, S. (2002). Thanks for asking. *People Management, 8(23),* 44.

Smith, D. (1991). Hermeneutic inquiry: The hermeneutic imagination and the pedagogic text. In E. Short (Ed.). *Forms of curriculum inquiry, 3* (pp. 231–237). New York: State University of New York Press.

Smith, J., & Hebius, L. (1986). Closing down the conversation: The end of the quantitative-qualitative debate amongst educational inquires. *Educational Researcher, 15(1),* 4–12.

Snyder, C. R. (1994). *The psychology of hope.* New York: The Free Press.

Snyder, C. R. (Ed.) (2000). *Handbook of hope: Theory, measures and applications.* San Diego and New York: Academic Press.

Snyder, C. R. (2002). Hope theory: Rainbows of the mind. *Psychological Inquiry, 13,* 249–275.

Snyder, C. R., & Lopez, S. J. (Eds.) (2002). *The handbook of positive psychology.* New York: Oxford University Press.

Snyder, C. R., & Shorey, H. (2005). The role of hope in effective leadership. In K. Christensen (Ed.). *Encyclopedia of leadership* (pp. 1369–1380). New York: Berkshire Publishers.

Soin, K., & Scheytt, T. (2006). Making the case for narrative methods in cross-cultural research. *Organizational Research Methods, 9(1),* 55–77.

Sousa, C., & Hendricks, P. (2006). The diving bell and the butterfly: The need for grounded theory in developing a knowledge based view of organizations. *Organizational Research Methods, 9(3),* 315–338.

Sparkes, A. (2001). Myth 94: Qualitative health researchers will agree about validity. *Qualitative Health Research, 11(4),* 538–552.

Sparkes, A. (2002). Autoethnography: Self-indulgence or something more? In A. Bochner, & C. Ellis (Eds.). *Ethnographically speaking: Autoethnography, literature, and aesthetics.* New York: AltaMira Press.

Sparrowe, R. T. (2005). Authentic leadership and the narrative self. *Leadership Quarterly, 16,* 419–439.

Spehler, R., & Slattery, P. (1999). Voices of imagination: The artist as prophet in the process of social change. *International Journal of Leadership in Education, 2(1),* 1–12.

Spence, D. (1984). *Narrative truth and historical truth: Meaning and interpretation in psychoanalysis.* New York: Norton.

Spicer, J., & Chamberlain, K. (1996). Developing psychosocial theory in health psychology. Problems and prospects. *Journal of Health Psychology, 1,* 161–171.

Spiegelberg, H. (1982). *The phenomenological movement.* The Hague, The Netherlands: Martinus Nijhoff.

Spilka, B., & Schmidt, G. (1983). General attribution theory for the psychology of religion: The influence of event-character on attributions to God. *Journal for the Scientific Study of Religion, 22,* 326–339.

Spradley, J. P. (1979). *The ethnographic interview.* New York: Holt, Rinehart, and Winston.

Spreitzer, G. M. (1995). Psychological empowerment in the workplace: Dimensions, measurement, and validation. *Academy of Management Journal, 38(5)*, 1442–1485.

Spreitzer, G. M. (1996). Social structural characteristics of psychological empowerment. *Academy of Management Journal, 39(2)*, 483–504.

Spreitzer, G. M., & Quinn, R E. (1996). Empowering middle managers to be transformational leaders. *The Journal of Applied Behavioral Science, 32(3)*, 237–261.

Spreitzer, G. M., De Janasz, S. C., & Quinn, R. E. (1999). Empowered to lead: The role of psychological empowerment in leadership. *Journal of Organizational Behavior, 20(4)*, 511–526.

Stake, R. (1988). Case study methods in educational research: Seeking sweet water. In R. Jaeger (Ed.). *Complementary methods for research in education* (pp. 253–300). Washington, DC: American Educational Research Association.

Stake, R. (1995). *The art of case study research.* Thousand Oaks, CA: Sage.

Stake, R. (2005). Qualitative case studies. In N. Denzin, & Y. Lincoln (Eds.). *The Sage Handbook of qualitative research* (3rd edn) (pp. 433–466). Thousand Oaks, CA: Sage.

Stanford, J., Oates, B., & Flores, D. (1995). Women's leadership styles: A heuristic analysis. *Women in Management Review, 10(2)*, 9–16.

Staw, B. M., & Ross, J. (1985). Stability in the midst of change: A dispositional approach to job attitudes. *Journal of Applied Psychology, 70*, 469–480.

Staw, B. M., Bell, N. E., & Clausen, J. A. (1986). A dispositional approach to job attitude. *Administrative Science Quarterly, 31*, 56–77.

Steiner, C. (2002). The technicity paradigm and scientism in qualitative research. *The Qualitative Report.* Retrieved December 11, 2006 from http://www.nova.edu/ssss/QR/QR7-2/steiner.html.

Stewart, R. (1999). Theorizing praxis: Processes for visual research. Unpublished manuscript. The University of Southern Queensland, Australia.

Stiglitz, J. E. (2003). *Globalization and its discontents.* New York: W.W. Norton & Company.

Stogdill, R. (1963). *Manual for the leader behavior description questionnaire—form XII.* Columbus, OH: Ohio State University, Bureau of Business Research.

Stogdill, R. (1974). *Handbook of leadership: A survey of the literature.* New York: The Free Press.

Stogdill, R., & Coons, A. (1957). *Leader behavior: Its description and measurement.* Columbus, OH: Ohio State University, Bureau of Business Research.

Strange, J., & Mumford, M. (2002). The origins of vision: Charismatic versus ideological leaders. *The Leadership Quarterly, 13(4)*, 343–377.

Strati, A. (1992). Aesthetic understanding of organizational life. *Academy of Management Review, 17(3)*, 568–591.

Strati, A. (1996). Organizations viewed through the lens of aesthetics. *Organizations, 3(2)*, 209–218.

Strati, A. (1999). *Organizations and aesthetics.* London: Sage

Strauss, A. L. (1959). *Mirrors and masks: The search for identity.* Glencoe, IL: Free Press.

Strauss, A. (1987). *Qualitative analysis for social scientists.* Boston, MA: Cambridge University Press.

Strauss, A., & Corbin, J. (1990). *Basics of qualitative research: Grounded theory procedures and techniques.* Newbury Park, CA: Sage.

Strauss, A., & Corbin, J. (1998). *Basics of qualitative research: Techniques and procedures for producing grounded theory* (2nd edn). London: Sage.

Strodtbeck, F., Simon, R. J., & Hawkins, C. (1965). Social status in jury deliberations. In I. Steiner & M. Fishbein (Eds.). *Current studies in social psychology* (pp. 333–341). New York: Holt, Rinehart & Winston.

Sturges, J., & Hanrahan, K. (2004). Comparing telephone and face-to-face qualitative interviewing: A research note. *Qualitative Research, 4(1)*, 107–108.

Suchman, L., & Jordan, B. (1990). Interactional troubles in face-to-face survey interviews. *Journal of the American Statistical Association, 85*, 232–241.

Sullivan, S. E. (1999). The changing nature of careers: A review and research agenda. *Journal of Management, 25(3)*, 457–477.

Sveningsson, S., & Alvesson, M. (2003). Managing managerial identities: Organizational fragmentation, discourse and identity struggle. *Human Relations, 56(10)*, 1163–1193.

Tajfel, H. (1978). The achievement of group differentiation. In H. Tajfel (Ed.). *Differentiation between social groups: Studies in the social psychology of intergroup relations* (pp. 77–98). London: Academic Press.

Tallerico, M. (1991). Applications of qualitative analysis software: A view from the field. *Qualitative Sociology, 14*, 275–285.

Tan, H., & Wee, G. (2002). The role of rhetoric content in charismatic leadership: A content analysis of Singaporean leaders' speeches. *International Journal of Organization, 5(3–4)*, 317–356.

Tandon, D., Azelton, S., & Kelly, J. (1998). Constructing a tree for community leaders: Contexts and processes in collaborative inquiry. *American Journal of Community Psychology, 26(4)*, 669–696.

Tashakkori, A., & Teddlie, C. (1998). *Mixed methodology: Combining qualitative and quantitative approaches* (Applied Social Research Methods, No. 46). Thousand Oaks, CA: Sage.

Tashakkori, A., & Teddlie, C. (2003a). *Mixed methodology: Combining qualitative and quantitative approaches.* Thousand Oaks, CA: Sage.

Tashakkori, A., & Teddlie, C. (2003b). The past and future of mixed methods research: From data triangulation to mixed model designs. In A. Tashakkori, & C. Teddlie (Eds.). *Mixed methodology: Combining qualitative and quantitative approaches* (pp. 671–701). Thousand Oaks, CA: Sage.

Tate, W. (1997). Critical race theory and education: History, theory, and implications. *Review of Research in Education, 22*, 195–247.

Taylor, S., & Bogdan, R. (1984). *Introduction to qualitative research methods.* New York: Russell Sage Foundation.

Terkel, R. (1972). *Working.* New York: The New York Press.

Tesch, R. (1990). *Qualitative research: Analysis types and software tools.* Bristol, PA: Falmer.

Thomas, J. (1993). *Doing critical ethnography.* Newburg Park, CA: Sage.

Thomas, K. W., & Velthouse, B. A. (1990). Cognitive elements of empowerment: An "interpretive" model of intrinsic task motivation. *Academy of Management Review, 15(4)*, 666–680.

Theus, K. (1995). Communications in a power vacuum: Sense-making and enactment during crisis-induced departures. *Human Resource Management, 34*, 27–49.

Tierney, W. (1987). The semiotic aspects of leadership: An ethnographic study. *American Journal of Semiotics, 5(2)*, 233–250.

Tierney, W. (2000). Undaunted courage: Life history and the postmodern challenge. In N. Denzin, & Y. Lincoln (Eds.). *Handbook of qualitative research* (2nd edn) (pp. 537–565). Thousand Oaks, CA: Sage.

Tilley, S. (2003). "Challenging" research practices: Turning a critical lens on the work of transcription. *Qualitative Inquiry, 9(5)*, 750–773.

Titscher, S., Meyer, M., Wodak, R., & Vetter, E. (2000). *Methods of text and discourse analysis.* (Trans: Bryan Jenner). London: Sage.

Tonn, J. (2003). *Mary P. Follett: Creating democracy, transforming management.* New Haven, CT: Yale University Press.

Torbert, W. R. (1987). *Managing the corporate dream: Restructuring for long-term success.* Homewood, IL: Dow-Jones-Irwin.

Tosi, H. (1991). The organization as a context for leadership theory: A multi-level approach. *The Leadership Quarterly, 2,* 205–228.

Travers, M. (2001). *Qualitative research through case studies.* Thousand Oaks, CA: Sage.

Treviño, K., Hartman, L., & Brown, M. (2000). Moral person and moral manager: How executives develop a reputation for ethical leadership. *California Management Review, 43,* 128–142.

Tsui, A., Zhang, Z., Wang, H., Xin, K., & Wu, J. (2006). Unpacking the relationship between CEO behavior and organizational culture. *The Leadership Quarterly, 17(2),* 113–137.

Tung, R. (2006). Of arts, leadership, management education, and management research: A commentary on Nancy Adler's "The arts & leadership: Now that we can do anything, what will we do?" *Academy of Management Learning and Education, 5(4),* 505–511.

Turnbull, S. (2006). Post-millennial leadership refrains: Artists, performers and anti-heroes. *Leadership, 2(2),* 257–269.

Turner, R. H. (1976). The real self: From institution to impulse. *American Journal of Psychology, 81,* 989–1016.

Turner, J. C. (1978). Social comparison, similarity and in-group favoritism. In H. Tajfel (Ed.). *Differentiation between social groups: Studies in the social psychology of intergroup relations* (pp. 235–250). London: Academic Press.

Turney, L., & Pocknee, C. (2005). Virtual focus groups: New frontiers in research. *International Journal of Qualitative Methods, 4(2).* Article 3. Retrieved January 12, 2007 from http://www.ulaberta.ca/~iiqm/backissues/4_2/html/turney.com.

Uhl-Bien, M., Marion, R., & McKelvey, B. (2007). Complexity leadership theory: Shifting leadership from the industrial age to the knowledge era. *The Leadership Quarterly, 18(4),* 298–318.

Umiker, W. (1988). Applied creativity. *S.A.M. Advanced Management Journal, 53(3),* 9–13.

UNDP. (1995). *1995 human development report.* New York: UNDP.

Urwick, L. (1935). The problem of organization: A study of the work of Mary Parker Follett. *Bulletin of the Taylor Society and of the Society of Industrial Engineers as members of Federated Management Societies, 1,* 163–169.

Välikangas, L., & Okurama, A. (1997). Why do people follow leaders? A study of a U.S. and Japanese change program. *The Leadership Quarterly, 8(3)*, 313–337.

Valle, R., King, M., & Halling, S. (1989). An introduction to existential-phenomenological thought in psychology. In R. Valle, & S. Halling (Eds.). *Existential-phenomenological perspective in psychology* (pp. 3–16). New York: Plenum Press.

Vandenberg, D. (1997). Phenomenological research in the study of education. In D. Vandenberg (Ed.). *Phenomenology & education discourse* (pp. 3–37). Johannesburg, South Africa: Heineman.

Van de Van, A. (1986). Central problems in the management of innovation. *Management Science, 32*, 590–607.

van Knippenberg, D., van Knippenberg, B., De Cremer, D., & Hogg, M. A. (2004). Leadership, self, and identity. A review and research agenda. *Leadership Quarterly, 15*, 825–856.

Van Leeuwen, T., & Jewitt, C. (Eds.) (2001). *Handbook of visual analysis*. Thousand Oaks, CA: Sage.

Van Maanen, J. (1979a). Reclaiming qualitative methods for organizational research: A preface. *Administrative Science Quarterly, 24*, 520–526.

Van Maanen, J. (1979b). The fact of fiction in organizational ethnography. *Administrative Science Quarterly, 24*, 539–550.

Van Maanen, J. (1988a). *Tales of the field: On writing ethnography*. Chicago, IL: University of Chicago Press.

Van Maanen, J. (1988b). Different strokes: Qualitative research in the administrative science quarterly from 1956–1996. In J. Van Maanen (Ed.). *Qualitative studies of organizations (ix–xxxii)*. Thousand Oaks, CA: Sage.

Van Maanen, M. (1990). *Researching the lived experience*. New York: SUNY.

Van Maanen, M. (2000). Phenomenological inquiry. http://www.phenomenology online.com.

VanWynsberghe, R., & Khan, S. (2007). Redefining case study. *International Journal of Qualitative Methods, 6(2)*. Article 6. Retrieved July 25, 2007 from http:// www.ualberta.ca/~iiqm/backissues/6_2/vanwynsberghe.htm.

Voelck, J. (2003). Directive and connective: Gender-based differences in the management style of academic library managers. *Portal, Libraries, and the Academy, 3*, 393–418.

Waddington, P. (1986). The Ansellsbrewery strike: A social-cognitive approach to the study of strikes. *Journal of Occupational Psychology, 59(3)*, 231–246.

Waldman, D., Lituchy, T., Gopalakrishnan, M., Laframboise, K., Galperin, B., & Kaltsounakis, Z. (1998). A qualitative analysis of leadership and quality improvement. *The Leadership Quarterly, 9(2)*, 177–201.

Walsham, G. (1993). *Interpreting information systems in organizations*. Chichester, UK: Wiley.

Walsham, G. (1995). Interpretive case studies in IS research: Nature and method. *European Journal of Information Systems, 4(2)*, 75–81.

Warren, M. R. (1998). Community building and political power. *The American Behavioral Scientist, 42(1)*, 75–93.

Wasserman, E. (2000). *The door in the dream: Conversations with eminent women in science*. Washington, DC: Joseph Henry Press.

Watrin, R. (1999). Art as research. *Canadian Review of Art Education, 26(2)*, 92–100.

Weber, M. (1947). *The theory of social and economic organization*. New York: The Free Press.

Weber, M. (1958). *The protestant ethic and the spirit of capitalism*. New York: Scribner.

Weber, M. (1964). *The theory of social and economic organization*. New York: Free Press.

Weber, R. (1990). *Basis of content analysis* (2nd edn). Thousand Oaks, CA: Sage.

Weber, R. (2004). The rhetoric of positivism versus interpretivism: A personal view. *MIS Quarterly, 28(1)*, iii–xii.

Weed, F. (1993). The MADD queen: Charisma and the founder of Mothers Against Drunk Drivers. *The Leadership Quarterly, 4(3–4)*, 329–346.

Weick, K. (1995). *Sensemaking in organizations*. Thousand Oaks, CA: Sage.

Weisner, D. (1999). *Step 7*. New York: Clarion Books.

Weiss, F. (Ed.) (1974). *Hegel: The essential writings*. New York: Harper & Row.

Weiss, J. W., Skelley, M. F., Haughley, J. C., & Hall, D. T. (2004). Calling, new careers and spirituality: A reflective perspective for organizational leaders and professionals. In M. L. Pava (Ed.). *Spiritual intelligence at work: Meaning, metaphor, and morals: Research in ethical issues in organizations* (Vol. 5, pp. 175–201). Amsterdam, The Netherlands: Elsevier Ltd.

Wells Swede, S., & Tetlock, P. (1986). Henry Kissinger's implicit personality theory: A quantitative case study. *Journal of Personality, 54*, 617–646.

Welsch, W. (1997). *Undoing aesthetics*. London: Sage.

Wengraf, T. (2001). *Qualitative interviewing: Biographic narrative and semi-structured methods*. Thousand Oaks, CA: Sage.

Wepner, S., D'Onofrio, A., Willis, B., & Wilhite, S. (2002). Getting at the moral leadership of education deans. *The Qualitative Report, 7(2),* June. Retrieved September 9, 2002 from http://www.nova.edu/ssss/QR/QR7-2/wepner.html.

Wertz, F. (1986). The question of reliability of psychological research. *Journal of Phenomenological Research, 17,* 181–205.

Wheatley, M. J. (1992). *Leadership and the new science: Learning about organizations from an orderly universe.* San Francisco, CA: Berrett-Koehler Publishers, Inc.

Wheatley, M. J. (1999). *Leadership and the new science: Discovering order in a chaotic world.* San Francisco, CA: Berrett-Koehler Publishers, Inc.

Whitman, E. (2007). "Just chatting": Research ethics and cyberspace. *International Journal of Qualitative Methods, 6(2).* Article 7. Retrieved June 26, 2007 from http://www.uaberta.ca/~iiqm/backissues/6_2/whitman.htm.

Whitney, D., & Trosten-Bloom, A. (2003). *The power of appreciative inquiry: A practical guide to positive change.* San Francisco, CA: Berrett-Kohler.

Whyte, D. (1994). *The heart aroused.* New York: Doubleday.

Whyte, D. (2001). *Crossing the unknown seas: Work as pilgrimage of identity.* New York: Riverhead Books.

Wicks, A., & Freeman, E. (1998). Organization studies and the new pragmatism: Positivism, anti-positivism, and the search for ethics. *Organization Science, 9(2),* 123–140.

Wiesner, D. (1999). *Sector 7.* New York: Clarion Books.

Wilkonson, S. (1998). Focus group methodology: A review. *International Journal of Social Research Methodology, 1(3),* 389–400.

Wind, E. (1937). Studies of allegorical portraiture. *Journal of the Warburg and Courtauld Institutes, 3,* 75–79.

Winter, D. (1987). Leader appeal, leader performance, and the motive profiles of leaders and followers: A study of American presidents and elections. *Journal of Personality and Social Psychology, 52,* 1996–2002.

Winter, D. (1995). Presidential psychology and governing styles: A comparative psychological analysis of the 1992 presidential candidates. In S. Renshon (Ed.). *The Clinton presidency: Campaigning, governing and the psychology of leadership* (pp. 113–134). Boulder, CO: Westview.

Winter, D. (1998). A motivational analysis of the Clinton first term and the 1966 presidential campaign. *The Leadership Quarterly, 9(3),* 367–376.

Wolcott, H. (1999). *Ethnography: A way of seeing.* Walnut Creek, CA: AltaMira Press.

Wong, A., & Slater, J. (2002). Executive development in China: Is there any Western sense? *International Journal of Human Resource Management, 13(2)*, 338–360.

Woolcott, H. (2002). Writing up qualitative research . . . better. *Qualitative Health Research, 12(1)*, 91–103.

Wrzesniewski, A., McCauly, C., Rozin, P., & Schwartz, B. (1997). Jobs, careers, and callings: People's relations to their work. *Journal of Research in Personality, 31*, 21–33.

Yin, R. (1994). *Case study research: Design and methods*. Beverly Hills, CA: Sage.

Yin, R. (2003). *Case study research*. Beverly Hills, CA: Sage.

Youngblood, M. D. (1997). Leadership at the edge of chaos: From control to creativity. *Strategy and Leadership, 25(5)*, 8–15.

Yukl, G. (1981). *Leadership in organizations*. Englewood Cliffs, NJ: Prentice-Hall.

Yukl, G., & Van Fleet, D. (1982). Cross-situational, multimethod research on military leader effectiveness. *Organizational Behavior and Human Performance, 30*, 87–102.

Zaccaro, S. J., & Klimosky, R. (2002). The interface of leadership and team processes. *Group & Organization Management, 27(1)*, 4–13.

Zaccaro, S. J., Rittman, A. L., & Marks, M. A. (2001). Team leadership. *The Leadership Quarterly, 12(4)*, 451–483.

Zander, R., & Zander, B. (2000). *The art of possibility*. Cambridge, MA: Harvard University Press.

Zawacki, R. A., & Norman, C. A. (1994). Successful self-directed teams and planned change: A lot in common. In W. L. French, C. H. Bell, & R. A. Zawacki (Eds.). *Organization development and transformation: Managing effective change* (pp. 309–316). Chicago, IL: Irwin.

Zellmeyer, V. (1997). When we talk about collaborative curriculum-making, what are we talking about? *Curriculum Inquiry, 27(2)*, 187–214.

Zhou, J., & George, J. (2001). When job dissatisfaction leads to creativity: Encouraging the expression of voice. *Academy of Management Journal, 44(4)*, 682–696.

Zimmerman, B. (1995). Self-efficacy and educational development. In A. Bandura (Ed.). *Self-efficacy and changing societies* (pp. 202–230). Cambridge, UK: Cambridge University Press.

ABOUT THE AUTHORS

Dr. Karin Klenke, PhD, has served on the faculty of Regent University as Professor of Leadership Studies and Director of Research, as a founding faculty member of the Jepson School of Leadership Studies at the University of Richmond, on the graduate faculty of the George Washington University, and on the faculties of Old Dominion University, Averett University, and the University of Pretoria. She currently serves as Senior Principal of the Leadership Development Institute (LDI) International, a consulting firm specializing in the development and design of customized leadership development and education programs as well as public leadership workshops and seminars.

Dr. Klenke holds a PhD in Organizational Psychology and has specialized in the study of leadership for the past 15 years. Dr. Klenke has published widely in leadership, management, psychological, and research methods journals. Her ground-breaking book entitled *Women and Leadership* received a national award. Dr. Klenke's current research interests include leadership effectiveness and positive psychology, women in leadership, e-leadership, leadership and spirituality, and multiparadigm and multimethod research in the study of leadership.

Frank Markow is Associate Professor at Life Pacific College in San Dimas, CA. His research interests include spirituality in leadership as well as areas of positive organizational scholarship which seek to understand personal identity and the meaning of work.

Acknowledgements: I thank Karin Klenke for her support and editorial guidance, as well as my colleagues and students at Life Pacific College. I also thank the participants in this study, who graciously and honestly shared their life stories with me to pursue my life's calling, education.

Suzanne Martin, PhD, teaches organizational leadership at Samford University in Birmingham, AL, and also serves as the Program Director for The Leading

Edge Institute, a program for college women in Alabama. Anchored in the data from this study, Martin plans to use a grounded theory approach to generate a model of leadership that is both post heroic and multileveled rooted in Follett's constructs. Martin's research interests include grassroots organizing, dialogic leadership, and qualitative research methods.

Acknowledgement: Dr. Karin Klenke provided invaluable assistance with the structure and content focus of this chapter.

J. Randall Wallace is the founder/director of Mustard Seeds & Mountains, Inc. He has lived and worked in an at-risk community in Appalachia for over 15 years and has over 25 years experience working in similar settings. He has an MA in Human Resource Leadership and a PhD in Organizational Leadership. He is interested in researching leadership in at-risk settings, focusing on grassroots leaders and leaders in the developing world. He has taught graduate courses in advanced human growth and development, leader as an agent of change, the creative leadership personality, educational psychology, qualitative research methods, and servant leadership at Azusa Pacific University and Eastern University.

INDEX

analytic generalization, 67–8, 70
appreciative inquiry, 374–5, 376
articulation of purpose, 311
ascendancy traits, 310
at-risk communities, 341–66
Atlas/ti, 291, 295, 299, 300, 304–308
authentic leadership, 13, 61, 95, 190, 196, 313,
    321, 338, 380, 381
authenticity, 38, 39, 43, 52, 192, 247
autocoding, 294, 295, 307
autoethnography, 201–202
axial coding, 93, 94, 148, 190, 196, 208
axiology, 14–15, 17–18, 27, 39

behavioral theory, 53, 312
being-in-the world, 224–5
between case analysis, 58, 68, 69, 148
bottom-up leadership, 342–3, 358
bracketing, 42, 227, 228, 232, 235

calling, 81, 279, 312, 317–39
catalytic authenticity, 39
categorical aggregation, 67
chaos theory, 315, 382
charisma, 113, 114, 143, 148, 166, 167, 168,
    176, 210, 216, 217, 310, 315
charismatic leadership, 58, 80, 81, 88, 96, 104,
    110, 113, 114, 115, 144, 147, 168, 213, 216
charismatic theory, 96, 114
co-operatives, 312
code family, 312, 353
code worthiness, 300
codes, 43, 49, 60, 68, 80, 81, 88, 89, 90, 91, 92,
    93, 94, 95, 96, 97, 100, 113, 118, 123, 125,
    148, 154, 167, 169, 177, 190, 192, 193, 212,
    291, 295, 299, 300, 301, 303, 307, 312, 347,
    348, 350, 352, 353, 365, 369
coding, 69
Cohen's kappa intercoder reliability, 100
collaborative ethnography, 201, 202

collaborative inquiry, 11
collaborative leadership, 72
"collective creativeness", 312
collective purpose, 314
common purpose, 310, 311, 314–15
complexity theory, 315, 380
compounding consciousness, 302
concurrent mixed methods
    designs, 159
confidentiality, 49, 50, 51, 52, 53, 122,
    149–50, 382
confirmability, 38, 43, 205, 231, 247
conflict management, 316
conflict, 9, 57, 58, 59, 69, 70, 111, 144, 157,
    251, 252, 277, 279, 292, 301, 311, 312,
    314, 315, 316, 327, 331, 332, 333, 334,
    335, 336, 338, 339, 344, 348, 354, 355,
    359, 360, 363, 364, 374
constant comparison method, 93, 149, 189,
    193, 198, 206
construct validity, 69–70, 90, 103, 158
constructive developmental models, 338
constructivism, 7, 14, 15, 16, 19, 20, 21–2, 27,
    29, 38, 64, 155, 371, 381
content analysis, 6, 10, 33, 35–6, 38, 44, 52, 65,
    87–115, 117–18, 139, 149, 160, 162, 175,
    177, 180, 189, 270, 271, 272, 274, 284,
    289–316, 347–8, 350, 351, 352–3, 381, 383
contingency theory, 13, 53, 316
coordination, 311
correlative validity, 103
creative citizenship, 303
creative energies, 314
credibility, 8, 38, 39, 43, 45, 48, 84, 130, 131,
    148, 188, 193, 205, 209, 231, 240, 246, 247,
    276, 379
critical ethnography, 201, 202
critical theory, 7, 14, 15, 19, 22, 24, 28,
    35, 202, 372
crowd mentality, 303

deconstructionism, 24
density data, 308, 309
density percentage, 308–10
dependability, 38, 43, 205, 231, 247
depersonalize, 298
descriptive case study, 62
dispositional resilience, 312
diversity, 33, 46, 51, 72, 146, 158, 160, 162, 276,
    312, 372, 378
dominance, 25, 35, 136, 310
dynamic sympathy, 315

educative authenticity, 39
empathy, 148, 166, 235, 278, 312
empowerment, 11, 12, 39, 111, 165, 280, 289,
    311, 312, 313–14, 348, 361, 363, 364
epistemology, 8, 14–15, 16–17, 19, 24, 27, 31,
    32, 33, 35, 38, 40, 45, 46, 52, 53, 69, 280,
    281, 285, 370, 381
epoche, 226, 227, 228, 235
essence of experience, 222, 223, 229, 230
ethnography, 33, 35, 136, 185–218, 260, 274,
    382
ethnomethodology, 22
evolving situation, 311, 315
explanation building, 67
explanatory case
    study, 62, 67
external validity, 37–8, 39–40, 70

fabula, 245
faith in humanity, 65–6, 312
falsifiability, 3–4, 14
focus group, 33, 35, 50, 89, 112, 131–3, 134,
    135–6, 151, 252, 376, 382
followers, 4, 32, 33, 35, 64–5, 66, 87, 89, 96, 97,
    111, 112, 113, 114, 118, 144, 180, 197,
    236–7, 239–40, 250, 258, 259, 268, 286,
    298, 300, 301, 309, 310, 311, 314–15
followership, 180, 240, 298, 301, 310, 312,
    314–15, 315–16, 321
foresight, 310, 311
frequency data, 299, 307
fully integrated mixed method designs, 159,
    274

generalizability, 4, 9, 11, 14, 16–17, 33, 37–8,
    46, 47, 65, 66, 70, 156, 158, 205, 274
Gestalt, 298
"great man" paradigm, 312
Gresham's law, 5
grounded theory, 6, 24, 35, 45, 69, 93, 94, 157,
    185–219, 284, 347, 348, 350, 356, 366
group principle, 302

hand coding, 98, 302, 304, 347–8
hermeneutic cycle, 231
Hermeneutic unit (HU), 290, 292–3
hermeneutics, 22, 23, 24, 28, 155, 223, 225
Highlander Folk School, 341, 342
historiography, 34
historiometry, 185–219
horizontalization, 235, 239
human strength (s), 61, 312–13
humility, 61, 316, 355

iconographical symbolism, 272, 273
iconography, 270, 272–4, 284
iconological symbolism, 272, 273
identity, 82–3, 97, 135, 151, 153, 162, 165, 169,
    176, 177, 194, 199, 201, 259, 264, 267, 280,
    317–39, 346, 355, 356–7, 363
ideographic method, 7
impoverished communities and poor
    communities, 341
incommensurability, 15
informed consent, 49, 50, 51, 52, 53,
    149–50, 382
inspiring movement, 300
instrumental case, 59, 69, 381
integration, 48, 96, 155, 181, 198, 227, 292, 328,
    334, 342, 370
integrative leadership, 312
integrative unities, 311
intercoder reliability, 90, 99, 100, 102, 103, 118,
    139, 251, 271, 307
internal validity, 37, 38, 44, 45, 67, 69–70,
    193, 218
interpenetration, 315
interpretivism, 7, 14, 15, 20, 22–4, 27, 45–6, 53,
    265–6, 381

intrinsic case, 59, 69
invisible leader, 310, 312, 314, 315–16

kenosis, 350, 362, 363, 365
Krippendorff's alpha intercoder reliability,
    100, 101, 102

latent codes, 96, 250, 304
law-dynamic, 303
leadership development, 173, 174, 196, 232,
    233–4, 239–40, 262, 346, 379
leadership lexicon, 315
League of Nations, 312
line-by-line coding, 295, 299
literal replication, 65, 68

macrolevel, 311
manifest codes, 92, 118, 304, 350, 365
member checking, 43, 67, 139, 268
memoing, 93, 190
memos, 94, 167, 190–1, 196, 226, 291, 294,
    300, 307
meta-ethnography, 211–12
meta-theme, 314
methodolatry, 35
microconstruct, 311
microlevel, 300–1, 311
ministers, 177, 211
ministry, 322–3, 325–8, 331–3, 335, 339
mixed methods, 7, 48, 153–82, 367, 370–2
moral purpose, 315
moral reasoning, 310
morality, 118, 337
Mothers' Against Drunk Drivers (MADD),
    57–8, 64
multilevel leadership, 303
multimethod conversion
    designs, 159

narrative analysis, 9, 136, 162, 165, 204,
    221–55, 270, 317–39, 367, 383
narrative identity, 321–2, 337
narrative psychology, 320
narrative synthesis, 9
negative case sampling, 43

networking, 295, 313
nomothetic method, 7, 205, 213–14, 234

ontological authenticity, 39
ontology, 14–17, 22, 24, 27, 29, 31–3, 35, 40,
    45, 52–3, 280–1, 381
open coding, 93–4, 148, 190–1, 193, 196, 294,
    299, 307
open-ended interviewing, 125
optimism, 5, 32, 87, 166, 308, 312–13, 348, 357,
    359, 363
organic leader, 315

participant observation, 11, 18, 36, 44, 66, 82,
    156, 159, 162, 196–7, 200–201, 203–204,
    226, 268, 372–4
pattern matching, 65, 67
peer debriefing, 43, 181
phenomenological reduction, 226–8, 235, 239
phenomenology, 6, 22, 24, 52, 136, 162, 187,
    218–19, 221–55, 284, 367, 381, 383
positive psychology, 65, 312, 316, 359, 377
positivism, 3–4, 14–15, 19, 22–3, 28–9, 32,
    46, 48, 53, 61, 114, 155, 223–4, 258,
    265, 276, 371
post heroic, 446
postmodernism, 7, 14
postpositivism, 14–15
poverty, 341, 342, 344, 345, 354, 355, 359
power over, 313
power with, 313–14
pragmatism, 15–16, 25, 26–9, 48, 64, 210,
    223, 381
predictive validity, 103
primary document (PD), 292
primary texts, 296
probing interview questions, 121–36
progressive business, 310
prolonged engagement, 43, 181, 185, 372
protection from harm, 49–50, 150, 382
purposive sampling, 64, 346

Q-methodology, 34
qualitative–quantitative debate, 52, 369–70

quantitative research, 5–6, 9–10, 14, 29, 33, 37–42, 44–7, 52–3, 62, 70, 155, 157, 161, 181, 261, 369, 371, 379

realism, 15, 19, 28, 64
reflexivity, 17, 42, 43, 173–4, 205, 234, 272, 277, 355, 368
repersonalise, 298
replicability, 4, 11, 14, 156, 274, 284, 369
researcher bias, 41–2, 104, 291, 307
respondent validation, 43, 67
risk of harm, 50

sampling validity, 103
saturation, 11, 67–8, 81, 94, 190, 198, 294, 301, 307, 348, 351, 373
Scott's pi intercoder reliability, 100, 102
selective coding, 93, 94, 148, 190–1, 196
self-directed work teams, 313
self-sacrificial leadership, 61, 65, 380
semantic validity, 103
semiotic analysis, 260, 272, 372
semistructured interview, 126–30
sequential mixed methods designs, 159
servant leadership, 13, 162, 165, 236
shared leadership, 136, 312, 313, 380
snow ball sampling, 176
social constructionism, 21, 38
spiritual leadership, 13, 32, 380
strange attractor of meaning, 315
structured interviewing, 122–5, 127
subjective career success, 318, 336
super codes, 148, 291, 348
symbolic interactionism, 25–6, 29

tactical authenticity, 39
team training, 313
thematic coding, 90, 93, 94, 95, 174, 351
theoretical coding, 93, 194
theoretical replication, 65, 68
theoretical sampling, 10, 64–5, 165, 193, 197, 226
theoretical sensitivity, 131, 187, 193–4
total quality management (TQM), 5, 312
total situation, 310
trait theory, 13, 53
transactional/transformational theory, 13
transferability, 38, 43, 205, 231, 247
transformative mixed method designs, 159, 377
triangulation, 44, 62, 65–7, 69, 155, 157, 170, 181, 246, 269, 370
trustworthiness, 38–40, 43–4, 52, 92, 102, 138–9, 194, 247, 276, 371–2

unstructured interviewing, 125–6, 127

virtual ethnography, 33, 202, 203, 382
visual anthropology, 258, 260, 270
visual content analysis, 270–1, 284
visual ethnography, 260
visual sociology, 258, 260
vocation, 317

we-power, 313–14, 316
within case analysis, 68
word crunching, 99, 114, 295–6, 316
word frequencies, 90, 290

zeitgeist leadership, 13, 35, 380